FUNCTIONAL BUSINESS COMMUNICATION

Third Edition

1983

WILLIAM JACKSON LORD, JR.

Texas Commerce Bancshares Centennial
Professor in Business Communication
The University of Texas at Austin

JESSAMON DAWE

Freelance Lecturer, Consultant, Writer

PRENTICE-HALL, INC., Englewood Cliffs, N.J. 07632

Library of Congress Cataloging in Publication Data

Lord, William Jackson, (date)
   Functional business communication.

   Rev. ed. of: Functional business communication /
Jessamon Dawe. 2nd ed. [1974]
   Includes bibliographical references and index.
   1. Communication in management.   2. Public
relations.   3. Report writing.   I. Dawe, Jessamon.
Functional business communication.   II. Title.
HF5718.L675 1983   658.4:5   82-9141
ISBN 0-13-332296-3   AACR2

Editorial/production supervision by Pam Price and Steve Young
Interior design by Pam Price
Cover design by Maureen Olsen
Manufacturing buyer: Ed O'Dougherty

Printed in the United States of America

10 9 8 7 6 5 4 3 2 1

0-13-332296-3

Prentice-Hall International, Inc., *London*
Prentice-Hall of Australia Pty. Limited, *Sydney*
Prentice-Hall Canada Inc., *Toronto*
Prentice-Hall of India Private Limited, *New Delhi*
Prentice-Hall of Japan, Inc., *Tokyo*
Prentice-Hall of Southeast Asia Pte. Ltd., *Singapore*
Whitehall Books Limited, *Wellington, New Zealand*

Contents

Preface vii

1 The Information System of Business 1

The Role of Communication in Operational Efficiency 1
Communication Media for the Business Entity 8
The Computer's Continued Impact on Communication 18
Information as the Prelude to Decision Making 27
Classification of Communication by Purpose 29

Part I
BEHAVIORAL TREATMENT OF HUMAN-RELATIONS
MESSAGES 31

2 Image Building: The Public Relations Function of Written
Communication 33

Appearance 33
What Is a Letter? 40
Readability 41
Planning 48
Goodwill Letters 61
Form Letters 74
Problem Situations for Writing Goodwill Messages 78

3   Systematically Imparting Information   86

Interaction of Communicator and Audience   87
Information and Instructive Communications Situations   89
Basic Considerations in Planning Communication Strategy   91
Designing Messages for Which No Resistance Is Anticipated   98
Informing Under Adverse Circumstances   109
Problems in Writing Informative Messages   117
Problems in Writing Informative Messages Under Adverse
  Circumstances   127

4   Persuading Toward Predetermined Action: Selling Ideas,
     Goods, and Services   135

Situations Calling for Persuasion   139
Anticipated Feedback   138
Making Use of the Tools of Persuasion   139
How Humans Assign Meaning to Words   140
Selling Ideas, Goods, and Services   143
Problems in Persuasively Selling Ideas, Goods, and Services   161

5   The Art of Refusing and Other Negative-Message
     Transmissions   173

The Psychology Behind Refusals   174
Business Situations Requiring Tactful Refusals   179
Planning Communication Strategy   192
Problems in Writing That Require a Tactful No or Contain a
  Negative Idea   200

Part II
DECISION-MAKING BUSINESS REPORTS   211

6   Constructing Short Operational Reports   213

An Overview of the Operational Report's Functions   214
Organization Strategy as the Focal Point of Your Message's
  Success   217
Choosing the Format for the Best Psychological Approach   221
Rebuilding a Procedure   230
Problems for Short Operational Reports   288
Suggested Topics for Other Short Report Assignments   314

7   Preplanning the Business Investigation for Long, Formal,
     Analytical Reports   317

Report Classifications   318
Categories of Research Activity   320
Agenda for Business-Decision Research Projects   324

Designing the Research Scheme 333
Problems for Writing Business Reports: Long, Formal, Analytical
    Investigations 336
Suggested Report Topics 360

8   Gathering Information for Business Decisions   363

Assembling Data from Secondary Sources 364
Collecting Data by Survey 371
Appendix: A Review of Formulas for Determining Sample Size 386

9   Shaping the Decision   395

Some Basic Ideas on Decision Planning 396
Decision-Making Techniques for the Yes-or-No Problem 409
Framing the Decision for the Comparative Evaluation 412
Decision Design for the Descriptive-Analytical Study 415
Appendix: Some Applications of Quantitative Decision Making 418

10   Preparing the Prefatory Report Parts   430

Page Format 432
The Title Fly 434
The Title Page 437
The Authorization Letter or Memorandum 437
The Letter of Transmittal 441
Organizing the Outline 444
The List of Illustrations 465
The Abstract or Epitome 465

11   Convincing Presentation of the Findings   471

Writing the Introduction 472
Report Format 479
Tabular and Graphic Presentation 484
Writing the Decision-Component or Content Sections 503
The Concluding Portions 515
Report-Writing Style 519
Scholarly Documentation—Footnotes and Bibliography 522
The Appendix or Appendices 528

Part III
RESOURCE MATERIAL FOR PERSONAL USE   533

12   Career Planning as the Focus in the Job-Getting Process   535

Appraising Yourself 536
Fitting Your Qualifications to the Job Requirements and the Hiring
    Entity 540

Selling Your Abilities   546
A Typical Problem Assignment in Application Communication   580

Appendix A—Useful Guide Forms   581

Index   587

Preface

The Eighties. Era of Communication! And aptly labeled—for this is a decade of communication technology brought on by continued developments and advanced refinements in computer capabilities. Increasingly, information is being created and stored in electronic form only. Over half the total U.S. labor force is now involved in the production, dissemination, and use of information in its various forms. Nearly half the gross national product is generated by information-related activities. Effective decision making at all levels, from the international to the individual, is based on the ready availability of complete, current, and accurate information.

Has the impact of those astounding facts really made its mark? Not yet, at least for those of us working in the area of business communication. Quite naturally, then, the question arises: "What about the continued need for employees trained both in the knowledge of and skill in *written* communication?" That need is ever present. It will continue to be.

As support, *Time,* reporting on "The Righting of Writing" (May 19, 1980), indicates that a wave of writing reform is sweeping through schools, colleges, and businesses all over the United States. In an age of talk shows, video cassettes, videodisks, and tape recorders, personal home computers, telephonitis, and declining educational standards, the clearly written word is swiftly becoming a lost art. The many new courses attempting to correct that drift are concerned not with creative writing but with something almost as rare: clear, usable, everyday prose . . . an aim of this book.

Communications training is one of the hottest areas in the corporate field today according to Nate Rosenblatt, a vice president of a new and thriving company called Learn, Inc. This firm sells a packaged seminar called "Power Writing." It is designed specifically for executives, for those MBAs also (as new employees) who still cannot write clear letters, memos, or reports even with degrees from prestigious colleges. A *Fortune* magazine report of its survey of a cross section of employers states that *all* wanted business schools to do a better job of teaching their MBA (and undergraduate) business students to write more effectively. (Effective communication skills *are being recognized* more and more as an important part of every graduate's management tool kit.)

Sun Institute for the Sun Company offers a course called "Write Up the Ladder."[1] It is tailored for employees, like those elsewhere, who suffer from lack of confidence and ability in writing basic memos, letters, and reports. And, as Gene Cartwright, a manager at Standard Oil of Indiana, puts it, "Companies are built around reports."[2] An official of the American Society for Training and Development (Robert Craig) goes further: "Poor writing," he insists, "is a significant factor in the whole drop in the growth of American productivity."[3] Virgil B. Day,[4] a vice president at General Electric, echoes a similar thought in his firm's attempt to learn more about communication. Members of industrial management, he states, *can*—and *must*—play increasingly important roles in communication in the light of new socioeconomic pressures to change our competitive enterprise system, and in the face of the bread-and-butter facts of increasing product competition at home and abroad.

Malcolm Forbes, president and editor-in-chief of *Forbes* magazine, has long been an advocate of better business writing. "Be crystal clear," he recommends. International Paper Company has gone on record (in *Business Week*) with its position on writing, believing that it is more important than ever for all of us to write and communicate better.

While at the University of Texas at Austin, graduate student Christopher Spicer, using an application of the Delphi method, conducted a study to identify the communication competencies required by future business people.[5] The study generated a list of competencies considered by experts in business and organizational communication to be essential for business persons in the 1980s. The sheer size of the list of required competencies dem-

---

[1] "Education," TIME, May 19, 1980, p. 89.

[2] Ibid.

[3] Ibid.

[4] In an address before the Annual Conference of the International Council of Industrial Editors, Denver, Colorado, n.d.

[5] Christopher Spicer, "The Communication Competencies Required by Future Business Persons: An Application of the Delphi Method," (unpublished Ph.D. dissertation, Graduate School of Business, The University of Texas, 1978).

onstrates clearly that courses designed to enhance one set of communication skills alone will no longer suffice as the sole communication requirement for undergraduate business and professional students.

Another study[6] of business graduates, done by Dr. Donald Zacharias to discover what additional competencies they would like to have gained from their courses of study, indicated that 17 percent wanted more experience in problem solving and 15 percent wanted more training in communicating technical information. A survey of graduate engineers revealed similar results.

The fact is that around the country a lot of attention is now being given to effective communication—and programs to accomplish it. Few of their suggested ways to improve writing, however, are truly new. What is new is the national conviction that something must be done about writing and the challenge of trying to spread writing skills widely throughout a society as diverse as that in the United States.

This spotlight, center-stage focus on writing skill improvement means one thing at least: students will write more. That fact alone is significant . . . whatever the quality of instruction and the classroom method. A Latin proverb thus seems relevant enough for repetition here: *scribendo disces scribere*. Translated it reads,

"By writing, one learns to write."

Some switched emphases and other changes must occur, however, in our era of communication technology. What is stored in the computer as data/information for processing must be retrievable without requiring wholesale changes, extensive editing, or reformatting entry to make it usable. It becomes even more important, therefore, for the communication specialist/information processor to be clear and succinct in developing written materials that are to be stored electronically, . . . *whatever* processing they may have to undergo later.

No one text—or course—can be all things to all users. Nor can a single volume treat (in reasonable length or adequate depth anyway) all facets of business communication. There is so much diversity now in the field: business communication, organizational and nonverbal communication, listening, making presentations, and so on. One text cannot be the panacea for all instructional purposes. This book like its predecessors makes no pretense at fulfilling all such needs. It still continues to focus on communication theory and its application in problem-solving strategies, organization techniques, and style in written messages, whatever the format demanded. Its concentration remains on sharpening problem-solving skills and enhancing writing competencies required to communicate decisions clearly, understandably, and acceptably to each recipient.

Some of the second edition preface predictions have come to pass; others

---

[6] Ibid (cited in Spicer study).

are in process. The time-tested, user-proven principles of effective written business communication set forth in earlier editions remain sound and usable. They are thus retained in this updated third edition. A notable switch in emphasis on and usage of short operational reports is evident, however, in business, industry, and governmental organizations. Chapter 6, therefore, has been enlarged considerably. Particularly significant is the expanded treatment of short, analytical reports. Many of the problem-solving, decision-making techniques associated with long, formal report investigations have been tailored for short analytical reporting. Updated examples plus additional ones have been included as applied illustrations.

In a 1980 ranking[7] of outstanding undergraduate business programs in the United States that reported the results of a survey of personnel executives from *Fortune*'s listing of the 200 largest industrial firms and 50 largest banks, financial institutions, insurance companies, retailing, and public utilities, and 92 deans in AACSB schools, the two areas of universal agreement where improvements in undergraduate business programs should be made were:

- more emphasis upon developing analytical and problem-solving skills, and
- more emphasis upon developing written communication skills.

This book is designed to help achieve both those ends.

WILLIAM J. (JACK) LORD, JR.
JESSAMON DAWE

---

[7] J. David Hunger and Thomas L. Wheelan, "A Performance Appraisal of Undergraduate Business Education," *Human Resource Management*, (Spring 1980), pp. 24–31. Published by the University of Michigan.

1

The Information System of Business

*The effectiveness of an information system depends
on the willingness and ability to think through
carefully what information is needed by whom for
what purpose.*

Peter F. Drucker

Business communication is applicable to the whole field of organized activity:
from the simplest inquiry and its response to the most lengthy, full-dress
business report; from the subtle soft-sell reminder letter to the elaborate
advertising campaign; from the single, rough graphic sketch to execution of
the "total package" concept. Its nature is the nature of the job to be done;
it adapts to the problem to be solved, to basic human psychology, and to the
recipient. But the study of letters, memos, reports, or any other communication medium is not an end in itself; the individual medium is only a *means*
to some administrative end. As such, the information system of business
through the written message continues to play a vital role in any organization.

THE ROLE OF COMMUNICATION
IN OPERATIONAL EFFICIENCY

Communication, in fact, plays several roles in the operational efficiency of
a business firm or organization: (1) that of a decision-making tool; (2) that
of providing the firm with knowledge of its identifiable publics—thus of

making it well informed, influential, prosperous, and highly competitive; and (3) that of making the firm a progressive, energetic pacesetter in the field.

Uppermost in the minds of the people who manage company or industry affairs is the need to operate a *successful* business. They see no way to avoid the truism that to be competitive means being competitive in *quality* and *service* as well as in price. If the firm cannot meet the challenge of keen competition over the long haul, it will fail to get new job orders and research and government contracts; it will fail to make the sales of goods and services that are the lifeblood of, and the reason for, its existence.

These facts are among the reasons one hears so much about efficiency whenever managers get together. Management also thinks about the work tempo in the firms and plants, and it worries because the tempo is often so slow. No company can be competitive under such conditions. Some workers feel that it is degrading to work briskly. We hear these views expressed by the question "Why should I break *my* neck?" and we see the same view in "featherbedding."

Management knows that slow tempo is not only the *result* but may often be the *cause* of such mental attitudes. The person who shuffles slowly through work all day, whether at a machine or a desk, usually goes home tired. The individual who hustles all day goes home feeling satisfied, proud of accomplishment—seldom as tired physically as is the loafer. *Attitude* is a big factor in the efficiency of people. And efficiency has much to do with staying competitive in business; yet the "right" attitude doesn't "just happen." It must be *made* to happen! Influencing the opinions, values, and behavior of audiences, then, should become the prime focus of all communication.

Communication is a basic process of organization. It is the "nervous system" that makes for cohesive organizations and allows their members to be cooperative and to coordinate efforts. Communication is not a secondary or derived aspect of organization but rather the essence of organized activity, the basic process out of which all other functions come.

All kinds of oral, graphic, and written communication are growing increasingly important to the person in business and to that individual's organization. Whether *internal*—and thus an employer-employee relation-ship—or *external*—where the concern is for the relationship of the company with its "publics"—letters, reports, and printed matter continue to play a vital role in the affairs of business and business people.

Today, numbers of business executives, joining the ranks of modern business communicators, are advancing the theory that the key to commu-nication problems can be found in devising an organization pattern that will maintain a flow of information up, down, and across all levels of the firm. There is hardly a major company in the United States whose plan of orga-nization has not been changed, or rechanged within the past decade. With such revised structures have come new jobs, new responsibilities, new decision-making authorities, and reshaped reporting relationships. All these factors combine to create new demands for information. As a result, many leading companies are suffering a major information crisis, often without even realizing it.

In the days before assembly lines and multioperation plants, all employees knew what orders were received, who the big customers were, whether materials were in stock, and how much was produced. They knew whether the business was prospering and, of course, could see when new people were added, when slack work forced layoffs. All knew when they did a good job and whether the shop produced merchandise of quality sufficient to maintain its reputation among competitors. Everyone knew whether prices met competition and whether wages were in line with those paid by other employers for similar work.

As businesses have grown larger and more diverse, the gap between employee and employer—between company and customer—has widened. Personal contacts have diminished or disappeared. The employer now has little or no knowledge of employees and their personal problems. And the employee has little knowledge of products, markets, competitors' activities, and other problems related to the conduct of the business. Production lines, complex operations, and specialization have narrowed the field of information readily available to the average employee. In view of these factors and the rising educational level of the work force, management is often hard put to provide employees with the satisfaction of accomplishment that is essential to best effort. Furthermore, the lack of knowledge regarding the reason for an action or decision has become a source of misunderstanding. This situation prevails at all organizational levels, from the vice-president who is not informed of an important action that involves him or her to the custodian whose routine is changed with the order "Do it this way now."

Everyone wants to be in on things, a part of the organization, and everyone has a strong dislike for surprise or change. To everyone at some time in business comes the question: "Why didn't I know about that before it happened?"

A chronic complaint from supervisors is that information which should emanate from them to their subordinates is too often received by way of the "grapevine" or, more embarrassingly, from the grievance committee whose union headquarters keeps them better informed than the company keeps its management members. Why does that happen?

Some executives admit that, despite their good intentions, they are forgetful and prone not to pass on all the information they should; others say that they are just too busy to do a consistently good job. It is equally true that management's procedures have not adequately taken into account the communication problem inherent in every organization in which there is more than a single supervisory person. Even the best writer cannot communicate effectively in a rigidly authoritarian organization; but it is equally true that communication will not rise above the mediocrity of poorly prepared employees even in the most "open" organization.

Improving the Information System of Business

One of the best ways to improve the information system of business is to master the basic techniques of problem solving and organization, the fundamental principles of written presentation, and the functions of effective communication.

Why, then, do communicators not achieve higher standards of performance? There can be many answers. One is that the goals of business have not been defined clearly for those responsible for informative reporting. Second, among the most important causes of misunderstanding and conflict that arise among people is the failure on the part of each person involved to understand the other party fully, to communicate effectively with the other. Especially in labor-management relations this is true, but it is true in any other field of business relationships as well. Management has long been aware of the importance of effective communication to operational efficiency and has taken many steps calculated to improve informational flow. Errors and mistakes have occurred, however, to cloud the issue.

Language usage itself is often misjudged. Whether language and thinking are purely rational processes is questionable. Emotion is always involved. We err in supposing that workers (or management) are solely creatures of enlightened self-interest and that they act in the work situation wholly in accordance with their reasoning. Any reflection on a person's ability to use the English language is a pretty touchy matter. Any suggestion that one's writing is inadequate bespeaks personal inadequacy, for language is a part of one's innermost self. The writer understandably resents the red-pencil treatment to his or her word creations, being told that the grammar is wrong, that slang is not permissible. What results is a half-guilty, half-resentful attitude toward language rules and language specialists. Such attitudes must be hurdled, therefore, by anyone who attempts to improve the quality of business communication.

Standards are so often presented as inflexible and arbitrary prescriptions, unrelated to practice, that the potential writer probably lacks any motivation to learn and comply with them. Knowledge of the standards and the reasons behind them, however, can enable the modern writer or business executive to face the problem of manipulating his or her environment with confidence. But to write and speak well requires hard work.

It is also easy to undervalue the context of what we write or say. The truth is, real communication is difficult unless the persons communicating trust and respect each other. Thus, we too often make the common error of writing "down" to our audience.

Another reason for lack of a better performance standard for writers is that the human-relation problems of business, industry, and government have been overcentralized. Too much authority has been taken away from those who have to deal directly with the recipient of messages. A final mistake is our failure to listen. We have assumed that people learn by being talked to, when in reality they often learn more when they talk. A change of attitude is thus called for in the communicator. Recipients should be recognized as intelligent, sincere, self-respecting individuals. Trickery and pretense have no place in effective communication if the organization is to operate efficiently, for effective communication depends greatly upon effective listening. In fact, management will find that one of its most useful tools is the proper and skillful use of nondirective counseling.

But the simple truth of modern organization still is that so much of what needs doing is done on and by paper. The occasions for handling objects are few, the chances of commanding people almost nil. No one, indeed, gives orders; rather, everyone "administers" public relations.

Consequently, writing needs to be managed just as production, marketing, and financing are managed. As a cost to present-day business, it is too sizable to be neglected. As a tool, it is too useful to be left unsharpened. This is an age of increasing paperwork. And from every business establishment pours a steady stream of letters, memoranda, reports—written communications of all kinds. Because more and more of one's decisions are necessarily based on the written or printed matter flowing across his or her desk, the business manager has come to depend less and less on what was learned formerly in face-to-face encounters with employees, suppliers, and competitors. The increasing complexity of business, vigorous competition, the continued demand for increased production and a better product, customer insistence on speed and service, the importance of good internal and public relations have all engendered an increasing concern with, indeed, *an increased need for* efficient communication.

Business and industry process thousands of letters and reports daily at a cost that staggers the imagination. Yet the actual dollar cost is the least of business's concern—the cost in misunderstood messages, hurt feelings, lost worker-hours, anger, inefficiency, irritation, disgust, ill will, and inadequate report information for sound decisions is far more costly to the firm than are the immediate expenses for paper, stamps, dictator's and stenographer's time, handling, and so on—costly as these are. The cost of a curt, harsh reply is a lost customer and perhaps his or her intimate friends' patronage as well. The cost of a confused, badly organized, poorly interpreted report is too often a less than sound decision or no decision at all.

Obviously, then, the goal of the business writer is to produce letters and reports that get results the first time around; to prepare these written communications in such a way as to attain their objectives and engender for the firm a reputation for integrity and fair dealing. Although more and more people are writing now than ever before, the *average* letter or report is no longer good enough.

The millions of words that are typed, printed, or penned annually as communications should make the wheels of the business world turn efficiently. Many of these words paralyze business activity. A true test of effectiveness in written communication is the creation of a message put on paper to be read, to be clearly understood, and to be accepted by each reader. Many messages call for action. Any respondent should be able to *act* on a message . . . intelligently.

Effectiveness of Message Presentation

The complexity of the business setting and the plethora of messages that are transmitted daily thus place increasing demands on the quality of communication. The rules of good diction and composition are important still, as is the requisite of friendly tone. Superimposed on these traditional bases, however, is the need to command attention, to establish confidence, and to induce action according to a predetermined plan.

There is no place nor use for the pompous, stilted, stereotyped message. Nor can business afford the luxury of rambling, have-to-read-them-twice messages buried in a mess of words that bring forth as many different interpretations as there are different readers. There is not even a comfortable niche for the dull, dry, monotonous, droning report that is often produced and seldom read. "Make it objective. Deal with the facts. Keep it brief and always to the point. Let your intelligent reader make decisions on the basis of it" are the pleas from business. Such treatment calls for a real job of fact presentation, not opinionated judgments. The report or letter then becomes a vital key in operational efficiency because the writer has a sound understanding of, and respect for, the nature of evidence. Reading audiences are becoming better educated and much more sophisticated, particularly at the executive level. Thus, the task of influencing opinions, modifying values, and changing the behavior of readers grows increasingly difficult.

Inadequate reporting leads to overflowing warehouses, orders returned to the factory, freight cars idle on sidings, extra correspondence, and mounting bills for long-distance calls as a harried sales manager tries to find out exactly how the customer wants the material shipped or to whom an order should be billed.

A board of directors or operating committee with many important decisions to make does not have time to decipher or untangle complicated, wordy reports. And they must have the facts to make instant decisions. The necessary information must be available in as efficient a form as possible. Specifications or orders for the production line must be concise and readable. If they are not, production lags in direct proportion to the time it takes to interpret them. Sales orders and reports must be complete and to the point.

In between must flow the endless letters, memos, and reports that inform and influence not only those closely related to the firm but those outside it as well. There are messages that must go to customers who regularly buy and expect service and products as needed, to potential customers who might be induced to enter the firm's books, and to the "publics" in whose minds are shaped the image and the goodwill of the firm.

Reports on research must be written so they can be understood—regardless of the background of the general manager or president. Consumer inquiries, complaints, and suggestions pour into business by the thousands daily, each communication requiring a tactful reply that will satisfy its recipient.

Proficiency in Communication Skills

Fortunately, management at all levels is becoming sensitive to the waste involved in inefficient communication and to the importance of keenly honed communication skills. Consequently, the college graduate who has demonstrated good communication capabilities is a step ahead of rivals in the job market. His or her rapid advancement will be geared closely as well to demonstrated communication competence.

The paradox is that those who tend to feel that writing is a secondary part of their jobs are usually judged by their superiors largely on the basis of what they do write. For many, promotion and the opportunity to grow professionally depend ultimately on a person who they seldom see but who judges their work by the written results.

Business wheels cannot turn if the bright young department head who assumes general managership cannot communicate adequately plans and ideas to capable subordinates, for this fact denies their coordinated strength and wisdom. The sales representative being promoted to the sales managership, and thus removed from direct contact with customers, who cannot write—ceases to be an asset and becomes a liability to the organization. So does the extremely capable engineer who cannot have his or her work recognized because of an inability to communicate results and make clear the importance of what has been done.

The communicator's real task begins, then, with a hard-nosed analysis of business problem situations, whether the vehicle conveying the solution is a letter, memorandum, or report. And the successful business communication will be one that shows the greatest respect for factual evidence marshaled to support points, free of distortion and persuasive gimmicks.

Consequently, as Dean John S. Fielden points out,[1] your job as a writer is to be so accurate in your treatment of evidence that no reader has cause to question whether a fact is "hard" or "soft" or whether supposedly solid fact is sheer opinion allowed to masquerade in fact's clothing. It is therefore your obligation to set forth clearly to your reader any assumptions you have made. After all, too many things in life are true "if only we assume that . . . ."

Successful leaders of all ages from Saint Paul at Corinth to Winston Churchill during the Battle of Britain to the recognized world leadership of today have found that effective leadership came about largely through effective communication. Its role is no less real in the operational efficiency of any business.

COMMUNICATION MEDIA FOR THE BUSINESS ENTITY

The mere mention of the word *communication* evokes a host of thoughts, running the gamut from the spoken word to the most literary work between hard covers. Communication can be looked at in many ways. A simple analysis of the process yields these components:

Source:	The creator of an idea or the developer and/or sender of a message.
Message:	Ideas, content, or subject matter to be communicated.
Medium:	Spoken or written language, codes, signs, signals, symbols, music, pictures, paintings, gestures.
Channel:	Printed texts, graphic displays, phonographic recordings, sheet music, films, radio, television, newspapers, the five senses.
Destination:	The receiver or receivers of a message, real or potential.
Context:	The physical, psychological, or sociocultural conditions or circumstances under which communication takes place.
Goal:	The purpose to be achieved by the message, the

[1] This paragraph develops an idea of John S. Fielden's "Classic: What Do You Mean I Can't Write?" cited in Phillip V. Lewis and John Williams, *Readings in Organizational Communication* (Columbus, Ohio: Grid Publishing, Inc., 1980), pp. 338–339.

anticipated results, the accomplishment, or the outcome of communication.

The business executive or the industrialist, however, needs an answer to the question, "What makes for the most efficient communication?" There's a need for answers to many questions: Are personal interviews and conferences more effective than written media in disseminating employee information? Is face-to-face communication worth the time and effort required? Advertisers, especially, want to know the impact of auditory copy versus the printed word, the superiority of animation, or other visual stimuli.

Oral and Nonverbal

The best communication tool that management has at its immediate disposal is the ability to talk to people face to face, where there is maximum possibility of getting from the recipient a quick kind of return signal. In communication terminology this response is called "feedback." It is the kind of communication with which humankind began. It continues to account for the major portion of daily communication.

We live in two kinds of worlds at the same time: one in which all things that are exist, and one in which we try to communicate about these things, using a code of symbols by which we can represent them. The problem of the communicator is to bring these two worlds together—to put "real world" and "word world" together in such a way that people understand each other. Words then become highways—or barriers—to communication. They can be both.

But the problems of oral communication are equally the problems of written communication. First, we have a limited number of words, with which we try to talk about a limitless number of things; yet, there is no real meaning in language itself. Written language is a language made up of letters. But language is not spoken writing. There is only meaning in language as someone uses a word and as someone else reacts to that particular word. Meaning does not exist in the word; it exists in the user; thus, we embark at once into the whole realm of semantics. Count Korzybski began the development of general semantics in modern education in his book *Science and Sanity*.[2] When interviewed by a reporter concerning his book, the count had an interesting way of stating his conception of semantics: "Language is a

---

[2] Alfred Korzybski, *Science and Sanity*, 4th ed. (Lakeville, Conn.: Institute of General Semantics, 1958). For additional reading in general semantics, see Stuart Chase, *The Tyranny of Words* (paperback) (New York: Harcourt Brace Jovanovich, 1971); S. I. Hayakawa, *Language in Thought and Action* (paperback) (New York: Harcourt Brace Jovanovich, 1972); and S. I. Hayakawa, ed., *The Use and Misuse of Language* (paperback) (Greenwich, Conn.: Fawcett Publications, Inc., 1962).

very tricky thing; words don't mean what you think. . . . It's like this. When a young lady says you are 'going too far' what she really means is that you are 'getting too close.' " Here is a simple collection of one- and two-syllable words. What do they really mean? Is "too far" actually "too close"?

The use of words is a very complicated procedure, for no two people will interpret a message in precisely the same way. The dictionary definition of words as a common ground is almost a total loss. For the dictionary is but a historical document. The communicator can use it to look up a word, but at once possibilities for deviation occur. All of us assign a meaning to a word in line with our own experiences, attitudes, and beliefs. Should a receiver look up the same word, his or her assignment of meaning may be entirely different because of his or her own peculiar background; so the only way that people can communicate with each other at all is through a sort of mutual agreement to assign the same approximate meaning to the same words. We *learn*, through the process of socialization, to assign the same approximate meanings to the same approximate stimuli. Who is responsible for generating this mutual agreement in the administrative situation?

The subordinate who receives administrative communications cannot be counted on for much help. It would be comforting to management to be able to say that its communications fell short of the mark because the receivers were stupid, disinterested, and/or had perverse personalities, or because its outside publics failed to react favorably to a message due to their own shortcomings. Such reasoning is an excuse. The reality of the situation is that people with whom we communicate expect *us* to exert ourselves, to create an interest in the communication that will result in favorable reception. The manager bent on becoming an effective manipulator of his or her environment must be armed with an understanding of people and their reactions so that his or her messages may be calculated to accomplish the desired purposes.

The second problem is that the "word world" in which we live is a relatively static world but the real world is dynamic. In any word-world description we face the problem of talking about something that ceases to exist, even before it can be talked about. Words are static; things are dynamic.

A third problem is that no word-world picture can ever be made complete. Any language picture, or even any symbol picture, is an incomplete and nonreal picture of the real world that does exist. But we often react to symbols as though they *were* real, a reaction that can lead us into further trouble in our attempt at effective communication.

The real problem, however, in oral communication is *listening*. To listen means that one has to think—the same problem one encounters in reading print. We *hear* a lot; we *listen* very little. We *read* or see a lot; we *think* somewhat superficially.

Consequently, the executive becomes obsessed with whether the message was *heard* or with how many people *saw* a certain cartoon depicting the safety point for the week—not with whether the message was listened to nor whether thought processes were stirred. Psychologists tell us that, as a result of hundreds of surveys, they have substantiated the fact that we retain or listen to much less than 50 percent (actually nearer 25 percent) of what we hear.

Behind all effective communications is the idea that "words make images." The communicator, therefore, must screen well the images released in the listener's, viewer's, or reader's mind, for one wrong symbol can render useless good intentions, sincerity, or a carefully planned strategy.

The management environment is largely verbal and its communications are mostly *purposeful*. An executive can scowl at the clerks to get them to mend their ways or beam at the secretaries to induce them to work harder, but most roadbed activities depend on words.

Hearing is something that comes naturally. Listening must be learned like any other skill; the more we concentrate on hearing and *grasping* the meaning of what we hear, the better listeners we become. Many times we may attend a meeting, a lecture, or conference and at the conclusion wonder what the leader spent an hour talking about. Why?

For one thing, it has been proved that, although we can talk at the maximum rate of approximately 125 words per minute and can read 1,000 or so words per minute, our minds are capable of comprehending accurately thousands of words per minute. When someone is talking, our thoughts may be like the hare and the tortoise. We race along with our thoughts far ahead of the slowly spoken words, stop to bring ourselves back to see what is happening, only to go off again thinking about something else. Each time we wander in thought, we stay away a bit longer before returning to the subject until finally the point of the speaker is missed, the meeting, lecture, or conference is over, and we have lost the meaning and purpose.

The dangers of oral and nonverbal communication become apparent. *Stereotypes* occur. We tend to "see" things as we think they should be (from past experience or from what we have read or heard) instead of as they actually are. For example, someone tells of a trouble we think of as being "the same old thing." We quit listening and begin working on a solution when actually the speaker may have been describing a new twist to an old problem. Similarly, we "hear" the general subject matter being discussed by another and start instantly framing a reply (so there won't be a deadly silence when she or he stops talking) before the speaker has made the point if, indeed, a point was to be made. We frequently do not hear what is being said because we have tuned out the person—an effect of the filtering process that is also very evident in *sharpening* and *mental set*.

Sharpening occurs because we tend to stress the things we feel are important—not those that necessarily need to be stressed. Suppose that we are looking at a painting of a landscape, for instance, with a farmhouse, a barn, an old-time well, a herd of Black Angus cattle, and a field of corn. Initially, a person will look at the picture in its entirety, *but* then will sharpen the view and pinpoint that which is of interest. If the person's father raises Black Angus cattle, she or he will likely pay particular attention to the Angus in the picture to the exclusion of almost everything else. If he or she is interested in raising corn or has a field of his or her own, close attention will be given to the stand of corn in the field. Or attention may be paid only to the dominance of color in the painting. As a result we often fail to consider the whole situation, whatever it is.

Mental set occurs because we have preconceived ideas of categories into which we conveniently place people and things. We have certain feelings toward women drivers, absent-minded professors, certain names, and occupations. Consider the four names and four occupations that follow. What name goes with each occupation?

O'Leary	Artist
Blumberg	Police officer
Wang Lee	Merchant
Von Bechner	Laundry worker

From experience and storytelling exposure we tend to associate the Irish with the police, the Dutch with the art world, and so on. Only through concerted educational efforts will we ever eliminate prejudices in the struggle for human identity, human integrity, and human rights.

Because we feel that everything we hear or read should have a logical ending, we simply add our own when it doesn't. We cannot tolerate inconclusiveness in *any* message medium; consequently, we *jump* to conclusions. The different interpretations and actions that might come from an inept message, then, are awesome to contemplate. That is one of the reasons industrial psychologists feel there is value in letting employees talk. Often troubled employees will talk themselves out of being angry or confused if they have an accurately informed listener who is willing to act as a sounding board.

Failure to listen can be a serious deterrent to upward communication, causing subordinates' hesitancy or reluctance to express any opinion. A similar obstacle is a superior's unapproachability. Key points, then, are a willingness to discuss a situation frankly and sympathetically, and a willingness to be influenced in making a decision. Without this attitude of willingness on the part of management, its policies are impractical and may be ignored.

Another type of communication problem arises out of the failure to develop and maintain constructive relations with the public, particularly in the communities in which the company's employees work and live and with whom the organization lives and does business. Schools, churches, civic organizations, and the individual on the street need to know about free enterprise, the firm's assumed ecological and social responsibilities, and the far-reaching implications of partisan politics. How are the facts to be made known? This question is fast preempting the attention of business people who realize that the answer must be obtained soon if our present economic system is to survive.

The starting point is, of course, with the employee. Every employee is an opinion molder at work, at home, in the community, and in the state and nation when he or she casts a vote. There are other ways of creating public opinion regarding the company and its activities that require directed management effort if a good job is to be done. The public in general is interested in the employment outlook at the plant in its community, what is being done there regarding safety and health—environmental and energy conservation— or other matters of interest. Similarly, the company has a vital stake in convincing the community that its organization is interested in community progress and that the company is a desirable place in which to work.

There is no substitute for the line supervisor who lives with employees in their daily work and who must share information and build understanding while managing the daily work routine. Particular attention should be paid to cultivating and satisfying the curiosity or interest of employees who are looked upon by their fellow workers as capable leaders, reliable bearers of news, and as competent interpreters of its meaning. The grapevine is one of the oldest systems of communication and must be taken for granted wherever human beings live, work, or play together. It is invisible, intangible, uncontrollable, unpredictable, but at times incredibly swift; therefore, it should be recognized as an agency by which information is always being carried to employees. Subordinates will listen to the informal communication of the grapevine with its inaccuracies and half-truths if adequate information is not provided officially.

If desired information could be obtained by an employee's asking for it, the grapevine would not be able to "sell" rumors. The supervisor's prestige and morale would be enhanced greatly if a fraction of the time spent trying to find out how and where the grapevine gets its information were devoted instead to transmitting timely and accurate material to those most concerned. Getting the truth fully and accurately and on time to management and employee alike is a major purpose of communication.

Communication, then, can discharge a most important role in the development and maintenance of morale. Availability of sufficient background information often makes the difference between monotonous performance and that extra effort that brings premium results. Communication programs can build and maintain sound working relationships by circulating information among employees about what is to be and has been done.

Closely related to disseminating appropriate information is finding out what is on the employees' minds. Unless special efforts are made, management will take for granted that many times it is in touch with employee thinking only to learn through costly error that it was mistaken. By securing the reactions of those affected by company practice and policy, management can evaluate past effort and improve future performance.

Management, therefore, has an important stake in developing an effective program for internal communication at the supervisory and general work force levels and in presenting business's viewpoint on vital issues to the public. To meet these problems, company forums, public service programs, house organs and bulletins, closed-circuit television, annual reports, and other devices have been developed in the past decade or two to assist management in transmitting information promptly and accurately to appropriate personnel throughout the organization and to the community. These media are as essential in helping management do a good job as is the telephone, the typewriter, computer, public address system, pocket pager, or any of the other new communication technology.

Top management sets the pace for communication at all levels through its policy formation. Organizational policies, of course, can either encourage or hinder communication. Essential is an atmosphere that encourages free, full exchange of information. A second requirement is providing lower management personnel with timely information to pass on to subordinates. Everyone is leery of "bypassing" either upward or downward in the organization or of simply being "dropped" from the normal distribution channel. Furthermore, a member of any organization is in large measure the kind of communicator that the organization compels that individual to be. The different channels for oral communication provided by various personnel should always be clearly recognized, respected, and used to the fullest advantage.

Written

Although oral communication is two way and thus more effective—though often less appropriate for a particular situation—the written message is one-way communication, with all its inherent weaknesses and problems. Written communication, however, is the concern of this text. It deals with letters, memoranda, and reports as the communication media of the business entity.

The writer, the specific purpose in writing, the situation, the subject, and the reader can and will affect the message. Wide variations among these elements pose a real problem in written communication. Trying to evaluate communication as good or bad, therefore, is at best a tenuous undertaking. What we often see as a *cause* of success in an organization, that is, good communication, may instead be an *effect*. Perhaps it would be more useful to consider the view that written communication is a medium or a catalyst in the process of achieving success in human enterprise.

Any written communication has two basic functions: to inform and to influence. Far too many writers seem to assume that, by merely sending a message, one has communicated. Mere emission of written words (or speech or graphic symbols) does not in itself guarantee that anyone understands or accepts the sender's ideas. One of the most prevalent and most dangerous fallacies concerning communication appears to be the supposition that ideas or thoughts are transmitted literally from one person to another through space. Only the physical signals are actually sent or received. The receiver must translate these signals into terms that are meaningful before the message "is communicated."

The mere physical reception of a message, however, is not the same as understanding it; yet, people *understand* a lot of things that they reject. For example, here is an interoffice letter from a headquarters executive to the business manager of a branch lunchroom. The reader will have little difficulty understanding it; how it is accepted is another matter:

Dear Bob,

You are doing a sloppy job on your inventory reports, and you are causing our office workers undue strain and loss of working time.

I will list all the things you are doing wrong:

1. You have been told repeatedly to write out any bill that looks illegible, but we are getting invoices that appear to have been written in a foreign language. I'm enclosing one of them.

2. You are transferring from one sheet to another improperly.

3. Here is a riddle I'd like an answer for. An invoice came in showing ten pounds of American cheese delivered to your operation. You did not list the ten pounds, but when you took inventory, it worked out that you did use seventeen pounds of cheese that week. How do you account for that?

The list goes on for a couple of pages, ending with the information that it takes three people to decipher his reports. No doubt Bob *understands* the message. The *effect* of it may be that he dons his coat and hat and walks out of his lunchroom without worrying about his replacement. Anybody can fire an employee. The superior manager uses knowledge of people and communications to make a good worker out of a poor one.

The writer of this wholly negative message might also have considered the effect it may have on Bob's sphere of influence. If he is popular—and even dullards have the built-in advantage of offering others an opportunity to feel superior—the executive may have other labor problems to worry about. For should the operation of the lunchroom falter because of Bob's having walked out without notice, the executive could have difficulties with his or her own boss, who may look upon that letter to Bob as being a little less than inspired. Inept!

For your letters, memoranda, and reports to inform and influence properly, you must take into consideration many factors other than the purpose of the message, the subject matter, and the nature of the reader. Among these is the style to be used for getting your ideas across. A clear, brief, simple, direct one is best, although this advice on language style is certainly not new to communication problems. But concentration on developing a "style" may give rise to the assumption that one has a simple, constant, homogeneous audience. *Brevity*, often confused with *conciseness* (meaning completeness, for example), may be "incompleteness" when one is discussing a new procedure or a policy of the firm. *Clarity* is not achieved in the message but in the mind of the receiver. Moreover, clarity may not always be desirable; ambiguity is a virtue in certain kinds of messages. Take, for example, statements on industrial disputes, layoffs, plant moves, consolidations, or other organization changes when, for confidential reasons or the need for proper timing, full disclosure is not feasible. Such disclosure without an adequate background for understanding on the receiver's part might bring adverse reactions from employees, unions, or the public. "Directness" may be nothing more than antagonizing bluntness when one is calling attention to a minor violation. Individuals and audiences differ so radically that we must continually adapt our means of communication and continually check for effectiveness. Language style, therefore, becomes a means—not an end—in written communications. *Communication* is the sending and receiving of messages, not the media or channels by which messages are sent.

Many business managers have become enthralled with the outward forms of communication rather than with the basic determinants of a message's effectiveness. But whether couching results in terms of profits or not, these managers would agree that overall company efficiency depends largely upon communication effectiveness.

"An organization comes into being," Barnard tells us, "when (1) there are persons able to communicate with each other (2) who are willing to contribute action (3) to accomplish a common purpose." The first executive function ... "to develop and maintain a system of communication"[3] ... remains as Barnard described it in 1938. Administration *is* communication.

If administration is defined as a process consisting essentially of decisions and if decisions are essentially communication phenomena, it follows that administration can be viewed as a communication process. A decision is conceived as occurring "upon receipt of some kind of communication consisting of a complicated process of combining information from various sources that result in the transmissions of further communication."

According to Peter Drucker[4] there are four fundamentals of communication:

1. Communication is perception.

[3] Chester I. Barnard, *The Functions of the Executive*, rev. ed. (Cambridge, Mass.: Harvard University Press, 1968), pp. 82, 226.

[4] Peter F. Drucker, *Management: Tasks, Responsibilities, Practices* (New York: Harper & Row, Publishers, Inc., 1974). Ideas for this section are from Drucker's Chap. 38, "Managerial Communications."

2. Communication is expectation.

3. Communication makes demands.

4. Communication and information are different and indeed largely opposite, yet interdependent.

It is the recipient who communicates. The so-called "communicator," the person who emits the communication, does not communicate. Unless someone reads (or hears), there is no communication. There is only noise. A communicator writes but does not communicate. Indeed, he or she cannot communicate. The writer can only make it possible—or impossible— for a recipient to perceive. Perception is not logic. It is *experience*.

We perceive what we expect to perceive. The unexpected is usually not received at all; it is misunderstood or ignored. Before we can communicate, therefore, we must know what the recipient expects to see (or hear), for communication makes demands. It always demands that the recipient become somebody, do something, believe something. It always appeals to motivation. If, in other words, communication fits in with the aspirations, the values, the purposes of the recipient, it is powerful. If it goes against his or her aspirations, values, or motivations, it is likely not to be received at all, or at best to be resisted.

"Where communication is perception, information is logic. As such, information is purely formal and has no meaning. It is impersonal rather than interpersonal."[5] Measurable information has nothing to do with meanings (that is, it has nothing to do with semantics in the broader sense). Walter Fuchs adds an understanding dimension to this concept:

> Language which has been completely transformed into information is the hardened tip of a not hardened mass. Nobody who talks about language should forget that one of the functions of language is information. Furthermore, nobody who talks about information should forget that language as information is only possible in the context of a language which has not been changed into clear-cut information.[6]

Thus a writer is concerned in information transmission with extralinguistic events—not with *measurable* information (which lies outside the language). Measurable information is a concern of information theory . . . a topic beyond the scope of this book.

A manager's skill in communication, therefore, must change if it is to be used successfully in problem solving, in organizational administration, and in interpersonal relationships. Change is the most important characteristic of the market and nonmarket environment in which an organization operates. Decisions involved in combining economic resources for the pur-

---

[5] Ibid., p. 487.

[6] Walter R. Fuchs, *Cybernetics for the Modern Mind* (New York: Macmillian Publishing Co., Inc., 1971), p. 142.

pose of production and sale must continuously take account of changes and must adjust to change. The business executive lives in an uncertain world that is in part his or her own making.

Managers *do* have access to a specific tool: information. They do not *handle* people; they motivate, guide, organize them to do their work. Their tool—their only tool—to accomplish these functions is the spoken or written word or the language of numbers. Administrators do not deal with the *things* of their world. They deal primarily with information *about* those "things." Communication plays the central role in all aspects of that administration. No matter how varied the activities, or how special the skills involved, in the final analysis the job of every executive or supervisor is communication. Essentially, the administrator must get work done through other people; and accomplishing this task requires an ability to communicate effectively.

Communication patterns are a significant influence on organization effectiveness. The job of mapping an existing network of communication even in a small company is a complicated and difficult one. But if we can map the pathways by which information is transmitted between different parts of an organization and by which it is applied to the behavior of the organization in relation to the outside world, we have gone far toward understanding the organization. Consequently, communication—especially in the written media—assumes a vital role in the operational efficiency of the business entity.

Our traditional ways of thinking about communication in this new technological era, however, will not solve our communication/information problems.

THE COMPUTER'S CONTINUED IMPACT ON COMMUNICATION

Some of the most far-reaching changes occurring in the 1980s—the era of rapid change in communication technology—are and will be in the information field. The typical *large* office today is a complex, distributed, highly interactive information-processing system. Techniques have been developed for describing, analyzing, and modeling the flow of information within offices. Unifying these techniques is a simple but mathematically tractable information flow model, Information Control Nets.[7]

Automation is a fact of life. Office automation is proliferating in large part because the costs of "computing power" are dropping so dramatically. By packing memory and logic functions of actual computers onto pieces of silicon no bigger than a cornflake, electronics engineers and designers have

[7] Xerox's Palo Alto Research Center studies, designs, and implements such office information systems.

been able to build computerlike intelligence into conventional office equipment. Silicon-chip technology is beginning to spawn such devices as typewriters that can recognize and identify misspellings; copiers that can memorize, store, and retrieve documents; and dictation machines that can translate a spoken message into a typed page. The biggest stumbling block to the use of the futuristic equipment appears to be the boss.

The office has not changed its essential procedures for over 100 years. Professionals become a bit wary when anyone tries to change what goes on. Managers have been reluctant to use the new machines, especially if the latter involve a keyboard.

In the U.S. service-oriented economy, the paper chase of the American office ties up 25 percent of the nation's work force, and by 1990 the figure is projected to rise to 40 percent. With a 10-percent shortage of office employees predicted by the end of the decade, white-collar workers will not be able to obtain and use all the information needed to run modern companies. Unless, of course, they have modern communication technology machines to help them. Spending by businesses to modernize the office, however, has so far been extremely low. Each American farmer works with an average of $52,000 worth of such labor-saving machinery as tractors, combines, and milking machines. The average American factory worker is supported by about $25,000 of capital investments in everything from computerized assembly lines to forklifts. Many, many office workers, on the other hand, are aided by a paltry $2,000 of capital investments that often amount to little more than a telephone, a typewriter, and a photocopier. Such offices will soon be as antique as those with stand-up desks and quill pens.[8]

One-third of total office costs—40 to 50 percent of the average company's total expenses—is accounted for in preparation, duplication, handling, and storage of paper. Office costs are not being offset by productivity gains. According to *Fortune* magazine, while factory worker productivity climbed 84 percent in the 1970s, office productivity improved a mere 4 percent.[9] Electronic office equipment offers one cost-effective way to meet the challenge of office productivity. Fast, reliable, and economical equipment that can improve productivity at both the secretarial and managerial levels is needed by most offices.

Office automation is and continues to be one of the fastest-growing areas of the computer marketplace, with annual sales of word- and information-processing equipment alone having passed the $1 billion mark in 1979. Tremendous growth lies ahead in a host of related areas—teleconferencing, electronic mail, facsimile transmission, information storage and retrieval, and computer-based systems designed to provide personal aid to management in decision making.

Some believe, of course, that we are never going to computerize the

---

[8] Christopher Byron, *Time*, November 17, 1980, pp. 81–82.

[9] IBM, *Data Processor*, 23, no. 5 (December 1980), 17.

office completely. But computers and new types of communication facilities certainly can be used to provide a quite different environment within which office tasks are undertaken.

The office of tomorrow is already on the drawing board today as psychologists and scientists study how the meaning of words are represented in human memory, and how people gain access to those memories. That information will prove extremely useful, not only in a better understanding of human thought (human information processing) but also in programming computers to understand human language. Yet few executives view the skilled writer's obsolescence or demise. Publications in increasing numbers continue to stress the importance of learning to write well while an individual is still in school and of the difference that that skill can make in a person's success or failure on the job.

Increased responsibility delegated to electronic storage, retrieval, and data-processing management, however, will compound the need for smoothly integrating the complex skills of the business communication expert, the office administrator, and the data-processing/information specialist. How, then, is this communication specialist to be prepared for handling such complexity? From the strides in teaching methodology and course contents (using a communication laboratory mode of instruction and selected multimedia technology), the next step must be the modular classroom. Modular classrooms will become the next laboratories for business communication to show how conferencing, board meetings, and remote-location data bases can be interlinked—teleconferencing. Modular classrooms can be combined along with data-processing and analysis use of multimedia and terminals and with business communication to provide completed analyses, setting forth clearly selected alternatives followed by "what if" simulation, among other possible approaches. There is a desperate need for better communication of complex issues and structures than is being taught today even at the graduate level. The need for academic computer and telecommunication developments is extensive, that is, how to show and display readily, in a meaningful way, complex statistical results or a decision (two-way communication technologies) given the new infrastructure that is emerging through the advances in computers and telecommunications. Information theory[10] is the underpinning of these concerns. Data-base developments—data collection,[11] data

---

[10] Information theory is a rigorous mathematical theory, a branch of the theory of probability. It is defined by concepts and problems. It deals in a very particular way with amounts of variation and with operations that have effect on such amounts. Information theory is applied readily to systems analysis, for information is the essential ingredient of any control system. The essence of the idea is that information is measured in terms of what *could have been* communicated under a defined set of circumstances rather than in terms of what actually *is* communicated at a particular moment. The yes-no decision is the smallest bit of information; each yes-no decision defines one bit of information.

[11] The process of gathering, verifying, and tabulating data, including sampling and surveying.

analysis,[12] policy analysis,[13] and policymaking[14]—are at best fragmented. Further strides are needed in integrating policy, operations, and controls. While these areas may not require a computer and telecommunications technology (e.g., specific equipment), it will be difficult to do meaningful academic and managerial research and teaching in the future without them.

Sufficient advances exist in microprocessors, distributed systems, minicomputers, digital switches, communication equipment, and the like to provide opportunities to train business specialists for the new industrial infrastructure. The latter provides one out of every six jobs in the United States. Shortage of communication specialists may be the limiting factor on some corporations' growth. A real concern now is with information systems management.

All too many graduates these days know almost nothing about the application of computers in business, or about systems analysis and design, or about privacy controls and user responsibilities, or about computer project management, or about data center management: information systems studies.[15]

The Information System Concept

Put simply, a "system" is a set of two or more components—people, things, and concepts—put together to accomplish a particular objective according to a predesigned plan. A system is a means for achieving purpose. Inherent in this concept are the ideas of interrelated elements, purpose, and strategy. Efficiently linking these components is the function of management, and implicit is the idea that the whole is something greater than the individual units considered separately. Today's progressive management, in providing organizational leadership and support for its members, must manage resources more effectively than ever in an increasingly complex environment. All resources must be related as a system. Information and communication are essential ingredients of this task.

An *information system* is a combination of people, data-processing equip-

---

[12] All further processing of data, including forecasting, mathematical modeling, and situation reporting.

[13] The identification of alternative ways of reaching goals; the assessment of their political, social, economic, environmental, and other effects; and the evaluation of ongoing programs.

[14] The process of deciding policy by weighing the alternatives and their consequences, as identified by the policy analysis.

[15] Ideas in the preceding sections were drawn from a discussion paper draft by Dean George Kozmetsky, Graduate School of Business, The University of Texas at Austin, entitled, "Computer and Telecommunication Academic Developments," undated.

ment, input-output devices, and communication facilities.[16] There are, of course, many information subsystems within a firm. Taken together they form a communication network through which timely information flows to both management and nonmanagement personnel—and in turn to the company's publics. Consequently, a total information system attempts to combine the various subsystems into an integrated network.

Information system research represents an approach toward studying a business organization or any part of a business organization. For the study, the system analyst attempts to group major decisions that business management must make (both formally and informally, explicitly and implicitly—thus all decisions) into categories that are based on a combination of (1) the general area that the decision concerns, (2) the time dimension of the decision process, and (3) similar requirements for information in the decision process.[17]

Prince states that

> A group of decisions possessing these three characteristics is the nucleus of an *information system.* The system analyst is concerned with tracing all information flows associated with this group of decisions and with the decision-making processes involved, regardless of the organizational boundaries that must be penetrated. This network of information flows that has been traced and charted for each group of related decisions constitutes a *system.* Since the focus of each network or *system* is upon "information flows," each network is called an *information system.*[18]

The information system approach is simply a special method for viewing and analyzing so that the system analyst can perceive each major information system within the business process. To perceive each major system, the analyst must be able to identify each major information flow. The latter represents the organization results of relating or matching the requirements for information with sources of data for each major decision. Management accomplishes this matching process by employing various sophisticated management-science tools and techniques.[19]

A management information system thus accumulates, processes, stores, and transmits data to "relevant" people in an organization, informing them and thereby becoming "information." But the present quest for "total systems" must be recognized as a hazardous quest for an ideal. If the use of the term "total systems" leads to the impression that integrating systems is easy—or if it is only a sales representative's slogan—then it should be discarded. It is better to think of a system as being only more complete or more comprehensive than an earlier process.

---

[16] Edgar C. Gentle, Jr., ed., *Data Communications in Business* (New York: American Telephone & Telegraph Co., 1965), p. 3.

[17] Thomas R. Prince, *Information Systems for Management Planning and Control,* (rev. ed.; Homewood, Ill.: Richard D. Irwin, Inc., 1970), p. 9.

[18] Ibid.

[19] Ibid.

The Computer and Its Role
in Information Systems

Although we are inclined to think of the computer as *the* one essential element, information systems are also necessary for small businesses that do not have or cannot afford computer hardware. For many companies it is axiomatic that management is not using one-tenth of the information that could be made available without a computer. At the same time, management of companies with computers seem to be deeply concerned that, unless they acquire additional computer capacity, the companies will be left behind. On the other hand, poor utilization of a computer does not automatically mean that the company has an ineffective management information system.

Management is concerned with the extent to which computers should be used to automate information systems. But a more vital concern, as Dearden points out, is the *adequacy* of the system in operation. It is vital to examine the quality of the system *first* and to consider automating it *second*. Not all management information can be improved by the use of a computer. Nor does all information generated by a computer qualify as management information.[20]

The most important consideration for the business manager, according to Dearden, is to have an effective management information system. To the extent that computers help in this task, one should use them. One should not make the mistake, however, of thinking that extensive computer use guarantees a good information system. For companies with computers, it is important that the computers be used effectively; but their effective use is less important than having an effective management information system.[21] The effectiveness of the one is not necessarily that of the other. After all, the computer is only a piece of hardware. It cannot think. Its efficiency depends on input and output. Humans determine the input and output through programming. For these reasons, management is forced to continue to struggle—aided by better tools—with many of the same problems of human communication that have occupied theorists from Aristotle to Whyte.

In an enterprise whose success hinges upon the coordination of the efforts of all its members, management depends completely on the quality, the amount, and the rate at which relevant information reaches it. The rest of the organization depends upon the efficiency with which management can deal with this information, reach conclusions, and make decisions. The goals an organization selects, the methods it applies, the effectiveness with which it improves its own procedures all hinge upon the quality and availability of the information in the system.

[20] John Dearden, F. Warren McFarlan, and William M. Zani, *Managing Computer-Based Information Systems* (Homewood, Ill.: Richard D. Irwin, Inc., 1971), p. 9

[21] Ibid., pp. 9–10.

No one needs to be reminded of the fantastic growth in computation brought about by the impact of computers. Calculation time is now measured in billionths of a second. Nevertheless, the information revolution brought about by technology created and continues to cause a severe management information crisis. Success or failure depends on how the boundaries between people and machines are joined. But such interface depends more upon experience with people, more specifically, with particular groups of people, than it does on technology. The computer enters the picture only as a means of improving the effectiveness of information systems. "The effectiveness of an information system," Drucker believes,

> depends on the willingness and ability to think through carefully what information is needed by whom for what purposes, and then on the systematic creation of communication among the various parties to the system as to the meaning of each specific input and output. The effectiveness, in other words, depends on the pre-establishment of communication.[22]

But, as with other management functions, a good program of information system control is not an event; it is an ongoing process.

Many managers admit that today's real problem is overall management (end-user based) and protection of automated information. New concepts are devised regularly by hardware and software suppliers in an attempt to help. For example, IBM's "Data System" concept is designed to give a more comprehensive approach to developing new applications faster and making them even more productive for the end users they serve. Data System is a larger concept than is data-base data communications because it uses more than data-base software merged with a data communication management system.

A data system environment also includes data administration and data delivery products, a number of interactive tools to help end-users solve problems, and a growing list of application products. Graphically, IBM's Data Systems Concept is conceived as illustrated in Figure 1-1. Such a data system is intended to mean more efficient administration of the data in a data base through a data dictionary, as well as improved delivery of those data to end-users through easy-to-use application development tools.[23]

We *have* an information explosion! Few would disagree. Every professional and executive suddenly have access to data in an exhaustible supply. Unfortunately, as the amount of the individual's information increases, the amount of his or her processing goes down—the net results of information overload. Drucker thus raises the question of what must be done to make this cornucopia of data redound to information, let along knowledge. Readily admitting that no one really has an answer, he concludes;

---

[22] Drucker, *Management*, p. 489.

[23] International Business Machines Corporation, *Data Processor*, December 1980, p. 25.

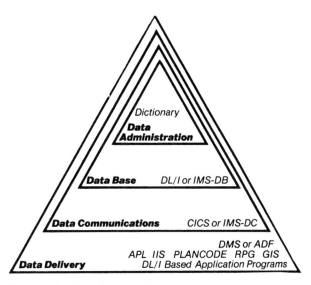

Figure 1-1   Data Systems Concept

Despite information theory and data processing, no one yet has actually seen, let alone used, an "information system" or a "data base." The one thing we do know, though, is that the abundance of information changes the communication problem and makes it both urgent and even less tractable.[24]

The management communication gap[25] resulting from the computer's impact (Figure 1-2) has more and more stifled the smooth flow of information between management and the generating sources of information. As the functions of management and computation has continued to grow in complexity, each has been unable to keep up with the other's jargon, techniques, and applications. More and better information does not solve the communication problem, does not bridge the communication gap, according to Drucker. He continues,

> On the contrary, the more information, the greater is the need for functioning and effective communication. The more information, in other words, the greater is the communication gap likely to be. The information explosion demands functioning communication.[26]

The gap can only be bridged successfully by a communication/information specialist—a person trained to know both management and end-user's needs

[24] Drucker, *Management*, p. 482.

[25] Coining of this phrase and the resulting diagram analysis are products of Harold J. Gallagher, president, Computer Logistics Corporation, Chicago, under the tutelage of William J. Lord, Jr., Graduate School of Business, University of Illinois, 1964.

[26] Drucker, *Management*, p. 491.

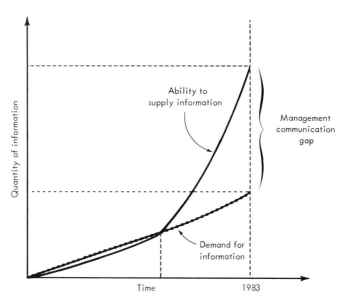

Figure 1-2   Impact of the gap between management communication and the demand for information

Here the quantity (relative) of information is shown as the dependent variable because of the great variability of supply and demand over the last few years.

Neither of the curves is intended to be similar to economic supply and demand curves. They differ in two ways: normal economic supply and demand curves have slopes of opposite sign, and price of the product is considered the independent variable.

The demand curve is slightly curvilinear because demand for information has increased at more than just a linear rate and certainly at more than a decreasing rate. This demand curve is a function of the knowledge of the (1) need, (2) source, and (3) use of information. Why? Because the more one is aware of what information is needed, where to get it, and how to use it once one has it, the greater one's demand for information will be. Therefore, demand = f (need + source + use).

The demand curve is drawn lower than the supply curve, not because management does not need the information, but simply because management does not yet know what to demand.

The supply curve is not "supply" alone. Rather it is the present "ability to supply" information. Supply curve is a function of (1) technological advances; (2) better educated, better trained personnel; (3) more complex organizational structures; and (4) available capital expenditures.

and the computer's capabilities. A person able to communicate effectively with both functions becomes in effect the information-processing center's cog—indispensable to the modern organization.

INFORMATION AS THE PRELUDE TO DECISION MAKING

No writing, whether transmitted as computer printout or by letter, memo, or report form, can be better than the information conveyed or the interpretation made. But two questions must first be answered if the information is to be useful in decision making: Who is the reader? What use will the reader make of the information?

Various types of information differ in aim: one is a by-product of routine activities; another is the result of investigations. Information becomes useful only (1) when it is aimed at some specific audience to whom the writer is responsible and (2) when it is verifiable fact or at least the conclusions of recognized specialists. Some information goes immediately to others in the writer's own field (to superiors or colleagues doing similar work) who use it as a basis for decisions (1) to continue a project; (2) to amplify a process in the firm's operation; (3) to stop, change, or abandon research underway; (4) to make a recommendation; (5) to try a different approach or a new technique, or one of a hundred other possibilities. Other reports go to readers not so familiar with the writer's field or subject or so well educated about it as is the writer. The writer's problem then becomes one of translating information into language that readers will understand.

Every reader is looking for something useful, to get it as easily as possible, to deal with the information quickly and efficiently, and to be free to go on with something else. The less time one forces a reader to spend on any transmitted information, the more valuable that person becomes as an information supplier.

Most people who work for a corporation, government, or industry are prime prospects for information reporting. The more responsible a person's job is, the greater the likelihood that informative writing will become an important aspect of it. Nearly all specialists become report writers or at least generators of vitally needed information for the firm's profitable functioning. Accountants; specialists in finance, marketing, production, personnel, transportation, and advertising; engineers; and researchers of all kinds usually discover that their reports represent the greater part of the work they do. Without good reports, their work may be wasted. Certainly no decision can be reached concerning such generators' efforts and contributions to the firm's progress if their reports are inadequate, vague, or unreadable.

Executives inevitably find reports and informative messages of all types and from all sources a necessary element in their work. They, too, must regularly report to others in the firm's hierarchy or to the stockholders. They must especially learn (1) how to gather information, (2) how to read and digest information reported by subordinates, and (3) how to summarize this quantity of information to make it meaningful for their decision making.

There is no room in the decision-making process, however, for two kinds of poor informational reporting assaulting business every day. One type is overloaded with facts but contains little or no interpretation. Masses of data are simply dumped in the reader's lap, and it is up to the reader to dig out the meaning. (Because most readers are busy people, they are never happy doing the work someone else was supposed to do for them.) The second type reads easily enough, simplifies, summarizes, and generalizes extremely well. Its only fault? No evidence to support any of the points reached. The report writer is responsible for the reliability and validity of what is reported. When evidence is rejected as unreliable, the writer must know why; often he or she should explain why to the reader. When the reporter accepts evidence and uses it to support conclusions, that writer is equally responsible for its truth and accuracy; usually the writer should justify the evaluations as well. Demand for efficient information handling is now so great that large corporations have communication specialists advising, instructing, and editing (in some cases ghost-writing) information that administrators must have and make use of. Those who have an ability to organize and write are in demand. A premium is paid for their services. If data are to help provide sound bases for the decision-making process, steps must be taken to assure their validity and applicability, such as checking the information against a prepared list of questions:

1. Are all the facts presented relevant to the problem?
2. Do they help to answer significant questions raised?
3. Is the evidence current or old? Is it adequate to justify the conclusions reached?
4. Have sources been investigated thoroughly?
5. Are the sources reputable, competent, reliable?
6. Have all important details been included?
7. Can a logical conclusion be reached from the information presented?
8. Would I feel safe in making a decision on the basis of the information presented here? Do I need more? Could I get more? Should I get more?

Readers expect facts and an interpretation of those facts. Decision makers must have the right kind of information fed to them at the right time; they simply cannot afford to sit idly by, nor can the complicated processes of industry halt while a writer takes a second try at providing more suitable information. Equally important, top management must know, recognize, and make use of the *key* communicators in their organization. They must have organizations conducive to proper information flow and must know the demands of their organization to plan for such flow. In short, decision makers must have an open organization—one in which barriers and bottlenecks are at a minimum—to ensure the right information at the right time for the right decision.

CLASSIFICATION OF COMMUNICATIONS BY PURPOSE

The further your education proceeds, the greater the tendency, and perhaps the need, to categorize your information. Categorizing may lead, however, to a rigidly "either/or" type of thinking, which sometimes is spoken of as "hardening of the categories."

Like most fields of specialization, scholars in business communication have attempted to find orderly means of classifying their subject matter and to simplify the analysis and study of it. Often the results have been the opposite. Numerous and overlapping classifications of letters and reports have caused confusion. Classifying reports, for example, calls for "both/and" thinking, since there is overlapping.

The tendency for letter classification by types (inquiries, orders, sales, credit, collections) has been extreme and has focused attention on minor makeup points rather than on major writing issues in the communication process.

Despite the fact that this text is not built around classifications, it may be helpful at this point to have a brief overview of how communications are classified according to *purpose*, the latter *the* basic key to any piece of effective writing.

For reports, title *key words* denote the piece's function: *progress, survey, study*—informational; *investigation, examination*—interpretative; and *advisability, feasibility, proposal, recommendation*—analytical. Any report research activity that seeks a solution to a specific business problem has the purpose of (1) *reaching a yes or no answer,* (2) *giving the better of two (or best of more) alternatives* in the comparative-evaluation inquiry, or (3) *determining how a phenomenon operates, what is desirable,* and *how to get there* in the descriptive-analytical investigation.

Letters and other informal messages, on the other hand, lend themselves basically to three categories, each with variations. First are those messages whose *primary* import is simply *informative.* Second are those whose purpose is essentially *persuasive.* Last are those messages that are *negative.*

Part I of this text is devoted to behavioral treatment of letters and other informal human relations messages on the basis of such a breakdown; Part II examines decision-making reports. Part III offers resource materials as reference services for the knowledgeable communicator.

Part I

BEHAVIORAL TREATMENT OF HUMAN-RELATIONS MESSAGES

The connection between experience, perception, and concept formation—that is, cognition—is, we now know, infinitely more subtle and richer than any earlier philosopher imagined.

Peter F. Drucker

2

Image Building: The Public Relations Function of Written Communication

*One cannot communicate just words . . . the whole
person always comes with them.*
Paraphrase of an old proverb

Goodwill is the priceless figure on a firm's asset ledger. It can be achieved in many ways for the business. Not the least of these is the image created by the company's letters. Whether the letter is sent internally to employees of the firm or externally to customers, suppliers, prospects, competitors—to anyone in any way concerned with the firm—part of that letter's function is image building. Sometimes the image achieved is good; often it is very poor.

What makes the right image?[1] Unfortunately, there is no one answer! Part of the picture is created by intangibles—just an impression. But we do know that many factors play a part in image building. Chief among these in letters are physical appearance, stylistic considerations, tone, and planning.

APPEARANCE

The quality and color of the paper; the preciseness of the fold; the placement of the letterhead and any items used along the top, down the side margins,

[1] For a broader perspective of image assimilation, especially as it relates to the corporation, people and society, the public, economic life, and so on, see Kenneth E. Boulding, *The Image* (Ann Arbor: University of Michigan Press, 1969).

or across the bottom; the placement of the copy on the page; and the style of the typeface—all are part of the physical impression.

When a person pulls a letter from its envelope, he or she forms an impression of it at once, whether favorable or otherwise, before reading a single word of copy. Subconsciously the eye appraises the physical aspects and the fingers register the paper quality. If mail has been received from this business house before, the receiver's mind neatly catalogs the present piece on the basis of previous experience. "Oh, yes, my college fraternity . . . wonder how much it is they want this time." Sometimes the receiver will glance at the return address on the envelope, guess what the letter is about, decide indifference to the contents, and throw the letter away without having read a word. It is important for a letter writer to have as many factors working in his or her favor as possible.

Attention to the smallest detail, which may seem unimportant at this stage of your study, goes a long way toward favorable reception of your letter. The more favorable the initial reaction you can elicit from your reader toward your letter, the more likely the receiver will be to read it and give attention to your message.

In your reader analysis (discussed later in this chapter), you will learn that the two greatest obstacles to overcome in your letter's success are not even part of the letter: first, you must recognize the reader's satisfaction with the status quo, and, second, you must be aware that every letter you write competes for the reader's time and attention and in many instances for his or her money. Also, if you originate the correspondence, your letter may be an intrusion on the reader.

Devices of all sorts have been created by business writers to add to the letter's personality, sophistication, and distinction. The distinctiveness should merely provide enough novelty to give your letter a better-than-average chance to attract attention and be read. We call it the interest-plus factor.

Some of the devices used are achieved with color and special layout on the stationery. If you choose to use color, you will need the advice of an expert. So much has been done in survey studies in recent years on the psychology of the right color for the right occasion, you will need more help than this text can offer here. Good taste in letterhead typeface (not too bold, not too demure) is more important than whether you used a colored stationery or not. An 8½ by 11 inch sheet of white, good-quality rag bond, 16 to 20 pound substance, is always proper. But the typeface on the letterhead must be equally in character if it is to create a feeling of pleasantness, care, and attention. It should be chosen with the image of the firm in mind. For such a "just right" letterhead you will need advice from your printer.

Many experts in the field of advertising and copywriting have played a large part in giving new impetus to the change in letter dress. Henry Hoke for years included in his *Reporter of Direct Mail Advertising* some of the more unusual and imaginative letter layout formats. The content of these letter illustrations always carried an explanation of the format and when and why it was used. Modifications were made in the customary salutation, complimentary close, layout, and conversational style in an attempt to achieve the naturalness and warmth you would hope to achieve if you were talking to the reader.

Dress in letters should be like that of an individual—enough to cover the subject interestingly and attractively but not so little or so gaudy as to call attention to itself. Whatever style you choose for letter format, it should always be in good taste. You never get a second chance to make a good first impression!

Rather than examine the various formats you could use, we believe it more practical to set up one of the popular conventional letter forms neatly and attractively and use it consistently throughout the text. Sample Form 2-1 is the modified block form. (Layout guide forms appear as part of Appendix A at the end of the text.) After you have begun to master your writing skill, you can begin to use your imagination in layout technique. Letter placement, indention, and punctuation are always decided as a matter of policy by the firm you work for. You will, of course, want to use the form and methods your employer prescribes.

If your letter is so long that it runs to two pages, equalize the copy on both sheets, using the same size block for both. Your second page needs identification in case it gets separated from the first. At the top of the selected block on page two (same line as for the date on the first page) repeat the first line of the inside address, followed by the date of the letter, and "page 2." Space four lines and continue the letter copy. An example of a two-page letter appears as Exhibit 2-1.

Although Sample Form 2-1 and Appendix A at the end of the text, present most of the standard letter parts and their proper placement, there are some additional aspects for you to consider to impress your reader favorably.

The *inside address* on your letter is the same as that used for the envelope and should be just as complete. It includes the name of the person to receive your letter (the addressee) with appropriate courtesy title—*Mr., Mrs., Ms., Dr., Professor*—and complete mailing address including the ZIP code. Part of the "right" impression your letter makes comes from spelling the addressee's name correctly; always check it carefully. If the receiver has a title indicating position—manager, president, executive secretary—you may add it (with an initial capital) following the recipient's name.

One of the newer trends for the inside address for formal and official correspondence is to place it at the end of the letter, double spaced below the typist's reference initials. Most of us continue to put it at the beginning of the letter, however.

The *salutation* is your greeting to the reader and is put a double space

THE UNIVERSITY OF TEXAS AT AUSTIN

COLLEGE OF BUSINESS ADMINISTRATION

AUSTIN, TEXAS 78712

Department of General Business
Business-Economics Building 600
Area Code 512, 471-3322

March 26, 19xx

Mr. A. B. Morrow
The Proctor & Gamble Distributing Company
301 East Sixth Street
Cincinnati, OH 45202

Dear Mr. Morrow:

Thank you for spending last Wednesday with the students in my nine
o'clock Business Communication class. These young adults were intensely interested in what you had to say, as I'm sure you noticed
from the number of questions raised.

Your very informative remarks were a welcomed break for all of us
from the usual class routine of studying principles and making
application of them to achieve more effectively written communication. It was pleasing to hear you stress the importance of good
writing on the job. While many of these college students have had
some part-time experience, the business world still remains "something out there" for a lot of others.

Your kindness in affording all of them an opportunity to interact
with a gentleman who is obviously very much on the way up the success ladder lent invaluable motivation and insight. Again we ap-
reciate your giving so generously of your time and expertise to
bring the business world into the classroom for an hour.

Sincerely yours

(Mrs.) Marjorie Jean Fuquay
Instructor

MJF:ss

Sample Form 2-1   Example of good letter placement, elite typeface, in the modified block format

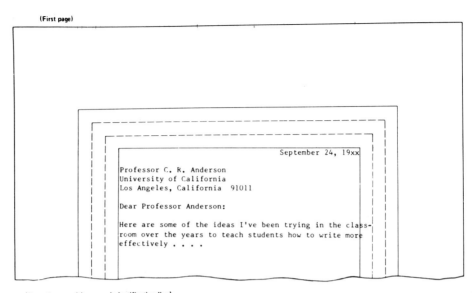

(First page)

September 24, 19xx

Professor C. R. Anderson
University of California
Los Angeles, California 91011

Dear Professor Anderson:

Here are some of the ideas I've been trying in the classroom over the years to teach students how to write more
effectively . . . .

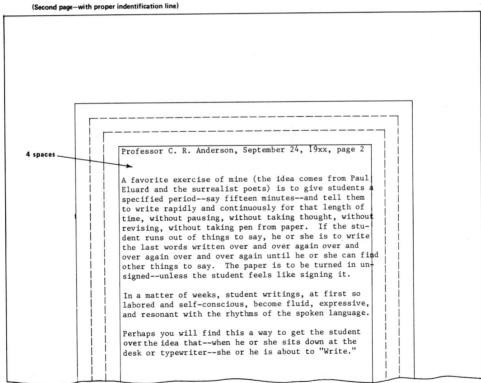

(Second page—with proper indentification line)

4 spaces

Professor C. R. Anderson, September 24, 19xx, page 2

A favorite exercise of mine (the idea comes from Paul
Eluard and the surrealist poets) is to give students a
specified period--say fifteen minutes--and tell them
to write rapidly and continuously for that length of
time, without pausing, without taking thought, without
revising, without taking pen from paper. If the student runs out of things to say, he or she is to write
the last words written over and over again over and
over again over and over again until he or she can find
other things to say. The paper is to be turned in un-
signed--unless the student feels like signing it.

In a matter of weeks, student writings, at first so
labored and self-conscious, become fluid, expressive,
and resonant with the rhythms of the spoken language.

Perhaps you will find this a way to get the student
over the idea that--when he or she sits down at the
desk or typewriter--she or he is about to "Write."

Exhibit 2-1   Portions of a two-page letter, with proper identification of the second page and
the copy divided about equally

below the inside address. By custom it has remained some form of "Dear [surname or given name]" followed by a colon as the preferred punctuation mark. Many good writers now feel that because this part of the letter should start conveying the naturalness and warmth the writer feels toward his or her reader, some change is in order. The basis for their belief is that the salutation can begin setting the tone for the entire letter. Thus the writer begins talking to the reader (just as though he or she might have walked into the office) with an appropriate remark that fits the situation. Such beginnings are referred to by the neologism *salutopenings*. Here are a few illustrations:

1. Your report, Mr. Seton,
    was superb. I certainly agree with the plans you've outlined for
    . . .
2. It's a pleasure, John,
    to answer your questions about . . .
3. Your request for credit, Miss Kirsopp,
    is receiving the careful consideration of our Credit Committee. You'll have their decision in three days.
    In the meantime, . . .

Possibilities for this type of letter opening are limited only by your imagination. And you can choose the form of punctuation following the reader's name to fit the occasion or mood. All these illustrations work the reader's name into the first line and replace the conventional "Dear——." If some of them look a little strange to you, remember that any change from the conventional is always a bit odd at first.

Although some of the standard *complimentary closes* will fit nicely with the salutopening, a little thought will provide you with a closing that fits the letter even better. Close with a friendly, personal statement; a question; an expression of appreciation; a positive idea; a strong suggestion; an appeal. If they are to fit in the normal complimentary close position, such endings should be only a few words long. For example,

Will I see you at the Convention?	Have a Safe Day!
Good luck on the campaign!	Let's grow with . . .
Call on us often.	Smile—you'll enjoy it.

Compliendings such as these are made to fit the occasion, not cut to a stereotyped phrase. Of course, you need to appraise the reader to know whether such use would be in good taste. If there is the slightest doubt that such a start or close would be offensive, use the conventional forms.

In using the standard salutation you should take care to match the complimentary close with it. Here are the main forms:

Dear [surname or given name]	Some form of *sincerely* or *cordially*. *Yours* is a part of this close with no punctuation after it. Capitalize the first word only.
With the impersonal (no name) salutation (Dear Sir, Gentlemen, Mesdames):	Some form of *truly*—Yours truly, Very truly yours, Yours very truly. (Same punctuation and capitalization rules apply.)

The main requirement for the *signature block* (blocked with the complimentary close line) is that your name be typed. Some penned signatures are almost impossible to decipher. Your title may go on the same line with the typed name if the title is short (separating the two with a comma) or on separate lines, blocked, with the comma omitted after the typed name. Typed signature lines—particularly for women's names—are needed to avoid problems that *might* occur for the person who replies. Some women correspondents use initials and last names only for their signatures on company correspondence. Others have names that are common to both sexes. In both cases the woman should have *Miss, Mrs.,* or *Ms.* typed preceding her name. Whether she uses the courtesy title in her penned signature is optional. No courtesy titles are ever used for men's signatures.

Sincerely yours   Cordially yours

(Miss) Katherine Anne Addams   (Mrs.) F. M. Colburn, Treasurer
Special Correspondent

Very truly yours

(Ms.) Pat E. Franks, President

The parts just treated are standard in almost all letters. Sometimes there are additional special parts used: the attention line, subject line, and postscripts. When a letter is addressed to the company and you want a particular individual to see it but do not know his or her name, you may use the attention line for the position, for example, Attention: Sales Manager. The attention line goes a double space below the last line of the address and just before the salutation.

Often the subject line saves words for you by telling your reader what your letter is all about and makes it easy to file for companies using "subject" files. Sometimes for emphasis the line is solid caps or underscored. It may be put above the salutation, on the same line with the salutation (if the subject line is short), or a double space below the salutation.

The *postscript*, according to *Webster's*, is "a note or series of notes appended to a completed letter, article, or book" (with or without the "P.S.").

But unlike the dictionary definition, the postscript is no longer used by modern writers "as an afterthought or to give supplementary information." A thoughtful writer plans the *entire* message from the first to the very last word to achieve a calculated effect upon the reader. Because the writer knows that the reader remembers most clearly and longest what is read last, the writer may place an important idea in the postscript to take advantage of this *impact* position. Frequent use of the device, however, especially to recurrent readers, will tend to dull its effectiveness.

WHAT IS A LETTER?

With thought given to the appearance of one's letters to create a favorable impression in image building, mention should be made of what a letter is before we consider the image impact of readability and planning.

The letter is the workhorse of business, the format of successful message sending for more purposes than any other single medium. Letters are the most adaptable, personal, flexible format that business uses. They can do a job by themselves or with almost any other media form. A letter can save a company money, or it can prove to be one of the most expensive media if thoughtlessly used. One particularly well-written, inclusive definition of a letter published years ago by St. John Associates, a top-flight New York letter shop (in *The Wolf Magazine of Letters*), puts it this way:

A LETTER IS MANY THINGS . . .

Ambassador and advocate, missionary and emissary, chronicler and counselor, salesman and statesman. It is as direct as a challenge, as disarming as a diplomat, as personal as a request. It can laugh, strut, amuse, assure, cheer, confront, congratulate, offer, urge, request. It can propose with the imperiousness of an emperor. It can ask with the diffidence of a courtier. It can leap boldly to a proposal, lie in wait for a foregone conclusion, whisper a suggestion, plead for a cause.

To the Postmaster General, a letter is most of the billion pieces of mail his department handles in the course of a year.

To the Salesperson, looking for a way to open a prospect's door, a letter is a chance to knock ahead of time.

To the Retailer, it is a way to let the best customers know that the store has something special for them.

To the Advertising Agency, it is a way to merchandise an idea, to announce a campaign, to register a favorable impression.

To the Business Executive, it is the way to say what he or she means and have it in writing—to reach the people he or she needs and wants to reach at the right time, at the right place, in the right way.

For the letter is, and always has been, *the next best thing to being there in person*. And in today's business world—when being there is as difficult as it is essential—as swift and inexpensive a device as a letter can put you almost anywhere you want to be by this time tomorrow.

READABILITY

Creating reader goodwill starts with the physical aspects of letters, but other factors are equally or more important. If appearance is the first test your letters must face, the second is that of readability. The ultimate success of a letter hinges on the tone and spirit in which the message is written. Although "tone and spirit" may be intangible, knowing some of the things that should or should not go into the letter makeup will help to achieve the all-important tone through style. A survey of generally applicable points as they relate to image building follows.

Your style should be unnoticed because of the clarity of the message. To write well and simply, train your mind to cut through surface details to get to your thoughts. You do not improve your writing by adding glittering gewgaws. Good writing comes from using the right word in the right place.

We are using the word *style* here much as we might were we discussing literary essays in which style is the reflection of the quality of the writers' ideas as transmitted through their personality and command of language. Your letters must reflect sincerity, tact, originality; they should be concise, interesting, easy to read, and understandable; they should be forceful, fluid, alive, warm, and friendly. Yet at the same time your letters should offer the greatest possible economy of the reader's time and attention.

No one wants to spend time reading your letter only to end with a puzzled expression of "What's that? What does it say?" If your reader does not understand what you say, he or she becomes irritated with you and *your* company for wasting time and imposing on his or her good nature. Nor does the reader want to read your letter only to be rebuffed or embarrassed by your thoughtless, harsh, sarcastic words.

Clarity of style cannot replace clarity of thought. Clear thinking (planning) leads to clear style. Style in letters is like the musical accompaniment to the words of a song—the music paints a picture of the words to convey a fuller meaning for the listener. So it is with the letter. The style paints a meaning to the message and like music should always be in *full* harmony for the most satisfying effect.

Modern writers prefer to rely mainly on the content of the message, using a simple, vivid, straightforward style rather than the artificial style of the person concerned more with *how* something is said than with *what* is said. Developing your own readable style is a matter of communicating your ideas to your reader by *arranging* your material, *selecting* the right words, and *constructing* your sentences carefully to achieve the desired results.

In *arranging* the material you want to convey to your reader, learn to depend upon the content to do the job by putting the emphasis where it belongs. Emphasis is achieved through (1) physical layout (copy arrangement, solid caps, enumerations, underlining) and (2) idea development.

Wilkinson et. al. suggest four ways of *emphasizing an idea:* (1) placement in the message, (2) amount of copy used, (3) types of sentence structure, and (4) choice of words.[2]

The points most favorable to your reader get first attention. You depend upon these to hold interest and need to place them in emphatic positions: the beginning and ending paragraphs of your letter. The reader remembers most thoroughly what is read first and last. Second in emphasis positions are the beginning and ending sentences of each paragraph.

Those points that you think need stressing get the most space in your coverage. For favorable points, select specific words and phrases conveying concrete ideas; for less stress and emphasis, use general or abstract words and phrases.

In sentence construction, dependent clauses give less emphasis than do independent clauses; therefore, to emphasize a point put it in an independent clause; for less stress, subordinate the point in a dependent structure.

Selecting the right words to convey your message also means eliminating those that do not work for you or that work against you. Avoid the stereotyped verbiage that too many business writers still use. Such words and phrases not only waste important space in your letter and spoil the "modern, efficient business" image but also destroy conciseness in your expression. Many are redundancies.

A list of some of the worst offenders follows. The "useless" words are italicized. In some cases you could eliminate the phrase and replace it with a single word (shown in parentheses beside some of the expressions).

a large number of (many)	during the time that (while)
at a later *date*	during *the year of* 1967
at all times (always)	enclosed *herewith*
attached *please find* (is)	enclosed *please find* (is)
at *the* present *time* (now)	feel free to (please)
cost *the sum of* $10	for the purpose of studying (to study)
due to the fact that (since, because)	fully cognizant of (aware)
duly noted	for this reason (therefore)

---

[2] C. W. Wilkinson, Peter B. Clarke, and Dorothy C. Menning Wilkinson, *Communicating Through Letters and Reports*, 7th ed. (Homewood, Ill.: Richard D. Irwin, Inc., 1980), p. 35.

hold in abeyance (postpone)

in accordance with

in a satisfactory manner (satisfactorily)

in order to

in regard to (regarding, about)

in response to, in reply to

in spite of the fact that (because, although)

in the amount of (for)

in the event that (if)

in the near future (soon)

in the neighborhood of (about)

in the same way (similarly)

is *at this time*

it is in recognition of this
fact that (therefore)

kind favor

kindly advise, kindly be advised

most of the time (usually)

of the above date

please *don't hesitate to* write

permit me to

pursuant to

re

recent date

regarding same

replying to

remember *the fact that*

the said policy, report

taking the liberty of

the writer

this is to

under separate cover

up to this writing

until *such time as* you

whether *or not*

with a view to

would like to . . . advise, state,
thank

with reference to

your letter of even date

Most verbal waste results from thoughtlessness and a reluctance to examine what you have written. It is difficult to be objective about your own letter compositions, but nothing will replace the willingness to apply commonsense criticism to your work. Here are other helpful suggestions:

1. Avoid faulty predication; use a *working* verb instead of the noun form expression:

give consideration to — consider

make an investigation — investigate

take into consideration — consider

may result in damage to — may damage

is indicative of the fact that — indicates

make the announcement that — announce

make an adjustment — adjust

come to the conclusion — conclude

come to a decision — decide

leave out of consideration — disregard

2. Don't qualify words needing no qualification:

winter *season*	*true* facts
exact replica	*two equal* halves (halved)
consensus *of opinion*	surrounded *on all sides*
merged *together*	*the month of* May
entirely completed	visible *to the eye*
hot water heater	eight *in number*
maximum *possible*	*qualified* expert
complete monopoly	*important* essential
neat *in appearance*	*first and* foremost
square *in shape*	*refuse and* decline
new innovations	red *in color*
absolutely essential	*the state of* Illinois
most unique	my *personal* opinion

3. Avoid worthless alternatives:

the purpose of this investigation *or study*
the purpose of this report *or paper*
any possible help *or assistance*
the value *and importance* of this effort
waste of power *or energy*
sincere and good wishes
appraise and determine the contract
deeds and actions
right and proper consideration

4. Watch compounds of *there, here,* and *where: thereof, therein, herein, wherein,* and so on:

An important factor in justifying an activity is the cost thereof.

5. Keep the needles in the sewing basket; think twice before using these words:

complain	inconvenience	misrepresented
complaint	misconception	mistrust
dissatisfied	misinformed	misunderstood
fail	misled	must
failure	unreasonable	neglect
uncalled for	unfair	unfortunately

Even the sentence context makes no difference:

We do not understand your *failure* to pay this premium.

Your *complaint* about the overcharge will have our careful attention.

We didn't think you were the *type* to *misunderstand* our intentions.

Although we could *ethically* deny your request, you may . . .

Frankly, we are *surprised* to see you take this attitude after we have tried so hard to please you.

We have your letter in which you *claim* you had already paid your account.

6.   Do not use up a good verb as the subject and then resort to a lifeless substitute such as *occurred, accomplished, maintained, effected, is:*

NOT: Cancellation of the notes was effected.

BUT: The notes were canceled.

Apart from deadwood words, doublets, needles, and wasted words, a simple writing style demands simple word choices. Not "we expect to *commence* work on the project immediately" but "we expect to *start* . . . ." Not "statistical range is used here because it *renders itself* easier to calculate than does the standard deviation" but "statistical range is used here because it *is* easier . . . ." If you equate simple words with the simpleton, we give this example of simple word choice with a style that vividly expresses the thought. Although the selection is 20 years old, and we have since put men on the moon, it remains a classic piece of good writing. It first appeared in a technical periodical.

Needed: More Talk, Less Communication*

Science—both the pure and the not so pure—is a vast book in which man writes all that he learns of the world that he can touch, see, hear, smell, or taste. At this hour in the life of Man, when he can hang in space to see the earth, and at the next stroke may touch the moon, those who write in this book must strive to use words that strike the minds of all men. For it may have come to this: to see is to live; to be blind is to die.

This is not to say that man will be saved by science. It *is* to say that each man must learn the lore of science, he must learn the thoughts of those who work in science, he must learn to put the fruits of science to their best use. But *if* he is to learn these things, the men of science must learn to speak to him in his own tongue.

*With thanks for the idea to Joseph A. Ecclesine's "Big Words Are for the Birds," in *Printers' Ink*, February 17, 1961.[3]

[3] A. Q. Mowbray, editorial in *Materials Research & Standards*, 1, no. 6 (June 1961), 447.

There is no law, so far as we know, that says a man must use short words when he talks and long ones when he writes. Nor is there a rule to force us to seek out the big word when our thoughts run deep. In fact, when the urge to tell burns in us, we turn to the short word. When we swear, we slash and bruise with the sharp, curt word. When we pray, our souls soar on wings of light, brief words. When we love, the sweet, spare words pierce straight to the heart. When we urge or drive, the words are pruned and clipped; they dart to the mind in one clean stroke. The long words bounce off the shell, weight us to the ground, probe in vain for the path to the heart or to the mind.

Each Man who takes his pen in hand to tell his peers what he has thought or done should make this pledge: "I swear that what I write will speak to men in words that they can seize and hold. I will shun the blunt, stiff, thick words that clot the brain and turn clear minds to sour ooze. I will cleave to the keen, terse, brisk words that bear true to the mark and shed a pure gleam in the dark. My one aim will be to see that those who scan my words can read my thought."

Quiz: Which word in this piece has more than one syllable?—AQM

Did you notice that only one polysyllabic word—*science*—is used in the entire passage? In your attempt to select the right word (the simple one) always use the familiar rather than the farfetched word, the concrete rather than the abstract word. You are writing to *express* thoughts, not to *impress* the reader with your mastery of a big vocabulary.

In *constructing* sentences for good functional prose and proper image building, learning to control their length is a basic requirement. Relatively short, simple sentences can make reading and understanding easier. Modern writers use great numbers of simple sentences to make their thoughts flow smoothly and quickly. A series of short, simple sentences in rapid succession tend to cause a choppy effect that may annoy your reader. The staccato effect of such sentence structure distracts the reader's attention, disturbs your copy flow, and in turn, affects your image as a writer.

Simple sentences, structurally equal to each other, however, may not produce clarity in the writing at all, for no one idea will stand out. To develop a central idea you will always need to use a balance of simple, compound, and complex sentence structures. Sentences must vary in length to save your reader from boredom. Every good writer maintains a balance in sentence structure although readers are rarely aware of it.

Here are some of the sentence techniques used in modern business writing to aid readability:

1. Preventing confusion and simplifying punctuation by using the "one thought-one sentence" formula.

2. Depending less on conjunctions to join separate ideas in a sentence and starting new sentences with conjunctions.

3. Reporting statistical survey findings in short, crisp sentences, like this:

> One survey set out to find whether matchbook messages made an impression on users. Approximately 5,000 people in 33 cities were asked whether they were carrying book matches. The 72.6 percent who answered affirmatively were asked to describe, without looking, the message on the matchbook in their pockets. Three out of eight were able to do so. Women fared better than men. People in medium and small cities fared better than those in large cities.

4. Deleting excessive prepositional phrases.

5. Using active rather than passive verb structure.

6. Avoiding overuse of verbal auxiliaries (would, could, should) and shifting to present tense whenever possible.

7. Eliminating elaborate windups at the start of sentences.

8. Keeping ideas moving swiftly and smoothly through strong topic sentence starts, connective words, and phrases.

9. Substituting participial phrases for relative clauses.

10. To would-be writers remarking, "I know what I want to say; I just don't know how to say it," we would respond with an old saying among writers: "Difficulties with a sentence mean confused thinking. It is not the sentence that needs straightening out; it is the thought behind it."

We have attempted to point out the limits of the permissible, to indicate the confines within which a writer may exercise choice in reporting that which custom and practice have made acceptable. It is not the business of the grammarian to impose personal taste as the only norm of good English.

A readable style comes from the "feel" one has for words and the way they go together. It is what comes "naturally" when you think of informal messages as your own *personal* communications to your readers. Style—like problem solving itself—cannot be acquired by slavish imitation of samples that you find in textbooks or in the files that you have access to in school or in business. For the important by-product of style is the mood created for your message's reception. A sales representative who is never heard, an ad never seen, a letter never read cannot get results.

Your reader brings to your writing limited mental power, using it in three ways: (1) in understanding the words you use, (2) in getting their relationships, and (3) in realizing the thought conveyed. You lose control[4] of your message when it is dropped into the mails. All you can depend upon for the message's right reception is the content, your preplanning, and the "mood" it establishes for the reader.

---

[4] By losing control we mean that you have no way of ensuring your reader's receptive mood for the message. For example, the reader who has just been promoted will approach the letter quite differently from the person who has just been laid off.

PLANNING

Planning is basic to any message's successful image building. You must decide *what* you want your communication to accomplish, *why*, and *how*. You can then begin implementing your objective. Since you must live with your decision, the planning process means, first, some tough-minded evaluation.

Analyzing the Situation

For success in your communication's mission, knowing what it is you are trying to accomplish is essential. The initial question to be answered is: *What is the message's purpose?* We get the answer through a series of additional questions:

    1. Is your purpose basically to convey positive information? (All communications are, or should be, informative. But we classify those messages whose major function is to inform—to make readers knowledgeable about something—as informative. We are therefore distinguishing between *intended* purposes of the message.)

    a. Will the message contain information that the reader will be pleased to have? Information that has been asked for?

    b. Will it indicate an action taken that the reader wanted done?

    2. Is your purpose basically persuasive?

    a. Will it have to convince the reader to do something you want him or her to do?

    b. Will it have to overcome the reader's resistance because of a likely unwillingness to act?

    3. Is your purpose basically to convey negative information?

    a. Will the message disappoint the reader? Not do what was asked?

    b. Will it likely make the reader angry, annoyed, or unhappy?

The specific strategies to be employed for handling messages indicated by these three purposive questions are the subjects of the following chapters.

Assembling the Facts

Once you have decided on your message's purpose, the next step is to gather *all* the necessary facts before you do anything else.

    A correspondent often picks up a letter, glances at it, and immediately begins to dictate a reply before having formed, either in mind or on paper, an outline of what he or she intends to cover. A letter written in this way can hardly be other than muddled. The writer may start with one thought, pass to a second, and then jump back to the first before going on to the third. The person who receives the resulting letter is confused and often irritated by such thoughtlessness, and loss of business may result. The impression created is not conducive to good image building for the writer or firm.

It is surprising how many facts do not get into a message even when they are known to the writer. The result of such failure to provide facts is that more communications are needed to clear up the situation. A message lacking all the facts is a luxury no company can afford. Part of the difficulty lies in relying on memory alone, but often it is just plain carelessness.

A simple procedure followed by many of the best correspondents in answering letters is to underscore the main points to be covered in their reply, to jot them down in the margin, or to use a pad for the list of essentials to be handled. These points can then be arranged in proper sequence according to the order of importance for the reader. For any complicated problem the procedure of outlining points and their subsequent arrangement for the best psychological effect is indispensable. The process also makes it easier to discard all irrelevant bits of information that will only occupy space, irritate your reader, perhaps cause confusion, and interfere with the conciseness of your message.

Analyzing Possible Reader Reaction

Equally important in determining your message's purpose is the question *"Who is your reader?"* What do you know about the intended reader? How will the recipient likely react to your message? What is his or her point of view on the subject you are writing about? How much does the reader know about it? What do you know about the reader from the letter? From the files you have on the reader? From your knowledge of behavioral research studies?

Perhaps no force in the interpersonal relations of business writing is more significant than that of persuasion. The American economic system rests in part upon the success of business communications in converting individuals to the points of view held by various business entities. A case might even be made that all business communication is persuasive, for persuasion takes many forms, from the emotional sales appeal to a straightforward presentation of facts in the informative message and in business reports. Objective reports, for example, can be defended as persuasive on the grounds that the objective presentation itself is aimed at convincing (persuading) the reader of its credibility through factual analysis.

As indicated already, the particular techniques and strategies employed for the various types of informal writing are discussed in the following chapters on the basis of whether the message intent is primarily informative, persuasive, or negative. At this point, however, we need to examine the concept of "persuasibility" as it relates to an awareness of the possible reactions of our readers toward written communication. One research study,[5] for example, indicates the presence of persuasibility as a content-free factor. It exists somewhat independently of the subject matter or of the appeals presented in any particular communication.

The treatise here is not intended to be exhaustive or all inclusive; yet there are many insights into a prospective reader's response that the writer can glean from a cursory exploration of behavioral research studies. Psychologists' and sociologists' explorations of what makes people react the way they do offer us much in understanding, appraising, and adapting to our readers when we write.

Promise of Reward and Ego-Involvement.

One who is persuaded anticipates a reward. It may or may not be realized; it may be fleeting or long lasting, socially acceptable or unacceptable, ethically right or wrong. Nonetheless, a reward is always anticipated.

What is the reward of being persuaded? It would appear from the studies[6] that one cannot be easily persuaded unless one anticipates some pleasurable experience as a result. It may be immediate and direct, or it may be a longed-for, long-range one, as in this illustration.

The attached outline of basic procedures used in our correspondence-improvement program is our sincere effort to help with your preliminary planning.	(Although the reader may anticipate an immediate reward, the long-range benefit comes from making use of what we have done.)

Thus a message (stimulus) is presented; the reader reacts positively to it; his or her reaction results in a pleasurable experience. When the reinforcement is not what the reader anticipates, the strength of the persuasion process is weakened, at least so far as future similar persuasion is concerned. We tend to build up an immunity to certain pleas (stimuli), or these same stimuli tend to elicit negative rather than positive reactions.

Promise of reward also makes the reader more attentive to what is read. That is why in informative messages we start with the heart of the message and emphasize *what it means* in terms of the reader's benefit. This procedure arouses the desire to read and understand the message. Early promise of reward (for reader emphasis)—even when only implied—helps to ensure careful reading of the rest of the message, too, as in this illustration:

---

[5] Irving L. Janis et al., *Personality and Persuasibility* (New Haven, Conn.: Yale University Press, 1959).

[6] James Deese, *The Psychology of Learning*, 3d. ed. (New York: McGraw-Hill Book Company, 1967), says, for example, that a reinforcement (a reward) is any stimulus that can increase the strength of a response when it is presented in close temporal conjunction with the occurrence of that response and that rewards are the most important determiners of learned behavior.

You're certainly right in your wish to preserve the fine protection your life policy has brought you for ten years.	(Agreement with reader's concern with an implication he or she can continue, but the reader has to read on to see how the reward is regained by reinstating the lapsed policy.)

By anticipating something pleasurable from reading the message, we are "set" to respond positively. In business writing terms this pleasure principle is simply the extension of the technique known as the *you-viewpoint*. It has its origin in the *id*.

The *id*—that part of our psyche that is regarded as the reservoir of the libido (the driving force behind all human activity) and the source of instinctive energy—is dominated by the pleasure principle and impulsive wishing. Its impulses are controlled through the development of the ego and the superego. That part of our psyche that, developing from the id, experiences the external world through the senses and consciously controls the impulses of the id, we call the *ego*. It is the individual's self-awareness.

When motivated intrinsically, therefore, we tend to act from the knowledge that accomplishment of a task is going to satisfy some goal. Such motivation is easy to make use of in business writing situations when there is ordinarily no balking anticipated in the reader's response to the desired action as in this illustration:

Will you please help us set up a correspondence-improvement program similar to the one that has proved so successful for your firm?	(Request for a favor, direct style, for which little resistance is anticipated.)

We anticipate that our reader will do what we ask partly because it is expected as a natural consequence of carrying on business or because of the position the reader occupies in business and partly from a sense of his or her feeling of accomplishment from helping us or of making a worthwhile contribution by what is done.

Extrinsic motivation, however, is aimed at getting an individual to engage in an action that, at the moment, might seem unappealing; thus, to persuade we use praise, promise, and ego-involvement. A letter trying to get a sales representative to submit weekly reports on time, for instance, might best begin:

Your fine record as a salesman since you've been with the firm, Bob, has no doubt convinced you of the importance of the *psychological moment*.	(Making use of the sales representative's sense of pride and planting a key idea around which the request may be built.)

Those individuals who are a part of the loosely knit social structure we may refer to as "upwardly mobile" are influenced positively when the illusion of prestige is present, whereas those in a relatively stable socioeconomic level may react negatively to such an approach. The difference lies in the concept of the future held by these two contrasting social entities. The upwardly mobile group often perceives of tomorrow as being better than today; their aspirations mold their actions. They like to conceive of themselves as surrounded by evidence today of that which will be real tomorrow.

On the other hand, members of the more stable, static working class often are likely to view tomorrow as a duplicate of today. Any approach to persuasibility should reflect immediate use of whatever the message proposes. If traces of an approach concerned with social upward mobility are apparent in the communication, the reaction on the part of the static group is likely to be wonder or frustration rather than acquisitiveness.[7] What this means in terms of a faulty situation and reader analysis (prior to writing) is that the communicator will hold one view, the reader another, and the views will be in direct conflict.

Readers' Perceptions of the Writer.   Persuasibility is dependent also upon how readers perceive the writer—on how credible the writer is. The writer's interest as perceived by the readers, his or her post or business designation and reputation play a cardinal role in the process of bringing the reader over to the writer's side. The writer provides readers with clues as to trustworthiness, intentions, and affiliations.

Merely perceiving a particular writer as advocating something new will be sufficient to induce acceptance in some individuals. Reader personality traits in this situation are authoritarian oriented. The reader places confidence in the writer and his or her opinion because the writer's position or designation deems that person to be an "authority."

If readers are inner directed, their value systems stress personal goals and standards, whereas readers who are other directed place more emphasis on group conformity and adaptation. Other-directedness is a part of insecurity, and individuals with such a personality trait have a need for group acceptance; they become acquisitive.

Unbiased, logical, authoritative, in agreement with my experience and ob servations—such words are related positively to persuasibility for the reader who perceives the writer as being sincere, versed in his or her subject (an authority), and not obviously biased. It is therefore important for the writer not only to present to the reader a worthwhile self-image, but to size up the reader's desires so that the message can reflect them. Any pretense at being something less than worthwhile leads to negative action or lack of action on the reader's part.

---

[7] These conclusions and others in this section are supported by Luther A. Brock's study "An Inquiry into Selected Factors of the Process of Persuasion with Emphasis on the Nature of Persuasion in Written Business Communications" (unpublished Ph.D. dissertation, Louisiana State University, Baton Rouge, 1963).

Persons with low self-esteem are predisposed to high persuasibility. Their feelings of shyness, personal inadequacy, and social inhibition in coping with everyday situations make them prone to change their opinions more readily than do others when presented with persuasive communications.[8] Their tendency to yield to the arguments and conclusions presented in the message is a form of social compliance that stems from an inability to tolerate anticipated disapproval for deviating from the opinion held by others. Such persons perceive in a writer the power to harm and are induced outwardly to conform to escape reprisal. Or they may perceive the writer as a power to help—a particularly potent source of influence—and such perception engenders hopes, heightens self-confidence, increases willingness to modify attitudes and behavior. At the same time such perception strengthens the reader's sense of dependency without directly stirring up conflicting emotions.[9] The ego thus uses a mechanism known as the "concept of compensation" to defend itself against anxiety caused by a feeling of insecurity through making extra effort in an area of real or fancied weakness.

Readers' Assumptions about Their Environments. A general agreement as a result of research studies is that individuals' actions are governed by their assumptions about the environment—from a continuum of experiences—in which they live. Through trial and error, through recognition of cause and effect, through frustration at the frequent lack of consistency in action and result, individuals impose some sort of order on their existence. In fact, for people to function at all, order and regularity must be imposed on the welter of experiences impinging upon them. From experience, people develop a set of more or less implicit assumptions about the nature of the world in which they live that enables them to help predict the behavior of others and the outcome of their own actions. Through conditioning people respond much the same way each time to the same stimulus.

Deep-seated emotional feelings and conflicts resulting from the reader's experiences account for remembering well, forgetting easily, or for an intermediate-stage reaction as the result of the stimuli presented through written messages. In the reader's mind there is constant tension between the desire for security and the desire for adventure. The reader's insecurity and an unorthodox or unrealistic "assumptive world" are partners. People who suffer from feelings of inferiority govern their activities according to certain untrue assumptions about themselves and the environment. These people compare their personal makeups with those of others, and the comparison often leads to an exaggerated (though real to the individual), negative personal estimate. People look for panaceas, yet often realize the futility of the

---

[8] Ideas are paraphrased from Carl I. Hovland, Irving L. Janis, and Harold H. Kelley, *Communication and Persuasion* (New Haven, Conn.: Yale University Press, 1961).

[9] Ideas paraphrased from Jerome D. Frank. *Persuasion and Healing: A Comparative Study of Psychotherapy,* rev. ed. (Baltimore: Johns Hopkins University Press, 1973), p. 34.

quest; thus, we, as writers, take the cue of offering hope, encouragement, and benefit in adapting our message presentation, as in this example:

Your life policy, protected by your 30-day grace clause, is still in force, offering you the full benefits applied for.	(Assurance to a worried reader who has passed up a premium-paying date and perhaps fears the company has canceled protection. After all, the person may reason, the policy is small and the company certainly is too large to be concerned about him or her.)

The desire to "belong"—an elemental human desire—is related directly to the individual's feeling of inadequacy. What peers accept, this person accepts. If a reader is more authoritarian oriented (as opposed to peer conscious), however, the message development on the basis of prestige and high credibility of information is likely to be more fruitful. Elements of the writer's prestige play an important role in the reader's reaction. So strong a factor is it, that readers sometimes accept the writer's word without giving adequate thought to the message. The prestige of the source of a suggestion provides a context for the statement from which the reader derives its meaning. The essential meaning of a message is tied so closely with the communicator in some situations that, if the recipients do not know who the communicator is, they fail to perceive the meaning. The situation is analogous to an artist's name on a painting. The amount of prestige associated with the artist determines the value of the painting. Similarly, dogmatic statements attributed to well-liked people (those with prestige) are more likely to gain acceptance than are those by disliked people.

Psychological Maturity.   The more psychologically mature the individual, the more successful the writer will be with developed rational approaches rather than emotional ones. Although mature individuals are still emotional beings, because of their psychological maturity they are susceptible to a presentation that respects intelligence and discretion. The contrary is also true. Because of a less mature personality structure, some individuals are more susceptible to emotionally geared presentations.

Make no mistake. Ego-involvement is not to be reckoned with lightly in your relationship with another through the written message. Failure to make adequate provision for it can doom your message from the start. For example, in writing to an intellectually mature person, one who takes pride in the ability to reason, to see through lightly veiled manipulations of sensory appeals, you are likely to offend rather than sway to your side if you choose highly charged language. The research of Hovland et. al. tends to support this point with two general conclusions:

    1. Because of their ability to draw valid inferences, persons with high intellect are more likely to be influenced than are low-intellect individ-

uals when exposed to communication that relies primarily on impressive logical arguments.

2. Because of their superior critical ability, persons with high intellect will tend to be less influenced than will those with low intelligence when exposed to communications that relies primarily on keenly thought out emotional appeals, unsupported generalities, or illogical, irrelevant argumentation.[10]

Members of higher-income families buy gourmet foods, spend more for costlier foods, and purchase much of the nation's luxury products. They have more time to devote to reading promotional literature and more leisure in looking and shopping.[11]

The Interplay of Reader and Writer Role Relationships.   In audience analysis prior to the actual writing, the communicator will do well to determine from the research tools possessed (opinion studies and market surveys, for example) how the reader may perceive the writer and the organization being represented. Firm records, simple observation, and reflection provide clues. If the writer enjoys a high reputation (e.g., trustworthy and creditable), the major problem is that of presenting the message in such a way that the image already existing will be perpetuated. If the analysis reveals that the reader may view the individual or the organization as less than completely credible, then the writer's chore of reversing the image is a sizable one.

Both writer and reader operate under multifaceted behavior relationships. Their reactions are the sum of their conditioning experiences *and* the interplay of their innate personality structures—extroversion, introversion, emotionalism, rationalization. What the individual writes for personal use is solely the expression of experience. When the person writes for a business concern, however, he or she looks to the company for work approval and for expectations of reward. The person tends to reflect company ideas and attitudes. (Similarly, the reader's reactions to the written message are influenced by his or her own firm's ideas and attitudes.)

In the classroom student-teacher relationship, on the other hand, the writer is not an independent performer. No matter who the assumed reader is for the writing problem, the student anticipates, first, how the teacher wants the material to be written. The person looks to the teacher for approval of this work and for his or her grade.

When entering the business world, the student is sometimes disillusioned, since what pleased the teacher is not necessarily what now pleases the employer. And what pleases the employer is not necessarily what will be most effective in bringing about the desired response from the reader; thus,

[10] Hovland et al., *Communication and Persuasion*, p. 183.

[11] Janet Wolff, *What Makes Women Buy* (New York: McGraw-Hill Book Company, 1961), pp. 17, 39.

the writer-employee finds it necessary to adjust performance to both the employer and the reader.

If an understanding of human nature and a watchful eye in observing reactions to certain stimuli in relation to the company's products or service use have been achieved, the writer can often gain insight into how best to approach the reader for maximum influence in the written presentation. By observing the merchandise returned to a store, the trend in claims and adjustments, the number and type of other complaints, trends in sales, and responses to various advertisements, for instance, the writer begins to comprehend the public image of the store. And with a clear understanding of the store's perceived image, the writer can gauge efforts accordingly.

An undue amount of effort in maintaining the image may influence negatively, however: the reader may perceive the writer as being defensive because the writer makes too great an effort to have the reader believe and trust in the writer and his or her firm. Is there something to hide?

Findings from behavioral research indicate clearly that enhancing a firm's image should be a part of the firm's total communication improvement effort. The better the firm's image, the better it can communicate convincingly. *A message will often be viewed and reacted to largely in terms of the credibility of its source alone.*

Some types of communication tend to be negatively classified by the reader. We tend to "categorize" or "label" certain messages (and individuals) to immunize ourselves against them, to protect ourselves from unwanted changes or associations. We perpetuate this stereotyping through such an action as reading newspapers whose editorial policies agree with our own. But we can accept or reject a message on the basis of more general characteristics. Poorly done third-class direct mail advertising is a good example. We feel an automatic negative response the moment we take it from the mailbox. And it has an associative effect with other media—newspaper, radio, TV, and magazine advertising.

Similarly, one should not take for granted that income level, social status, avocation, or any other stereotyping category automatically means that the individual is a particular personality type. There are many exceptions to the generalized label. When the business writer assumes that because the reader is a low-income individual and should automatically have the "common person" approach, the writer may be making a mistake that produces a negative response. For example, if the writer knew more about the reader, which is very possible in writing to employees, the writer might realize that the recipient would be more susceptible to persuasion by an authority-figure than by a peer-figure approach.

Many people who earn low salaries and who are not highly educated feel no inadequacy nor are they highly emotional. To assume from an initial audience analysis that certain readers fit a certain label will likely result in ineffective communication. For the individual who is leader-follower oriented and who is concerned about today, whereas yesterday is only a memory, tomorrow simply a hope, timing the communication to coincide with the exact time of this person's decision and action is vital to the message's success. If the communication arrives too far in advance, it will be ignored or forgotten. If it is overly delayed, the recipient may have already been misinformed or have taken an opposing position on the basis of information acquired from other sources.

The fact is that all humans are not created equal. They are not equal in emotional development or in persuasibility. A writer must accept the chore of doing as keen an audience analysis as possible. The message can only be as effective as the writer's realization of the roles that the writer and the reader play in the total process.

Added to the difficulty of sizing up your reader is the semantic problem that the writer must deal with in conveying a message to the reader. The writer must not only know what to say but must also find a suitable set of words to give these thoughts expression. Giving precision to the message's purpose is one problem; it is yet another for the writer to couch the thoughts in terms of interest, warmth, conviction, and proper image building that will bring the desired response from the reader. With the knowledge of the processes of influencing people, the writer makes use of suggestion (testimonials, creating a favorable image), imitation (toward the herd instinct for support after the image is created), exhortation (emotionalism), argumentation, promotion, logic, and correct timing to enhance a favorable communication image and reception.

Pressures exerted by the writer's organization; the writer's attitude toward the subject matter of the message, toward himself or herself and toward the reader; the writer's limitations of vocabulary; sense of style; and usage are all part of the interplay of forces making the job of writers a difficult one. The message's content is chosen on the basis of such factors as purpose, the reader's needs and expectations, the amount of information available, the organization's customs and policies regarding its written communications, the medium that carries the message, and the timing. And the writer couches that message in the language that is anticipated to be conducive to the reader's favorable response.

Some business writing theorists and practitioners suggest that the writer should develop emotional appeals for action first and then reinforce these appeals through the development of rational ones. The rationale is that emotional appeals cause the reader to desire to do that which the writer wants done, and the logical appeals give the reader a means of rationalizing emotional desires.

What the writer intuitively knows or assumes about the reader will have much to do with the success of the message as well, for, as already pointed out, the reader's attitudes and actions, like the writer's, are governed largely by the employing company. In an attempt to understand, explain, and anticipate the behavior of a reader, the writer may benefit much from making inferences from personal experiences. There are times, however, when the writer has no experience to match that of the reader. Reader concept—and the reader's probable reaction—must then be drawn on some other, more sophisticated basis. Empathizing with the reader's position, the writer needs to know a good deal about his or her own emotional makeup, the reader's, and the situation involved in the particular communication.

Adapting to Your Specific Reader

The most successful writers are those who are able to visualize the person to whom they are writing, to reconstruct that person's mode of living and habits of thought, and to adapt their messages to that individual. The writer's own self-centeredness, insincerity, outspokenness, stubbornness, and tact-lessness in writing are a few of the reasons why adapting the letter to the reader is often ignored.

Writing good letters requires imagination, but, by taking a safe middle-of-the-road stand, a correspondent *can* write in exactly the same tone and spirit to everyone with whom the company does business and not give offense. The latter is, therefore, quite the reverse of reader adaptation. Can you imagine a letter suitable for a small retailer in a town in the Midwest making a favorable impression on a large retailer in New York, or a letter that one might send to a New England farmer being appropriate for an attorney in Chicago? Letters written so that they might be intended for anyone often have interest and appeal for none.

Only when you have a mental picture of your reader are you ready to think about jotting down the points of your message in some order and phrasing those thoughts for a message that will receive a favorable reception.

Positive versus Negative Phrasing.   A negative attitude toward a reader, product, or service may paralyze a writer's imagination to such an extent that the entire letter is negative. A pessimistic outlook, an overcautious, indecisive, or insecure attitude toward a situation will likely result in a helpless or grudging tone. The positive approach, of course, is more forceful and effective than a negative one. The letter that can say "yes" is the easiest kind of letter to write; but many business situations demand that the writer often say "no." Saying "no" in positive words usually is simply a matter of changing a negative thought to a positive one, as illustrated in these examples:

Negative:	We cannot ship the chaise longue until June 1.
Positive:	Your chaise longue will be shipped June 1.
Negative:	We cannot quote a price on the contract until specifications have been completed by our engineers.

Positive:	We shall be happy to quote you a price on the contract just as soon as specifications have been completed by our engineers.
Negative:	The inconvenience and undependability of an old-fashioned water heater . . .
Positive:	The modern miracle that delivers every gallon of water steaming hot the way you want it . . .

Excessive negatives work against the promotion of good human relations and tend to destroy a good image of the writer and the firm. It sounds begrudging to write

Drivers are not eligible for safe driving awards until they have completed two years of company driving.

A slight change to positive emphasis will ensure a more favorable reception:

Drivers are eligible for safe driving awards after completing [or when they complete] two years of company driving.

When a customer writes to learn about joining a mutual fund and receives a reply that starts out with negative emphasis—

You cannot join our mutual fund until you contribute a minimum of $300

—the prospect's interest in joining the fund is likely to curdle. By rewriting, we raise the human quotient of that sentence, this way:

Your membership in [name of the fund] is automatic when you contribute the initial $300-minimum fee.

All of us respond more readily and more favorably to positive ideas than to negative ones. We like cheerful, pleasant, positive thoughts because they give us a feeling of well-being. The unpleasant, unhappy, awesome aspects of the negative spell out failure. And we want our name and actions associated with success. Expressing the positive rather than the negative, then, means, for the business writer, staying optimistic, always seeing the brighter side of every situation, and superimposing the positive picture over the negative. How? Sometimes we can completely eliminate the negative altogether; other times to minimize its import we subordinate it. We stress what something *is* rather than what it *is not*. We emphasize what a service, product, or firm *can* and *will do* for the reader instead of what it *cannot do*. We let action and explanation replace inaction and apology. And always we avoid words that carry uncomplimentary insinuation or unpleasant connotations. For example, a cemetery monument manufacturer wrote a customer to thank him for an order. In the letter was this familiar close:

We hope to serve you again in the future—and often.

The writer might as well have said, "Many Happy Funerals to you!"[12] Whether they are purely negative in connotation or simply tactless word choices, they often defeat the purpose of the letter. To see whether a word or a phrase in your writing might humiliate, belittle, or chasten your reader, try putting yourself in the receiving position. How would you feel if you had been the policyholder receiving this letter written by an executive of a large insurance company?

> As you know, your policy provides . . . etc. Consequently, no benefits are payable under this claim.

The policyholder, burned to a crisp, replied:

> Obviously, we did not know, nor did your agent know, or we would not have spent the time and trouble to make out this claim. In effect, what you are saying to us is this: you are just plain stupid—you know you didn't have a claim.[13]

Advertising copywriters long ago took the cue in avoiding the denied negative. It is still good advice for modern-day writers who would build good images through writing. No matter how strong your statement denying that your product or service is *not* such and such, the fact that you put the negative idea into words (or feel defensive enough to make a statement about it) plants the seed of doubt in your reader's mind. The fact that you write "Latho-Supreme will not dry out on your face like other ordinary shaving creams," invites your reader to challenge this denial. The challenging question—a special form of the negative—should be avoided as well, since it, too, invites the reader's denial. "Wouldn't you rather . . ." will perhaps elicit several more promising alternatives in the reader's mind than the one you propose. To the question, "What could be better than . . . ," the reader can probably think up at least two that are better and maybe even a half dozen if the mind is really set to the task. The fact that you have flung the challenge with "Why not get . . ." may be all the reader needs to begin thinking up reasons for not doing what you propose or suggest. The writer's use of such negatively invited responses causes the reader to fight against the idea the message attempts to convey.

Service for the Reader: The You-Attitude.   Your attempt at positive rather than negative statements, your word choice, controlling sentence length, planning, and adapting your language and style to your reader are a culmination and visible demonstration of one of letter writing's chief principles—"the you-attitude." This technique is a matter of seeing and presenting ideas from the reader's point of view. It is the expression of *your*

---

[12] From *Better Letters*, a publication of The Economics Press, Inc., Fairfield, N.J., BL 30, n.d.

[13] Ibid.

attitude toward the reader. And, as far as the reader's reaction is concerned, it is often more important than what is said.

It is far easier to write from your own vantage point than to be concerned with your reader's interests, personality traits, and particular needs. Quite without the writer's realizing it, this self-centered feeling creeps into the letter. Just how selfish the average human is is a subject of endless debate, but there can be little question that you are the person who means the most to you.

We are naturally self-centered. We tend to think in terms of our own selfish interest about everything that makes up our world. This YOU is the writer's YOU. But it is *YOU*, the reader, with whom the writer must be concerned in business writing. All writers have a group of interests centering in their own welfares, those of friends, of family, and of business. Writers and readers are self interested. Writers forget that all-important principle of influencing people to think, to feel, to act as many want them to, to present what they desire in terms of the self-interest of the reader.

When you write to a banker you *are* a banker; when you write to a homemaker you *are* a homemaker; when you write to a business executive you *are* a business executive. The test of genuine imagination is the power to step across space and put yourself into the reader's shoes—to be empathic. How would you react to what you have said if you were the reader of your message? What does the reader want more than anything else? How can you make that person feel good? What should you do to avoid annoying?

GOODWILL LETTERS

Each letter you write offers you a chance to display your imagination, your thoughtfulness, your concern for your company's success, and your ability as a letter craftsman. Dashing off a batch of routine letters is a trap into which many have fallen. The writer does not stop to think that what he or she is really doing is talking on paper to another human being.

Goodwill, of course, is not restricted to the special type of letter known as the "goodwill message," for goodwill has its rightful place in whatever is written. Certain situations, however, call for letters that have as their sole purpose the expressing of thanks, extending condolences, or offering congratulations: goodwill letters. They can be, and often are, the chief means a firm uses for image building.

Goodwill is achieved in letters by using the fundamental principles already pointed out in this chapter. An effective writer also gives attention to these points:

1.   Remember that it is the reader who counts; make it a personal—not a form—message.

2.   Be sincere.

3.   Make the person think well of himself or herself.

4.   Meet the recipient "face to face."

5.   Be serious but not deadly serious.

6.   Be confident but modest.

7.   Be cordial.

8.   Be interested.

9.   Make the letter radiate warmth and friendship.

10.   Wherever possible, have the goodwill letter signed by someone in authority. A letter signed by the president, vice-president, general manager, or other ranking officer will create more goodwill than will one that is signed by a person holding a modest title or no title at all.

Letters to Established Customers

A few words of appreciation and thanks to an old customer can be written at any time. Such letters should express in simple, direct language the sincere appreciation of the writer *without some ulterior motive* (a chance for a sales talk, for instance). More and more companies are realizing that they have been taking their regular patrons too much for granted and have overlooked opportunities to retain the goodwill of established, steady customers.

Many companies seek accounts that they have lost with letters aimed at recapturing lost goodwill but, while accounts are active, neglect to write letters that would have kept them from becoming inactive. Customers like to be flattered, to be made to feel important, and to be given special attention by any company. Although it is not practical to pamper each customer as though the person were a spoiled child, business is afforded many opportunities for writing to established customers. One such opportunity is the appreciation for the customer's patronage when the customer has met all obligations under an installment purchase contract, an extended payment plan, or an open account—paid consistently on time. The example that follows is typical of such goodwill notes:

Dear Mr. Goldsmith:

This is the kind of letter I enjoy writing most. Your fully paid Accommodation Coupon Book account has just been placed on my desk, and my personal thanks go to you for the prompt way you've cared for this responsibility.

We hope to enjoy the privilege of serving you again soon. Our facilities of credit are always here for your use.

Sincerely yours

A letter of appreciation, however, can be written at any time to anyone, whether it is a thank you for prompt payment, a thank you for a large order, a gift, a favor, or just an excuse for writing to let the person know that he or she is important to you.

The objectives of the thank-you letter are these:

1. To place a value on the favor or gift in warm, fresh phraseology that removes it from the realm of routine.

2. To support the open expression of gratefulness with specific reasons for gratitude as a means of establishing the writer's sincerity.

3. To maintain the proper restraint so that the reader is not embarrassed with an enthusiasm out of proportion to the size of the gift or favor.

4. To make the reader feel like a nice person, with a carry-over to any other individuals involved in the favor.

5. To avoid spoiling the reader's pleasure in the act by pointing up specifically what the writer expects to do in return.

Compare the two versions of the letter that follow on the basis of the objectives just set forth:

Writer Crowding into First Position
Dear Sir:
On behalf of the members of the School Board and the administrators of Arlington Public Schools, may we take this opportunity to thank you for the Edna Lucas Journalism Scholarship so generously donated by you?

Your continued support of educational activities through the years is indeed appreciated.

The Reader's Act in the Spotlight
Dear Mr. Huntington:
Your generous gift of the Edna Lucas Journalism Scholarship is but another evidence of your fine public spirit, which has benefited Arlington citizens for many years.

You'll be quite proud, we feel sure, of the first winner, John B. Sax, whom you afforded the opportunity to develop his talents at the University of Missouri.

We of the School Board and Administration of Arlington Public Schools certainly appreciate your fine gesture.

Here is a goodwill message (to be bound with those from other people) to be presented to a good friend and colleague being honored upon retirement:

"The reward of a thing well done is to have done it"—*to quote Emerson*—

And, Gene Nelson,

you have done it! Much, much more than you can be aware of even in your age of reflection . . . called "retirement."

You've been colleague, supporter, counselor, spirit booster, comforter— but most of all, a friend! It has been a pleasure for me to have worked with you, to have taught two of your sons, and to have you and Rose as friends over the years. Indomitable in spirit, you've kept a calm head while those of us about you were losing ours. I've never known you to lose your fine sense of reasoning because you lost your temper; in fact, I've never seen you really angry. Those traits, along with your keen sense of humor, have given me and others a great role model to emulate. And there's more . . . much, much more.

Your advice has always proved to be first rate; I've tried to heed and follow it. Your scholarship is enviable. Your deep concern for students, the Department, the College, the University . . . for academe in general . . . is really admirable. And there's more . . . much, much more.

The respect you've gained from students, peers, and superiors is a worthy hallmark of accomplishment for each of us to seek. You are admired and loved by us all. But there's more . . . much, much more! Words alone, however, simply cannot express the deep meaning "Gene Nelson" has for me. I can only hope I've enriched your life for a portion of what you've done in enriching Shirley's and mine. We appreciate you so very much for that.

My wish is that you find your days of retirement all you've dreamed them to be . . . contentment, fulfillment, and Peace.

Congratulatory Messages

Another real opportunity for building goodwill with customers and enhancing the image of the writer and firm is the congratulatory note. Everyone appreciates recognition, for the desire for praise is a basic human craving. People are proud not only of the honors they win, but also of anything outstanding done by members of their families or associates in their businesses. By watching the local newspapers, trade periodicals, TV news, and public service programs, writers can easily find many opportunities for building goodwill by congratulating customers upon their accomplishments or upon the success of those closely related to them.

Such events as a business promotion, an election to office in some civic or social organization, publication of an article or book, election to public office, personal accomplishments, graduation of children from school, the purchase of a new home are but a few of the activities worthy of a friendly note of goodwill, like this note from the heating subcontractor on a new residence:

Dear Mr. and Mrs. Dowe:

Our sincere wish is that you find your new home as enjoyable and comfortable as you hoped it would be.

The enclosed box of note paper is sent with our compliments. We thought you might like it to help establish your new address with your many, many friends.

Cordially yours

Here are additional points to keep in mind when you plan a letter of congratulations:

1. Keep yourself out of the opening words, if possible, moving straight to the nice thing that has happened to the reader.

AVOID: "May I take this opportunity to congratulate you."

"I was quite happy to read of your promotion to the vice-presidency."

2. Try to give what you say an original, conversational slant which makes the reader feel it couldn't have happened to a nicer, more capable person.

To a young lawyer recently associated with a prominent law firm:

"Congratulations are in order to Baker, Potts, and Sanders—and to the city of Memphis—for getting the services of such a fine lawyer."

To someone recently promoted to the vice-presidency of a friendly, competing firm:

"With you in charge of the Sales Division at United, we'll surely have to watch our step to keep abreast of the competition. Congratulations on the vice-presidency!"

For the more conservative:

"Your promotion to the vice-presidency of United is a recognition of talent we take pleasure in. Congratulations!"

3. Play up concrete, specific reasons why the reader deserved the honor with enough restraint to avoid embarrassment.

Not the clichés, please:

"Nobody could have been more deserving of this fine honor."

Nor extravagances:

"To the best go the richest rewards—and unquestionably you are the best to join the firm in many a year."

But with specific, restrained, and believable words:

"Your knowledge of people, your talent for quick decisions, and your immediate grasp of the important aspects of a situation no doubt all contributed to the favorable choice of the Board of Directors."

4.   End with gracious, optimistic comment.

Perhaps a little overboard:

"We're looking forward to even greater things from you in the future."

Simple, conversational:"We hope you're happy in your new job."

"Let us hear from you occasionally, for we watch your career with great interest."

Congratulatory messages in general offer no real problem in writing. The mere fact that the honor has been noticed is more important to the person receiving the message than the form in which the praise is worded. The only indispensable quality is sincerity.

Constructive Notes of Condolence and Apology

If letters marking happy occasions are such mighty builders of goodwill, even more significant are letters offering sympathy and help in misfortune. But the latter are difficult to write. Most of us tend to evade this responsibility by choosing instead a printed card at the stationers that comes close to saying what we'd like to say ourselves. Sympathy letters can be an intrusion if they are not simple and straightforward. They should be brief, not philosophic or too flowery; they should not be mechanical, blunt, cold, or formal. True sympathy is not an emotion that can be expressed by following specific directions in a letter-formula strategy. Here are a few selected pointers, however, especially noteworthy in writing death condolences, followed by con-trasting samples for your analysis:

1.   Point up a hopeful aspect of the grievous situation instead of mak-ing the reader feel worse by recalling too many doleful details. Focus the attention on "it's wonderful that he lived" rather than "it's dreadful that he died."

2.   Make any references to the deceased general instead of emphasiz-ing concrete details, such as "nice smile, charming way," which might only send the survivors into more tears.

3.   Avoid any sharp emotional words, such as "shock," "a void that cannot be filled."

Dear Mr. Roe:

We were shocked and saddened to hear of Jimmy's death. I had known that he was very sick, and that his chances of

Dear Mr. Roe:

Your son was a wonderful person with a great many friends who will miss him.

While grief is something that must be

recovery were not too good, but his passing leaves a void that cannot be filled.

Jimmy had been a friend of mine for many years and was a man whom I respected and admired very much. We shall miss him a great deal.

Our heartfelt sympathy goes out to you at this time.

suffered alone, it is nice that your memories of Jimmy's life can be so pleasant and rewarding.

As time passes, your pride in him will certainly make up in a measure for your immediate sense of loss. In the meantime our sympathies are with you.

The effect of the letter on the right comes from word choice and the way the words are put together to convey the feeling of sincere concern. Note the sincerity of the following illustration written in a somewhat lighter vein:

Dear Mr. Henry:

Mr. H. H. Brown, our sales representative, tells me you went to the hospital a week ago for major repairs. He relates that everything turned out fine though you will be in bed another two or three weeks.

Knowing how strong you have been physically, I think you may fool these doctors, but just in case time passes slowly, I am mailing you today two good books I've read recently and liked a lot. Perhaps you'll enjoy them as much as I did.

Best wishes for a quick recovery!

In spite of better-than-average efficiency of an entire organization, embarrassing mistakes will happen. If the business firm is to keep its fences mended, the note of apology must be written. The objectives of an apology are these:

1.   To focus the reader's attention on positive action taken to rectify the situation rather than on the bad things resulting from it.

2.   To explain how the mistake happened (if an explanation will help) as briefly and positively as possible.

3.   To make the reader feel important enough to the writer that his or her goodwill is valued.

4.   To apologize with action rather than words.

5.   To reassure the reader with a statement that minimizes the possibility of a recurrence (if the situation warrants).

To understand and appreciate fully one store's supreme efforts at atonement, you will need this background of the situation: A gentleman of some affluence bought a mink stole to be delivered to his wife on her birthday—his current wife. His former wife still used his name: Mrs. W. T. Cannon. By one of those unhappy coincidences, the stole was delivered to the first Mrs. Cannon instead of to the second Mrs. Cannon, whose birthday it was to make delirious. Here is the store's effort at making amends:

	Dear Mr. Cannon:
Action taken to rectify the situation	Your wife is no doubt by now luxuriating in the beautiful Satincraft mink stole delivered to her by special messenger this morning.
Brief and positive explanation	Because we value your patronage, the store makes every effort to provide quality merchandise and dependable service for you. In spite of our diligence, though, a package is sent occasionally to the wrong address. We eagerly ask your indulgence for the delivery of your wife's present a day late.
Minimizing possibility of recurrence	The delivery desk has been alerted to check carefully the address for every package directed to you or your family so that your merchandise will be certain to reach you—and on time, too.
Positive situation instead of regret	We sincerely hope that the beauty of the stole makes every day a birthday for your wife.

Seasonal Greetings

Many firms that do nothing about goodwill all year long will invariably stir themselves when Christmas rolls around. But despite a popular belief to the contrary, it is not easy to dash off a Christmas letter. There are two reasons for the difficulty. First, it is difficult to make one Christmas message different from the many others the reader is likely to receive; the other is the difficulty of conveying a sincere thought without having it take on the form of sentimentality.

The Christmas message to customers is not just a formality to be rid of as quickly as possible; it is a real opportunity to offer a friendly hand, to make up for former indifference, and to let the customer know the company is sincerely grateful. But because a good Christmas letter, or for that matter any other seasonal greeting, must come from the heart, no one can tell another precisely how it should be written. Like the thank you letters for patronage, it should omit any real sales message. Other suggestions that may prove helpful for writing seasonal greetings are these:

1. Find a quiet moment when you can relax and write the message with serious thought and concentration without interruption or pressure.

2. Think of something you would like to read if you were getting the letter instead of writing it. Then say it in the simplest way possible.

3. Don't try to be clever, cute, or spectacular in the message.

4. Remember, you can be a little more personal in a Christmas note than in almost any other kind.

5. Shorter letters seem best, though there is no rule on length.

Notice how the examples that follow keep in line with the suggestions above. Their sincerity of tone and their simple language reflect a genuine spirit of friendship, a natural warmth and glow.

Dear Mr. Inglis:

Christmas means more to us than holly, cards, and pretty sentiments neatly embossed. When, on Christmas morning, we find candy and candles on our tree, we realize that there would not even be a tree but for the goodwill and patronage of you and all our other good customers.

And, we are truly grateful.

Just counting our own blessings leads us to wish you and yours the most prosperous New Year you have ever known and a Christmas as happy and joyous as our own.

. . .

Dear Mrs. Miller:

Thirty years ago, when this business was founded, I used to enjoy a friendly chat with each of our patrons at this season of the year.

But the rapid growth that has made this a larger, better organization has necessarily deprived me of the opportunity to shake hands with all our friends, to thank them personally for their confidence and goodwill, and to wish them the best of everything at this holiday season.

I am well aware of the substantial part you have played in making 19xx such a successful year for us. And, since I have not had a chance to greet you personally and wish you a Merry Christmas, I'm taking this occasion to do so by letter—to express to you my deep gratitude for your friendship and patronage.

Christmas at your house I sincerely hope will prove a fitting climax for 19xx, and may the coming year bring you more success and happiness than any which has gone before.

There is no reason why seasonal messages of appreciation should be confined to Christmas and the New Year. In fact, many experts believe that almost any other special day of the year will prove more valuable to the business house in building goodwill than will Christmas time. The rationale is that at Christmas the organization's customers are receiving more personal mail and season's greetings from acquaintances and other businesses than at any time of the year. Your message has to work twice as hard to make an impression on the reader. Of course, businesses do not want to take a chance of offending the customer by not sending greetings, particularly if the house has done so in past years.

But a letter mailed in connection with some other event or day, such as the anniversary of the company, Thanksgiving, or the Fourth of July, will probably carry the advantage of having less competition and offer a perfectly natural lead for writing.

> Happy Birthday to you!
> Happy Birthday to you!
>
> Well, maybe it isn't your birthday, Mr. Young . . . but have you forgotten? It's your shop's birthday!
>
> Yes, just one year ago we helped bring your smart, sparkling new building into being by doing the plumbing, heating, and insulating. We hope it has given you a full year of prosperity, comfort, pleasure, and enjoyment, and that it will continue to do so.
>
> It seems only fitting that today—on your firm's first birthday—we should say "Thank you" once again for letting us help serve your needs. We know you are very proud of your shop, and we are equally proud for you.
>
> Best wishes for another prosperous year.

Invitations to Special Events

Most people like to be invited to go places and see interesting things, especially if the invited group is limited or select. Much goodwill can be created by such invitations if they are not an overt sales effort. Even a letter simply announcing better facilities for service may be a goodwill builder, like this off-the-beaten-path invitation:

> Did you know, Ms. Snider,
>
> that we've expanded? And here we are ready to do your work better than it was ever done before.
>
> You've probably been to formal openings where the men got mechanical pencils that didn't work, and the ladies, withered gardenias with a "gone with the wind" odor. We thought about having one like that, too, and then we decided POSITIVELY NOT.

We've made a lot of new friends!

And many of these have been kind enough to tell others about our services and reasonable costs. That's why we had to take over next door.

No flowers!

We had no formal opening, gave away no souvenirs. Still, we'd like to have you come in and see our enlarged place, for we have already found it makes for increased efficiency. It's not the most beautiful shop in Chicago . . .

But it's ours and we like it!

Drop by soon.

Cordial Contacts

The cordial contact letter, sometimes called the "reminder letter," is used primarily to keep everlastingly in touch, with prospects of the business house. The firm's name, its values, its image, and the availability of its product or service are kept continually before prospects through this type of message.

Characteristically, the "copy should be restrained, erudite, dignified. But it should also come up off the page with the warmth of storytelling, slip quietly into the commercial, ride through a wisp of soft sell—and be on its way. Its impression is one of quiet, soft-spoken sincerity,"[14] to give the reader confidence in the firm and its people.

Cordial contact pieces are often planned as a series to achieve message consistency for periodic mailings throughout the year. In this respect, they resemble a direct-mail campaign.

Frequently a letter begins by telling an interesting story built about historical landmarks or little-known facts of the city in which the reader lives; it may be tied in with a current TV or newspaper campaign. It is sophisticated copy at its best. But one's reminder letters do not necessarily have to be smooth to be effective. The fact that you are interested enough to write regularly is important. Good cordial contact mail, sent month after month to good prospects, will produce business.

Perhaps we can best characterize reminder letters by reminding you that "little drops of water wear away the hardest stone," or of the old adage that it isn't the one-thousandth blow of the hammer that breaks the rock but all the 999 that have pounded it before.

Using the soft-sell approach, the reminder letter (it can even be a leaflet insert, postcard, or self mailer) *makes no attempt to complete a sale by mail . . . frequently not even to promote an inquiry.*

The essence of reminder advertising is that it must remind, preferably

---

[14] John D. Yeck and John T. Maguire, *Planning and Creating Better Direct Mail* (New York: McGraw-Hill Book Company, 1961), p. 262.

on a regular schedule and in a pleasant way. Jack Carr, author of *Cordially Yours*, is famous for his success with cordial contact pieces. His formula is simple: write to a list of good prospects regularly, once a month. Begin your letter with a story, a joke, an interesting experience. And in a light-hearted way lead into a recital of some of the benefits of your product. Carr continues,

> Mail these month after month, for the sole purpose of establishing and maintaining a constant contact on a concentrated group of people, and I can tell you in exact figures what such letters will do. If the average legitimate, reputable merchant or manufacturer will compile a mailing list of 1,000 names, we'll say, names of actual potential prospects for his product, one hundred and forty out of each thousand will respond by the end of the first year. And about an equal number for each succeeding year. Until, at the end of five years, 70 percent of the total list will have made inquiry, come into the store, or actually become customers. The other 30 percent of the list will have died, moved elsewhere, or through some change, no longer remain prospects.[15]

Cordial contact mail builds a reputation, makes friends, and predisposes the prospects in your favor. It is good to use between sales representatives' calls when they cannot call as often as they should. The reminder letter does not try to take the place of a sales representative; it just makes another "cordial contact" for the writer. It builds goodwill for the business, too.

Here are examples from the Charles W. Groves Division (Services Industries Group, Rexall Drug and Chemical Company), Michigan City, Indiana, a firm devoted exclusively to providing mailing lists of American school teachers and college students. The first letter utilizes Labor Day as the focus of this cordial contact piece. As usual with the Groves's copy, the letters radiate the warmth, the sincerity, and the theme-oriented approach the company writers are noted for.

> The first crisp, cool night, Dr. Lord,
>
> has already come to Indiana. The frost isn't on the punkin' but it soon will be. Somehow, Labor Day has come to mark the end and the beginning.
>
> The real meaning of Labor Day to a working nation is the pause that represents, despite what the calendar may say, the ending of one year and the beginning of another. It is a time curiously out of time. A time for saying farewell to the year that has faded into summer and looking forward to the quickening tempo of a new year.
>
> It is with this new marketing year in mind that we send you the enclosed materials. Here, for your handy reference, is a powerful direct mail file. Powerful, because it acquaints you with a market made up of

---

[15] Jack Carr, *Cordially Yours* (Garden City, N.Y.: The Reporter of Direct Mail Advertising, n.d.), p. 35.

nearly 30% of all Americans, for whom education is a full time occupation.

May we help you include them in your advertising program for this coming year? Please phone (collect) or write for more information.

Cordially,

CHARLES W. GROVES division

Another thought, Dr. Lord.
Our computerized coverage of teachers and college students at their home addresses, is the only professional medium that enables your advertising to penetrate in depth.

. . .

CHARLES W. GROVES

427 Willard Avenue   Michigan City, Indiana

IT WAS EARLY WHEN SHE REACHED SCHOOL

and she was surprised to see a child hovering near the door. "It is locked," he offered bleakly as she tried the knob. She fumbled for her keys and immediately he grinned. "You are a teacher," he announced. "What makes you think that?" she asked, and he hesitated just for a moment before replying softly, "You have the key."

Those four words make clear that her philosophy of education must meet the needs . . . the longings   the hopes and the pleadings of all little boys and girls who wait at the door for someone with the key. We have this teacher's name and home street address and those of her 1,500,000 colleagues on magnetic tape, incorporating the latest refinements in scanning input, programming, and zip coding techniques.

Do you want your advertising presented to people who use the key to better living, better citizenship and progress? Then ask us for more information about our authentic and accurate listing of American school teachers. We'll be happy to answer your questions.

With a smile, too.

CHARLES W. GROVES COMPANY

Letters to New Customers

The loyalty of a new buyer is perhaps not so fixed as that of one whose name has been on the ledger for a long time. The patron is forming an opinion of the firm the moment he or she enters its place of business and makes the first purchase or telephones the initial service call. Mental attitude is that of uncertainty; the company is on trial as to the goods sold and the quality of its services. Extra courtesy through a welcoming letter may go a long way toward winning the goodwill and confidence generated through cordial contact pieces that lead to repeat orders.

FORM LETTERS

So numerous are the occasions for goodwill messages that organizations find it advantageous to rely in part on a form-letter file to handle them adequately. Form letters play a large part in the volume of business mail annually.

Time, expense, recurring situations, and the desire to give faster service are factors making it necessary to resort to form letter use. There is nothing wrong in a business firm's using form letters if care and attention are given to them. Often, however, the form letter is a hastily done, carelessly planned, sloppy job. Its effect on image building could not be worse. A good form letter, for example, should not be readily recognized by the reader as a form. With modern, inexpensive methods of excellent reproduction (multilith or multigraph offset printing) there is little excuse for any business's form letters not being first rate. Unless equal care is given to the form-letter message itself, however, good physical appearance alone will not do the job.

A reader may object to a sloppily done form letter, to a form message that does not give the information wanted, or to a form letter that ignores answering questions the reader raised. Neither time nor economy is justification for such a practice. Consequently, readers build up resentment and ill will toward the firm that attempts to cut corners through such thoughtlessness or inattention.

Form letters or printed cards decrease the cost of correspondence by cutting down on dictation and transcription time, handling costs, and filing even though something may be lost in effectiveness. For repeated inquiries about a product, acknowledgments of orders or information requests, confirmation of reservations, a message similar to the following can work well for the business:

Thank you for your recent order, which is in the process of being filled. You can be sure we are carefully following the billing and shipping instructions exactly as you gave them.

We do appreciate this opportunity to serve you. And, it will be our pleasure to do so again any time you choose to send the perfect gift for that special occasion . . . from the House of Margot.

(You must, of course, adapt the content specifically to meet the situation calling for repeated message use.)

A series of form paragraphs, too, can work well for you in cutting down dictation and typing time if these paragraphs are on file and numbered for selective use in message building. (Some companies are largely automated in word-processing cards or go so far as to put entire paragraphs and letters on computer cards or magnetic tape for automatic retrieval.) Any competent office worker can compile a complete answer to an inquiry or confirm a reservation request simply by your dictating "Paragraphs 2A, 3B, 1C," "Letter Number 401"—or whatever the appropriate material is to fit the particular situation. Though an individual printout or typed job, the finished product is nonetheless a form letter.

The time and cost involved in typing an envelope and tucking the well-prepared form letter into it is minimal compared with the extra goodwill the firm gains from a prompt reply.

But personalizing is difficult in form letters, for the writer must be able to say the same thing to a wide audience of readers. Resale on goods and services is often impractical, especially if the firm offers a wide range of products. Frequently, the inquiry is likely to be too restrictive for any general message to be adaptable to any one particular reader's letter unless it is computerized. Including dates and figures manually is illogical unless you are using a blank fill-in, in which case you have automatically identified your letter as a form.

The writer can promote the firm, however, in any form message used. And even completely processed letters can do much for the firm's goodwill image. Such messages use a headline lead to take the place of the salutation or an attention block device to replace the inside address. The letter includes as well a printed, simulated signature of the writer. You can, for example, in such messages (1) tell the reader what is being done about the inquiry, (2) express appreciation for the communication, (3) convey your desire to be of help, and (4) look forward to future relationships by leaving the way open for future communication. Here is a sample reply incorporating all four aspects:

A REPLY WILL BE
ON ITS WAY
TO YOU SHORTLY . . .

giving you the information you've asked for. A few days will be required to assemble all the materials we think you need for the information to be of greatest value to you.

Thank you for writing and letting us explain the new tax procedures on investment trusts. [You would of course insert whatever the recurring situation calls for here.]

Please write again should you need additional material before making your decision.

B. H. Ryan

B. H. Ryan, Counselor

A SUMMARY CHECKLIST FOR THE BASIC FUNDAMENTALS IN GOOD WRITING

Tone, Style, Appearance

Appearance and Style

AS 50   The first-glimpse impression of you is gained from the reader's initial reaction to the overall effect of your layout.

a.   Here that impression can be improved by closer attention to:

(1)   more attractive typing.

(2)   eliminating messy erasures.

(3)   avoiding strikeovers.

(4)   other points as marked.

b.   Your placement of the copy on the page shows carelessness:

(1)   too high.

(2)   too low.

c.   Frame your copy in adequate white space for a more pleasing effect.

d.   Balance letter parts and space them properly:

(1)   the date.

(2)   inside address.

(3)   subject line.

(4)   complimentary close.

(5)   signature line, title.

(6)   others as marked.

e.   Give attention to paragraphing (eight typewritten lines is average length):

(1)   Break up heavy paragraphs for better emphasis, speedier reading.

(2)   Compact information needs frequent paragraphing.

(3)   Vary the paragraph lengths.

(4)   Paragraph whenever the subject aspect changes.

(5)   Combine paragraphs to avoid a scattered, choppy effect.

f.   The quality of your paper is unsatisfactory.

AS 51   For two-page letters:

a.   Identify second page with addressee's name, date, and the page number.

b.   Divide the copy on both pages approximately equal for better psychological effect.

Readability and Tone

RT 60   Your contact with the reader must be reasonable, logical.

a.   Here you're on a point too far afield of your subject.

b.   Keep your reader in the forefront and talk to that person, as one single, important individual:

(1)   Here you've made the reader merely a member of a group.

(2)   Here you've told the reader that he or she is an abstraction—that you are not thinking of him or her as an individual person.

c.   Don't go on the defensive:

(1)   The reader's honesty should be taken for granted—not challenged or even called into question.

(2)   Respect the reader's judgment and intelligence by avoiding the obvious as if the individual didn't know.

(3)   Respect the reader's feelings by complimenting his or her good taste and by avoiding needless buffeting.

RT 61   Save your reader's time:

a.   You need to cut, condense without sacrificing content. Here you are too wordy, detailed, drawn out.

b.   Here you're asking too much of your reader.

c.   Here you've been too scant. Have you provided enough information and details for reader understanding and intelligent response?

d.   Wording is repetitious, overlapping; use synonyms.

e.   Vary your sentence patterns:

(1)   Break up this string of subject-

verb-object forms (choppy, staccato).

(2)   Intersperse short sentences with longer ones.

(3)   Avoid so many sentences starting with the same word.

(4)   Too much telling, not enough asking here.

f.   Choose more forceful, colorful words for your copy.

g.   The stiff "Business English" style is no longer acceptable if it ever was. Avoid clichés and stereotyped language.

h.   Work for greater rhythm in word and/or sentence "flow" for coherence, smoothness.

i.   Write in active voice.

j.   Make your talk more conversational, natural.

k.   Make a smooth transition from one idea to the next; one paragraph to the next.

l.   Avoid wordy, ambiguous windups to the main idea of your statement. "I would like to . . ." hints but never really does what you want to.

m.   Connotation is poor. Stay positive.

n.   Be aware of misspelling, diction, syntax, form as marked.

RT 62   Get involved in the situation.

a.   Is this a businesslike treatment?

b.   Isn't this statement or treatment illogical?

c.   Work for better reader adaptation.

d.   Be more tactful, positive; soften the effect of this phase.

e.   Minimize references to yourself.

f.   Be more enthusiastic in what you have to say.

CHECKLIST FOR GOODWILL MESSAGES

Opening

GWM 10   The first sentence is a critical point for strictly goodwill messages. Your lead (topic sentence function) should suggest the tone and subject for the entire letter.

11   The cue for a successful opening comes from trying to identify yourself as the reader. Think of something you would like to read if you were getting the letter instead of writing it. Then say that something in the simplest way you can.

12   Clever, epigrammatic writing is fun to try, but it may tend to alienate the reader by making too much of an issue, or it may fall entirely flat.

13   A slogan-type opener probably won't quite do the job. Don't try to be clever, cute, or spectacular in this type message.

14   Allay any reader doubts or suspicions of why you are writing.

15   *Sincerity* is the keynote of whatever you say. Work for better reader adaptation.

Coverage

GWM 20   Lead smoothly into a development of the subject (the reason for writing) that can make use of illustration, analogy, even personal reminiscences.

21   Here the turn is disconnected, annoying.

22   Opportunities abound for building goodwill—appreciation, congratulations, recognition and the like. In your development,

a.   Treat the subject tastefully, personally.

b.   Don't overplay the point.

c.   Avoid patronizing talk.

d.   Avoid commercialism; it is *not* to be a sales message.

e.   Make your compliments subtle, believable.

f.   Avoid any appearance of a form letter.

23   Wouldn't a shorter version have a more pleasing effect on your reader?

24   Isn't this one too scant or just too brief to really accomplish what you're trying to do?

25   Fair coverage of the particular assignment should include specific points. (Your instructor will provide details of what else is to be included for adequate treatment of a specific case used in the assignment.)

Close

GWM 40   Cordial warmth is especially called for in this closing paragraph. Rework your phrasing to achieve it.

41   Give the letter in the close a sense of finality. Here you seem to trail off, leaving the reader somewhat suspended in air.

42   The graciousness in tone you want cannot be achieved through using hackneyed, worn-out, meaningless expressions.

43   Fit the close to the particular situation—in character, in wording.

Tone and Style As Marked

Your Grade _____

PROBLEM SITUATIONS FOR WRITING GOODWILL MESSAGES

Because of the news they bear, most goodwill messages usually begin directly with the subject. Some, however, follow promotion-message strategy by leading off with a novel, interest-arresting topic. There are such great differences in goodwill messages that no single plan or strategy of presentation will apply for them all. Characteristically, however, these goodwill messages have a friendly, warm conversational style— sometimes lighthearted. All are sincere always. Throughout they emphasize the positive side of things. They are almost devoid of negative expressions. Focus is upon the reader. These letters are perhaps more subject to the imagination and creative talents of the writer than are any other kinds of messages written.

1.   *Writing a note of appreciation to one of Your City's Civic Clubs.* When your **BBA** fraternity (Alpha Kappa Psi, Delta Sigma Pi, Phi Chi Beta, Pi Omega Pi—whatever one you are a member of or know something about) was making plans recently for its annual banquet to honor newly elected members and to install new officers, a problem arose in finding a suitable place to hold it. The Campus Union facilities were already reserved for the Friday night your fraternity had chosen. Your limited budget prohibited renting a public place. Recalling the civic interest, nonprofit-making programs to which the civic clubs are dedicated, you, Pat Higgins, chairperson of the social committee of your fraternity, contacted one (Rotary, Lions, Kiwanis, Knights of Columbus—select whichever might have a clubhouse in Your City). You made arrangements to talk with a member of the local chapter. He in turn presented your request for the use of the club facilities for your banquet to the proper committee for approval. Because your banquet was a scholastic activity, you were granted the use of the clubhouse without charge. Of course, your fraternity arranged for the food, but the kitchen equipment, silver, tables and chairs, and linens were all made available to you by the club. It was only requested that the clubhouse be left in the same good condition in which it was found and that the linens used be laundered and paid for.

The banquet was truly a success, not the least reason being the pleasant atmosphere of the tastefully decorated and appointed (___civic group___) clubhouse. You and the members of your fraternity appreciate very much the courteous favor the civic club granted you. At your last fraternity meeting it was voted unanimously that a letter of thanks be written to the president of this civic club, Perry N. Myers. You will include a fraternity check for $25.65 to cover the laundry bill on the linens used.

Now, for Pat Higgins, write a short, sincere, thank you message for the fraternity, signing your name as chairperson of the social committee, addressing the message to Mr. Myers at his office, 1102 Perry-Brooks Building, Your City, Your State.

2. *Writing a sincere thank you for an interview trip.* Assume that you are registered with your college's placement service and that you have had several on-campus interviews with various recruiters sent by their companies to seek new executive-trainee personnel. One interview produced a two-day, all-expense-paid plane trip to the firm's home office in a Metropolitan City, Another State, so that you might have a firsthand inspection of the company's operation, talk with company personnel, take the battery of company tests given to all prospective employees, and so that home office executives could get to know you and your interests and abilities better.

As is usually the case, you were given the red-carpet treatment—quartered in a fine hotel, wined and dined, and shown about the city by Jenks Renfro, the company executive serving as your host and guide. Although Mr. Renfro said that it would probably be two weeks before you heard from the company (you were aware of several other candidates being interviewed in the same way during your visit), you were much impressed by what you saw and by the people with whom you talked.

Write a thank you letter to your host expressing appreciation for all the courtesies extended to you.

3. *Winning goodwill for your bank—and maybe some interest.* The First National Bank of your city suburb of Kingston was the First State Bank until three years ago. Ten years before that there was no bank at all in Kingston. But in a growing metropolitan-area suburb like yours, the swelling population and income have brought a rapidly growing demand for modern banking facilities.

The First National has expanded just as swiftly as the payrolls in the aircraft and chemical plants on the edge of town. And with warmer, more personal service than the nearby city banks can offer, First National has won a good many accounts away from the major competitors.

Every day you sign your name, John Bracken, vice president, to several personal letters that include carefully worded goodwill elements. You feel, however, that the time has come for a general goodwill letter to be sent to all your checking-account clients. You want to express your appreciation for their business in the most direct, natural terms you can find. Also, full-page advertisements in the city paper remind you that local automobile dealers are starting to receive next year's models. You might drop a hint in your letter, then, that First National can probably save its customers some money on new-car financing costs and at the same time help them establish their credit records for future use. It's up to your letter to help maintain your bank's reputation for excellent service and personal attention to the needs of its depositors.

4. *Writing a goodwill message for an organization in response to a generous donation.* You are Adrien Sheftal, a professional staff member in a large corporation, Your City, Your State. It has been your observation that goodwill letters are usually written on a one-individual-to-another basis or as a business firm to an individual (customers, prospects, community leaders, and so on). Your situation for writing a goodwill message is different.

In your community service role, you've been working with the physically and mentally disadvantaged in one of Your City's community centers. The center, of course, is staffed by a few professionals but does not have enough people employed (budget restrictions) to handle all the activities and number of participants making use of the center and its programs.

An appeal for citizen volunteers and involvement in the center's activities two months ago brought a small response. You were one of half a dozen people who volunteered. Because of your fondness for art and the aesthetics, the center's director asked you to work on the arts festival that she was putting together as a mainstreaming activity. It would include all kinds of handcrafts: painting, sculpture, macramé, woodwork, and metalwork. These finished objects were to be displayed at the center over a weekend for public view.

The Arts Festival proved to be one of the most successful events for the center since it opened two years ago in its own facilities, due in large part to the extra effort you put in on it.

What really made it outstanding for viewers and participants alike—apart from the beautifully expressive artwork—were the recognition prizes awarded in each category. You contacted trophy dealers in town and finally persuaded one of them to go "all out" in designing special trophies for each entry class and in meeting the fast-approaching deadline you had, too.

Mr. John LaRue, LaRue Trophies, Inc., 4617 Duval Avenue, made a real concession in his charges when he learned the particulars of this event. The invoice for 15 trophies—a first, second, and third place award in each class—you realized could barely cover Mr. LaRue's costs. Naturally, you expressed your appreciation and that of the center's also when you picked up the trophies late on Friday afternoon. Good manners now, of course, call for your writing a personal thank you for this entrepreneur's generosity.

5. *Writing a cordial goodwill note of support to a struggling but promising FM-stereo station.* You place high value on spot-news programs when the news is interpreted from the viewpoint of a resident of your own community, and you can safely stomach a network commentator or so when the attendant commercials are not too long and insipid, but for radio appreciation your vote goes for "music that lives," music that does not leave a dull hangover when the last intonation has echoed into the past— particularly in the evenings, when the pulse of life is slowing in this world of cold reality.

The old quip, "There's a time for everything," might have its value, but where pop, rock-and-roll music, and western hoedowns all day and all evening are broken only by an occasional semiclassical or swing music program, the effect wears pretty thin on the eardrums.

You thus appreciate the viewpoint, though seemingly idealistic, and herald the bravery of the new FM-stereo radio station owner in your city who is playing down sensationalism and playing up, quite, quite literally, the appreciation of *good* music. It is a case in point, you think, which needs your verbal support—and the vote of those like yourself who want to see the fledgling station make a go of it. From the scant news stories you read in the local paper, however, you gather that it's only a question of time before the decision to "give up" on this new venture is made. It would be a real loss to the citizenry, and especially to the university student population, if the station were forced to abandon operations from a lack of interest.

So pull up your chair and write a letter, to Timothy L. Brite, president and general manager of station BHVN, that will place your vote alongside those who do care—a vote which you sincerely feel will help put new life into a sick industry and give radio a right and a will to live a worthwhile life.

   6. *Writing a dual-purpose goodwill letter.* As recently elected executive secretary of the Jaycees (Junior Chamber of Commerce) in Your City, Your State, you take upon yourself the project of writing a welcome letter to each new member. The fresh interest of the joiner is there—so why not capitalize on it as a means of inspiring wholehearted participation in the many activities of your organization? What do you wish to accomplish by the letter? Your objectives seem to be (a) to make the new member feel through warm words of appreciation he is a part of the organization, (b) to reimpress his original interest by pointing up ways in which he may benefit from being a Jaycee, (c) to suggest activities of the local club in which he might be interested and actively take part.

As you start to draft your letter, it occurs to you that you might be able to do a better goodwill job if it were possible to get acquainted with the new member in some casual social setting. Will you get much of a response to the conventional "Drop in some time and I'll buy you a cup of coffee?" Would it be advisable to invite him to join you and other Jaycees in the new Friendship Room at your bank for free coffee and a chat? The president, 35 years old and a Jaycee himself, says yes. You might offer a personal tour of the fastest-growing young bank in the city—but you do it subtly and in a secondary way. You do not want this message to be obviously a public relations mailing for your bank, but you would like it to serve that purpose too. Will you write it on a bank letterhead—Commercial Bank, Throckmorton at Sixth—or would it be better to use a Jaycee letterhead? Will the Jaycees object to your sending out such a dual-purpose letter under their name? Or will you have to make it a bank letter signed by you, Wilfred Dewey, assistant cashier, with the Jaycee angle a secondary one?

Make your decisions and write a form letter that will accomplish your objectives for each new member. A fact that might be useful is that the 35-year-old president is the oldest officer and you are the youngest, at 27.

   7. *Writing a cordial contact as the first step in competitive job application elimination.* Graphic Service, 202 Talbott Building, Dayton, Ohio, is an organization run by Beck & Beck—John Beck and his son. Both writers of the first rank, they have been producing lively direct-mail advertising copy for years for a long list of highly satisfied clients. Their letters are medal winners. The firm also offers a full line of printing

and mailing services. (John is author of one of the best selling books in the direct mail advertising field.)

Business is booming . . . so much so that Beck & Beck have decided to hire an additional copywriter to help take over some of the copy-composing chores. That's where you come in.

One of Graphic's clients is S. Rose, Inc., a Cleveland, Ohio, firm whose business is buying, selling, or renting everything in the way of office fixtures, furniture, and equipment. The Becks have turned out the copy for the first of a series of six "reminder" letters for S. Rose, Inc., using the pseudonym of s. mouse. Here's the copy (with letterhead):

S. ROSE, INC.

i am s. mouse of s. rose, inc. and im the boss.

when bob rose and dick rose leave at night im in charge.

if i want i can put my feet up on dick roses desk and squeak my head off.

but im in trouble now for answering the phone.

last night a man called up and said send me out 10,000 filing cabinets, 23 used comptometers and 341 new and used desks and chairs.

well, i said, o.k., and he said, to whom am i speaking. and i said, this is s. mouse of s. rose, thats whom.

and he said, oh, well be sure to tell dick or bob what i want. and then he hung up.

so i feel like a rat.

if i tell dick rose somebody wanted 10,000 filing cabinets he would just laugh at me. because i didnt get the guys name or address.

so im writing you on this electric typewriter they left plugged in and i hope youre the guy who talked to me last night.

but even if you arent, why not order something from dick rose or bob rose. theyll give you a good deal. and theyve got everything in office fixtures, furniture, and machines. just call them up at 471-1600 and tell em i sent you.

p.s. the roses will treat you right. if   cordially yours,
you dont want to buy it theyll
rent it to you. and if you dont
want to buy or rent you can sell   s. mouse
em your stuff.   signed by hand

You are one of the prospective applicants for the Beck & Beck position and your job is to write the second of the six-letter series, keeping in character with the one the Becks have already produced. You, of course, have a clear field of what you'll say and the "theme" you'll attempt to develop. John and his son figure on hiring the bright, young copywriter who they feel can fit into the Beck & Beck image easiest. This second letter—yours—will be the elimination point for many, the passport to a top-paying job for one. You've decided you want that job very much. So, go after it!

The slow, soft-sell idea you want to put across is the same as that in the example letter: S. Rose, Inc. sells, rents, or buys everything in office furnishings; so when the reader has a need for fixtures, furniture, or machines that person will just naturally think first of S. Rose, Inc.

8. *Cordially inviting good ex-customers in the area to reactivate their accounts.* With the erection of the new Town and Gown subsidiary of A. B. Mason's, a large department store in your city, in the new Highland Park shopping center, you have moved over to the managership. One of your first projects for promoting trade is that of going through the ledger sheets to find the names of residents of the northwest area who had accounts with Mason's but who have not used them for a year or more. You bring the list up to date by checking in the current telephone directory and plan to get back into the fold these good customers whose credit capacity has already been established. You'll prepare a one-page letter to be individually typed that will invite them to the week-long party the store is having (May 18–23 from 10:00 A.M. to 5:00 P.M. each day) to celebrate the opening of the suburban store.

You'll think up a novel way of saying that the store has missed them—and wants a chance to renew a business friendship in plush new surroundings. You'll enumerate enough of the conveniences and new features to lure them in if only out of curiosity. You'll describe specific merchandise that would interest people of different ages and sexes. You'll assure them that their accounts are still in good standing and offer them a 5-percent discount on any purchase up to $125 if they'll bring this letter along.

Your assignment is to compose a goodwill letter to accomplish Manager Burton Perry's purpose. The store's address is Town and Gown, In the Heart of Highland Park, Your City, Your State. (In some way you'll have to connect the new store to A. B. Mason's. The letterhead will carry it, but you'd best say something in the letter, also.)

9. *Writing a goodwill, good-neighbor message for the holiday season.* Porter's, a prestigious department store in San Antonio, Texas, does a substantial volume of business with customers from Mexico, many of whom fly in for a day's shopping or for a weekend from time to time.

Your task is to wish these prosperous good neighbors a happy holiday season—without attempting to sell anything but the friendly image of the store itself. Your letter will be translated into Spanish by an experienced interpreter. (Please don't write it in Spanish, however, even if you are justifiably proud of your fluency in that language.)

The letter will go mainly to customers in larger cities, such as Mexico City, Monterrey, and Guadalajara, and also to the closer border areas. It will be read, in other words, by sophisticated shoppers, not to be patronized as if they were coming in from the provinces.

Of course you'll want to keep in mind that Christmas customs are a bit different in Mexico. For example, Santa Claus is certainly not unknown but doesn't play as big a part in holiday imagery south of the border. On the other hand, the three Magi, the wise men, are emphasized somewhat more. (Remember, they originated the custom of Christmas gift giving.)

Without specifically suggesting purchases in your store, you will perhaps want to point out some of the special services that may be helpful to "guest shoppers" in your store:

- An agent of your store sees goods through customs at Laredo–Nuevo Laredo and arranges for their delivery in Mexico, usually by air express.

- A service representative in your store will make hotel reservations for visitors and secure tickets to concerts, ball games, operas, polo matches, and Fiesta events.

- One of your personal shoppers reads letters and receives telephone calls in Spanish and is familiar with the Mexican market—what is available and what is not.

10. *Writing a note that gets your representative an appointment to demonstrate your new Electronix Display-Riter.* As Marian C. Gates, you went to work as a sales representative for Electronix Business Machines, Inc., the day after you received your BBA degree from Your University, Your City, Your State, in May. After a series of assignments in various parts of the country and several gratifying promotions, you were given the opportunity to come back to your home state as manager of the Teleprocessing Division of the regional office (916 Frost Building, Your City, Your State).

You are quite pleased with your office and everything about your new job, including three personable sales people who are to help you. When you feel you have just about learned your way around, you begin to concentrate on promotion ideas designed to demonstrate your worth to the company. One idea you play around with is that of writing a personal letter to a select list of business offices in your city, which should furnish you with interesting leads.

You look over a sheaf of such letters the company furnishes on a national basis with a view to getting an idea as to what has been done and possibly an inspiration for a new approach. Most of the company letters are directed to executives, with the central appeal the prestige accruing to the firm from messages that are "letter perfect." A plausible new approach occurs to you: Why not play up the advantages to firms of keeping their staffs happy with new Electronix Display-Riters? So you look over the promotion material for cues with which to push this angle:

- Almost effortless operation in individually hooked-up pieces of equipment apart from CRT screens can be done on a 92- or 96-character keyboard.

- The Display-Riter can use any one of three available printers with speeds of 15.5, 40, or 60 characters per second (cps).

- There's a choice between single or dual diskette units.

- Five licensed programs, prerecorded on diskettes, provide flexibility and variety in performing tasks associated with originating, processing, and distributing information.

- Each program uses "prompts" in everyday English to guide an operator through the required steps of a task—so easy!

- An exclusive function of the Display-Riter is spelling verification. Users can add their own 500-word custom "dictionaries" (special terms, unusual words, etc.) to the 50,000 electronic dictionary of standard words.

- The Display-Riter can be used as a stand-alone unit and printer or as a cluster of up to three work stations. Each operator can tie into the other work stations and the computer as well.

- Document editing on a full-page, display screen makes for a completely correct, finished copy *before* printing.

- Rough drafts, of course, can be printed for complex copy editing and the electronic draft stored for later additions, corrections, and changes after this manual editing process is completed.

- The Display-Riter eliminates the typist's agony of seeing the finished copy returned, marked beyond salvaging short of retyping: cost effective! And happy employees.

You'll take over for Gates and write a letter around the central theme described here that will have business managers mailing in their appointment cards for demonstrations. Of course, your copy will be done on the Display-Riter as visual proof of its effectiveness.

3

Systematically Imparting Information

For everything . . . there is a system of order.

The only part of a language one can use in writing, if purpose is to be accomplished, is that part which is the same as the audience's. Nothing written
is any good at all, no matter how beautiful the prose unless it is in the same
language as that of the person to whom it is written. And its usefulness
frequently depends upon the timeliness of dispatch (having the right information at the right time) as well as upon how easily understood the content
is.

Getting ideas from the writer's mind to that of the reader—the essence
of communication—means knowing *what* to transmit and *how* to transmit
it effectively. The business writer must become a role player: he or she must
understand and play the role of communicator while visualizing the receiver's, for the message will be influenced by

1. The situation making the communication necessary.
2. The reader's knowledge (both generally and specifically as related
to the message circumstance).
3. The relationship between writer and reader (established by
interaction).
4. The favorable or adverse information that the message contains.

Since a writer's communication is a form of behavior and since behavior is caused, the impact, the evaluation, and the response to one's message are all a part of the information-imparting process. By way of background, let us examine first the facet of behavior known as interaction.

INTERACTION OF COMMUNICATOR AND AUDIENCE

The individual and his or her surroundings are in a constant process of influencing each other. Surroundings are a stage on which the individual plays a role and the acting out of this role affects the stage itself. The role is played directly or indirectly in relationship with other people. It may be played in person-to-person relations (one writer, one reader) or in person-to-group relations (one writer, a group of readers).

Our environment provides a setting for interaction, a process in which the individual not only reacts to other individuals, situations, and objects but also influences his or her surroundings. There is a dyadic systemization of behavior, for the actions of one person produce the environmental events for another. One's behavior (part of which is role taking) is a process of interaction with one's environment. The individual's modes, or responses to and influences upon others, are determined to a considerable degree by the nature of the relationships one has and has had with others. Thus, by interaction of two individuals we mean that the writer reacts to the reader and the reader to the writer in such a way that the response of each is a reaction to the other's behavior which produces a change in the behavior of each. Each brings to the happening (leading to and causing the interaction) a certain role prescribed by the situation.

On the basis of evaluations, the reader reacts by responding to the communicator, and the communicator in turn from his or her observation and evaluation comes to understand what he or she *means* to the reading audience. Meanings are the framework upon which roles and mutual expectations are built.

Expectations serve the writer and reader as guidelines for their behavior toward each other and as values by which to interpret each other's behavior. Expectations also determine the future of the relationship and the resultant behavior in communication exchange. How the writer expects the reader to react to a message may have considerable influence not only on the reader's actual behavior but also on how the reader's behavior is eventually perceived by the writer.[1]

When a reader receives the writer's message (see Figure 3-1), the words

---

[1] For a more extensive treatment of this subject, see Lee O. Thayer, "The Nature of People," in *Administrative Communication* (Homewood, Ill.: Richard D. Irwin, Inc., 1961), Chap. 2.

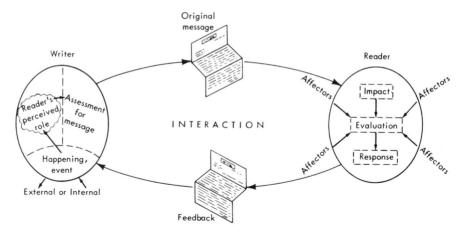

Figure 3-1   The interaction process between writer and reader

act as visual stimuli to his or her nervous system. The reader evaluates and interprets these stimuli and then responds to them. The response may be a nod of the head in agreement; a frown or a shrug of the shoulders in perplexity; vocal utterances of joy, disgust, annoyance, or confusion; or a written reply to the writer's message. The reader's response then serves as an impact on the writer who in turn evaluates and responds, repeating the process. The entire written interaction sequence takes place in business many times daily. (Obviously, this sequence occurs more overtly, more spontaneously, and more often in oral communication than in writing.) Participants to the situation (each happening, event) take each other into account, are aware of each other, identify each other in some way, and make judgments and appraisals. Their interaction is something more than a mere addition of the actions of the two individuals. Taking another into account becomes a control over one's own developing act and gives stability to an ordered business life.

Interaction, therefore, may be thought of as a cause-and-effect relationship—the process in which the writer's behavior acts as a stimulus for the reader's, whose behavior in turn acts as stimulus for the writer, and so on. The individual events are interdependent and difficult to isolate in the communication process. One must, however, recognize that the interaction process necessarily implies feedback. Such feedback allows the participants in the communication process to act with an awareness of the thoughts, feelings, and intentions of other participants. With feedback, the reflected behavior may lead to cooperation in the organized process of imparting information or may act as a barrier to the communication process itself.

But what affects one's evaluations of a communication? Partly it is the reader's perception of the particular situation. *Meaning* (drawn from the reader's experience) enters the picture as well. Fallacious and unconsciously held assumptions that the reader has developed in part through the language system also affect the evaluation process and, consequently, the behavior response.

Language becomes the universal tool to interaction. To know what to say and what not to say, one must have some conception of what the other person knows or does not know or written communication will be ineffective. One must take the role of the other individual through language, and it becomes more difficult when the language symbols are transmitted on paper. Organized attitudes must then play a part.

The individual acquires thought and judgmental habits largely through interaction with other persons. It is by no means entirely fanciful to suppose that one assumes certain problem-solving functions that are observed when performed by others. For example, one may assume a "critic" role in the sense of learning to apply to one's self the same standards and rules of critical evaluation that another person has previously manifested in interaction. One may assume the role of informant, instructor, director, or mollifier from previous experience with others. The businessperson in the course of activities learns to assume many roles, to evaluate, and to interact with readers in the process of imparting information to others.

INFORMATIVE AND INSTRUCTIVE COMMUNICATION SITUATIONS

A large body of the communication of any business is made up of those messages, written voluntarily, that go out to tell somebody something that the recipient needs to know. The writer's readers may be company representatives, suppliers, fellow members of an organization, firms that regularly do business with the company, new customers. The main purpose is to get an idea across so that the reader may act upon it properly.

Informative and instructive communications are just that—*primarily* informational and instructive. We communicate informatively when we explain, describe, clarify, report, analyze, ask questions, or answer inquiries and requests. Such messages *tell* (or ask) the reader about an idea, an organization, a meeting, a product or service. They inform the reader of a report or other publication of interest, of a policy of the organization, of an entitled benefit, or of a project the firm has underway or is contemplating. They point out pertinent research including gathering and disseminating techniques. Such messages also *instruct* the reader on work standards, jobs to be done and performance levels expected (the letter of authorization, for example), operational and training procedures of all kinds, and changes or decisions affecting the receiver. They *appraise* individuals, products, and service projects. All affirmative answers to inquiries and requests, such as acknowledgements of orders and reservations, letters of transmittal, the granting of a customer's claim or granting credit, sending information requested—all are informative and instructive communications. (Certain kinds of reports, news releases and bulletins, manuals, and brochures are additional examples.)

Sizing up the Situation—
Anticipating the Reaction

Inquiries, Requests	*Replies*
All messages asking for routine information; requests for printed materials, reservations, changes in procedure (payment schedules, address changes, etc.), and assistance where the reply is likely to be positive rather than negative.	All affirmative answers to routine inquiries and requests.

Orders		Acknowledgements
Claims		Adjustment grants
		Credit approval
Letters of authorization		Letters of transmittal
Procedures		Recommendations
Job descriptions and work standards	See Chapter 6	Progress reports
Regulations, policies		Credit reports
Directives		Research results
News releases, bulletins, manuals		See Chapter 6

The form of the message (letter, memo, or other format) is determined largely by the subject matter, the intensity of treatment given to it, the preference of the organization or writer, or the circumstance making the communication necessary. The writing style is direct, succinct, forceful, and understandable so that the information will have less chance of being distorted because of the evaluations, misconceptions, misassumptions, and interpretations that occur in the interaction between writer and reader.

The information transmitted must be meaningful and useful to the reader; it must be *acceptable*—fitting in with the reader's own beliefs, needs, and attitudes. It must be instructive—the reader must *learn* from it. "Facts in themselves are not information," Lee O. Thayer points out. He continues,

> . . . To the person who accepts a fact, it is indeed information. But to the person to whom we are trying to communicate a fact, it is not information unless he accepts it as such.

> We too frequently overlook this simple but pervasive point. We get angry or disgruntled when someone does not agree with us. We attribute his failure to agree to his stupidity when we should attribute it to our own, for not realizing that *the facts upon which we base our own conclusions are not common knowledge.* They are private. We accepted them, and

now act upon them, but does the other fellow? If we kept in mind that facts in themselves are not information, we would likely avoid many disagreements and many more misunderstandings.[2]

Informative and instructional communication is *intentional* communication; that is, the content, purpose, and import *intended* by the writer. The reader, however, may not distinguish (indeed, it may not be possible for the individual to distinguish) between what you, the writer, intended and what the reader gets out of the communication. For there is a fundamental, pervasive barrier to any communication: the crucial differences in what people will attend to at any moment and in the values they will assign to aspects of their individually perceived worlds.

Writers will think and believe on the basis of the intended content or import of the message; readers are never so restricted. Actually, we have little or no control over the reader in the reception of our communication; thus, as communicators, we must always be aware of the pitfalls for the communication and sharpen our own thinking, attitudes, and techniques to increase the probability of getting the desired information across. Sound thinking and planning must precede any writing of such messages if our communication is to be effective.

BASIC CONSIDERATIONS IN PLANNING COMMUNICATION STRATEGY

The heart of your informative communication is its main thought. Therefore we begin with the basic question established in Chapter 2: What do you want the communication to do? Your problem is how to pack the core idea of your central thought into a tight, condensed presentation to convey that information to your reader.

We have to plan and prepare for most of the things we do. Getting up in the morning, a Sunday drive, a picnic, your job, or even your studying must have *some* thought. The same principle applies to writing informative messages. We must take time to think about what we are going to say if we want the best results. People often complain that they do not have time to compose good copy, that getting the work done will not permit them to think too much about what they are going to say. Production pressure, they report, simply demands getting the work out in any shape or form. To such an argument, we raise this question: Why is there never enough time to write a good letter but always time to do one over if necessary?

Before beginning to write or dictate the first paragraph of your message, therefore, a good plan (already pointed out in Chapter 2) is to gather all the

[2] Thayer, *Administrative Communication*, p. 139.

needed information, to visualize the message as a whole, and to make an outline if necessary. This process will take only a few minutes, but they will be minutes well spent. Such a procedure may also be the means of saving the writer the embarrassment of realizing, when rereading the finished communication, that an important point has been omitted or the further embarrassment of receiving from the reader a second message saying "Your reply was unclear."

Facts alone, however, are not the answer. The facts must be related so that the reader will understand them. The following letter from a mail-order house shows a misuse of facts. The reader had ordered some shirts:

Dear Friend:

Enclosed is our refund check for the merchandise you did not receive.

You may cash this check locally, or if you wish, you may send it to us with your next order.

When your order was received we must not have had the merchandise. But your refund check should have been sent to you with the papers, and you still may get it. Or perhaps the order was shipped and the package still may arrive. We are investigating to see just what happened, and you may hear from us again.

Should you get two checks and no merchandise, please return one of them. If the shipment has arrived since you wrote and you decide to keep it, please return the check and this letter.

Should you receive only this check and no merchandise, no reply to this letter is necessary.

Yours truly

If there are several facts to be mentioned, as there were in this letter, the writer must be sure that not only have they been related but also that they are presented in the order of their importance. There is only one way to be sure: jot them down *before* you write. The time spent in writing out the points also gives you a chance to organize your ideas and to avoid the confusion in the letter sample above.

If only one or two facts are to be conveyed, the average writer should have little trouble in relating them without writing them down first. Sometimes, however, it is with the one- or two-point message that we become most careless, as was the writer of the reply to the following letter from an insurance policyholder.

Gentlemen:

My policy with you and all receipts in payment are in Midland

City with the beneficiary. It is essential that I have the number of my policy by next Monday. Will you please furnish me this number?

Thank you.

Very truly yours

This letter requires an answer to only one fact, but here is the reply the policyholder actually received:

Policy No. 1364667

Dear Mr. Brown:

The following information is in reply to your recent postcard.

Premiums on this policy are paid to November 28, 19xx, and approximately 15 days before that date a semiannual notice will be sent to you.

If you have other questions about this policy, we invite you to write us.

Cordially yours

We can assume that Mr. Brown was intelligent enough to see the number he wanted in the reference block. The rest of the information was merely fill-in. The writer felt something needed to be added and, in attempting to make it "appear" like a letter, lost sight of the one thing the policyholder wanted to know. The very short reply that follows could have done the job nicely.

Policy No. 1364667

Dear Mr. Brown:

As you see, your number is 1364667.

We hope the information reaches you in time.

Cordially yours

Certainly the writer will have some definite ideas about what he or she is trying to accomplish. If thoughts are orderly and facts are known, the writer should have little trouble in influencing the reader. This assumption alone, however, does not always result in an effective informative communication. For example, the president of a loan company thought that he had a clever way of making a client pay his bill. He had all the facts—except one. He did not know his client! His letter went like this:

Dear Mr. Siminovich:

What would your neighbors think if our truck were to drive up to your home and remove all of the furniture that has not been paid for yet?

The head of the loan company received this reply:

Dear Mr. Smith:

I asked my neighbors about what you said in your letter and they told me if you did such a thing it would be a lousy trick.

Do not try to be clever at your reader's expense.

Because the informative message gives or asks for information, pacifies, or explains, one must use an approach that conforms to the type of communication being written. How do we begin?

Get Off to a Good Start.   Make the opening of your message say something significant by starting with the heart of the message. The purpose of most opening paragraphs of constructive, informative communications is merely to indicate subject matter and perhaps to express a word or two of thanks or appreciation; the subject is then developed in the succeeding paragraphs. For this reason, openings are usually short, and, to make every word count, you need to give special attention to your expression. It should be positive, friendly, and enthusiastic.

For most informative and instructive communications, you can anticipate little resistance on the part of your reader to the subject you are writing about. That is why you will most often choose to begin with the direct style of writing—sometimes called the "headline" approach—rather than with the indirect or "narrative" form. Use the direct approach when you have something pleasant to say. It can also be used as an attention-getter. Without the attention-getting factor, especially if you initiate the message, your informative communication has an uphill struggle. Perhaps it will not even be read. A provocative question often gains the reader's attention and interest from the start as in this illustration:

Gentlemen:

May we please have information to serve as a base for a decision to provide private plane service for our company?

When possible, subordinate routine acknowledgments, identifications, and review of the letters you are answering. An opening that begins "In reply to your letter of the 16th" uses the most important space in your letter to tell your reader an obvious fact. Your own reply is visible evidence that you got the letter and are answering it.

Give Only Essential Information, Couched in You-Attitude Terms. Conserve your reader's time by writing clearly and concisely. All readers dislike cluttered writing. You will need to leave out unnecessary words to make room for others that have a greater contribution to make in relaying your ideas in the simplest way. As writer, you may sometimes have to give a brief orientation to help your reader become familiar with the subject, for readers cannot be expected to agree with something they do not understand. Following the example just given, for instance, the next paragraph might read this way:

> Your Model 310 Howerton seems to be the answer to our problem of getting key people to outlets in scattered parts of the United States and Mexico and back to the plant in a minimum of time. Since a $125,000 investment is critical at this stage of our 5-year-old growing business, however, we'd like to know these things:
>
> 1. Is it possible to lease a plane for a trial period to determine whether real economy of money and time results?
>
> 2. May all or part of the lease fees be applied to the purchase price, should we decide to buy?

Simple words and short sentences help to build understanding in a natural flow from sentence to sentence, idea to idea as you develop the subject. Technical and unfamiliar words build barriers. Using words to impress your reader rather than express the real thought may result in rejection of your message.

Let your information, phrased in a spirit of helpfulness, offer a *real* service to your reader. Whatever you have decided to include should always show consideration for *reader* interest, *reader* needs, *reader* wants. Your reader wants to be treated as an individual.

Providing material from which the reader can reach logical conclusions, using familiar points (easy reference), and arranging your material in a varying pattern of questions and answers, statements and explanations help move your message along on its mission. Simultaneously, these techniques save words and the reader's time. Keep focused on your purpose throughout the communication.

Design Your Closing Paragraph to Build Goodwill. Writing a good closing is sometimes one of the most difficult things to do well, particularly in short letters. Many writers think that they *have* to say something at the end of the letter or it will not sound right. Perhaps so, for it is much like walking away from someone you have been talking to without any word of farewell. Reread the suggested reply to Mr. Brown's letter on page 93. Notice how the rewrite has adapted the closing to fit his request. He needed the information quickly!

Of course there is nothing wrong in closing a letter when everything has been said, particularly if you carry on extensive correspondence with the reader. Using trite phrases detracts from the value of the informative communication and adds nothing to the reader's knowledge. Your closing should be something that adds emphasis to what has been said or is a sincere statement of your feelings toward your reader. Closings can be useful, but you have to *make* them so. Often they may be a plus value in goodwill. The close for the message on private plane service, for example, might read this way:

> Lease costs and the basic services provided are, of course, of interest to us. We'll certainly appreciate any information that will help us arrive at a satisfactory solution.

Try phrasing your close to fit the communication. Your choices may be to

1. Indicate continued interest in your reader.
2. Resell your business or organization.
3. Look to future dealings together.
4. Reemphasize the central theme of your message.

The good close is always friendly, natural, and sincere. It should never be negative, contrived, or trite, and it should always leave the channel open for further communication.

Appraising the Receiver's Position

With a background established for planning informative communication strategy, let us now examine specific considerations in appraising the reader's position. The intellectual and cultural level, the reaction to the nature of your message, the relationship to you, and the nature of the reader's environment and yours must be assessed if your message is to be effective.

Evaluating the Reader's Intellectual and Cultural Level. *What do you know about your reader's intellect and culture that will help you to adapt your material and word choice?* That is the first question you must answer to be able to visualize the reader as an individual and thus to write *to* a person.

Is the recipient a professional? If so, the reader's education is likely to be above average and his or her cultural background a bit more diverse and sophisticated than that of the nonprofessional. In what part of the country does the recipient live? A large metropolitan city or a small town? A cultural center, an industrial hub, or a poverty-stricken wasteland? With the mobility of twentieth-century America, a residence can at best be only a guideline to the intellectual and cultural level. Nor is the person's vocation any sure-fire indication of those levels. But vocation, coupled with location, is likely to give you your first insight in appraising the receiver as an individual.

Is the recipient a recognized authority or expert in a particular field? The reader's accomplishments are likely to be a matter of record. A quick search through current trade periodicals, association and professional directories, or the public library will often provide useful bits of information about your reader. Do any of your staff or business associates know the reader personally?

What has the reader told you about himself or herself in the communication to you? Is the writing that of an educated person? Is the word choice indicative of broad educational and cultural exposure? A polished writing style? Or is the writing dull, confused, hard-to-read prose? Enthusiastic? Sound like a person you would like to know? To have as a friend?

What previous association have you had with your reader? Do you have a file on the person—a credit or job application, a personal history, a ledger sheet? Have you had occasion to associate with the individual socially or through civic endeavors?

Answers to these and similar probing questions are needed if you are to evaluate your reader adequately.

Anticipating Reader Reaction to the Nature of the Message. The second basic question in appraising the receiver's position is: *How would you react to the information you are sending if you were the reader?* If you know, for example, that your reader is well educated and culturally sophisticated, your choice of words, phrasing, and subject coverage can be planned in a manner different from that employed for the less educated or illiterate individual. Your tone for both will be different, however, if the information you are conveying is pleasant rather than unpleasant.

If you are conveying complicated or technical information, you will have to take extra care to make it clear, readable, and understandable for either type of reader. The fact that you have a well-educated reader does not mean that you need to be less careful in your planning and presentation than you would be for a less-knowledgeable reader. Always try to conserve your reader's time and effort by anticipating the reception of your information; plan it to achieve the best psychological effect from the *first* quick reading. Should you not have evaluated properly and anticipated receiver reaction, you are likely to emphasize points of your own interest, to assume knowledge where knowledge is absent, or to present information irrelevant to reader use.

Measuring the Influence of the Reader's Relationship to the Communicator. A third basic question has a direct bearing on the role playing and interaction process: *What is the sphere of relationship between writer and reader?* The reader's reaction to the nature of the message may have far-reaching effects on this relationship. Measuring this influence means having correct answers to the two preceding basic questions. If your reader is an authority, for example, has asked you for information, and you respond with no thought to reader intellect or reaction, you will assume a role of little or no significance for the person. Should the reader be seeking your help and you do not give it as expected, you have in effect indicated that this individual is not worth bothering with.

Is your reader in a position to exert influence in your favor sometime in the future? Are you likely to need reciprocal help? There is nothing like a selfish interest to produce care and consideration in the writer's attempt to convey information effectively. Whether or not the reader can return a similar service, however, should make no difference in the care and attention you give your message. The fact that everyone exerts *some* influence in his or her sphere of personal associations should be sufficient incentive for you to do your best job on every informative communication you write. A disgruntled reader's idle talk against you and your firm can easily spell trouble.

Assessing Environmental Conditions.   Allied closely with the sphere of reader-writer influence is the consideration of environmental conditions. *What are the internal and the external conditions that have a bearing for the writer's appraisal of the reader's position?*

For the writer's performance level, he or she needs to *be* a part of the firm or organization, to be involved in the issues, to know that people depend on his or her skills. Management, in turn, needs to provide for the employee the environment conducive to happy involvement, from which motivation and creativity come. People who keep looking outside themselves get fresh ideas and new approaches to problem solving.

Employees have four basic psychological needs: a feeling of security, an opportunity for advancement, humane treatment, and the realization of doing something useful. An environment set by management to meet these needs is conducive to effective communication.

Which conflicts and pressures in your environment will erect barriers to successful communication with your reader? Does policy prevent being open with your reader? Will management back you up on promises you make? Will it follow through? Will it fail to take an action you indicate? And is your reader likely to have similar conflicts and pressures? To make effective use of the information you impart?

DESIGNING MESSAGES FOR WHICH NO RESISTANCE IS ANTICIPATED

If you initiate the inquiry or request, the possibility for a future sale is all the motivation the firm needs to respond to it. Some inquiries or requests mean business for the firm; some do not. A company or organization that wants the goodwill of the public will answer all *reasonable* inquiries promptly.

Many now have a standing rule of "in and out" in three days (some in 24 hours), which means that any message coming into the firm and requiring a reply will get it promptly—or at least an acknowledgment that it is being worked on. Most organizations welcome inquiries about their products, services, research activities, personnel, and operations. They expect these inquiries as a part of "doing" business. Many inquiries are good referral leads for company sales representatives. Claims indicate weaknesses in services or products that the company needs to improve for better customer relations. Firms are often in need of similar kinds of information themselves—the principle of reciprocity.

Probably the easiest of all messages to write—whether we are explaining, describing, asking, or answering questions—are those our readers will receive favorably. Designing such messages involves specific application of selected techniques you have already been introduced to at this point in your study. Now we will see how giving the crux of your message in the opening words, organizing for the best sequence, framing ideas constructively, and winning support for your message with the proper tone apply in imparting information effectively.

Giving the Crux of the Message in the Opening Words

In asking for information that you expect to receive as a matter of course, begin directly with the request—as specifically and concisely as you can frame it. Similarly, whether you are placing an order, filing a claim for damaged or malfunctioning merchandise, authorizing an investigation, or making an inquiry, step briskly into the subject. The first five to ten words are considered the most important—by position and emphasis. They should get at the very heart of the informative communication without ceremony or detour. Alerting the reader to the purpose of the message in the subject block or in the opening words focuses attention. Your reader will appreciate this time-saving technique.

Nine out of ten people want to begin such requests or inquiries with an explanation—to "back into" the message. If a sales representative on the road is about to run out of order blanks and writes the home office for a new supply, should this writer move right into the request? Certainly. The person in charge of supplies will have no objections to sending new blanks. So the writer could well begin with

> Will you please send a new supply of order blanks to reach me at the Statler-Hilton, Chicago, by Friday?

That is direct, polite style. To save time, it is better to tell the reader what you want immediately and *then* proceed with any necessary exposition as to why you want it.

There are occasions, however, when to launch point blank with what you want or need may be a bit unrealistic, too blunt or perhaps offensive to the reader. This may occur (1) because of a time lapse between writings (such as the lag between the time an authorization is written until a report is transmitted), (2) because of the time that has elapsed in exploring possibilities of a research project and the actual authorization to proceed, or (3) because of your reader's lack of familiarity with your reasons for writing. Your letter thus needs some legitimate basis for being written.

Take, for example, the authorization for an investigation. Suppose that you have had preliminary negotiations by phone and personal conference on a proposed research topic. Two weeks later you reach your decision and are ready to proceed with the study. The "please investigate the feasibility of" approach gives the impression your reader has never heard of it until just this moment. Thus, *in dependent structure* you need to pick up previous negotiations or purpose before stating the authorization, like this:

> In line with the plans outlined in the past few weeks, will you please proceed with the investigation of . . . ?

Or

> So that we may have a sound plan for consideration, please start your comparative-evaluation study of mobile-home park operations in the Northwest, which we've discussed in the past few weeks.

Notice, too, that these examples are written with the utmost degree of directness in sentence structure. There is no reason for slowdown approaches to the subject by such beginnings as

> "Is it possible for you to send me . . . ?"
> "I should like to have information that will help me get started on . . ."
> (the hinting type that never asks)
> "You are hereby authorized to . . ." (pompous, cliché)
> "This is your authorization to . . ." (mechanical)

If you are making a claim, your opening sentence should identify the difficulty, at least in general terms. However, it may be more diplomatic to cushion the complaint by leading into it with a dependent structure that expresses a verbal pat on the back.

> "In view of our good experience with _____ in the past, it was surprising to find that . . ."
> "Although our last order for a _____ was filled promptly and correctly, this latest one . . ."

The ultradirect request for remedial action in claims—

"Will you please refund . . ."

"May I have a replacement for . . .?"

—perhaps suffices when the situation is clear-cut and routine and when there could be no doubt as to the justness of your claim.

The same reasoning holds for favorable replies—acknowledgments, adjustment and credit approvals, and transmittals. Make your "yes" encompass as much of the subject as you can.

There are two kinds of direct-style answers—one that grants a favor or request and one that pleasantly supplies information asked for. The psychology behind the favor-granting answer is that if you have good news to tell, tell it immediately. Only a person with a mean character streak will keep the reader dangling to find out whether the request has been granted. The good news is the most positive element in the message and should be emphasized by

1. Position in the *first main clause* of the message.
2. An enthusiastic tone.
3. The use of colorful, forceful words.

The same writing principles apply for the information letter supplying answers that you are glad to give. A constructive answer to some main phase of the reader's inquiry deserves first position. (You will, of course, apply the laws of emphasis to any portions of your answer that might be displeasing to the reader.)

Here is an example of two ways of saying "yes."

An Actual Letter	*A Revised Version*
Dear Sir:	Dear Mr. Leslie:
We are in receipt of your favor of April 12 in which you request that we furnish you a copy of our current Grayvale directory with certain notations and emendations. In reply I wish to assure you that we are very much interested in your proposed directory of Texas manufacturers and believe it is a project that should be supported by Texas industry in every possible way.	Yes sir; we'll gladly help with your manufacturers' directory, just as you've asked in your April 12th letter.
	To get the names and classifications up to directory exactness, Mr. Stanley Foraker of our own directory staff has already started a by-name check of each listed industry. He will label carefully the exact goods produced or processed; and he will mark the sales agents as such. You can expect his report by the 20th, I'm sure.
In order to ascertain whether or not a particular manufacturer listed in our directory is a producer or processor or is only the sales agent for goods manufactured outside the state, it will be obviously necessary for us to put a	Your completed directory will certainly help Texas industry to get a measure of itself and will help to sell Texas as a ripe

responsible and capable clerk on the assignment to contact by telephone each manufacturer listed and to request information direct as to his classification and the nature of his operations. We are quite willing to do this, despite the extra work involved, and in fact we have already selected the man and assigned his duties to him. He will start to work at an early date, and we will notify you in due course as to his progress.

Assuring you of our continued interest, and trusting that you will not hesitate to call on us in the future at any time we may be of service to you in any way, we are

Yours very truly,

field for many types of new enterprises. It's a fine job you are taking on. We'll be glad to see the book.

Yours sincerely

You will notice in the examples a progression of directness in sentence structure from the slowest,

I believe I can do what you ask (fraught with uncertainty)

to the future,

I will do what you ask (fraught with probability)

to the present,

I am doing what you asked

through the accomplished action,

I have already done what you asked.

Skilled writers take the progression a step farther. An adjustment opening that starts "The attached check, No. 9167, replaces . . . " not only states the action accomplished but shows the check performing its intended function.

Remember, too, that in most cases reader deference is preferable to the I-viewpoint:

"Well, here I am" as contrasted to "Ah, there you are!"

"I had a wonderful time" to "You are a wonderful hostess!"

If the date of the request has significance, or if you feel you need to make an acknowledgement, pick it up incidentally in a dependent structure or push it down in the sentence—possibly all the way to an end phrase as in the revised version sample on the preceding page. Frequently, however, acknowledging the reader's letter *by date* is an utter waste of words and space in your message.

Orienting the Reader
with Background Material

Once you are launched on the subject and the reader knows the purpose of your informative communication, your next step is to tell why—*if* additional exposition is necessary. The decision to explain further is always yours to make. But remember that readers cannot be expected to agree with something they do not understand.

Such orientation begins as you proceed from the opening paragraph into the main body of the message. Simple words and short sentences and natural flow from sentence to sentence, idea to idea help to build understanding. Good writing leads from one phase to another without any jarring effects. The question here is: How can you make the explanation a smooth one and a logical outgrowth of your opening remarks?

The technique is to make the sentence a you- rather than an I-oriented one. We look for a service-to-your-reader benefit; a helpful attitude—your wish to furnish accurate, dependable, useful information; some sort of compliment on the person's business sense; appreciation of the individual as a good customer; a courtesy or goodwill remark; or some identification that makes the request or information given natural in this situation.

Here are some examples:

"To help you make the best use of the enclosed material, we've made marginal notations with suggested cross-references."

"Only as businesses like yours continue to demand the highest ideals in education can we as teachers expect students to reach these same levels in course performance. That is why . . ."

"Because the five years just ahead are likely to be the most critical in our challenge for industry leadership, you as a valued employee will . . ."

"Every day more and more people are realizing, as you have, the financial gains to be made by . . ."

"In order to clarify the situation . . ."

"To keep you informed . . ."

"Accustomed as you are to having the right information available for making the right decision, you can appreciate . . ."

"Phases that seem pertinent to my problem are these: . . ."

"As a business report writing student investigating the growth potential for the insurance business in three selected cities, I am assembling data to . . ."

Topic-Sentence Leadoff

In helping your reader become familiar with the subject, you can move your writing along by using a topic-sentence leadoff at the beginning of each paragraph. The topic sentence expresses the main idea of the paragraph and is used as a foundation for building a larger thought unit. (Although the topic sentence is best placed at the paragraph beginning, it may occur in the middle or as a summary statement at the end.)

At the beginning of a paragraph, the topic sentence focuses attention on the content and lets your reader know the plan to be followed in your writing. For example,

"A tax-sheltered annuity offers many unique advantages." (The advantages are then named.)

"Our program consists of two plans—a Savings Fund Plan and a Retirement Thrift Plan." (The two plans are in turn described in detail.)

Not only are sentences such as these helpful in orienting your reader with background material and in giving a leadoff to subject matter, but they can serve as transitional devices as well. Pointing in two directions, these sentences can remind your reader of what has been said and prepare him or her for what is to follow.

The topic sentence is a control of ideas in directing the reader's flow of thought. You develop these controls by descriptive detail, cause and effect, illustration, example, definition, narration, comparison, contrast, or analysis. Each paragraph of your message represents a logical thought unit that has a distinct bearing on the progress of the message toward its objective. Such logic is established through the use of the topic sentence to achieve unity of purpose. Topic sentences, therefore, help to achieve unity and coherence in your message.

Selecting an important idea and expressing it in a sentence clearly, accurately, and forcefully, and then developing it into a thought unit of a paragraph, helps the reader to understand. The technique is especially effective in informative writing to emphasize a point by stating the topic sentence, following it with supporting or developing details, and then summarizing it. Care should be taken in employing this approach since the mechanical application of it is readily apparent even to a casual reader.

If one sentence is all you need, however, it is better to start a new paragraph, rather than to pad the one you are writing or to cover two topics in a single paragraph. Some writers mistakenly believe that they should avoid one-sentence paragraphs, but a one-sentence (even a one-line paragraph) can be used effectively to give greater emphasis to a point by setting it apart. Certainly you will want to avoid two topics in one paragraph, for the rule of one idea, one sentence is even more applicable to paragraphs: one topic, one paragraph.

Organizing Aspects of the Message for the Best Sequence

With your opening paragraph established and your orientation begun, next you will have to present the facts necessary for your reader's complete understanding if you originate the message or choose the best psychological sequence for the items of information you present if you are replying. For either case, the question is: What will you need to tell?

In your thinking and planning prior to writing (Chapter 2, pages 48–61), you will have decided already what points are relevant and what information to include. It is a matter now of ordering those points for presentation as constructively and tactfully as possible.

For your own originated inquiry, request, claim, order, or authorization—just as for constructive, informative replies—you will need to arrange your ideas for the best sequence. You should consider whether the reader will react more favorably to a descending scale (the most important things first and tapering off) or whether a climactic arrangement is preferable (leading up to the most significant phase somewhat dramatically). It may be possible to retain interest more effectively by putting a highly significant detail at the first and last (a combination of descending-ascending) with the less important material in central positions. Different arrangements work better in different situations. The essential thing is for the *effect* to be calculated. Knowing which choice to make for the sequence of points is easier if you have, at this stage, appraised your receiver's position, for then you will be able to adapt your material to the intellectual and cultural level of the reader. Here is a combination-order-of-points example:

Main idea in first sentence with supporting reasons.

DATE: August 23, 19xx
TO: All Centex Representatives
FROM: The Sales Manager

From here on, we'd like all of us to think and talk of our 8-ounce cans as "Individual" sizes instead of 8-ounce sizes for this reason: the can may occassionally contain a little less than 8 ounces. We'd rather have the customer happily eating an "individual" portion than suspiciously checking the ounce content.

Benefit-to-reader lead into second phase—the advantages of the vacuum process.	Your vending-machine operators should be pleased with the keeping qualities of the new vacuum-packed individual sizes, samples of which were sent to you recently. Our vacuum process outdistances the competition, we think, in preparing food to withstand the prolonged heat of vending machines.
Direct appeal for reader action on third phase.	Will you please channel any remaining stocks of individual cans packed before July 19xx to regular grocery stores and obtain new vacuum-packed stock for vending machines?
Positive statement of reason for reader action.	That way we'll make the best use of both lots.

In your replies you will want to select the same order as the inquiry you are answering: ascending order, descending order, or mixed, according to the nature of the information conveyed, *and* your appraisal of the reader.

Framing Ideas Constructively

In framing ideas constructively for the reader (after you have made the decision for the order of presentation), you will need to adapt your language to express these ideas appropriately. How often have you seen good news mutilated the way this sentence does it?

Effective January 15 your workday will be one-half hour *longer* to facilitate your expressed wish for the elimination of a half day's work on Saturdays.

Why not begin with the main phase of the good news this way:

Beginning January 15 your Saturdays are your own, for on that day Carlton Company goes on a 5-day schedule.

And follow it up as a bond with your reader:

Your Board of Directors is happy to grant this request made by your Employee Council.

Then make clear the aspects of the message:

Following up your own expressed preference, you will arrive at the office at 8:15 A.M. instead of 8:30 A.M. on January 15 (and on all subsequent work days) and will leave at 5:15 P.M. instead of 5:00 P.M.

You might also close on a goodwill-plus value:

Make pleasant use of your longer weekends!

Of course all the questions you ask must be framed for an easy reply; they must be considerate of your reader's time and effort. Ask for no information you could get conveniently elsewhere even though it might require *your* time and effort. (The reader should be the most logical source to seek information from, thus providing a legitimate basis for your request.) Additionally, you ought to limit the number of questions asked or the amount of information sought to a bare minimum.

You must write so that you can not only be understood but so that *you cannot possibly be misunderstood.* Your ideas are thus stated clearly, concisely, and succinctly in terms of reader consideration: How the recipient fits into the situation, how he or she is benefited or how the reader helps, how he or she is served or how this person can serve, how his or her needs and wants are met or how the reader contributes for the betterment of all concerned.

All questions asked deserve an answer.

Explanations of terms, procedures, or operations are made not as flat assertions as though the reader were unenlightened but from the viewpoint of natural assumption, inference, and logic. Take, for example, the granting of an adjustment to a customer's valid claim. What is back of the company's policy of a 90-day guarantee against defective products? The policy obviously is set up to protect the firm against would-be chiselers who might take advantage of the company. But the policy is also set up as well to guarantee customers better products at the lowest cost, to protect us against error in mass production (usually, under normal use, a defective product will show up within this 90-day period), and as a matter of convenience in replacement. These latter customer benefits provide the basis for framing an explanation constructively.

Simply writing "Our policy is to replace all products showing a defect within a 90-day period after purchase," or "Your 90-day guarantee is still in force and our policy is to replace all unsatisfactory products during that period" offers no explanation. In such statements the attitude of the adjuster comes off second best also.

Granting credit affords you a chance to educate your reader on handling credit obligations properly as you establish the basis for your own credit policy procedures and operations, terms, and payments.

The low-priced, top-quality lines you'll find at Sexton's are made possible only by having all credit customers pay bills regularly when due. Prompt payment coupled with our low collection costs in turn allows us to take advantage of discounts which we pass along to you as a customer.

Handling price (creating value equal to the cost of the product or service), reselling the firm in the reader's mind (leaving an impression that it is a good place to do business), reselling products and services and stimulating new sales (the best place in town to get your money's worth) are ideas that must be framed from the reader's point of view for effectiveness.

The same approach is continued as you phrase each idea positively to benefit the reader's needs and the uses to be made of the information.

Winning Support of the Message with Proper Tone

The enthusiasm, warm feeling, and natural word flow introduced in your opening paragraph sets the tone that prevails throughout the entire informative communication. How can you expect an enthusiastic reception to a message that is dull, mechanically written, cliché ridden—an uninspired effort?

All the techniques, instructions, and illustrative application of points covered thus far in designing messages for which no resistance is anticipated have been couched in terms for achieving proper tone throughout the communication. Go back and reread them.

You will notice in the examples used as direct openings an absence of clichés ("Enclosed please find"), verbiage ("I am submitting herewith, Check No. 9136 to replace") and negative references ("The attached ———will take care of the difficulty you've been having"). The same holds true for orienting your reader with background material and framing ideas constructively.

Not all business writing is terribly exciting, but it need never be boring. Writing, like every other job, is only as interesting as you make it. So give better to your reader than you get. Do not answer in kind to a thoughtless writer. Address yourself to the reader's feelings, not the words used, for letters—like people—have personalities that attract or repel.

Refrain from changing your personality when you begin to write. Make an effort at being friendly. To preserve a personalized, efficient image of the company in your messages, be careful in your phraseology. Readers know when they have been manipulated, and they resent it.

No less important than winning support of your message is the wording and tone of your closing paragraph. The end of the informative message should be just that, without any evidence of rambling which weakens the message's effect. Your close can accomplish a great deal for you. It can

1.   Leave a good impression of you and of your company.
2.   Prompt the reader to do the very thing you wanted done.
3.   Leave no doubt as to the action you want taken.
4.   Give the reader the implication that you know you've done what was wanted—and willingly.
5.   Offer more than your reader asked of you.
6.   Give you a chance to say something genuinely pleasant.

7. Help you—if your message is a long one—to sum up, to bring into focus all that has gone before.

Phrase your closing remarks (the last paragraph should be just one or two sentences long for the best psychological effect) as a polite suggestion, friendly advice—never as an order. Require of your reader a minimum of effort; promise only what you are sure you can do. Pay a compliment, appeal to pride, give an alternative, leave the way open for further communication with your reader.

Some short messages do not require a separate closing paragraph. You will help win your case by not manufacturing filler at the end of your informative or instructive communications.

INFORMING UNDER ADVERSE CIRCUMSTANCES

Not all messages whose *intended import* is informative or instructive are entirely positive. Often they involve some information that your reader will not want to receive. The right technique in this situation is to calculate carefully the sequence of ideas, bypass communication barriers, give your reader a way out of the situation, and gain acceptance of your message through understanding by emphasizing constructive rather than destructive aspects.

Let us take a typical problem and follow through to its solution. Suppose, for example, that you are managing editor of *Business Horizons*, a monthly journal of business and economic conditions in Indiana. In each month's issue you publish a tabular statistical section, "Local Business Barometers," that gives various business indicators for most of the cities and large towns in the state. Among the key statistics appearing there are dollar figures representing end-of-month bank deposits and total monthly bank debits in each city.

In a letter you received today, a bank vice-president from Lafayette takes exception to the bank data for his city. Mr. Martin W. Lang of the Farmers National Bank put his question this way:

The deposits shown for all Lafayette banks as of the end of February are $24,194,000. Since the deposits in our bank alone have averaged about $18,000,000 through all the past year, that would leave only $6,000,000 as the total for the other two banks here. Although they are smaller banks, they certainly have much larger funds on deposit than that figure would indicate. I should like to arrange to have your statistics corrected. Although I do not know where you get your information, we should be glad to supply you with our data directly.

The embarrassing fact is that the figures are supplied monthly by a cashier in Mr. Lang's bank. All your data come from cooperating banks in Lafayette and throughout the state. A quick check of your files shows that the deposit total reported by the Farmers National Bank on the date in question was $11,189,476. It also appears that there has been no marked change in the level of deposits in this bank during the past year.

Mr. Lang's letter continued,

Because Lafayette and West Lafayette are so close together both physically and economically, it seems to me that it would make sense for you to show combined statistics for the two cities; they really function as one.

The suggestion is interesting, but you cannot adopt it. *Business Horizons* does publish aggregate figures for the Standard Metropolitan Statistical Areas, as defined by the U.S. Bureau of the Census, as well as separate statistics for the cities in those areas. Nevertheless, Lafayette–West Lafayette is not an official SMSA, mainly because its total population is not large enough. You do not have space in your journal to publish both separate and total statistics for all cities that happen to be situated close together. Anyone who wants totals has only to pick up a pencil and add a few numbers.

Thus this problem (as is true for any informative communication containing adverse information) not only involves applying the principles set forth in the previous section, "Designing Messages for Which No Resistance Is Anticipated," but it also requires special consideration of the reader's response to some embarrassing or unpleasant ideas.

Calculating the Sequence of Ideas

In calculating the sequence of ideas to be presented in such messages, the questions you will have to find answers for are: What are the areas of information that must be clarified? What order of presentation will have the best psychological effect?

For Mr. Lang, two areas need clarification: *bank deposits* and *metropolitan areas*. Mr. Lang is confused on what demand deposits *at the end of the month* include. This information is the total owed to depositors of the bank at the close of business on the last day of the month for which the report is being made. It is the same figure appearing on the bank's balance sheet for the end of the month. It is *not* the amount of money deposited by customers during the month nor does it include the accounts of other banks or time deposits.

Metropolitan areas are urban zones that meet certain socioeconomic criteria set up by the Census Bureau. Why would a business journal restrict certain statistical coverage to SMSAs? (Because it is assumed that they are qualitatively different from other urban areas.) What qualitative differences set SMSAs apart? (Research on central place and metropolitan functions suggests that there are certain economic functions concentrated dispropor-tionately in large cities. For that matter, an increasing share of the population lives in metropolitan areas.)

If you were to respond to this letter, how would you begin? Essentially there are two alternatives:

> 1. Get the unpleasant matters out of the way in the beginning in order to clear the air, relieve tension, and permit the letter to continue along more ingratiating lines.
> 2. Convince the reader of your appreciation for his interest, your goodwill, and your common sense *before* revealing that the questions must be resolved on your terms.

Which of these tactics would you prefer if you were the reader?

Some professional writers feel that the second, indirect, approach is an affront to the reader's intelligence. They base this opinion on the fact that indirection is widely recognized today as a deceptive tactic. Will Mr. Lang be offended by your playing tricks on him? Possibly he may if he is a so-phisticated communicator himself or a realist. Nonetheless, if the trick is well played, even the worldliest reader is likely to see it, at worst, as an innocent effort to spare his feelings. In this case, the information should be excluded from both the opening and close since it is potentially irritating.

There are hazards, and perhaps greater ones, in the average writer's presenting unpleasant information directly at the beginning of a letter. The direct approach requires writing skill and imagination for adverse infor-mation messages. In this case, if we launched directly into the bank's re-porting procedure, we would be in danger of embarrassing our reader. After all, it is his cashier who has given us the information.

Perhaps by keeping the talk brief, *impersonal*, and emphasizing what-ever positive aspects might be found, we would carry off the direct approach reasonably well. It is probably safer, however, to begin with the indirect method—some expression of the common interest you have in the journal would do—to bypass the communication barrier inherent in your reader's instant negative reaction to unpleasant information.

It would also be unfortunate, after a short, pleasant opening paragraph, to lead abruptly into the negative issues. So we would attempt to cushion the beginning of our second paragraph. But which of the sticky issues comes first? They should be dealt with separately. Since the matter of the deposit reports is the simpler of the two and surely the more hazardous, why not deal with it first? The banker is undoubtedly more concerned with his first question; the second seems almost to be an afterthought. Stalling on the main topic is likely to be recognized as just that—stalling.

Bypassing Communication Barriers

There are many barriers to clear and effective communication. The individual's habits of thought and action, among others, may prove to be serious obstacles. That is why we first gave attention to calculating the sequence of ideas. The channel used to communicate information may act as a barrier to successful communication. (Certain kinds of information are best communicated in person, other kinds by letter, still other kinds by report, telephone, telegraph, and so on.) Poor writing habits constitute another barrier to transmitting information. You should also recognize that you and your reader may have conflicting attitudes and values that will act as barriers.

To bypass communication barriers, you must know how to handle ideas, how to perceive correct relationships between you and the reader, how to think positively, and how to take proper action. Distortion and misunderstanding lie in wait for the unwary writer.

Allowing the Reader to Save Face
Through Understanding

As we continue to explore the answer to Mr. Lang, you will see how we attempt to bypass these barriers by allowing him to save face and by gaining his acceptance through understanding.

Having decided to begin your information coverage on the matter of deposit reports, you will of course give the banker the facts. You do receive reports directly from his bank and the deposit level last reported is as the problem indicated—$11,189,476. But you want to keep this informational talk as impersonal as you can. To keep from putting Mr. Lang into an untenable position—one that he would be *forced* to defend—avoid speaking of "your bank," "your cashier," and "you." Perhaps resorting to passive constructions are best here. For example,

> Banks cooperating in our monthly survey send us their deposit and debit figures directly. Ordinarily the information is prepared and sent to us by a bank cashier.

Without speaking of *errors* or *fault*, you will want to invite whatever corrections may be necessary. You might introduce this subject by suggesting that the kind of data you want may have been misunderstood, but avoid saying by whom.

Ordinarily, the next subject, the possibility of combining Lafayette and West Lafayette, should be discussed in a separate paragraph. It is distinct from the bank data discussion. Both paragraphs should end and begin as gracefully as you can manage and not on a negative note in either case.

As to the combined statistics, you can share your reader's interest in making the published information more useful and representative. Surely there is no need to apologize in speaking of this topic; an apology would only imply that your policy was questionable. Note, too, that the term *policy* sounds bureaucratic and arbitrary to many readers; it would be best not to use the word at all in this communication.

You can avoid negative talk by explaining clearly just what you do; not what you don't do. Your combined statistics represent economic measures of Standard Metropolitan Statistical Areas, which are determined by the Census Bureau. The responsibility, then, really is not yours, is it?

Further, you would not want to speak of SMSAs as if this banker had never heard of them. He probably has. But you might indicate briefly what the main criteria are. Actually it would be pleasantly optimistic to see metropolitan potentials in Lafayette–West Lafayette, perhaps within this decade? That notion might provide a cheerful conclusion to your explanation.

It would be in order to express your thanks for the banker's interest in your journal. Beyond that, possibly casual appreciation for the bank's cooperation, as long as the mention of it is too vague to be taken for sarcasm, or looking forward to some pleasant encounter, offers you a goodwill note for the close.

Frequently when a person criticizes, it is because the individual does not understand or does not know certain basic facts. We attempt to convey these facts merely as *news*, without showing the reader up as stupid, foolish, or ignorant. Using the disarming technique, we express understanding of the point of view held and grant that on the basis of known facts the person's stand was perfectly natural. We then give additional information that will allow the reader to save face in changing his or her position and to accept ours through his or her own understanding.

How you enlighten your reader to gain that person's acceptance is a true test of your ability to write effective informative messages even under adverse circumstances.

Playing up Constructive Rather Than Destructive Aspects

Expressing understanding of your reader's position, building up the ego in any reasonable way, offering additional information—a way out of his or her untenable position were you to confront the reader directly—are all constructive aspects in informing under adverse circumstances. Without such you force your reader into further defense of the position already assumed. An individual cannot be expected to change an opinion of you or your procedure—nor will a person have cause to do so—unless you offer a sound reason why that should be done, and thus a logical way out of the situation.

Looking for positive points on which to hang your ideas, avoiding any point-blank negative assertions ("we're right—you're wrong" attitude)—even a negative implication—and playing up your role as a reasonable, *helpful* person are ways in which you set forth the constructive rather than destructive aspects to win your case.

As a further illustration of the technique, suppose that you worked as a correspondent for a life insurance company and this request came to your desk:

Please quote me the rate of insurance for a person 32 years of age.

The request for information is made without giving full details of the writer's needs. Naturally, your first question is: What kind of insurance? You cannot please your prospective customer by answering "You dope, don't you know we have dozens of kinds of policies, different rates for different types, and that rates for some of the same type coverage differ according to the sex and health of the insured?"

Rather than writing to ask the reader what kind of insurance he or she had in mind—a situation fraught with destructive aspects, by the way (because you take the chance of embarrassing the reader for failing to tell you in the first place and because the additional delay in providing information is likely to cool the desire for insurance from your company)—you look for some constructive way to help. So you tell the reader about *a* plan that applies to all people age 32. Like this:

> Thank you for your inquiry on rates of insurance for a person 32 years old.
>
> From experience, we've found that most purchasers this age buy the ordinary life policy. This type of insurance gives a young person with large insurance needs the greatest amount of permanent protection for each dollar of premium paid. The rate for it—for man or woman— is $250.40 a year on each $10,000 of coverage. Rates for other amounts, larger or smaller, are in direct proportion.
>
> Of course, we offer many different kinds of policies designed to meet individual needs. You will find it very helpful, we believe, to talk personally with a well-trained life underwriter who can give you the information on which to make your decisions.
>
> Therefore, we are asking a representative of the Company to call on you when he is next in Oldham. May we look forward to serving your needs soon?

And here for your final analysis are contrasting versions of "keeping people on your side" through the office memo, which at times also must inform under adverse circumstances.

TO: Department Heads, Division and
      Subsidiary Managers
FROM: H. J. Dowdy, Safety and Claim Department
      State Public Service Company
SUBJECT: Progress Report on Accident-Prevention Program

Preachy, Formal Tone	*More Tactful and Friendly*

Preachy, Formal Tone

Our report for March will soon be ready and in the mail. It will contain statistical data showing your standing for the first quarter of 19xx, as compared with last year.

In general, the program has had an excellent start. With a very few exceptions, employee committees have been organized, have held their own meetings, and have conducted employee meetings. Response from supervisors and other employees has been wonderful. We couldn't ask for better cooperation.

There are two points we would like to call to your attention.

The first is that some of the meetings we have attended show lack of proper preparation. If a meeting is to be successful, *it must be prepared carefully.* An agenda should be prepared in advance—elements or points to be stressed should be decided before the meeting. Ten to fifteen minutes of preparation can make a big difference in the success of your meetings.

The second point is to *STRESS SHORT ON-THE-JOB MEETINGS.* They really pay off. The departments and divisions with good records have good on-the-job meetings.

We are grateful for your excellent cooperation. Please call on us for any assistance we can render.

More Tactful and Friendly

You will soon be receiving your first quarterly report on our Accident Prevention Program. The effects of the program are certainly rewarding: the overall company accident record is down 10% from that of the same period last year! How your own group contributed a measure of effectiveness is apparent from the comparative figures in the report.

Each of you may well feel proud of your part in making State Public Service Company a safer place to work. Will you please pass on to your employees our appreciation for their excellent response? The way they organized their own committees promptly and conducted their own meetings made a great contribution toward getting the program under way.

Now that the preliminary steps are completed, even greater progress may result in the next quarter. Two ideas for better success occur to us from our own appraisal of program activities:

1.   Encourage committee chairpersons to plan each stage of each meeting well in advance so that all the time may be used purposefully.

2.   Stress short on-the-job meetings— the very best kind of safety instruction right at the source of possible trouble.

Thank you for doing such a nice job! We'll be glad to help any way we can.

CHECKLIST FOR CONSTRUCTIVE, INFORMATIVE MESSAGES

Opening

CIM 10   First-sentence directness is at the heart of positive, informative, constructive messages. Start your communication that way.

11   Your point of contact is illog-

ical or you begin with too minor a point.

12   This one is contrived or too superficial.

13   Try for a more sincere, original opening.

14   Isn't some identification missing that should be included for completeness or for orientation purposes?

15   Subordinate this reference information, however.

16   Avoid the cliché starts.

17   Too much is crammed into the opening paragraph. It tends to lose all sense of direction.

Coverage

CIM 20   Make the sentence leading into your coverage a logical, smooth one. It should continue with the idea begun in the opening paragraph.

21   You have an abrupt break in subject matter treatment. It irritates.

22   Make clear what it is you are doing; why you are writing.

23   The information you give your reader must be meaningful and acceptable to him or her. Is the point you make here instructive? Can the reader learn from it?

24   You've presented non-essential information.

25   Better ordering and adaptation of points is possible. Give thought and planning to the sequence of your idea development for better coherence.

26   Organize your material to show usefulness to reader—a mere listing of points (even of questions or answers) without elaboration often is not enough to get the job done.

27   In the comments you make, reflect your own wish to be of help to your reader. Phrase the information in terms of offering a *real* service to, or consideration of, the reader.

28   Write constructively—no negative inference or reference.

29   Scant coverage; won't the reader still have questions?

30   Is this statement quite accurate?

31   Special points of coverage raised by the individual problem assignment call for a good proportion of these ideas. (Your instructor will provide specific points of expected coverage according to the case problem selected as assignment.)

Close

CIM 40   A goodwill pleasantry is needed.

41   Adapt the close to fit this one case. It should be something that adds emphasis to what has been said or is a *sincere* statement of your feelings toward your reader.

42   Throw away the clichés and ready-made filler statements.

43   Let's end on subject, not off it.

Tone and Style As Marked

Your Grade _____

CHECKLIST FOR INFORMING UNDER ADVERSE CIRCUMSTANCES

Opening

AIM 10   To avoid the reader's instant negative reaction, indirection may be called for as the start of informative messages with unpleasant aspects. Of course, if you have any good news, start with it!

11   Begin on some common point of interest you both have in the subject matter, or

12   Show pleasant appreciation for the reader's interest.

13   You are too close to the adverse information. Your reader will either be embarrassed or suspect that bad news is in the making.

14   Don't even hint at what is wrong or why you are writing at this stage.

15   Try for a more sincere, original beginning.

16   Your point of contact with the reader is illogical. Orient the reader.

17   Avoid the cliché starts.

Coverage

AIM 20   You've shifted abruptly into the negative issue. The effect is disastrous after a short, pleasant opening.

21   Cushion the point—possibly through using passive voice—as you make the turn into the explanation.

22   Don't lecture your reader on things that he or she should already know.

23   Explain the facts clearly without patronizing the reader to gain acceptance.

24   Shouldn't you leave room for face-saving doubt here? There may be some "misunderstanding" about the matter in question.

25   Won't you need to invite from your reader whatever corrections may be necessary to put things in proper order?

26   You've gone into seemingly unnecessary details. Cut them.

27   You've treated issues together that should be handled separately.

28   Is this statement quite accurate?

29   A better ordering of points for adaptation to the situation is possible.

Reorganize for better sequence of idea flow.

30   Build up your reader's ego in any reasonable way:

a.   Express understanding for the reader's point of view.

b.   Treat the additional facts you give merely as news to aid understanding.

31   Too scant coverage.

32   Specific points of coverage indicated by the problem require a good proportion of these issues. (Your instructor will provide specific points of expected coverage according to the case problem selected for assignment.)

Close

AIM 40   Avoid any negative issue in the close.

41   Let your closing remarks positively *infer* the reader's acceptance of your information without putting this idea into specific words.

42   Avoid   empty,   stereotyped remarks.

43   Look   to   future,   pleasant relationships.

44   Keep the channels of communication open.

Tone and Style As Marked

Your Grade _____

PROBLEMS IN WRITING INFORMATIVE MESSAGES

1. *Developing cordial directness in an explanation of your "Letter and Report Writing Workshop."* As Albert W. Schroeder, seminar manager, yours is the problem of explaining your upcoming workshop to Mr. Harry R. Starr, training director, Olympiad Insurance Company, Box 1298, Some City, Any State. He has seen your announcement in a summer issue of *Training in Business and Industry* under the column, "Training Calendar."

November 15–16–17 5th Annual Management Training Workshop to put more zip into your own writing. Latest techniques offered by two industry powerhouse leaders for motivating others you supervise. Sponsored by The Bureau of Industrial Relations, 703 Haven Street, Ann Arbor, Michigan 48104. Contact Albert W. Schroeder, seminar manager.

By virtue of his position, Starr is vitally concerned with keeping up to date on what is happening in the business writing field. He is responsible for the training and supervision of 175 full-time correspondents in the home office. His other duties require much writing as well, for he serves as liaison in setting and maintaining correspondence standards from the larger field offices of his insurance firm. "The brief workshop notice sounds tailor-made for my needs," he writes, "If it's as action-packed as your announcement indicates."

So, what are the particulars you have to offer Mr. Starr through this workshop? The two leaders—Dr. Dugan Hayes and Mr. Joseph Laird (senior and staff instructors, respectively, for the National Airway Lines)—are topnotch. Their aim is a "how to" clinic for modernizing and improving the participants' business writing. Attendees at the workshop will actually work on their own letters, reports, and memos during the session, for each participant is requested to bring

- Some letters or reports that the participant has written.
- Letters that the participant must answer soon after the seminar is over.
- A report on which the participant is currently working.

A fact Starr obviously already knows is that letter and report writing can be hard, time-consuming work. For some people it's a distasteful part of the job. And, it's costly work, too—as much as $6.63 a letter, according to one recent survey. Damage to the company's image, although impossible to calculate, may be even more costly. Thus, whether Starr's aim is to cut costs, to pick up some valuable pointers on supervising others' writing constructively, or simply to make his own business writing a less onerous task, the workshop can help make his writing activities easier and more productive.

Participants in each of the four previous workshops have been enthusiastic in their praise of the course.

Because registration is limited to 25 participants, you'll perhaps want to suggest that Starr complete the seminar registration form you're enclosing and return it without delay. The $350 fee for the three-day, twelve-session clinic includes tuition, course materials, luncheons, and one-year subscriptions to *Management of Personnel Quarterly* and *Personnel Management Abstracts*. Full fee is refundable for registrations canceled one week or more in advance of seminar date; otherwise a $25 charge is required.

You'll also enclose a descriptive outline of the twelve sessions: (a) Current Trends in Business Writing, (b) How to Organize Your Ideas, (c) Reorganizing Participants' Letters, (d) How to be Understood, (e) How to Create Readable Writing, (f) Communicating Unpopular Messages, (g) The Mastery of Rhetoric (Self-help), (h) How to Draw Up a Report, (i) Applying Principles and Techniques, (j) Advanced Writing Clinic, (k) How to Supervise and Edit, and (l) Summary Panel and Critique.

2. *Gaining readability, brevity.* The letter that follows is filled with repetitious and

unnecessary words. But what message does it really convey? Obviously a problem exists. Just what that problem is may be debatable. A shortage in gas supply? Accelerating inflation? What?

As executive assistant to Mr. Jones, there are several avenues open to you. You can

- Go through and cross out redundant words and phrases, repetitious and unnecessary words.

- Rewrite the letter so that readability and brevity are both achieved, despite a certain lack of clarity.

- Scrap the project and start from scratch again, presenting your completed effort for Mr. Jones's signature.

Your instructor will make the appropriate assignment in line with what goal is to be achieved at this stage of your learning:

United Gas Corporation
P.O. Box 1618
A Major City, Your State
Gentlemen:

We wish to acknowledge receipt of, and to thank you very much for, your recent letter dated June 10 and the very complete thought and consideration you have given to this matter.

It is the consensus of opinion that if we all cooperate together we can greatly minimize our mutual problems which we share in the marketing of our products.

My own personal opinion is that the survey of cost and expense should be done over again due to the fact that shipping rates and costs are increasing upward.

Enclosed herewith you will find a carbon copy of the true facts and basic fundamentals of this perplexing problem which we will have to face during the winter months of January and February.

You may, or you may not, agree with this idea. However, we are most anxious to discuss it together with you at a meeting on Monday morning at 10 A.M.

Thanking you in advance, I am,

Very sincerely yours,

L. Q. Jones, Manager

LQJ/jl
Enclosure
xc G. Hatmaker
Executive Vice President

3. *Conveying cordial directness in providing Video-Pix information to a good prospect.* As Charles M. Arnfold, sales manager, Sonex Corporation, 1935 Armacost Avenue, Los Angeles, California 90025, you have the task of answering an inquiry from E. L. "Mack" McConathy. Mr. McConathy is in charge of training engineers at Tracor, Inc., 6500 Tracor Lane, Any Large City, Your State. His reading in *Training in Business and Industry* probably prompted his letter, for one of your recent ads in this magazine carried the banner: HOW TO MAKE A SALES REPRESENTATIVE OUT OF AN ENGINEER.

Here is what your ad said:

> Engineers are too smart to be sales people. They know so much about their specialties that they usually talk right over the customer's head. So you have to train them. And with the new $1,345 portable Sonex Video-Pix unit, you can teach anyone how to sell in just hours. With instant replay of both video and audio, you can show sales representatives exactly how they look and sound to customers. You can show them how their technical details get lost. What they do wrong. And what they do right. There's no easier, faster way to show key people what happened at a presentation they missed. Or to show managers how to improve a business meeting. And because it's packaged in three luggage cases, you can take it anywhere and train anybody. Even your experienced sales people. The smarter they are, the more they can learn. Write for our free brochure, Sonex Corporation, Visual Communication Products Department, 1935 Armacost Avenue, Los Angeles, California 90025.

Making a good salesperson out of an engineer is only one of the many accomplishments your Video-Pix is capable of achieving. The Video-Pix can tell things to an executive that nobody has the guts to say. It isn't after a person's job. It's not afraid to be honest. It's not afraid of being fired. It's not human. It's a mechanical conscience. The quintessential fink. It can tell executives who think that they're hypnotic speakers that they're right, that their jokes aren't funny and their little stories have a built-in lullaby. That they have this little nervous habit of . . .

In short, a Video-Pix can coldly, methodically rip a person to pieces. But once the person knows the whole story, he or she can regroup with the good parts left in, the bad parts left out. Sophocles could have had just such a thing in mind when he said (406 B.C.), "One must learn by doing the thing; for though you think you know it, you have no certainty until you try."

Mr. McConathy asks for the brochure and the nearest dealer outlet. But his letter also reveals that he's doing some comparative shopping since you catch traces of ad copy in it used by your two biggest competitors: G X with its Video Tape Recorder Tri-Pack and KonKord Electronics with its VTR-600. The three companies have similar tripack units: a video recorder, TV monitor screen, and camera—all priced competitively. The Sonex Video-Pix unit retails at $1,345, the G X at $1,395, and the KonKord VTR-600, $1,295.

What concerns Mr. McConathy is the amount of training actually needed to use the Sonex Video-Pix, the special lighting equipment required, parts service, and maintenance costs. Sonex Video-Pix, like its competitors, requires only a few hours briefing for the operator to become an expert TV telecaster; all systems use normal room light; parts service is provided by your outlet, Electronics Center, Inc., 2929 North Haskell Boulevard, Metropolitan City, Your State, currently on a one-day basis. You have no figures on maintenance costs yet because of the newness of this sales training aid. Indications are that $35 is the average repair job cost for the few units that have needed attention thus far. Tracor with its highly skilled technicians would probably be able to service most of its own needs. You are contemplating offering a service contract soon for your units but no price has yet been set.

Sonex's real advantage, aside from competitive pricing, is its smaller screen—22½ inches—with sharper detail than the 25-inch monitors of your competitors. And you offer a full line of Video-Pix units—at higher prices—all kinds for all kinds of uses. Your competitors have only one unit on the market so far.

Like your competitors, too, your Sonex Video-Pix unit records audio and video simultaneously (*live* programs with the camera can also be shown right in the user's own layout), plays back instantly on the TV monitor. (The G X unit is the only unit that plays back on any standard TV receiver.) Any frame can be held as a "still" for close study. Tapes can be replayed indefinitely or erased for reuse.

Write the letter as Arnfold. Make full use of a vivid imagination on training engineers to be *real* Tracor sales representatives through the Video-Pix method.

4. *Ensuring cordial directness in an explanation about garment manufacture.* As Executive Secretary S. L. Simpkins, Garment Manufacturers of America, The Mart, Chicago, Illinois, you'll do what you can to help President A. Y. Baker of the Braunfels Gingham Factory, Any Small City (population 30,000), Your State, to make an expansion decision. You'll limit yourself to facts and to statements of those in the field for him to evaluate, for you certainly don't want to appear to be selling him on doing something that might turn out badly.

In the ten years that Baker has been a member of your organization, he has enjoyed a phenomenal growth and achieved an astounding financial success manufacturing cotton cloth on the banks of one of Your State's rivers. His markets now extend into all 50 states, Canada, Mexico, and two South American countries. He employs 400 people and his annual volume is around $8 million gross. Baker is seriously considering expanding his operations to include garment manufacture. His inquiry asks for any available statistics you have relative to the size of business that can move over into garment manufacture most successfully and what type of clothing, according to retail price, is the best bet for the beginner. In addition, he wants to know whether the small producer can compete with the big-mill operator with greater financing and larger markets already established, whether there's less risk for women's wear or men's wear, what percentage of loss due to fashion change the small operator can profitably absorb, and whether the added markup at each stage of the process of complete manufacture offsets the loss from style change.

Baker has made, quite successfully, the transition from manufacture of gray goods to conversion of material into piece goods of various colors and patterns. According to statistics available to you, his may be just the type of business to manufacture low-priced garments profitably. Within the last ten years two of the textile giants, Sanders Mills and Sun-cron, Inc., have practically sold out their finished-goods operations and have returned to being primarily gray-goods concerns. The first to go were the women's synthetic outerwear divisions. Fashion, of course, is the all-important factor in the volatile women's wear field. "Once you get above the very-low-price brackets in women's wear," states an official of one textile concern, "everything sells on taste. The converter and the manufacturer have to suit many different kinds of tastes with a myriad of patterns, colors, and styles. Sometimes the color trend changes every few weeks. The small independent operator is more flexible in keeping attuned to the changes."

This information should in part answer Baker's question as to the size of factory that can expand profitably in this way. The small independent manufacturer also has a distinct competitive advantage, particularly in women's wear. The chancy aspects resulting from style obsolescence make it impossible to plan too far ahead. That's why it's done best by small operators who can deal in hundreds of yards of cloth and take orders on a short-term basis. Big organizations have to get orders far ahead, requiring millions of yards. While some big producers certainly combine phases profitably, the small business is better set up for complete finished-product manufacture.

You can safely tell Baker that women's blouses and dresses are the most subject to loss from the whims of fashion. Men's sport shirts and slacks are less affected by sudden drastic style changes. You're not willing to quote him any figures as to what percentage of loss due to style change a business such as his can absorb or how much of the loss may be offset by successive markups on finished garments. You might suggest, instead, that he write Mr. David Ungent, owner-president of Ungent Mills, Tallahassee, Florida, who has made the transition with about the same original setup as Baker's. Your price for surveys and recommendation reports, which he also asked about, is based on a $50-an-hour labor cost, with a minimum guarantee of $6,000.

You'll send Baker, along with your answer to his inquiry, a copy of *Fifty Years of Garment Making*, the most recent publication of your organization.

   5.   *Inquiring about a prospective job applicant.* As O. C. Wingo, recruiting representative, Salary and Wage Administration Department, Lane-Jantz Fibre Company, 301 Elam Avenue, Erie, Pennsylvania, you are reviewing applications, carefully screened and filed over the past three months, for positions in production. The positions in production require people with diverse educational backgrounds—mechanical, electrical, chemical, ceramic, and industrial engineering, as well as general or liberal arts. The yardsticks by which employees are chosen for those positions are the abilities to manage and direct effectively the efforts of others, to learn from experience, to assume responsibility, and to delegate authority. A strictly specialized background is not preferred. The position that you are currently considering applicants for is in the industrial engineering group at your Shreveport, Louisiana, plant. The incumbent will take an active part in all phases of industrial engineering assignments, including plant and process layout, material handling, motion and time studies, and incentive-payment planning. The applicant may be called upon to help lay out a whole assembly line.

The application you are looking at now is that of Raymond E. Linart, currently employed by Liberty National Manufacturing Company, Any City, Any State. Your records show that in the spring last year, when Linart was graduating from Your College or University with a BBA degree, engineering route, one of your staff interviewed him along with a number of others through the university placement office. There are some notations on his application, made by the interviewer. Mr. Linart was a pleasant, quiet fellow, slow in speech, but apparently thoughtful about what he was saying, carefully choosing his words. His grade average is mediocre. The confidential reports that the placement office supplies are from the students' professors, and the interviewers have access to them. The Lane-Jantz interviewer made brief summaries of the three reports on Linart. In general, he was considered likeable, pleasant, cooperative, and conscientious. One statement which is underlined—apparently significant to the interviewer—reads: "Is inclined to overrate his capabilities and intelligence." You wonder if this failing has proved true during the past six months since he's been with Liberty National. This feature could be the key to continued failure, if it's correctly concluded, or, in some situations it could mean success. You will need to inquire specifically about this point. Linart's background and training are good, but for some reason he was screened out right there at the university. Since that time, Linart has written your office, indicating his sustained interest in Lane-Jantz. With some practical experience acquired, he may now be a good prospect for the Shreveport job. He lists Mr. P. K. Smith, his supervising engineer, as one of his references in his letter.

Write a reference-inquiry letter to Mr. Smith at 4828 Haines Boulevard, Any City, Any State.

6. *Writing an informative message about a community bank's services with goodwill overtones.* The Highland Lakes National Bank of Kingsland, Your State, has been offering the people in the community blue-chip banking services for almost four years. For the past year it has been the proud occupant of a modernistic building in the midst of a new shopping center. The shopping center, with the usual assortment of retailing establishments, is a gathering place for the young community.

Kingsland, with its water sports, fishing, hilly terrain, and a delightful Sunbelt climate, is a mecca for tourists and is rapidly achieving status as one of the prime retirement centers in the country. Permanent residents number 4,000 to 5,000, with the shopping center drawing customers from a larger area of about 10,000. The tourist season runs from April 1 to September 1. The permanent residents live in lake cottages ranging in value from $30,000 to $125,000; thus it might reasonably be assumed that they are classified in the middle- and upper-middle-income brackets, with some possibly in the upper bracket.

While Highland Lakes National Bank has enjoyed rewarding asset growth during its four years of operation, there are still a number of permanent residents who bank elsewhere—in nearby towns or in the cities from which they came prior to retirement. The officers and directors, naturally interested in obtaining new bank customers, are confident that they have enough to offer in first-rate service and convenience to make a new banking connection for these people a highly satisfactory experience. In addition to the safety afforded by the bank's competent management, the customer receives full banking services: the highest maximum interest rate for time deposits allowed by federal regulations, compounded quarterly; protection by the Federal Deposit Insurance Corporation for individual accounts up to $100,000, with numerous combination accounts insured separately up to the maximum; safety-deposit boxes; loan service; drive-in facilities; and so on. In addition, the bank has a coffee room for conferences and visiting, and its top floor is a community room available for civic and social meetings. *Convenience* to the customer is likely the bank's major attraction—but we'll leave the figuring out of the aspects of convenience to you.

Mr. John B. Selman, chairman of the board and a graduate of your own College of Business Administration and of the University Law School, has requested that you compose a goodwill note inviting people in the area who have not used the services of Highland Lakes National Bank to become new customers. Since the volume of such letters will be comparatively small, each letter will be addressed and typed individually so that you may insert the customer's name at any spot in the message where you think a personal touch might be helpful. As a bonus for new customers, the bank is offering an unusual set of eight gold-coin glasses, described in promotional literature as "12-ounce glasses with many uses . . . clean, simple in design. At home in colonial, contemporary, or modern decor. A truly unusual set. These are yours when you open a Certificate of Deposit Savings Account with a minimum deposit of $500. You will be proud to own and use them." So that the management may estimate the return on the mailing, you'll tell the customer in some tactful way to bring the letter along when coming in to open the account. Address your letter to Mr. M. H. Singletary, Kingsland, and send it out under the signature of W. F. "Woody" McCasland, president.

The bank plans to mail invitation letters to likely prospects periodically; so composing a letter that may be mailed at any season of the year is likely the best approach. Success in preparing this mailing piece, then, will depend on the originality and applicability of the theme chosen for it rather than on a seasonal gimmick. Your presentation will need to attract favorable attention from a rather sophisticated and presumably well-educated group of people.

7. *Conveying courtesy and directness in a request.* As Thomas P. Noble, personnel executive of The Public Service Company of Your State, with headquarters at 1215 Public Service Building, 615 Akron Street, A Major City, Your State, you sum up your employment possibilities for your offices throughout the state with an eye to completing your force with the best of the fall graduates from Your State University or from a group of former graduates who have a little experience behind them and are ready to move on to better jobs. You need at least one person, and perhaps several, for each of the following positions, if they are highly qualified candidates: engineer, accountant, sales representative, marketing analyst, data processing and systems analyst, dietician, correspondent, and administrative assistant.

Your organization is a large utility corporation providing transportation, electricity, gas, and water to the people in 27 State towns and cities. Additionally, it handles sales and service of electrical supplies, gas stoves, patio grills, yard lights, refrigerators, and air-conditioning units. You decide that the simplest way of reaching personnel of such varied preparation and capacities as will meet these job requirements is to write to Dr. J. O. Ondrey, director of placement, GSB 2.114, Your State University. You do not know Dr. Ondrey personally, but you have used several of his textbooks on personnel management for your in-training programs and have had intermittent correspondence with him over matters of policy. He is a well-known authority in the field of personnel work.

You ask Ondrey to have three candidates for each job classification write you application letters for positions as "business interns" in your company. These "interns" are trained in your department for positions as junior executives. Training consists of six periods of three months each. Each period is devoted to a different department function in the organization. Beginning salary is $1,475 a month, with a $50-a-month raise at the end of each three months until the training is completed. Your preferences is for former students with from one to three years' experience.

You've been highly pleased with Your State University graduates as employees in former years. Perhaps you'll want to tell Ondrey so when you write this message.

8. *Making clear a company claim that will result in accurate reparation.* As head of the adjustment department of the Bobbitt Flying Service, regional distributor of Thunderwing Airplanes, you have the job of straightening out by mail a claim to the home office, Thunderwing Aircraft Company, Thunderwing Building, Kansas City. Recently the Bobbitt Company sold a new Thunderwing 170. Two days later it installed a remanufactured E-225-8 engine in a customer's Thunderwing 190. Predelivery inspection of the new 170 revealed a crack in the oil pan of the engine. To make delivery on time, you explained to the customer that the defect was minor, since no leak was apparent. He could take the plane, and you would replace the pan as soon as you could get another from Kansas City. You wrote a letter to Claims Adjuster Sam A. Turner at the home office, asking for a replacement pan 0-430-A, costing $163.44, with a labor allowance of ten hours at $10 an hour.

The run-in and subsequent inspection of the remanufactured E-225-8 engine on your customer's Thunderwing 190 revealed a crack in the attached oil sump. Since the sump was leaking, you removed it and replaced it with one from stock at a cost of 14 mechanic labor-hours at $10 an hour—$140. You wrote another letter to Turner, listing the parts by catalog number and unit cost—a total of $196.50—asking for reimbursement and a labor allowance of $140. You boxed up the cracked sump and mailed it back to the company.

In about ten days you receive a new pan (0-430-A) for the new Thunderwing 170 under Invoice No. 62227, for $163.44, which lists the parts used for the sump—and no labor allowance. Now $163.44 was the cost of the pan. Evidently the home office has confused the two cases, listing the parts for the sump on the 190 and using the price of the pan for the 170. You box the cracked pan and get it off by express, wondering just how you'll straighten this mess out.

As Adjustment Manager Oscar Tarrant, get an accurate reparation for the Bobbitt Flying Service, Bobbitt Field, Your City, Your State.

9. *Making your own just claim for an equitable adjustment.* For this assignment you are to write a claim letter for a situation in which you believe that you have a just case for getting full reparation. Perhaps you may even have made an earlier claim and the firm or service facility responded, in effect, that there was nothing it could do for you under the circumstances . . . a polite brush-off. So you gave up. Don't! It's worth another try. Studies show that most people have a max of seven negative responses in them before giving in. Persistence pays off.

See if you can't get the reader into your shoes . . . to *experience* the frustration, annoyance, disappointment, disillusionment—whatever emotional experience you had.

How would that person have felt under these circumstances and what would *she* or *he* have reasonably expected the firm to do about it? Your role is that of a reasonable person—what a reasonable person could expect in the course of doing business with this firm. For example, a reasonable person would expect a product sold, used by the buyer, and then cleaned according to instructions to stand up and still be usable. When it doesn't, that is just cause for a claim. A shirt that comes apart at one or more seams after only one wearing and laundering *is not* a reasonable product. A tablecloth or bedspread that, after the first washing, shrinks out of shape or puckers is not what a reasonable person expects to get in a product for his or her money from a reputable retail establishment. You get the picture?

So, make your request for adjustment. You don't have to specify what you want done, just that you want or expect an appropriate settlement.

When this letter has been marked and returned to you, polish and edit it, type it up in good layout, *and mail it* to the president, store buyer, or other firm official. By all means, use his or her name.

10. *Writing a follow-through message to reinforce the impression you made at an interview.* Yesterday morning you were one of several prospective May graduates who were granted interviews with Mr. H. G. Blodgett, personnel director, American Aluminum Company, Pittsburgh, Pennsylvania, at his suite in a local hotel.

Blodgett was a personable man, around forty-five, dressed in a well-cut oxford-gray business suit, white shirt, and black shoes. His tie and handkerchief were in matching muted grays. His voice was deep and cultured with sharp enunciation of final "t's" and "g's." He was on his annual tour of the colleges to obtain for his company promising prospective employees for the home plant in Pittsburgh and the new branch in A Large City, Your State.

You answered the Placement Office's call because you were particularly interested in going to The Large City, Your State. But you would, of course, go to Pittsburgh if the prospects were pleasing enough to make the move feasible. Blodgett's company offers employment in many lines: engineering, industrial management, public relations, transportation, accounting, statistics, sales, office administration. Each employee begins work with AAC through a six-week training period at the headquarters' offices at company expense. Snatches of Blodgett's talk drift back to you as you sit down to compose that letter he asked you to write and send along with your application form.

"The important thing with us," Mr. Blodgett stated, "is getting people who will stay with us. The best way to do it is to fit the person to the job as carefully as possible, not only for now but for the future. Consequently, we're not interested in getting only 'A' students. For a long time I made a bid for the top-ranking only for my company. Experience has shown us these individuals want to get to the top too quickly. The head jobs, of course, are already filled with old-timers like me, who've been with AAC a long time and have a thorough groundwork behind them. An 'A' average won't prove a handicap naturally . . . but qualities other than scholarship carry weight with us. What does your education mean to you?"

Well, you flubbed around with that one; so you're glad to have time to mull it over and come up with a better answer. Did he intend to trap you into saying that your BBA degree entitled you to an executive post? Just what does it mean to you in relation to AAC? All the people he talked to have the minimum bachelor's degree. What else did your study afford you that the others might not have been alert enough to capitalize on?

"Our starting pay is competitive, we think—in Pittsburgh and in the branch offices. You will receive regular increments according to a merit system which enables you to pile up points toward selection for executive positions as they become vacant—a slow process. The sales division offers the greatest opportunity to make money. Salary plus commission. Right now we especially need editorial assistants to work in the publications office. . . .

"Since AAC has numerous government sensitive contracts, we have to be certain of the integrity of our employees. . . . At times we are prone to put personality factors ahead of skill; for example, we want even our secretaries to be able to type adequately, take shorthand, and operate transcribing machines, but we'd prefer that they be also cultured representatives of the company. That's the main thing . . . each employee in any particular niche should be a public relations asset to AAC."

Your conversation with Blodgett was a pleasant experience; so let's just suppose that you're eligible for a job with this company and write an application for Blodgett's files that will recall you to him favorably enough that you'll be considered.

PROBLEMS IN WRITING INFORMATIVE MESSAGES UNDER ADVERSE CIRCUMSTANCES

1. *Developing an informative customer-service angle under adverse circumstances.* The mail-order general wholesale house of Scott-Huber, Inc., 2120 River Road, St. Louis, Missouri 59001, has just finished a thoroughgoing, in-depth study of its operating costs and other factors affecting the price structure of its merchandise. The unit cost of handling orders has increased more than 185 percent in six years, it finds. This problem is accentuated particularly in the handling of small-lot purchase orders. In terms of numbers, 18 percent of its orders account for 4 percent of its sales volume but absorb 29 percent of the order-filling costs (opening, routing, assembling, packing, shipping, and billing).

Here, then, is one point of attacking the price-squeeze bottleneck that is so disturbing to merchandisers right now. If these occasional, fill-in, small-lot-buying customers will save up their orders and keep them above $75 a unit, savings can be realized all along the line. Thus Scott-Huber, by cutting down on order-handling costs, will be able to combat other factors pushing up prices.

How to suggest this improvement to customers, though, is a problem in tact. Most of the customers are profitable over a period of months. Their annual volume of purchases is important to you. And you certainly don't want to drive them away.

They are small retailers scattered widely, and their goodwill is a cumulative asset. So the Scott-Huber sales manager, Roy G. Herberger, decides to present the policy as a request for cooperation instead of a flat statement of policy that orders under $25 will not be handled except in emergency or rare exception cases.

Take over for Herberger and write a form message that he can use to send to all his list of small-lot-buying retailers. Address your message to the first name on the list: Nolan Dry Goods and Notions, 123 Main Street, Some Small City, Your State.

2. *Encouraging the prompt handling of a shipping error.* Mr. R. R. Edwards has been reading those American Paper ads about printing forms to cut down errors and save office time, and now he's pretty sure of a form he ought to set up for telephone orders in the Arklatex Builders' Stores main office in Texarkana. There ought to be a pad with carbon sheet attached right by the main telephone so that two copies of telephoned memoranda can be made on the spot. If he had such a system working, then the slip-up in service to the promising new customer, Mr. Jerry Gilbert, over in Magnolia, Arkansas, wouldn't have happened. Better see about that order pad, he says to himself.

But the slip-up did happen. Gilbert, after agreeing to accept a new-type door closer as a change to his order he was placing by phone, reduced the number of the large No. 3 size to a dozen and a half. The universal hold-open catch he was told about seemed to make duplicate stock unnecessary. He also ordered a dozen each of the sizes 1 and 2. The closers, delivered promptly by Panther Motor Freight Lines, checked out okay on the two dozen smaller ones, but the other case contained only a dozen of the big fellows. Then the following day, Gilbert got Arklatex's Invoice G884 showing one dozen each No. 1's and 2's and *one and a half dozen* No. 3's. That shortage and overcharge was disturbing enough, but the real hitch is that Jerry needed fourteen No. 3's for a local contractor who's in a hurry to install them at the new consolidated school building and turn the key over to the trustees.

So Mr. Edwards, the sales manager, tells you to fix things up immediately and cordially. Since actions speak loudest, you hand the hardware department a memo to make quick shipment of the six delinquent No. 3 Falcon All-way Door Closers by sending special messenger over to put the box on the 11:10 A.M. Panther truck east. Thus do you complete the invoice G884.

Next, you prepare, for Mr. Edwards's own signature, a letter that will tell Mr. Gilbert what you have done about the closers and will try to make him feel that he may safely telephone his instructions and orders in the future and expect to get his full shipments. To accomplish the latter, you will need to be frank to admit what happened, without emphasis, and to back up your assurance that "it won't happen again" (but not in those forbidden words!) with something tangible and plausible.

What actually happened, of course, is that the clerk who took Mr. Gilbert's phone call made a memorandum that the Falcon closers would be okay on his order of Wednesday and also noted that the No. 3's would be cut down a dozen. By your usual routine, the order would have gone to the billing department for quintuplicate typing. One of the five copies would have gone to the order fillers.

To speed up the shipment, however, oral directions for the modification were given the order fillers. Somebody looked at Mr. Gilbert's order and observed that the universal hold-open catch would make the No. 3's and the 3h's the same—and so sent him a dozen of each size only. The invoice, typed from the phone memorandum, was correctly made. The special speed-up got the shipment off one whole day early—but it wasn't all there.

Well, fix it up the best you can. Remembering that Mr. Gilbert's store is one of the new wholesale accounts you are trying to cultivate, pick up all the points of Gilbert interest (including things about Magnolia) that you can make plausible.

3. *Trying to keep a good customer on back order for a sizable supply of cans.* As Assistant Sales Manager Hal Bennett in the new location of Con-Can Company, 6215 Alameda Drive, Dallas, Texas, you have some bad news for Mayo Barnes, purchasing agent, Burton Coffee Company, 596 Nueces Street, Any City, Any State. On March 25 you sent all your good customers a letter (and you suppose Burton's got one) notifying them of the dismantling of the South Bend Plant on April 1 and a gradual moving of equipment to the new plant during the remainder of the year. Your message invited customers to get orders to you covering the period from May through October before May 15 so that their requirements might be processed, fabricated, and warehoused to carry them during this interval.

The Burton Coffee Company, a regular purchaser of about $20,000 worth of cans yearly, made no response to your letter—nor has it sent in any orders since then. Today, however, you get an order from the company for 10,000 No. 209 2-pound round friction-top containers ($1,000 value) with a 10-day scheduled delivery time. It will be about 10 days before Con-Can goes into full production, and, with a backlog of orders, you can't deliver the Burton cans sooner than November 10.

Your assignment is to write an informative letter of the situation, making the message convincing enough to keep this customer on back order for his containers.

4. *Asking for an adjustment on a badly packed shipment.* You, as Earle A. Norvelle, owner and manager of Norvelle Home Furnishings of 320 Market Street, Any City, Your State, have been rather busy the past few days making plans for your year-end clearance, with the main purpose of boosting business for at least a week and clearing your stock for inventory on June 30 at the same time.

Everything was running smoothly enough until today's delivery of the 30 outdoor serving tables (leaders for a summer sale) from the Keber Furniture Manufacturing Company of a Major City, Your State. You had placed a repeat order for this backyard chef's dream after having been assured by the Keber people that delivery could be made within two days after receipt of the order. This morning, however, when the State Fleet Lines unloaded the crates at the Norvelle warehouse, it was discovered that two wheels, one on each of two different cart tables, had been broken to such an extent that each complete assembly was damaged (obviously the result of undue pressure of the tight packing crates) and that 16 of the serving trays were not included in the crates. Apparently, a Keber shipping department employee's hammer was as heavy as his eyelids at about closing time yesterday.

You are more concerned at the moment about those missing trays than about the broken wheels, however, because your quarter-page ad in two of the local area papers and 2,000 direct-mail pieces featuring the tables *with the serving trays* at $113.75 (you bought them at $88) have already gone to press.

You have been buying more and more of those Keber casual furnishings since the factory started its cedar processing six months ago. Your customers have been coming back for extra pieces of the beautiful long-life wood from the Texas hill country. You realized, even before your customers did, the unusual combination of quality and utility of the Keber pieces—hence your plan to use the lunch cart as a leader.

But now, with the sale starting in three days (on Saturday) and with the demand building up as it undoubtedly will, you have the problem of getting a letter off to the Keber Company, as a follow-up to your hasty phone call, telling them about the damage and repeating your request for a speedy replacement of the wheels along with the rest of those serving trays. You will return the damaged carts, of course, but not until the replacements arrive.

Make your letter do the job—courteously, firmly, tactfully.

5. *Completing the reparation on a just claim.* Friday's mail delivery brings to you, Walter W. Keber, in your Chicago office of Keber Furniture Manufacturing, the just claim of your good customer Earle A. Norvelle, owner of Norvelle Home Furnishings. Norvelle's claim is a just one—the error lies solely with the Keber Furniture Company.

But you're not surprised. In fact, you've been expecting something like this to happen ever since reliable Dan Whiteside had to leave his shipping clerk duties for an emergency appendectomy. Dan's temporary replacement, old Moses Hunter, tried hard to do the work well, but he has too many years behind him. Dan is back on the job now, but that doesn't square things with Norvelle.

Of course you'll take Norvelle's word about the two broken wheels on the patio cart tables, and the letter certainly clears up the mystery of the sixteen extra trays found in the shipping room (see problem 4). But today is Friday—too late to get the goods to Some City, Any State, in time for that sale. A fast check with State Fleet Lines gives you assurance that you can have the two wheels and sixteen trays in Norvelle's store by Monday noon. It's a ticklish situation, but you must maintain the friendship of this good customer.

Write Norvelle the letter, granting the claim, explaining the error, convincing him that the mistake won't happen again, and keeping him sold on the products of the Keber Furniture Manufacturing Company.

6. *Carefully giving additional information on a customer's inquiry with an order for candy boxes.* To your desk as Assistant Sales Manager Hal Bennett, Con-Can Company, 6215 Alameda Drive, Dallas, Texas, comes a first order for 100 No. 6291 1-pound Christmas candy boxes, a check for $8.95 to pay for them (parcel post charge of 95 cents included), and a generous sample of Mabel's Almond Toffee. Mabel (Mrs. G. H. Sandry, Mabel's Candy Shoppe, Lockhart, Texas) writes that she is planning to wholesale this toffee through grocery and department stores in Texas, Oklahoma, and New Mexico and wants you to send her a sample vacuum can suitable for marketing it. She also submits a sketch done in water colors (nasturtium yellow, brown, and gold with a motherly picture of Mabel) that she wants on the cans. She'd like some figures

on cost and assurance of a delivery date in time for her to get the candy in the stores to supply Christmas shoppers.

You can ship Mrs. Sandry the 100 candy boxes from open stock right away (it is now October 17), but you'll have a good many problems fixing her up with candy cans. You have packed (along with the fiber candy boxes) a sample vacuum can that you usually sell for 1/2-pound coffee. Since the toffee is slightly heavier than coffee, you think perhaps a 1-pound can of this type may be what Mrs. Sandry has in mind. She gave you no idea, however, as to how much candy she wants to pack in a unit.

You can supply her this special-order 1-pound can with her sketch lithographed on at 25 cents a unit (minimum single order $500, minimum yearly total, $5,000). It is possible that in the early stages of her wholesaling, Mrs. Sandry's requirements may fall below these figures. Too, all the containers your company produces require the use of a closing machine, which Mrs. Sandry possibly doesn't have. Should she decide to use your can, the Closing Machine Department will be happy to furnish her with one at a cost of around $250 delivered. You're attaching a leaflet picturing and explaining the closing machine.

The toffee she sent is quite good and should build her a profitable business, once it catches on. Write her a letter that gives her the information she wants. If you are to do business together, she will have to submit an initial $500 order and promise of the required yearly total. With confirmation in your hands right away, you can assure her of delivery by November 15. Perhaps you'd best send along a credit application form so that you can get an idea of her financial condition, too.

1. Writing a letter to Olan Wigstaff—and may it do more good than harm when introducing Digby Sayers. Maybe it's true that some people do talk too much, you think; but they certainly don't have a monopoly on such pastime. Evidence? The way you opened your big mouth and bragged to Digby Sayers, a junior executive in your firm (Toltex Oil Company).

Actually you did happen to sit by Olan Wigstaff at a banquet in New York City two years ago. The oil royalty from three continents gathered at convention that spring, and it fell your lot to sit by the kingpin, Olan Wigstaff, at the kickoff dinner. You leaned over and said, "I'm Jim Tolney." Wigstaff, smiling broadly, said: "Yes. To be sure."

After that he seemed rather distracted, developing a dishearteningly detached air. You'd tell him your best Texas stories, and he'd focus a vacant but determinedly polite attention toward you; you were convinced, though, he never heard a word you said.

Then, one sad morning back in Houston you just happened to mention your meeting with Wigstaff to Digby Sayers, the most promising of your young employees. Well, maybe you were bragging a little. The expansive grin on Digby's face was a sort of challenge to you. Ordinarily you're a comparatively honest fellow, but that glint of disbelief did something to you. So you elaborated on your acquaintance. True, you weren't guilty of calling him "Wiggy," but somewhere along the line you did leave the impression you were a guest at Wigstaff's home and at a party of his at the Long

Island Yacht Club. (The convention delegates did make a tour of his home and grounds; and there was a party at the yacht club—for the whole convention.)

This morning comes the payoff. Digby is going to New York to read a paper before the Independent Geologists Association of America, and he wants an introduction to Wigstaff, hoping that he, too, may be invited to Wigstaff's home and to the yacht club.

Now, you sit munching your fingers. How can you write a letter to Wigstaff that won't give you away either to the mighty man or to your Digby?

You do it! Your letterhead is Toltex Oil Company, 2615 Midway Mart Building, Some Major City, Your State. Address your letter to Mr. Olan Wigstaff, president, Tri-Continent Oil company, Tri-Continent Building, 298 Fifth Avenue, New York, 10019. (You are vice president of your company.)

8.   *Making a full-reparation offer to hold a customer while trying to regain a lost sale.* As an adjustment correspondent for the Crenshaw Mail Order Company of Chicago, you receive today a stern note from Mrs. Carlton Brannon of 2301 Pleasant Hill Drive, Some City, Any State. The lady writes;

> Two weeks ago I ordered an Eastern Electric Switch Clock at $32.50, but you sent me a Time-King clock that your catalog lists at $20.50. I'm sending the clock back to you. I expect you to send me back my money. Just cancel this order.

Apparently, Mrs. Brannon has a just claim, but it's hard to see how a mistake like that could be made. So you mark her claim for further investigation and proceed through the remaining mail. A few letters later you find a note from a Mrs. Carl Brannen of Fort Smith, Arkansas. This lady reports that she, too, received the wrong clock—an Eastern Electric Switch clock instead of the Time-King she ordered.

You see the whole thing now. The name similarity somehow caused a slip up in the shipping department. May be you can make Mrs. Carlton Brannon understand and possibly regain her goodwill. It's worth a try anyway.

You decide to begin your letter to her with a full-reparation opening, giving her a check for the money right off. You'll have to make some explanation for the error, of course, but be certain to convince her that future checking of shipments against orders will prevent a recurrence of this slip up. Then you reason that she probably is still in the market for a clock. She had been sold on the Eastern model. Wouldn't it be possible to kindle once more that unfilled desire? So you plan to employ your best sales strategy to get her to endorse your check and send it right back to you as payment for an Eastern Electric Switch Clock.

In planning your sales presentation, you review the literature supplied by the Eastern Company. The Switch Clock, they say is

> a clock with a "brain" that automatically turns lights, radio, roaster, coffee maker on and off. It's simple to operate. Just plug the electric appliance into this Switch Clock, set the time indicators, and this silent, portable electric servant does the rest. It will make coffee for you before you get up, cook a roast for you while you're shopping, and turn your radio off after you've been pleas-

antly lulled to sleep. And besides being a perfect time piece, it's a thing of beauty with its angular, modern lines and stylish aluminumized case.

It's truly a remarkable clock. The satisfaction it would give Mrs. Brannon, you believe, would go a long way toward regaining the goodwill that has been lost for the present. The odds for your letter's success aren't too encouraging, but let's see what you can do.

9. *Getting a difficult customer back on a systematic payment program.* As credit sales manager for the leading department store in Your City, you find that you have no trouble with 80 percent of your customers. These people manage their affairs well. If they cannot pay promptly, you usually hear from them. They come in, write, or phone. They tell you when they will pay, and they fulfill their promises. Their attitude is mature. "Future oriented" describes them well because they look ahead and plan.

The other 20 percent give you trouble. "Present oriented" would describe them. They tend to overbuy because they want what they want when they want it. Often they cannot pay promptly. There is no question of their basic honesty; if there were, you would not have them as credit customers in the first place. There is, however, some question as to their skill in managing their affairs and real doubt about their judgment when debt is involved. In some ways they are immature and childlike.

Childlike describes Pat Monroe, 25 years old and a successful manufacturer's representative with a good income and a job that means being away from home often. However, he did see a collection reminder you sent and was in your office the next day, not to apologize but to berate you for the "needless" annoyance you caused. He pointed out what you knew well—his ability to pay his account. You felt like pointing out that it was not his ability but willingness to pay that was in question.

When he wants something, he buys it. If he buys too much in a month, he simply lets the account go and pays only part. In the past year the account has been building up, and he has fallen into a pattern of sending you a small payment every three months. (Your collection reminders and letters begin after an account has gone unpaid for 90 days.) Because of the little run-in you had with him, you have not wanted to do anything more than send statements.

You checked with the credit bureau, and there was nothing alarming in the report; yet the account is getting larger than you think is desirable, not but what you could collect it if you had to, but you want to build a good account rather than lose one. Finally, you decide to face the issue squarely and write to Mr. Monroe firmly, recommending that regular monthly payments be resumed.

10. *Reminding a good customer of the values of discount taking.* As B. C. Darnall of Tibbett Wholesale Drug Company, 918 La Salle Street, Chicago, Illinois, you honored a first $6,000 order from Marvin Caster, Caster Drug Mart, Another City, Another State, making shipment on April 30 under 2/10, n/30 terms. The size of his order and several questionable features in his situation have caused you a little worry. If Caster's business (he has just moved into a new $200,000 plant at a new location) proves slower than he has anticipated, a number of creditors may soon be dunning him. You'd like very much to get him started with you on a sound footing; so you decide,

five days after making shipment, to write him a novel letter pointing up the advantage of discount taking.

A fine business manager like Caster is well aware of such advantages. The information you have indicates that he makes use of this advantage on at least half of his purchases. You'll have to make your treatment subtle enough in order not to appear to be talking down to him. Perhaps your best attitude is one in which your letter appears to be a routine customer service notifying dealers of the impending discount date. You might like to add importance to this particular discount by interpreting it as something timely and tangible. In any event you won't want to leave the impression you're worried about payment.

Today you'll write this letter as Darnall in such a way as to accomplish a twofold purpose: (a) to make Caster feel you appreciate his patronage and (b) to inspire him to mail you a check on or before the deadline date.

4

Persuading Toward Predetermined Action: Selling Ideas, Goods, and Services

Communication . . . always appeals to motivation.
If it fits in with aspirations, the values, the purpose
of the recipient, it is powerful. If it goes against the
recipient's aspirations, values, motivation, it is
likely not to be received at all or, at best, to be
resisted.

Peter F. Drucker

"Every letter is a sales letter" is an aphorism often touted by business writers. And why not? After all, even in the blandest goodwill note or informative message you are still trying to persuade the reader that you are considerate—a nicely mannered individual who always thinks of others—that you are knowledgeable, worthy of the time and effort to read your words, that you have done a real service by doing what the reader wanted, by providing useful information willingly and enthusiastically.

Any communication is thus persuasive to the degree that it succeeds in influencing the attitude of the reader toward the writer, the message, and the writer's organization. It is *not* persuasive when the message is so perfunctory that it is disregarded or so tactless that it arouses antagonism.

When reader and writer are in agreement, a letter between them dispatches its business quickly and clearly and with friendliness. The message is fast and direct (as you learned in Chapter 3).

But when reader and writer are not together in their thinking, the message has to *reach out* to the reader, *set up* a tone of friendly sincerity, *pave the way* for the point it needs to make, and *swing the reader over* to the writer's point of view. Thus, truly persuasive communications must *change* the reader's way of thinking or feeling and convince the reader that the writer's proposal is to the reader's own benefit. We call this technique the "inductive" style of writing.

George Baker was talking about just such a technique in 1902 when he said, "The exact nature of the task a speaker or writer sets for himself will, of course, affect the order of his persuasive work." He continued,

> When a man wishes simply to persuade people to continue in a course of action, or to carry out a purpose already formed, he may arrange his persuasive work in climactic order, for even a very slight amount of persuasion will probably move his audience in the right direction, and he will leave them stirred to immediate action by his final effort. If, however, he wishes to urge men to give up doing something to which they have become accustomed, or a purpose already well established in their minds, he must naturally, as in the case of refuting long-established ideas, bring forward his strongest appeal first. When he has stirred his audience by his first strong appeal, he can maintain his effect with other appeals, each of which would not have been strong enough, if given alone at the outset, to rouse his audience.[1]

This philosophy set the stage for the modern psychological approach to business writing, particularly as it concerns persuasive strategy. Attention-getting information *is* presented at the first of the message, but often that information is not as important to the description of the idea being presented as is the information presented further along in the communication. Rather, the attention-getting beginning is merely a means of positively inviting the reader to read on.

In 1950 Hovland et al. theorized that "in the case of persuasive communication . . . the recommended opinion generally consists of a single statement which is within the memory span of most individuals and in many instances, a single communication is sufficient to induce opinion change."[2]

Since 1902 business writing theorists and practitioners have devised, tested, and distilled a psychological plan for successful, inductive request making to include these points:

1.   Make use of some of the reader's own emotional drives by building the persuasive message around them. For small requests, begin with an explanation of the situation.

2.   Condition the reader's mind for the message through opening material about which the recipient can feel good or at least neutral toward. Introduce a key idea around which the proposal may be developed.

3.   Lead the reader to accept the proposition before it is actually stated, by a buildup of reasons why it should be granted. (Your first

---

[1] George P. Baker, *The Principles of Argumentation* (Lexington, Mass.: Ginn and Company, Publishers, 1905), p. 366.

[2] Carl I. Hovland, Irving Janus, and Harold H. Kelley, *Communication and Persuasion* (New Haven, Conn.: Yale University Press, 1961), p. 16.

reason given will be the strongest—from the reader's point of view—in favor of what you are proposing.)

4. Make an open bid for reader action on the request in the form of a question when the reader is prepared to accept it (about halfway through the message or later). Do not emphasize the request by placing it at the beginning or end of the paragraph.

5. Place a value on the reader's efforts—his or her compliance—in a gracious leave-taking or close with a pleasantry.

With over 2,000 years of traceable literature available on the subject of persuasive talk and writing, this chapter attempts only to point out the wide uses of the style and to show how to make it work in selling ideas, goods, and services.

SITUATIONS CALLING FOR PERSUASION

The first use of persuasion you will probably think of is mass communication persuasiveness: radio and television. In print, it is advertising. In letters, it is the tons of sales letters that have sold millions of dollars worth of goods and services—with other tons of letters that have collected the money for those same goods and services. Through mass media, persuasive writing gets people elected to offices. In other uses in business and in professional and personal life, it requests favors of people they might refuse if asked for bluntly; it asks for credit and gets special credit extensions; it gains favorable adjustment responses—it has dozens of uses initiated *by the writer.*

A pressing private or public issue, solidifying or changing people's opinions, a point of controversy, and fund raising require persuasive writing since all must appeal not only to reason but also to the emotions.

Disappointing answers to requests require letters that anesthetize the inquirer against the pain of being refused, that state the refusal as kindly as possible, and that allow the reader a face-saving, self-respecting exit from the encounter. If the message is constructed wisely, the reader will actually be on the way with a feeling of kindliness for the sincere writer who had to turn the reader down.

Persuasion, therefore, is a writer's conscious effort to affect the reader's behavior in a specific circumstance or at a specific time. Although the situations demanding persuasive attempts vary in their degree of difficulty, so too does the degree of resistance of individuals. Some people are more easily persuaded than others. For example, a national survey trying to determine the characteristics of successful sales people (with the sample made up of a group of the most successful in the United States) some years ago established the fact that 90 percent of the most successful find it virtually impossible to resist the sales pitch of other sales representatives.

ANTICIPATED FEEDBACK

In formal reports, persuasion comes into play largely by the writer's anticipating reader resistance to the subject matter, getting on common ground with the reader, and identifying his or her own course of action with the reader's. You anticipate that the factual report will create belief from its contents and respect for you as a writer because of your objective treatment and that it will not arouse skepticism or scorn.

For informal persuasive messages—letters and memos—the reader's anticipated reaction is likely to be negative. To anticipate what the reaction (feedback) to your request will be, you almost have to know more about other people than they know about themselves. If you were your reader and were to receive the request you are about to make of that person, how would you react? Would you register an immediate "no" if the request were made directly? An *instant* negative response crystalizes in the mind to such an extent that, no matter how persuasive or logical you may be in the rest of the message, your efforts will be wasted on the reader. Just doing what comes naturally, you will tell the reader how it looks from *your* side. But little or no persuasive selling is done by telling another "I have a book I want to sell you," "I want you to help me canvass for United Way," "I want to buy my opening stock from you on six-month terms."

Anticipating the feedback you will get from your persuasive message means, therefore, getting your timing right: Pave the way for your request *before* making it or even letting the reader see it coming. This cue is the very heart of the whole "inductive," or persuasive, process. Of course, you can worry with that idea at length because it is easier to say it than do it. But all the "paving the way" has to be done in the bright, warm light of the other person's interest if it is to work at all.

What other factors will you have to anticipate and overcome in changing reader response from resistance to acceptance?

In addition to those barriers discussed in "Informing Under Adverse Circumstances" (Chapter 3), you must anticipate an indifference factor (your reader is not interested in or is unimpressed by the subject of your message) and a predisposition factor (the reader's attitude is highly contrary to the nature of the action that he or she is being asked to take). Both factors must be overcome if you are to persuade your reader. In anticipating such obstacles to the action you desire from your reader, you thus plan strategy in light of techniques of persuasion gleaned from a study of the nature of people.

MAKING USE OF THE TOOLS
OF PERSUASION

The power of positive suggestion has long been a recognized tool in persuading others to your way of thinking. Sales people take the cue in asking a prospective customer to make a choice between "something and something" not between "something and nothing." They do not ask *whether* you want it or not; they ask *which* do you want—the regular or large, economy size. This technique is also a verbal demonstration of the principle known as "success consciousness"[3]—the confident assumption that you have presented your case convincingly; have stopgapped all likely negative reactions and thus anticipate your recipient's doing what you ask, of his or her accepting the decision you must make in answer to the person's own persuasive request.

In selecting the proper language style, skillful persuasive writers use the same technique as does the successful salesperson. They avoid *if, hope,* and *trust* sentence constructions, for these words too often imply the writer's unsureness of his or her explanation, reasoning, or conviction; they undermine writer confidence. Similarly, attempts are made to personalize and adapt the message by deliberately keeping selfish interests in the background while concentrating on the reader's stake in the proposal.

Examples abound of business writers' attempting to influence readers in terms of the writers' own self-interest. Applicants for jobs fill their letters with explanations of how badly they need jobs, how they prefer to live in a certain city—or a certain part of the country—how they wish to be employed by the firm that will give them the greatest opportunity for their own advancement. Sales letters begin: "We have put on the market a new computer that we feel will meet the approval of businesses everywhere. We have spent years researching and perfecting this machine." Collection correspondents ask for payments on the grounds that the store needs money. An adjustment letter begins: "We are surprised that you find fault with this clothing bought at such a reasonably low price." Such attitudes *will not* get desired results, for they ignore behavior patterns, the use of reason, and the emotional drives of individuals.

Behavior Patterns

An employer will hire an individual when that individual has convinced the prospective employer of the value that he or she can contribute to the firm. Readers buy products and services when sales writers make readers visualize

[3] C. W. Wilkinson, Peter B. Clarke, and Dorothy C. Wilkinson, *Communicating Through Letters and Reports,* 7th ed. (Homewood, Ill.: Richard D. Irwin, Inc., 1980), p. 90.

things in terms of reader enjoyment, comfort, benefit, profit, satisfaction, well-being—provided that readers can afford them. Your readers will pay their bills (assuming that they have the money) as soon as you show them that it is to their own self-interest to do so.

A reader reacts—agrees with you, the writer, and takes the action you suggest—only when you have made that person believe it is to *his* or *her* advantage or betterment to do as you ask—or that it is the only reasonable course of action under the circumstances.

Knowledge of human nature is thus the necessary qualification of the successful business writer in employing the *you*-attitude persuasively. Adaptation is the adjustment of what one says and how one says it to a reader to make both pleasing. Rare is the person who is governed by reason rather than by feeling. You get people to do things by making them *want* to do them. And, what do people want? They want

1. To be well thought of.
2. To do more work in less time with less effort.
3. To get ahead in business and in their own social world.
4. To make more money.
5. To be a friend.
6. To be believed—and to believe in.

From anticipating the reader's attitudes vicariously, the writer may conceive alternative approaches to a communication problem, imagining how the individual in his or her world will react to each before making a selection. Although every individual is different, certain general guideposts about human nature will help the writer plot a course: (1) the way an individual assigns meaning to words and (2) the effect of his or her beliefs on the impact of the message.

HOW HUMANS ASSIGN MEANING TO WORDS

The meaning that an individual assigns to words comes first from one's own background of experience, education, and place in society. And words can trigger memories out of this background that are destructive to any purpose. Or the words may be entirely unfamiliar because of educational limitations so that no meaning at all or a distorted concept results. Even ungrammatical expressions may be more communicative than the most erudite. If a person pushes an old automobile into a service station and says "This here car won't run no more," the attendant knows what is meant. If another individual pushes the car in and says "This vehicle lacks the facility for self-propulsion in a forward direction," the attendant might mop his brow with a greasy chamois trying to grasp the meaning. The apt business writer always adapts language to the estimated educational and cultural level of his or her readers.

A person's social status has a great influence on the meaning attached to messages. Since all of us strive for better things, the status an individual has not quite achieved may be more important than the slot into which he or she now fits. If your message implies to the reader that you consider that person in the class to which he or she aspires, either socially or intellectually, you may have won support for your point, no matter how opposed the individual may have been at the beginning. If you think of and write to someone as an honorable person who habitually performs effectively, you are playing right into that person's own self-image. And the reader will go to great lengths to protect that self-image.

The opinion you have of others influences their behavior. If you think well of them, you may give them something to live up to. If you think poorly of them—and say so—you may destroy their initiative for improvement or you might stir them to the determination to make you change your mind. The latter situation is rare, however. For these reasons, too, all good writers provide a way for reader face saving in the encounter when they communicate with individuals whose performance, intelligence, or understanding is in question.

The consistency of your behavior also contributes to the assignment of meaning. If a hard-nosed supervisor suddenly transmits a message that is friendly and ego-building, the immediate reaction may be: "Well, what is the old goat up to now?" If a customarily nice person comes up with a harsh directive to field representatives, the recipients may develop all sorts of fears, such as that pressures are developing from above or that layoffs are in the offing.

The timing of a message may be poorly chosen for effective meaning as well. For example, suppose that the afternoon paper carries an editorial showing the need to cut costs in city government and that the very next morning an interoffice memo makes the rounds in the city hall asking for an updating of each employee's qualifications and job record. The data may only be intended for giving merit raises; yet more than one employee will likely get the feeling that "heads are about to roll."

The Role That Beliefs Play

What a person believes is what that person is—no matter how erroneous the beliefs may be. The business writer who cuts across the grain of beliefs will encounter difficulties that might have been avoided otherwise. Beliefs can change in the light of changing experience and conditions, but because of human inertia such change is a slow process. People believe what they want to believe, what works to their benefit, and turn deaf ears to things that do not fit advantageously into their personal scheme. The average human seems satisfied with the status quo. Since people are reluctant to change, frequently the proposed change your message suggests is not worth the effort. Your reader is not too excited about getting your message in the first place. Instead of reading it and doing what you suggest, most would rather go golfing, go fishing, or do nearly anything else. Lots of people have a tendency toward mental inertia.

Your persuasive approach to them in writing must attempt to jolt them out of this laziness—to arouse at once their own self-interest. Their approach to any message is selective: they accept readily any evidence showing that you believe as they do, and any contrary ideas are either entirely wasted or produce an adverse emotional reaction.

Many readers resist seeing both sides of an issue. If your reader can be led to accept the idea that what you are proposing will benefit instead of act as a detriment, you have made great headway. If you can also attach your reasons to some of that person's emotional drives, you stand a good chance of winning your case completely.

The selectivity process also carries over into rationalization. People are inclined to think of their own behavior as logical and that of others as illogical. When you call readers to task, they begin to rationalize, to convince themselves that the way they behaved was the only way they could have behaved under the circumstances and that you are the one who has misjudged them. Consequently, we use a positive rather than a negative approach when the reader's performance is the subject of the message.

Another form of belief that is valuable for the business writer to consider comes from the herd instinct: the tendency of people to believe what others in their group believe. And this is the most dangerous kind of belief to oppose, for there is courage in numbers. The adept writer makes it a point of knowing the common beliefs of the group to which a reader belongs.

The vestments of authority are usually advertised in the business setting. The boss has a private office, a larger desk than others do, a choice secretary. No matter how reluctant people may be to recognize authority, they know that as civilized, social beings they must accept it. So the emotional reaction to a message from the boss is different from that evoked by the same message from someone not possessed of the authority to give it. Thus the roles of the communicator and the recipient play an important part in a message's meaning.

To combat reader inertia and to compete successfully for the reader's attention, time, and money, there are other tendencies about human nature worth remembering. People think that they think, but very few really do. Most buy or react because of what they *feel*. And when you get their attention and their proper feeling toward you, people like to get information that does not make them think too hard. People want personal adequacy, romance, the promise of longer life, and vitality. Some people like to be asked for their advice, for they love to talk. People forget easily. (Psychologists claim that 80 percent of what we read or hear is forgotten in the first hour.)

People will not look far beyond their own self-interests. They resent change, dislike newness, forget the past, and remember inaccurately. Some will not fight *for* things when they can find something to fight *against*.

Others will follow a habit until it hurts. They will accept ready-made beliefs and stick to them. With minds already made up, they do not wish to be "confused by the facts." They will follow leaders with their eyes shut and mouths open and stand by them even when their faults are known. Most people yield to suggestion when flattered, work hard to establish superiority in the eyes of equals, find greatest interest in their own emotional kicks, love low prices—but dislike economy intensely. That is the contradictory public you write to—strange breeds indeed, requiring you to visualize each person as an individual if you are to employ the tools of persuasion effectively.

Emotion and Reason

When you need to change your reader's way of thinking or feeling regarding what you want done, therefore, make your choice in light of the nature of your proposal and what you know of your reader's beliefs or feelings about it. A music conservatory buys practice pianos through a logical, rational procedure. To an ambitious pianist, however, the piano may be "an instrument of dreams," a purchase that leads into a world that takes color and form from countless emotional associations. One executive may hire an employee on a dollars-and-cents calculation of the money that person can bring to the firm. Another may put a part-time college student on a job as an investment in human values.

Usually, of course, the nature of the proposal or request governs the choice. It is hard to visualize selling a tractor to the operator of a large farm on the basis of emotional motivations. The important thing is to decide which appeal to use and to stick to the decision. The appeals do not mix well.

SELLING IDEAS, GOODS, AND SERVICES

Thus, with the idea that the tools of persuasion are reason and emotion, the secret of the inductive plan of writing is (1) to open with some interest-arresting talk closely related to—but not directly on—the subject,[4] (2) to build up reasons why the request you are about to make (or the disappointing

---

[4] Because of the "cushioning" effect of this material, it is often referred to as a *buffer*.

decision your message announces) is in the reader's self-interest, (3) to state the request (or decision) in definite form—a question, and (4) to drive for action in closing with a favorable goodwill idea or with some positive expression of outcome contingent upon the reader's granting the request.

The process is that of leading the reader to accept your point of view in gradual stages so that, when you finally present your request or decision, the reader is prepared for it. Strategy calls for postponing the reader's reaction until you have built your argument. Such strategy begins at the point of contact—arousing reader interest.

Arousing Reader Interest

To gain your reader's attention at all, or to have your reader even look your way, you need to revert for a moment to the preceding discussion on what people are like and to recall (1) that mental inertia and (2) the crowded day that person may be fighting. You are on course when you begin to study what your reader is thinking and how he or she is feeling. Perhaps these pointers will help you get that start.

Start Talking as Close to Your Point as You Can Without Giving away Your Purpose.   Unrelated "attention getters" can get momentary notice but can either make a long, tedious trek to your real subject matter or can break off with a jerk that irritates when you move from your opening remarks.

Come as Close as You Can to a Statement or Question That Brings up a Picture of a Personal Benefit to the Reader.   Is there some work the reader needs to have done well (if the reader is an employer)? Might a promotion come faster with computer expertise (if the reader is an employee)? Might the reader really like to sell a large bill of goods to a new retail business (if that person is a sales-minded credit individual)? The writer wants advertising to hit people just right and not ram headfirst into ingrained prejudices of people (if a promotion person)?

Attribute a Worthy Motive When You Mention "Benefit."   That "come as close as you can" leeway has to be there because you will often be making a request that simply does not immediately touch the reader's benefit. What money will be made, for example, by a businessperson's canvassing for you in the United Way drive—or by contributing money to it, either? The time-and-money output is specific and formidable; the advantage input is harder to see. But it is there if you look for it! Will the person get some wholesome publicity? But you would never suggest doing altruistic things for selfish reasons, would you? Dig a little deeper, then, and let the reader feel good and self-respecting in doing something to help less-fortunate people. (If the

publicity benefit enters the mind and helps sway the reader's decision, well
. . . so be it.)

You can draw up a graduated list of benefits that one may enjoy from
doing things that people ask of people in business:

1. Immediate tangible benefits to the individual or the business or
organization he or she represents.

2. Secondary benefits from the betterment of business in general—
the basis on which business people are asked to cooperate with academic
advancement.

3. General good to all or some sector of society.

4. The basic good feeling of doing something without reward.

5. Maybe just plain sympathy for the writer who asks help.

Respect Reader Intelligence.   It is better to ask or suggest instead of
telling someone a commonplace fact as if it were unknown. And when you
ask, do not underestimate the reader. A letter that begins "Have you ever
heard the old saying 'A chain is no stronger than its weakest link'?" will find
it hard to get much farther than that.

Even more important, *do not tell a person what that person thinks or
feels.* All your reader has to do is to respond mentally, "I do not, indeed, either
think or feel the way you say." It is usually irritating also to imply that the
person or something about him or her is lacking in some way if he or she
does not think the way you said. The plodding counterpart of that approach
is to come right out and tell a person what he or she *should* think, or feel,
or do.[5] Be careful not to make the person fight back.

The more your reader has to believe in—goals, ambition, home, success—the more powerful is the desire to achieve and the easier it is to motivate
that person to these desires by hooking your message appeal on them. Obviously, when you scatter your appeals like buckshot, you may hit the target—
and then again you may not. The strategy of persuasive writing calls for
having *one* major appeal and building your entire case around it (including
the interest-arousing beginning).

Human interests are predicated on desires, and these are much more
than the basic needs of survival. Interest is achieved when people feel that
what you offer is important or beneficial to them, or to those persons, things,
or ideas in which they are interested.

[5] The predicament-to-remedy, straw-man technique, or jaded-appetite appeals are
to be avoided. They set up a situation for which only your product, service, or proposal
is the logical solution. But such beginnings as "Are you tired of serving the same old fare
at every meal to the loving members of your family? Try . . ." make your reader feel
entrapped. The reaction is negative, for the points are criticisms of present performance.
Approval motivates better response, greater effort than criticism ever can.

Your motivation in arousing reader interest in persuasive writing is to *gain* a reading so that a person *believes* in what you are proposing and *acts* as you want. People do some things better for others than for themselves because their identification (a main problem in life after survival) is to them a reflection of their own impact upon the world. The reflection of one's impact on the world, measurable in material things and in psychic rewards, is the basis of meaning or identity. You as writer can build your central message appeal around the reader's attempt to adjust successfully within a social group—the need for status and recognition. You can appeal as well to reader need for self-preservation within the economic structure.

To one's basic need for attractiveness to the opposite sex, the appeal "in style" satisfies the desire for high-class appearance . . . for subtle "admiration." To role-playing in one's relationship to one's colleagues and associates, a person's own self-estimate as he or she wishes to be *seen* by others is the key. For the business executive's own self-estimate, the interest appeal is likely that "of a person of decision . . . of analytical ability and action . . . confidence . . . poise . . . good judgment." For the reader's role and need for measurable status, the interest appeal is through material ownership. It is the most obvious role through which one seeks identity in the world. Why? Because identity, position, or status in society is measured in large part on the basis of material rewards. And one wants symbols that indicate the ability to perform—visual evidence of status and capability. Many products lend themselves to this need adaptation.[6]

To arouse your reader's interest and cater to the desire for saving time by doing things efficiently, your product, service, or proposal must in some way help the recipient cut corners on time and shave minutes on doing a job. In turn, the time saved gives the reader the ability to stay relaxed, to keep in good health, and to live longer—to get more out of life.

You can think of dozens of ways to begin your persuasive messages by appraising your reader and the particular writing situation. Some will offer a smoother launch than will others. All the attention-interest factors in the world that you might choose for persuasive messages are useless, however, unless they lead toward *and through* the conviction phase in swaying the reader to your proposition. Therefore, whatever the appeal or approach you choose, the opening should arouse the reader's interest with favorable material allied closely enough to the subject to serve as *an opening wedge* for your message—some key word or phrase around which your inductive strategy may be built.

---

[6] It is impossible in a text of this nature to cover in detail all aspects of sales writing. Entire college courses are devoted to this subject. For an expert treatise on selling by mail (from which only a brief introduction to the many ideas are presented here) see John D. Yeck and John T. Maguire's *Planning and Creating Better Direct Mail* (New York: McGraw-Hill Book Company, 1961).

Building up Your Case

Paving the way for the point you wish to make—by immediately enlarging upon the proposal and upon what good comes from it for the reader—occupies the greater portion of the persuasive message. Some writers are able to stay with the reader's interest only through a well-wrought attention-grabber, and then they shift to writer interests. Having held out a promise, a benefit (even a valuable, sound, prospective idea), having established tentative favor, a point of agreement, understanding, goodwill, satisfaction—in short, a direct benefit or an indirect one—that captures your reader's interest, your letter must now *convince.*

Your sure-fire hold on the reader's continued interest is to keep that person clearly in focus as you make the transition from the opening to *proving* your claims. And, if in the opening you can plant the basic idea around which to build your case, or if the material you choose to use ties in with the request you will presently make, your transition will be all the easier. Suppose, for example, that you were a small-town jeweler and that you wanted to persuade a manufacturer to grant you a dealership for his brand-name silver flatware. The *key idea* or *wedge* planted in the opening might center around (1) the beauty of the product itself, (2) your town, a good market for silver flatware, or (3) the amount of interest being expressed by potential purchasers. Hence, an opening with a wedge idea in it for this situation:

> The natural beauty of Centurion silver flatware undoubtedly accounts in part for its universal appeal to modern-day brides.

Notice the words *universal appeal* (the wedge) tie in with a reader-interest opening on "beauty of the product." These words can now be used to build on for the turn in to the heart of the message. They would be easy to pick up as you start developing your first reason why you should be allowed to sell the product because of your "well-above-average" silver sales (for a town your size), even though the manufacturer's current distribution policy does not permit small-town dealerships.

Timing, in its subtleties, however, is the structural skeleton of the persuasive body of writing. The basic clue of "paving the way" for introducing a formidable idea is only a door-opener: It gets an attentive ear and keeps a reader listening to suggestions or ways in which to improve his or her status or ways of doing, leading the reader to ask "How?" The writer's proposal is thus invited into the reader's consciousness instead of being forced in against resistance. Obviously, we cannot talk long about *advantages* of our proposition without revealing what it is. For most letters in the inductive pattern, the specific suggestion of what we want the reader to do (buy our product, set up long-term credit for us on open account, help with the United Way campaign, modify an objectionable advertising policy, or give us a job) has to be known in perhaps the first third of the letter. From there on, our persuasive talk continues to keep the reader in the foreground with amplification of the positive values suggested in the beginning and maintained in the transitional shift.

If the specific proposal is delayed too long, two undesirable things may occur: the buildup (through logical proof or emotional picturing) may attach to other competing proposals, or the reader may demand in exasperation, "What's this all about, anyway?"

In planning any persuasive argument, your first need is to line up the elements in your favor and those against you. From this point on, you have the problem of setting the positive counterpoints against the anticipated negative aspects your reader might raise. Let's look at a typical problem to see how the technique works:

Your company, Diron Plastics Corporation, 4800 Essex Expressway, Detroit, Michigan, specializes in plastic products for industrial and commercial use. Your location in the city is not by accident because much of your work is for automobile manufacturers.

As Neil W. Kerwood, section head of the Automotive Trim Division of Diron Plastics, your work is devoted largely to the development and production of plastic molding and plastic parts to be used in decorating new automobiles. A current project—the development of a plastic molding from Direx plastic for use in the interior trim of automobiles—is giving you trouble.

You hope to develop a molding that can be used for trimming the dashboards of cars decoratively and that will also provide maximum safety. Direx, a plastic developed by your company about three years ago, is ideal because it acts as an excellent color base and is spongy. There's just one problem: Direx does not adhere consistently to the metallic sheeting of the dashboard. The Direx molding will cover the dashboard for a few days; then the molding comes loose. The problem has you stumped.

You need the services of Franklin Judd, former head of the Automotive Trim Division, to help you find a solution. Franklin was instrumental in the development of Direx. He knows this plastic inside and out. Mr. Judd is no longer with your company, however. Diron Plastics Corporation has a policy of optional retirement at age 60 with mandatory retirement at age 65. Mr. Judd chose to retire early at 62 and live on his company-provided pension. He retired about eighteen months ago and is living at 32 Sunshine Lane, Sarasota, Florida; at least, that's where he spends his winters. He and his wife still maintain their home in Detroit and return in May to be near their grandchildren for a few months.

You want to persuade Mr. Judd to return to Detroit about February 18 (today is February 1) and spend six weeks consulting with you on the solution of the Direx problem. Your argument must be developed carefully because Judd left your company early partially because of his dislike for Michigan winters and partially because he was "tired of working so hard." Select some persuasive appeals you believe would be attractive to Mr. Judd. Money of course may not be a major point, but you will pay him $3,000 for his efforts.

Close examination of the problem will probably produce, among others, these positive elements and negative points:

Positive Elements	Negative Points
1. Judd was one of the developers of Direx and probably still thinks of the material as his very own.	1. Judd is probably basking in Florida sunshine, and it is colder than the dickens in Michigan.
2. Judd will be complimented by his know-how being sought.	2. Judd said he quit early because he was tired of working. There may have been other reasons.
3. The consulting job offers a relief from the boredom that sometimes sets in for retired but active people. (This is a negatively positive point.) The job does not require him to be active for too long a period if he does not wish.	3. The retired couple may be in the middle of an important fishing project or some other pleasant distraction. You know nothing of Judd's present activities.
4. Mr. Judd's efforts will make it possible for the company to advance in automotive trimming.	4. Diron's retirement program is providing nicely for the Judds' financial needs.
5. Diron Plastic's contributions to automotive trimming will result in overall improvement in the appearance of automobiles—something the whole world can appreciate.	5. The $3,000 is only a token payment; the contribution he can make is invaluable, but he'll receive little reward beyond that.
6. The return to Detroit would make it possible for the Judds to be reunited with their grandchildren a little earlier this year.	6. You haven't written Judd in 18 months; he's likely to be suspicious.
7. The $3,000 stipend could be used in many ways by a retired couple.	

The negative elements (and some positive ones) will probably not appear in the letter you write; you merely line them up to get an estimate of what the situation is and what you must overcome in order to persuade the reader. Although there may be fewer negative than positive points, as so often happens, the negatives weigh *heavily* in this case.

With the arguments now structured, you can begin to see possibilities for your initial point of contact with Judd. The "close enough to the subject talk" serving as an opening wedge must have, as all persuasive requests should, some legitimate basis for being written to allay his suspicions of why you are writing to him after all these months.

Sometimes it is possible to ask for cooperation on a project of mutual interest (or to imply that that is what you are doing) with the specific request held off until the way is paved. But better buffer ideas for this problem seem to be

- Some bit of news about activities at Diron Plastics. (Judd was with the company for years and might enjoy being kept posted on what has been happening. The news item should not be directly on the subject of the letter, however.)
- Some kind of idea that might introduce the element of challenge without indicating that this letter is to provide any sort of challenge to Judd.
- A compliment of some sort. (This approach can be overdone easily, but a subtle compliment can be effective.)
- Talk about the automotive industry in general (trends, plans, etc.)
- Some other phase of mutual interest; perhaps you were good friends while Judd was here at the plant.

As already suggested, your opening, too, should contain some key word or phrase around which your inductive strategy can be built, yet should not give away the fact you are asking for Judd's help in the form of his return to work.

From here you begin to build your case by moving toward your request, giving it a logical background of interest to your reader. *Introduce* your reasoning by telling what further development and experimentation with Direx is necessary and why you need Judd's help. (The transitional turn, written in the you-viewpoint, of course, is dependent on the buffer opening material you select.) You need a planned sequence of items telling Judd the importance of the work on Direx and the contributions Direx could make to automobile interiors. In explaining as many details of the situation as necessary, tell Judd enough for him to get an inkling of the problem. When you have given your convincing argument and established your plan, definitely ask Judd to come to your aid. Phrased as a question, the request is placed—for the best psychological effect—in the middle of a paragraph. And you follow up the request immediately by suggesting additional advantages to Judd, perhaps playing up the contribution he can make to the entire automotive industry.

The final point of timing strategy in the persuasive letter is the deft shaping of your suggestion that the reader act on your request or proposal.

The Request for Action

Effective persuasive writers use a structured plan of proportion and emphasis in the material presented for the ultimate objective—*controlled reader action.* Because you have confidently presented reader benefit or contribution, have made clear what is wanted and why (minimizing the reader's objections by pointing out advantages in complying), you should now just as confidently seek your reader's definite compliance by asking for it.

The really skillful writer clinches the close for action by positively assuming—in tone, wording, or both—that the reader will do exactly what is asked. Apologetic expressions which imply that you know your request is unreasonable or unwarranted (which stress the inconvenience or trouble you cause) should always be avoided. Nor will the effective writer suggest a negative alternative by using an *if* construction at this vital point in the message.

Instead, if you are selling a product, the appeal-for-action close

1. Centers on the choice and one choice only.

2. Tells the reader how to make it.

3. Traces the steps to take—checking an order card, dialing a merchant's store—by minimizing the inconvenience (but definitely not using that negative aspect).

4. Supplies an incentive (appeal) to immediate action.

5. Attaches a recall of the values that will accrue to the reader from securing the product.

If you are selling an idea or making a request of the individual, the action

1. Avoids any negative alternative choices.

2. Places a value on reader compliance that serves as a final suggestion to act.

3. Pictures good things coming from reader action and effort

Persuasive strategy in informal writing closely parallels the syllogistic research model[7] used in report writing (see Chapters 6 and 7) with a slight difference in wording:

Major Premise:	(a) If you can state and get agreement on the principle of your argument, and
	(b) If you can present facts in detail to show the reader's position and/or responsibility, the reader should act in a certain way.
Minor Premise:	You can state and get agreement on the principle of your argument by presenting facts in detail to show the reader's position and/or responsibility.
Conclusion:	The reader should act in a certain way.

[7] The syllogistic form of reasoning is as follows:

Major Premise:	If A is true, B will occur.
Minor Premise:	A is true.
Conclusion:	B will occur.

The inherent fallacy or weakness of syllogistic reasoning is covered in the discussion on its use in report writing.

In your persuasive message, then, *you request* that the reader act as your logic indicates. To see how the suggestions made here for the Judd case are embodied in a unified, persuasive approach, here is one solution:

Yesterday during a coffeebreak, Frank,

the discussion turned toward the original group you were a part of who were so instrumental in the beneficial contributions that have advanced Diron Plastics to its present leadership position.

The results and potential of your work are still very much in evidence around here. It appears that your invention, Direx, is just what the automotive industry has been looking for as an excellent interior trim that offers maximum safety. As its developer, you know the potential of Direx better than anyone else, of course.

Its good looks, excellent color base, and spongy nature make Direx a natural for beautiful interiors and for meeting the continued emphasis on government safety standards. Direx is so pliable, however, it has us stumped on how to make it stick to the dashboard metal for longer than just a few days. Since I know you're still interested in its future, will you consider returning to the plant for about six weeks, starting February 18, to help solve the challenge Direx presents us? Your consulting services in perfecting the product to adhere to metal will be invaluable in making Direx a universally accepted material for the entire automotive industry. You'll also have the satisfaction of knowing that your invention is responsible for saving countless lives from another great advancement of yours in the plastics industry.

Of course, we believe both you and Mrs. Judd will welcome an early return to Detroit for an extended visit with those fine grandchildren of yours. The company wants to fly you both here, pay you a $3,000 honorarium for your services, and fly you back home when you're ready to return.

Won't you, therefore, please let us know the date you can leave Florida? We'll make all the arrangements for a pleasant, enjoyable trip for you. It will be great having you back on the Direx team, Frank.

The Power of Words

There is a saying often quoted by writers that "words are half the problem when one tries to write, speak, or talk." People who use those words are the other half—the two are inseparable. Words are but fragments of experience.

Masters of word imagery, Yeck and Maguire, have this to say:

They [words] are mere elusive wisps of memory, symbols for the many experiences which have had impact on a human nervous system. As a person matures, a word gathers more and more meaning. . . . And the word is merely the skeleton of the experience. A person may not remember the "flesh" of the actual experience. But the skeleton which brings forth a reaction—the meaning of the word—*is* there.

The meanings of words are like the drip of water which adds length to an icicle. A little bit more meaning is added to a word as a person builds contact with life. And, as the icicle of experience increases imperceptibly, so does belief grow.

Words and their meaning are like an iceberg. The part above the water is the word, merely the symbol for the huge mass beneath the water. And, like an iceberg, a word may plumb the depths deeper than one realizes.[8]

Because your readers have been conditioned to the use of certain words that have greater meaning than other words, you must be extremely cautious in your selection—particularly when you seek to create *belief*. The impact of the words must not set up conflicts in your reader's mind.

We use Yeck and Maguire again to illustrate the point.

... Remembering that words gather meaning as mankind marches through time, take this sentence:

Jesus wept.

The *meaning* to Christians of the word *Jesus* goes *clear back*, all the way through recorded Jewish history, *clear back* to those hazy, misty times when the promise of the Messiah was made. When you consider the iceberg of meaning beneath the word *Jesus*, when you consider the importance to the Western world of the word *Jesus*, can you imagine using any other word than *wept?*

Because of the human experience with the word *Jesus*, back through the long shadows of time to the crucifixion and beyond into the ages of darkness when the Messiah was promised to man, *Jesus* calls for the *dignified sorrow* implicit in *wept.*

If the sentence had been written *Jesus cried*, the word *cried* would have been in conflict with the lower part of the iceberg of meaning in the word *Jesus*. *Cried* would make Christ sound like a neurotic, immature child. Because people have been *conditioned* to such a depth of meaning in the word *Jesus*, they wouldn't *believe* it.

If you used these words, *Jesus spilled tears*, what would you get? The result, unfortunately, is comic. And comedy doesn't fit in with the deep ... deep ... meaning of the word *Jesus*.

And people wouldn't *believe* it.[9]

When you are faced with the problem of words meaning different things to different people, remember there are classes of words that more nearly approach universal application than others—those that are picture making.

---

[8] Yeck and Maguire, *Planning and Creating Better Direct Mail*, pp. 130–131.

[9] Ibid., pp. 131–132.

What are the picture-making words in the language? We may consider that Adam and Eve were the first to feel the need of conversation. In the process of building a language, what did these lovely new people talk about first? We might guess they talked about the things they could see: *man, woman, dog, apple*—the names of things: *nouns*. Next, they might have talked about what these did: *eat, run, bark*—actions: *verbs*.

According to some authorities, nouns and verbs are the words of *fact*, and adjectives and adverbs are the words of *opinion*. If you say "It is *extremely* important that you submit your purchase requirements on time," that is a matter of opinion. If you say instead "Filing your purchase requirements by the tenth enables us to have supplies available for you when you need them," the reader has tangible evidence of *importance*. Words that make pictures are far better than abstractions for getting an idea across, for creating belief.

Nouns that name things the senses can know, adjectives that catch up their exact characteristics, and verbs that keep things moving help the reader to keep awake. They move the writer's ideas into the reader's consciousness with greater accuracy than do nouns that suggest mental concepts or abstractions (those ending with *-ness* or *-tion*, for example) or verbs that indicate mere existence (forms of *to be*).

Most of us are sun worshippers in one way or another. We like the *look* of sunshine even though we may air condition ourselves against its heat. Clouds and rain are gloomy and droop the spirits. They do not give an atmosphere for action, for vigorous thinking, or for decisions. Since we deal with words in a letter, and since we know from reading about human nature the feelings that words can evoke, we need to refine our techniques for writing positively, cheerfully, and constructively.

A superficial level of negativeness to be avoided is one that momentarily oppresses one or more of the senses with screechy sounds; acrid smells; creepy or slimy touch; bitter tastes; ugly shape, form, or color; or pain of any kind. A deeper level of negatives to be avoided is in pictures of ugliness of human character and human relations: *dishonesty, corruption, oppression, exploitation, infiltration*. Any of these can create feeling-tone environments that are hard to shake off, and they are ineffective in getting people action minded.

The more subtle negatives are those that attach to readers or to their ways of doing things. And the ones that really drag the sled are those that inadvertently condemn the writer's own proposition or request. The tar bucket is a dangerous paintpot.

The denied-negative trap—the fallacy of trying to create a forthright positive picture by denying its opposite—trips up some writers. The denial word (*no, not, none, avoid*) is short, colorless, and lacks the power to reverse the image created by a colorfully negative word. "This is not a mere flimsy carton" is an ineffective way for conveying the reassurance: "This sturdy carton will carry your crystal intact." "We are not questioning the honesty of your advertising intent" really tells the recipient that we *are indeed* questioning it (otherwise, why even state the point?)

The convincing writer of persuasive copy needs to study diction with a keen ear to hear the subtleties of connotation or mental association in attempting to create the right emotional tone.

Here for your appraisal are two illustrations in designing the persuasive request to accomplish its mission:

The first situation concerns the ever-present problem of getting sales reports into the company in sufficient time to make them useful to an efficient operation. Obviously, the sales representative understands that he or she must make weekly reports as a part of the job and the rule for timing their arrival has been in effect for some time. He or she *makes* the reports; they simply arrive *too* late.

AN ANALYSIS OF THE SITUATION

Positive Points in the Writer's Favor	*Negative Elements That Must Be Overcome*
1. Sales representatives are obliged to comply with the request or be penalized in some way.	1. The outgoing nature of the sales personality makes sales people productive but indifferent to detail and red tape.
2. The assistant is in a position to report the sales representative to the boss at any chosen time.	2. Good sales people are too valuable to lose.
3. The rule for timing the arrival of the reports has been in operation for some time, and the representatives understand it.	3. Human beings resent being called to task for their shortcomings.
4. The summary made at the right time enables headquarters to provide for the representatives' needs more efficiently.	

A CALCULATED WAY TO GET
FAVORABLE ACTION

	TO: All Acme Representatives FROM: The District Sales Manager Dear Bob:
Making use of the salesperson's sense of pride	Your fine record as a salesman since you've been with the firm has no doubt convinced you of the importance of the *psychological moment*.
Planting a key idea around which the request may be built	
Advancing further the key idea introduced in the opening. Injecting a sense of rightness	Being right there with the right goods when the customer is in the right mood can mean the difference between a large

Placing time on the table	commission and a small one, can't it? Your sense of *timing* must certainly be pretty good in view of your outstanding performance.
Conversion to headquarters; showing the big stick—but not wielding it	Here at headquarters the boss has a good appreciation of the psychological moment, too—and the right moment for those fine reports of yours seems to be precisely Friday morning. With your re-
Why writer profits from compliance	ports in my hands by then I'm able to present a summary to him by Monday noon—and he carries the ball from there in keeping inventories ahead of the de-
Why reader benefits	mand, speeding up deliveries, and in all the many things he does to keep those customers of yours happy. So won't you
Requested action in the form of a question, internal position	please post your reports each week by midnight Wednesday in order that we may give you the best of service? I'll be sure to get them by Friday from any point in your territory with that sort of timing.
Gracious leave-taking, which ties in with the salesperson's sense of pride	The sales index went up 1 point last month on an overall company basis. Keep up the good work!

As background for the second situation, John H. Morris, age 22, has a roving heart, restless feet, and a hankering for beverages that on occasion befuddle his judgment. Recently, a commercial pilot presented a $2,000 check, bearing young Morris's signature, at the window of your bank. The check was to be used to defray expenses for one chartered plane from a metropolitan city to a distant rural town. A few days later your bank honored a $3,600 check to provide a pleasure boat for this Morris hero to launch on Lake Travis. Morris, who is supposedly running the Morris Oil Well Supply Company for his father, doesn't have that kind of money in your bank, but his father carries a steady $30,000 balance; so of course you have honored the boy's checks. It's time now, you think, to call a halt.

For Your Critical Analysis	*A Psychologically Planned Way*
Dear Mr. Morris:	Dear Mr. Morris;
I am writing to you in regard to your checking account, which in the past has been overdrawn several times. I was happy to honor your recent checks although you did not have sufficient funds in your account, thus creating an overdraft. This I knew was in violation of the Banking Law, and it leaves me open for	Serving the banking needs of you and your family over the years has been a source of real pride to us. We've always tried to do our best to make your relations with us pleasant and profitable by giving you the best possible service in line with good banking practice.

You know without my mentioning it the |

criticism from the bank examiner the next time an audit is made of this bank.

Recently when this bank was examined, the overdraft received special attention by the auditors, and I was asked to discontinue this practice. Therefore I suggest that in the future you call at the bank and make arrangements before issuing checks that might cause you to be overdrawn.

Your cooperation in this matter will be personally appreciated by me.

confidence we have in you and your family, both as to your moral and your financial standing; so you can easily understand our concern over the state of your account in recent months. Our interest in the situation centers around protecting, first, the depositors of this bank and, second, your good name and my own as a banker in Pioneer City.

The granting of an overdraft by a bank, as you know, represents the extension of credit for which proper arrangements have not been made and terms of repayment have not been clearly specified. Overdrafts are thus not good business for the borrower or for the banker, are they?

Because of that fact the banking regulatory agency insists that banks refrain from such a practice. Won't you come by to see me soon so that we may make satisfactory arrangements to cover your present overdraft and to keep within the principles of sound banking? We'll be happy to discuss your credit requirements at any time.

I enjoyed matching shots with you at the Club last month and am looking forward to a return round soon.

As a final illustration of a communication that blends the informative techniques (Chapter 3, "Adverse Circumstances") with those of persuasion discussed in this chapter, look carefully at the following letter. The message is an acknowledgment of the reader's order and requires a correction of one item, a substitution of size on another. Basically, the letter is persuasive, for it attempts to get the reader's *acceptance* on both, thus culminating in a contract between the two parties.

APEX FOODS, INC.
Any City, Any State

Mr. X. R. Tarlton
Purchasing Agent
Town House Hotels
Metropolitan City, Any State

Dear Mr. Tarlton:

Reference to original order for records, confirmation of accuracy

Subject: Order No. 58–2157, December 12, 19xx

Pointing toward arrival of entire order; picking up delivery date	So that you may be sure of having your complete shipment of Apex foods available for use on December 20, as you specified, will you please confirm the following changes?
Making clear the first necessary change	*Item No. 1.* According to the new price list issued on December 1, Bulletin No. 58–7, your requisition should read—

> 24 cases No. 26 Apex chili
> with beans, 24-oz., at
>
> $20.80 .... $499.20
>
> instead of
>
> 24 cases No. 26 Apex chili
> with beans, 24-oz., at
>
> $18.75 .... $450.00

Resale on merchandise to ensure authorization	In order to maintain the quality of our foods, it is necessary for us to keep prices in line with the increased costs of the prime beef we insist on. You'll find this price comparable to that of competing brands—with the plus value of superb Apex taste.
Persuading toward the substitute on Change No. 2	*Item No. 2.* The Apex barbecue sauce No. 194, 15½-oz. size, was replaced with No. 196, 24-oz. size, on November 1. The larger size for institutional use was the result of a preference study made by the Market Research Division. Hotels, schools, and military procurement offices found the 24-oz. size so much more economical, it's the only large one we're making now. At $6.00 a case, your shipment of 15 cases would come to $90.00.
Easy way to confirm changes	By authorizing these changes on the enclosed order card immediately, you can be sure of our delivery at the desired time.
Low-pressure suggestion for the next sale	The enclosed leaflet describes the new Apex institutional-pack tamale, tasty as ever and more generously proportioned. On page two you'll see the specifications of the two sizes designed for hotel use.
Appreciation of customer's business	We're pleased to have the opportunity to provide your good customers with quality foods. A new price list will reach you the first of next month.

At times no amount of persuasive effort produces response to your message and no amount of follow-up seems to bring the desired result either. What do you do to get action? There is no known cure, but sometimes resorting to a light treatment of the situation will appear to work a miracle. The letter that follows is an actual example of how an innovative, creative company sought—and got—action after three previous messages had been ignored. It is an application of selected strategies and techniques set forth in this chapter.

FROM: *Cyndi Mathews*   DATE: *Later Than You Think*
TO: *The Convention Coordinator*   SUBJECT: *"Idea Starter" Catalog*

My name is Cyndi Mathews and I work for the "big wheel." Someday I figure I'll be vice president of the company—but you're not helping me establish my reputation one bit.

Several months ago, Mr. Riceman (he's the man who wrote you last) asked me to be on the lookout for your request for our free catalog offer. "Yes, sir!" I replied, burning your name deep in my brain.

A few days ago, he said, "Cyndi" (we're very informal here—he calls me Cyndi and I call him Mr. Riceman) "could the catalog request have been mislaid?" I told him I'd check. I did. It hadn't!

So, Mr. Riceman sent you another letter. Still no request. Finally, Mr. Riceman sent you a third letter. No soap!

Yesterday, a very disappointed Mr. Riceman walked over to my desk. "Cyndi," he said, "You're an avid believer in Idea Starters, aren't you?"

"Yes," I agreed.

"Do you believe it's the best darn (he's very careful of his language out of respect for my age) Idea Catalog there is?"

"It sure is," I exclaimed, my voice firm and clear with the knowledge that I spoke the truth.

"Do you think it still brings its readers the kind of actual, factual, power-packed idea starters that has made us *the* idea company?" he persisted.

"Gosh, yes sir!" (even firmer and clearer than before).

"Then why in hell (I guess he forgot my age for a moment) hasn't that request arrived?"

"Well, sir, how the hell am I supposed to know," I stammered— (I forgot *his* age for a moment).

"It might be that it arrived with other catalog requests." He looked at me and walked out, taking with him all hopes of my getting to be vice president of the company at age 23.

Now, you and I both know your catalog request never arrived.

Won't you fill out the enclosed reply form and mail it back to my personal attention ... for the sake of your next convention ... and my career?

Cyndi

Cyndi

CHECKLIST FOR PERSUASIVE MESSAGES

Selling Ideas, Goods, and Services

Opening

PM 10   Your buffer beginning—closely akin to the subject but not on it—should catch the immediate interest of your reader.

11   What you have is too far off the subject.

12   Your letter will be easier to develop if you can plant a wedge idea here on which to build later.

13   This one hints too much at what your message is all about (what you will presently ask of your reader) or gives you away entirely too soon. It violates the strategy of the inductive style of writing.

14   Frame your ideas positively, not negatively.

15   Wording moves the reader too slowly.

16   You've attempted too much in the opening.

17   Make believable, not high pressure.

18   Keep zeroed in on the you-viewpoint.

Coverage

PM 20   Concentrate on the reader as you turn into the discussion. Work at a reader-interest idea for this position.

21   Make the transition from the opening smooth, perhaps by picking up here the key idea set forth in the opening.

22   Introduce the material that is to follow by giving reasons, background.

23   No hint still at your purpose in writing.

24   Your reasoning—framed in terms of reader benefit—should lead up con-vincingly to the heart of your message.

25   Don't just tell the facts. Frame them in terms of reader adaptation.

26   Make your point—in definite, clear phrasing—a third to halfway down the letter, buried position.

27   Follow up the specific point of your writing with at least one other con-structive advantage growing from it.

28   This point is needlessly negative.

29   No apologies are called for.

30   Too much emphasis is given here to your own interests in the matter.

31   Too scant coverage to be con-vincing, persuasive.

32   Too much detail is presented.

33   A good case is made from an adequate treatment of these points. (Your instructor will provide specific items of expected coverage according to the case selected for assignment.)

Close

PM 40   Subtly assume positive accept-ance of your message's content by reader.

41   Picture good things resulting.

42   Show promptness on reader's part as being desirable. Place value on reader's compliance.

43   Avoid high-pressure endings.

44   Avoid negative inferences in *if* phrasings.

45   Make any action called for easy on the reader.

Tone and Style As Marked

Your Grade _____

PROBLEMS IN PERSUASIVELY SELLING
IDEAS, GOODS, AND SERVICES

1. *Persuasively requesting an executive to serve on an advisory committee.* In your job as administrative assistant to the chairman, Department of General Business, Your University, Your City, Your State, you must frequently write messages for your boss's signature. Such is your task today.

After three years of work, an endless number of hearings and votes, the department has received final, official approval for a new degree program. The Coordinating Board of Higher Education has agreed with the College's wisdom in offering a major in Data Processing and Analysis (DPA) for the undergraduate business student.

The U.S. Department of Labor's forecast for the next decade is that job openings for computer programmers, analysts, and related data-processing job functions will exceed vacancies in accounting annually. That condition foretells bright opportunities for graduates of your new DPA program. Courses have been designed to provide a foundation in the integration of hardware, software, and business functional analysis for business systems.

Thus, DPA graduates will provide a link between the rapidly developing machine and software capacities being generated by information technology and the managerial talents needed to solve fundamental business problems (e.g., inventory control, production, forecasting, finance, cost accounting). The DPA degree is intended to prepare a professional who can fully appreciate the complexity of data-processing system design and the need for easy system maintenance and user satisfaction.

Student demand is already high for this new degree major—100 the first semester the program was approved. Projections are that majors in DPA in the next five years will outstrip the number of accounting majors (2,500) currently enrolled. Such a dramatic impact means that you will constantly need outside inputs if you are to provide businesses with the most knowledgeable, computer-trained business graduates possible. For example, field people are needed (a) to monitor and evaluate the adequacy of your DPA program, (b) to act as ambassadors for this program's emerging end products (your graduates), being sure that they are employed strategically, and (c) to be active contributors that keep your College of Business on the cutting edge. To provide efficiently for such inputs would therefore be the responsibility and *active* function of the advisory committee that your boss—E. W. Jordan—is trying to put together.

Dr. Jordan has given you the names and addresses of five business executives whom he would very much like to have staff this advisory committee. All of them are heavily involved in the field of mini/microcomputers. The majority of these individuals are also loyal supporters of your College, contributing money regularly to the CBA Foundation. Perhaps some may feel they are already "doing their share." Your request will be written, however, to serve as an individually typed form message for all five executives.

You may also assume you are enclosing information sheets that you regularly provide interested students inquiring about the DPA program:

- The degree program description and checklist.
- A sheet of descriptions of the topic courses offered—business data base design, applied data communication systems, commercial software systems, data processing project management, COBOL with business applications, computer system utilization in business, and system design and evaluation.
- An advising guideline of electives for DPA majors.
- An advising guideline of DPA elective courses for nonmajors.

Take over this writing task and address your first letter to Mr. Don E. Stewart, president, Office Products Division, Amdahl Corporation, 3131 Pond Drive, Any Metroplex, U.S.A.

2. *Clinching the deal on multipack packaging for citrus juice.* As Sales Manager Barney Thompson, Modern Packaging, 9216 Burnet Road, A Major City, Your State, you'll try to sell Mr. A. B. Follett, owner-manager, Follett Citrus Products (in the Rio Grande Valley), 5492 Port Road, Brownsville, Texas, multipacks for his frozen and canned fruit juices—and perhaps later for fowl. He writes that he's considering the possibility of boosting sales with the use of multipacks for his fruit juices if the cost doesn't bite too deeply into his profits. He'd like cost estimates on two-, three-, and six-pack paper cartons similar to those used for soft drinks. Since the price of citrus fruit fluctuates, is there any way to make the cartons so that they may be broken into smaller units should consumers shy away from quantity purchasing when prices necessarily reflect rising fruit costs? Has your company done any research to determine the size of multipack which moves best?

Follett processes orange, grapefruit, papaya, pineapple, and tomato juices. He wonders whether it's preferable to package juices of all one kind or to collect assortments. Could you be of any help to him on that problem?

You check the itinerary of Harvey Dale, your Valley sales rep. Dale will be in Brownsville next Tuesday. When you catch him at a hotel in Alice, your telephone conversation with him reveals the fact that he calls regularly on Follett, but has been unable to sell him a thing in five years. Follett operates a thriving business, buying his cans in large quantities from Modern Can Corporation in Houston. You give Dale instructions to do his best on Follett, promising to send him a copy of the letter you're mailing today.

In terms of volume, you can practically assure Follett of a boost in sales. Golden Glow Corporation has used multipacks of concentrated orange juice in some areas of the country. "Generally," says Sales Promotion Manager Richard H. Tobe, "when we market our juice in multipacks, sales increase around 20 percent." Tobe admits, though, that distribution of Golden Glow multipacks is spotty. Volume falls off if the price of oranges goes too high. "We have to cut back on the price of packaging if orange prices increase," he goes on to say. "We can't put the increase in orange prices into the selling price to the consumer." You can partially offset this price-fluctuation difficulty by assuring Follett that you can design packages for him that can be broken like egg cartons into smaller packs.

From the study you've made of the problem, seven-packs are the largest that consumers will accept. Too, experience of companies dealing in other food lines indicates that it's better to stick to a single type than to deal in assortments. The A. J. Bainz Company has experimented with soup assortments. Ad manager C. A. Milsap explains: "We have 16 different kinds of soups. If we try to preselect by putting, say, tomato and cream of mushroom in a two-pack, then we run into the customer's personal taste. That knocks out our whole idea of assortments." The Bainz people have been quite successful, however, with six-packs of strained orange juice for babies.

The cost of the packaging is the prime negative feature—and one that will weigh heavily with Follett, you feel sure. The cost of the packs will vary with size, of course, from 5 to 10 cents, a big bite into profits that will have to be absorbed in volume. You can't quote him a definite price, since it varies with quantity. You'll let Dale handle the price angle for you, frankly telling Follett that multipacks are costly but in many ways profitable. They cater to the preference of consumers for once-a-week shopping. They are well adapted to the introduction of new lines, since the longer the item is around the house, the stronger the brand preference is likely to become. The theory behind multipacks is that the larger the home inventory, the greater the frequency of use.

Proponents of multipacks think that these cartons help sales by billboarding the product on the bulging supermarket shelf, making it easy to integrate package design with advertising.

Write a letter for Barney Thompson that will pave the way for a sale for Harvey Dale when he calls on Follett next Tuesday.

3. *Persuasively bidding for the services of an organization expert.* The architectural and engineering firm of Mason, Jorgensen, Dent, and Struball Company, 1200-1209 Trade Mart Building, Some Metropolitan City, Your State, is suffering from truly adverse conditions. Founded four years ago by a seasoned practitioner and three top-notch architecture graduates, the partners currently find almost all their combined savings gone and two of the partners with ulcers. At no point in the company's life has it been solvent. It has done well in obtaining contracts, for Metropolitan City and its environs as well as the state continue to enjoy a building boom. Last year with contracts totaling $15,000,000, the company lost $30,000 on fees amounting to $540,000. Industrial work in the United States makes up about half of the gross with the other half coming from jobs outside the United States.

Morris Mason, president, who started the firm after ten years' experience with one of Metropolitan City's prestige architectural engineering groups—and miraculously still without an ulcer—suggested to his partners that they call in an outside consultant to prescribe a remedy for their woes. Upon the recommendation of Universal Management Consultants, a firm with an international reputation, they hired Alan L. Fowler, a 35-year-old Harvard Business School graduate (married, with a boy, 12, and a girl, 10), to study company operations for two months. His report was anything but complimentary. According to Fowler, the only good thing about the firm was its architecture and its engineering. The organizational setup was scrambled, the lines of authority were haphazardly defined, management was inefficient and costly. Utilization of company talent was extremely poor. What MJDS needed was a manager, Fowler said, and a keel-to-mast overhauling. He seemed confident, however, that with proper management the firm could be converted to a very profitable operation.

It is difficult to like anyone with such a degrading opinion of one's business; yet the partners were so impressed with Fowler's acumen that they offered him the managership the day he delivered the bad news. People with Fowler's ability, though, aren't easy to pick up. With his customary economy of motion, he gathered up his briefcase and said he was leaving for New York and was going to work in Panama in about three weeks. Various disparaging remarks about the distasteful living conditions in Panama—as compared with the amenities of Metropolitan City—had little effect. Fowler was gone without waiting for the partners to offer terms.

Mason knows of a multimillion-dollar dam project in the making for the Australian government at Canberra (not yet released to the bidding public) and would like to send a representative right away to put in a bid. The company's limping condition, however, seems to make liquidation a more feasible move. With an optimism born of necessity and fired by discussion, the partners decided to make an all-out effort to get Fowler at the helm. Other capable managers were likely available somewhere, but the screening process takes time. They agreed to pay Fowler a salary equal to the partners' stipend—$40,000, if the money is available for them—plus 10 percent of the profits.

A telephone call to Fowler might get the job accepted. But Morris Mason has confidence in his persuasive writing talents. In addition, a letter to Fowler, Mayfair Hotel, New York 10029, will give him time to mull over the offer and arrive at a decision in deliberate stages instead of perhaps rushing into an answer.

For your assignment, do your best as Morris Mason to get Fowler on his way to Metropolitan City to manage MJDS.

4.   *Writing a promotion piece for Scully's, Inc.* You, as Harold A. Walker, hold a rather special position, not long occupied, for a unique clothing store in Kansas City. The history behind your position explains it. Scully's, in its original and rather unfashionable location, was a landmark in the city. Primarily a men's clothing store, it did have small departments featuring women's sportswear and boys' clothing. The interior was very much that of a small-town store; there were no carpets—only runners—and the old board floor creaked underfoot. The long-time atmosphere of Scully's was that of genuine friendliness. The service, both on the floor and in the credit department, was superior. When a man walked into Scully's, he always had the feeling that he was going into the home of an old, casual friend. He could depend on sincere advice in the selection of a tie, suit, or gift and buy on credit as casually as borrowing a dollar from his brother.

During the past year, the three Schafanar brothers have had constructed in the heart of Kansas City one of the most ultramodern buildings in the city. It is across the street from one of the largest department stores in town, and Scully's now has one entire floor devoted to ladies' exclusive fashion. There is also the young men's College Shop and the Young Miss department. The building itself, three-storied, with its two-level, glass-display frontage, black marble exterior, and windowless walls, presents a very glamorous appearance. The interior is all plush carpets, spun aluminum, sunburst chandeliers, and expensive scents, pervaded by soft music. It is about as different from the shabby gentility of the old Scully's as Africa is from Newfoundland. Scully Schafanar, president of the corporation and mastermind of the promotional policies of the store, is not concerned with sales and profits (that will be established, what with the prime location and the name brands in stock) as much as he is in preserving the old Scully's atmosphere—very difficult with all this glamor. Whereas in the old store it was only a question of properly chosen and directed personnel, putting across that old feeling is going to be a real advertising and promotional problem in this new location. He fears that many of his old and true customers may shy away from this breath-taking new store. He has created this advertising position and carefully chosen you as the one to fill it. Your first task is to get out a mailing to all of Scully's customers, primarily to assure them that they should feel just as much at home at the new Scully's as they did at the old store.

You ponder over your approach to this letter. Wouldn't it be very much like a family, perhaps, who had acquired an advanced station in life and was in a position to buy an elaborate new home? You, as this family, would hope sincerely that all the old friends of days gone by would not feel that they were left by the wayside, that you now wished to travel in a different, more glamorous circle, leaving them out of your life. Maybe that family would decide to hold an open house, inviting all the old friends over for an informal gathering, not to preen the new advancements, but to show its desire to have them *share* it and that everything was still just the same between you. This letter, the essence of informality, will definitely accomplish the objectives of a commercial store, however. Scully Schafanar is not just a host; he is a merchant. He wants to put over a warm appreciation for his good friend-customers, reimpress those customers with their original desire to make Scully's their favorite store, point up benefits from trading with Scully's, and slip in a little sales on some of the merchandise they may be interested in. Scully Schafanar has always had his clerks keep a card file on their customers, for previous sales mailings, and now you make use of the information. It's a big project, but you know that Scully will appreciate your efforts; you decide to write separate form letters to carefully grouped customers. Those files as well as the credit records show whether a customer has bought primarily in the men's, women's, or boys' clothing lines. There will be something specific in the newly enlarged and enhanced lines that will be a sales feature to each group.

Take over for Harold Walker and write a letter that Scully Schafanar will feel good about. His ulcers have been taking a beating over the new store's opening. For assignment purposes, choose one of the specific categories (ladies, men, young men, young miss) and write the first of the form letters.

5. *Persuasively stimulating out-of-state organizations to try Your City as a convention site.** A letter is currently being sent by Your City's Chamber of Commerce to out-of-state groups in an appeal for their convention business. The results have been discouraging. Your City ranks third in the state in the number of conventions it hosts. But the bulk of this business comes from state-based organizations. Your City's Chamber of Commerce wants to strengthen its out-of-state trade.

Why is it state groups prefer Your City? One big reason is geography. One group advocate recently observed that Your City's central location contributed to a large

* Former Teaching Assistant Stonewall Jackson Fisher contributed the idea for this problem.

attendance. Another individual noted the abundance of historical sites of interest to natives of the state as a drawing card.

The reason for the lack of national interest can only be hypothesized. An initial observation is that Your City is competing in a much larger, more diversified market. It necessarily lacks the glamor of New Orleans, Las Vegas, or San Francisco. Nightlife here is not outstanding, even by the standards of other cities in the state. Furthermore, Your City is not located centrally relative to the nation as a whole, nor does it have any landmarks of national interest nearby (other than a former president's ranch, a library in his honor, which can hardly be classified as national "drawing cards").

In short, we have a "good, clean, fairly quiet town." Is it marketable to a convention planning committee? Definitely so, but the right sales pitch is going to have to implicitly recognize Your City's obvious shortcomings and focus upon its attractive selling points.

What does Your City have to offer? Well, for one thing, the prices can't be beat; it is one of the top 14 most desirable U.S. cities in which to live. Even a cursory glance at a travel guide will tell you the average hotel room costs several dollars a day less than in the traditional tourist meccas. The same economy goes for food, too. Further, Your City has an abundance of convention facilities located in remarkably close proximity to each other. What's more, Your City is richly endowed with intellectual and political talent. It's hard to imagine an organization that could not find suitable guest speakers to fill its program. And what about the climate? In Chicago and St. Louis and such places to the north, it is likely to be nearly freezing with ice and snow everywhere—foul weather, to say the least. Finally, you have a lot of friendly, down-to-earth people here who are anxious to be of service because they appreciate the value of convention business.

So how do you get all this across to the convention planning chairperson? At the outset you should recognize that your biggest enemy is going to be apathy or, even worse, ignorance about the opportunities of Your City. Your job is to get the reader's favorable attention and inform that person about Your City's potentialities.

Then you will need to round out your discussion with a positive appeal for action. Remember when you draft this letter that it may be competing with dozens of other messages each extolling the virtues of some town eager for convention business.

6. *Sending a profitable customer back to your wholesale outlet for a novel Christmas present for a man.* To your desk as sales manager of Novelty Manufacturing Company, 9299 Solomon Avenue, Chicago, Illinois, comes a letter that requires some careful handling. Miss Agnes Littlefield, a free-lance promotion agent, wants five of your toy Indian Chief trucks for her Christmas show. For two years during the two weeks before Christmas, she has rented the auditorium of the Community Playhouse for a full-dress showing of gifts for men. Her selections have included everything from traditional neckties to outboard motors, for which merchandise she has made deals with local stores to sell on a consignment-commission basis.

So successful has Christmas House been that this year she's making a widespread, year-long search for unique gifts to be sold with ideal promotion tactics: a movie cartoon at regular intervals, Christmas music, and intermittent floor shows. She wants your Indian Chief trucks as a drawing-card item to play up a man's penchant for electric trains and other intricate items on Junior's gift list—and on a consignment basis! You think that perhaps you should hire the young woman right off for a permanent post on your promotional staff—but first there's the matter of getting your trucks into Christmas House as the best advertising offer you know of. You distribute your merchandise only through wholesale outlets; so you can't set yourself up in competition with A. B. Sanger Company, your dealer there in Your City. A quick check of the Sanger file reveals the fact of a sizable order for Indian Chiefs scheduled for December delivery.

You see various advantages that you can point out to Miss Littlefield in making a deal with Sanger's—cheaper freight costs, quick replacement should the trucks meet with rapid-fire sale, inspection of and choice from your two models. (Both retail for $45. Perhaps there's no need to quote her any wholesale prices, for you can't speak for Sanger's. Then, too, her commission might be figured on the selling price.)

You promise to pave the way for Miss Littlefield with a persuasive letter to Carlton Simpkin, sales executive down there at Sanger's. In the letter you'll write to Miss Littlefield urging her to make contact with Simpkin, you'll have to do some reselling on your Indian Chiefs to keep her from getting the idea of bargaining with your principal competitor, the Sinbad Manufacturing Company in A Major City, Your State.

Your toy trucks come in two models: C-1628, a transfer truck, with cab, chassis, and gadgets of actual trucks reproduced to the minutest detail; and C-1629, a convoy truck. Both trucks are operated by remote control and are painted red with black lettering. (Use your imagination to make them appear real.) You write the letter for C. P. Bodine, sales manager of Novelty Manufacturing Company to Miss Littlefield at 2962 Elsmere Place, Your City, Your State.

7. *Making a full-reparation offer to hold a customer while trying for a larger sale.* You, as Cesare Boldin, have a flourishing business with personally designed women's clothes in your own shop, Boldin's, at 1692 Midway Mart, Any Metropolitan City, Your State. You intermittently insult your clientele in a phony French accent and shower them with outrageous compliments only they could believe. Usually you have them convinced the only way to social or marital success is through clothes by Boldin.

Two months ago Miss Agatha Drew of Box 621, Route 2, Any Small City, Your State, came in from the ranch country to be outfitted for a year's finishing at Briarcliffe on the Hudson, a select girls' school in New York. You designed for her a tuxedo coat in palomino suede cloth with a dyed-to-match muskrat collar—for the handsome sum of $805. Today you got an irate letter from Miss Drew saying that she is returning the coat express collect. The coat she received had a leopard collar, and the bill was for $850.

You check with the workers in the sewing room to find that the tailor had been in the habit of combining leopard with palomino suede cloth and had made up Miss Drew's coat that way instead of following specific instructions.

Your business has been built on the idea of focusing your talent on individual designs for the individual woman; so you have no use for a stock coat. But you've had dealings with ranch-style temperament before. You know that Miss Drew will pay well for what she wants but will probably be very difficult about having something put off on her. You decide to give her her money back—a credit memorandum for $850 attached to the letter you'll write her. But you want to employ your best persuasive strategy to get her to keep the coat. You'll explain to her that the extra $45 is the difference in price between leopard and muskrat and try to convince her that the exotic leopard skin will lend excitement to gala occasions that will certainly compensate for the extra expense. Getting the coat back is as easy as endorsing the credit memorandum and returning it at once.

8. *Writing a specialized invitation to reactivate accounts.* The Style Shoppe, dealing exclusively in distinctive clothes and shoes for men and women, is about to begin its gigantic pre-Christmas sale. You, as Stanley A. Petty, credit manager, are sending an advance notice to all your present revolving-charge patrons to inform them of a special presentation. On Saturday, November 17, from 1 P.M. to 5 P.M., they will be the only customers admitted to the store. At this time they will have the first chance to look over the sale offerings before the rush begins on Monday.

As you look over the present status of your charge accounts, you find that 223 of your credit customers have not used their account within the last six months. Because you think the patrons represented by these dormant accounts need personalized treatment, you decide to draft a special mailing piece. This letter will utilize the announcement of your special privilege sale to tell these customers that The Style Shoppe has missed them and welcomes their future credit purchases.

While describing to them the exceptional values that will be encountered at the sale, you will subtly weave in a barrage of goodwill pleasantry to convince each lady and gentleman to become a regular charge customer again. *Some* of your more eye-catching sale items are these:

- Your entire fall line of Country Club unisex heels is reduced 40 percent.
- A wide selection of Ms. Mort, G. Piloti, Fashion Spa, B. Blas, and L'Petite dresses and suits features reductions ranging from 20 to 50 percent.
- Beauty-Rest portable hair dryers, regularly $49.95, are now reduced to only $21.50.

From your desk at 809 Latrobe Avenue, Your City, Your State, draft this specialized mailing piece. Instead of an inside address, you will create in its place a catchy attention block. Let's get those accounts active again.

9. *Keeping a good customer on back order for a supply of Satin-Kraft backing.* As sales manager of Gwathmey Brothers and Long, St. Louis, you sent out on May 2 the following memorandum to all your regular customers:

We have received our annual notice from the Belmont Mills regarding their vacation schedule. The Fabrics Divisions at Albany, New York, and Hartford, Connecticut, will be closed from July 1 to July 16, inclusive.

During this closing their production operations will be unavoidably restricted, but the mill will maintain services at both plants on the finished-product lines they normally stock. On other items that require complete manufacture at either plant, they will necessarily have to have orders and specifications in their hands on or before June 10 so that they can schedule the orders for completion and shipment before July 1.

Should there be any special items that you might require, won't you send us the specifications promptly so that we can forward them to the mill for processing and shipment before the vacation closing period?

Today, July 10, you receive a special-delivery order for 5,000 yards of Satin-Kraft backing, gold, satin sample included, at 32 cents a yard for backing and laminating (a process of sticking the satin to the backing) and 65 cents a yard for the satin—a total of $4,850. The order comes from Mr. Gable Sargent, purchasing agent for the State Engraving Company, Any Metropolitan City, Any State, one of your best regular customers. He wants immediate delivery of the backing for a rush job on a brochure for the Petroleum Club in Metropolitan City.

Belmont Mills supplies the backing and laminating at 32 cents a yard in lots of 5,000 and allows customers to select their own satin from a swatch of samples—clearly a custom job that requires complete manufacture at the Hartford Fabrics Division. You call in your secretary to see whether the State Engraving Company was sent one of your Belmont vacation notices. A check has been placed by the company's name on the mailing list. It is possible, however, that the secretary might have checked the name without actually mailing the duplicated memo. Too, Sargent might not have read it, even though he received it. In any event, you cannot give him immediate delivery on his backing. Belmont has six more days to run on its vacation schedule. You make a special long-distance telephone plea to your friend Tom Aimsworth, production chief at the Hartford Division, for priority handling on this order when full-scale production resumes. He assures you that shipment straight to Metropolitan City can be made July 19—nine days from today. Sargent can expect delivery by express by July 21.

In a special-delivery letter you'll explain the circumstances to this good customer, trying to keep him on back order for Satin-Kraft backing. Is it possible that he might direct his efforts toward other phases of manufacture of his brochure in anticipation of certain delivery of the backing by July 21?

Since you hope to keep him from going to a competing market, you'll need to sprinkle expert resale on Belmont Satin-Kraft at strategic points throughout the message. Satin-Kraft has superior loft and spring to that of comparable products, and Belmont satin retains its luster and sheen throughout the life of a book. Made of the finest twisted nylon yarn, this satin resists wear at all vulnerable spots and may be washed with a damp cloth without altering its appearance. It's true, Sargent probably knows these features. Try to give them a thoughtful, new slant.

10. *Exhibiting salesmanship in applying for credit.* Get the viewpoint of R. M. "Rock" Brady, Some Small County Seat Town, Your State, who, after six years of traveling as a sales representative for athletic and sporting goods, now feels that he should settle down and make a home. His vocation practically determines the type of business he wishes to undertake. Being an athlete and a good fellow, he returned in 1969 from three years of military service to finish his education and resume his athletic career at Central State University. Five years later, with a background highlighted by varsity

letters in football and basketball, a bachelor of arts degree in business, and a natural ability to make and use friendships, he became successful as a representative for a major independent sporting-goods house in selling athletic equipment to south and central state high schools and colleges. Further, he continued to call the Small County Seat Town his home, kept up many public contacts, took time out for many a fishing trip with the "old gang," married a hometown resident, and just naturally likes the town anyway. Now, at the end of this year, he has a big plan cooking.

As County Seat Town still has no exclusive sporting-goods store (the needs of the townspeople and college students being supplied by limited lines in two hardware stores and the general school-supply stores near the campus), Brady decides that he can build up a good business in these lines—if he only had the money to start. He talks a local building owner into an agreement to equip a well-located shop with showcases, tables, shelves, and adequate fixtures and rent it at $375 a month. For his initial inventory he sets down a tentative assortment of items estimated to total $14,150 at wholesale prices. He has $3,500 in the bank to start with and thinks that he'd better reserve $1,200 for his initial expenses and closely budgeted family expenses before the store begins to pay. With the remaining $2,300 as bait, he determines to ask the Stitsen Company, Chicago, to grant him a line of credit up to $11,900, to be repaid in parts in 90, 120, and 150 days, respectively. This figure will cover the initial inventory except for fishing equipment and a few other items not handled by Stitsen Company.

In the role of Rock Brady, study this situation until you become enthusiastic about the store; then write the letter that will get you this extraordinary extension of credit. Canvass the picture for your talking points, considering your knowledge of merchandising these lines, your local contacts, and your personal contacts with Stitsen Company and other athletic-goods sales representatives in the field.

11. *Keeping a close check on a credit customer.* As credit manager of the Stitsen Company, Chicago, you are proud of your treatment of R. M. "Rock" Brady's persuasive application for an unwarranted line of credit. Your artful letter proposing to extend Brady credit up to $2,000 on his first order and persuading him to take advantage of your introductory 4-percent cash discount by raising the remainder from local sources, was, to say the least, successful. (See Problem 10.)

Less than two weeks after your letter was mailed, Stitsen had filled Brady's first order totaling $8,195.50, including items amounting to $1,945.50 (by Invoice No. N92Rw6) on open account with the company's usual retailers' terms, 2/10, n/60. As a special courtesy to Brady, the invoice was dated September 1—ten days after the date of shipment.

On October 9 a Stitsen sales representative dropped in and took Brady's order for a special tennis racket for a friend of Rock's and a fill-in assortment of hunting clothes, the entire bill totaling $197.30. Because the sales representative reported that the business seemed to be brisk enough, the new shipment was made on the regular terms. On October 28 a statement of the forthcoming due date of Invoice N92Rw6 was sent. When no remittance had been received by November 10, a second notice was mailed, with a sticker requesting special attention. By November 20 you, having marked this account for personal attention, sit down and dictate a note designed to get Brady to pay this bill promptly and feel better about it. What will you say?

12.   *Adapting a letter to land the job following an interview.* This morning you had an interview with Mr. P. B. Colfax, assistant director of personnel, Sun Steel Corporation, Cleveland, Ohio, in which you fared rather badly. Mr. Colfax came to your college's Placement Office for the purpose of enlisting midyear graduates as employees for his firm's Junior Executives Training Program. The Placement Office arranged for you to see him. You introduced yourself nicely, you thought, and prepared to wait for Colfax to take the initiative. He did.

"Is it hard for you to say 'no' to a salesman?" he began.

"No," you said, "It used to be. But my education here in the College of Business Administration has—sort of—built up a sense of values. I like to feel that I know what I want—and—well, I can say 'no' now."

"Interesting," he said. "Some pretty valid studies show that 90 percent of successful salesmen find it hard to say 'no' to another salesman. On meeting someone, do you wait for the other fellow to say 'hello' first?"

"It all depends. If I know him pretty well, I'd say 'hello' first. If I'd just met him, I'd probably wait for him."

"I see . . . Would you speak up or let the incident pass if someone pushed ahead of you in line?"

"I certainly wouldn't make much of an issue of it, but—yes, I'd call attention to the fact he was a pushing sort of a fellow in some courteous way."

Colfax just sat for what seemed like a long time. You were getting more nervous by the minute. Were your answers wrong or right? There wasn't any way of knowing. Perhaps you were being taken through one of those "stress" interviews that management books talk about.

When it began to look as though Colfax were through with the whole affair, he came up with: "Would you rather make a decision yourself or have someone help you make it?"

"I'd like to review the opinion of everyone competent to speak on the subject, but make the decision myself."

You were rather proud of that one—but not for long. Mr. Colfax said: "I'll play the role of a customer who, for some reason, has stopped doing business with your company. You have to win the business back."

Then he sat and waited for you.

You took one gulp and plunged: "Mr. Colfax, I haven't had an order from you for some time. I've been wondering . . . is anything wrong?"

Colfax:	"No. Nothing's wrong."
You:	"Well—I mean, when steel was short, you sent us quite a few orders. We took care of you, didn't we?"
Colfax:	"Are you implying I'm under obligation to you?"
You:	"I wouldn't say that. I just mean that we always took good care of you."
Colfax:	"Didn't you make a profit on every ton?"
You:	"All I mean is, I'd like to be fair about this deal."

Colfax:	"Then you mean I'm being unfair!"
You:	"Oh, no! I don't mean that at all. But, well . . . steel might be short again some time."
Colfax:	"Do I hear a threat in that statement?"

When your ears were red enough to catch fire, Colfax laughed. "Being able to manage people through resourcefulness is perhaps the most important requirement for our management trainees. Most college graduates are technically competent in their major fields. 'Know-how' is 90 percent for a rank-and-file worker. For promotion to supervisor, 'know-how' is 50 percent. For promotion to executive, 'know-how' is 20 percent and human relations 80 percent. We are looking toward a person's long-term progress. We want to develop people who can fit into future vacancies, take jobs that don't even exist yet. We can look at a person's record and fit a square peg into a square hole. But we want to know what kind of wood the peg is made of, what quality, how durable.

"In our Executive Trainee Program we employ accountants, statisticians, salesmen, engineers, trainees for almost all business major fields. Fill out this application blank, please, and write me a letter of application for my files."

And that was that. Do you think you have a chance to recover from such a disastrous showing? You may be thinking that you'd have certainly done better than the unfortunate whose experience is recounted here. No doubt you would have. But analyzing this situation and presenting yourself as being a person worthy of consideration is a real test of your writing skill. Use your own major field and write a letter to accompany the thoughtfully filled-in application blank that will land you in Sun Steel's Junior Executives Training Program.

5

The Art
of Refusing
and Other Negative-Message
Transmissions

*Bruising another's ego comes naturally for many
. . . stroking it effectively has to be learned and
cultivated.*

Among the most valuable talents a person in business can have for maintaining good customer and employee relations is an ability to say "no" or to transmit any other adverse information tactfully, acceptably, and positively! Anything unpleasant to your reader is negative; the reaction is against you, consciously or subconsciously. As an effective writer and a successful individual in a business or organization, you want your reader's goodwill. To get and keep it, you will need to avoid the negative when you can, to subordinate it when you cannot.

Although you have already been introduced to communication involving negative-element handling and the positive versus negative viewpoints,[1] this chapter is devoted primarily to the principles and techniques generally employed for messages whose major purpose is the transmission of a wholly negative communication.

In handling negative messages, remember that your position is disadvantageous. On the one hand, your reader is *expecting* a "yes" answer—a compliance with a request—that you cannot give for some valid reason. On the other, the reader may not be expecting any communication from you at all, and the message you originate carries only disappointment. The advan-

[1] Chapter 2, "Planning: Positive versus Negative"; Chapter 3, "Informing Under Adverse Circumstances"; and Chapter 4, "Persuasion."

tage in either case is usually to the writer's benefit, not to the reader's. Therefore, you must put more thought into this type of writing than into almost any other kind of informal communication.

Softening the effect of a refusal is largely a matter of applying the laws of emphasis in writing: subordinating the negative message and highlighting the positive, hopeful features.

THE PSYCHOLOGY BEHIND REFUSALS

Fortunately for the writer, most readers are susceptible to a *convincing explanation* for a rejection or other bad-news messages. The reader's frustration or anger and the resulting ill will occur when he or she does not understand clearly what necessitates the negative information. When a person is frustrated, the ensuing reaction will almost always be negative. You will have to strive to convince the reader that you do have his or her interest at heart if you are to win support for your message.

Psychologists tell us that the ego needs strengthening before it is asked to perform and that the ego should be reinforced beforehand if it is to withstand frustration. To keep or make a friend, then, the writer needs to reinforce the reader's ego before giving any disappointing news.

You will recall at this point that ideas in which the reader is assumed to be interested are used to begin and end your communication. They should usually begin and end paragraphs as well. Most of the space in the communication is given over to these ideas. They are phrased specifically; they enjoy the benefits of independent rather than dependent sentence construction, active rather than passive grammatical voice. Conversely, unwelcome or unpleasant ideas are generally imbedded in the middle of paragraphs, dwelt upon just enough to establish their true meaning, and stripped of the emphasis of concrete, specific words.

How can you make a refusal reasonably pleasant? The technique is that of stressing the positive aspects—what you *have* done, *can* do, *will* do, or *are* doing—rather than their negative counterpoints.

We call again upon the inductive style of writing and begin to think about neutral material with which the reader might agree or at least might not resist. The reasons for the refusal are thought out with care and are designed so that, when they are presented to the reader, the logic of each one in sequence is apparent. Thus, when the refusal is actually made, the reader will be prepared for it and may even feel that it is inevitable. Two types of reasoning are used:

1. How the reader stands to profit from your refusal, if possible. These are the most potent sort of reasons if they can be made to seem plausible

and logical. But we do not risk insulting the reader's intelligence by *manipulating* advantages for that individual.

    2.   The reasons why the refusal is necessary from your viewpoint.

If you can get on common ground by agreeing with the reader, in some way, you will of course have established yourself as a reasonable human being. But the problem at this point is not to be so optimistic in tone that you mislead the person into thinking the answer is to be "yes" or that the reader misinterprets your position from the start. Take, for example, the following illustration (the opening paragraph of a refusal to a request made of a telephone company for a specialized classification listing of all manufacturers served by the telephone company):

> Your directory of manufacturers and industrial services should be a big help to [the State's name] businesses and good advertising for the state as well.

If the writer stops here, the reader's interpretation may well be that the writer is going along with the request made when actually the answer was to be in effect "I'm sorry, but we are unable to provide the kind of listing you specify." Getting the reader around to the refusal and making that person accept it gracefully is all the more difficult under the circumstances that the illustration sets forth.

    How might the example have made a proper springboard for the refusal that is ultimately to develop from it? Let us try adding a qualifier after the opening remark this way:

> Your directory of manufacturers and industrial services will be a big help to [the State's name] businesses and good advertising for the state as well, particularly if it is to be done in the highly specialized manner your letter outlines.

The phrase "particularly if it is to be done in the highly specialized manner your letter outlines" serves as a turning point into the reasons for the refusal (the telephone company has no *economical* way to provide the *specialized* listing the reader seeks).

    Phrases such as "You are right," "We agree that you should," "From the facts you had, we can understand your reaction to," "It is obvious as you say," and similar expressions set the writer on the same side of the fence as reader critic. When you have established friendly feelings for such a reader, that person is much more likely to listen with an open mind to whatever else you have to say. The psychology behind disarming the reader is that, by expressing understanding of his or her reaction (in any *reasonable* way, remember), you take away reader defense. (How can you continue to argue with someone who *agrees* with you—even though perhaps on a minor point?) These same kind of phrases are often useful, too, in introducing reader face-saving comments necessary to your negative message's success.

    Because negative words or negative inferences psychologically work against success in transmitting and gaining reader acceptance of negative messages, the writer makes a deliberate effort to exclude *all* negative words and negative references. The writer is just as deliberate in phrasing *all* ideas in the messages as positively as possible.

You cannot say "I'm sorry" about something without recalling the initial unhappy experience. You cannot write "unfortunately" without restating some gloomy aspect of the circumstance you are trying to make acceptable to your reader. Nor can you write in terms of *delay, broken, damaged, unable to, cannot, inconvenience, difficulty, disappointment,* and others of negative character without stressing some element of the situation that makes your reader react *against* you rather than *with* you. Similarly, phrases that some writers use to precede a negative as a *softener* effect——

"As much as we would like to"
"As sound as your proposition appears to be"

—already give away the fact your answer is to be "no." What must inevitably follow such phrases?

As your reader moves with you through your explanations, and as the soundness of your reasons soaks in, ideally the reader sees that you are logically justified in refusing. (In fact, the reader would have to do the same were he or she in your place.) The recipient perhaps only infers the turndown. But he or she is more likely to accept your decision so presented without ill feelings. Mere implication of the refusal is never enough, however. Your refusal must be unmistakably clear. Otherwise, there is danger of a misunderstanding of your *real* message.

In actually stating the "no," it need not be brutally harsh. In fact, it need not be negative at all. By using a limiting word, such as *best, only, exclusively, solely, concentrate on . . . instead of, confine to . . . rather than,* and others similar in connotation, the negative answer can be made *clear.* For example, when something is done for *other* people but not for the immediate reader, the writer can deemphasize the "no" by using such words (yet make the answer clear). A reader is told that a requested manual cannot be sent by the writer's saying "it is for use *only* in training company employees."

Reserving at least one reason to immediately follow your refusal allows you to bury the disappointing news and to reduce the psychological impact of it on your reader. The mind has less time to dwell on the buried negative answer than would be the case if you ended the paragraph with the refusal itself. Paragraph-end emphasis tends to *spotlight* the bad news, not lessen it.

Keeping your reader in step with you, therefore, as you attempt to inform and to gain acceptance of your message as the only logical course of action open to you is the psychology used in refusals.

In summary, the techniques for writing negative messages are these:

1. Begin with material the reader may feel good about, and try to relate it to an important emotional drive.

2. Relate the opening buffer to a key idea around which the negative message may be built.

3. Win the reader's support through a buildup of reasons for the negative issue:

>   a. Why it is necessary (phrased impersonally in some situations to keep the heat off—particularly if the reader is at fault).

>   b. Why the reader may profit from the refusal or from correcting inappropriate performance.

4. Frame the heart of the negative message as positively as possible in an internal paragraph position, followed immediately with some constructive remark.

5. End with goodwill material unrelated to the negative issue.

You can say no pleasantly but firmly by employing one of several psychological approaches prior to the statement of the negative idea itself:

1. Giving your reasons first—at least the one most favorable to the reader—then saying or implying "no." Following psychologists' advice of reinforcing first, the writer gives *reasons* for the negative reply before the negative answer. With the reader prepared ahead of time for the "no," that person is better able to withstand possible frustration. If the reasons given are good enough, the reader senses the negative that logically follows but is prepared to accept it.

2. Partially agreeing with the reader—the "yes . . . but" approach. An agreement with the reader on some minor point is followed by the negative idea that must be conveyed. Because the "yes . . . but" approach has been used widely in business writing, many people recognize it at once; therefore, use it carefully and sparingly.

3. Explaining "company policy" as a basis for refusing. When an explanation is needed for the writer's inability to comply with a request or when the writer is reinforcing directives, the words "company policy"—or any other subterfuge—are not enough. But if the *why* behind company policy can be explained to show how the reader benefits (even indirectly), he or she is more likely to accept the explanation. Such explanation must be in terms the reader can understand and appreciate—the positive approach.

4. Deemphasizing the "no." Placing the negative idea in a subordinate clause or phrase is one way of deemphasizing it. Care must be used, however, so that the negative is not so inconspicuous that the reader fails to recognize it for what it is.

The really skillful writer may even begin the message with the turndown and still make it positive:

It's a pleasure to explain to you, Mr. Simmons,

why Johnson Construction Company makes only one Fund Campaign drive from its employees annually rather than for each individual charity agency as requests are received.

Can there be any doubt in the reader's mind about the company's refusal to make another fund-raising drive however worthy or persuasive the reader's cause is?

If the reader is left dangling after the negative answer, the impression received is not likely to be a pleasant one. The writer therefore tries to get the reader's thinking back to the positive side by following the no answer with something positive. An abrupt change of content, however, is not logical, and the reader would suspect and even resent an obvious attempt to get his or her mind off the negative situation that way.

Here are a couple of examples employing the techniques we have been discussing.

TWO WAYS OF REFUSING AN UNKNOWN PERSON

Consumer Credit Refusal

The Iron Hand Showing	*A Politer Way*
Dear Mr. James:	Dear Mr. James:
Since investigating your recent application for a charge account, *we find* it will be *difficult* to open the account for you just now.	The customers who purchase from us on a charge basis are generally the ones who visit us more often; so naturally we appreciate your interest in becoming one of our charge patrons.
The information *does not quite* come up to the *requirements* of our company in opening new accounts.	As a price protection to the many people on our charge ledgers—and to our own operation—we follow an exclusive credit policy. In the process of our usual credit investigation of your record, we will need to discuss your application further, preferably in person.
Although we are *unable* to serve you as a charge customer at this time, *we hope conditions will be* such in the near future that our credit department will *be permitted to accept* your application for credit.	
In the meantime *we hope* to receive a liberal share of your patronage.	Won't you please come by the credit office the next time you are in the store? We'd enjoy talking with you.
(90 words; 8 negative references)	(99 words slanted positively)

REFUSING THE REQUEST OF A WELL-KNOWN PERSON

	Dear Bill,
Pacifying reader with agreement as to validity of request	Prices certainly are high, and I can readily appreciate your need for a larger drawing allowance.

Introducing basis for refusal—mutual benefit of policy	As you know, the Sales Division sets the beginning allowance figure at a point that preserves the best interests of the whole company. At the same time, the amount affords new sales people a measure of security while learning the job. The six months' timing that precedes the first increase is a sort of trial period for all of us. For sales people it is a chance to decide on a permanent connection with the company. For us, it's an opportunity to evaluate productiveness before we increase our investment in new personnel.
Reader's benefit from policy	
Writer's benefit from policy	
Overall reason for refusal—impartial treatment of representatives	Naturally, we have to maintain a uniform allowance figure for all new representatives with individual effort rewarded on a commission basis. So the best we can do for you now is to make available new sales aids and counsel designed to help you up those commissions. The sales-manual supplement we're sending includes a digest of the techniques advanced by Elmo Roper at the convention last month. You might find some of his ideas quite profitable.
Refusal in positive rather than negative terms	
Suggested remedy to his problem	
Off-subject close	The new Tolby self-sharpening paring knives pictured on page 6 of the supplement should provide your dealers with a real drawing-card item during the upcoming fruit season.

BUSINESS SITUATIONS REQUIRING TACTFUL REFUSALS

Is the customer always right?

Marshall Field & Company, Chicago, maintained for many years—perhaps they still do—a policy of making adjustments on goods bought in other stores, if the merchandise came from a line or brand handled by Field's.

In Texas a woman bought a fur coat from a large specialty house. Later, taking advantage of one of the store's services, she left the coat for summer storage. When she came to reclaim it in the fall, she insisted the coat given her was not the one she had put in storage. The case went all the way to the store president, who was impressed with the customer's patent sincerity (and also with the size of her account). A new coat was made up to the customer's specifications at a cost of $9,000. The used fur coat, which the store kept, had relatively little value; the store does not sell used furs.

But the customer is not always right despite these stories . . . all true. The business house must decide when to say no.

"To err is human" is the basic assumption underlying most good claim letters, for errors are not uncommon in business. If, like thousands of other Americans, you have had an occasion to write an angry letter to an erring corporation, you can be sure that your name and letter now reside in a neat manila folder marked "Customer Complaints." The letter may have brought prompt action, a satisfied correction (the positive, informative message), or it may have brought you a negative response.

Although most businesses do not enjoy them, there are situations requiring communications whose sole message spells bad news for the receiver. At the top of the list are the answers that must refuse all kinds of requests made of the firm, or organization, or individual. Obviously there is good reason—so far as the writer is concerned—for turning the reader down. As for the reader, there may be little or none. The request may be unreasonable, for instance, in its demands on the writer's time, money, or participation, such as the request made of an individual to come at his or her own expense to be a convention speaker, or of a company to send (at company expense) an employee to participate in an association's convention not connected with the business in any way.

Or, the request may be (1) unwarranted because the product or service for which a claim is made falls outside the warranty period, (2) unjustified because of the abnormal treatment or abuse given the product for which no guarantee could be expected to cover, (3) unreasonable in the sheer "economic size" of the request made, or (4) something the organization feels sincerely it is not responsible for.

The following illustration, contrasting two ways of refusing a consumer claim, has as its basis "no responsibility on the part of the company."

Are Customers Lost This Way?	*Are They Kept with Special Treatment*
Dear Mrs. Devillbiss:	Dear Mrs. Devillbiss:
Your pink taffeta evening dress purchased from the French Salon on September 5 was received at our claim desk this morning. Thank you for writing us about your unsatisfactory experience with it.	With the combination of unusual new materials, fabrics for evening clothes get lovelier all the time, don't they? Such a complex designing process no doubt contributed to the original beauty of the pink taffeta dress you returned to us yesterday.
A thorough examination of the material indicates that it was not cleaned properly—washed instead of drycleaned. The directions on the garment at the time of	The new fabrics make necessary extra care in the choice of cleaning fluids designed to keep the garments looking

purchase clearly stated that under no circumstances should the material be placed in water.

We are herewith returning the dress so that you may refer your claim to the cleaner. It is indeed unfortunate that such a thing should have happened.

beautiful. Manufacturers pretest the fabric and attach cleaning directions to all luxury clothes. As an extra precaution, the National Institute of Dry Cleaners distributes process information to first-class establishments all over the country.

When we received your dress, we took it straight to the Institute laboratory for an appraisal. Their report indicates that under no circumstances should the dress have been subjected to wet cleaning—which it apparently was. So you see, Mrs. Devillbiss, we can only guarantee the true color of our clothes when they are cared for with the cleaning process designed for them. We are returning your pink taffeta so that you may take the claim up with your cleaner for a decision as to what may be done.

We've enjoyed having you come to Bardon's for clothes over the years. Our personal shopper will be glad to help you with any rush orders for special occasions any time you are unable to get in to the city to shop. Just let us know

Sometimes the basis of the refusal, as already pointed out, is simply company policy *against* doing whatever the reader has requested—sending confidential information that is intended for company use only, for example, or not contributing gifts for door prizes or providing personnel to aid or staff a worthwhile group activity, be it cultural, civic, or social. Worthy though the request may seem, from an economic or physical standpoint, the company or individual is prohibited from granting *all* demands made; thus, the answer must be "no" for any single one.

Similarly, orders must be declined for one reason or another; for example, the dealer may be an unacceptable outlet for the company's merchandise. Among the reasons for such a refusal may be that the prospective dealer is shaky financially, is unethical in pricing or discounting, or is unwilling to offer follow-up servicing on products. You can see that there are few, if any, reader advantages or benefits to be conveyed in such a situation. And the decline would require all the finesse a writer could muster to maintain good relations with this reader. The writer would want to maintain good relations for a number of reasons. The primary one is that sometime in the future this particular prospective dealer could well be a profitable outlet for the firm's products. And, too, a disappointed, angered prospective dealer has a wide sphere of influence on others that could prove detrimental to the wholesaler or manufacturer.

Orders may be filled improperly or incompletely. Who is at fault? Not necessarily the seller. The goods may be mislabeled or defective, and the responsibility lies with a third party.

Other orders from a consumer to manufacturer or wholesaler have to be declined and rerouted to proper marketing channels because the manufacturer or wholesaler policy is one of not competing with its retail distributors for consumer sales. The customer is likely to be offended and certainly disappointed at the delay and added inconvenience by not getting the wanted and expected product. Any reader is likely to find it hard to understand, too, why the firm is so arbitrary.

A supervisor's appraisal of an employee's job performance may often result in a negative communication to the employee concerned. Perhaps the person being appraised is not doing a bad job and, for the most part is performing regular duties as required, perhaps even doing some problem solving, although not of the innovative type. The individual is simply not introducing new ideas into the organization (innovation being a new way of doing old things as opposed to invention, which is something completely new and different). Apparently, then, this person is not the sort who "willingly accepts change when suggested or introduced from above." This antichange or at least the lack of a prechange attitude is a common one and results in a negative appraisal. The positive points to stress to the employee might be:

1.   The person who introduces the change or innovation will help the company through increased efficiency and profits.

2.   In turn, the person reaps similar tangible rewards: bonuses, increased salary, promotions, or other tangible benefits.

Here are two illustrations—each with a contrasting way of getting the negative idea across—for your analysis of the points just presented:

TWO WAYS OF WRITING THE BAD-NEWS MESSAGE

TO: The Office Staff

FROM: The Office Manager   DATE: April 15, 19xx

I am faced with the *unpleasant* duty of saying that so much *wasted* coffee time will have to stop.

Happy employees are certainly the kind we like best.

Perhaps you *fail to realize* the spot you place me in when I *can't* find anybody to put on rush jobs, when I fail to meet deadlines, when I'm *forced* to pay over-

Because of a sincere interest in seeing that you find your work here pleasant, the company does its best to provide comfortable surroundings, good pay, agreeable hours, and spaced rest periods.

time for work that could easily be done as regular routine.

Fifteen minutes is certainly ample time to get to the first floor and back. I *shall expect* from here on out a *fairly strict adherence* to the time limit.

Thank you.

Locating the coffee room on the first floor was part of our plan to provide you with refreshments in the 15 minutes available for that purpose. The prosperity of the business is reflected in benefits to all of us. Thirty minutes a day for coffee breaks contributes to the firm's prosperity in the form of more and better work and higher morale all round. Much more time than that for each of us adds to the cost side of the ledger sheet. For these reasons, it is to everyone's advantage to keep rest periods within the time allotted. Most of you do, it's true. Can't we make it 100 percent?

Thanks a lot . . .

Cards-on-the-Table Fashion to a Factory Drop-Shipper

Recently we sent you a bulletin on our policy on minimum shipments and freight allowances on pickups, *which you apparently did not read.*

If you will review that bulletin, you will find that the minimum delivery under *absolutely all circumstances* is 10 cases of Amigo canned goods, or a minimum quantity of 100 pounds. Your order of April 5—at hand today—for drop-shipment to Baden Supermarket, Tallahassee, Florida, is *below the minimum permissible pickup.* You also *neglected to add* the 10 cents per case for drop-shipment on this order.

Do not fail to make sure that your customers and your staff understand our policy on minimum release and prepaid freight.

If Baden can't use 10 cases, there will be additional charges on this order—and *don't forget* the 10 cents per case drop-shipment charges.

We are truly grateful for this order.

(145 words; 8 touchy references)

A Goodwill Way

In order for drop-shipping to be profitable for all of us, we established the minimum shipments and freight allowances outlined in Bulletin No. 6281, February 4.

So, in accordance with the terms of that bulletin, your April 5th order for Amigo canned foods, destination Baden Supermarket, Tallahassee, Florida, would need to be for at least 10 cases, or a minimum quantity of 100 pounds.

Will you please see whether Baden would like to take advantage of the 10-case offer and send along the requisite 10 cents a case for pickups?

We will be happy, of course, to ship less for an additional charge.

Enclosed are 15 copies of Bulletin 6281 for distribution among your staff should you need them.

(119 words; no accusations)

In mercantile trade, unearned discounts on invoices are frequently taken by the buyer. An aggressive, profit-minded, customer-concerned manufacturer or wholesaler simply cannot afford to allow such practices to go unchecked. Over the long run, the practice would prove detrimental to business, and, too, such permissiveness on the manufacturer's part is unfair to other customers who pay on time and do earn the discount. So this message in essence is a no—the buyer did not earn the discount that was taken.

CONTRASTING WAYS OF RETURNING THE UNEARNED-DISCOUNT CHECK

June 28, 19xx

Gentlemen:

Thank you for your check for $912.38 in payment of our Invoice No. 3321 of June 15, amounting to $980.00.

According to the invoice you were entitled to a quantity discount of 5% and also a cash discount of 2%, if you paid within ten days from the date of this invoice.

The quantity discount, or 5% of $980.00, is $49.00, which brings the amount of the bill to $931.00. From this amount ($931.00) you could have deducted the cash discount of 2% or $18.62, had you paid the bill before June 25. This would have brought the amount of the bill to $912.38.

Unfortunately, your remittance was neither made out for the correct amount, nor did it reach us in time to allow us to give you the benefit of the cash discount of 2%. Now, if we were to allow this discount under the present circumstances, it would only be fair to make similar exception in the case of our numerous other customers. Such practice, once adopted, would, you will readily see, soon disrupt our entire credit system. For these reasons, and also because the net amount of the bill will not be due until July 15, we thought it best to return this

June 28, 19xx

Gentlemen:

Your check for $912.38, clipped to this letter, is our friendly effort to co-operate with you in making the most of your money.

In all phases of a business transaction, a mutually helpful attitude between the manufacturer and the jobber allows each to realize the full profit margin. The 5% quantity discount on your Invoice No. 3321, for example, is helpful to you in a price advantage and to us in the distribution of our products. Thus full payment of this June 15th invoice amounts to $931.00 with the quantity discount deducted.

In addition, the 2/10, n/30 terms indicated on the invoice are designed to reward you for prompt payment—a plan which actually adds up to 36% interest on your money for a year—and to give us the use of 98% of our money for an extra 20 days each month. The arrangement is truly effective, of course, only when the manufacturer and jobber adhere closely to the terms. To be eligible for the cash discount, your check should have been postmarked no later than June 25. So that you may have the use of your money until July 15—when $931.00 falls

check to you. Please send us one for the correct amount in due time.

Yours truly

due—we are returning your check post-marked June 28.

A catalogue supplement will be sent to you in a few days featuring fall specialties we think you'll find particularly attractive as new price leaders.

Yours truly

Misunderstandings may arise over discounts, bills, credit terms, or exchanges. The surest mark of an inexperienced businessperson is the promise that mistakes will never occur—and the anger when they do.

In some situations quick, emotional reactions are appropriate. If someone gives you a cheery greeting in the elevator, it is fitting to smile in return, perhaps without even being sure whom you are greeting. Decision makers often encounter occasions that call for trusting their first hunches rather than trying to postpone action. In most business situations, however, the faster the reaction, the less successful the communication usually proves to be. This aspect of the communication problems in negative-message handling simply means you need to anticipate the hurried reactions in others.

When you have to tell a person something that you know is going to be displeasing, you prepare in advance for the reaction. If you want your reader angry, you prepare either to stand up to this anger or get out of the way. If you want the person to calm down as soon as possible, you try to mitigate his or her anger. Although anger probably is the most common cause of too rapid reactions, it is by no means the only one. It is also possible to anticipate and allow for overoptimism, sorrow, and other such reactions from others.

One of the most important aids, therefore, to your success in communicating is the awareness that there is the possibility of such reactions. The greatest difficulty comes not when you can foresee clearly a quick and vehement reaction. It comes from taking your reader by surprise.

Angry reactions, of course, are the most difficult to cope with because they tend to provoke anger in response. If you are right, you can afford to keep your temper. If you are wrong, you cannot afford to lose your self-control.

You also need to be careful how you give one of your subordinates good news if his or her tendency is to get so excited at the first hint that the *if's* and *maybe's* are missed.

Seasoned business managers develop a tolerant rather than a complacent attitude toward the errors of others and an understanding that there is an irreducible minimum of error. Less experienced consumers, in making claims or writing complaints, are likely to be less tolerant. Both sides of this communication situation are at times wholly negative in nature. In business, such customer complaints are frequently referred to as "fire-and-brimstone" letters. The writer gives vent to negative feelings with the first words, quickly identifying it for the reader as a fire-and-brimstone situation. Here are two examples:

> That television set your store sold me last week is a *disgrace!* The picture is distorted and flops around like a pan of frog legs. You've sent your repairman out twice, and each time the set is worse after he tinkers with it. I think you knew it was no good when you sold it to me; that's why you kept saying you were making a special price to me. You may have hoped I wouldn't have sense enough to complain. I'm writing the network, too. This is the last time I'll ever buy anything from your store.
>
> . . .
>
> What is wrong with you screwballs?
>
> I sent you a note telling you that after the policy was delivered I paid it all up in full for the whole year and here I still get these damn notices.
>
> You better get this straightened out before it is due for the next year. For I might go and cancel it because there are other insurance companies, you know.

You will notice, too, the negative-laden closing threats in both illustrations. Although businesses are anxious to avoid such feelings on the part of customers, a little thought will show it is to the writer's advantage to be more even tempered. Will the reader of these letters be inclined to do better for the unhappy customer? The claimant, too, should always avoid negative words of accusation, such as *complaint, disgusted, dishonest, false, fraud, unfair, untrue, worthless, no good.* Far more is to be gained by focusing the reader's thoughts on what can be done to restore goodwill. It is better to assume that the firm you are writing to will want to do the right thing—as you see it—even though its reply may have to be a refusal of an adjustment because of extenuating circumstances.

If you want fast action, send your complaint to the public relations department. If the company that made that lemon of yours is small, the public relations department may consist of one overworked employee. But you have paid the company a compliment by assuming that it has a PR department, and in many cases, the company will accept the compliment gratefully, handling your complaint with extra care and attention. Keep in mind that the individuals paid to read and reply to your letters are strangers. If the language you use is abusive, your letter may well be ignored, tossed in the wastebasket, or put at the bottom of a big stack to be answered later.

Answers to persuasive requests for credit terms on initial purchases or for an extension of credit term payment once you are on the firm's books can, at times, mean negative responses, also.

The following refusal of an extension-on-credit term arrangements (partial payment) employs techniques presented for you in this chapter. The letter additionally serves to carry the unpleasant message of "a final notice" to collect in as constructive a vein as possible.

THE REFUSAL TO ACCEPT PARTIAL PAYMENT

Dear Mr. Hilbert:

Subject: Loan No. 16–191–43

Beginning with the only favorable aspect	Your passbook is being returned with a credit entered for the money received today.
The reasoning behind the refusal	Pioneer Savings and Loan has a twofold purpose: (1) to facilitate home purchases through loans, and (2) to protect the interests of investors who trust us with their savings. With both purposes in mind, we make our plans around contractual obligations that must be met on time if we
Alarm at the status of Hilbert's account	are to succeed. So you can understand our alarm, Mr. Hilbert, when your payment today still leaves three monthly installments past due on your home loan. Our loan committee feels that you have had ample time to bring this account up
Threat of drastic action	to date. Unless you do so by Tuesday, June 25, steps will have to be taken to
A hopeful alternative	protect our investment. It is possible you might prefer to make arrangements to sell this property yourself.
Last chance to clear account, self-interest	We are indeed looking forward to your taking care of this obligation in such a way as to protect your own interests before the 25th, at which time it will become necessary for us to refer your loan to our attorney for action.

If it is mercantile credit—business house to business house—the creditor's decision for a "no" answer usually is based on the prospective debtor's financial ratio of assets to liabilities. As an indication of the soundness of the debtor's operations, this ratio should ordinarily be at least 2 to 1. Exceptions, of course, are made according to current economic conditions: how tight the money market is, what the financial picture from credit reporting agencies reveals about the applicant, how tied up the creditor's capital is, and other factors.

The Credit Research Foundation, for example, lists ten factors influencing the credit decision:

1. Size of the order received.
2. Size of the potential volume of orders.

3. Company credit policy.

4. Whether the customer is new, established, or has been inactive.

5. The risk inherent in selling to the class to which the customer belongs.

6. The risk involved in relation to the gross profit margin in the merchandise.

7. Whether the product is perishable or seasonal.

8. How much time is available to reach a decision.

9. The unit value of the commodity to be sold.

10. Total credit exposure related to the particular customer.

Rules of thumb in deciding to refuse or grant credit are sometimes as clumsy as thumbs themselves, but they have a certain utility. Four conventional criteria employed in evaluating a credit applicant are called the "Four Cs."

Capital:	The applicant's financial condition, amount of cash on hand, amount of easily convertible assets, outstanding obligations, and so on.
Capacity:	Ability and experience as a businessperson; in other words, apparent potential.
Character:	Reputation for fair dealing, integrity, prompt payment habit, stability.
Conditions:	The external factors influencing the credit extension, such as business conditions at large and in the particular line of business under consideration, the current phase of the business cycle, local economic factors.

You can thus see how the Credit Research Foundation's factors are employed by the prospective creditor's Four C's rule-of-thumb evaluation for decision.

Dun & Bradstreet is the principal reporting agency for mercantile credit. Many lines of business have their own agencies, including the wholesale grocers, jewelers, hardware dealers, manufacturers, and so on. The Credit Interchange Bureau will furnish a list of a firm's sources of supply, which are also useful for credit checking.

Consumer credit is kept score on by the Associated Credit Bureaus of America, which has about 1,700 members, with files on more than 70 million persons. An authorized business may ask for a brief report or a complete one with all details on you to make the decision for or against credit extension. Details will include family status, education, business history (often with relevant details of social life), police record, resources, paying record (top credit limits and terms of payment), health, and other pertinent factors. Such information comes from your previous applications for credit with other businesses, from your employer's records, bank records, and other sources.

Consequently, there is usually no lack of information sources for the prospective creditor's decision to refuse credit or to refuse an extension of payment terms, although the answer to the one applying will be disappointing, and perhaps can offer little solace in the refusal. It should be readily apparent that, to keep from receiving such refusals yourself, your own credit reputation needs to be managed with the greatest of care.

Employers at times face the unpleasant task of having to turn down prospective job applicants. Often the turndown occurs after lengthy negotiations. Much time will have been expended by both the employer and the prospective applicant in exchanging communications, completing application forms, testing, investigating references, and traveling to an interview. Obviously, the firm is looking for the best possible candidate as its employee: the one who can offer the most to the company, who is the easiest to train, and who is best able to start on the pay back after training. The reasoning used is, of course, that the one turned down will understand these basic economic facts of business life if the writer presents acceptable information.

Here is an example from a large employer of college graduates that follows the basic inductive style of writing with neutral buffer opening.

> Thank you so much for the time and effort you've given us in providing a most complete set of credentials as applicant for the position of executive trainee.
>
> This year there have been an unusually able group of candidates showing interest in our program. Evaluating their relative potentials has been a rewarding, yet at the same time, an extremely challenging job. You are aware, I am sure, that it is to our mutual benefit to select only those applicants particularly suited to the program. We have now filled all positions with candidates having a bit better qualifications than yours. Because of the definite promise your training and experience shows, we know you will have much to offer an employer as you seek to take advantage of another opportunity.
>
> In the meantime, we intend to keep your record on active file in case a suitable opening occurs that you might consider. Your interest in applying for work with our organization, and your cooperation in completing the necessary requirements requested of you, is indeed appreciated.

For the new college graduate in today's highly competitive employment market, there are occasions for job-offer turndowns—another refusal situation. Frequently, from the interviewing process through placement offices, the graduate may receive two, three, or more specific job offers. (If the offers do not come together, the graduate may want to postpone making a job commitment until results from all the interviews are in. But that is a case for employing persuasive writing techniques, not a negative reply.)

The problem of refusing an offer without giving much thought to the process may be as simple as writing "I appreciate your offer, but I've decided to accept another position." What's the harm in that? Maybe none; company recruiting personnel know they will not get *every* promising candidate they go after. But suppose that after the candidate has been on the job things are not so promising as she or he had been led to believe. The person is not promoted, or lives too far from work, or does not get along with the boss, or the climate does not agree with his or her allergies; so this individual begins to look around for another job. What happened to all those companies so eager for his or her services a few years earlier?

It is at this point that the writer may wish he or she had been less curt, less final, in the turndown letters. Could the door have been closed not quite so definitely and still have been fair to the hiring company?

Suppose that those rejected companies still have a file on this person? A personal history, letters of recommendation, an account of this interview, *and* the letter rejecting the offer are easily accessible. What might the letter have included that would now stand the applicant (a second time around) in good favor? To begin with, some words of appreciation ought to have been mentioned for the company's time and expense (including the payment of travel costs for the interview if that was involved), a word of praise for the company and its plant personnel, treatment on the visit, some expression of the favorable impression received. An indication of interest in a special aspect of the company's work may be a personalizing touch that will help make the letter memorable and leave a favorable impression with the employer. The delicate problem is leaving the door slightly ajar instead of slamming it in a possible future employer's face. Whatever is said must be said tactfully and sincerely, with ideas developed from reflection of the whole problem of keeping one's self employable.

By all means the writer should offer a brief explanation or reason for accepting the job offer decided upon. A statement should then be added such as

> Should conditions change, I would welcome an opportunity of placing another application with you later.

This statement is not an insult to the one employing nor will it be offensive to the one turned down. In fact, it may remind the employer who was turned down to save this letter and the person's file as a possible future employee.

Additionally, the writer may point out tactfully his or her increased value as an employee after experience elsewhere. Take care in this approach. No employer likes to be made the stepping stone to an employee's success in some other place. A legitimate basis for rejecting an offer, however, is the applicant's sincere feeling for the need to gain additional experience, for educational or other "broadening" reasons, before being of ultimate value in the job being turned down. In the letter of resignation, too, there is always something complimentary you can find to say about the company or its personnel.

Unsolicited suggestions and ideas regarding slogans for company use, advertising and the like, for which the submitter probably expects compensation are still other occasions calling at times for a polite, goodwill refusal. A slightly different situation calling for refusals occurs in the "public utility" concept—a request for the *free* services of writers or other professionals regarded as expert or authoritative in their fields. Constant demands are made upon writers to "knock off" (the term is an exact reflection of the view of the writer-as-magician) a few hundred or a few thousand words to be used in some undeniably excellent government project. Back of such requests lie two assumptions. The first is that the writer is a wonder worker and can therefore produce petty miracles without labor. The second is that inasmuch as everybody can "read" and "write" we are not asking the person to do anything we ourselves could not do if we merely put our minds to it. These assumptions are in conflict with each other.

Here is how one person slides out of the predicament according to Sydney J. Harris:

I admire and envy a writer friend of mine, who takes the proper stance on a matter I feel strongly about, but rarely have the courage to enforce.

Sitting with him in his study a few weeks ago, I overheard a telephone conversation between him and a man from a radio station. The man had called my friend to participate in a round-table program; as he had a loud, clear, radio-type voice, I could hear both ends of the conversation.

"I get the picture," said my friend. "What fee are you prepared to pay for this job?"

"Well," said the radio man, "it's a sustaining, public service program, you see, and we don't have any money allocated for speakers."

"Are you being paid for your work on it," asked my friend, "or are you contributing your services, too?"

"Naturally," said the man, "I'm getting my regular salary. It's part of my job."

"It's not part of mine," said my friend. "What about the engineer in the control booth for the program. Is he getting paid?"

"Well, certainly," said the radio man. "It's his job, too."

"I thought that perhaps he was volunteering after hours, as a gesture of generosity and goodwill," my friend remarked. "Now tell me this—what about the announcer, the producer, the director, and the man who comes and sweeps the floor afterwards? Are any of them doing it as a public service?"

"No, of course not," admitted the radio man. "But we just don't have anything in our budget for speakers. There's no money available."

"I can go along with that," said my friend. "I'm not greedy for money. But I'm sure you don't want charity either. Since you're asking a service of me, why can't you reciprocate with one for me?"

"Such as what?" asked the radio man.

"There is a lot that needs doing around my house—the walls need washing, the basement should be calcimined, and some bookshelves have to be put up. Why don't you come around on Saturday, or send someone around, to do these chores—and then I'll gladly let you have my services for the program."

"I've never heard of such a thing in my life," sputtered the man.

"Neither have I," purred my friend, "but I think it's high time we both heard it.

"You'll let me know, won't you? Thank you . . . and goodbye."[2]

PLANNING COMMUNICATION STRATEGY

In all the situations portrayed here, essentially it is the individual involved—or a firm's policy—that determines the negative decision. The writer's appraisal of the facts, concern for the reader's feelings, any alternative approaches, and the constructive aspects that he or she can devise guide the writer in planning an effective negative communication strategy.

Perhaps at this stage it would be easier to understand the art of refusing if we trace through the stages of planning and make application of the principles and techniques involved in a typical case. Let us take the following problem for analysis.

The booming industrial development of Corpus Christi and its resultant population growth has brought many problems to your desk. You're James T. Overton, customer service director for Gulf Coastal Gas Company, Box 17, Corpus Christi, Texas.

Some of your thorniest problems have to do with new customers from other parts of the country—customers not accustomed to using natural gas for home heating, much less for air conditioning. Many of your customers express delight at their low heating bills in winter because of low gas prices and the mild Gulf Coast climate. But some complaints always follow your summer month billings. A few householders always conclude that their meters are defective or that the gas company is taking advantage of them. They cannot understand that in this warm climate, air conditioning is more expensive than heating. One of your assistants just left this letter on your desk:

[2] Reprinted by permission of Sydney J. Harris and the *Chicago Daily News.*

Gentlemen:

My gas bill is going up every month. What are you people trying to do? See how far you can jack it up before I yell? You Texas companies brag about your cheap gas, but I never had a July bill in Wisconsin half as high as the $81.60 you are trying to charge me here.

I've had enough of these exorbitant bills! You utility monopolies just try to gouge small customers like us; I've seen in the papers how many millions of dollars you make. If you're honest about this thing, you'll send someone out to repair my meter, which obviously runs even when the gas isn't on. And I want you to check, too, to see if gas isn't leaking and about to blow my house sky high. You'll cut this ridiculous bill in half, too.

Yours very truly,

Jim Sorenson, Jr.
1276 Oneda Drive

One of your service personnel has already checked Mr. Sorenson's meter and found it in perfect condition and noted, too, that the residence is equipped with a 4-ton gas air-conditioning system.

Your job, as of August 11, is to write Mr. Sorenson a conciliatory letter pointing out that he did indeed use $81.60 worth of gas, a fairly modest amount considering the air-conditioning capacity installed in his house and the cost of present-day energy.

Gauging the Message to the Reader's Personality

Since you cannot comply with his request to halve his gas bill, your letter really constitutes an adjustment refusal; however, it should be considerably more than that. You have an opportunity to design an effective customer relations message selling this disgruntled man on the idea that gas power is a better buy than any other domestic necessity.

In appraising your reader to gauge a likely reaction, you have little doubt from reading his letter that he is upset, uneasy, and frustrated. But you believe Mr. Sorenson to be basically an intelligent person—one whom you can reason with through an adequate explanation of the facts.

First, on what point do the two of you agree? Certainly that Sorenson wants dependable, convenient gas service, and you are looking for this common point of agreement to establish yourself in Mr. Sorenson's eyes as a person of goodwill. There is really no place for apologies—you do not owe him one anyway—or for empty acknowledgments, the "we got your letter" type of beginning.

His letter indicates he does not feel he is getting his money's worth. So a major consideration for this message is to convince Sorenson that he *is* getting his money's worth in terms of summer comfort for the entire family.

How can you plant the idea of how much he gets for his gas dollar in Corpus Christi? It would be well to start on this point early in the message, although you would not want to give away the fact of refusing him in handling the issue. Perhaps, too, you would want to inject a note of welcome to this Texas newcomer if he is one. In doing so, you could suggest that you are proud of the Texas Gulf Coast and of booming Corpus Christi, but that the area does have one major drawback: its hot, humid summers. Certainly you would not want to emphasize the unpleasantness of weather in conveying the idea; it can be implied without calling attention to it. For example, "I'm sure that you and your family are going to like Corpus and the friendly Texas folk here, even though you'll surely miss those delightful Wisconsin summers." With such a beginning you have already begun to plant the basis for later discussion on the fact he is getting his money's worth in cool, comfortable air conditioning.

Throughout the letter you would want to avoid the defensive or contentious tone. Consequently, in telling Sorenson what a good job your company does, you would avoid letting it seem you have a chip on your shoulder.

Will you want to refer to the "high bill?" No, that is the real negative issue. The constructive side is to avoid saying "we cannot charge you less or refund part of your bill" for you believe by giving a clear explanation first, he will see the point.

In an attempt to design an effective customer relations message to Mr. Sorenson, therefore, the question is: What would you have done as a result of receiving his complaint? You probably would have taken prompt action in sending an expert out to check the Sorenson's meter; so we can begin with that point as introduction in the turn to our reasons for refusing. Your qualified expert rushed to the scene and found everything in perfect working order. You thus believe there is a reasonable explanation for the situation, and you proceed to give it in the best sequence of constructive ideas you can devise.

Mr. Sorenson also needs a little face-saving exit in this encounter. Frequently, a counteroffer is used to soften the refusal effect. What can you use here? You might invite him to call your service department for a free check of his air-conditioning equipment to make certain it is operating at top efficiency. Or you might suggest ways to maximize use of the cool air circulated in his home: leaving the blinds closed or draperies drawn instead of opening them to the pleasant, morning sunshine, or leaving the fan running continuously rather than having the thermostat set on automatic, for example, to maximize circulation of the cooled air.

Since Mr. Sorenson does not think much of your service already, you do not want to dwell long on the discussion of the company. You make a mental note not to let a paragraph close on a negative note, *not to compare Wisconsin unfavorably with Texas!* Trailing off, then, into some pleasant topic unrelated to the negative issue should stand you in good stead with this customer. It is probably not desirable to try to sell Sorenson more gas-burning equipment while he is in this frame of mind. Perhaps some additional "Corpus Christi talk" would be appropriate.

Estimating the Worth of Alternative Approaches

With the kind of thinking and planning done as outlined for you above, you are now ready to choose your approach for writing the message. What are your alternatives? There are three. You could simply write Mr. Sorenson that his meter is accurate, that there is no leak, that he used $81.60 worth of gas, and that you can make no adjustment on his bill. Is he likely to have any change in feelings about your "gouging" small customers from that kind of negative reply? Quite the contrary. You would tend to strengthen his current belief that your giant monopoly utility company thrives on "robbing" customers who have no recourse of action but to pay what *you* say they owe.

There's no goodwill to be gained from a direct, negative turndown here, nor have you offered him any reassurance that his home is not "about to blow sky high" in your assertion that his bill is correct. That insecure feeling comes largely from his unfamiliarity with using gas in the first place. And he is unaware of the safety devices built into your system from years of experience, tests, and trouble-free service.

Your second alternative would be to ignore the letter entirely, chalking it up as "one of those crackpot complaints" every business receives at times. But the same criticisms as for the first alternative—the direct "no" answer—are even more valid for this wastebasket solution. Most organizations take great care *not* to ignore letters however cranky they seem. Operating under the philosophy that resolving complaints is one of the surest ways of improving service and maintaining customer goodwill, private and public organizations assume the complaint legitimate so far as the writer is concerned, worthy of their time and effort at conciliation.

Thus, the company's third alternative—and best approach—is to employ the inductive strategy for the refusal, seeking to gain customer understanding and acceptance of the inevitably unpleasant news your message must convey. Such an approach logically focuses on constructive aspects.

Focusing on Constructive Aspects of the Situation

Without sounding too defensive, you would like to show Mr. Sorenson your side of the picture, tactfully *refusing his request for convincing reasons*. Above all though, you would want to emphasize the dozens of ways in which Mr.

Sorenson and his family benefit from the convenience, safety, and reliability of gas service. The technique is to convince him that when he pays for a thousand cubic feet of gas, he is paying for a cool afternoon for his family during summer's heat—or for enough heat to cook several days' meals, keep the house comfortably warm when crisp fall days return, provide endless supplies of hot water. And in case Mr. Sorenson is thinking of a switch to electric heating and cooling service, you may want to plant the idea that natural gas is his most convenient, economical source of energy in Corpus Christi—without overtly mentioning the competitive public utility.

Would you not want to do a little institutional advertising—public relations—too, in terms of reader advantage? For instance, you might want to invite Sorenson to consider that many of his neighbors in Corpus Christi are utility employees and stockholders—emphasizing the meaning of *public* in *public utility*. The truth is that the yield on gas utility securities is generally lower than it was ten years ago and that the dividends are steady but fairly modest. You can point out, too, that your rates are only 40 percent higher than they were in 1935, while the cost of living, as indicated by the Bureau of Labor Statistics consumer price index, has more than quadrupled since 1935. Probably the reason he thinks in terms of tremendous profits is that the gross revenues of your company and others like it are large. Mr. Sorenson perhaps does not consider that you employ more than 1,500 persons and are obligated to pay dividends to an even larger number of shareholders. Those "millions of dollars" he mentions are divided among thousands of persons.

Checking your rate book, you find that the amount of gas for which Mr. Sorenson was charged ($81.60) would have cost him roughly $105 in most Wisconsin cities. Of course he would not have used that much gas during a normal Wisconsin July, but that is the fault of the Corpus Christi climate, not of your company. Remember, too, that Mr. Sorenson's August bill is likely to be even higher; so you would want to do your best to keep him from being too unhappy about that.

To recap, then, your message would move from the common agreement viewpoint decided on for the opening rather quickly into the basis for the refusal—an idea planted in the opening around which you can build. Your transition to the subject begins *introducing* your reasons—what you first did as a result of receiving his letter (sending the expert to check). You proceed next with an explanation of the situation—the positive (constructive) aspects in the case just pointed out. Inject in the middle of a paragraph the refusal, clearly stated—that is, his bill, therefore, is correct and quite reasonable under the circumstances. And follow up with the counter suggestion to soften the effect, ending pleasantly "off subject."

Frequently, totally negative messages hold no countersuggestion possibilities like that just suggested for Mr. Sorenson as a way of letting the reader save face in softening the refusal effect. The case of Mrs. Nelda Wright, owner-manager of the M & M Motel, Hot Springs, Arkansas, will illustrate:

Nine months ago Mr. Richard Holman, sales manager of Ozark Canvas-Plastic Awnings Services, Little Rock, sold the material and made up one dozen extralong shower curtains for Mrs. Wright's motel baths. The heavy-duty duck material, guaranteed mildew-proof and shrink-resistant (4 percent or less) was from a run you purchased from Canvas Fabrics, Inc., Chicago, Illinois. Ten days ago you got a letter from Mrs. Wright along with one of her curtains—spotted and shrunk. You in turn immediately mailed the curtain with a letter of your own to the Chicago firm asking about the guarantee on the material. Back came a prompt refusal on the basis that the curtain was abused by laundries—too strong a bleach and too much hot water. Moreover, you were reminded that the material was guaranteed by Canvas Fabrics for six months of use—not nine. Since the Chicago firm will not back up the material, you cannot afford to replace the curtains at your own expense. Your letter to Mrs. Wright must refuse the adjustment.

Using the same approach of analysis as that for Mr. Sorenson, you would begin on some common agreement point with Mrs. Wright at the same time trying to establish a basis for the refusal to follow. The idea of your agreement with her on "expected satisfactory service from your products under *normal* use" would leave no doubt in her eyes that you are a person of goodwill, good intentions—and still would not mislead her. The use of the word *normal* will serve as your basis of refusal later after you have explained the follow-up action you took to be of service to her. Part of the positive material you might also use as you move into the discussion is the fact your guarantee *protects* the customer. It *ensures* the customer of getting top-quality material and workmanship. (The point is that you think she is basically honest and will accept a reasonable explanation of why you must refuse her.) Your policy of replacing material *only* under the circumstances you outline should be clear and convincing enough for her to understand and appreciate.

Additionally, she is still going to need some shower curtains and you have a chance here—after you feel you have gained her acceptance of the refusal—to try and sell her some new ones, but with no high pressure, please.

Nowhere in this letter would you be apologetic in any way since that tends to put you on the defensive and reinforces the justness of her claim in her thinking.

A second alternative to the totally negative problem would be a somewhat humorous approach. If deftly done, Mrs. Wright will see your position in the matter and still not take offense at the lighthearted treatment of *her* serious situation. Humor, however, is never to be used at your reader's expense.

Dear Mrs. Wright:

We here at Canvas-Plastics had a rather strange visitor a couple of weeks ago. A poor, spotted, shrunken shower curtain from the Ozark resort area came by and filed some unusual complaints. It seems that some ole' laundry had inadvertently doused our nine-month-old friend in strong bleach and too hot water. It caused his fine finish to spot and shrink, and his owner to send him away.

Since part of our firm's success, however, is owed to so many of his shower curtain friends, we decided to try to help our visitor out and sent him with a referral letter to Chicago where all of his shower curtain kin are loomed. Chicago, although sympathetic, explained that no replacements would be in order because the guarantee on all materials is for six months (our friend, you'll recall, was nine months old) and has to exclude such uncontrollables as laundry abuses.

Needless to say, our shower curtain pal was disheartened. Knowing he could never return to his former place of service for his owner, he pleaded with us to help his showering comrades back at the M & M Motel.

That's why we're writing you, Mrs. Wright, knowing you'll understand our saddened friend's dilemma, and believing you'll want to assist him by purchasing some new shower curtains for his motel buddies. Seriously, Canvas-Plastics will be very pleased to help you in making a new selection—under the same guarantee and prices—from the enclosed catalog.

When there is a compliment to pass on, a skillful letter writer will make it personal for favorable effect; but if an accusation is to be made the writer will cast it in an impersonal statement rather than offend needlessly. Indeed, this is one of the rare occasions in which passive voice is preferable to active if the active voice leads to personal accusation. That, too, is why the humor in the preceding illustration can work effectively. The writer can talk about the curtain without talking directly about or to its owner.

Avoiding Words and Ideas with Poor Connotation

The connotation (emotional associations) of words or entire sentences is a quality of the language every writer needs to master, especially in handling negatives. Be sensitive, and thoughtfully employ the you-attitude. Remembering that a negative, as defined in business writing, is anything unpleasant and that it is always a stumbling block to good relationships, the letter-writing specialist's code of action is to avoid the negative when possible and to subordinate the negative when it cannot be sidestepped. Such accusations as "You failed to oil" will almost always destroy rather than rebuild goodwill. Nobody likes to be accused of things that he or she should not have done, even if guilty.

"We have noted the complaint you make about the error in your account" may be a correct statement of fact, but the reader will not want to be called a complainer even though that person has a right to be upset about the mistake.

"We regret you neglected to sign the signature card enclosed in your letter of June 5" is a pretty direct way of saying "you are a careless individual." This writer, too, may be laboring under the false impression he or she is being courteous in beginning the sentence with "we regret."

"Our knowledge of economic conditions leads us to conclude that your proposed investment would be unwise" implies that the reader lacks financial judgment and that the writer's judgment is superior.

The term *company policy* has been used so much as an excuse by high-handed correspondents or timid adjusters with no good reason for not complying with a request or granting an adjustment, that most people now take it to mean about the same as "None of your business" or "I'm afraid to tell the reason why." When a person thinks that he or she has a just request or claim, that person feels entitled to an explanation or reason (not an excuse) before the refusal. Unless a reason is forthcoming, he or she is not going to be happy with the writer or firm.

Using the face-saving principle—in focusing on constructive aspects of the situation—is also extremely important to a business or organization's goodwill when you are correcting or differing with someone. For example, a busy doctor sent a second check for his department store account several weeks after it had already been paid. The store correspondent wrote

> We are in receipt of your remittance of $227.56. You have sent us this in error. Our records show that your account was paid on April 2.

Such a point-blank negative assertion of the doctor's mistake can hardly please him. Would a little face saving like the following bring a more favorable reaction on his part, do you think?

> Thank you for sending your $227.56 check. Since the account was paid on April 2, 19xx (possibly by the bookkeeping service you use), we are returning your check.

Face saving is a device to be used in many situations. It is indispensable to effective negative-message handling.

CHECKLIST FOR NEGATIVE MESSAGES

Opening

NM 10   Begin with some general point (about the subject if possible) both you and your reader can agree on.

11   Establish yourself in the reader's eyes as a reasonable person. (Aren't the most reasonable people you know the ones who agree with you?)

12   You've given away the fact that your message is bad news. It violates the inductive strategy of writing.

13   Empty acknowledgments or apologies are out of place.

14   Don't mislead or deceive your reader with overly enthusiastic tone or wording.

15   Your opening should establish the basis—a key idea—on which you can

build the development of the negative message in the body.

16 Avoid negative words or any statement that puts you on the defensive.

17 Your tone and words should leave no doubt in the reader's mind that you are a person of goodwill, good intentions.

Coverage

NM 20 Lead the reader into a cooperative review of the facts with sincere, on-target conversation.

21 Material should begin to shift the discussion toward an explanation of the negative situation.

22 An abrupt subject-matter shift here lacks smoothness, or connection in the turn; it irritates.

23 Sentence shift tips off the bad news too soon.

24 Enough constructive discussion to gain understanding and acceptance—to convince the reader of the reasonableness of your stand—should precede the actual negative message your copy delivers.

25 Sequence of ideas leading up to the disappointing news must be logical, smooth.

26 Make the decision your message carries unmistakably clear—though not harsh—halfway down or later, buried position.

27 The skillful writer attempts through positive implication to phrase the bad news without resort to any negative wording.

28 Follow the disappointing news with some constructive aspect.

29 Isn't it possible here to present the reader a face-saving exit from the encounter—

a. Through some phrasing which relieves him or her of guilt feelings though not of responsibility?

b. Through some form of compromise or counterproposal?

30 Avoid negatives at the beginning or end of paragraphs.

31 Your treatment should deliberately attempt to rebuild, to restore goodwill through concentration on the bright side of future relationships.

32 For an adequate handling of this particular assignment, work in enough of these facts to gain understanding. (Your instructor will provide specific points of coverage according to the case selected as assignment.)

Close

NM 40 Trail off on some pleasantry unrelated to the negative issue.

41 If you've made a counteroffer, quietly suggest here that the reader take it up.

42 No high pressure, please. No imperatives!

43 Above all, make your closing gracious and sincere, not tactless, hackneyed.

Tone and Style As Marked

Your Grade _____

PROBLEMS IN WRITING THAT REQUIRE A TACTFUL NO OR CONTAIN A NEGATIVE IDEA

1. *Refusing an unwarranted purchase attempt politely.* As Jack English, sales manager, Sew King Company, 207 Market Street, Any Metropolitan City, Your State, it is your task to give an enterprising customer the "kid glove" treatment.

Part of your company's spring advertising campaign has been a radio program on which you gave a $40 certificate to be applied on the cost of any regularly priced Sew King to the identifier of the Mystery Song of the day. Three months ago one of your certificate awards went to Mrs. Fred Nolle, Any Rural Town, Your State. You never heard from Mrs. Nolle. Today you realize what she's been up to. This week you ran an ad in *The Chronicle* (your metropolitan city's leading daily) offering a Sew King portable which regularly sells for $182.50 at the phenomenal price of only $149.95. On your desk is a letter from Mrs. Nolle asking that you deliver her machine. She has copied down the number (S-305) of the portable advertised for sale, enclosed her $40 certificate, and included a check for $109.95.

Planning your defense, you check Mrs. Nolle's certificate. It reads in part: "This certificate is good for $40 on the purchase of any of our regularly priced machines." Mrs. Nolle should have known you couldn't let one of those fine portables go for little more than half price. Still, your business sense makes you aware you can't tell her she's a "so and so" for trying. She probably has a lot of friends and relatives in her rural area who could get the impression from Mrs. Nolle that the Sew King Company doesn't stand behind its word. Misunderstandings of this sort can prove rather costly.

You write this letter for English with words chosen carefully to make Mrs. Nolle understand your company's position, to make her feel good about the whole thing, and to induce her to send you another check that will result in her being the proud possessor of an $182.50 Sew King portable.

2. *Turning down a job offer and winning a customer.* The job offered you by the Triad Research Institute, 1315 North Forman Road, A Major City, Any State, sounded good. After concentrating through your last two years in the College of Business Administration on statistical mathematics and computer programming, it was just what you wanted. You would have set up advanced research problems to be fed into complex computing machines, including one full-scale electronic "brain." But now you've been offered something better.

The district manager of the company that made the "brain" called you in this week. It didn't take you long to know that his opening in business machine sales was what you had really been waiting for. You would have the opportunity to show how the larger machines built by Stevens-Point Corporation could be used. You would demonstrate programming techniques and sell the capabilities of the machines to business and research organizations all through the Midwest. Besides, Mr. Sperry, the Stevens-Point manager, was able to offer substantially more money than the Research Institute could hope to match. The corporation also held out fringe benefits, including a yearly training program, increasingly long vacations, a generous retirement and insurance plan, and other inducements.

You would have accepted Mr. Sperry on the spot except that you were already committed to go to work next month for Dr. Hans Castorp at the Research Institute. This fact complicated the situation considerably. For nearly three years you were one of Dr. Castorp's prize students at the university before you graduated and he moved to directorship of the Triad Research Institute. Moreover, you would be expected, as a Stevens-Point representative, to deal frequently with Dr. Castorp and his colleagues at the Institute since it is a major Stevens-Point customer.

Dr. Castorp is certainly human enough to appreciate your situation. The problem is to write a tactful refusal of the research job that will keep Dr. Castorp's goodwill toward you and toward Stevens-Point as well.

3. *Transmitting a firm but tactful "no."* As M. K. Hague, district sales representative for the Vamco Music Corporation, 2120 Sculler Avenue, Jacksonville, Florida, you have to make a refusal of a request by a student at Florida State University, Tallahassee, Rodney E. Skopinski, of 115 Meadow Lane.

Two weeks ago you received a letter from Mr. Skopinski requesting that the manufacturer refund his $114 down payment on a $565 Vamco Stereophonic Recorder. Mr. Skopinski stated in his letter that this was not the equipment which he had intended to buy. It had been described and represented to him, by the local dealer in Tallahassee at the time of purchase, as exactly the type recorder he asked for. He stated that he had wanted a stereophonic recorder but that this instrument was not a stereophonic recorder and was not doing the job for which it had been represented. Furthermore, he had spent $55 on stereophonic tapes, which he now claimed were ruined by virtue of the machine's being a mere standard Vamco Recorder. Mr. Skopinski wants you to return the down payment along with the money that he had spent for what he now terms worthless tapes.

Upon checking with the local dealer in Tallahassee, you found—as is often the case—that it was apparently a pure and simple matter of operator difficulties rather than a faulty machine. The dealer related the following facts to you. Mr. Skopinski is a sophomore who had, on a previous occasion, purchased a new FM table-model radio at the regular retail price of $99.50. After using the radio for approximately six weeks, he returned it and stated that he could no longer use this radio because of its inferior tone quality. At that time the dealer allowed him to apply his $30 down payment on the radio toward the down payment on the Vamco Stereophonic Recorder. Thus, for an additional $84, the dealer allowed the student to take the Vamco Stereophonic Recorder out of the store and use it for two months. When Mr. Skopinski failed to make the payments as he had agreed to do under the conditional sales contract, the local financing institution that had bought the sales contract and promissory note came back to the dealer. The Easy Loan Company reported that it was unable to obtain the regular payments promised by the student and wanted the dealer to make good the outstanding balance. By virtue of his arrangement with Easy Loan, the dealer made full restitution and immediately checked with the student. It was then and only then that Skopinski made a claim concerning the operational status of this machine. He refused the dealer's request to bring in the machine for checking and additional instructions concerning the operational procedures involved.

You will write this letter for Mr. Hague, refusing as tactfully as possible, this unwarranted claim.

4. *Tactfully refusing a good customer's unwarranted claim.* As Advertising Manager Allen B. Conroe for *Home Beauty Magazine*, Constitution Square, Philadelphia, Pennsylvania, you receive in the morning's mail two facing pages of the latest issue of your magazine and an irate letter from Mr. Harvey Doolittle, advertising director, Cape Cod Shipbuilding Company, 981 Ocean Drive, Wareham, Massachusetts.

"Your magazine," Mr. Doolittle writes, "reaches just the sort of upper-income people to buy my fiberglass boats—and your 4,250,000 circulation figures guarantee that my $21,250 full-page, 3-color, center-spread ad will reach a lot of them. But the company my ad is keeping—as you can see from the facing pages I'm sending—practically destroys the effectiveness of the appeal.

"The artwork is fine—pretty folks enjoying a boat ride against a background of blue water. But who wants to pay $2,885 for a sloop when he looks at the starving individuals in the accompanying article at the same time? My national sales feel off 10 percent in the 30 days following the ad's appearance. A survey by the research department establishes the cause of the slump as the depressing company this ad was keeping. So you can well see why I'm asking that you refund the $21,250 cost."

You look at the two pictures Doolittle sends and realize reluctantly that he might have a point. *Home Beauty Magazine* prides itself on the variety of its articles, on its wide coverage of news of interest to sensitive, affluent people. The first page of the article that Mr. Doolittle finds so destructive to his ad pictures the miseries of Calcutta. On this page, a powerful treatment of human degradation executed by a staff of master craftsmen, you see a beggar, a 16-year-old mother with her dying baby, and a starving man in the gutter. It is easy enough to see that some readers, confronted with so much misery, would turn away from expensive pleasure craft and resolve to make a contribution to the appropriate charity.

You approach the makeup department, fully prepared to accuse the staff of gross stupidity. The explanation is a logical one. A full-page advertiser canceled some weeks back when the magazine was being made up. A last-minute adjustment resulted in the pushing together of the boat ad and the article. Still you're within the rights of your contract. Mr. Doolittle got his full-page 3-color story of fiberglass boats in the exact center of the magazine, just as he'd asked. With television biting a great hunk out of the volume of magazine advertising, your department can ill afford a $21,250 loss. Despite the work of the research department, Doolittle can scarcely prove that his sales slump resulted entirely from the ad. It is possible, though, that he might not have got so good a return from this ad as he might from another one more fortunately placed. So you decide to try to make Doolittle happy with a 10-percent discount and a letter in your best goodwill vein. You'll enclose a company check for $2,125.

5. *Communicating a foreclosure threat to a customer who has missed three home payments.* On March 15, Harold A. Bingham of City Mortgage Loan Company feels that he must protect the interests of his firm by taking drastic action against John Sampson of Cresthill Road—now delinquent four payments on his home. On January 15 when one payment was fifteen days delinquent, Bingham sent Sampson a nice little reminder note. On February 1 he mailed a somewhat stronger message pointing up the delinquency and reminding Sampson that two payments were now due. On February 15, Bingham wrote a rather strong letter based on defense of an investment and urging payment or an explanation. On March 1, when the third payment came due, an even stronger note, pointing up the acceleration option went out. Now on March 15 you will write a letter for Bingham that gives Sampson one last chance before you institute foreclosure proceedings. The deadline date is March 25.

Sampson will very likely know what will happen as a result of this drastic measure. Perhaps you'll play up the eventualities, though, for the psychological effect. He is subject to loss of part of his equity in a foreclosure sale. The purchaser gets immediate possession; so he may have to find suitable housing on very short notice. He'll have difficulty, too, in ever getting another home loan and will suffer loss of business and personal prestige. You may add any sad circumstances of your own that will help this case.

You'll write this last letter to Sampson in a sympathetic vein with the attitude you're sure he'll avert the consequences by paying.

6. *Tactfully postponing acceptance of a "third choice" job offer.* Let's assume that three months have passed since you initiated your career-launching venture with a prospecting-application-letter approach. From the dozen or so letters you mailed, four produced enough interest to gain you a response and a request to complete company application forms. Subsequently, three of these follow-ups resulted in expense-paid interview trips—all of which you felt were pretty successful. In each case, the personnel director's parting words to you were, "You'll hear from us within the next two weeks."

Immediately upon returning to your school, you wrote each person who'd played host to you on these trips a warm thank-you note for the courtesies and the time spent with you while you were at the company being given the red-carpet treatment. In each note, too, you'd managed to work in a sincere expression of your interest in becoming an integral part of that firm. You felt that each offered a career opportunity (though somewhat different in each case) for an ambitious, enterprising person willing to work at making a meaningful contribution to the firm's advancement. After the interviews, however, it was a fairly simple matter for you to rank these three firms in your mind as first, second, or third choice of employment.

Monday you received a firm job offer from Mr. E. D. Swift, recruiting coordinator, Spectar, Inc., P.O. Box 7096, Any Metropolitan City, Any State (choice no. 3—a job opening outside your major area). Mr. Swift's letter offering you the job states, "Please let us know your decision right away; it's imperative that we fill this position as soon as possible." That was five days ago and still no response from choice no. 1 or no. 2. With your future perhaps at stake—and because good manners dictate it—you dare not delay responding to Mr. Swift's communication any longer. Yet you'd like to postpone your decision (that is, making a definite commitment to this job offer) for two more weeks so that you might have a chance to hear from the other two firms.

Your reasoning is that you've known people who started to work in an area that did not relate to their *greatest* interest (with hope of moving later into their major field) and who never got back on the track. You, therefore, think it only fair to yourself—and to Spectar—to explore all possibilities available so that, when the commitment is made, each party benefits to the fullest degree from that commitment.

The work at Spectar would mean becoming an executive trainee in a two-year program designed to acquaint the new employee with the total company operation. Eventual placement would be in whatever division the firm's need for personnel was most crucial. Spectar is one of the new companies in the ever-growing innovative electronics field.

Mr. Swift is perhaps considering other candidates for this job if you turn it down; so what sort of reasoning can you give him which won't ruin your chances altogether? That is your tough assignment.

7. *Acknowledging a difficult order situation.* You are Holt Minkleton, managing editor for Clifton Publishing Associates, 930 Lexington Avenue, New York. Your firm is involved primarily in publishing textbooks and other academic papers for distribution to colleges and senior high schools. Of course some fiction, biographies, and other trade books are published, but at least 85 percent of Clifton's net sales are from academic sources.

Today, September 5, you received a memo from the distribution department. Their problem is that a large number of complaints have been received from college accounting departments around the country. Apparently, a large number of college bookstores have notified the complaining accounting departments of an insufficiency of elementary accounting textbooks. The last edition of the textbook, *Basic Accounting Principles*, by Dr. Thomas B. Ardbilt, is out of stock, and a large number of current orders have not yet been filled. You are aware that this situation has been caused by a printer's union strike which is expected to end within the next 10 days. Thus, the striking workers should be back at their jobs by September 15 at the latest. Since all work has been completed on the revision of this text (typesetting, galley proofing, and so on) except the actual page printing, binding, and distribution, all orders should be filled (the books in the stores) by September 30. Of course this date is beyond the usual date on which most fall classes begin; however, the relatively short wait for the text should be more than compensated for by the fact that

- Ardbilt is a national authority in accounting theory whose practical experience as research associate for the American Institute of Certified Accountants (a practicing accountants' organization similar to the American Medical Association for doctors) has enabled him to insert many up-to-date, practical aspects of elementary accounting theory into this new edition of his book.

- The text has a large number of illustrative problems, many of which are adaptations from the AICPA's nationally uniform accounting examination (e.g., they reflect realistic situations that are important to practicing accountants).

- The book is revised every year, thus always being an up-to-date text (many textbooks are revised every two, three, or more years).

Your problem, therefore, is to write a letter which is completely personalized for one particular accounting department (the chairperson, Department of Accounting, Your University, Your City, Your State). The letter will then be sent to all colleges planning to use this text, the name of the department being changed to fit the case. This job is critical since Ardbilt's book has many acceptances from accounting departments across the United States. If the departments were forced to change to more readily available texts, they might never return to Ardbilt. This situation would result in a large loss of revenue. You believe that, since the book should be in the students' hands no later than October 2, there will be little loss of instruction. (Actually the first week or two of elementary accounting is involved with the basic accounting equations and the nature of accounts, the trial balance, the general journal, methods of posting, and so on. In other words, the student is being given simple material easily handled in a lecture—material not necessarily dependent on a text and elaborate problems for student understanding.)

The letter you write will be an acknowledgment for this negative situation in which you attempt to reinforce the value of this text for reader and students . . . enough so to retain placement of that initial order.

8. *Handling Brady's slow-pay tactics with friendly firmness.* On December 9 an itemized statement reminded R. M. "Rock" Brady of the 40-day-old balance of $1,945.50 from his first invoice and of the currently due items totaling $197.30 from the purchase of October 9, the entire statement thus covering $2,142.80. When December 19 came and still no word from Brady, you wrote him this letter:

Dear Mr. Brady:

Because of the off-with-the-gun start you had made in selling Stitsen goods, as Bill Simms reports it, we were glad to allow the additional two weeks you told him you would need to clean up the remaining $1,945.50 on your original stock of goods.

We matched your confidence with our own and set December 9 as the date when your check would come in along with that for Invoice N92Rw6 for $197.30.

Certainly we want to play ball with you and help all we can. Is there any way we can help push things along? Bill said you were having your own initiation into the credit business at the time. That's fine, of course, as your credit customers are your best friends and your solid support in expanding your sales volume. Do you mind a friendly tip from an old hand, though? Most of those boys can pay promptly just as easily as not—if you ask them. And don't mind asking them. They'll respect you more for a businesslike handling of business. If you'd like a little experienced help, we have a set of right smooth collection reminders adapted to retail sports shops which several of our customers have used profitably. Shall we send you a set?

High business standards in the use of credit work both ways, of course, and it is immediately important for you to keep your own paying record in the clear by sending your check for $2,142.80.

Put it in the mail today, won't you?

Sincerely yours

That should have stirred him up, of course; since it didn't, you followed the prompting of your tickler file and talked the situation out more forcefully in this letter, dated January 4:

Dear Mr. Brady:

With spring only a few weeks off, the school down your way will soon be coming alive with sports-minded students—and so will Brady's Sports Shop.

Bill Simms's schedule will bring him to your place in a day or two to help you get your seasonal lines of Stitsen goods. When he gets there, won't you please meet him with that Stitsen payment ($2,142.80) over which you shook hands on his last visit?

I'm asking you to do this, Mr. Brady, because I'm honestly interested in seeing you keep on the inside track at this first crucial turn. A clear credit record will allow you to buy confidently and keep your stock up to attractive levels. But it's worth more than that. I've been in this game long enough to know that the "slow pay" mark fastens to a new business quicker than to an old and strong one . . . harder to rub off, too. At this crucial stage for you, the reputation value of straining a point to keep a "prompt pay" rating is worth a long sight more than the meager interest from using the other fellow's money overly long.

A way back last August I confidently put Stitsen's money on you in this race. I'm still confident that you will do the thing that will make us both winners now.

Sincerely yours,

No success with that try either; nor was Bill Simms able to pick up Brady's check. Bill did reinforce the urgency for Brady's clearing up this account. So, today, January 15, you'll make one last try at getting your money and letting Brady save his skin. Unless you've received full payment for the account by January 22, you'll be forced to turn over Brady's name and past-due status to the Retail Merchants Credit Association. As well, you'll turn the account over to your lawyer who's prepared to institute suit to collect.

9. *Tactfully refusing credit to a doubtful risk who might become a profitable one.* It's mid-January—and at your desk as credit manager of De Hoyle Sporting Goods Company, Buffalo, New York, you are getting acquainted with the footwork of Rock Brady in Some Small County Seat Town, Your State. His very persuasive request for $496 worth of competition-priced baseball equipment on 60-day terms sounded good until you got Your State Salesrep's confidential wire report on the Brady store.

It seems that Brady's credit sales have been booming—almost as fast as his delinquent accounts. Likewise, Brady's own credit payments have been lagging, although the one reference he listed (Wiggins and Barnes) did give a fair report. Your salesrep got it straight from the Stitsen Company representative that Brady is long past due on a large payment to that company. A look at Brady's financial statement, which shows that the Sports Shop is well below the 2-to-1 ratio of quick assets to liabilities usually required for safe credit buying, supports your sales representative's observations. So, in spite of Brady's persuasive efforts, you will have to say "no."

Remember, though, that Brady probably is a fundamentally honest person who is off to a poor start in his entrepreneurship. There's a good chance that he may pull out of his present slump, and, if he does, you want to get in your share of the sales. So don't just say "no" and leave it at that. Instead, drive for a cash sale now. Offer him a 5-percent discount to help him build toward that 2-to-1 ratio he needs to become a good credit risk. Above all, make him feel that you're a person with his best interest at heart . . . doing him a favor by refusing.

10. *Protecting your distributor's territorial rights with a direct-to-dealer letter.* For Calway Goode, sales manager at Gordon Appliance Manufacturers, Broad and Salem Streets, St. Louis, Missouri, it is your task to protect one of your local distributor's territorial rights and, at the same time, to preserve a new retail outlet for a unique new product. Mr. J. R. Tampke, manager, Baldwin Hardware Company, Sheffield, Alabama, orders six of your new Liqui-Blenders to be shipped to him direct. Attached is his check for $135.96, the correct amount at your factory price, plus shipping charges. And the check is pinned to one of your current mimeographed *distributors'* lists. How he got the list is a disturbing point, which you decide not to mention in the letter.

The main point is that you cannot sell to him direct (at $22.50) or at the distributor's wholesale price ($25.00), list or no list. You must keep your agreement with your exclusive distributor for the district—the Banks Wholesale Hardware Supply, 892 Clairmont Avenue, Birmingham, Alabama.

Of course you want Mr. Tampke to buy—and sell—your Gordon Liqui-Blender; so you write him a letter, returning his check and asking him to place his order with the Banks Supply. Analyze your policy in the light of its ultimate advantage to retailers and derive from this analysis a presentation that emphasizes Mr. Tampke's advantages rather than your own or your dealer's.

As you prepare to write this letter, you look over one of your recent quarter-page ads appearing in the current issues of *Ladies Home Journal, The Saturday Evening Post,* and *House Beautiful.* From it you pick out some sales points that will appeal to Tampke's customers:

> Blends faster! Cuts quicker! Blends! Chops! Grates! Pulverizes! Mixes! Purees! Liquefies! New Gordon Liqui-Blender, complete with recipe book for $37.50. Amazing "Cut-'N'-Fold" action. New "Cut-'N'-Fold" action is so quick you'll prepare meals in minutes! It makes 60,000 cuts a minute! Drop in a few vegetables and milk—zip! Cream soup, ready to heat. You'll change leftovers into treats; blend cakes, sauces; purée vegetables. You'll surprise everyone—save time, money, and energy.
>
> EASY TO CLEAN: Container opens at both ends and cutting unit comes apart completely. No food traps!
>
> 2 SPEEDS: Top speed gives you a true purée. Low speed is for coarse cutting.
>
> NO-SPLASH TOP: Center of top section slips out; ingredients can be added while blender is on.
>
> CANNING-JAR THREAD: Replace container with a fruit jar for speed in home canning.

Your advertised retail price allows Mr. Tampke a 50-percent markup over cost. So popular has this mixer become in the six months it's been on the market that you have had to double production. Write a letter to Tampke that will have him sending in his order right away to your Birmingham distributor.

11. *Making a bid for a customer's business while tactfully refusing credit.* As Richard Kerr, credit manager, Montana Electrical Supply House, Missoula, Montana, you have decided against granting credit to Western Appliance Store, Clara, Montana, for $500

worth of miscellaneous electrical household goods. Trade agency reports that came in response to your inquiries show excellent performance on credit terms until two years ago, but the present picture looks a bit unstable. The financial statement submitted by the store's owner, Lafe Sorensen, with a $500 order shows strong fixed assets and a generous sum for goodwill. The Pacific Credit Exchange report lists three accounts marked "Closed" and another marked "Cash Basis Only." Other sources of information indicate that Sorensen's customers of two years ago are moving along with an oil-exploration crew and reforestation projects. The mobility of customers does not bother the enterprising Sorensen too much though—following the idea of the rural Bookmobile Library, he loads up a truck of miscellaneous merchandise and electrical appliances at two-week intervals and follows the trail of the transient families. This reversal of customer traffic, however, makes his buying of stock more of a guess than a forecast.

You'll base your refusal on the requisite 3-to-1 ratio of current assets to current liabilities which your supply house requires of merchants in communities under 10,000 population. In spite of Sorensen's being under this ratio, you see that he has present and future value as a retail outlet for your heating pads, toasters, percolators, hotplates, and steam irons. A man with such vision and vigor is probably a better potential customer than is one already using your credit terms of 2/10, n/30.

Take over for Kerr and keep Sorensen's friendship as you offer him a 5-percent discount on this first shipment if cash accompanies his authorization to fill the order.

12. *Tactfully refusing a customer's heated request for money back on radio equipment.* As Dean H. Barton, newly appointed head of the adjustment department of your state's branch of Alloyed Radio Corporation, 305 Walmsley Avenue, Your City, Your State, you tackle the tough problem of refusing to take back some radio equipment from John McDuff, a hot-headed nouveau-riche customer from A Rural Town, Your State. You've known the man for some time but have had no occasion to do business with him until seven months ago.

McDuff had always worked pretty hard in his small moving van business and earned just enough to keep his wife and three boys, aged 12, 10, and 7, in food and clothes. Then it happened! The plot of land left him by his uncle Ephraim was found oozing with oil—the beginning of a new oil boom in a field over in Midland County. McDuff soon began raking in the greenbacks from his royalties and was finally able to have the country home he'd always wanted.

He built a beautiful 12-room house in a setting of trees 11 miles southeast of town, establishing his family there in record time in a lavish life of aristocrats. The only drawback was that they weren't used to such luxury; so they ran wild and the servants had their hands full keeping their place in order.

John saw an advertisement in *Millionaire*, showing ultramodern, custom-built radio equipment by Alloyed Radio Corporation. He called your office with a sizable order. The next day Jack Warner, the serviceman, was in the rural town with a panel truck full of equipment and two men to help with the installation. A color TV screen and tuner plus an AM-FM tuner with two speakers were placed in the living room. The game room was set up as a central control base, with a two-speed, high-fidelity phonograph, a microphone, and an amplifier. Speakers in every room were connected to this amplifier. The cost of the complete system was $1,800 plus $234 for installation charges.

Warner tried to impress on his customer the delicate nature of the mechanism, instructing McDuff to call the office in case anything went wrong and under no circumstances to attempt any repairs himself. One afternoon the two older boys were playing catch with a baseball in the living room and not only broke the TV screen but also the dial of the AM-FM tuner. The penny-pinching habit of a lifetime was still with McDuff; so he decided at least he could repair the tuner—he'd made a crystal set when he was a boy, and certainly that project qualified him. The net result was tuner parts all over the floor and a call to serviceman Warner.

When Warner arrived, he found the tuner completely out of alignment and the cathode TV tube broken. Since the installation had been an expensive one with a wide profit margin, Warner did the repair work free of charge. But he tactfully warned McDuff again that the equipment should not be tampered with and that the phonograph in the game room must receive careful treatment if the best service were to be obtained.

The last repair job was on April 5. The 90-day guarantee period ran out the last of May, at which time McDuff reported no mechanical deficiencies. But today, August 10, you receive a burning note saying the TV broadcasts are completely distorted, the speakers have a loud buzz, the records are scratchy, the tuners won't bring in anything clearly, and that he wishes you'd take the blank thing and throw it in the river and bring him a new outfit.

By the symptoms he describes, you figure at least a $60 repair job is indicated, with service charges on the truck and servicemen amounting to $25. You tactfully tell McDuff you cannot replace the equipment—it is perfectly good if given the proper care. The only adjustment you can make is a repair job at the reduced price of $65. You write the letter for Barton.

Part II

DECISION-MAKING BUSINESS REPORTS

Researchers do not stumble over mountains, but over molehills.

Poetic license with Confucius

6

Constructing Short Operational Reports

A report's function is to provide the right information to the right person at the right time. The analyst's problem-solving consists of determining the needed action, searching for alternatives, evaluating the probable consequences of each, and making rational choices among those alternatives in light of complex organizational objectives.

Chapters 7 through 11 trace in detail the methods, procedures, and writing techniques for handling long, formal analytical report problems. As prelude this chapter on the reporting process is concerned with the real workhorses of day-to-day business functions—short operational reports.

The thinking and planning processes are basically the same for all report problem solving; for short operational reports, however, the writing style is more informal, the format different, and the content less intensively treated. In this chapter, therefore, we are concerned with an *organized* approach for adaptive management as we examine those aspects of short operational reports you will need to learn and master to perform effectively in the business entity:

1. The functions of operational reports.
2. Organizational aspects.
3. Writing considerations.

AN OVERVIEW OF THE OPERATIONAL REPORT'S FUNCTIONS

For any sizable organization, there are generally three levels of management needing short operational reports of some kind. At the first level—commonly called *operative*—are those managers whose concern and responsibility lie in the problems arising with employees in performing the operations of individual jobs. The *departmental- and supervisory*-level managers (middle management) deal with problems in supervising and coordinating the employees. At the *administrative* (or *executive*) level, the problems are those of group management. The reader-writer relationship for operational reports at whatever level may be either internal or external, superior or subordinate.

Internal reports move vertically upward or downward, from a non-executive or subexecutive to top management or from an executive down to lower officials or employees. They move horizontally or diagonally from one department to another within the firm, or from one employee to another in departmental structure. A short report submitted by an outside consultant (external relationship) to the employing firm takes on the aspects of the staff report as well.

A staff report is an internal report prepared by a member of the staff (or by an employed consultant) for another staff member or for a department as an administrative tool. Thus, lest there be confusion in terminology at this point, we consider all reports *of whatever size or format* that are written for *internal operation of a firm* as staff or administrative reports. These reports may be of many kinds:

Policy statements	Statistical analyses
Periodic reports	Product analyses
Sales reports	Process analyses
Committee minutes	Attitude surveys
Reports on interviews	Readership surveys
Advertising reports	Justification reports
Employee bulletins	Improvement reports
Examination reports	Progress reports
Accounting reports	Analytical reports
Market surveys	Research reports
Management newsletters	Recommendation reports
Procedures statements	Employee appraisals

External reports, *prepared for readers outside the company*, usually to inform or sell the company to specified publics or prepared by an outside consultant for a fee, may include:

Periodic reports to stockholders, to the public through news releases, articles in magazines	Annual reports
	Progress reports
	Information reports
Credit reports	Brochures
Personnel reports	Public relations releases

Staff operational reports are further classified as to physical characteristics according to the form they take to suit the importance of the problem:

Printed forms built to some predetermined plan

Memorandum reports

Letter reports

Short, analytical reports (under ten pages)

Long, formal reports (ten pages or more of text with all the formal prefatory parts)

Short operational reports, written for informal situations, may assume varying degrees of informality. Suppose, for example, that the advertising manager of a company needs to have a record of sales over a period of time to relate advertising costs to profits. All that would be needed from the sales manager would be an informal memo recording sales, broken down monthly, annually, and so on.

Or, because the user may need this information provided weekly (for monthly reports) or monthly (for quarterly reports), the departmental manager designs a printed form requiring a minimum of writing. The report is provided simply by an employee's filling in blanks with appropriate figures or brief comments. Inventory control reports; plant housekeeping (production) details; sales reps' reports of calls, changing conditions, and competitors' activities; production records; absentee and turnover reports; mileage logs; performance reports; and personnel appraisal forms from supervisors and recruiters are typical examples. Progress on manufacturing processes or job constructions, exit interviews with employees, employee clearance records, repair orders and shipping records, daily settlement sheets (cash receipts and disbursements), self-inspection reports (housekeeping), and records of employee training are other logical uses of printed form reports built to a predetermined plan.

Strictly informational, these reports offer few writing problems, although they are indispensable to the operation of business concerns. The only report-writing tasks involved are for those who devise the forms originally, or who must devise a change in a form once it is in use. Designing printed report forms thus requires a thorough knowledge of the information needed and of the interpretation anticipated from it.

More appropriate for our concern here, however, are those operational reports generated by the organizational problems which staff specialists are generally called on to help solve. These short informal reports vary in length from one to ten pages of text. They are often written on subjects of temporary or current interest and speed up the process of keeping someone else informed or of supplying vital information to someone concerned with adapting to a problem and solving it. They have neither table of contents nor cover, because there is no need for them. The pages are usually clipped or stapled, top left-hand corner. A short transmittal letter may go along with them. They are a less finished product than are long, formal reports, but the two are alike in that they require the same process of organization and care given to subject matter treatment.

Some companies give uniformity and continuity to all of their reports—whether short or long—by specifying basic makeup, color of paper to be used, and the assigning of consecutive numbers to each report. The same part of every report is placed in the same position within the report so that anyone analyzing a succession of these reports always knows where to look for any particular aspect. In support of this procedure, Commonwealth Edison Company some years ago in an attractive, illustrated pamphlet entitled *How to Write a Report* made this statement:

> The reader of your report
> Does not expect a masterpiece
> But he does want
> A well-planned report
> With time-saving arrangement of essential points, and
> Readable writing.

We believe this advice is equally appropriate for current short operational reports, whether they are written as part of a continuous series or as independent efforts. If they don't get the desired results, short operational reports are a waste of time and effort. Because they go to people inside the same company, we often take too much for granted; our short reports are unclear. Internal short reports are as important as messages to people outside the organization. Every letter, every memorandum, every short report that passes within an organization is important, for each carries possibilities for errors, for arousing resentment, for failing to succeed in its purpose. In many respects it is more difficult to write internal messages than it is to write messages to outsiders. Because such messages are written to associates, there is greater danger of being careless, curt, or less explicit than one should be.

Internal messages of every sort face as many requirements as do messages that go to customers or the public at large. They are part of the intricate problem of human relations. They must be clear and complete; they should be concise; yet they cannot ignore the emotional impact that written words always have on people. The right kind of written messages gets the results that are desired; there is no confusion, no friction; no wasted time or energy through misunderstanding of facts or intentions.

The writer of a short report can seldom be certain that the one who receives it will read the report carefully or that any systematic method of checking will be used to be sure that all important points are noted and remembered. The competent writer anticipates this problem. The message is organized and presented in such a way that important points and special details are made to stand out sharply from the context (language redundancy) that surrounds them.

ORGANIZATION STRATEGY AS THE FOCAL POINT OF YOUR MESSAGE'S SUCCESS

All readers—business executives included—have certain similar expectations regarding written messages. For your reports, they want you to

1. Follow some visible method of organization—some recognizable pattern of structure.
2. Make each sentence go somewhere.
3. Provide transitional signposts.
4. Be concise.

Just as with the long, analytical report problem, you must of course first have a clear understanding of what it is you are up against, spelling out your objective(s) and isolating the factors you will need data for in solving the difficulty. The steps in problem solving—by way of review at this point—are these:

1. Determine the problem.
2. Gather the needed data.
3. Organize the information collected.
4. Interpret the facts.
5. Reach a solution.
6. Communicate the results.

How can we best make use of these steps in constructing short operational reports?

Unless the writer's content is clear, complete, and accurate, little will be communicated. The subject matter is the heart of your message; the written presentation is merely the clear expression of orderly, organized thought.

A good suggestion for beginning, therefore, is to write out a specific statement of the main idea you want to convey to your reader. You should not worry about the wording or brevity of this peg sentence, for it may not even appear as such in your finished copy. The idea is to make it as *specific* a statement as you can in line with what it is that you want to transmit to your eventual reader.

With this statement in writing where you can examine it, you are then ready to start detailing (in outline fashion) to a limited extent *how* the idea is to be developed. This detailing will both indicate the objectives of your report and tell you what kinds of data you will need to collect for an adequate presentation.

Suppose that you wanted to issue an *informational memorandum* on Celcos, a chemical fiber. Your main idea might be written something like this:

> Celcos, a chemical fiber combining the best features of acetate and viscous staple in ease of processing and ability to cross-dye and absorb resins, is produced commercially by the Celanese Corporation of America.

Your jotting down of objectives for this kind of informational report might then proceed along these lines:

1. Description of the product (i.e., properties of the fiber)
2. Possible end uses
3. What its producer says about it
4. Merchandising and pricing information
5. Availability of product

} The kinds of things you will need to cover for an adequate treatment of the subject

Of course, if the report were to be other than informational on this same topic, the peg would have been stated differently. The outline content and arrangement would be different also—because the objectives hinge on the ideas generated by the specific peg statement.

Having set forth the objectives of your report, you are ready to deal with the needed data for a concise treatment of the subject. Because your objectives spell out clearly the kinds of information you will require, a minimum of effort is expended in collecting, organizing, and interpreting pertinent data for the problem solution.

The actual writing up of the investigation begins with reshaping your peg statement. Professional writers call this statement the *lead*. It becomes a summary statement, the overall conclusion, or a recommendation line, the first thing in your report draft. It comes first in your thinking because

1.   Whether your reader goes beyond the first sentence or paragraph, the main thing you wanted to get across will have been presented.

2.   A crisp statement of the main idea is the best possible way to interest your reader in going further.

3.   The reader is immediately aware of the structure of the piece of writing that follows, thus is able to readily understand each of the succeeding paragraphs.

In everyday writing we just don't have the time or space to "build suspense." Most of us—and your readers are certainly included—are usually pressed for time (or think we are at least) when we are presented with letters, memos, or short reports to read. We thus read with a let's-get-on-with-it frame of mind. As a test for your own reaction, try answering this question: "How long will *I* stay with a piece of writing that I have to read without being let in on the writer's main idea?" Not long . . . correct?

A recent paper on "Technical Writing," begins

> We would like to tell you in a general way what our experience in industry has been on the subject of technical writing.

To find out what that experience has been, the reader is required to plow through 23 printed pages of text and look at 10 or 12 additional pages of example supplements. More of this writer's potential readers would take up that 23-page task if, in the beginning, they had been given a reasonably specific idea of what the author had to say. If, for instance, they had been confronted at once with a lead sentence that read

> Our experience in technical writing in industry leads us to suggest that
>
> 1.
> 2.
> 3.

Stating the main idea clearly in the beginning of the report helps to ensure unity, emphasis, and coherence for the piece of writing as a whole and makes actual writing of the short report much easier as well. The body of the writing becomes added exposition, amplification, or presentation of examples of the summarized idea of the lead.

In the process of analyzing the data you have collected for the problem you are dealing with, you are supporting your interpretations with the facts. On the basis of these interpretations of the analyzed data, general conclusions are drawn by means of logical processes of inference and reasoning, from which your recommendations grow if warranted by the situation. It is at this point that your organizational strategy can pay off for your report message's success.

Although the suggested approach already indicated is a good one for you to use in roughing out your problem solution, the finished presentation hinges on several things. Among your considerations, of course, is the reader: how familiar that person is with the subject and what the immediate reaction is likely to be to your proposed solution. If it involves a drastic change in procedure or the expenditure of a large sum of money, the reader's instant response might be negative if the solution is read first before proper background and understanding of the facts behind your proposal are made known. What the report is to be used for—as a record for the files in information accumulation, or as the basis for an immediate decision—will also have a bearing on the way your information is organized for the finished presentation.

So, basically, you have a choice of three organizational patterns, whatever the short report format called for. These are the logical, psychological, and chronological arrangements for data presentation. The *logical arrangement* of information lays the groundwork in an introduction, presents the main factors in order of importance in the discussion, and from this analysis draws conclusions and makes recommendations wherever appropriate. The *psychological arrangement* (also known as the *inverse order* of presentation and epitomized in the "peg" or "lead" line) puts the conclusions first, followed by an introductory statement setting forth the necessary identification information of the problem. This paragraph is followed by the detailed discussion of factors. (The psychological pattern of arrangement is finding increasing favor with executives whose time is especially limited.) The *chronological arrangement* presents the facts as they happened in order of time. It is slow moving and may bury important points in the middle of the report. The format, however, is suitable for periodic informational reports and for those in which an active sequence of doing a thing is important.

Variations on these three basic organizational patterns may appear in your finished letter, memo, or short report under the following headings (or others similar you devise to fit particular circumstances):

(1) Identifying information	(2) Investigation	(3) Problem
Summary statement	Analysis	Factors
The problem or objective	Interpretation	Discussion
Supporting facts	Recommendation	Conclusions
Discussion (analysis)		Recommendation
Conclusions		
Recommendation		

(4) Purpose	(5) Purpose and needs	(6) Introduction
Procedure	Conclusions	Present situation
Results	Discussion	Proposed solution
Conclusions		Conclusions
Recommendation		Recommendation

(7) Proposal	(8) Suggestion
Need	Reasons behind it
Supporting facts	Advantages
Results	Disadvantages

The universal criticism of these suggested headings, however, is that they can be used for almost any short operational report but fit none specifically. *Far more is to be gained if your captions can help tell the story for your reader.*

CHOOSING THE FORMAT FOR THE BEST PSYCHOLOGICAL APPROACH

Just as the reader, content, purpose, and use are prime considerations in initially organizing the information, so too are these elements important in selecting the physical format for channeling your message properly. You have a choice of three formats: the memorandum report, the letter report, or the short analytical report form.

The Memorandum

The term *memorandum* has in the past been taken to mean interoffice or intracompany communication. That distinction, however, is no longer valid, since some memo messages now go outside the company. It is still the least formal of the three formats and finds its greatest use in down- or cross-channel reporting in the business organization.

The memo is just another way of transacting official business by the written word when precision, care with detail, reference, and orderly handling are necessary. Oral instructions or orders too often lead to misunderstandings or rely too much on memory for getting things done properly and at the right time, and thus one resorts to memoranda to set the record straight and to pinpoint responsibility.

Generally, memos are used when the material

1. Is to be widely distributed.
2. Should be "on record," though not too permanently.
3. Is of immediate interest.
4. Contains difficult names, figures, or specifications that could be distorted over the phone.
5. Needs to have time allowed for compilation or additional research.
6. Requires a "hard copy" file.

Any memo performs one of two functions: (1) a narrative message transmission or (2) a solution to a problem. A *narrative* memo's basic purpose is to keep the recipient(s) informed, to give instructions, make requests, and the like. In that respect, it is just like an ordinary letter in text presentation.

Only the format is different. The *problem-solving memo,* as one might expect by its designation, offers a recommended solution to some problem in the organization. While the narrative message rarely makes use of internal headings for the paragraphed text, the problem-solving memo always uses effective captions. Both kinds, however, are concerned with transmitting information about one, two, or all of the following events: (1) history—what has happened, (2) status quo—what is happening, or (3) expectation—what will happen.

During the development of a difficult problem solution (long report), whether it is a survey, a manufacturing procedure or process, marketing study, or an experimental research project, certain preliminary results are achieved. These partial solutions of the complete problem are significant, and the vehicle for transmitting such results to the person in charge of the project is the memorandum report. Serving the important function of keeping the administrator informed on the progress of the work insofar as tangible and useful data become available, such memos also provide an opportunity to suggest changes or additions to the problem under study. When the final report is submitted, the reader is then somewhat familiar with the contents and is in a position to better evaluate and understand it.

Additionally, memos cover almost every conceivable facet of business, but, like all reports, deal with only one subject. Maybe you want to prepare the way for a conference—to get a quicker meeting of minds. And after the conference, a memo might be needed as a reminder for the record on what was accomplished and what is planned. Maybe you want to tell subordinates of a new policy or procedure affecting their operations. A memo establishing procedure puts the policy on record and specifies responsibility. The justification for a purchase or change in procedure is tailormade for the problem-solving memo presentation. Your response to an administrative request for information, possibly concerning some phase of operations, will likely take memo format as well. Or the memo may be a summary report for the record, or concern suggested changes on some activity just completed. It may be simply a record to the file for clarifying and confirming some agreement reached should a question about the matter arise later. Sample Form 6-1 is a narrative memo message.

There are no established types per se, for memos range all the way from a hastily hand-written message of a few lines to several pages of typed copy. The usual distinguishing elements appearing on the first page, however, either typed or printed are

DATE: _____

TO:	The reader of the report
FROM:	The writer's identification
SUBJECT:	What the report is about

Some printed memo stationery carries only these elements, in which case complete identification of reader and writer, including titles and addresses, is necessary. For memo forms within a company and on letterhead stationery,

THE UNIVERSITY OF TEXAS AT AUSTIN
COLLEGE OF BUSINESS ADMINISTRATION
AUSTIN, TEXAS 78712

Department of General Business
Business-Economics Building 600
Area Code 512, 471-3322

M E M O R A N D U M

DATE: TODAY

TO: DATA PROCESSING PERSONNEL

FROM: W. J. LORD, JR., WORKSHOP INSTRUCTOR

WILL EACH OF YOU PLEASE PROVIDE ME WITH INFORMATION ABOUT
YOUR WORK AND DIVISION RESPONSIBILITIES?

OF PARTICULAR CONCERN ARE THE TYPES OF WRITING THAT YOU ARE
REQUIRED TO DO REGULARLY, PERIODICALLY, INFREQUENTLY . . .
EVEN THAT THAT YOU HAVE DONE ON A SPECIAL, ONE-TIME BASIS.

SINCE MY ROLE IS TO HELP YOU IMPROVE YOUR WRITTEN COMMUNI-
CATION SKILLS, ANSWERS TO THE FOLLOWING QUESTIONS WILL HELP
MAKE THIS WORKSHOP MORE MEANINGFUL TO YOU:

    1. WHAT DO YOU BELIEVE IS THE SINGLE GREATEST
        PROBLEM YOU HAVE WITH WRITING?

    2. IS THERE ONE PARTICULAR TYPE OF WRITING YOU
        HAVE TO DO THAT YOU FIND DISTASTEFUL? IF SO,
        WHAT TYPE? WHAT ABOUT IT IS DISTASTEFUL?

    3. WHAT PORTION OF YOUR WORK TIME IS SPENT IN
        WRITING ACTIVITIES?

ANY ADDITIONAL POINTS THAT YOU THINK RELEVANT TO MY BEING
USEFUL TO YOU WILL BE APPRECIATED. YOUR FRANK ANSWERS AND
INFORMATION, OF COURSE, WILL BE KEPT IN STRICT CONFIDENCE.
MY AIM IS TO SHARE WITH YOU SOME VERY PRACTICAL COMMUNICA-
TION TOOLS AND TECHNIQUES.

Sample Form 6-1   A narrative memo message

only the names and titles (or departments) of reader and writer are needed for identification purposes. Some forms, too, carry the department name—printed just over the date line or otherwise balanced with the firm name—making it unnecessary to repeat this information in the FROM line. For a typical problem-solving memo, see Sample Form 6-2 for format setup.

Memos are usually not signed, although writers may add their initials at the end of the last page just below the last line of type or following their typed name on the FROM line. Some companies require all memos to have a typed signature line four or five spaces below the last line of copy and require as well the writer's penned signature over it. The signature line is used particularly in those cases in which the memo report has been dictated by someone other than the person whose name appears as originator in the FROM line, and when the writer wants to show special interest and responsibility, such as the memos used by accountants during an audit; employee evaluations; or recommendations for dismissal. No complimentary close, however, is used on memos—signed or unsigned.

Numerous variations on the memorandum headings of TO, FROM, and SUBJECT (with additions like FILE NO.—, and COPY TO:—) and variations on internal paragraph captions are quite acceptable. Your goal, however, should be to keep your report format uncluttered, attractively spaced and balanced, and easy to read and understand. Two specific memorandum "forms" deserve special attention: the playscript technique and the justification report format.

The Playscript Technique.   Some network of procedures or procedural duties—written or unwritten, simple or complex, carefully developed or casually improvised—exists in every business or organization. These activities are the step-by-step means by which all repetitive business functions are coordinated. They are the kinds of activities so often termed as "red tape" by the people involved in them—but without which no business of any size could operate.[1]

In their desire to be helpful to the departments and individuals involved, some procedure writers list together all procedural duties for an individual or department. When they have finished with Department A's functions, for example, they list separately the actions that are the responsibility of Departments B, C, D, and so on. All duties are gathered together neatly, but the *team pattern* has disappeared. And the language usually turns out to be complicated and indirect as well. Such a technique fails to show the work relationships between the involved departments or individuals. The resulting document actually is not procedural but is a mere recital of department duties as they relate to a procedural subject. Such information is useful only in the writer's work folder as "procedure description"; the procedure's basic job is to integrate "action" relationships as Figure 6-1 illustrates.

---

[1] Robert D. Hay, *Written Communications for Business Administrators* (New York: Holt, Rinehart and Winston, 1965), p. 447.

ACME MANUFACTURING CO.

Plant # 4 – Milwaukee, Wisconsin

Planning Memo No. 21
November 2, 19--

TO : Mr. Byron J. Thomas, President
Chicago Office

FROM : E. W. Eldridge, Plant Manager

SUBJECT: Installation of Time Clocks in the Milwaukee Metal Works
Division

Summary

Installation of time clocks in the Milwaukee plant would result in
greater efficiency in the Accounting Department, considerable savings
in time computations, and a reduction of tardiness among employees.

←— (1¼″) —→   ←— (1¼″) —→

Recommendations

1. Install an appropriate number of time clocks within the
   plant (one each at the four entrances).

2. Reduce the accounting department staff.

3. Conduct an employee orientation program to coincide with
   installation of the clocks.

Discussion

1. The rapid expansion in the number of employees in the last two years
   (from 500 to the present 1,012) has worked a hardship on the
   Accounting Department. Because a great number of daily reports are
   required, numerous errors have been occurring in time computations.
   As a result, wages have been incorrectly determined and workers are
   disgruntled.

   A survey of twenty-two companies of comparable size within the city
   reveals that eighteen are now using time clocks, and the others plan
   to install them soon. All companies using clocks report that errors
   in time computation have been reduced to a negligible figure.

2. Twelve of the companies using time clocks have been able to reduce
   the number of payroll clerks needed. Our own chief accountant estimates that using time clocks will allow him to reduce his staff by
   five.

   Additionally, the use of time clocks will relieve department heads

   ↑
   (1-1½″)
   ↓

Sample Form 6-2 Typical memo format for problem-solving short reports of the chore of compiling daily time reports. Each man now spends an average of 2½ hours daily on such reports, and the time saved could be profitably used by them on other job activities.

3. Several of the companies surveyed reported dissatisfaction among employees when time clocks were first installed. The employees particularly resented having to punch a clock while their immediate supervisor was not required to do so.

Only three of the companies surveyed had conducted an orientation program prior to installing the clocks. Our employees can be fully informed of the advantages accruing to them through a short orientation program. Time clocks will provide:

(1) Correct time and wages.

(2) No favoritism in reports of tardiness by supervisors.

4. No information is immediately available for determining installation costs for the clocks. The survey of companies now using clocks, however, points up the fact that savings can be made in time reporting, and greater efficiency achieved in the process.

Triple space,
followed by a
wrapup statement
for the report

Because the number of employees in each company surveyed approximates our own and these companies are profitably using clocks in their operations, we ought to expect similar results at reasonable costs.

Sample Form 6-2   Continued

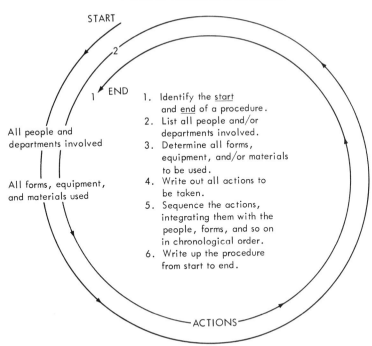

Figure 6 1   Graphic concept of a procedure: a systems cycle that sequences a team's actions

In the *Systemation Letter* by Leslie H. Matthies, executive director of the Foundation for Administrative Research, published by Systemation, Incorporated, Colorado Springs, Mr. Matthies describes a technique that he has developed to simplify procedures writing. The technique is called "the play-script procedure" and borrows ideas from the playwright. Here is how he makes it work.

Because procedures writers can only make team patterns clear when they write in normal work-step sequence, they make all the people taking part in the procedure "actors." Each actor has definite lines (work to do or steps to take)—all in a unified, single-thread sequence. In real life, the logical time sequence is natural. The "flashback" technique, often used in books or in motion pictures, is not real life. By placing the procedure in a logical time sequence, the action pattern becomes more understandable. It is merely a matter of numbering each work step in your playscript procedure in its natural order using these characteristics:

1. Tell only *how to proceed.* All other matter is out.
2. Reveal the *actors,* the people in the organization who get the action.
3. Write within a definite *systems cycle.*

4. Write in *logical time sequence,* starting with the first action, ending with the last, and numbering each step.

5. Commit a specific person to a *specific responsibility.* (This requirement pains people who really love disorder and vagueness.)

6. Start each sentence with an *active verb* such as *sends, prepares, designs, authorizes.* These are "go" words.

7. Use ample white space so the names of the actors stand out easily.

Only after you have written down the exact systems cycle or activity you plan to cover should you begin to write the procedure. Ask yourself, "Where does this action start?" That will be step 1. Then ask, "What happens after that?" That will be step 2. Continue with the next steps—all in their logical time sequence—until you have come to a point that you consider a "logical end" for that particular cycle or activity.

The playscript procedure is a format that tells people "how to proceed in an activity or to do their work." It also tells in exactly what sequence each of the "actors" does his or her part. It is possible to have actors in your procedure, use work words, and use short sentences—but still *not* have *playscript.* You must add the vital factor of *when,* for it is *the* factor that binds the people and their work or activity into a team in the sequence. When any procedure is revised, always put the revision date on it at the bottom of the first page, as in Sample Form 6-3.

Some procedures writers go out of their way to avoid mentioning people. They can't bring themselves to speak plainly and say *supervisor, manager,* or *employee.* Here is an example:

All requests will be submitted on form BGT-316, Request and Authorization for Travel Status and must be approved in accordance with Standard Practice Memorandum 113, Revised 4/7/81, Subject: Administrative Approval Authority. In all cases sufficient time must be allowed, not only for the required approvals, but for the necessary ticketing and reservation arrangements which must follow.

A procedure may require three degrees of coverage: (1) for the company, (2) for the department, and (3) for the individual. Don't mix them. If your company procedure goes to 300 people, why tell them about detailed steps that only 30 people in one department need to know. If your department procedure is of interest to 30 people, why ask those 30 people to read the detailed work steps that any *one* individual follows? Write each procedure with your exact "audience" in mind.

Other suitable subjects for playscripts are the procedures for using company cars in the firm, handling transfers of personnel from one department to another, filing hospital or accident claims, handling budget adjustments of personnel, and so on. If a policy statement governs the procedure, that statement is incorporated into the playscript technique as well, right after the subject line (see Sample Form 6-3). For a comparison of the two styles

Date: _____

Subject: Personnel Transfers

Policy: To transfer employees from one department to another when work loads change.

Responsibility	Action
Requesting Supervisor	1. Fills out and signs 3 copies of Form 457, "Transfer Request," for each employee required.
	2. Sends all copies to Budgets and Planning.
Budgets and Planning	3. Adjusts budget and work-load records.
	4. Sends all copies of Form 457 to Personnel.
Personnel	5. Finds available employees, in consultation with Budgets and Planning.
	6. Secures releasing department supervisor's signature.
	7. Adds effective transfer date to all copies of Form 457 and.
	a. Files one copy in each employee's personnel folder.
	b. Sends each No. 2 copy to requesting department.
	c. Sends each No. 3 copy to releasing department.
	8. Posts permanent records to reflect change.
Releasing Supervisor	9. Sends department personnel record folders to requesting department.
Requesting Supervisor	10. Posts permanent records to reflect change.
	11. Files employee record folders in locked personnel records cabinet.

Rev. 4/7/81

Sample Form 6-3   The playscript technique for procedures writing

of procedures writing, the listless, bogged-down prose usually characteristic of procedures writing is presented first as Sample Form 6-4 and the rewrite of the same procedure using playscript format follows as Sample Form 6-5. How Sample Form 6-4 is analyzed and converted into Sample Form 6-5 is traced for you by Mr. Matthies in the following section, "Rebuilding a Procedure."

REBUILDING A PROCEDURE

INSTRUCTIONS: To improve a procedure, first take it apart—find out what is in it. To analyze the returnable containers procedure, do the job in five steps.

Step 1—Finding the Exact Systems Cycle. Spell out the cycle. *Include all steps.*

1. *Starts* when the user decides materials are needed that will come in a container that is to be returned.
2. Tell how these items are to be bought, and who is to record them. Consider the variation that will take place if somebody changes the purchase order.
3. Tell how the containers are to be handled within the plant.
4. Cover the sequence of returning the containers to their owners.
5. *Ends* with the adjustment of charges or credits.

Logically the systems cycle starts with the discovery of the need and with the decision to buy.

Step 2—The Actors. By combing through the procedure example, you will find (expressed or implied) the following actors:

Purchasing	Using department
Matériel	Salvage & Disposal
Shipping	Employees
Transportation	Vendor
General accounting	Receiving

Step 3—The Actions. The individual actions you can find include

1. Deciding that the materials are needed.
2. Buying the materials in returnable containers.
3. Receiving the materials.
4. Telling how containers are to be handled in the department.
5. Moving the containers.
6. Keeping records on the containers.

```
                    P R O C E D U R E


Subject:  Responsibility for Returnable Containers

It has been determined advisable to establish a procedure to delineate
the manner by which the Company shall insure that internal organi-
zational units accept and discharge the responsibility for controlling
drums, reels, crates, carboys, part-boxes and/or other species of
similar containers for which the company is deemed responsible.  To
indemnify the Company and/or the vendor(s) from any subsequent for-
feiture of such equipment is the Company's objective and to further
implement such objective this procedure is established to facilitate
reimbursement for minor discrepancies as such may occur between the
book and physical inventories.

Departments that bear the aforementioned responsibiltiy include
Purchasing, Materiel, Shipping, Using Departments, Internal Transpor-
tation, Accounting and Salvage and Disposal.  The containers shall be
sorted by vendor after transporting from department out areas to the
Salvage and Disposal yard in the north end of the building until
determination has been made that lapsed time and/or quantity accumu-
lation indicates that shipment of the containers should be made.
Shipping Instructions, Form 442, shall be prepared and containers and
Shipping Instructions forwarded to the Shipping Department.

It shall be incumbent upon the user to determine first the need for
the material that must be furnished in subject containers and later,
that there is always attached to each empty returnable container, a
Delivery Tag Form 277, with each container.  When empty the container
shall be removed to an out pick up area.  Employees shall be admonished
not to cause container(s) to become irreclaimable or to re-employ such
for their original purpose.

The potentially contingent liability nature of a returnable container
should be recognized and identified as a situation in which the Company
has made a contractual agreement and which may or may not be the
property of the vendor(s) but precludes restitution should such objects
become irreclaimable, lost, damaged, non-identifiable, or otherwise
mishandled.

It is mandatory that all concerned  adhere to the explicit instruc-
tions given in DSPP 452, Issuance of Shipping Order.  Upon returning
empty returnable containers to the supplier, three copies of Packing
Sheets shall be forwarded to General Accounting pertaining to any
returnable items.  If any Change Order information has been issued,
it also shall appear on all Packing Sheets.

The control records for returnable containers and charges, as well as
Company purchases of these containers to which title has passed to
the Company (and which can be resold to vendor(s) ), shall be maintained
by General Accounting which shall submit Debit Memos or Invoices to
cover related transactions.
```

Sample Form 6-4   Prose-style, difficult-to-follow procedures writing

On all Purchase Requisitions and on all Purchase Orders, the amount of the charge or deposit of returnable containers, or purchase price (in cases where the container is a part of the total purchase price) shall be set out as a separate item on these papers including any empty gas cylinders. Further, these provisions shall apply to any subsequent Purchase Order changes. Include on such papers the return shipping address. In all cases, each returnable container shall have affixed firmly to it, a stencil or Tag, Form 227, which shall contain information attesting to the returnability of the item, giving the vendor's name, the vendor's return shipping address, the Purchase Order number, the contract or Company material number, the quantity capacity (in gallons, weight, size, pounds, feet, etc.).

It shall be compulsory to notify Purchasing and General Accounting should the vendor's Packing Sheets indicate returnable containers without Purchase Order agreement upon receipt of such containers.

Sample Form 6-4   Continued

Subject: <u>Handling Returnable Containers</u>

Responsibility   <u>Action</u>

Using Department   1. When material needed comes in a return-
                                able container, notes this fact on the
                                Purchase Requisition.

                            2. Sends approved requisition to Purchasing.

Purchasing Department   3. Shows any returnable containers as a
                                separate item on the Purchase Order.

                            4. Includes the amount of charge or deposit
                                and the vendor's return shipping address
                                on each order involving returnable con-
                                tainers.

                            4a. If, after issuing the Purchase Order,
                                changes are necessary, shows any re-
                                turnable containers as separate items
                                on the Purchase Order Change Form.

Receiving Department   5. Upon receipt of any material in a return-
                                able container, attaches a tag or uses a
                                stencil to identify the container.

                            5a. If the vendor's packing sheet shows
                                returnable containers, but the
                                Purchase Order did not, advises
                                Purchasing at once.

                            6. Sends returnable containers to using
                                department.

Using Department   7. Uses material.

                            7a. During the time the container is in
                                the using department, supervisors <u>see</u>
                                that employees don't use the con-
                                tainers, remove them, or damage them.

                            8. When container is empty, fills out and
                                attaches Delivery Tag, Form 227.

                            9. Places container in "pick-up area" adja-
                                cent to the department.

Internal Transportation   10. Moves containers to the Salvage &
                                Disposal Yard.

Salvage & Disposal   11. Sorts containers by owners, following
                                instructions on Salvage Department's
                                copy of Purchase Order.

Sample Form 6-5   Procedures revised in playscript format

12. When elapsed time limit shown on Purchase Order has been reached, or when the quantity of the containers is large enough to justify shipment, prepares Shipping Instructions, Form 442.

13. Places containers, with Shipping Instructions, with the weather proof envelope attached, in the "ship out" area.

Internal Transportation 14. Moves containers, with Shipping Instructions, to the Shipping Department.

Shipping Department 15. Includes the original Purchase Order number (or any Purchase Change Number) on the Packing Sheet, Form 86.

16. Returns containers to vendor.

17. Sends two copies of the Packing Sheet to General Accounting.

General Accounting 18. Keeps up-to-date control records on all returnable containers and on charges and deposits relating to these containers.

19. Uses Purchase Orders, Receiving Reports, Purchase Order Changes, Packing Sheets, and Shipping Instructions as source data for up-dating records.

20. Issues any required debit memos or invoices.

_____

From Issue Nos. 17 and 114, 19xx-yy.

Sample Form 6-5   Continued

7. Sorting containers by vendors.
8. Returning containers to vendors.
9. Collecting a deposit.
10. Issuing debit memos or invoices as needed.
11. Not using containers for other purposes.
12. Not damaging containers.
13. Checking containers for identification tags.
14. Identifying the containers.

In the original procedure example we found no logical time sequence. These actions were scattered. Some of the earlier actions are given after later actions. This confusing "flashback" technique makes it hard for the reader to find the real-time sequence of action.

Step 4—Subjects of the Procedure. The general subject (returnable containers) includes such items as

Drums	Reels	Gas cylinders
Crates	Carboys	Parts boxes
Barrels	Engine boxes	

Step 5—The Forms Used. By combing through the procedure example, we can identify these different forms:

Purchase order	Purchase order changes
Requisitions	Stencil
Packing sheets	Tag
Credit memos	Delivery tag
Invoices	Shipping instructions

So much for analysis. The result appears as Sample Form 6-5.

The Justification Report. As one of several patterns of the short operational memo, the justification report developed at The University of Texas[2] warrants individual treatment. This report is written to justify a decision, recommendation, or proposal. It does these three things:

1. Draws conclusions.
2. Makes recommendations.
3. Presents facts to justify them.

The justification report is a deductive presentation that gives the recommendation immediately and a summary of the most important considerations before giving detailed explanations. The emphasis of the report is on the evidence for the recommendation.

[2] W. P. Boyd, *Good Style and Form in Business Writing*, 3rd. ed. (Austin, Tex.: Hemphill's Publishing Co., 1965), pp. 19–20.

More often than not, such a report is unauthorized, and the person for whom it is intended does not know it is being prepared until it is received. It is also used when immediate action is called for and when justification is sought for a request for new equipment, construction, or a *change* in procedure.

An argumentative style of writing is tactfully followed so that the reader recognizes the validity of each argument and is ready to say at the end, "Yes, that's right." Care must be taken that the reader is never put on the defensive. Often, justifying an action or expenditure involves presenting the arguments *for* and *against*, showing that advantages far outweigh the disadvantages or vice versa—a comparative-evaluation report—evaluating two things or more to say that one is better. (An illustration of the complete justification format and content appears as Sample Form 6-6.)

The reader should be able to review the report in thirds according to individual need for conviction. The heading tells what the report is about: THE RECOMMENDATION. If further assistance or evidence of the justness of the decision is needed, the reader can review the parallel arguments *for* and *against*. If the recipient is still not convinced of the wisdom of the recommendation, the writer has a third chance at reader persuasion in an analysis of the outlined pro and con arguments—the third level.

Particular points to keep in mind as you construct the justification report are these:

1. Word the recommendation as a sentence or noun phrase, with a benefit at the beginning of it. The benefit is made up of eventualities that the decision hopes to gain or to avoid.

2. Arrange parallel columns, heading them with captions which say that one side is *for* and one *against*. These captions should say something constructive—no one- or two-word caption will do that.

3. Line up four to seven graphic-style arguments which tell your story, working significant figures into your arguments. For each one *for* you'll need a corresponding one *against* on the same issue, just as in debate.

4. After you have formulated your arguments, examine them for excess words:
   a. Cut out all the words you don't absolutely need.
   b. Eliminate any that may be inferred from context or implication.
   c. See whether you can make one forceful word take the place of several words.
   d. Use forceful words and picture-making nouns.

5. Make a center caption that tells a more complete story of your supporting arguments.
   a. Number your paragraphs to correspond to the reasons you have listed in the parallel *for* and *against* columns in the preceding section.

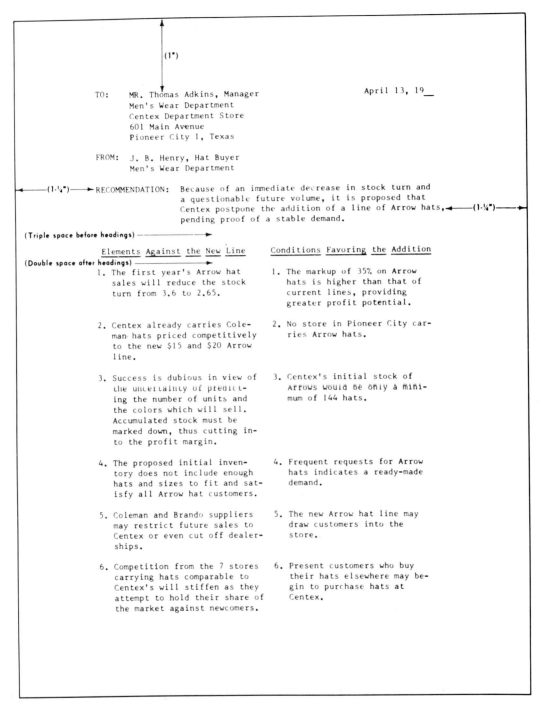

(1")

TO: MR. Thomas Adkins, Manager   April 13, 19___
       Men's Wear Department
       Centex Department Store
       601 Main Avenue
       Pioneer City 1, Texas

FROM: J. B. Henry, Hat Buyer
       Men's Wear Department

←——(1-¼")——→ RECOMMENDATION: Because of an immediate decrease in stock turn and
                              a questionable future volume, it is proposed that
                              Centex postpone the addition of a line of Arrow hats, ←——(1-¼")——→
                              pending proof of a stable demand.

(Triple space before headings) ———————————→

                Elements Against the New Line   Conditions Favoring the Addition

(Double space after headings) ———————————→

1. The first year's Arrow hat   1. The markup of 35% on Arrow
   sales will reduce the stock   hats is higher than that of
   turn from 3.6 to 2.65.   current lines, providing
                                            greater profit potential.

2. Centex already carries Cole-   2. No store in Pioneer City car-
   man hats priced competitively   ries Arrow hats.
   to the new $15 and $20 Arrow
   line.

3. Success is dubious in view of   3. Centex's initial stock of
   the uncertainty of predict-   Arrows would be only a mini-
   ing the number of units and   mum of 144 hats.
   the colors which will sell.
   Accumulated stock must be
   marked down, thus cutting into the profit margin.

4. The proposed initial inven-   4. Frequent requests for Arrow
   tory does not include enough   hats indicates a ready-made
   hats and sizes to fit and sat-   demand.
   isfy all Arrow hat customers.

5. Coleman and Brando suppliers   5. The new Arrow hat line may
   may restrict future sales to   draw customers into the
   Centex or even cut off dealer-   store.
   ships.

6. Competition from the 7 stores   6. Present customers who buy
   carrying hats comparable to   their hats elsewhere may be-
   Centex's will stiffen as they   gin to purchase hats at
   attempt to hold their share of   Centex.
   the market against newcomers.

Sample Form 6-6   Brief-form justification report, memo format

Topic sentence lead
picking up both sides

Relative Weighting of the Issues

1. Even though the 35% markup of Arrow hats is higher than that of the lines now carried, Centex must recognize the less advantageous position resulting from a decrease in stock turnover. Expected Arrow sales of $2,400 for the first year alone would result in a stock turn of 2.65, down from 3.6. The higher profit margin realized from Arrow sales would not offset the drop in stock turn.

2. In spite of the absence of competition in Arrow hats from other stores in Pioneer City, Centex would be competing with itself by bringing in this new line. The Coleman hat now carried is in the same $15 to $20 price range. If Centex must diversify it should buy a different type of hat or price range instead of introducing a competing product within the same store.

3. It is very difficult to estimate accurately the total number of Arrow hats that will sell during the first year or the colors that will be in demand in each season and price range. Accumulated stock must be carried over to the next season, resulting in extra storage costs. The late-season maneuver to clear inventory by sales and markdowns results only in cutting down the profit margin. A favorable light in this gloom is that the initial introductory order would include only a minimum of 144 hats. This limited beginning inventory would minimize losses in the event of failure.

4. In order to satisfy the expected demand for the Arrow hats, Centex must have the goods. Lately, frequent requests for Arrows have been made by customers who think the new line is superior to the hats that Centex now carries. The initial order that would bring the new line into the store is lacking in coverage. The sizes of 6-3/4, 7-1/2, and 7-5/8 have been completely left out, and all sizes to be purchased are regulars, with no thought of long-oval sizes at all. This inadequate supply will seriously affect the sales success of Arrow hats.

5. For years Centex has carried Coleman and Brando hats on good terms with the respective suppliers. With the introduction of a new line in the store, antagonism will surely develop with the present manufacturers. It is quite possible that Coleman and Brando would institute sales restrictions to Centex or even prohibit further trade at all. The present contracts with the two companies should be closely examined before buying Arrow. The new hat will surely draw customers into the store, with the possibility of their buying something besides Arrows--perhaps even Colemans or Brandos. If antagonism develops, these customers may have only one hat to buy-- the Arrow.

6. When newcomers attempt to break into a market, stiffer competition arises from the already established firms and products. In this case,

Sample Form 6-6   Continued

the 7 other stores that carry hats comparable to Centex's will surely grasp their part of the market with tighter hands. Present customers who have been buying their hats elsewhere may begin to purchase their hats at Centex, but the result will be stiffer all-round competition from the other stores concerned.

As a result of the analysis given above, it is the considered opinion of this report that the introduction of a line of Arrow hats is not now economically feasible and the step should be postponed until stable success is assured.

J. B. Henry

Summary statement or paragraph at the end not numbered

Sample Form 6-6   Continued

b. Without using a side heading, let a strong topic sentence at the first of the paragraph show what you are talking about and what you want to say about it.

c. The purpose of the third level is to weigh the conflicting evidence and elaborate on and interpret the facts of the situation. Not all the issues in the third level will come out the same way your overall decision does. *Don't load the evidence the way you think the decision should come out.* Here again you will emphasize important figures. Your coverage in the third level will be three or four times as long as the second level. Don't sell your arguments short.

d. End each weighting with a concluding sentence that carries the significance of your treatment to show which side wins.

6. Triple space and present an unnumbered sentence or paragraph to conclude and wrap up your argument.

7. Skip four to five spaces, type your name, and sign without a complimentary close.

In the third level where arguments of each side are weighed, *elaborate as fully as you feel necessary* to convince persuasively with factual evidence.

The Letter Report

Many reports—operational or evaluative—are submitted in letter form, both within an organization and in business generally. Running two to five pages in length, such a report is usually the result of a minor special investigation or of the writer's own knowledge and experience. More commonly it is a combination of both.

A direct communication from one person to another, the letter report is written more often in an informal than a formal style, though the writer-reader relationship is the determining factor. The letter report, on the whole, is set up exactly the same as any good business letter.

Following the style of a complete report in abbreviated form, the letter may, in a single sentence, state the objective, the authorization for it, the scope of the coverage, and the method used. When the letter report is long—or when the writer needs to give the reader some organizational cues to the presentation because of the number of points covered—the various sections are given center or side headings as well. The letter report is just as carefully organized as is the analytical short or long report.

Like the memo, the letter report puts the findings at or near the beginning unless the material is controversial or the reader needs certain facts before the findings will become clear. Very likely, a subject line is used also. An example letter report appears as Sample Form 6-7—making an oral report.

Because a responsible manager in any organization must function effectively through planning, organizing, acquiring, coordinating, and evaluating information before reaching a decision and putting the results into action, he or she relies on letter reports as one means of performing this control function. That is, it is one way an executive has of making sure that plans, policies, and directives are being carried out. Measuring performance

---

SAGAMO ELECTRIC CORPORATION
1910 Garner Avenue
Schnectady, New York

Public Relations Department

November 2, ----

Mr. Abe C. Murray
Midwest Divisional Manager
2121 River Road
Cleveland, Ohio

Dear Mr. Murray:

Subject: A PLAN FOR PRESENTING AN ORAL REPORT

Following the instructions you gave me on October 15, I have compiled
some timely tips on successful speech making. To serve your purpose
as material for conducting a clinic with the Regional Sales Managers in
Indianapolis in mid-December, I've set up my findings as though direct
instructions to the speaker himself.

Opening Remarks

Your opening words should make a specific bid for audience interest in
what you have to say. Here are some suggestions you may use in the
order of your choice:

1. Orient the listener to the material by working in essential background of the writer, the company involved,
   or the reason why what you'll report is important, timely,
   or novel.

2. Condition the listeners into a receptive attitude with
   an appropriate comment about the audience, a bit of humor of
   the situation, or by bringing out into the open any hostility
   the audience may feel toward you or the subject.

   Some suggested attention-getters are these:

   a. A well-told story if it applies to the subject--not
      a joke, necessarily. (Humor of the situation is better.)
   b. An illustration that strikes at the heart of the unusual
      feature of your report. (Visual aids are often helpful
      here.)
   c. The shock treatment which makes the listener realize the
      importance of the problem.
   d. An apt quotation from an authority.
   e. The establishment of elements that speaker and listeners
      have in common.
   f. The use of a thought-provoking question.

Lead-pointer Orientation

A one-sentence statement of the purpose of your report should come at the
end of the introduction: What you hope to accomplish for your listeners.

Sample Form 6-7   A short report in letter format

against standards and objectives is essential for such evaluation and may lead as well to additional action—corrective or complimentary.

Other variations on the letter report format may take the form of the management newsletter, generally in the way of some informational an-

---

Mr. Abe C. Murrary, November 2, ----, page 2

(The only time you'd skip this opening statement of purpose is when you feel sure your listeners would react unfavorably. In such case, an inductive treatment is in order.)

Essentials of Coverage

Make the listener aware that you're talking by points and which point you're on so that he may follow your organization plan. Fewer points well covered achieve a greater response than many points inadequately covered. Bear in mind the reader will try to remember what you say, and he can't remember too many points. Hunt for the interesting part of each phase and play it up. Audiences are hard to hold. A good device is to present the most important phase first and the second-most-important last.

If you're reporting an article, don't just digest the material--though that's part of it. Evaluate the information according to criteria known to the audience, according to the use which might be made of it, according to its difference from usual practice, according to the future of the material in the light of certain trends, and so on.

Winding it Up

Effectively finish your report instead of just trailing off. Make the closing vivid--the last thing you leave in the listener's mind. A summary may be necessary, but summaries are usually dull. It is better to make internal summaries at each point than to summarize the whole speech at the end. Such summarization throughout may be accomplished in transitions from one phase to another. Your close may be a vivid statement of your own reaction to the material, a quotation which aptly points up the theme of it or echoes your own viewpoint. The closing words should be the most effective in the whole speech.

Ensuring an Effective Presentation

Practice your speech, preferably in front of a mirror, until it is as effective as you can make it. You owe your audience an interesting, well-organized presentation that ends when it is supposed to. Chances are the listener would rather sleep at home!

Your managers, I believe, will find these suggested techniques helpful in our concerted drive at improving the firm's image in the year just ahead.

                    Cordially yours

                    William C. Spencer

                    William C. Spencer
                    Staff Specialist - PR

Sample Form 6-7   Continued

nouncement—concerning a demonstration the company plans to hold or almost any kind of activity involving all or some employees. The letter report, Sample Form 6-8 is an example of this type.

```
FLIC                                          MANAGEMENT LETTER

                                                   Number 11

                 19xx UNITED WAY CAMPAIGN

        The 19xx United Way Drive will be run exactly as it has been
    for several years.  It will not be necessary to have meetings as all
    of you are thoroughly familiar with the procedure.  On October 7,
    supervisors and department heads will receive pledge cards and pins.
    The booklet, Here Are the Facts, and the reminders listed here
    should assist you with the campaign in your department.

        1.   The United Way Drive will be held October 8, 9, and 10.  All
             cards should be cleared up by Wednesday, October 15.

        2.   There are no payroll deductions for United Way; however,
             pledges can be made and employees will be billed at a future
             date by the United Way Headquarters.

        3.   Supplies of blank pledge cards will be included for new hirees
             and employees recently transferred into your department.

        4.   All cards should be returned and the following notations made
             on the face of the card where they apply.

             a.  Separated.
             b.  Absent (hold card until Monday, October 13, if you feel
                 employee might return by that date).
             c.  Leave of absence.
             d.  Transferred (do not forward cards for employees
                 transferred out of department; the supervisor in
                 the new department will originate the new card).
             e.  No pledge.

        5.   Please check all cards carefully for name, address, and correct
             contribution.  If it is a future contribution, make sure the
             month or months for which the United Way should bill the
             subscriber is correct.

        6.   Cards and contributions should be delivered daily to the
             Cashier's Department, Room 121.  It will be open from 8:30 a.m.
             to 4:30 p.m. daily during the week of the campaign.

        7.   If you have questions or need additional supplies, please call
             Ray Swartout, 432.

        The quota set for Franklin Insurance employees is $25,000, the
    same as last year, and if they give as they did last year, this amount
    will be reached.  Everyone can contribute to the United Way with the
    assurance that these dollars work for a necessary, humane cause.

    September 30, 19xx                          Personnel Department

             THIS CURRENT INFORMATION IS FOR YOUR PERSONAL CONVENIENCE--
             PLEASE DO NOT POST.
```

Sample Form 6-8   A management newsletter

The Short Analytical Report

The short operational analytical report (sometimes referred to by the acronym SOAR) is concerned with decision making just as is the long, formal research endeavor. Unlike the long, formal analytical investigation, however, the short analytical report is 10 or fewer pages of text. As a rule, the short report deals with a single purpose or objective *with restricted scope*. The long, formal report (Chapters 7–11) deals comprehensively with a problem of major significance and broad scope. Thus, the short report's depth of investigation lacks the intensive, detail treatment so much a part of the longer, formal version. Prefatory and appended pages are minimal for the short report as well.

The only prefatory item usually a part of the short analytical report is the title page. It is stapled to the report proper in the top left corner. A note of transmittal (sometimes doubling as a synopsis) is clipped to the report when the writer is ready to submit the finished project to its intended reader.

As with the long, formal report, numerous research, survey, investigation, test, and evaluation problems can be studied and reported on by following an established procedure in conducting the search or test, marshaling the data, and writing the report. Yet these studies may require complex techniques in assembling the basic information, and the ensuing short reports at times will challenge the writer's ingenuity in arriving at conclusions and in making appropriate recommendations.

Summary tables, curves, diagrams, charts, and illustrations are inserted into the text at their appropriately introduced places to assist in the interpretation of the report data and in substantiating the conclusions and recommendations—just as in the long, formal report. (Occasionally, original data are placed in an appendix as well.) Original laboratory test data and field observations are used only when they are essential to the short report investigation. They then are placed in an appendix in order not to interfere with the smooth flow of thought in the report text. Frequently, the long, formal analytical report is a culmination based upon a number of short reports which were written and approved as the study of a major problem progressed toward an ultimate solution.

To make interchange of information easier and more effective, some organizations have devised particular short report formats for their employees' use. A noticeable trend in organizational practice by supervisors is definitely toward having "decision making" shared. Management theories contend that an organization is run most efficiently when there is an attempt to equalize power by letting all employees participate in the decision-making process. Authority is not a commodity to be taken for granted by supervisors and managers, contend behavioral scientists such as Renis Likert of the University of Michigan and Frederick Herzberg of the University of Utah. Supervisors have to earn respect and have to be willing to let their employees grow. As a concept, the supervisor as the absolutely autocratic (or parental) monarch has fallen into disrepute. Subordinates' input to decisions will become the accepted mode of operation in most organizational subsystems in the future, for employees are the manager's eyes, ears, and scouts! Employees, therefore, will want some say in decisions affecting their work and work conditions. They will likely insist on work that is challenging and interesting.

New employees learn quickly that when they want to sell an idea to management they must be prepared to give sound answers to such questions as why? who? how much will it cost? and what are the benefits? Learning how to write effective recommendation reports will get this idea across better than will almost any other known method. Actually, there's no better method for an employee's gaining visibility in an organization than by submitting high-quality business reports.

If you want a job that challenges your intellect and abilities and that allows you to win promotions quickly, you will have to make substantial contributions to the ongoing success of your organization. Not only will the productive employee convey crucial information in assigned and completed reports, but that individual will also be an interpreter and processor of the numerous reports that person receives. The quality of the firm's operations, therefore, ultimately hinges upon the quality of the short operational analytical reports produced. Ineffective reports are the result of overemphasis upon form. The careful writer will instead devote his or her energies to collecting information, solving problems, and presenting ideas clearly and forcefully in language readily understood by the reader(s).

Consequently, one of the most useful tools available to you is the knowledge of, and skill in,

- problem solving, and
- subsequent communication of those decisions in defensible written and oral reports.

While the patterns for developing the short report may differ in format among various private and public organizations, there are certain common characteristics all decision-making reports share.

Decision-making reports are by nature analytical; that is, a course of action is indicated for the report's recipient. That condition is true whether the report's format is a memo recommending some current-action proposal, a short operational report on some issue of monetary concern, or a long, formal research investigation whose time horizon is measured, if not in terms of years, certainly in multiple months.

An average or so-so report writer can produce a very usable document for the action-taking manager if that writer has mastered some very basic techniques and strategies in decision making. For the short operational analytical report writer, there are four basic steps in an organized approach to decision making:

1.   Defining the problem in an effort to locate the specific factor that must be changed.

2.   Defining expectations so that there is some means of measuring the decision outcome—success or failure.

3.   Developing alternative solutions to the problem to make sure that opportunities are not overlooked.

4.   Getting the decision ready for action taking by making it clearly understood to those charged with the responsibility for carrying out that decision.

Additionally, the decision-making report writer needs to keep in mind that all the factors of good communication and the essentials of sound management come into play:

1.   Accuracy and completeness in handling data.

2.   Logic and emphasis in presenting ideas.

3.   Adaptation of language and style to reader interest and preference.

4.   Restrained persuasiveness in creating credibility.

5.   Effective data display for easy reading and interpretation.

The four basic steps, the factors of good communication, and management essentials are explored in the remaining pages of this chapter.

Types of Information.   Effective managers are concerned with four types of information (Exhibit 6-1). A short analytical report can be produced readily on task, human, or maintenance factors where problems exist for every organization. To make the organization run smoothly, a manager needs constant information on these areas of control. For the fourth type—planning information—either a short operational analytical report or a long, formal report may be appropriate. These reports are infrequent: one time only or on a more periodic, special basis than are control reports.

The Five-Step Model in Problem Formulation.   Because prose and graphics are more meaningful than are mere words alone, a series of exhibits is offered in the following pages. These are designed to help your understanding of the research process, to span the spectrum of decision-making reports according to the nature of the decision to be reached, and to provide useful tools on the job. We begin with a five-step model in *problem formulation* drawn from the scientific method of research; more than just defining the problem is involved. The model is the basis for any soundly conceived analytical investigation. Each step accomplished provides a basis useful farther along the way in producing a sound decision in a quality report. All five steps are part of the preplanning phase for both the short operational analytical report writer and the long, formal report investigator.

FOUR TYPES OF INFORMATION

control $\left\{\begin{array}{l} \\ \\ \\ \end{array}\right.$

1. TASK (job, on-going)

2. HUMAN (relations)

3. MAINTENANCE (procedural, operational, legal)

4. PLANNING (mainly external, future)

Exhibit 6-1   Data sources for management reports

Step 1—stating the problem as a question to be answered by the investigation—is simply an attempt to define the problem precisely. It is inconceivable how anyone can expect to produce the most usable solution possible—for that matter even to come up with an answer for management—if the problem to be solved is not crystal clear in that reporter's mind *and from the start* of the investigation. Yet many a report writer launches out to "solve" a problem without having gone through this first essential step. If the person authorizing the report does not have a clear understanding of the problem, either, there can be nothing short of muddled results ahead for both writer and reader. To get a clear understanding of the problem, therefore, the short report writer may find the series of Exhibits 6-3 through 6-6 useful.

The *key* to defining the problem effectively, then, lies in phrasing it according to the nature of the decision you will be trying to reach (see Exhibit 6-3). As the writer you certainly will have a "feel" for the problem because of close association with it and/or the familiarity provided by a background information search. By the process of elimination, then, you can identify the *nature* of the problem decision even if it is a descriptive-analytical inquiry

A FIVE-STEP PROBLEM-FORMULATION MODEL

1. STATE THE PROBLEM AS A QUESTION TO BE ANSWERED BY THE INVESTIGATION.

2. ISOLATE THE DECISION CRITERION (THE OVERALL MEASURE THAT ULTIMATELY CONTROLS THE DECISION).

3. STATE THE WORKING HYPOTHESIS FOR THE PROBLEM.

4. DETERMINE THE COMPONENTS FOR THE DECISION CRITERION.

5. PUT THE ELEMENTS OF THE PROBLEM INTO THE SYLLOGISM FRAMEWORK:

   MAJOR PREMISE: IF A IS TRUE, B WILL OCCUR.
   MINOR PREMISE: A IS TRUE.
   CONCLUSION: THEREFORE, B WILL OCCUR.

Exhibit 6-2   Five-step research model, problem formulation

(the toughest to identify readily). For example, from what you already understand about the problem, simply ask yourself this series of questions:

1. Am I trying to decide to do something or not to do it? (If the answer to this question is "yes," then the report is the yes-no study and you'll phrase your question according to the cue for this type, Exhibit 6-4. If the answer is "no," then move to the next question.)

2. Am I trying to decide between two or more apparently equal alternatives to see which one should prove to be superior as a solution to

DEFINING THE PROBLEM . . .

THE <u>KEY</u> LIES IN PHRASING

THE PROBLEM AS A QUESTION

ACCORDING TO THE NATURE OF

THE DECISION TO BE REACHED.

NATURE OF DECISIONS . . .
IN ANALYTICAL REPORTS

1. YES-NO ANSWERS

2. COMPARATIVE-EVALUATIONS OF
   TWO OR MORE ALTERNATIVES

3. DESCRIPTIVE-ANALYTIC INQUIRIES

Exhibit 6-3   Vital phases in Step 1 of the problem formulation model

```
┌─────────────────────────────────────────────────────┐
│                                                      │
│        1.  FOR YES-NO ANSWERS . . .                  │
│                                                      │
│                                                      │
│   START THE QUESTION WITH SOME                       │
│   FORM OF THE VERB TO BE:                            │
│                                                      │
│                                                      │
│      A.  "SHOULD OR SHALL"                           │
│      B.  "WOULD OR WILL"                             │
│      C.  "IS OR ARE"                                 │
│                                                      │
│                                                      │
│   EXAMPLE: WOULD IT BE PROFITABLE                    │
│                                                      │
│   FOR ACME, INC. TO ADD X PRODUCT TO ITS             │
│                                                      │
│   WHOLESALE MERCHANDISE OFFERINGS?                   │
│                                                      │
└─────────────────────────────────────────────────────┘
```

Exhibit 6-4   Cue for phrasing yes-no studies question

the problem? (If the answer to this question is "yes," then you have a comparative-evaluation investigation and, you'll phrase your question according to the cue for time, place, or method/choice, as presented in Exhibit 6-5).

3.   If the answers to the questions raised in 1 and 2 are both negative, then, by the process of elimination, you've identified the problem as a descriptive-analytic inquiry. You will know, therefore, to begin the statement of the problem as a question to be answered by the investigation with *what*, *how*, or *why* (see Exhibit 6-6).

See how simple it is! The cue words are used here arbitrarily simply to provide you with a consistent, systematic approach to problem identification and statement. They provide a system that is easy to remember and use every time the same way until you gain skill and confidence in this approach to

2. FOR COMPARATIVE-EVALUATION STUDIES . . .

THE ALTERNATIVES ARE CONCERNED WITH TIME, PLACE, OR METHOD/CHOICE.

A. IF TIME, START THE QUESTION WITH WHEN.

EXAMPLE: WHEN IS THE IDEAL TIME TO PUT THE NEW X PRODUCT ON THE MARKET—SPRING, SUMMER, OR FALL, 19xx?

Exhibit 6-5 Cues for stating the comparative-evaluation report as a question to be investigated

problem solving. But a note of caution is in order. Problems of any of the three types can be phrased by using some of the cue words associated with some other specific decision. "What," for example, can be used in the method/choice (instead of which) of the comparative-evaluation decision (what method of acquiring a new product—making or buying—is most profitable in the long run for Ajax, Inc.?) And, within the descriptive-analytic type, additionally, a question could be phrased as a "how" rather than a "what," as a "what" instead of "how," or "why," and so on. You, therefore, may want to try stating the problem with each key word suggested to make certain that you have it worded as precisely as possible. In fact, making several tries at

B. IF <u>PLACE</u>, START THE
    QUESTION WITH <u>WHERE</u>.

EXAMPLE: <u>WHERE</u>— WESTVILLE,
CENTERVILLE, OR EASTVILLE—SHOULD
THE NEW BRANCH OF MORGAN SAVINGS
AND LOAN BE LOCATED?

C. IF <u>METHOD/CHOICE</u>, START
    THE QUESTION WITH <u>WHICH</u>.

EXAMPLE: <u>WHICH</u> METHOD OF
ACQUISITION—MANUFACTURING OR
PURCHASING—SHOULD SALEM-
HARCOURT, INC. USE TO ADD AN
ADDRESSING MACHINE TO ITS
PRODUCT LINE?

Exhibit 6-5   Continued

stating the problem as a question—whatever the nature of the decision—will
prove helpful. With each phrasing, you'll begin to sense just how well you
understand what the problem *is*.

With step 1 accomplished (the question statement later will be useful
in framing the report title), you are ready for step 2.

Step 2—isolating the decision criterion—concerns "Just what is it (singularly) that *ultimately* will be instrumental in deciding the answer to the question?" As an example, *yes*, it is *financially feasible* for Sutton Industries to acquire an auxiliary enterprise (a horizontal integration decision whose ultimate answers must prove the financial feasibility of the project). Or, Z firm's *manufacturing* product X to add it to its offerings is *superior* to buying it from another supplier *as a long-range profit producer* (a make-or-buy comparison decision whose ultimate choice must prove its long-range profit superiority over the other method).

Step 3—the working hypothesis—is a tentative answer to the problem. Characteristically, working hypotheses are stated as declarative sentences and embody—implicitly or explicitly—the decision criterion. Note the two examples just given. Both state explicitly the decision criterion and are working hypotheses as well. Some may feel that stating a tentative answer would tend to bias the report's outcome. The report writer's responsibility is to not let that happen. Thus, that same objective mind will allow the writer to change his or her belief (about the tentative answer) when the facts assembled convince to the contrary as the data are being analyzed on the way to the report's decision.

Step 4—the components—involves the writer's answering the question, "On what areas will I need to assemble evidence for the working hypothesis to hold true and for me to be able to reach a *defensible* answer?" Three or four *major* aspects of the investigation are usually sufficient; each will have its evidence—the favorable *and* the unfavorable—weighed against the decision criterion to determine the component's influence on the decision outcome.

Step 5—syllogistic reasoning[3]—brings the elements of the problem formulation into perspective. You have a chance at this stage to test the logic of your thinking and to establish not only the extent of each component's existence but the conditions under which each must exist for a favorable decision to be reached. That "B will occur" in the hypothetical syllogism equates to step 3—the working hypothesis—of your problem formulation. "If A is true" equates to step 4—*favorable* components. You thus are establishing the assumptions concerning the components that you are willing to make at this point prior to collecting data.

With the major premise established (the conditions and extent of the components), you will have also established a basis for judging the relevancy or irrelevancy of all data that you dredge up in the subsequent data search. A bit later in this discussion you'll also see how you've achieved a major step toward a well-organized report with all that has been accomplished to this point.

---

[3] The syllogism is discussed more fully in Chapter 7, p. 330.

3. FOR DESCRIPTIVE-ANALYTIC INQUIRIES . . .

THE GOAL IS TO DETERMINE THE STATUS QUO AND/OR PROBABLE FUTURE OF SOME PHENOMENON. THUS, THESE REPORTS ARE ANSWERS TO <u>WHAT</u>, <u>WHY</u>, AND/OR <u>HOW</u> QUESTIONS.

A. IF SOMETHING IS WORKING WELL FOR THE FIRM BUT PRECISELY HOW AND WHY ARE UNKNOWNS, PHRASE THE QUESTION AS <u>WHAT</u>.

EXAMPLE: <u>WHAT</u> ACCOUNTS FOR THE SUPERIOR PERFORMANCE OF TEC-CRAFT'S SUBASSEMBLY DEPARTMENT?

Exhibit 6-6   Cues for stating descriptive-analytic inquiries problem as a question to be answered by the investigation

B. IF SOMETHING IS WRONG AND MANAGEMENT WANTS TO FIND OUT AND CORRECT IT, START THE QUESTION WITH WHY.

EXAMPLE: WHY DOES STANDARD, INC. SUFFER FROM EXCESSIVE MIDDLE-MANAGEMENT TURNOVER?

C. IF THE STATUS QUO NEEDS TO BE KNOWN AS A MEANS OF PREDICTING THE FUTURE, STATE THE QUESTION AS A HOW.

EXAMPLE: HOW CAN ALLIED STORES BEST COMBAT THE ENTRENCHED COMPETITION IN CENTOWN?

Exhibit 6-6 Continued

SOAR Problem Illustrations. As an application of the model to short operational analytical report problem solving, examples of the three types of problems according to the nature of the decision to be reached are offered in the following pages. Each problem is traced through the five steps. We begin with the yes-no study.

The Westside Roofing Case.

Westside Roofing Company does repair work on a time-and-materials basis, but the average customer will not pay for a second call by the company if the original effort to repair the roof failed to be effective. This peculiarity is one of the reasons why major roofing concerns are not attracted to repair work. Obviously, roof repairs must be analyzed carefully and done by the very best craftsmen.

Westside's competitors are not usually interested in repair work for the reasons stated. And rival firms are not generally equipped to service these calls to any greater extent than is Westside. Only a few of the smaller independent concerns actually solicit repair contracts, and they usually handle this work with the services of the owner-operator and one or two additional roofers. Although these independents often consider themselves specialists in repair work, they are not often found to be reliable. Consequently, they are not generally called by the owners (customers) unless the major roofing companies are unable to get to the work.

The most important factor in handling repairs is the time normally required to inspect the roof and determine the cause of failure. At Westside, the partners, under the existing policy of management, do all the estimating, planning, inspecting, selling, purchasing, and supervising the training program. This effort does not leave time for unprofitable or policy (insured roofs) calls. In fact, it leaves little time for the actual profitable selling and supervision of the larger roofing contracts.

Repair calls coming into the office during the periods in which the company is engaged in larger, productive construction disrupt the work schedules if the repair work must be accomplished within any reasonable time. Normally, repair calls are emergencies at the time they come into the office and need to be completed without delay to serve the customer as that person needs to be served. Repair calls that are not serviced promptly will discourage property owners more quickly than will a delay on completing new roofing orders.

To service repair calls, however, Westside is forced to pull certain skilled roofers from the larger, productive jobs, using the supervisor and one roofer and dismissing three or four other workers for the time required to complete the repairs. In many cases, the rush of larger productive work is such that these people cannot be pulled out for repairs. Although the customers want and need immediate service, a forced delay of their repair needs for unreasonable periods may be necessary, even to the extent of not being able to get to the work until the customer becomes discouraged and employs someone else for the job. Westside has lost several customers that it wanted to keep because of such conditions.

Repair work, from the company's experience, could be developed into a profitable operation. But much of it is handled now at a loss in both money and customers because it is very difficult in 75 percent of the attempted repair jobs to analyze the source of the failure correctly. Necessarily, then, charges for repairs must be higher, as a percentage, than for regular contracts and larger jobs. A fair anticipated average would probably be 50 percent.

A separate repair crew would not necessarily be limited solely to this type of work. Some of the crew's time could be used in clean up, work too small for larger crews, small waterproofing jobs, and numerous other tasks requiring small crews.

One of the senior partners believes that any arrangement involving repair work should be planned as a separate function to take up the least time of the partners. The problem is tossed in your lap for investigation.

The Problem Formulation.   Remember, before taking off at high speed, to state the problem as a question to be answered by the investigation but first make sure of the *nature of the decision to be reached.* Are we trying to decide to do something or not to do it? For this case, the answer is "yes;" so you are assured that the problem is a yes-no study. Therefore, the question starts with some form of the verb *to be:*

> 1.   Should Westside Roofing Company establish a separate repair department and crew to provide better service for its customers?

This question incorporates the cause and effect behind the problem: obviously the firm is not doing a first-rate job in repair service.

What overall measure will likely control the answer to this question? Profitability? Hold on; let's think that through. Recall that the firm has said a 50-percent return. Suppose that the separate repair department and crew cannot produce a 50-percent profit. What answer are you forced to for the study? A "no," right? But suppose also that even if the separate function produced only a 25-percent return—or less—that its efficiency allowed *other areas* of the company to perform more profitably. Would you not want to produce a "yes" answer in that case. Had you set up *profit* as your decision criterion, logically you'd have to answer "no" *if* the separate repair department and crew could not produce a 50-percent payoff. Thus, it is wiser here to select some other controlling measure that will allow a positive decision to occur *if the facts lead that way.* (You recall as well that next you'll state the working hypothesis. And, it should always be a *positive,* declarative statement. Negative hypotheses are more difficult and messy to deal with.) You could, of course, qualify the profit angle . . . say, *long-range* profitability. But a better approach is to use a decision criterion that gets at the cause of the problem—customer dissatisfaction. What would relieve this situation? A more efficiently run operation maybe? Then, a workable decision criterion is

> 2.   Increased efficiency in the firm's operation.

The working hypothesis—the tentative answer to the problem (your belief about the outcome at this point)—will incorporate this decision criterion, stating it specifically or by implication:

> 3.   Establishing a separate repair department and crew will permit Westside Roofing Company to operate more efficiently, leading in turn to more profitability.

Now, from what you know about the problem, on what facets of it will you need information for this working hypothesis to hold true? These facets will be the components of the investigation—specific areas of the data search.

Certainly, you will have to look at the volume of repair work that a separate repair department and crew will be able to handle on a full-time basis. And, whether it is reasonable for the firm to think it can get that much work (market share). Another consideration is that 50-percent profit the partners think ought to be minimal. How realistic is it? Yet another concern for the investigator here would be the changes that have to occur in the firm's organization with a repair department and crew operating as a separate function. What would the organization be like? Who would be doing what? Therefore, minimal components of this problem investigation emerge as

4. A. Volume of repair work requirement/capacity.
   B. Return in relation to cost.
   C. Use of the firm's work force.

In the data search, it is conceivable that the investigator might uncover another component or two, not thought about at this point. Such discoveries can always be incorporated as the analysis proceeds. The important thing in step 4 is to set up sufficient components to give goal and direction to the data search.

With the essential four steps accomplished, we can now put the problem elements into the syllogism framework, testing our soundness of logic and establishing the conditions which the components will have to meet for a "yes" answer to occur. Here is how the syllogism would read for Westside Roofing:

5. MAJOR PREMISE: If (A) the volume of work Westside Roofing may reasonably expect to acquire is sufficient to keep a repair crew fully employed, (B) the return on investment in relation to cost is acceptable to management, and (C) maximum use and efficiency of the work force occurs, then (D) the firm should establish a separate repair department and crew to provide better service to its customers.

MINOR PREMISE: A. Sufficient and continued volume of repair work exists to warrant a separate department and crew.
"A is true"   B. Return in relation to cost is acceptable.
                 C. Proper use of the full work force results.

CONCLUSION: Therefore, (D) establishing a separate repair department and crew will permit Westside Roofing
"B will occur"   Company to serve its clientele more efficiently, leading in turn to increased profits for the firm.

The Working Outline.   As a follow-up to the completed problem formulation while it is still fresh in your mind, now is a good time to construct the *working* outline for the report. You have all the pieces needed; but a working outline is just that—*flexible*. Any part of it is subject to refinement in wording right up to the final typing . . . or to a complete replacement of a caption if that proves necessary. Constructing a working outline also allows you to understand further the problem's ramifications as you test and weigh the significance of each part. The outline's parts will appear in the short report *only as section captions*, never as a separate page of contents. Each part of the outline is a statement of writer intention at this point, another tool in the skillful researcher's intellectual resource chest.

Any good piece of writing has a beginning, a middle, and an end. A short analytical report is no exception. Its beginning is an introduction; its middle, the body; its end, a conclusion. But these labels are so general as to make them useless in a tightly organized, succinctly written, meaningful structure for either writer or reader. So let us see what elements from the problem formulation can be used where in the working outline. (Since the report will have to have a title and since the working outline is just a working tool anyway, start by formulating a title for the report right on the working outline page. The statement of the problem as a question to be answered by the investigation provides relevant information for this task. The suggestions made for structuring titles in Chapter 10 should provide ample guidelines here. Also see the title in Sample Form 6-9.)

The introduction caption (I) should state what you intend to accomplish in the report. When this caption is transferred to the report text later, it will give the reader an initial orientation to the investigation. Your cue for structuring a working caption for the introduction comes from step 2 of the problem formulation—the decision criterion. What is it that is hoped for when the problem is solved? Better operational efficiency. So incorporate that idea into the caption along with words to indicate that, indeed, this is the beginning. In parentheses below the introduction caption (and for all captions of the outline), you will need to state just what it is that you must write about when this section is put into rough draft later on. All introduction sections of short reports have specific requirements. Minimally, these are *purpose, background information, data sources*, and *factors of coverage*. (In text, the latter element is an identification for the reader of the analysis sections plus words to indicate a conclusion is drawn from these sections' findings.)

From the problem formulation, step 4 provides the body of information. The components you have determined for the short report (A, B, C) will each provide a separate section (II, III, IV) of the report analysis. These should be arranged in the working outline in the order in which they will be presented in the report. It is the same order of logic used in syllogizing these factors in the major premise of step 5. Each component caption again is phrased in terms of the writer's intention (notice in Sample Form 6-9 the participles used—*establishing, determining, assessing*) and incorporates the condition(s) that the component must meet for this factor to prove favorable to the problem solution. Parenthetically, the writer indicates what sorts of data must

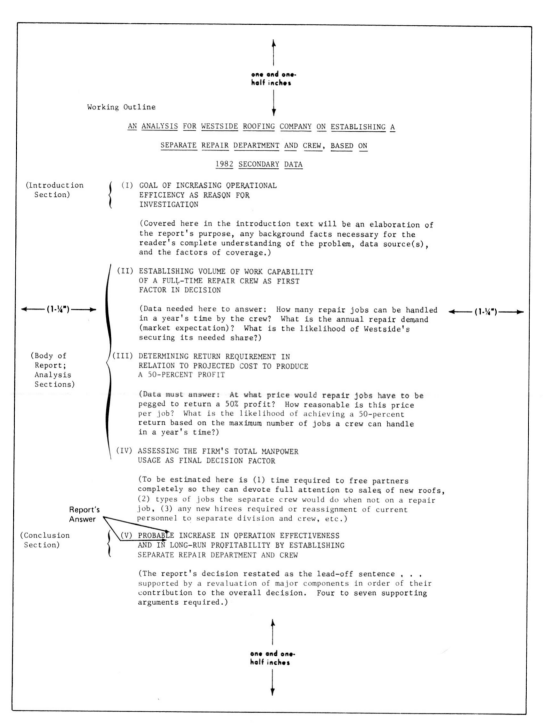

Working Outline

<u>AN</u> <u>ANALYSIS</u> <u>FOR</u> <u>WESTSIDE</u> <u>ROOFING</u> <u>COMPANY</u> <u>ON</u> <u>ESTABLISHING</u> <u>A</u>

<u>SEPARATE</u> <u>REPAIR</u> <u>DEPARTMENT</u> <u>AND</u> <u>CREW</u>, <u>BASED</u> <u>ON</u>

<u>1982 SECONDARY DATA</u>

(Introduction Section)

(I) GOAL OF INCREASING OPERATIONAL EFFICIENCY AS REASON FOR INVESTIGATION

(Covered here in the introduction text will be an elaboration of the report's purpose, any background facts necessary for the reader's complete understanding of the problem, data source(s), and the factors of coverage.)

(II) ESTABLISHING VOLUME OF WORK CAPABILITY OF A FULL-TIME REPAIR CREW AS FIRST FACTOR IN DECISION

(Data needed here to answer: How many repair jobs can be handled in a year's time by the crew? What is the annual repair demand (market expectation)? What is the likelihood of Westside's securing its needed share?)

(Body of Report; Analysis Sections)

(III) DETERMINING RETURN REQUIREMENT IN RELATION TO PROJECTED COST TO PRODUCE A 50-PERCENT PROFIT

(Data must answer: At what price would repair jobs have to be pegged to return a 50% profit? How reasonable is this price per job? What is the likelihood of achieving a 50-percent return based on the maximum number of jobs a crew can handle in a year's time?)

(IV) ASSESSING THE FIRM'S TOTAL MANPOWER USAGE AS FINAL DECISION FACTOR

(To be estimated here is (1) time required to free partners completely so they can devote full attention to sales of new roofs, (2) types of jobs the separate crew would do when not on a repair job, (3) any new hirees required or reassignment of current personnel to separate division and crew, etc.)

Report's Answer

(Conclusion Section)

(V) <u>PROBABLE INCREASE IN OPERATION EFFECTIVENESS AND IN LONG-RUN PROFITABILITY BY ESTABLISHING SEPARATE REPAIR DEPARTMENT AND CREW</u>

(The report's decision restated as the lead-off sentence . . . supported by a revaluation of major components in order of their contribution to the overall decision. Four to seven supporting arguments required.)

one and one-half inches

(1-¼")

one and one-half inches

Sample Form 6-9   Working outline for yes-no study, captions phrased as writer's intent

260

be assembled, questions the data must answer, any probabilities that must be determined, consequences of any kind that may arise, and so on. The writer's perspective should be: "What data, what aspects will I have to have answers for for the component to prove favorable?" (If in the data search that follows, of course, you cannot generate such information, that lack becomes a negative for the component. But at this stage you are positively optimistic—"A is true" remember—and you are concerned with thinking *through* all the ramifications of the question just raised.) This same approach is used for *each* of the components.

The caption for the conclusion (Part V in Sample Form 6-9) is a restatement of step 3 in the problem formulation—a recasting of the working hypothesis. It is in phrase form (unless you are using a complete sentence outline *throughout*) which reflects the anticipated answer to the problem. That is, it is a positive achievement of the goal stated in the introduction caption. You do not know at this point which component will be most influential in the decision's outcome. The parenthetical remarks, therefore, simply indicate that (1) the report's decision is restated as the leadoff sentence of the conclusion section, (2) the answer is then supported by a revaluation of the components findings, and (3) the results are put in descending order of importance of the component's contribution to the decision.

With the working outline thus completed, you have the superstructure of the report in place. What remains to be done is to assemble the data, to set them up in appropriate data displays, to analyze and interpret each piece of evidence the data search generates—its *effect*, and to determine the significance of each component as a whole. (Later in writing the conclusion, the significant aspects—major findings in the various components—will be weighed and evaluated in terms of their influence on the decision outcome.)

Note that the captions in the sample working outline use only half the writing line width—the way they will be set up in the typed report. Sample Form 6-9, therefore, is set up as though it were a page of finished report manuscript with proper margins shown. The roman numerals of the various report sections are placed in parentheses on the outline but do not appear in the finished report—no numbers, letters, or roman numerals are used with short analytical report captions as a rule. Thus it is vitally important that your wording in the caption reveal for the reader what function (introduction, factor of analysis, conclusion) each caption represents.

The Salem-Harcourt Office Equipment Problem.

Salem-Harcourt, Inc. is a manufacturer of postage meters and related pieces of office equipment. Currently, the firm accounts for 90 percent of postage meter sales; profits are quite satisfactory. The executives view with some concern, however, a detectable trend in the office equipment business of offering entire office systems to customers—not just one product or another. The company product lines currently include all the related equipment for mailing a letter (machines to fold the letter, inserters for putting it into an envelope, sealers, stampers, and the like) except an addressing machine.

The firm's executives also know that only one-third of all potential customers in the market area have installed postage meter machines. In the never-ending search for new profits, therefore, the company faces the question of whether it would be better (1) to plow a budgeted amount of money into promotion designed to more completely saturate the postage meter market or (2) to go into the addressing-machine-manufacturing business, thus adding the missing link to a complete "office systems" offering. You are asked for an answer.

The Problem Formulation.   Again, questions need to be raised as a way of determining the nature of the decision of this problem. Is the report writer here trying to decide to do something or not to do it? No. The firm has decided to do something already, but the "what" is unknown. Is the reporter trying to decide the better of two or more apparently equal alternatives as solutions to the problem. The answer is "yes;" there are two methods to choose between to determine the superior one: a comparative-evaluation study. The alternatives are not concerned with time or place. The question thus begins with *which:*

> 1.   Which method—increasing promotional expenditures or manufacturing a new, complementary product—will prove superior in generating new profits for Salem-Harcourt, Inc.?

Because the question statement incorporates the decision criterion, it isn't difficult to isolate it for this problem:

> 2.   Superior new profit generator (long range).

The working hypothesis incorporating the decision criterion would thus be

> 3.   One of the two methods is superior to the other as a generator of new profits for the firm.

To name one of the alternatives as the superior choice here may bias the researcher's approach in solving the problem. Particularly is this fact true when the number of alternatives is three or more. With only two, the situation is not so serious if one choice is selected and it does not prove out. Obviously, the other does in a thorough comparative-evaluation report. It is always the better course of action for the report writer to refrain from selecting a specific alternative in comparative-evaluation studies regardless of the number of alternatives. You guard against an unnecessarily biased approach; you remain objective for the data and subsequent analyses of facts to lead you to the proper selection.

What components would come into play to establish the superior choice in the Salem-Harcourt office equipment problem?

> 4.   A.   A comparison of the costs associated with the two courses of action.

B. A comparison of the expected rates of return from each.

C. A comparison of the time intervals necessary to realize expected return rate from each method.

D. A comparison of the probabilities of achieving expected goals (competitive considerations) of the two choices.

Thus with the elements of the comparative-evaluation study completed (steps 1–4), we can now put them through syllogistic reasoning to test the logic and completeness of our results. In syllogistic form, this problem's elements are

5. MAJOR PREMISE:	If (A) the costs for the two courses of action can be determined accurately, (B) the expected rate of return for each can be estimated reliably, (C) the time interval necessary to realize expected rate of return for each can be pinpointed, and (D) the probabilities can be established for achieving the expected goal by each method, then (E) one course of action will prove to be superior to the other in generating new profits for Salem-Harcourt, Inc.
MINOR PREMISE:	A, B, C, and D can be accomplished.
CONCLUSION:	Therefore (E), one of the two methods will emerge as superior to the other in generating new profits over the long run for Salem-Harcourt, Inc. That's the choice the firm should select.

The Working Outline. When the problem formulation is completed for the comparative-evaluation study, the report writer is ready to draw up the working outline. The same approach and reasoning as that used in the preceding yes-no investigation is again used here. Each caption has a function. The goal is indicated in the introductory caption, the writer's intention is stated for each component of the body, and the conclusion caption is an achievement of the objective indicated in the introduction. Thus, the working outline for the Salem-Harcourt comparative-evaluation decision will look something like that shown in Exhibit 6-7.

After the research has been completed, the data have been analyzed, and each analytical section has been written in rough draft, the report writer can easily recast each component caption of the working outline to show *which choice* is superior for each factor before the report is typed in final form. For example, suppose that for component A (II, Costs) the analyst reaches the subconclusion that manufacturing a complementary product will be far more costly overall than will be the cost for increased promotion expenditures—even over an extended time interval. The final version of this caption in the finished report, therefore, might read: "INCREASING PROMOTION EXPENDITURES AS LEAST COSTLY CHOICE IN GENERATING NEW PROFITS." When all four analytical sections have been completed, their captions rephrased to

A COMPARISON FOR SALEM-HARCOURT, INC., OF TWO METHODS--
INCREASING PROMOTION EXPENDITURES OR MANUFACTURING A
COMPLEMENTARY PRODUCT--TO DETERMINE THE SUPERIOR
MODE TO NEW PROFITS, BASED ON SECONDARY DATA

(I)   GOAL OF MAXIMIZING PROFIT AS

      IMPETUS BEHIND THE INVESTIGATION

      (In the report text, this Introduction section will
      expand on the study's objective; give any background
      facts needed by a reader to understand the problem;
      identify the major data source(s) and specific pro-
      cedure, if applicable; and present the elements of
      coverage. Other items beyond these four requirements
      may be added.)

(II) DETERMINING THE LEAST COSTLY OF

      THE TWO CHOICES AS THE INITIAL

      DECISION COMPONENT

      (What will have to be present if one choice is to be
      proven less costly than the other? What kinds of
      costs are associated with each method? Is one choice
      more costly in the short run? What are the total
      costs of each?)

(III) ESTIMATING THE LARGER, MORE RELIABLE

      RATE OF RETURN FROM EACH METHOD

      (What will have to be present for one method to
      prove superior to the other in rate of return?
      Price a new product would have to sell for to
      break even to produce additional revenue? Ratios
      of additional expenditures required to generate
      additional revenues?)

(IV) PINPOINTING THE CHOICE ACCORDING TO

      TIME REQUIRED TO REALIZE EXPECTED

      PROFIT

      (What will have to be present in each choice for
      the realization of profit within a reasonable
      time frame? How long to achieving impact on market
      with each? Time required to gear up manufacturing
      process before a new product could go on the market?
      etc.)

Exhibit 6-7   Working outline for comparative-evaluation short analytical report, captions phrased to
reveal writer's intent

(V) ESTABLISHING THE PROBABILITIES FOR

EXPECTED GOAL ACHIEVEMENT BY EACH

MODE

(What will have to be present if the goal achievement
probabilities are assessed for each choice? New
marketing procedure and distribution system with new
"system" product? Likelihood of achieving X-percentage
increase in sales with 90-percent of total already?
Maintenance of firm's image by either choice?
Internal/external changes necessary?)

(VI) LIKELY EMERGENCE OF ONE ALTERNATIVE

AS SUPERIOR MODE IN MAXIMIZING

OVERALL PROFIT

(Lead-off statement reiterates superior method of
new profit generator, followed by words to the effect
that the answer is supported below by significant
findings--facts and figures--from the various components in the order of their contribution to the
decision. Since the two choices will have already
been ranked according to each factor analyzed, the
conclusion is a matter of judging, weighing, indicating significance of the component in terms of the
choice ranked superior.)

Exhibit 6-7   Continued

reflect the superior choice by each factor, and the draft of the conclusion section is done, the latter's caption can also be recast to reflect the overall answer of the superior mode to maximize new profits for Salem-Harcourt.

A State Department Employee Turnover Case.

In your job as assistant director of personnel (you split your working time between Personnel and Data Processing), it is your job to ascertain why the State Budget, Systems and Planning Department (SBSP) has been losing so many of its middle-management personnel, in the last three years in particular, and what to do about the situation.

Director of Personnel Y. A. Tuttle makes available to you for study the personnel records, including exit interview statements as to why the individuals left. Since neither of you considers the reasons given as entirely dependable, you'll need to work out a scheme for determining the real difficulty. The percentages of turnover for the three years in question *are* consistently higher than the 6.5 percent average quoted for middle management for the nation by the American Management Association:

19xx (two years before)	19yy (year before)	19zz (latest year)
8.0%	10.0%	11.5%

A look at population forecasts by age levels to 19-- (six years from 19xx) adds to the seriousness of your problem:

Age Level	Percentage of 19xx Figures
10–14	+43.5%
15–19	+54.0
20–24	+25.0
25–41	−1.2
42–65	+17.0
66–	+23.0

From this forecast, it is apparent that the age level of the bulk of middle-management people is the only one for which a decrease is expected. What does that signal for the future of SBSP?

When you have analyzed the problem from every angle you can think of, it occurs to you that what really seems needed is a formalized system of administration better tailored to recognizing middle-management personnel abilities than does the current step-classification/step-advancement system. That is, a definite program for figuring out how much a person should be paid by determining what he or she is supposed to be doing, how much the job is worth to the state, and how well the person is doing it.

As a means of testing the validity of your conclusion, you informally obtained the opinions of several top-management people in various state offices on formal systems of administration for select groups of people with the promise that you would not identify them should you decide to use information they disclosed. You got a mixed bag of opinions. But you still believe that a formal system of administration is your best answer under the circumstances; so you'll write up your report and recommend that a study of special salary and administration plans be made toward the end of selecting one that will work for the State Budget, Systems and Planning Department. There of course may be other alternatives that you believe should be examined in the process of this reporting situation.

The Problem Formulation.   Once again, we begin with questions in order to decide the type of problem according to the nature of the decision to be reached. Are you trying to decide to do something or not to do it? "No"; that decision is a "given" in this case. Thus, it is not a yes-no decision problem. Are you trying to decide the superior alternative from among several choices? "No"; you don't know what alternatives are available at this point. So, it is not a comparative-evaluation study.

By elimination, therefore, you know that the nature of the decision here is the descriptive-analytic inquiry. A *what, why,* or *how* problem statement is thus in order. The entire five-step problem formulation follows in Exhibit 6-8.

The Working Outline.   When the components of the decision criterion have been determined and syllogistic reasoning of the problem elements has occurred, the working outline is ready for attention. A typical working outline for the State Budget, Systems and Planning personnel case is detailed in Exhibit 6-9.

When the report analyst has the problem formulated and its working outline structured, the overall operational pattern or framework (research design) of the project is well in hand. These two vitally important preliminary elements stipulate what information the report writer must subsequently collect for a valid answer to the problem. Additionally, the two provide a blueprint that ensures that the assembled data are relevant. The boundaries are set, the problem fenced in. Goal and direction are laid out.

Data gathering methodologies are treated in Chapter 8 and setting up displays of the data in Chapter 11. These procedures are identical for either a long or short report investigation. Many report writers would prefer skipping the task of devising the data displays under the mistaken belief that a short report does not require them. Data displays, however, must be set up for the short analytical report, just as they are for the long, formal investigation, for they are the bases from which analyses are to be drawn. Those analyses mean *writing* interpretations, pointing out relationships, trends,

1. **THE PROBLEM STATED AS A QUESTION TO BE ANSWERED BY THE INVESTIGATION:**

   WHAT CAN BE DONE TO CURTAIL THE HIGH RATE OF TURNOVER AMONG SYSTEMS, BUDGET, AND PLANNING MIDDLE-MANAGEMENT PERSONNEL?

2. **ISOLATION OF THE DECISION CRITERION:**

   AN EFFECTIVE RECOGNITION SYSTEM.

3. **STATEMENT OF THE WORKING HYPOTHESIS:**

   INSTITUTING A FORMALIZED SYSTEM OF ADMINISTRATION THAT RECOGNIZES AND REWARDS MIDDLE-MANAGEMENT PERSONNEL'S ABILITIES WILL HELP TO CURB THE TURNOVER RATE.

4. **DETERMINING COMPONENTS OF THE DECISION CRITERION:**

   A. CAUSES OF CURRENT TURNOVER.
   B. TYPES OF RECOGNITION SYSTEMS.
   C. COST EFFECTIVENESS.
   D. ADVANTAGES AND PROBLEMS OF SPECIAL-GROUP TREATMENT.

5. **PUTTING THE PROBLEM ELEMENTS THROUGH SYLLOGISTIC REASONING:**

   MAJOR PREMISE: IF (A) THE REASONS FOR CURRENT TURNOVER OF MIDDLE-MANAGEMENT PERSONNEL CAN BE PINPOINTED PRECISELY, (B) THE WORKABLE TYPES OF RECOGNITION SYSTEMS CAN BE DETERMINED, (C) PAYOUT-COST EFFECTIVENESS OF A RECOGNITION SYSTEM CAN BE ESTIMATED, AND (D) THE ADVANTAGES AND PROBLEMS OF SPECIAL-GROUP TREATMENT CAN BE ASSESSED, THEN (E) INSTITUTING A FORMALIZED SYSTEM OF ADMINISTRATION THAT RECOGNIZES AND REWARDS MIDDLE-MANAGEMENT PERSONNEL'S ABILITIES WILL HELP CURB THE TURNOVER RATE.

   MINOR PREMISE: A, B, C, and D CAN BE ACCOMPLISHED.

   CONCLUSION: THEREFORE, A RECOMMENDATION CAN BE MADE TO THE DIRECTOR OF PERSONNEL (1) THAT A SELECTION STUDY CAN BE CONDUCTED OF THE MOST LIKELY WORKABLE PLANS IN SALARY AND ADMINISTRATIVE RECOGNITION SYSTEMS AND (2) THAT THE ONE PROVING ITS SUPERIORITY FOR STATE MIDDLE-MANAGEMENT PERSONNEL BE PUT INTO OPERATION IMMEDIATELY TO CURB THE RATE OF TURNOVER.

Exhibit 6-8   Problem formulation for the descriptive-analytic inquiry

A STUDY FOR STATE SYSTEMS, BUDGET AND PLANNING TO DETERMINE STEPS FOR CURTAILING THE RATE OF MIDDLE-MANAGEMENT TURNOVER

(I) GOAL OF RETAINING VALUABLE, QUALIFIED PERSONNEL AS REASON FOR INVESTIGATION

(STATEMENT OF PURPOSE AND/OR ELABORATION OF OBJECTIVE; ANY RELEVANT BACKGROUND INFORMATION NEEDED FOR READER UNDERSTANDING OF THE PROBLEM; DATA SOURCES AND METHODOLOGY; AND COVERAGE, E.G., ORGANIZATIONAL PLAN OF REPORT.)

(II) VERIFYING THE REASONS FOR CURRENT HIGH RATE OF MIDDLE-MANAGEMENT TURNOVER

(WHAT EXIT INTERVIEWS REVEAL; PRESENT PERSONNEL'S BELIEFS OF WHY OTHERS LEFT, ETC.)

(What will have to be present to verify the reasons for current high rate of turnover?)

(III) DESCRIBING VARIOUS SYSTEMS DESIGNED TO RECOGNIZE A PERSON'S WORTH

(TYPES OF SITUATIONS PARTICULAR SYSTEMS ARE DESIGNED TO FIT; SYSTEMS CURRENTLY IN USE BY OTHER STATES; SUCCESS RATES STATES HAVE EXPERIENCED; ETC.)

(What will have to be present for a system to recognize adequately an employee's worth?)

(IV) ESTIMATING PAYOUT/COST EFFECTIVENESS OF A RECOGNITION SYSTEM

(ACTUAL DOLLAR COST ESTIMATES OF MOST LIKELY WORKABLE SYSTEMS; PROJECTION OF RETENTION RATES; PREDICTED WORKFORCE CRUNCH EFFECT; ETC.)

(What will have to be present for the additional dollars required to become cost effective?)

(V) ASSESSING THE ADVANTAGES AND DRAWBACKS OF SINGLING OUT ONE GROUP FOR SPECIAL TREATMENT

(ADVANTAGES CLAIMED; PROBLEMS LIKELY TO BE CREATED; TOP MANAGEMENT'S VIEWS TOWARD SUCH A PROGRAM; ETC.)

(What will have to be present for the advantages to outweigh the drawbacks in singling out a group for special treatment?)

Exhibit 6-9 Working outline for the descriptive-analytic inquiry

(VI)   **RETENTION OF MIDDLE-MANAGEMENT PERSONNEL
THROUGH SELECTION STUDY AND CONSEQUENT
IMPLEMENTATION OF A WORKABLE SYSTEM THAT
REWARDS THEIR EFFORTS**

(STATEMENT OF THE OVERALL CONCLUSION
FIRST THING; FOLLOWED UP WITH A
REVALUATION OF COMPONENT ANALYSES--
SPECIFIC FACTS AND FIGURES--ARRANGED
IN DESCENDING ORDER OF THEIR
CONTRIBUTION TO THE DECISION;
STATEMENT OF RECOMMENDATIONS)

Exhibit 6-9   Continued

exceptions, highlights, lowlights, averages—significant information, defensible information. *Writing!* But the writing discipline is a problem area for many also. Emory offers these points,[4] summarized from the work of Barzun and Graff:

1. Do not wait until you have gathered all your material before starting to write. Nothing adds to inertia like a mass of notes, the earliest of which recede in the mists of foregone time. On the contrary, begin drafting your ideas as soon as some portion of the topic appears to hang together in your mind.

2. Do not be afraid of writing down something that you think may have to be changed. Paper is not granite, and in a first draft you are not carving eternal words in stone.

3. Do not hesitate to write in any order those sections of your total work that seem to have grown ripe in your mind.

4. Once you start writing keep going. Resist the temptation to get up and verify a fact. Leave it blank. The same holds true for the word or phrase that refuses to come to mind. It will arise much more easily on revision, and the economy, in time and momentum, is incalculable.

5. When you get stuck in the middle of a stretch of writing, reread your last two or three pages and see if continuity of thought will not propel you past dead center.

6. Since the right openings for sections or chapters are difficult, special attention must be paid to them. As you collect your materials, be on the watch for ideas or facts or even words that would make a good beginning.

7. Often the rereading of an opening paragraph of writing will seem alien to what follows. What has happened is that the first paragraph was simply the warming-up, and the true beginning was set down in the second. You were priming the pump, choking the car, and the sputter is of no consequence. Discard that first paragraph.

8. A writer should become aware of his or her peculiarities and preferences regarding the mechanics of composing as soon as possible, namely, pen versus typewriter, size and color of paper, physical arrangement of notes and books, and even what kind of clothes and postures to assume for work. This advice is consistent with our underlying principle: indulge yourself so that you will have no excuse for putting off the task.

---

[4] C. William Emory, *Business Research Methods* (Homewood, Ill.: Richard D. Irwin, Inc., 1976), pp. 428–429, citing *The Modern Researcher*, rev ed. (New York: Harcourt Brace Jovanovich, 1970).

Readability Rules

Additionally, a number of suggestions have been distilled over the years to help ensure any business communication message's effectiveness. They are presented by way of chapter summary here for your guidance in writing short operational reports.

1. Tell your reader why you wrote the report and give the facts needed to focus his or her mind on the problem. A good business report gets down to business quickly. If your first sentences are reflections about the problem, you are probably wasting the reader's time. Even the most unbiased reader gets an impression—good or bad—from the first page read in the report. The point of contact must always be logically established.

2. Write as you would if you were doing a news story. Pack the condensed story in as rapidly as you can put it across. C. R. Anderson, long recognized as a leading authority in report writing, years ago drew the analogy of the short operational report and the news story. He states,

> Your short report has lots in common with a news story. Both should be completely organized, both add up the facts on both sides, and a balance is struck to indicate the stronger. Human interest is essential to news stories and frequently adds interest to reports. The writer stands midway between the facts and the reader and gets them together. Much research and checking go into both . . . sifting, sorting, condensing, and explaining. Both the news story and the report are adapted to the reader.[5]

3. Vary your sentence structure and length. Keep a balance between long and short sentences, and try for an average of no more than 17 to 20 words per sentence.

4. Avoid an arbitrary, bossy tone. Your statements should be written simply, tactfully. In this sentence—

> Beginning Wednesday, November 5, all visitors will be barred during working hours.

—the word *barred* is psychologically bad and defeats whatever purpose management may have had in mind for instituting the policy.

5. Avoid negative wording that tends always to generate opposition—to pit one department against another. For example,

> Complaints have come from the Purchasing Department that work is being delayed there because of failures of requests to come through promptly from your division.

[5] C. R. Anderson, A. G. Saunders, and F. W. Weeks, *Business Reports*, 3rd ed. (New York: McGraw-Hill Book Company, 1957), p. 85.

6. Keep paragraphs short—eight to ten typewritten lines should be about maximum. Margins should be ample, pages uncrowded, to make reading easier.

7. Use common, familiar words—not farfetched ones. When you must include technical or difficult terms, always define them.

8. Use concrete words, not abstract terms. What is *practical* for one reader may be impractical for another, but if you set forth the facts involved, your reader can draw the abstraction of *practicality* independently.

9. Adapt to your reader. Using the first person is common in some short reports, although this use is governed by the relationship between writer and reader, as well as by policies in the organization.

10. Let your finished report "incubate" for awhile—overnight if possible. Then revise and rewrite, cutting excess words and irrelevant information.

11. Watch for these specific weaknesses as you write your short report, especially as you edit it:

a. Broad generalizations not related to the specific problem.

b. Generalizations based on the writer's own limited experience rather than the available facts.

c. Mere repetition of the facts of the problem.

d. Listing of pros and cons without appraisals.

e. One-sided argumentation, in which the only points stressed are those favorable to the writer's decision.

f. Failure to consider one or more of the major areas of the problem.

g. Failure to consider the problem in relation to other problems.

h. Too precise estimates of needs, instead of recognition that projections into the future are at best close approximations.

i. Naïve acceptance of statements without any critical appraisal or reading between the lines.

j. Oversimplification.

12. Write to express your thoughts, not impress your reader with how really educated you are. The reader will *know*, understand, be convinced by, and act on the basis of your short operational report message.

Although there is no guarantee that any short operational report you write will result as a successful communication in every instance, you can increase its probability by using the suggestions, techniques, and approaches discussed in this chapter. They have been tested—their merit proved. Sample Form 6-10 is a fairly complete short operational analytical report using the techniques of directness and conciseness discussed in this portion of the text.

AN ANALYSIS FOR NATIONAL OIL COMPANY OF THE REASONS FOR

VARIANCES IN VOLUME AMONG ITS SERVICE STATIONS,

BASED ON A 19-STATE-AREA SURVEY

Submitted to

Mr. John P. Baker, Vice President

by

Ray H. Stephens, Research Associate

Philadelphia, Pennsylvania

October 21, 19xx

Sample Form 6-10   A short analytical report

AN ANALYSIS FOR NATIONAL OIL COMPANY OF THE REASONS FOR

VARIANCES IN VOLUME AMONG ITS SERVICE STATIONS,

BASED ON A 19-STATE-AREA SURVEY

GOAL OF DETERMINING WHY SOME
STATIONS ARE SUCCESSFUL AND OTHERS   *(Point of Contact--elaboration*
ARE NOT AS BASIS FOR STUDY   *on report's objective)*

To determine why some National Oil Company service stations
enjoy high-volume sales while other, very similar stations do   *(Purpose)*
not, this report compares and analyzes the operations of 200
manager-owned NATOCO stations in the 19-state area served by
the company. Authorized on September 16, 19xx, by Mr. John
P. Baker, Vice President in charge of sales, this report, submitted on October 21, 19xx, was prepared by Ray H. Stephens,
Research Associate, Home Office.

(Methodology
& Data
Sources) As a means of collecting the data for analysis,[a] the stations
were first observed by members of a research team who, posing as customers, visited 100 successful (high volume) and
100 unsuccessful (low volume) stations. These were selected
by Mr. Baker on the basis of their similar physical facilities
and locations. All are about equal in traffic flow passing
the station; all are predominantly community stations; that
is, they are not on main highways; and all are nearly equal
in number and nearness of competitors. Following their observations as customers, the team members conducted interviews
with the individual station managers to get information on the
managers themselves, the employees, and specific phases of
station operations. *(Organizational plan of the report)*

Four main aspects of all stations are examined in this report.
First, the stations are compared on the basis of their outward characteristics--the first things customers see. Next,
the comparison centers on the ability of the personnel at each
station to satisfy customer demands. Then, the services and
accessories offered by the stations are evaluated in terms of
their being what customers expect. Finally the extent of
station promotional activities are analyzed regarding the
stations' effectiveness in attracting customers. Conclusions
are drawn from the significant findings revealed by these
four area comparisons to account for the differences in station performances.

(Concluding statement for Introductory section,
giving it a sense of completeness)

[a]
 The data on which this report is based were generated by Dr. Raymond V. Lesikar.

1

Sample Form 6-10   Continued

DISPARITY IN STATIONS' OUTWARDLY
OBSERVED ASPECTS AS A POSITIVE
MEASURE OF CUSTOMER PREFERENCE

(Topic-sentence lead giving signifi-cance of first component)

Since the physical appearance of a station itself forms the basis for the customer's first impression, it is logical to focus first on the station's outwardly observable attributes. Highly significant is the fact that no correlation exists between the age of the building and a station's ability to attract customers (Table 1).

(Supporting Data Display)

TABLE 1

COMPARISON OF NATOCO STATIONS' PHYSICAL APPEARANCE
INSTRUMENTAL IN CUSTOMER FIRST IMPRESSIONS

Area of Observation	Percentage of Stations*	
	Successful	Unsuccessful
Overall Appearance:		
Clean, neat	82	10
Fair	18	62
Dirty	0	28
Stock Display:		
Neat, orderly	68	11
Fair	30	63
Poorly arranged	2	26
Restrooms:		
Clean	92	22
Fair	8	47
Dirty	0	31
Age of Building:		
Less than 5 years old	31	33
5 - 10 years of age	41	47
Over 10 years old	28	29
Pricing Policy:		
Higher than others in area	9	23
Equal to stations in area	74	47
Lower than others in area	17	30

*Based on observations of 100 high-volume and 100 low-volume stations.

SOURCE: Survey data

Sample Form 6-10 Continued

(Topic Sentence) → Of all service stations less than 5 years old, about one in three is successful; one in three is not. In fact, the age range of the buildings and the percentage of successful and unsuccessful stations within each age range are very evenly distributed. These facts stongly contradict the popular assumption that a newer facility makes the difference in attracting customers and increasing sales.

(Topic Sentence) → The marked disparity in other physical aspects of the stations, however, does show a definite relationship to sales volume. Eight in 10 of the successful stations observed received the highest rating given for overall cleanliness; only one in 10 of the unsuccessful is so ranked. Nine of 10 successful stations have clean restrooms. None are dirty. To the contrary, three-fourths of the unsuccessful stations have dirty--or only fairly clean--restrooms.

(Elaboration on topic sentence-- supporting figures)

(Topic Sentence) → An orderly stock display is yet another appearance characteristic differentiating the high-volume and low-volume stations. A majority of the successful ones have neat and orderly stock displays. Only about 1 in 10 of the unsuccessful operations rate the same way . . . a sharp contrast between the two.

(Topic Sentence) → Even pricing policies do not explain the differences between high- and low-volume stations' ability to attract customers . . . whether prices were displayed on a large signboard or only on the pumps. Three of every 4 successful stations meet the going price in the area (staying highly competitive). In contrast, almost twice as many low-volume as high-volume producers undercut going-rate prices.

(Concluding paragraph for first component) → Thus, apparently there is little or no connection between newness of the facility, the station's pricing policy, and customer preference in service stations. A neat, orderly, and clean facility, on the other hand, is an associated characteristic of successful stations. The degree of cleanliness, neatness, and orderliness clearly set the high- and low-volume stations apart.

(Wrap-up Statement for first section)

DIFFERENCE IN PERSONNEL'S
ABILITY TO PLEASE CUSTOMERS AS
FURTHER DISTINGUISHING FACTOR

(Topic-sentence lead giving most significant finding of second component) → From their observations, researchers posing as customers found attendants at successful stations markedly more courteous than those at the unsuccessful stations. Only 6 percent of high-volume stations employ personnel who could be described as less-than-courteous. More than 9 of every 10 high-volume station attendants are courteous or unusually so. In contrast, fewer than 3 in 10 low-volume station attendants are rated high in courtesy; more than 3 in 10

Sample Form 6-10   Continued

are actually unpleasant. This wide difference in personality traits seemingly directly affects the ability of the stations to satisfy their customers.

(Interpretation)

When the backgrounds of the attendants are examined for qualifications, several significant aspects emerge (Table 2). Of the attendants employed at the successful stations, 66 percent are youthful (21-30 years of age). Unsuccessful stations show a marked preference toward older--perhaps more mature--attendants; more than half of their personnel are between 31 and 50 years of age.

TABLE 2

(Supporting Data Display)

COMPARISON OF QUALIFICATIONS OF NATOCO SERVICE STATION
ATTENDANTS AND MANAGERS

Area of Observation	Percentage of Attendants[a]		Percentage of Managers[b]	
	Successful	Unsuccessful	Successful	Unsuccessful
Grades on NATOCO's Aptitude Test:				
Below 40 (not qualified)	10	34	0	9
40 - 59 (acceptable)	47	57	17	43
60 - 79 (good)	36	7	42	30
80 - 100 (outstanding)	7	2	41	18
Age:				
Under 21	13	14	0	3
21 - 30	66	33	14	31
31 - 40	17	31	51	36
41 - 50	4	20	19	20
Over 50	0	2	16	10
Experience:				
Less than 1 year	16	21	0	1
1 to 5 years	49	26	52	41
6 to 10 years	27	39	36	38
Over 10 years	8	14	12	20
Education:				
Grade school or less	18	27	2	12
Some high school	43	57	28	44
High school graduate	39	16	56	42
Some college	0	0	14	2

[a]Based on 216 at successful stations; 184 at unsuccessful stations.

[b]Based on 100 successful and 100 unsuccessful stations.

SOURCE: Interviews with station managers.

Sample Form 6-10   Continued

Attendants at successful stations are markedly better educated than are those at low-volume stations. Not surprisingly therefore are their better scores on aptitude tests as well. Only 1 person in 10 scoring in the unqualified range is employed at high-volume stations; a third of those employed at low-volume stations scored below the acceptable level.

(Analysis & Interpretation)

For station managers, the results of the company's aptitude test again demonstrate a correlation between ability and success. The picture of station manager qualification is a replica of the attendants' profile: Successful station managers are characterized as more mature than low-volume station managers, better educated, about equally experienced, and none are unqualified as measured by scores on aptitude tests. Almost 1 in 10 managers at low-volume stations scored in the unqualified range and an additional 4 in 10 are just barely acceptable. The successful stations, then, are run by better qualified managers than are unsuccessful stations. As well, they are staffed with highly qualified attendants.

(Concluding Statement)

CONTRASTS IN SERVICES AND
ACCESSORIES OFFERED AS THIRD
MEASURE OF HIGH-VOLUME SALES

(Topic-sentence lead giving significance of subject matter)

Since a large part of a service station's business is service, it is important to examine the areas of customer services and accessories to determine their effect, if any, on sales volume. Successful stations lead unsuccessful stations in giving every type of driveway service normally expected by the customer (Table 3). Apart from cleaning windshields, the most-often performed services are battery, oil, and water checks. These services are provided by the successful stations for 7 customers out of 10. Fewer than 3 of every 10 customers receive such service at low-volume stations. Apparently, customers prefer to trade where their cars are automatically checked whenever they pull in for service.

(Analysis & Interpretation)

A definite distinction exists between the two classes of stations for off-driveway services, also. The line of demarcation between light and heavy auto services is clearly drawn for the successful stations. Services such as tune-ups, fuel system and carburetor services, and heavy repairs are not available in more than 8 of every 10 successful stations. Instead, those services that can be performed quickly and easily, such as cooling system inspections, wheel, shock, and brake checks, are offered, and by every other high-volume station. A third of the low-volume stations, on the other hand, tend more toward garage/service station combinations, offering all types of heavy work.

Sample Form 6-10   Continued

TABLE 3

COMPARISON OF NATOCO SERVICE STATIONS
BY TYPE OF SERVICE OFFERED

(Supporting data display for 3rd component)

Type of Service	Percentage of Stations*	
	Successful	Unsuccessful
Driveway Services		
Windshield cleaned	99	78
Floorboard swept	18	3
Oil checked	89	62
Battery checked	74	27
Tires checked	71	30
Water checked	84	38
Off-driveway Services		
Light work:		
Cooling system	62	34
Wheel and shock	62	34
Brake	58	40
Heavy Work:		
Tune-up	14	38
Fuel system	15	34
Carburetor	14	32
Other heavy repair	3	27

*Based on 100 successful and 100 unsuccessful stations

SOURCE: Survey data

Additionally, a surprisingly significant distinction between
high- and low-volume stations occurs in four service-
complementing accessories. Eighty-four percent of successful
stations offer seat covers, floor mats, and tire chains.
Almost 100% of such stations have mirrors in stock. These
four items are available at less than a third of the low-
volume stations. The reason for the popularity of these four
items is unclear. Whatever the reason, the stations that sell
them are definitely more successful than those that do not.
Characteristically, then, high-volume stations limit auto

(Concluding statements)

Sample Form 6-10   Continued

service to routine maintenance. They carry a line of accessories that customers normally expect to find available . . . items specifically shopped for or bought on impulse.

EXTENT OF PROMOTIONAL ACTIVITIES'
INFLUENCE ON SUCCESS OF STATIONS

(Topic-sentence lead giving significant finding)

Two significant aspects of annual advertising expenditures by type of station emerge. First, the total amount of money spent on advertising has little or no influence on sales volume (Table 4). A majority of both successful (57%) and unsuccessful (89%) stations spend $600 or less annually on promotional efforts. In each of the $200-increment ranges up to $600, the percentages of high- and low-volume stations are fairly evenly divided except for the $200-400 range. Though total promotion expenditures are not large for either type station, it is true that three to four times as many high-volume as low-volume producers spend more than $600 each year. But even the expenditures in excess of $600 annually were insufficient to reverse the low-volume sales experienced by 11 percent of such stations.

(Analysis & Interpretation)

TABLE 4

COMPARISON OF TOTAL ANNUAL ADVERTISING EXPENDITURES
BY TYPE OF SERVICE STATION

(Supporting Data Display)

Range of Expenditures	Percentage of Stations*	
	Successful	Unsuccessful
Under $ 200	22	31
$201 - 400	14	36
401 - 600	21	22
601 - 800	17	3
801 - 1000	16	5
Over $1000	10	3

*Based on 100 successful and 100 unsuccessful stations

SOURCE: Survey data

(Topic Sentence)

The second important finding from promotional activities is that the medium employed does not equate with success. Both classes of stations concentrate efforts on personal contact with customers. The most-often-used methods--direct mail and novelty items--are fairly proportional for both types of stations (68 percent high-volume and 48 percent low-volume stations use direct-mail campaigns). Similarly, stations that

Sample Form 6-10   Continued

distribute pens and calendars to their customers are fairly
equal in numbers between high- and low-volume stations (64 and
53 percent, respectively). No real correlation exists between
type of advertising used and the ensuing success--or lack of
it.

The fact that these stations are all community stations helps
explain why the amount spent on advertising has little influence on sales. People in a community know the station is
there already; it is customary to trade in one's own neighborhood. Novelties and direct-mail are ineffective tools for
pulling in a lot of new customers to the area. They are token
appreciations to customers and an attempt by the user-stations
to keep the same customers coming back.

Bonuses such as trading stamps are a regular enticement used
by retailers to bring in new customers or to hold on to regular ones. But only a third of the successful stations at most
use them. Still, that is more than twice the number of unsuccessful stations that use stamps. Discounts are available
at only 10 percent of the high-volume stations; 11 percent of
unsuccessful stations offer discount purchasing. These facts
clearly indicate that such promotional efforts do not directly
account for differences in volume sales of the two types of
stations.

The lone hint at a correlation between high-volume sales and
promotion activities occurs in participation in company-
sponsored contests. Better than 9 of every 10 high-volume
stations take part. Only 6 in 10 low-volume producers do.
Yet, the fact that such a large percentage of unsuccessful
stations participate diminishes the positive relationship that
might have helped explain the differences in sales volume.

(Concluding Statement) Apparently, then, none of the promotional activities, nor advertising methods, nor amount of expenditures are instrumental
in determining sales volume for a particular station.

(Analysis & Interpretation)

ABILITY TO MEET CUSTOMER EXPECTATIONS
AS REASON FOR HIGH-VOLUME STATIONS'
SALES SUCCESS

(Report's Conclusion-- Answer to the problem) The overall distinguishing factor between successful and unsuccessful NATOCO stations is the ability of the high-volume
stations to provide what customers expect. High-volume stations' physical appearance, personnel, and services set them
apart from low-volume stations as the following facts indicate.

(Summary of reasons why)

Overall cleanliness and orderliness--those outward, prime appearance aspects that influence customers to stop in--are the
trademarks of high-volume stations. Eighty percent of them
rate at the top in cleanliness (none have dirty restrooms)

Sample Form 6-10   Continued

and all are orderly in stock and equipment displays. Low-volume stations, on the other hand, are dirty or only fairly clean (75 percent); disarray is the impression given by these stations. Neither newness of the facility nor pricing policies are instrumental in distinguishing low-volume stations from high-volume producers as to variances in success.

Courtesy of the attendant is a characteristic associated with high-volume stations as well. Ninety percent of high-volume station attendants are rated such. Only a third of low-volume station attendants are courteous to customers; an equal number are actually unpleasant in manner. No customer wants to be treated to that by choice. The older, less-well-educated attendants typically employed at low-volume stations are perhaps set in their ways, less likely to hustle than are the younger, more eager-to-please attendants at high-volume stations. Only 10 percent of successful station attendants scored in the unqualified range on company aptitude tests. One-third of those employed at low-volume stations rank as "unqualified" by the same tests.

Managers at both type stations present a profile like that of attendants. High-volume station managers' aptitude test scores demonstrate a correlation between ability and success. These individuals are more mature, better educated, and qualified by aptitude tests than are low-volume station managers. Ten percent of the managers employed at low-volume stations are totally unqualified. Another 40 percent just barely rate the "acceptable" level. Good management obviously makes a big difference for those stations with large sales volume.

Customers expect normal driveway services--windshields wiped, battery and oil checked, and so on--and they get it at high-volume stations 75 to 95 percent of the time. Not so at low-volume dealers where fewer than 3 in 10 customers are given such service. Off-driveway services for the two types of stations differ drastically, also. The majority of high-volume stations provide only light service (brake, cooling system, wheel, and shock checks); few offer any heavy garage-type work. Only about a third of the low-volume stations perform the usually expected light service, but the same proportion engage in heavy work . . . a garage rather than service station operation.

More than eight in every 10 successful stations also carry a line of accessories which customers expect to find when such items are needed. That is not the case with low-volume stations where few, if any, accessory items are available for customers.

Despite the fact that advertising is supposed to increase sales for the user, promotion activities wield little influence in accounting for the disparity in sales of low- and

(Significant findings and figures re-evaluated & presented in descending order of their importance to report's decision)

Sample Form 6-10   Continued

high-volume stations. A majority of all stations--high and low-volume--spend $600 or less annually in promotional efforts. The medium used--direct-mail, flyers, etcetera--seems to make no difference in attracting customers to the station. Twice as many high-volume stations as low-volume ones use trading stamps, but only a third of all stations use them. Though 90 percent of successful and 60 percent of unsuccessful stations participate in company-sponsored contests, this activity does not explain the difference between the two in terms of sales either.

(Reiteration of the answer, giving a sense of completeness to the report)

The overall conclusion reached in this report, therefore, is that successful stations differ from low-volume stations in three significant ways, and these differences account for high-volume sales. High-volume stations--

1. Are staffed with highly qualified managers who employ customer-oriented attendants,

2. Create favorable first impressions on the customers with clean, orderly facilities, and price their products competitively, and

3. Provide customarily expected services and accessory items for potential customers.

Sample Form 6-10   Continued

CHECKLIST FOR THE JUSTIFICATION
REPORT

Wording of Recommendation

JR 10   Word the recommendation in a sentence or noun phrase, with a benefit at the beginning of it.

11   The quality of your benefit needs improvement.

12   Pare your wording for clarity, conciseness—no extra words.

13   Make the recommendation complete.

Coverage

JR 20   Line up four to seven graphic arguments which tell your story.

21   The quality of your arguments is judged on

   a.   Suitable talking captions.

   b.   Adequate coverage of the main issues.

   c.   Arguments exclusive, nonoverlapping.

   d.   Sufficient figures, concrete illustrations to play up the points.

   e.   Logic.

   f.   Unbiased, equally *for* and *against.*

   g.   Parallel structure.

22   The quality of your exposition is evaluated on

   a.   Suitable talking captions.

   b.   Direct topic sentence introduction of each issue.

   c.   Full use of supporting figures.

   d.   Adequate illustrative material to cover the points raised.

   e.   Quality of summary statements at the end of each issue to show which side wins.

   f.   Quality of the final summation.

Format and Style

JR 40   Arrangement of memo heading properly includes

   a.   Date.

   b.   Full identification of reader (TO line).

   c.   Full identification of writer (FROM line).

41   Triple space before and double space after centered heads.

42.   Set up the parallel columns in proper arrangement: one argument *for,* one *against* for each point at issue.

43   Arrange spacing so that the number against starts on the same typing line as the corresponding number for.

44   Cut out all words you don't absolutely need.

45   Eliminate any word that may be inferred from context or implication.

46   Use forceful words and picture-making nouns.

47   Side margins are 1¼ inches; top and bottom, 1 inch.

48   Number successive pages on line five at the right-hand margin; double space and continue writing.

49   Work for better coherence, variety, originality, force in your presentation.

                Your Grade _____

CHECKLIST FOR THE SHORT
ANALYTICAL REPORT

Transmittal/Synopsis Functions

Delivery/quality of decision and supportive evidence, smoothness, tone, style; adequate support; arrangement.

TS 1   This instrument delivers your work; make your opening words say so, direct style.

2   Synopsis function starts answer to the problem early in the opening as well.

3   In case recommendations are made, the principal recommendation should be introduced early also.

4   Let your attitude and treatment create an interest in the reading of the report.

5   Brief essential phases of the introduction for proper reader orientation.

6   Condense each of the component areas proportionately, relating findings to the problem.

7   Include essential figures and concrete highlights—the essence of the investigation should be here, independent of the report itself.

8   Abstract the conclusion section proportionately.

9   Close your synopsis with an idea that gives a sense of completeness to your presentation. You seem to trail off.

10   Your coverage is scant.

11   This version is too generalized for the reader to get the essential reasoning behind your decision.

12   The closure for the letter should be one of warmth, sincerity, naturalness.

13   Tone needs improvement.

14   Writing style needs attention.

Your score _____ (40)

Title Page

Proper coverage; identification details; arrangement; economy of word usage.

Your score _____ (10)

Problem Identification: Introduction

Logic in point of contact; purpose/objective statement clear; necessary background for even a casual reader's understanding; data sources/methodology explained, limitations; elements of coverage in investigation; style; smoothness; arrangement.

PI 1   Caption, properly phrased, should be descriptive of introduction section.

2   Point of contact with the reader lacks logic.

3   State purpose clearly; why the need for study.

4   Identify data sources; assumptions.

5   Your method of data treatment needs to be explained.

6   Identify the components of coverage, weaving in the reasoning for their choice.

7   Indicate conclusions to be drawn from component analyses—some statement to give your introduction section a sense of completeness.

8   Inadequate coverage for proper problem orientation.

9   Wordy, drawn out.

Your score _____ (20)

Critical Discussion Areas

Topic sentence leads; adequate coverage; logical development of points; adequate support for generalizations; introductory statements where needed; unbiased presentation; full disclosure and use of figures, if applicable; transactions; comprehensiveness and clarity of subdecision or summary statements; documentation; format and style.

CDA 1   Captions should be phrased descriptively to identify component *and* intention of each section.

2   Topic sentence lead *introduces* the section either by identifying the significant topic *or* by revealing a major finding.

3   Support each finding or argument with the facts or figures behind it.

4   Interpret the findings in terms of their meaning for the problem being investigated, component's significance.

5   What appears here is mere data reporting; little or no analysis. Show how the data support, influence, and affect the component and your stated intention in the caption.

6   Round out each factor with a concluding statement which shows what

you have accomplished and how such relates to the overall problem.

7   Coverage is too scant to carry conviction.

Your score _____ (100)

Conclusions, Recommendations

Adequacy of coverage of the conclusions, recommendations; quality of overall answer statement; supporting facts, figures for conviction; logic; completeness.

CR 1   State overall answer for the problem and indicate supporting evidence follows as the leadoff statement for this section.

2   Caption, of course, should reveal the answer also.

3   Present supporting evidence in descending order of importance to the report's decision.

4   Include adequate fact and figures to carry conviction; this portion of the report is a revaluation of the significant findings from your analyses.

5   Too generalized.

6   Too scant treatment.

7   End the section smoothly; give reader a sense of report's completeness. (If a recommendation is being made, it logically grows out of the conclusions and offers a natural ending itself, though more logical to put it in transmittal for this problem.)

Your score _____ (30)

Graphic and Tabular Support

Adequacy of coverage; suitability; comprehensiveness of captions; technical correctness; placement; properly introduced into text before its appearance.

GT 1   Too many illustrations interfere with the continuity of your text.

2   An overall evaluation of illustrations is based on adequacy of coverage; clarity; emphasis on vital points; suitability; technical correctness; appearance.

3   Improperly arranged.

4   Make illustration captions self-identifying: The who or what, when and where as they apply to the subject matter.

5   Place the illustration close to the text reference to it.

6   Don't split a table on two pages if it's small enough to place on a single page.

7   Similarly, don't put a small table on a page all by itself. Include some text.

8   What is the source of the illustration?

Your score _____ (30)

Writing Style, Overall Presentation

Readability; ease of understanding; variety in sentence structure; coherence; force; proper paragraphing; correct language use; third-person style; conciseness.

1   Don't put the caption at the bottom of the page, with the first line of the text on the top of the next page. If you can't get two lines of text on the bottom of the sheet following the caption, make the page short.

2   Keep tense sequence consistent.

3   Make the message, not the graphic illustration or table number, the subject of the sentence.

4   Compress here without sacrifice of the content.

5   No contractions, please, in scholarly style of writing.

6   Write in impersonal, third-person style: no first- or second-person pronouns or imperatives.

7   Writing style is dull, monotonous, boring; needs improvement.

8   Language error.

9   Unclear, incomplete.

10   Logic.

Your score _____ (20)

Recap of Score Parts		Total	_____
Transmittal/synopsis	———	Less: Penalties	_____
Title page	———	Your grade	_____
Introduction	———		
Components	———	*Scale of Values:*	
Conclusions	———	225–250 = A	
Graphic/tabular support	———	200–224 = B	
Writing style; overall presentation	———	175–199 = C	
		150–174 = D	

PROBLEMS FOR SHORT OPERATIONAL REPORTS

1. *Informing personnel of a new, quality product.* You are A. K. Baker, business manager for Myron Corporation, Any Metropolitan City, Your State. And you believe that you've finally gotten the corner on cutting increasing costs from overuse of copiers in the firm. Costs have really been getting out of hand since no one seems to use carbon paper anymore when multiple copies are needed. Instead, an original is typed—whether a letter, a multipaged form, a memo, or a document—and the needed number of copies for distribution and filing are simply reproduced on one of the copier machines.

The product you've purchased in limited quantity for trial use is Permalar.™ Permalar utilizes a new scientific breakthrough that makes it superior to carbon paper in many, many ways. It's a high-technology product, made to exacting specifications by skilled craftsmen. It won't rip or tear no matter how many times you use it. It won't wrinkle or curl even if you twist it. It won't strike through like ordinary carbon paper . . . it isn't carbon *paper* at all! Here's what the manufacturer says about the product:

> Permalar's basic ingredient is genuine DuPont Mylar polyester, and that's what gives it toughness and resilience. When used it releases a controlled ink flow that gives you clear, clean, perfect copies. The Mylar re-inks itself like a sponge with each use; so it lasts and lasts.

> That's why Permalar won't wear out like carbon paper. In fact, we guarantee that 50 sheets will give you up to 5,000 clear copies or we replace it free of charge!

> Permalar outperforms carbon paper in every way. And because of its long-lasting qualities, Permalar is actually economical to use. Over 180,000 offices are now using Permalar.

What really sold you on an initial order of eight packs (50 sheets, each pack) at $11.58 per pack is the fact it won't smear or smudge hands or paper! Everyone, you think—company management as well as secretarial and typing personnel—will be delighted with Permalar. Hands and papers stay clean! Each sheet makes up to 100 copies. And you saw a demonstration where the hundredth copy still looked better than most copies made on ordinary carbon paper.

Permalar, you're convinced, will save the firm money week after week, month after month. But you'll have to convince personnel to use it, to give Permalar a fair trial. Instead of wasting time and money making photocopies of correspondence and records, you feel they ought to use Permalar selectively to duplicate typed copies. Photocopies, you've calculated, cost 5 cents, 6 cents, 8 cents, and up for each copy depending upon which copier and materials are used. Permalar copies cost less than half a cent each. It's convenient to use.

So your task is to compose a memorandum to be sent to all office personnel. You'll tell them, of course, about Permalar's fine features. More importantly, however, you'll need to make your presentation convincing enough to get them to give Permalar a fair-trial usage for two months. At that point you should have sufficient data compiled to make a real cost-saving comparison.

 2. *Handling employee morale decay at Trans Electronic Laboratories.* You are personnel manager at Trans Electronic, a firm producing transistors and other components used in electronic equipment.

Started just three years ago by two electronic engineers (Drs. Robert A. Stott and James H. Hardy), the staff has grown from 20 to 260 employees. A year ago you moved from your original location on the second floor of the Rochester Industrial Building in the center of Your City to a new, modern one-story plant just outside the city limits.

With the exception of your engineers and department heads whom you have imported from distant cities, almost all the factory and office personnel live within a radius of 25 miles of the plant. A high percentage of them are women who've joined that swelling number of two-income families. At present you have 225 production workers and 35 office employees. This number is sufficient to take care of your government contracts and orders from private industry. With the arrival of two new manufacturing plants to the area in the last two years, however, competition for labor is much keener. Your policy has been to select your employees carefully, offer salaries and wages comparable to, or slightly higher than, those paid by other plants and businesses; to provide hospitalization and group insurance; and to offer an attractive pension plan and bonuses.

Trans Electronic is nonunion. Espirit de corps in the organization has always been high. Of late, though, there has been a gradual falling off in production and a lessening of efficiency among personnel. You cannot point your finger to any one particular cause, but management realizes that its team is not showing its customary vigor and fight. Letdowns such as this one often take place in the best of industrial families.

At a meeting of the executive committee yesterday, it was decided that appropriate action should be taken now to "head off" the situation before a really serious demoralization occurs. The question, of course, is what action should the firm take? Obviously, management wants to boost morale, step up production, and get the entire work force back to peak efficiency.

Many of the employees may not know the history of the organization . . . the inception and rapid growth that Trans Electronic has enjoyed. But the loyalty, enthusiasm, and hard work of the personnel are the principal reasons for the goodwill the firm now enjoys with its customers and throughout the trade. The need for "getting back on the ball" is perhaps a theme worth plugging.

Although the situation is not alarming to management just yet, the time is ripe for a "pep talk." (The foregoing paragraphs are intended to provide you with necessary background upon which to base an intelligent solution. Draw upon your good judgment in making your decision of what must be done and present your solution in a memo to Dr. Stott.)

3. *Using good human-relations psychology in the office memorandum.* As personnel director of the Acme Corporation, you have surveyed its 650-member office force in an attempt to better working conditions and increase company morale. One frequently mentioned point has been the objection to working on Saturdays. Your current workweek is 8:30–4:30 Monday through Friday, with one hour for lunch, and 8:00–1:00 on Saturday.

In executive session, the administration has agreed that a five-day workweek is possible. It will mean a change of hours to provide employees with free weekends, however, and calls for cooperation on their part. First, the five-day workweek will begin at 8:00 A.M. sharp and will end promptly at 5:00 P.M., with the customary hour for lunch. Second, the new schedule will mean having all the week's work completed by 5:00 P.M. on Friday of each week instead of using Saturday's half-day for catching up; otherwise it will be necessary for overtime work to see that everything is in order to start out on Monday. The firm will not pay for any overtime necessary to accomplish this task.

A third aspect concerns a change in the lunch hour. In the past all employees except one or two supervisory personnel in each department have taken the hour 12:00 to 1:00 for lunch. This policy has created problems in answering phones, receiving unexpected callers during the lunch hour, long lines in the company cafeteria, and in some cases tardiness in returning from lunch. So a rotation system will be instituted whereby a third of the office force will each go to lunch at 11:30, 12:00, or 12:30. Each department will work out its own schedule. With the institution of the earlier lunch shift, the last coffeebreak in the morning can be no later than 10:45 to allow time for cleanup and for getting the cafeteria food lines set up for the lunch hour. The staggered shifts should make it possible for each employee to be served without the customary long wait.

Write a memo concerning the new policy for distribution to all employees. You may supply additional facts which logically can be assumed for the situation described.

4. *Conveying information clearly in the memo report.* As supervisor in Your City warehouse of the Nationwide Grocery Company, you receive this note from R. D. Smith, warehouse manager:

Denver wants us to increase our shipment of bananas by 100 boxes a day.

At present you handle 2,700 boxes of bananas a week in Your City warehouse where they are ripened and prepared for distribution to stores in Your City area and Denver. You ship 250 boxes six days a week to Denver and distribute the rest locally. You have six ripening rooms in the warehouse with a capacity of 10 cars a week (roughly 425 boxes to a car). Processing costs run $1 a box. Increasing the volume by 600 boxes would reduce the cost to 87 cents per box.

You will require two additional people to do a good job and maybe a third during peak periods. The need for closer temperature control, ripening around the clock seven days a week, plus possibly some night cutting and packing as well as split shifts make additional help necessary.

Shipping 2,100 boxes a week to Denver reduces the maximum number of boxes in any week that could be processed for local distribution. During special promotions, it might become necessary to find additional supplies from an outside source; that is a possibility. At such times would Denver be willing to agree to a pro rata cut in shipments? If so, you think that you could supply the requested 600 additional boxes of bananas a week.

Put your reply in good memo form. If you can create a table to take care of some of the figures, do so.

5. *Designing a recommendation memo report.* You are adjustment manager of the Yarrow Shirt Manufacturing Company, which makes and sells men's dress shirts.

The company had been using the same type of button on the shirts for several years, Stock No. 580. In may, the Style Department recommended the adoption of a new "square shape" (rounded corners) button, Stock No. 685, which has a more pearl-like appearance. The new button was used exclusively after June 15, even though it cost 25 cents a dozen more than No. 580.

On July 16 your department received a request from one of your New York dealers for 2 dozen buttons. These were to replace buttons broken on recently purchased Yarrow shirts.

A letter received July 17 from a customer in Michigan included this statement: "After the Yarrow shirt I bought last week was laundered by hand yesterday, four of the eight buttons were broken. Please send more buttons."

The next day three more complaints were received, one of which said: "The two cuff buttons on my new Yarrow shirt broke the first time it was laundered."

During the next two weeks, July 21–August 4, you kept a close count of all complaints about broken buttons on recently purchased shirts. There were 65 requests for new buttons and 16 complaints about broken buttons. In addition, 12 shirts were returned to have buttons sewed on, and 7 shirts were returned for credit by stores whose customers were so angry that they refused to keep the garments.

One of the customers wrote, "I shall never buy another Yarrow shirt. There's no excuse for your using such cheap buttons on a $16.95 shirt."

Shirt sales average 10,000 monthly. Complaints of all kinds during the first five months of last year averaged 0.2 percent of sales.

Write a memorandum report to the production manager making a recommendation based upon these facts.

6. *Proposing a change in pricing policy.* As Stanley Tucker, sales representative for

the Superior Distributing Company, wholesalers for auto parts and appliances, you receive a note from the Meade Manufacturing Company, 9902 McGraw Street, Chicago, congratulating you on the good work that you have done promoting sales of Meade specialties. You recognize the tell-tale earmarks of the form memo on this note that brings you words of praise. The president of your firm (Superior's address is 2309 Travis Street, Your City, Your State) recognizes it as an opening for some well-placed words of criticism for Meade's practice of allowing only a 4-percent markup to the distributor. Several companies whose lines Superior handles give an 8–10-percent markup.

Your president, T. Y. Bodkin, points with pride to the fact that your sales for Meade represent a larger figure than that produced by any of your fellow representatives. A memo from you just might carry some weight in persuading the Meade outfit to change to a 10-percent markup for distributors. In turn, this larger markup would allow the distributor to give discounts on large orders, thus encouraging volume purchases in the place of orders now by the dozen or partial dozen lots. You can point out that the increase in sales would make up for the difference in markup very quickly, as the specialties are "sure fire" sellers.

Do your best to bring about this change in policy which would benefit you and your company and many others in your line of business.

7. *Developing an orderly presentation for a completed task.* The management of Elliott Oil Company Refinery, Metropolitan City, Any State, authorized and you then engaged Henderson, Jones, Aton & Company to investigate the attitudes, beliefs, and feelings of the technical staff toward their work situation in the refinery and in the Elliott Laboratories. Conferences were held between HJA members and refinery representatives to select the persons to be included, the techniques to be used, and the time schedule to be followed in the investigation. As part of the complete survey, personnel psychologists of HJA held interviews with a sample of eighty technical personnel in the company.

A basic introductory statement was given at the beginning of each interview:

> Please tell me about yourself and your job situation: what you like about it and would like not to have changed; what you dislike about it; and where you would like to have some action taken.

The interviewer then sat back and listened, perhaps asking at times for amplification or clarification of a point but never asking a direct question. Detailed notes were taken. But this fact was never concealed from the interviewee. Attempt was made to cover areas such as promotion, salary, "how you stand," recycling, use of abilities, work load, supervision, recognition, confidence in management, and training.

From these interviews several points emerged. Some of them dealt with grievances, some with satisfactions. Without any statistical tabulation the following points are worth noting and considering further:

> a. Information on changes in company policy was disseminated orally by supervisors, notices or letters, and group meetings. One-third of the group felt that the messages were neither clear nor complete. Group meetings were voted

the least effective and the supervisors' personal discussions the most effective media of communication.

b. "Recycling" means rewriting correspondence or reports to make content and language acceptable to superiors. Reportedly, material was passed up the entire chain of command and rewritten to satisfy each person's objections until it finally passed the level responsible for sending it outside. Half the staff reported that they wrote material at least twice and sometimes from three to five times. Common reasons given for rewriting letters and reports were that the information given was not always complete and supervisors were picayune concerning petty details. Other comments were that the message became obsolete as it went up the line and that there were mechanical errors in the finished report.

c. None of the staff signed their reports and thus felt cheated of credit for them. Sometimes reports were held up until they were out of date.

d. The overall attitude of the technical people was favorable. The company's provisions for security of jobs and generous benefit programs were widely appreciated. Pride was taken in being a member of a select group. Office buildings were comfortable and attractive. Apparatus, equipment, and materials for work were readily available. The orientation program received praise. Lack of regimentation was liked; employees were grateful for a certain amount of freedom. They liked to say, "My job is what I make it."

e. Metropolitan City was highly regarded as a desirable place in which to live.

f. Engineers in the equipment inspection department objected to the lack of adequate locker rooms and shower facilities, which were necessary because of the dirty jobs they performed. Process engineers showed more enthusiasm for their work than did other engineers. Mechanical engineers were more vocal than were those in other departments in their complaints. They complained of long hours of work, of "being pushed" by their supervisors, and they were discontented with recent promotions following resignations.

g. Most of the employees indicated a feeling of unimportance in their jobs. Many jobs were designated for *immediate* attention (RUSH!). Some said, "Every job I'm given is a rush job." They no longer felt that quality of work was important, simply that it be done in a hurry. A few employees found themselves responsible for work which they lacked authority to carry through to completion. None of these workers seemed to feel a part of management.

h. Individuals who had received promotions were more favorable in their attitudes. Those with longer length of service tended to identify themselves with the company. Older personnel who had not been promoted were critical of the company. They concentrated on criticisms of salary, selection of supervisors, and promotion policies.

Organize this information in outline fashion for presentation to Elliott's executive committee. (Your instructor may also specify that you write up the notes and present them in memo format.)

8. *Fulfilling the last procedural requirement prior to employee dismissal.* When you

had a vacancy for a full-time secretary open up recently, one of the six applicants interviewed was Ms. Cyndi Mota. Her conduct during the interview, resumé of qualifications, personnel test scores, and her immediate supervisor's comments on your follow-up investigation were exemplary. She was selected and subsequently transferred in the middle of the workweek to your department from another division in the organization where she had prepared order forms. That was four months ago.

What turned out to be "habit" began her second week on the job as secretary. Cyndi called in sick. The following week it was the same pattern—two or three days at work, then no Cyndi. You inquired of other staff members in the office if they knew what Cyndi's problem might be. One of the other secretaries said that Cyndi mentioned low blood pressure and that she was going to see a doctor about it.

During her first partial month (two and one-half weeks), Cyndi was out 2½ days; the second month, she was absent 4½ days. Her immediate supervisor—your administrative secretary—always explained Cyndi's no show as "sick again!"

You had a talk with Cyndi at the end of her first month's service with you, asking how she liked her job, whether she was happy working in your department, how she got along with the rest of the classified personnel in the large outer office where she was stationed. She replied positively in all instances. You then inquired about her health; she said fine, no problems. She did state that she was taking medication on doctor's orders. You expressed hope that she had her medical problem under control and wouldn't have any more days out. And you explained to her what being dependable meant in your operation: being at work everyday, showing up on time, ready to shoulder her share of the responsibilities. You also told her that her work was quite satisfactory—when she was there to work—but that her absences placed a great burden on the others who had to fill in for her, doing work she was supposed to be doing.

After that talk, Cyndi put in the first full, five-day work week since she was hired. You breathed easier. Then, she went on vacation (earned because of total service in her former department), and you prepared your second monthly sick leave report accumulation showing her (for the first time) with a negative balance: −3½ days. (You'd give her the break of one day which maybe she will have made up by the end of next month, or if she wasn't absent anymore it would balance off against the day she earned for the month.)

The Personnel Office put out a memo shortly thereafter to all employees stating that any employee with negative sick leave time reported would be docked on the next paycheck.

Cyndi returned from vacation and worked four days before she was absent again. This time she did not call in. Her mother called to talk with her; your administrative secretary explained that Cyndi had not reported in, that she had been late several days this week, and that she had been trying to contact Cyndi herself. "Oh," her mother replied, "I guess she's moving into her new apartment today."

When Cyndi came to work the next day, your administrative secretary cautioned her that she was pressing her luck in her erratic work attendance, in her tardiness, and particularly in not keeping the office informed when she's out.

Cyndi's check for the month was docked for the previously reported negative 3½ days, but she said nothing about it to you. She did mention casually that she was making up the time. You then explained patiently to her that she couldn't possibly make up all the time she'd missed at her "half hour extra"-a-day pace . . . not with her attendance record.

The third month's sick leave report showed Cyndi with a $-1\frac{1}{2}$ days accumulation. A week ago, she was out one afternoon for a doctor's appointment. Then, this past week when she was absent again following a staff holiday, it was the last straw so far as you are concerned. You explained to Cyndi that

- her dependability record was anything but good,
- her job was a five-day-a-week one, not four,
- she had not improved her work attendance record despite several oral warnings, and
- the next time she was absent, you'd issue her a written notice (a required procedure of your organization prior to firing).

The written notice would indicate that unless her record of work attendance improved markedly within the next month and a half, she would be dismissed from her job as secretary in your department, within the six-month-probation period for a new employee. (No justification for dismissal has to be given.) However, Cyndi has worked for the organization for over a year in one department or another and thus does not come under the 6-month ruling for a new employee in the firm.

When you arrived at work today, your administrative secretary informs you that Cyndi has called in sick again. So now you must carry through on the last step of dismissal procedure—the written warning. Write the memo to Cyndi that documents the attempts made to help her become a more dependable employee, that sets forth clearly and as positively as possible the expectations and conditions for future employment with you, and that can't possibly lead you into a grievance hearing on charges of discrimination against a minority employee now . . . or when you fire her if it comes to that.

9. *Exhibiting tolerance in an employee evaluation.* The morning's mail brings you, at the personnel manager's desk of the Reed-Merkel Mills, Salina, Kansas, an inquiry about Harold H. Wardleigh, an employee who has been with you since the company was organized in 1979. The letter, signed by Frederick R. Zeeb, personnel director, Crescent Metal Products Company, Wichita, Kansas, reads in part as follows:

We need a young man with college training in accounting and computers who is able to establish and maintain cost accounting records for us and help an ambitious company grow up rapidly. Since these projects in cost accounting wouldn't take his full time until we have expanded quite a bit, he must be willing to carry his share of the more routine work. Additionally, he'll be expected to develop a data-processing system for the company. Thus, he should be somewhat innovative and possess a solid understanding of the data analysis side of the process.

Our head accountant is a practical person of good judgment and experience, but not technically trained or knowledgeable in data processing. The candidate must be one who can fit into this situation harmoniously.

Although Mr. Wardleigh doesn't list your name as a reference, the employment record that he submitted shows that he has been working with you for some time. Will you please tell us in strict confidence just how you think he would fit into a new department under the conditions I've outlined and whether there is a possibility that he did not intend to give your name as a reference (and if so, why)?

Wardleigh's case has been worrying you a bit since the Reed-Merkel Mills started growing up itself, and your first reaction is that of pleasure at the chance of losing the man. Your second thought is a sense of responsibility to the Crescent Company and then to the person under consideration. You appreciate having someone who can solve the problems related to any phase of your accounting work as its complexity has changed through a complete data-processing system. His cynical sense of superiority, however, and his failure at times to cooperate in doing work outside his immediate province are in sharp contrast to his proved ability (backed by a **BBA** degree with a major in accounting, minor in data processing and analysis) and his efficiency when he does work.

Possibly a "practical person of good judgment and experience" who knows his line of work can get the best of Wardleigh's worth; so you decide to give him somewhat of a boost for his being able to do the work well. In all fairness, you have to cover the issue of attitudes. A little speculation tells you that if the man were to get into the right situation he might improve measurably.

Review the facts as you know them, study the Crescent situation as outlined in the request message, and write a report that will be fair to Wardleigh and to the young Crescent Company in Wichita. Your instructor will specify format for this written presentation.

10. *Producing a clear set of instructions for less than nimble-fingered representatives.* As R. Painter Felman, copywriter for E M R I Imports, Inc., Any Major City, Any State, your job is varied, sometimes challenging, often demanding . . . requiring at times all the imagination you possess. E M R I Imports is a U.S. distributor for a line of Far Eastern imports. Motorcycles and sewing machines are the backbone of the firm's business success. It is the sewing machine line that causes you some headaches.

Sales representatives for the firm are quite knowledgeable of the various lines they sell. They know, too, that the sewing machine they represent is sound; a quality product, durable, and dependable. One of the machine's most salable features is its zig-zag stitchery, a boon to putting in a "blind hem." But to E M R I sales representatives who know little of the basics of sewing to say nothing of the finer points, demonstrating a "blind stitch" is a nightmare. How do you, as Felman, explain to the representatives how to demonstrate the "blind hem" to prospective retailers? The latter's sales people in turn will have to demonstrate to the buying public.

A "blind hem" is the professional tailor's way of cuffing trousers, pants suits, sleeves in shirts and blouses, hems in dresses, with never a single stitch showing through in the finished garment. Here's the set of instructions provided by the Far Eastern manufacturer to the E M R I firm:

- Lift the right side of the demonstration material and fold over about ½ inch of the right edge.
- Again lift the right side to your left and make fold 2 about an inch from fold 1.
- Turn fold 2 under and crease the material so fold 3 is about ¼ inch to the left of fold 1.

Clear? Hardly! To one familiar with sewing—certainly to the person who wrote this three-step procedure for "blind hemming"—these directions are clear. But E M R I's sales representatives say those words are so much Greek so far as they are concerned, that the "home office" had better produce something the reps *can use and leave* with the prospective buyers. Obviously, something needs to be done to bring meaning into the directions if the representatives are to be successful in pushing the zig-zag's top feature.

And that's where you step into the picture. What can you do to make the instructions of "blind hem stitchery" understandable enough to your firm's sales representatives so that they, in turn, can explain it clearly to prospective buyers? Give it your best shot!

11.   *Writing a procedure for handling plant tours.* The Buckhorn Brewery, an old established distilling plant in your town, three months ago completed an expansion program adding extensively to the plant facilities and operations. Already a point of interest for out-of-town tourists to the city, the firm is now experiencing an increase in requests to tour these new facilities from local groups as well.

Mr. J. R. Queens, general manager, deems it advisable to establish some procedural guidelines for handling these tours which are encouraged, of course, as part of the total public relations program of the company. He wants to make the tours as interesting and educational as possible but to accomplish his objective with a minimum of interference to operative personnel.

Mr. Queens, thus, has hired an official company host who is to receive all tour requests and is to be in charge of all tours. The host, acting as coordinator with the personnel department, secures written approval from all department managers concerned in any individual tour. The personnel department makes arrangements for assigning guides and handling transportation needs. When department managers and the personnel department have all the details worked out for a specific tour—agreeing to the date, time, number in the group, and so on—the host is notified that the request is acceptable as outlined. The host in turn advises the requesting group that the tour has been approved and makes final arrangements for the tour. On the day prior to a scheduled tour, the host will remind (either by phone or memo) those departments involved of the next day's upcoming tour.

Step into the role of executive trainee at the Buckhorn Brewery and set up this procedure for Mr. Queens's approval. You decide to use the playscript technique, including a short statement of policy governing plant tours.

12. *Presenting the case of the unhappy worker.** As director of labor relations for Richardson Aircraft Company of San Diego, California, your major responsibilities are confined to happy workers and smooth management and union relationships. As a matter of fact, Richardson is highly regarded by other members of the industry for the outstanding program it provides for employees. Wages are comparable to, if not a little higher than, the industry average. Two-week paid vacations are given to employees who have worked for the company a year or more. In addition, eight days out of every year are paid holidays. Working conditions are good with ample lighting, heating, and air-conditioning facilities throughout the plant. Richardson sponsors a group life insurance, hospitalization, and medical-surgical insurance plan. The company pays monthly insurance premiums for each worker.

Robert A. McKendree, former president of a smaller aircraft company, has just become president of Richardson. He has not had an opportunity to become completely familiar with the company's labor agreement with the United Automobile, Aircraft, and Agricultural Workers of America, but some recent rumors have caused him concern. The grapevine has it that Richardson is mistreating its employees. The source of the gossip lies in a grievance filed by the union for a former employee, Marvin Brubaker. The charge has been made that Mr. Brubaker was wrongfully dropped from the group insurance plan as a result of illness. The conflict has progressed until it seems likely that the problem may have to be turned over to an arbitrator for settlement. Mr. McKendree wishes to know the full story behind the case and the probability of the outcome if the situation is referred to an arbitrator. He asks you to investigate and report to him.

The material is at your fingertips, but the outcome is uncertain. It *does* seem certain that the case is headed for arbitration; neither side is willing to concede. The problem would ordinarily be thought of as insignificant, but the precedence and the new interpretation of the contract that might be forthcoming are important.

The grievance presented by the union states that

> the Company is in violation of its agreement dated December 2, 19xx, in laying off the Aggrieved [Marvin Brubaker] while the Aggrieved was on sick leave, and in discontinuing the payment of its contributive share to group life insurance, hospitalization, and medical-surgical benefits, as provided by Article XIX, Section 4b of said agreement.

The company and the union are in agreement on part of the facts. Marvin Brubaker entered the employ of the company on February 10, 19yy. On or about July 9, 19yy, Brubaker requested and secured from the company a leave of absence as a result of illness. The leave was granted on the basis of a qualified doctor's certificate. The leave of absence indicated July 24, 19yy, as the expected date for him to return to work. Additional leaves of absence were granted—the last one expiring October 15, 19yy. On June 19, 19yy, a number of employees were laid off as a result of lack of work in accordance with the plantwide seniority.

---

* Adapted from Case # 1–25766 CLE–L–96–59, Bureau of National Affairs, *Labor Arbitration Reports*, Vol. 34, pp. 18–21.

The layoff was severe enough to affect employees hired on February 10, 19yy, including Marvin Brubaker. The company notified Brubaker that, because of lack of work, a reduction in force was necessary and that he had been laid off. The company then discontinued payment of Brubaker's hospitalization and medical-surgical benefits.

With these facts the unity ends. The union holds that on June 19, 19yy Brubaker was properly absent from work based upon a leave of absence as a result of sickness; that he was not subject to be laid off in line with his seniority; that the company was in error in seeking to lay off Brubaker while on sick leave; and that the company was in violation of Article XIX, Section 4b, in discontinuing the payment of the company's contribution to Brubaker's hospitalization and medical-surgical benefits plan.

The company feels that, under the terms of the agreement, it was required to lay off Brubaker when the layoff was sufficiently extended to reach his seniority date and that no further obligation rested upon the company to make contributions to the hospitalization and medical-surgical plan for any employee on layoff, even though the employee might have been on sick leave at the time of layoff.

A brief analysis of the situation is required. It is necessary to distinguish between the rights of an employee who has been laid off and the rights of an employee on leave of absence because of sickness. The individual on a leave of absence is still considered to be employed even though he is not on the active payroll. Such an employee continues, for a time at least, to accumulate seniority, to vote in union matters, and to have the right to return to his job within the required period of time.

An employee who has been laid off because of lack of work also changes his payroll status to inactive payroll. He is still a member of the union and may return to work when the work is available. He forfeits his right to return if he does not return according to the terms of the agreement.

One of the chief distinctions between an employee on leave of absence and an employee on layoff is that the former is entitled to his job back at the time he, at his own election, returns to work provided it is during the leave of absence. Whereas, the employee who has been laid off, returns only at the election of the employer.

Segments of the Labor Contract

Article XIX, Section 7. "Those on sick leave or compensable injury leave, when they return to work from such leave, shall be entitled to the job they held prior to the leave of absence, provided that they are able to perform the work, and subject to Article V, Section 2."

Article XIX, Section 4b. "Sick leave may be granted on request of an employee certified by a qualified doctor—not applicable for illness of one (1) to five (5) days, for a period not to exceed eighteen (18) months, and with the understanding that contributions to group life insurance, hospitalization, and medical-surgical insurance by the Company will be discontinued after one(1) Year."

Article V, Section 2. [This section, entitled "Seniority," provides for the procedure to be followed on layoffs and recalls. Brubaker was recognized as an employee and would, therefore, be subject to these provisions. Plantwide seniority is practiced with layoffs when lack of work justifies it.]

Article XI. [This section, entitled "Insurance," specifically limits insurance payments to "employed seniority employees." What is meant by employed seniority employees is not clearly defined.]

If this case is allowed to go to arbitration, the arbitrator would have the authority to make rulings based on the content of the present labor agreement. His decision would be binding on both parties to the contract if they have agreed to take it to arbitration. (Mr. McKendree is well aware of this.)

You must convey the necessary information to Mr. McKendree along with your estimate of the ruling if the case is given to an arbitrator.

13. *Resolving an internal conflict at Texas-Built Elevators.* Texas-Built Elevators, Inc. is an independent manufacturer of hydraulic elevators for passenger and freight use, and is located at 4300 Parkway Drive, Dallas, Texas. The company now employs approximately 220 persons and builds and distributes elevators throughout the United States. There is a smaller branch plant located in Indianapolis, Indiana, but Dallas is the home office. President of the corporation is Franklin W. Mann.

As Nolan B. Stalker of Pattersson, Stalker, and Williams, management consultants, you are associated directly with the Texas-Built home office because you are permanently retained as staff consultant. Mann calls you in frequently to investigate problem areas and to make recommendations on situations where problems exist.

On April 2 Mr. Mann called you in and confronted you with the company's latest problem of a major magnitude. Some disagreement had arisen between two members of the management team, and Mr. Mann wanted you to get at the root of the trouble and bring back your findings with accompanying suggestions concerning a course of action. From the oral briefing given by Mann, plus a folder of material he had had assembled by his secretary, the following story emerged.

In May of 19xx, after Fred Allyn had been production control manager at Texas-Built for five years, the plant superintendent resigned to take another position. Harold Nelson, vice president in charge of manufacturing, discussed with Mr. Mann the problem of filling the position, and it was decided to promote Allyn to superintendent from production control manager.

The five supervisors in charge of production departments reported to the superintendent. It was the superintendent's job to supervise the supervisors in operations; one of the major requirements was personnel administration. The superintendent reported to Nelson.

As production control manager, Allyn had also reported to Nelson. While Allyn's job had been only to set overall production schedules, he had cultivated a broad outlook in his five years as production control manager. He had studied plant operations and had gained a good understanding of technical production problems, although he had never had actual production experience. Allyn seemed to get along well with the supervisors and with the other workers with whom he came in contact in administering his job. Supervisors and workers often came to him with personnel problems that ordinarily would have been handled by the superintendent; so, when the larger job became vacant, Allyn appeared to be the logical choice.

Nelson, who was 53 years old and 11 years Allyn's senior, subsequently came to have some doubts about the move. Nelson had been a lathe operator in his early days with the company and had worked up through the ranks to his position of vice president in charge of production. He began to think that Allyn lacked a technical background adequate for the position of superintendent.

After Allyn had been superintendent for several months, friction developed between Allyn and Nelson. Last October Nelson told President Mann that Allyn was opinionated, gave snap judgments, and knew little about technical processes. The split has now grown wider and has been aggravated by work pressures caused by a growing volume of business. Nelson has complained that Allyn does not have the technical background to meet the problems arising in connection with the new work. President Mann has not dismissed or transferred Allyn because he has always thought that he was valuable as a personnel administrator. However, the situation has reached the point where some action seems necessary. Mann asks you to investigate the matter and to make the appropriate recommendations.

For the past week you have been out in the plant talking with the executives and key people through the rank of subsupervisor. You have discussed with each what his or her job is, what is required from other departments or key personnel, what types of problems come up, and how the problems are solved.

Conferences have been held with both Nelson and Allyn. Each discussed his job and responsibilities in a businesslike manner.

You are beginning to formulate the opinion that Allyn's judgment is excellent and that he has a keen sense of human understanding in dealing with the personal problems of his subordinates. His workers like him, and, although he does not know all the technical aspects of operations in the manufacturing departments, the subordinates say that he is helpful in solving technical problems by suggesting possible ways for performing tasks. Many of his suggestions are not practical, but the workers often get new ideas from just talking over the problems with Allyn. He does not try to force his unworkable ideas on the workers. They say that he is exacting in finding out why an idea is not good and that often, in trying to explain why it is impracticable, they find that their first reaction is wrong and that the method suggested would work, although they had never tried it before. The supervisors say that between Allyn and the methods engineer, whose job it is to design tools and specify methods, they feel that they have adequate technical assistance.

From observations of Nelson's work, it seems that he is an executive who is fair in coordinating the efforts of those reporting to him. It was observed that Nelson frequently gives instructions to his subordinates regarding rather minor administrative phases of their departments. Those reporting to Nelson are the superintendent, the production control manager, the methods engineer, the industrial engineer, the maintenance supervisors, the chief inspector, and the purchasing agent.

On a few occasions Nelson and Allyn met in informal conferences affording an opportunity for you to observe them working together. Allyn generally could analyze a problem in a fraction of the time it took Nelson, and it seemed to you that his judgment was usually better than Nelson's, even on problems that Nelson had thought over prior to presenting them to Allyn. Often Nelson would call Allyn to his office and ask him whether they should make a certain move. Allyn would frequently react in a flash and inform Nelson why such a move should or should not be made.

What should be done? Take over the task as Stalker by evaluating the material. Using your best managerial abilities, draw justifiable conclusions and outline the actions that you would recommend. Brief Mr. Mann sufficiently on findings you think he needs to know.

14. *Presenting a purchase decision in justification report format.* Should Budget Systems and Planning install a photographic typesetting machine in its Data Processing Division? The decision is yours to make and to recommend in a justification report.

The BS&P office is already equipped for photolith printing. Informational and instructional materials for state offices and agencies is computer printout or typed copy which is pasted up on master sheets with appropriate line drawings and large-type headings. These masters are reproduced photographically on mats, which are then run on a small offset press. Each mat will provide as many as 5,000 printed copies.

Because all materials should look professional, it has been the practice to have headings and captions set in type by a commercial printer. A proof copy pulled from the type is pasted up on the master for photoreproduction.

Recently, Mr. Donnigan asked you to investigate a newly developed machine that will produce nearly perfect printing on a small scale. This device, called the Headliner, can be operated by an office worker after one hour's instruction. The operator merely dials the letters to be printed, and the machine photographs images of the letters on a sensitized tape, spacing them automatically. After feeding the tape through a developing solution, the machine issues its finished product—printing ready to be pasted up on the master copy. The style and size of type may be varied by changing type discs in the Headliner. Each disc represents one typeface and includes a complete set of capital and lowercased letters, numbers, symbols, and punctuation marks.

The most conspicuous deterrent to installing the machine is its initial cost: $1,535. In addition, each type disc costs $35. (You believe that the office should have five or six styles of type for a beginning, perhaps more later.) The operating expense, on the other hand, is fairly modest. The tape on which the lettering is printed costs $10 per 100-foot roll (the manufacturer says that 20 percent should be allowed for waste), and the developing and fixing solutions cost about $2.50 for an average week's work. The machine could be operated by a $3.65-per-hour drafting assistant already on the staff. Each hour's work will produce some six to eight feet of lettering in a heading type of the size you ordinarily use.

Experience with office machines has taught you to consider closely the probable maintenance needs of such complex equipment. You are assured, though, that guaranteed repair service is available on a contract basis for $45 a year. The factory-trained service representative is located 30 miles away.

The alternative is to continue having type set by the cut-rate Bottomly Printing Company, which does business down an alley several blocks away. A quick examination of the work you had done by Bottomly last year shows that about one thousand feet of heading type was set (measured by total length of lines), at a cost of $945.16. The work from Bottomly is reasonably good, though the choice of typefaces is far smaller than that offered by the Headliner. Bottomly makes no charge for corrections, although there is sometimes an inconvenient delay when copy must be returned to the shop for changes.

Clearly, there are advantages and disadvantages on both sides of the question. Now it is up to you to reach a decision as to whether you should buy a Headliner and to report your decision as convincingly as you can.

15. *Deciding whether Valley Canning Company should adopt a money-back premium offer to build sales?* Valley Canning Company, a 10-year-old family business with headquarters at McAllen, Texas, has enjoyed rewarding growth since it was founded as a sort of hometown cannery by David B. Hendershot with a $10,000 initial investment.

Located in the midst of the Winter Garden district, the enterprise has competed successfully against the numerous canning interests in the area as well as with the national distributors stocking supermarket shelves. It has progressed steadily from local to regional and ultimately to distribution through retail chain outlets in Houston, Dallas, Fort Worth, San Antonio, and El Paso. Originally setting up his operation to process citrus juices, Hendershot subsequently steered his product mix away from this highly competitive field toward the canning of green and wax beans, peas, beets, onions, stewed tomatoes, and the bottling of tomato catsup. At present, orange and grapefruit juices comprise only approximately 20 percent of total production.

Hendershot, the company's major stockholder and only president, notes that sales for the last four years have reached a plateau, with figures running rather uniformly like those for last year:

Gross sales		$3,500,000
Cost of goods sold	$2,793,000	
Selling and administrative costs	483,000	3,276,000
Before-tax profit		$ 224,000

The total advertising budget, including radio and newspaper promotion and salesrep's aids, amounted to $127,995.

In the search for ways to boost sales and develop brand loyalty for his products, this industrious president has had the company chemist busily working on the details for processing Valley Gourmet Fruit Salad, made of orange, papaya, and pineapple tidbits, watermelon and cantaloupe balls, and maraschino cherries, laced with apricot brandy. (The brandy is merely for flavor—no alcoholic content.) He is now ready to launch this gourmet's delight.

In a series of conferences with you, Sales Manager A. B. Collie, Hendershot has advanced various novelty ideas designed to push sales past the level that customary advertising has been able to produce. Today he asks you to investigate the possibilities of a 30-day, money-back offer for the promotion of Valley Tomato Catsup (currently commanding about 7.9 percent of total gross sales) and Gourmet Salad. Valley catsup, developed from his grandmother's personal recipe, is sufficiently unique in flavor to have won high brand loyalty from the households in the sales territory, according to Hendershot; so he is of the opinion that people who like his catsup will like his salad even better.

Under his plan shoppers purchase one 20-ounce bottle of catsup for 81 cents and one 30-ounce can of salad for 98 cents, send in the two labels along with their names and addresses, and receive in return a shiny, new half dollar. The offer will run through the next three months. Hendershot has read (he cannot remember where exactly) about a successful campaign of this sort for the promotion of catsup. With the addition of his gourmet salad to the package, he thinks his scheme is surefire. Besides, he argues, none of the other canners in the area have tried it.

He wants your recommendation within two weeks as to whether the company should launch this money-back campaign. He is willing to augment last year's advertising budget by the amount necessary to cover the premium, with a $5,000 allocation from the regular budget to cover auxiliary newspaper and radio expenditures necessary for effective promotion.

Your assignment is to take over for Collie, evaluate the pros and cons of the project, and provide him with an answer in a well-written, brief-form justification report. The following are some working notes on which to base your argument.

As a marketing major graduate of the College of Business Administration, your attitude toward Hendershot's pet project is ambivalent. Certainly it has merit—but it has numerous disadvantages as well. Your first effort to get dependable information is rewarded with a letter from your college roommate, Harper Hollyfield, who has been for five years a vice president with a national advertising firm in Chicago: Mitchell, Marwick, and Albritton. He gives you permission to use any of the data from his company's files, so long as they are not released outside your own business.

In the first place, this form of promotion has been found most effective, in Hollyfield's experience, for launching a new product that is within itself rather glamorous. Very likely Valley Gourmet Salad meets this test. Hendershot's belief that a brand preference prevails for Valley catsup may be a bit optimistic. No brand-preference studies have actually been run on it. Your own idea is that 45-percent brand loyalty is a good estimate. Even though the recipe is different enough possibly to radiate an aura of glamor, it still must be branded as a "convenience" item, as must other products in the Valley line with the exception of the salad yet to be introduced.

In the second place, promotions of this sort work best for products that can be fixed together in a convenient package or that can be at least picked up by the shopper from shelves in close proximity. It would be difficult to join a bottle of catsup and a can without considerable additional expense; and, the way grocery stores are laid out, catsup and fruit mixes are usually placed in different departments. This is, however, a popular form of promotion for grocery items and, according to Hollyfield, has been successful in raising individual product sales for client national manufacturers by 15 to 25 percent during the premium-offer period, with a subsequent average increase in sales of 3 percent during the remaining 11 months.

One particularly pleasing feature is that only a small percentage of the offers is redeemed. Shoppers buy the products with every intention of claiming their half dollars, but for one reason or another they never get around to sending in the labels within the deadline. Hollyfield shares with you these company statistics from last year's files:

Number of Campaigns	Percentage of Offers Redeemed
16	3
10	4
3	5
1	7
Total 30	Average 3.6

Your next step is getting together some cost and sales figures. Last year Valley sold approximately 1,200,000 bottles of catsup—roughly 100,000 bottles a month. McAllen Business Aids Service has quoted you a price of 10 cents a redemption (including notice forms to attach to catsup bottles, envelopes, coin-safety cards, and clerical service) to handle this phase of the campaign for you. In addition, you will furnish the half dollars and the 10 cents for postage. Thus the total cost for each redemption will be 60 cents. Valley catsup sells direct to the retailer for 55 cents and salad, for 75 with a gross profit of 10 and 20 cents, respectively (30 cents on the combination).

Figures from company files indicate that the average consumption of catsup per household in the area is 9 bottles a year. A study recorded on page 91 of the February issue of the *National Food Manufacturers Bulletin*, "Median Advertising Appropriations for 100 Food Manufacturers," cites the median percentage of advertising dollars to net sales as 4.3 percent. Your own experience with direct-mail promotion points toward $3 in sales for every dollar of advertising money as profitable. Valley operates at 75 percent capacity, with production for an upsurge of sales no real problem.

In the preparation of your report, you may draw on your own fund of marketing knowledge or use any references at your disposal, in addition to analyzing the material given in the assignment.

16. *Designing a recommendation report that determines the future of a symposium.* Last year, your firm, Organizational Media Seminars, a leading management consulting group specializing in cost-effective communication planning, sponsored a symposium for businessmanagers and educators in the area. Its purposes were (a) to spread knowledge of the latest methods and techniques available in "teleconferencing" for users and prospective users, (b) to focus attention indirectly on the services, equipment, and facilities of Organizational Media Seminars, and (c) to build the firm's reputation and prestige in a highly competitive field. Because such symposia are usually sponsored by educational institutions, there was some question as to whether you would reach, through a business-sponsored meeting, all the people you wanted to reach. Furthermore, your management had decided that the seminar ought to be virtually self-supporting—even though this venture was largely educational and thus a promotional cost write-off. You charged a $35 registration fee for attending the two day-long sessions.

The program was this:

Thursday

Morning session 9:00–11:30	"Teleconferencing Economics" and "Satellites, Land Lines, and Microwave—Buy or Rent?"

Lunch (11:45–1:15)

Afternoon session 1:30–4:00	"Current Services and Their Cost" and "Coming Services and Their Cost"

Friday

Morning Session 9:00–11:30	"How to Design Facilities" and "Preparing for a Teleconference"

Lunch (11:45–1:15)

Afternoon sessions 1:30–4:00	"A step-by-Step Planning Procedure" and Tour of OMS headquarters and service facilities.

(The workshop leaders were all experts, well known and with national reputations. Some were members of the management consulting group; others were those whom the organization brokers to firms across the country.)

This first symposium drew 105 people, many of them in top management of important companies. A cost analysis of the project broke down as follows:

Expenses.	
Speaker fees	$1,837.50
Lunches and dinners	1,995.00
Printing and mailing	1,000.00
Other expenses	559.60
Subtotal	$5,392.10
Registration fees	
105 persons @ $35 each	3,675.00
Cost	$1,717.10

In addition to news stories and pictures in the local media—television, radio, and newspapers—the symposium produced a lot of favorable publicity in trade journals and resulted in a number of requests for brochures and technical assistance by firms whose representatives attended the meetings.

You have now been asked by Clarence Toole, president, Organizational Media Seminars, to prepare a report answering three questions:

- Should we sponsor another symposium this year?

- Does this type of activity belong more appropriately under the sponsorship of a local college or university?

- If we do sponsor another symposium, should we make any changes in it? Should we charge a registration fee? Should we do more direct selling on Organizational Media Seminars' facilities and skills? Should we invite our competitors, Comtech Telecommunication Systems and Future Systems Incorporated, to be co-sponsors with us?

To guide you in your report, here are the comments from various people about last year's symposium:

The chairman of the General Business Department of a major university in your city:

Thank you for inviting me to this excellent program. Quite candidly, I believe that such a workshop should in the future be under the sponsorship of our College of Business Administration. After all, education is our business; we have the facilities and staff to do a good job, and we can do it without seeming to sell anything but education. When such projects are sponsored by business firms or groups, there is always a feeling that the conference is so much propaganda for the organization's sales efforts. This symposium dealt with a single topic— teleconferencing. We have been devoting increased research efforts and allocating more resources to this area over the past few years. New courses have resulted. Our modular classrooms are now the laboratories for business communication to show how conferencing, board meetings, and remote location can be interlinked. The modular classroom can be combined with the STAT/OR Division's use of multimedia and terminals with business communication to impart completed analysis, set forth clearly selected alternatives followed by "what if" simulation, and so on. We would have liked an opportunity to share a status report at least, perhaps even to have entered into a "friendly" debate on differing viewpoints.

The service manager of Organizational Media Seminars:

If this affair cost us $10,000, it was well worth it. People in my department have been getting all kinds of favorable comments about the symposium. It built more goodwill than anything we've done in recent years. (In this firm, the service department is made up of artists, copywriters, photographers, layout experts, information system specialists, language specialists, and others who provide technical services to clients.)

The sales manager of Organizational Media Seminars:

My people report that the conference undoubtedly resulted in a lot of goodwill and publicity for our organization. However, it's almost impossible to say whether any new or additional business came to us as a result of the workshop.

Since the workshop, OMS representatives have landed four new major accounts, two of whom had representatives at the symposium. All these accounts are using Organizational Media Seminars' services in a rather small way now, but they can be expected to develop into quite profitable accounts within a few years, provided they continue to do business with us.

On the other hand, three old customers have ceased to use the firm's services. Two of these accounts were fairly large ones, one of which had a representative at the symposium. The third account was a comparatively small one with City Community College. The administration of the college was apparently rather hurt that it had not been asked to sponsor, or at least to assist with, the symposium.

Sales are up 2½ percent in dollar volume over last year's, but I want to re-emphasize the fact that this increase could be the result of many factors other than the symposium.

The head of Public Relations and Production for your firm, Jon Wells:

My one regret is that we did not make a more conscious effort to focus attention on all that our firm is doing. The brief tour of our facilities should be supplemented by exhibits showing costs and services of all we do, plus a sales pitch by someone within our organization. Next time, we should not charge a registration fee and let the "commercials" justify the cost of the workshop.

The advertising manager of Organizational Media Seminars, Ron Ely:

The company received more intangible goodwill and prestige from this conference than I expected. In fact, both competitors in this area are a bit jealous of the favorable results we got. We should plan early to make this a bigger and better affair this year, and we should start lining up key speakers immediately. Perhaps we could minimize the feelings of our competitors by giving them a place on the symposium format.

Executive vice president of OMS, Dianne Downing:

We maintained a high level of excellence throughout the symposium. My one concern is whether we can duplicate it another year . . . keep it at the same high level, since we should aim to vary the topic and the speakers. I believe that it would be better to have no symposium at all than to let the quality deteriorate. I would suggest holding such a program once every two years."

How would you organize your report to Mr. Toole? What decision as to specific recommendations would you make? On what basis would you make these recommendations? In arriving at your decision, keep in mind that this is an actual situation, typical of much reporting in business where certain data such as costs, attendance, and publicity can be quantified but where there is also an area of opinion—qualitative judgment at best—often contradictory or inconclusive. Yet a decision *must* be made as logically as possible. For that reason, you ought not to duck your responsibility as a report writer by saying that "you don't know enough about the situation." In this instance, you know as much as did the actual person who had to make the recommendation.

17. *Selecting the proper periodical for a large, new account.* For this report assignment, assume that you are director of research for the Bycliff-Wiggins advertising agency.

Bycliff-Wiggins is a comparatively small but rapidly expanding agency that is just now moving into the big-account class. The new account responsible for the agency's latest good fortunes is that of Moroccan Crafts, Inc., manufacturers of a line of fine-quality luggage.

Moroccan Craft's current advertising plan calls for more than the usual dealer co-operative campaigns used in the past. This time, a nationwide campaign is to be run in a major periodical. The periodical that will carry the Moroccan Craft story to the buying public hasn't been determined as yet, but here is where your agency is brought into the picture.

At the request of Mr. Charles H. Kappi, account executive for the Moroccan Craft account, you are to make the analysis which will point the way to a sound decision. Your analysis is limited to two periodicals—*Adventure Travel* and *Southern Outdoors* (or any two magazines selected by your instructor)—the others having been eliminated by Mr. Kappi for one reason or another. Stated more specifically, it is your assignment to get a picture of the advertising characteristics of the two magazines that will show where the Moroccan Craft advertising would be most appropriate—fitting in harmoniously with the style and image of complementary advertising.

Normally, such studies involve extensive survey investigations. At the moment, however, Bycliff-Wiggins cannot afford a costly study (in time or money); so you set about doing the next best thing. Working on the assumption that the bigger agencies long ago have made similar studies, you conclude that an analysis of the advertisements they place in a magazine would reveal their findings concerning that magazine. Thus, your objective is to obtain a summary picture of the advertisements in *Adventure Travel* and *Southern Outdoors*. Your study will get at the facts that will help you make a sound decision: information as to classes and price levels of goods and services, the buying motives to which the advertisements appeal, the techniques used to present these appeals, and so on. These facts can be made to portray the readers they are written for. That is, they will give a good indication of such things as the typical reader's age, sex, family status, and economic and intellectual level.

You begin your investigation by getting copies of each of the two magazines in question (issues for fall and spring; each quarter; whatever time coverage your instructor decides is an adequate number of representative issues). Then, based on what you believe to be the major points which reveal the magazines' readership, you construct a tally sheet for your data assembly. Next, you make an ad-by-ad check of the magazines, summarizing your findings after all ads have been checked. Then you will be ready for an analysis that will point the way to the correct choice of magazine. This analysis and the data upon which it is based will be written up in an easy-to-read and eye-pleasing report.

When at last you are ready to write the report, you'll face the decision as to scope, tone, and form. You decide to use the impersonal style (no *I*, *we*, or *you*; just consistent third person throughout), to include enough identification to make the report readily understandable to anyone up the line from Mr. Kappi who might have occasion to read it, and to set the report up in proper format.

Although you will break up your data from the large tally sheet into smaller units and present adequate data displays in the report, you will have to translate their story into words. Do not shift the burden of analysis of your graphic illustrations to your reader. Instead, seek out concrete words and specific instances to keep away from statistical jargon and gross generalities of talk. You will, in short, work to make the report a readable, understandable, meaningful document.

NOTE: This problem may be assigned as the long, formal analytical report, particularly if more than two issues of each magazine are used. In addition to the title page (that would be stapled on the short analytical report), the long, formal report requires a left-side binding cover, a title fly, the title page, a *copy* of the authorization instrument, a personal letter of transmittal, a table of contents (in organized outline form), a list of illustrations, an epitome (in direct style, beginning with a succinct statement of the main finding, then shifting back to its real job of compressing each section—introduction, component analyses, conclusion—proportionally), the report proper, an appendix, and possibly a bibliography (if secondary sources are used in the research).

18. *Comparing Tacoma City Lumber Yard operating data with those of other lumber-yards.* Your first job as the newest addition to the accounting department of Tacoma City Lumber Yard, Your State, is that of preparing a comparison report of your firm's cost of doing business last year with the average cost of the 42 lumberyards in your classification (net sales of $400,000 to $800,000). A survey was recently completed. The chief accountant, H. Y. Marlin, handed you the survey results of "Retail Lumber Dealers Survey of Cost of Doing Business" to use as the base for a staff report on the subject.

Your initial step is that of assembling the requisite information from the company records and filling in the accompanying worksheet. Next, you'll make the necessary computations to supply the missing columns. With your comparison figures set up, you'll appraise them for aspects in which your firm did well and for those for which improvement might be indicated. (With your material well in hand, you'll prepare your report in the format outlined by your instructor.)

Questionnaires were mailed to 1,226 members of the Lumbermen's Association, Your State, and information for the survey was furnished by 199 independent yards and line yards reporting individually. Six line yards submitted consolidated reports covering a total of 122 yards. The independent yards and line yards reporting individually were divided according to the annual volume of net sales. Your company came under Group C, sales of from $400,000 to $800,000, with operating data assembled from 42 reporting yards.

Summary of Operating Ratios of Lumberyards with Net Sales of $400,000 to $800,000*

	Gross Margin	Total Expenses	Net Operating Profit	Profit Before Taxes
Highest	34.4%	39.9%	13.3%	13.4%
Median	25.0	22.6	2.2	5.1
Average	24.4	23.2	1.2	4.4
Lowest	12.5	10.0	−9.7	−0.9

*All percentages are based on net sales.
Source: Latest-year survey data, Your State's Lumbermen's Association.

A Comparison of Operating Data of Tacoma City Lumberyard with Average Figures of 42 Other State Dealers

		42 Dealers		Tacoma City		
		Average	% of Net Sales	Data	% of Net Sales	Comparison Percentages
1.	Sales, net	$564,596	100.0%	$574,404.52	100.0%	
2.	Cost of sales, material only					
	a. Inventory, beginning of year	125,452	22.2	151,380.68		
	b. Purchases	417,090	73.9	396,446.02		
	c. Total (a plus b)	542,542	96.1	547,826.70		
	d. Inventory, end of year	115,874	20.5	149,273.26		
	e. Net cost of sales (c less d)	426,668	75.6	398,553.44		
3.	Gross margin (1 less 2e)	137,928	24.4	175,851.08		
4.	Salaries of owners, officers	27,922	4.9	25,000.00		
5.	All other salaries and wages	45,562	8.1	90,348.74		
6.	Truck and auto expense	6,182	1.1	4,934.42		
7.	Depreciation, all	6,478	1.1	5,086.44		
8.	Insurance	4,076	0.7	6,073.46		
9.	Taxes (no income tax)	5,410	1.0	7,575.38		
10.	Advertising	5,076	0.9	7,452.84		
11.	Bad debts	2,956	0.5	3,618.32		
12.	Interest expense	4,054	0.7	6,054.56		
13.	Discount allowed	4,390	0.8	5,802.76		
14.	All other expenses	18,760	3.4	27,504.76		
15.	Total expense (add 4 through 14)	130,866	23.2	169,451.38		
16.	Net operating profit (3 less 15)	7,062	1.2	6,399.70		
17.	Discount earned	4,390	0.8	7,872.12		
18.	Other income	13,276	2.4	35,932.14		
19.	Net profit before tax (16 plus 17 and 18)	24,728	4.4	50,203.96		
	Inventory turnover: 3.54 times					

19. *Resolving a departmental problem of troublesome employees.* The general office of the Baxter Metal Works, Your City, Your State, employs 155 people. Employees are hired on the basis of interviews and tests. Successful applicants are then on probation for three months while they are given on-the-job training under the direction of their departmental supervisors. Each person in the office is considered every six months for a pay increase, but an individual may be passed over if the department head fails to give a recommendation. When a pay increase is allowed in the plants of the company, a corresponding increase is attempted for the general office force. The plants are completely unionized.

In the Cost and Factory Accounting Department are nine employees: four women and three men who have been with the company for five to seven years and two men who have been in their positions for less than a year. The last two, the senior cost accountant and the factory accountant, are the supervisors of the department. These positions have been changed twice in the past three years. In each case the positions have been filled by younger people from outside the office staff. The management, although recognizing the worth of the older staff members, has felt that the employees in the department were not eligible for promotion.

The female employees of this department have been particularly displeased with this action. It has had a noticeable effect on their work. The department supervisors and the company office manager have conferred several times to discuss the excessive amount of talking and visiting that has been going on between the older members of the accounting department. The topic of conversation of these older members is well known to the rest of the office force, and it is feared that a general morale problem will develop if the situation is not corrected at once.

The general office manager of the Baxter Metal Works, Mr. O. E. Yates, has asked you to write a short report recommending the action he should take under these circumstances. You are a "troubleshooting expert" newly hired by the company.

In researching the problem, draw on your knowledge gained from other areas of study, especially management, psychology, and sociology. Submit your report in the form specified by your instructor.

As a start toward deciding on a possible solution, you will want to ponder the alternative courses of action open to you. Would a wage-incentive program work to alleviate the trouble? If so, what system should be recommended?

Naturally, there are other courses of action, and you will perhaps want to consider arguments for and against some of these proposals before making your recommendation: (a) discharging the offending employees, (b) writing a memorandum or letter to all employees (for the general office manager's signature) asking that they refrain from excessive talking and visiting, (c) having the general office manager call in the personnel concerned and ask them to discontinue this practice, and (d) transferring some of the employees to other departments, thus attempting to break up the "talking and visiting" klatches.

20. *Recommending a coupon campaign to introduce a new product.** As Bill Ross, market research assistant at Porter Coffee Company, 1200 Astro Parkway, Some Metropolitan City, Your State, you've been at work for some weeks planning the initial test marketing of a new Porter product: freeze-dried Cupp, another instant coffee (or "soluble coffee," as it is known in the trade), but one with a vastly improved taste and aroma.

You've helped design point-of-sale display advertising and have worked with the advertising agency, Brass & Fustian, on a 30-second TV spot commercial, which shows Cleopatra serving a cup of Cupp to Marc Anthony. The company plan is to give Your City consumers the first chance to appreciate the new product and its advertising—for Your City has long been known as an excellent test market.

The question has arisen whether to introduce Cupp in Your City groceries at a reduced price or to mail Your City residents an advertising leaflet with a coupon good for a

---

* R. H. Ryan of the Business Communication staff contributed the idea for this problem.

price reduction on each consumer's first jar of Cupp. You feel rather strongly that the coupon offer is preferable for a number of reasons. To support your point of view, you've decided to present to your boss, Market Research Director Keyes Clark, a justification report outlining for his evaluation the case for and against couponing.

Cupp will be delivered to Your City grocers at a unit price of $4.39 a jar, with a suggested retail price of $5.49. You believe that it is preferable to let consumers see Cupp for the first time marked at the regular price rather than introducing the product at a promotional rate and apparently raising the price later. On the other hand, some special inducement is in order to persuade shoppers to try Cupp. Reduced-price coupons would provide just such an inducement.

The Brass & Fustian people have offered to produce a simple four-color mailing piece extolling the glories of Cupp and to mail the leaflet to Your City households along with a coupon, all for an estimated cost of $105 per 1,000 addresses. The coupons will be punched cards, coded to show the area of the city to which they were mailed. The distribution cost will also include the use of a mailing list that covers slightly more than 75,000 Your City households, most of them known to be permanent homes within the city limits. The mailing list is guaranteed to be free of duplications and to include no more than 3 percent of undeliverable "nixies." For a slight extra charge the envelopes can be marked "Return Requested, Postage Guaranteed," to provide an accurate count of "nixies" and to remove undelivered coupons from circulation. The direct-mail specialists at the advertising agency estimate that about 20 percent of the coupons will be redeemed, almost certainly between 16 and 24 percent.

You tentatively plan that the coupons will be good for a $1 reduction on the regular price, that is, the $5.49 jar can be purchased for $4.49 and a coupon. (In addition to paying each grocery $1 for each coupon redeemed, you will have to pay the usual 5-cent handling fee per coupon.) The Brass & Fustian people suggest that valuable marketing information can be derived from statistics showing area by area how many households redeemed the coupons. Socioeconomic data on each area will give clues as to the types of households where Cupp has been tried. Further, the agency executives suggest a follow-up telephone survey of a sample of the households from which coupons were redeemed, to determine consumer reactions to the product and to get some indication of probable repeat sales.

While the coupon scheme is admittedly expensive, it can assure maximum, controlled coverage of the market, and it will produce information on consumer characterisitics and product response that would otherwise be difficult to secure. Advertising support on television, at point of sale, and probably in newspapers will add to the cost of the campaign; however, those expenses would probably be necessary in any case. It will be difficult to set up the entire campaign in less than six or seven weeks, though the Porter executive committee would like to have Cupp on the market in Your City early in the spring. They believe that summer is an unpromising season for the introduction of a coffee product. One of the company officers with whom you discussed couponing felt that the possibility of coupon theft was a serious disadvantage. She also mentioned that, when coupons are delivered to large apartment buildings, janitors, trash collectors, or children are sometimes known to gather coupons for sale at cut rates to unscrupulous dealers.

Even with these drawbacks, and some others that may have occurred to you, it seems worthwhile to introduce Cupp to Your City through the use of a coupon campaign, and it is such a campaign that you are recommending in your justification report to Mr. Clark.

20a.   For instructors who use a team approach in short analytical reporting, this problem lends itself to market-area profile analysis. As an example, a team of four might divide Your City into quadrants with use-redemption rates of 16, 19, 21, and 24 percent. Using the latest Your City census data, they can construct consumer profiles for Cupp.

SUGGESTED TOPICS FOR OTHER SHORT REPORT ASSIGNMENTS

1.   Do a justification study for modifying some classroom in your building as a "Communication Laboratory" in which you establish (a) the need for it, (b) the room desired and why, (c) specifications the facility must have—flexible seating and type wanted, lighting, storage cabinets for video and other visual and audio equipment, and (d) guaranteed usage of the facility once it is operational.

2.   Establish the need for a change in some policy, procedure, or requirement in your college or university.

3.   Recommend a revised procedure (for one that currently is not working satisfactorily) in your college or university, such as registration, filing for office in student government, drawing tickets for cultural entertainment or athletic events where seating capacity is less than student demand for the activity.

4.   Recommend a solution for some internal conflict problem in a department store, ad agency, discount house, or other business or industry in your area.

5.   Make a comparison report of the Qatron 48H Home/Office Music System (company owned) versus Piped Music (commercially charged) for some office building in your city.

6.   Make a leased versus company-owned piece of equipment study for some firm in your city.

7.   Do a feasibility study of a volunteer "You-lock-it, you-carry-the-key" storage facility in your city.

8.   Do a feasibility study of a volunteer business student advisory service for businesses in underdeveloped or economically deprived areas of your city.

9.   Arrive at a suggested solution for solving the parking problem on your campus.

10. Do a recommendation study for starting some student-owned, student-operated, student-staffed business for your city, such as

   a. home-cleaning service,

   b. lawn and yard care service,

   c. fresh-cut flower vending,

   d. day nursery care for children of married students,

   e. day excursions for school-aged children during the summer months,

   f. delivery and errand service,

   g. crafts and art, and so on.

11. Select an "ideal site" in your area for a company-owned employee recreation facility.

12. Determine the best copying machine (repography) for an office that requires copy reproduction in excess of 100,000 pieces annually.

13. Decide whether or not a local product firm should adopt a *money-back premium offer* to build sales for a new product. (The new product to be introduced would be packaged with one of the firm's current top sellers.)

14. Determine the feasibility of profit sharing for a sporting-goods store (or some other business in your city) as a means of reducing the job-security fear for its hourly wage employees.

15. Do a survey report of the faculty in your school to determine if their undergraduate major was a factor in their becoming professors.

16. Do a comparison of the merit-rating practices of a selected firm or association (bank, savings and loan, insurance agency) in your city for salary increases with effective merit-rating bases as revealed in research articles.

17. Perform an analysis of placement data from your school's placement service (three years or some other selected time period) for comparisons, trends, implications.

18. Determine the feasibility of automated data processing in a moderate-size business in your city.

19. Should some service industry (gas station, dry cleaning, savings and loan) use trading stamps as a means of increasing its business?

20. Make a justification report for an additional mobile maid service in your city.

21. Do a survey study of the banking, savings and loan, or insurance business in your town to determine its communication improvement program.

22. Determine the most-needed public recreational facility in your city.

23. Where in your city is the best location for

   a. a luxury mobile home park?

b.   a storage locker facility for personal effects (the 24-hour access, "you-lock-it, you-carry-the-key" type)?

c.   a new, public swimming pool, tennis courts, or similar recreation facility?

d.   a garden center to serve *all* the various garden clubs and their special interests?

e.   a new convention center?

7

Preplanning the Business Investigation for Long, Formal, Analytical Reports

*The start of any exciting journey into the unknown
begins by taking that first step.*

The business enterprise, regardless of its magnitude, is involved at one time or another in solving certain basic problems. In the beginning there are the decisions as to what goods or services it will offer to the public and from what headquarters. Next are the determinations of the inputs necessary to generate the output product or service and the economic cost of procuring them. Then are the matters of settling on the optimum volume of the operation, the most feasible distribution system, and the range of competitive pricing. Fourth are the hazards of the success cycle: the decision to expand, how and where, and how to capitalize the expansion. The entrepreneur or the seasoned manager may occasionally be successful with decisions made by hunch in any of these areas, but for long-run survival decision makers must depend upon reliable information about a particular situation to guide them. Additionally, they must have comprehensive records for evaluating the results of past decisions and for improving the quality of future ones. Business reports accumulated as part of repetitive routine operations or initiated to solve a pressing, unusual difficulty become the information system by which executives plot their strategies—the indispensable ally of economic management.

This chapter is designed (1) to orient you to the types of reports written in business and (2) to suggest procedures for planning research activity toward the solution of a specific business problem. The following areas are explored:

1. Report classifications.
2. Categories of research activity.
3. Agenda for business-decision research projects.
4. Defining the problem.
5. Report organization sequence.

REPORT CLASSIFICATIONS

A two-way division of reports designates them as *internal* or *external*. *Internal* communications are those concerned with the operational and administrative details of the enterprise. Most of them are staff written, with the superior as the writer and the subordinate as the reader or vice versa. They may originate at any level of command and move vertically, horizontally from department to department, or diagonally from a department on one level to a department on another. Occasionally, however, management may feel the need of specialized knowledge not available within the organization, in which case an outside professional consultant may be employed. This effort results in a report that may be considered *external*. Other external reports are those that go outside the business to inform the stockholders, to build or maintain the company image through news releases or house organs, or to promote the organization in other ways. Reports may be written with periodic regularity or on a single-occasion basis to meet special needs.

In the business scene internal reports justify their existence in one way or another through their relationship to management's decision-making prerogative. They assume various functions and are presented in various forms.

Types According to Decision-Making Status

Reports are first classified according to their degree of contribution to the decision process in the following way.

Informational Reports. The informational report is written merely to keep management aware of the status of the operation. Production, sales, inventory, and other sorts of statistics are compiled for administrative analysis—the catalyst of the enterprise that speeds up the reactions of the business mix so that management may map its course in a timely, competitive way. Several steps removed from the decision process, informational reports still serve a vital function in its realization.

Interpretative Reports.   A bit higher in decision-making status are those reports designed both to inform and to interpret. The writer of such reports, for example, *explains* unusual sales slumps or upsurges in the light of the environment that created them or *interprets,* for example, delays in the progress report for a construction project. Often called the *examination* report, it does what that name implies: it *examines.* The report writer may be sent to examine a phase of operations and return with the facts plus an opinion.

Analytical Reports.   At the peak of the decision-making pyramid is the analytical report with the components of the decision recorded in its pages. This type of presentation makes full use of the writer's reflective thinking. Its preparation calls for the assembling of information on which to base judgment of alternatives, for evaluation and interpretation of data, and for the final weighing into a conclusion. The analytical report may advance even further and recommend a course of action. Recommendations are usually made, however, only when the writer is authorized specifically to do so.

The Forms a Report May Take

The physical format of the report varies with the extent of management's vested interest in the outcome, the use to be made of it, and the formality of the situation. Format classifications are these:

1. *Filled-in blanks,* with the content and sequence predetermined by the designer.

2. The *memorandum report,* usually in TO, FROM, SUBJECT style, which makes up a part of day-by-day operations. (Company policy may dictate that all internal reports be written in this fashion. If not, this format is best adapted for down-channel or interdepartmental reporting.)

3. The *letter report,* which is a little more formal than the memorandum. Business etiquette might indicate the letter as a preferable form to the memorandum for up-channel communications.

4. The *short, informal report,* which is usually ten pages or less. Such reports are typically staff written and are of temporary or current interest.

5. The *long, formal analytical report* prepared with all the aspects of full-scale formality. Such reports generally involve decisions of great moment to the business requiring them. (The makeup of the long, formal report is developed as the chapters of Part II progress.)

CATEGORIES OF RESEARCH ACTIVITY

The search for data to solve problems makes up a major portion of the report writer's activity, for an investigator may have little or no knowledge about the problem topic and company files may not produce any readily available information. Such research activities fall into several classifications.

According to Prevailing Goal—Pure or Applied

In line with the investigator's primary goal, research is categorized as *pure* or *applied*. If the researcher's purposes are intellectual—gathering information merely for the sake of knowing, with no applications in view—*pure research* is the end result. Large pharmaceutical or chemical companies maintain research laboratories for the purpose of producing discoveries. Independent research institutes, with no economic pressures, undertake research merely to accumulate knowledge. The investigator involved in pure research hopes to arrive at generalizations or laws of universal value.

If the purposes are practical—finding a better way of doing something, of putting to good use the discoveries of the pure researcher, or of readying a substance for the marketplace—the investigator is engaged in *applied* research. Chief concern here is *action*. A large share of business investigations falls into this category.

By Type of Data Employed—Primary or Secondary

According to the source of the data the investigator employs to solve the problem, research is classified as *primary* or *secondary*. If the researcher creates his or her own data through a carefully planned and controlled activity, this person is carrying on *primary* research. In pursuit of primary data, the analyst may implement a *survey* through the questionnaire, the telephone, the interview, or panels of respondents. Or the researcher may find out what is needed through *observation*—by watching the activity surrounding the object of investigation according to thoughtfully preplanned criteria. *An experiment* may be conducted in a meticulously controlled environment, theoretically and traditionally, with all the variables kept equal save one. The computer and probability theory, however, afford greater variable flexibility.

If the analyst chooses the use of data already recorded at the time the investigation gets underway, the analyst is pursuing *secondary* research. The researcher has no part in creating the data. They are waiting to be found in printed sources, in company records, in the minutes of board meetings, or in other informally recorded documents. The analyst's job is that of assembling the data and analyzing them.

The data the analyst pursues may be further categorized in three ways: (1) historical, (2) survey, or (3) experimental. The records of a company, compiled continuously, furnish *historical* data that may well serve as the base for many business decisions, with no capital outlay involved. In addition, historical data may be thought of as any information of record prior to the investigation. It may have been preserved formally or only in the minds of eyewitnesses or of receivers of eyewitness accounts. Historical data may be gathered through primary or secondary means or through a combination of the two, whereas survey and experimental data are acquired through primary research.

In Line with the Research Method

The plan of attack the investigator applies to the problem, whether primary or secondary data are used, may be termed the *research method*. Five kinds are pertinent to business studies.

Descriptive Research.   Inquiry as to the current status of practices, policies, operations, or any phase of business activity is termed *descriptive* research. The analyst is concerned with determining how the object of investigation operates and the accent is on one point in time—usually the present. Such investigations are often initiated for diagnostic reasons: What is wrong? Part of their work may be prescriptive: What should be done to remedy the difficulty? A final step may be prognostic: What is the future of the business phenomenon examined?

Historical Research.   The *historical* researcher perhaps looks for the same things as does the descriptive researcher, but with a suitable time period involved. This researcher is concerned with how the object of investigation has operated from a chosen point in the past up to the present with predictions for the future. The primary interest is in change, growth, and development and the causes of such change and their implications. Management studies the past as an insight into the present and for anticipating activity not yet realized.

Sociological Research.   In the business setting *sociological* research deals with groups; the interaction of people, the impact of policies or practices on company employees and vice versa, or the effect of one or several aspects of the business environment on the people involved.

Prognostic Research.   An educated "guesstimate" of future trends is necessary for business prosperity. Management must know when and how much to produce, the possible future cost of inputs, and any trends in the environment that might alter plans. *Prognostic* investigation may be implemented through statistical measures (the most valid and universally accepted research techniques) or through the application of the researcher's analytical powers.

Operations Research.   A relatively new method for business is the systems approach for plotting *operational* strategies. In such an approach the elements of the system are segregated and decisions involving the parts are made in terms of their impact on the system as a whole. The advent of the computer has opened vast avenues of systems exploration, many still in the formative stage. Through the mathematical models of linear programming, an anlyst may derive a sound scheme for controlling inventories or capital budgeting. Simulation of an operation in a mathematical model may enable the investigator to revise a distribution system scientifically. A year's run on a computer printout may be examined with different configurations of components being applied until the best system becomes apparent. Dynamic programming, game theory, and probability assignment are additional tools for augmenting the accuracy of decision techniques.

In reality, the research methods outlined are not clearly defined nor mutually exclusive, for more than one research method is present in practically all studies.

According to the Nature of the Business Decision

Gearing the research to management's greatest need is the final guiding factor for investigative effort. The type of problem to be solved gives the study its initial direction. This text explores three major types:

Problems with Yes-or-No Answers.   Studies involving yes-or-no answers (often labeled *binary* decisions) generally arise with the hypothesis that something is true: the addition of a new product will boost lagging sales; the establishment of a branch in another state will prove profitable; the construction of a $10 million plant will be feasible; or the cost of an electronic data-processing installation will pay out in a specified number of years with increased efficiency. The executive authorizing the study wants a yes-or-no answer. A 50 : 50 answer is not much good since action will result from the findings of the investigation. Rarely are sufficient data available to provide a clear-cut yes-or-no answer; consequently, a set of weights and balances, supplemented with derived data, is often necessary to achieve at least a

60 : 40 answer—the best odds, at times, that management may expect. Such studies are descriptive in establishing the current environment affecting the decision and prognostic in anticipating the success of the proposed venture for a projected period of time.

The Comparative-Evaluation Investigation.   Determining the better of two ways of doing things or the best of several is a pervading part of the management hazard: Is it better to issue stock or borrow money to finance a costly project? Which of three cities would make the best location for a branch factory? Is it better to concentrate on products characterized by style and luxury connotations or on those affording economy and large volume? Such comparative-evaluation studies are descriptive in that they describe the operation of the alternatives and prognostic in that they predict which will operate the most efficiently for the future.

Descriptive-Analytical Inquiry.   In the business enterprise numerous occasions arise in which management needs to know precisely how and why an operation or practice is working as a base for future company plans. How well is the new electronic data-processing installation paying off? What are the new problems arising from it? What is the state of employee morale as the result of the wage-job evaluation plan? What type of individual makes the best insurance sales representative? What type of advertising campaign will best launch a product in a specified market area?

At other times the executive knows that something is wrong and seeks a remedy. Why does the company suffer from excessive middle-management turnover? What is at the root of poor labor-management relations? Who is at fault in the dispute arising at the supervisory level? Such studies describe the status quo, diagnose the difficulties, and prescribe the remedy.

If something is working unusually well, management likes to know why as a means of perpetuating the good: What accounts for the superior performance of a department? What are the outstanding characteristics of a good plant superintendent?

At still other times the executive is interested in knowing the status quo as a means of predicting the future. How do actual sales compare with budgeted sales? What is to be done about the finished-goods storage problem resulting from a poor sales quarter? Large operations and small ones in increasing numbers look to the computer and to linear programming for the solutions to such questions.

It is evident by now that overlapping among the classifications of research activities exists and that the analyst had best abandon an either/or type of thinking in favor of a both/and type. So long as the investigator has an insight into the research processes, clear-cut distinctions are not essential.

AGENDA FOR BUSINESS-DECISION RESEARCH PROJECTS

Whether the analyst will seek a mathematical or computer answer to a business problem or will apply his or her own decision-making powers toward a solution is probably a matter of economics and personal preparation. In either case, the approach is much the same: the essential features of the problem must be determined in all of its many aspects. The agenda for decision-making research projects illustrated in Figure 7-1 is a step-by-step guide from the germ of an idea to be investigated to the finished long report. It is designed so that you can adapt it for any particular analysis technique. Formalizing research plans according to the stages suggested in the agenda and elaborated as the chapters in Part II develop will enable you to proceed on a project with little lost motion.

Defining the Problem

Research activity in the business enterprise is usually authorized at some level of command; thus the investigator receives the problem already partially analyzed in the mind of another person, possibly with a better background on the subject than the researcher's own. To orient himself or herself to the situation, the analyst moves into step I of the agenda—a comprehensive exploration of all facets of the problem that could influence the ultimate answer. Questions should be asked unashamedly until one is sure what is expected.

If the authorizer's statement of the problem is in the form of a hypothesis, the investigator should mull it over, tentatively testing its soundness, and enumerate the objectives of the proposed investigation as they appear at this point. For step II, the analyst may well follow the stages of defining the problem outlined in the following paragraphs as springboards for thought in adaptation to his or her specific inquiry.

Appraising the Company Situation. The analyst can become acquainted with the internal and external environment of the problem by asking questions such as these:

1. Financial aspects

   a. What is the company's financial picture currently? For the last five to ten years? The outlook for the future?

   b. What capital is available for the new project? Will it call for a

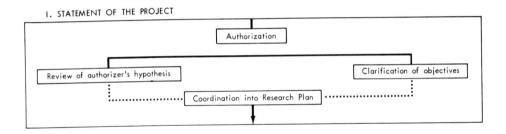

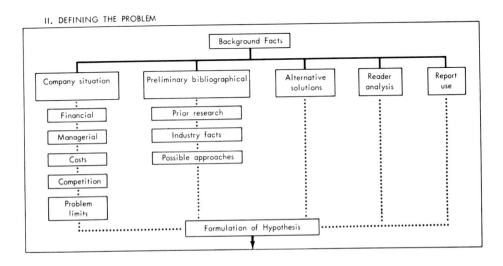

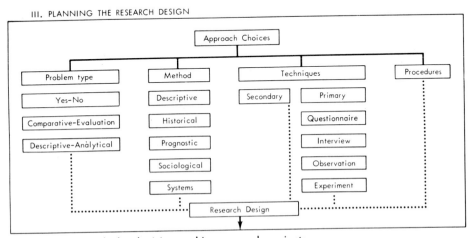

Figure 7-1   Agenda for decision-making research projects

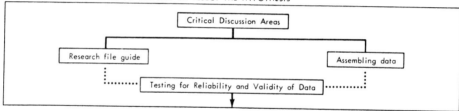

IV. SEARCH FOR DATA TO SUPPORT OR REJECT THE HYPOTHESIS

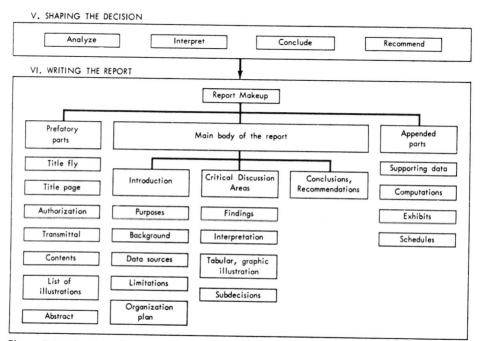

V. SHAPING THE DECISION

VI. WRITING THE REPORT

Figure 7-1   Continued

stock issue? If so, what are the plans for it? Is borrowed capital proposed? If so, what are the arrangements? Other financing proposals?

c.   Are there any particularly advantageous or disadvantageous features about the company assets?

d.   What sort of profit percentage does the company strive for? What profit percentage does it expect of the new project? How soon?

2.   Managerial features

a.   Are the company's current operations efficient?

b.   What management, labor, and other personnel are provided for the new venture?

c. What labor and personnel problems are or might be evident?

d. Is the operation located well to make efficient use of its resources, raw materials, or other input ingredients? For the marketing of its products or services?

e. Are the necessary input resources readily available in adequate quantity and at economical cost?

f. What are the credit terms? What influence do they have on the proposed activity?

3. Costs of doing business

a. How much will it cost to manufacture this product or create this service? Is the cost compatible with the going sales rate?

b. How much promotion money is planned? How does the budgeted amount compare with that employed in other similar situations?

c. Are transportation costs excessive or reasonable?

d. What are the possible hidden costs?

e. What are the peculiar tax problems?

f. What seasonal variations are anticipated?

g. What is the anticipated break-even point?

4. The competitive climate

a. Who are the known competitors of this business or project? Where are they located? What about their size and market stronghold? Is this industry dominated by giants? Or is it made up of numerous relatively small factors?

b. Is the pricing of this product or service competitive?

c. What government regulations affect the proposal?

5. The problem itself

a. What previous efforts has the company made to solve this problem? What efforts have other people made?

b. What work has already been done on the current project?

c. What limits has the company set on the investigation?

c. How much time is allowed for it?

e. What expense money is available? What assistance?

Exploring the General Literature in the Field. Because the researcher does not know the answer to the problem—or perhaps even the significant aspects of it—he or she may be the victim of false moves. Evidence may be tracked down that later has little bearing on the problem; it should be ignored. Any measure that can cut down on the wasted effort is worthy of consideration.

A universally helpful early step in any investigation—whether the researcher will create primary data or gather it from previously recorded sources—is a cursory examination of the general literature in the field. Armed with notetaking cards, the researcher goes to the best available library. The intent at this point is not to make an exhaustive study of the literature but to survey it generally as a help in formulating the problem.

Overall industry material is sought first to accomplish these things for the analyst:

1. to give an idea of what has already been done on the subject
2. to clarify the nature of the industry and the size and power of the principal factors
3. to discover any problems peculiar to the industry, particularly if the researcher is writing the report as an outside consultant
4. to give an initial insight as to the significant criteria upon which the overall decision might hinge
5. to provide bibliography clues
6. to open up possible avenues of approach to the problem.

If the industry under investigation is well established and of importance nationally to investors, *Standard & Poors' Industry Surveys* and the *Survey of Current Business* are excellent sources for this preliminary reading. After the principal factors in the industry are discovered, a rather thorough financial rundown on them over a period of time is available in *Moody's Investors Service.* Since most established industries have developed trade associations, a very good source of industry economics may be obtained from the annual statistical issue of the association's publication.

If local inquiry does not produce the names and addresses of the trade association in question, libraries have fairly current directories available. Trade associations are generally most cooperative in providing selected copies of their publications on request. If the industry studied is rather new—as quite frequently it is—*The New York Times,* with almost every item listed in a specially prepared index, is an excellent source, as is *The Wall Street Journal,* with an index for the New York edition. State divisions of trade associations and chambers of commerce provide data and clues for sources on the local level. Directories for manufacturers, banks, insurance companies, and so on are available in most states. *Fortune, Business Week, The Nation's Business, Forbes* and other periodicals frequently contain colorfully written industry accounts.

The best advice for any researcher is to carry on a continuing love affair with the library—the fountainhead of learning—and to maintain at least cordial relations with the librarian, a specialist in tracking down information. When the investigator gets this general economic picture in mind, library research pauses for a while. The next step is to pin down as closely as possible the limits of the problem.

>   ***Posing the Alternative Solutions to the Problem.***   Knowing that a business decision hinges on the study, the analyst concentrates on alternative solutions to the problem. Not only may he or she be called upon to defend a solution arrived at, but the investigator may also find it necessary to say that it is better than other solutions. So, as many possible solutions as seem reasonable are written down for reflective thought. The nature of the alternatives will differ according to the type of decision to be reached.

In some cases, finding the alternatives and evaluating them is basic to the solution of the problem, as in the following example. A furniture manufacturer is plagued by lagging sales with the result that warehouse capacity is completely filled. Something must be done immediately. The person involved in solving the problem would begin to list possible solutions in this way: (1) maintain scheduled production and rent warehousing space until sales catch up with production, (2) shut down the whole operation until sales catch up, (3) cut production on slow-moving merchandise and step up production on fast movers, (4) cut overall production by the amount of finished goods in the warehouse, and so on.

In other cases, considering the alternatives early in the study adds insight, even though the alternatives are not a part of the study itself. For instance, activated by the hope of expanding profit, a Virginia manufacturer of low-priced shoes for men and women believes that a branch for production of women's high-priced shoes would be a moneymaker. He wants a study conducted to prove or disprove his thesis. By assignment, then, he wants only one solution to his quest for added profits investigated. It is well, nonetheless, for the researcher to list alternative solutions to the problem as part of the background for the study and to begin to list alternatives such as these: (1) locate the plant in Metropolitan City but stick to the manufacture of low-priced shoes, the realm of company experience; (2) add a women's high-priced line but expand the home plant, where many problems are already settled, to produce it; (3) stick to present lines and initiate an aggressive sales campaign with part or all of the money allotted for the Metropolitan City plant; and so on. Although the focus of the study will be on the evaluation of the already-decided-upon location, a knowledge of the alternatives will help the researcher evaluate the data gathered subsequently to formulate a decision.

>   ***Analyzing the Possible Readers.***   Before deciding on the true purposes of the study, the analyst needs to examine critically the chief reader and any possible auxiliary readers. A beginning might be to ask this question: "What rank does the chief reader hold in the company?" If the main reader is the president, a bead on the size of the report is immediately drawn. Highlight

presentation of the essential issues is the writer's welcome gift to the president—and the details of the presentation widen as the target level of command falls.

"Through what chain of command will the report move on the way to the ultimate reader? Will this report receive consideration from the board of directors? Who is on the board?" The more readers of different types that are added to the brew, the more complicated the selection of ingredients becomes. Considering the readers calls for other inevitable questions: What do the readers know about the subject? Will they understand the technical language, the lingo of the trade? What is their intellectual and cultural level? Should the possibility of future, as well as present, readers influence the way the report is prepared? With these questions answered, the report writer summarizes the characteristics of the readers as another step in giving his or her work direction.

Clarifying the Use to Be Made of the Report.   If management asks for a decision as a result of the study, it is the writer's obligation to make one. A fine line exists between drawing conclusions and making recommendations, but there is one. The researcher's position is less vulnerable if he or she says "The evidence points in this direction" than if he or she says "It is recommended that this step be taken." The final substance of a study might be "There is insufficient evidence of the success of this move now to warrant the expense involved in implementing it." If all research required a definitive answer, vast assemblages of time, money, and effort devoted to inconclusive research would have to be looked upon as waste. Certainly no one would look upon the inconclusive decades of cancer research as waste, for each experiment very likely pushes back the frontiers of ignorance a little farther.

If the report is part of the company's long-range planning, an inconclusive answer might be the right one. If action must be taken immediately, a conclusion one way or the other must be drawn. Business is highly competitive and time is its dictator. With threatening forces pushing toward a deadline, there is no place for a fence-riding individual. Management, in a state of doubt before the study began, may feel fortunate with a 60-percent answer on which to base a decision.

If management plans to use the report for a preliminary decision, with a later, larger study in the offing, the writer knows that a beeline to the most significant issues marks the course. If the report is primarily directed to one reader, but with the possibility that its substance may later serve as the base for a petition to charter or to convince the Securities Exchange Commission that a stock issue is feasible, the report writer has cues as to the direction the study should take.

By way of illustration, the case of Harley Flour Mills, a plant considering the addition of ready mixes to the product line is presented here much as a researcher might record it in the preliminary planning stage.

DEFINING THE PROBLEM OF HARLEY FLOUR MILLS

Surveying the Company Situation

Financial Aspects

1. Harley Flour Mills, a three-generation family business, has experienced a steady slump in sales for the last ten years.

2. The land, buildings, and equipment are currently appraised at $1,625,000, although it is doubtful that the company could be liquidated at that figure.

3. Machinery is in good operating condition, despite the fact that some of it is ten years old.

4. The loss of about $88,000 in the last two years leaves operating capital almost nonexistent from company funds, except for tax rebate.

5. The new president, Thomas Y. Bentley, recently married to the great-great-granddaughter of the founder, has unlimited personal capital for investment in the company, if such procedure seems desirable.

6. The addition of ready mixes to the product lines, Bentley's hopeful solution to the net-loss position, must realize 8 percent of gross sales if the venture is to prove profitable.

7. Machinery for manufacturing ready mixes can be provided for an additional $150,000.

Managerial Features

1. Harley Mills was founded as a sole proprietorship by August Harley and has continued as a family business up to the present.

2. Originally manned by 10 employees, the company saw ups and downs until ten years ago. During the post–World War II years, the number of employees swelled to around 250; subsequently production slowed down until 100 people now carry on the operation.

Production Facts

1. The present 24-hour capacity of the mill is 2,700 100-lb sacks of flour and 90 100-lb sacks of meal, with a 300-day operating year.

2. Five years ago was the last time that as much as 80-percent capacity was maintained.

3. The last two years saw production to orders, with operation at approximately 50 to 60 percent of capacity, respectively.

The Competitive Climate

1.   Known competition consists of three independent flour mills making ready mixes and branches of large national operations that have infiltrated the state.

2.   Dry ready-mixed products must compete with other similar products as well as with frozen and refrigerated lines.

The Problem Itself

1.   President Bentley wants an investigation of the feasibility of ready mixes as a means of bolstering lagging sales.

2.   He has eliminated from consideration frozen and refrigerated lines for the present, hoping to take his market a step at a time.

3.   Initial distribution will cover a 600-mile radius of the home plant.

A Survey of the Economics of the Industry

Standard & Poor's Industry Survey of the flour-milling industry and *Northwestern Millers Almanac* indicate that

1.   The ready-mix business is dominated by giants who have been able to force smaller operations to withdraw through minimum pricing and extensive advertising.

2.   The introduction of 30 to 50 ready-mix lines by the giants is fairly common.

Alternate Solutions to the Problem

1.   Liquidating the company at the going rate and investing the money in some suitable way.

2.   Converting present equipment, with necessary additions, for the manufacture of a product with more sales appeal at the lowest change-over cost.

Analysis of Possible Readers

1.   Bentley is young, enthusiastic, optimistic, with the daring to take chances. He is intelligent and, despite his background of wealth, is dominated by the profit motive. He is well educated, but not particularly well versed in the flour-milling industry. He has attempted to make up for this lack by a rather intensive study of operations in the brief time he has been president.

The Use to be Made of the Report

1.   Bentley will use the report as the base for an immediate decision to add ready mixes to the product line or to look for another way of using company assets.

2.   The board of directors will study the report before giving final sanction to the project.

3.   President Bentley wants conclusions as to which way the evidence points, but he will make his own recommendations.

DESIGNING THE RESEARCH SCHEME

With the broad aspects of the problem defined by the authorizer (or by the analyst if the study is self-initiated) and the aspects of the investigation hewed into shape from analysis of background facts, the researcher is ready for step III on the agenda: planning the research design. The analyst has likely already decided whether the problem is a yes-or-no, a comparative-evaluation, or a descriptive-analytical type. No doubt already determined also is whether the inquiry will be primarily descriptive, historical, prognostic, sociological, or mathematical, and in what ways the research methods will be combined. The remainder of the research design is embodied in three stages: (1) a formal statement of the working hypothesis, (2) the definition of the critical discussion areas, and (3) the selection of appropriate research techniques and procedures for locating facts and statistics to support the hypothesis.

Statement of the Working Hypothesis

If the problem is assigned to the reporter by a superior, a tentative answer may already have been formulated. President Bentley of Harley Mills, besieged with financial troubles, notes the success of other millers with ready mixes, examines the possibilities of his own operation for producing them, and settles on the tentative answer that they would be a solution to his difficulties. Research will tell him whether or not the answer is right. Or a bottleneck develops in an assembly line. The supervisor enumerates all instances of exactly what happens up to the bottleneck. She or he applies reflective thinking to the difficulty until a probable solution is conceived. Subsequent testing will verify or disprove this belief.

This examination of specific instances for a cause-and-effect relationship and for other discernible patterns with the hope of arriving at a generalization is a form of inductive logic; the generalization or tentative answer is known as the *working hypothesis.* Hypotheses in the behavioral sciences are rather pseudoscientific in contrast with those of the physical and biological sciences and are only in effect verifiable; yet their formulation gives direction to investigations based on them. The analyst may find it necessary to think up several hypotheses for a problem and submit them to critical analysis before accepting one of them as the base for study. Subsequently, the analyst will search diligently for data that support or reject this thesis, perform elaborate tests, engage in extensive observation, and carry on interrogation to discover the truth of the original belief. *This starting with a generalization (the hypothesis) and looking for specific instances to defend it or discredit it is known as deductive logic.* The final answer, derived from evaluation of specific instances, will be a rephrasing of the original premise or a rejection of it. This combination of inductive and deductive logic forms a pattern for building a research design.

A final stage in clarifying the problem might well be the framing of its elements into a question to be answered by research: Will the addition of ready mixes to the product lines of Harley Mills be an economically feasible means of rebuilding the company's financial structure? Will it be profitable for Braddock-Sperry Shoe Corporation to manufacture women's high-priced shoes in the selected location?

The Definition of the Critical Discussion Areas

Underlying the working hypothesis selected to serve as a base for a business investigation is a key idea or decision crieterion, either expressed or implied. In the Harley Mills problem, the decision criterion is *profitability*, as it is for many commercial projects. With the key idea or determinant in mind, the analyst next tries to define the kinds of data needed to prove profitability, financial feasibility or whatever overall decision criterion is embodied in the hypothesis. The kinds of data needed may be isolated deductively through a pseudoscientific form of syllogistic reasoning: What must be present if the hypothesis proves to be true? The simple hypothetical syllogism reads like this:

Major Premise:	If A is true, B will occur.
Minor Premise:	A is true.
Conclusion:	Therefore, B will occur.

The working hypothesis in the syllogism is B; what will have to be present for B to occur is symbolized by A.

The Research for a Yes-or-No Answer.   Business decisions calling for yes-or-no answers are easily translated into syllogistic form. Let us consider here also the hypothesis for Harley Mills. What must be present for financial feasibility to result? A little thought may produce a simple syllogism such as this:

Major Premise: If (A) there is sufficient *demand* for the company's ready mixes, (B) the competition can be met, and (C) the manufacturing costs are compatible, (D) the addition of ready mixes to the product line will be profitable.

Minor Premise: (A) There is sufficient demand.
                    (B) The competition can be met.
                    (C) Manufacturing costs are compatible.
Conclusion: Therefore (D) the addition of ready mixes will be
                    financially feasible.

Determining whether or not minor premises A, B, and C are true makes up the research activity.

The components of the minor premises may be determined in the same way: What will have to be present if the demand is to be sufficient, if the competition can be met, and so on. If there is adequate demand, for example, such things as these might have to be present:

1. The current and future population in the market area must be adequate.

2. The present and future per-capita income of the population should be such as to encourage the purchase of ready mixes, which are more expensive than breads made by baking from flour.

3. The eating habits of the area should point toward acceptance of convenience foods.

The organization of a research design for a yes-or-no answer is pictured in Figure 7-2. The analyst begins at the bottom of the design, deciding what kinds of evidence (such as the three items just listed for demand) will be needed to support the minor premises A, B, and C, according to the reasoning described. The search activity may unearth data more relevant to the problem than that set up in this preplanning. If so, the design can be readily altered. Consciously planning the research in line with this design assures the analyst of obtaining data with maximum relevance to the yes-or-no decision he or she hopes eventually to arrive at; consequently, where the analyst is going is "a known." Techniques for formulating the yes-or-no decision from data gathered in this way are elaborated in Chapter 9.

A Research Model for the Comparative-Evaluation Inquiry.   In the comparative-evaluation study, the hypothesis is virtually that one choice of two or of several will be more *efficient* in achieving the analyst's purposes than will the alternatives. The overall decision criterion, then, is *efficiency*, translated into what the chosen alternative is supposed to do. The investigator will likely have gone through an inductive analysis of a number of possible alternatives before selecting those for further investigation. Suppose that a corn-producing factory in Iowa is looking for a city in which to locate a sorghum-processing branch, since sorghum serves many of the same purposes as corn at a cheaper production cost. The investigator considers all the cities that might be suitable sites and selects three for further study. The

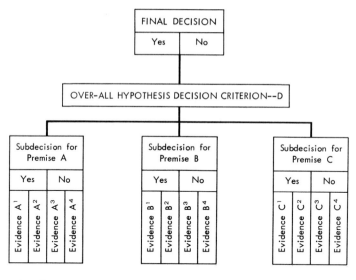

Legend
D = The key idea or criterion for the ultimate decision found in the hypothesis.
A, B, and C = The premises as to what must be present for the hypothesis to prove true.
Evidence 1, 2, 3, and 4 --Data to support the Premises A, B, and C.

NOTE: The model is planned from the top down. The data are gathered and filled in from the
bottom, serving as a base for the Yes-No Decision Design in Chapter 9.

Figure 7-2   Research model for a yes-or-no decision

criteria for the ultimate choice are the criteria for this specific type of plant location: sorghum availability, adequate resources such as gas and water, transportation facilities and satisfactory rates, community acceptance, and so on. These criteria become the components of *efficiency*, the bases of the major premise: that choice 1, 2, or 3 will be superior to the others as to the presence of criteria A, B, and C.

In comparative-evaluation studies (illustrated in Figure 7-3), the bases of comparison make better divisions for the research effort (and for the final report) than do the things compared. If the researcher begins with city 1, compiling statistics for raw-material availability, production resources and transportation facilities and proceeds to do the same thing for cities 2 and 3, no real comparison results until he or she gets to the conclusions. Such a concluding section will in effect call for a rewriting of the entire report. The analyst operates more effectively by beginning with raw-material availability, the first plant-location criterion, gathering data as to each city's capacity according to this measuring stick, and then following the same procedure for other criteria. The researcher thus piles up data fuel for subdecisions on the cities compared that are eventually blended into the final choice. This research model forms the bases for the Decision Design for the Comparative-Evaluation Study given in Chapter 9.

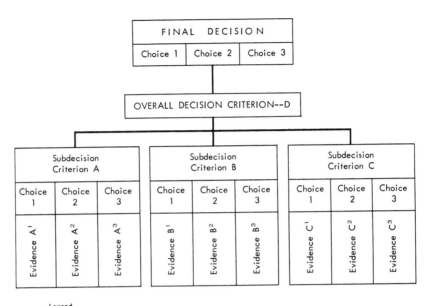

Legend
Choices 1, 2, 3 = The items to be evaluated.
Criterion D --The key idea, the summation of criteria of performance for the chosen alternative.
Criteria A, B, C = Elements which must be present for the chosen alternative to perform efficiently:
A + B + C = D.

NOTE: The model is planned from the top down. The data are gathered and filled in from the bottom,
leading to subdecisions ranking each of the choices according to Criteria A, B, and C.

Figure 7-3 Research model for a comparative-evaluation study

Research Scheme for the Descriptive-Analytic Investigation. For studies designed to determine how a phenomenon operates, what might be desirable, and how to get there, the analyst prepares the research design around the aspects of a working hypothesis, which are arrived at inductively. For example, Company X is plagued with excessive middle-management turnover. The analyst examines the exit interviews of those leaving the company over a period of time in an attempt to discover a pattern; such things as lack of promotion opportunities, necessity for apple-polishing, or low salary levels may show up—the bases for further investigation. How well an electronic data-processing system is functioning may be divided according to what the system is supposed to do: cost saving (aspect A), increased efficiency (aspect B), good employee morale (aspect C), and so on. Linear programming for warehouse, inventory, or budget control and other forms of operations research so prevalent today may well fall into this category of business problem.

The report developed from the findings of a descriptive-analytic study (illustrated in Figure 7-4) may end with conclusions that describe the operation, diagnose the bad features, or pinpoint the good ones according to the purpose of the study. The report may go a step further with recommendations that suggest remedies or implementation plans, or forecast the future

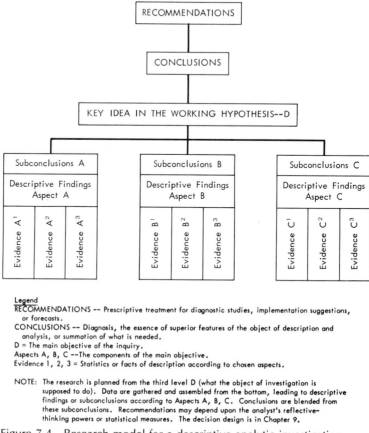

RECOMMENDATIONS

CONCLUSIONS

KEY IDEA IN THE WORKING HYPOTHESIS--D

Subconclusions A

Descriptive Findings
Aspect A

Evidence A^1 Evidence A^2 Evidence A^3

Subconclusions B

Descriptive Findings
Aspect B

Evidence B^1 Evidence B^2 Evidence B^3

Subconclusions C

Descriptive Findings
Aspect C

Evidence C^1 Evidence C^2 Evidence C^3

Legend
RECOMMENDATIONS -- Prescriptive treatment for diagnostic studies, implementation suggestions, or forecasts.
CONCLUSIONS -- Diagnosis, the essence of superior features of the object of description and analysis, or summation of what is needed.
D = The main objective of the inquiry.
Aspects A, B, C --The components of the main objective.
Evidence 1, 2, 3 = Statistics or facts of description according to chosen aspects.

NOTE: The research is planned from the third level D (what the object of investigation is supposed to do). Data are gathered and assembled from the bottom, leading to descriptive findings or subconclusions according to Aspects A, B, C. Conclusions are blended from these subconclusions. Recommendations may depend upon the analyst's reflective-thinking powers or statistical measures. The decision design is in Chapter 9.

Figure 7-4   Research model for a descriptive-analytic investigation

of the phenomenon described. The decision design based on this research model is given in Chapter 9.

Selecting the Appropriate Research Tools and Procedures

When the analyst has set up the critical discussion areas for the investigation, the broad outlines of research activity are crystallized—as well as the skeleton outline of the report to be written. To be decided next is whether data will be gathered from secondary sources or whether the analyst will create them independently and the techniques to employ creating them, the remaining phases of Step III on the Agenda.

For a substantial number of business studies, a fairly dependable answer may be derived from economic analyses of printed data. A preliminary decision from secondary sources may be valuable to the analyst, even though a primary investigation is planned for the ultimate answer. For those business problems for which data are not available from printed sources or company records, the researcher in most cases will institute some sort of survey. The questionnaire and the interview are tools of proved efficiency for establishing a market profile, for determining consumer preferences, or for describing the company image. Motivational research and the depth interview are highly valid approaches for assessing the *why* of human behavior. Panels of respondents are widely used in marketing circles, as are telephone surveys for limited amounts of data. Observation is a means of recording incidents that, together with other incidents, may produce a generalization on the way toward the final decision. This method of research is often used in grocery stores for the examination of customer habits, on street corners for traffic patterns, or in factories for appraising the efficiency of plant layouts. The opportunities for business experiment are many and profitable—but generally the most costly and time-consuming research form. It is not often that a student researcher has a chance to go into a business and actually conduct an experiment. It is equally difficult for students to gain entry into a company for other forms of original research. For these reasons, the emphasis of this text is on the research techniques presumed to be the most widely feasible—the survey and research from secondary sources. With the accent on analysis and writing, the investigator may lend depth to her or his experience by vicariously working through preassembled data (the case method) or through the rich educational rewards of mastering the techniques of bibliographic inquiry.

Since putting thoughts in writing is a further step in clarification, the analyst does well to finalize the research plans by recording the following items.

1.   A statement of the project derived from formal authorization and preliminary assessment of objectives.

2.   A listing of background facts derived from

   a.   Appraising the company situation.
   b.   Reviewing the literature in the field.
   c.   Posing alternative solutions.
   d.   Analyzing the possible readers.
   e.   Clarifying the use to be made of the report.

3.   Formulating the working hypothesis.

4.   The aspects of the research design growing out of

   a.   A decision as to whether the inquiry is a yes-or-no, comparative-evaluation, or descriptive-analytic type, with a consequent selection of the appropriate research model.

b. A choice of research method or methods to be used and how: descriptive, historical, prognostic, sociological, operations.

c. The choice of techniques to be used: secondary or a specific form of primary research—the questionnaire, telephone survey, interview, observation, experiment, or such.

d. A concrete outline of procedures to be followed, including a time schedule.

e. A delineation of the critical discussion areas and the types of data needed to support them.

f. The preparation of a research file guide, recap sheet, or punch-card code for recording and storing data as they are assembled.

When you have settled on a project, you may find it profitable to carry your analytical thinking through the three steps on the agenda outlined in this chapter: I. Statement of the project; II. Defining the problem; and III. Planning the research design. Then, with your preliminary planning done, you will be ready for step IV, Search for data to support or reject the hypothesis—the subject matter of the next chapter.

PROBLEMS FOR BUSINESS REPORTS: LONG, FORMAL, ANALYTICAL INVESTIGATIONS

An attempt is made here to provide problems for class or individual assignment that are suitable for analysis in whatever college or university might use this book—a task virtually impossible of realization. One solution considered was that of basing all proposed decisions on national statistics, an approach deemed shortsighted in that it would orient prospective entrepreneurs for big business only. Student appraisals of the report-writing classes in which the procedures outlined in this text have been followed often rank new knowledge of the local, state, or regional economy as one of the most desirable outcomes; consequently, research problems that lend themselves to area adaptation were elected for major emphasis. The adaptation process is necessarily yours. Laws in the several states differ. The difficulties a type of business encounters in different locales vary. Effort was also exerted to supply situations of interest to writers with different fields of specialization.

As you read the cases, you will notice that they involve solutions of varying degrees of difficulty. Such variety was provided so that individual classes could make choices in line with the emphasis to be placed on Part II in the makeup of course content. Some of the problems may well be set up for a joint research activity. When the class or classes in preliminary planning sessions have determined the kinds of data needed to solve the difficulty, a director of research may be selected. This director subsequently assigns to individuals or groups the task of locating certain data and of duplicating them for class distribution. Then each class member prepares an individual report on a competitive basis.

We bring you the problems that our students have found the most absorbing and challenging. It is our hope that you too find them a rewarding educational experience. In each of them you and your instructor will fill in the locations, where needed, and make other appropriate changes.

At the end of this section is a list of suggested topics for the three major types of business problems to serve as springboards for developing cases dealing with real or hypothetical companies. Going out into the business environment to investigate actual situations and propose solutions to difficulties is indeed a rewarding report experience. Quite often, though, access to a business is understandably denied. With some ingenuity you may create a hypothetical company background with an imagined difficulty that your report may in a measure solve. That is the kind of investigation you will want to plan, rather than the term-paper variety, to utilize the decision-making techniques explored in this chapter and others in the text.

1. *Determining if Some City, Your State, is a likely site for a profitable, exclusive mobile-homes park.* Seton Enterprises, Inc., 2115 Ricker Building, Chicago, owns and operates a chain of prestige hotels and motels—the Arrowheads—located at carefully chosen spots in various parts of the United States. Three years of making surveys, drawing plans, and selecting ideal site sizes have led the officials, under the presidency of Mr. John T. Seton, to the decision to expand into luxury mobile-home park operation. One of the first sites he has selected for extensive examination is Some City, Your State. Mr. Seton has chosen you, Ronald Hendrix, and your firm, Some City Research Associates, 917 Colorado Street, to make the study for him at your quoted fee or $5,000. He has in mind a park costing $450,000 on which capital he expects at least a 17-percent yearly return by the end of the third year of operation.

During your several phone conversations and one hasty trip to Chicago, Mr. Seton has set forth certain specifications for your consideration. He envisions a tract of some eight acres as the initial development, with additions or subdivisions to come later, as the demand warrants, in an adjoining ten acres on which he has an option to purchase. The initial park would be complete with streets, curbing, patios, 100-amp electrical service, underground utilities, automatic sprinkler system for lawns, landscaping, swimming pool, car wash, coin-operated laundry, and hobby and storage areas. Water would be furnished. The kind of park Seton has in mind would be modeled after some of the luxury installations now thriving in California, Arizona, and Florida.

Zoning regulations in Some City would impose certain restrictions as to the minimum amount of space for the lots; a reasonable figure might be 3,000 square feet, of assorted shapes and sizes so that different models of mobile homes could be accommodated. Streets would have to be at least 36 feet wide to take care of large mobile homes. Easy access to a state or U.S. highway is also a rather uniform requisite.

At present the typical mobile home is an 850-square-foot unit with two bedrooms, a bathroom, kitchen-dinette, and living room that sells, fully furnished, for $17,000 (10 percent down and $250 a month). Luxury carpeted, air-conditioned models sell for up to $30,000. (These figures may need to be modified. They are given to indicate the types of housing with which they might compete.) Suggested initial costs for the park are given. You may choose to substitute timely, local figures, as well as to change the amount of the total investment:

Eight acres of land at roughly $12,500 an acre	$100,000
Option to purchase an adjoining 10 acres	25,000
Curbing and streets	50,000
Patios	25,000
Electrical service, all underground utility connections, sprinkler systems	125,000
Pool, hobby area, car wash, laundry, and storage areas	110,000
Contingency fund	15,000
Total	$450,000

In addition, these overhead figures are provided, to be modified in line with local conditions, if you choose:

Manager's salary, in addition to the privilege of occupying one unit free	$8,400
State and county taxes	1,250
City taxes	7,965
Repair, maintenance, improvement	2,400
Utility costs	5,000

Caretaking and protection service will likely run $60 a year for each lot. Depreciation will need to be figured in accordance with some selected method. On the basis of this background, you may write report A, B, or both A and B, in line with your instructor's preference.

Report A. *Should Seton Enterprises Build a Mobile Home Park in Some City, Your State?*

If you choose to write only this portion of the problem, assume that a suitable site in Some City has been chosen prior to your investigation, with the land option already assured for 90 days. Then you will proceed to determine whether the $450,000 should be invested here for the chosen purpose. As with Report B, you will need to establish the characteristics of the people most likely to patronize the park and decide whether enough of the right sort are already located in Some City or could be induced to come here with the right sort of promotion. Is the climate good for this form of living? Are there adequate entertainment, cultural, or recreational facilities to serve as a lure? How much would Seton have to charge each month for each mobile-home lot to make the operation profitable? Would the rental fee be right to ensure patronage from the people most likely to want to live in the park? What phases of the economic future of Some City might affect the decision? With what other types of accommodations, such as low-cost or low-rent housing, would the park have to compete? Could it do so successfully? With those ideas as springboards, you'll size up the critical determinants of your decision.

Report B. *What Is the Most Likely Site in Some City, Your State, To Locate an Arrowhead Mobile Home Park?*

If you choose to do this assignment, your first task is that of determining the zoning regulations of Some City, Your State, having a bearing on your location. Then, with a city map in hand (perhaps supplemented by scouting trips in the environs) you will choose two or three possible sites for intensive study. Mr. Seton's authorization memo points up certain aspects for possible investigation: (a) What are the characteristics of the people most likely to patronize the mobile-home park? (b) What location will be best for them from the standpoint of access to their main pursuits, such as education or work? (c) Which spot provides the best access to the recreational activities of the area? (d) Which site provides the most pleasant living surroundings, taking into consideration freedom from noise, excess traffic, smoke, or other pertinent handicaps? (e) Which is the best placement in relation to the location of competing parks? (f) Are there any predicted city plans (such as the construction of a new highway, a dam, or a lake) that would make one site preferable to others considered? (g) Would ready access to shopping centers prove to be a problem for any of the sites? (h) Would variations in land costs exert demonstrable influence? Mr. Seton of course instructs you to investigate any other phases that might prove vital to the solution of your problem. Land availability might be the crucial element. You may make your problem realistic or you may assume that 18 acres are available at each of your sites, according to your instructor's preference.

Suggested References

The Trailer Coach Association, 607 South Hobart Boulevard, Los Angeles, California. (This association at the time of this writing has a publication entitled *Mobile Home Parks as an Investment*, that probably will be updated periodically.)

Mobile Home Dealer magazine, Chicago, Illinois.

Construction Review

U.S. Department of Commerce publications.

Mobile Home Park Management, 909 South First Street, Arcadia, California.

Census Bureau publications.

Articles in current periodicals and newspapers.

2. *Deciding where Lariat, Inc. should locate a new restaurant.* Tom Rolfe, a hopeful example of the American success story, in 25 years has nourished his original hamburger-type eating place in Metropolita City, Your State, into a chain of luxury restaurants in five major cities. Along the way he has plowed a substantial portion of the profits into ranch holdings, where the makings for his specialty—steak—are grown. Today Lariat, Inc. is a closed corporation, with Rolfe as president and headquarters at the main restaurant, 9251 Morningside Drive, Metropolitan City. Still in his early forties, he plans further expansion with his customary verve.

Rolfe has been convinced for some time that smaller cities have enough people with the money and the epicurean taste to appreciate the fine food his restaurants offer and that the quality of the menus in most small-city establishments is customarily poor at prices almost as high as his own. He also believes that these places have need for the entertainment centers he plans to provide. He feels that the community would welcome an attractive site for bridge parties, luncheons, teas, rehearsal dinners, and the like. A first-class taproom, possibly on a membership basis, would also be an appreciated addition to community life. In a way his operation will compete with local private and country clubs, but with the democracy of the wallet as the main participation requirement. He is willing to allocate $150,000 to the project to cover land, building, and equipment costs and three months of operating expenses.

With 70,000 set as an approximate population figure for his target cities, Rolfe and the board of directors have selected three possible sites for the first additional restaurant: Eastport, Midland, and Westville, Your State. If the first venture reaches, at the end of three years, the 25-percent net-profit percentage attained by his current restaurants, he will move a restaurant at a time into other similar cities.

Some time ago Rolfe, aware that his operation has assumed big-business proportions, approached your firm, Tarlton Advertising, 2696 Apex Towers, Metropolitan City, Your State, with the possibility of employing you to handle all of his publicity, including the launching of the new locations. As David D. Hambrick, research director, you have had numerous conferences with Rolfe concerning his expansion plans during the past three months. Today you receive from him an authorization to make a pilot economic ranking of the three cities he has selected, with a more thorough study of the top-ranking city to be initiated later. An examination of the Yellow Pages of the telephone directories for the three cities reveals three or four quality eating places in each of them. Rolfe, a highly confident personality, thinks the uniqueness of his own new Lariat will not suffer serious competition from existing restaurants; so he says you may skip the competitive aspects for the present. He will pay your firm $7,500 for the pilot study upon delivery on the date indicated on your class calendar.

NOTE: Adequate data for three hypothetical cities which provide a good opportunity for statistical analyses are assembled for you. A more interesting study, of course, would result from your assembling similar data for three cities in your own state, from which environmental interpretations might be made. The years in the study are labeled A through J, with J representing the year just finished prior to your undertaking the project, I the year before last, H three years ago, and so on. You will probably find it desirable to fill in appropriate years.

POPULATION ESTIMATES
(As of January 1 of the years indicated, in thousands)

City	Year									
	A	B	C	D	E	F	G	H	I	J
Eastport	72.0	67.3	67.3	68.2	68.8	69.4	69.3	69.3	69.5	69.7
Midland	58.1	64.6	67.7	64.5	64.5	68.5	69.3	70.1	69.7	69.5
Westville	67.0	59.3	60.3	60.9	61.6	62.8	63.8	64.5	65.5	67.6

Source: U.S. Bureau of the Census, population, years A through J.

EFFECTIVE BUYING INCOME
(net dollars in thousands)

City	Year				
	A	B	C	D	E
Eastport	$265,620	$267,988	$240,414	$249,922	$255,814
Midland	270,526	321,062	336,482	332,450	335,852
Westville	234,462	222,794	215,854	225,212	231,820

City	Year				
	F	G	H	I	J
Eastport	$270,598	$287,920	$301,352	$332,506	$355,488
Midland	374,422	404,558	434,178	469,006	525,830
Westville	248,542	270,974	290,344	321,712	357,522

Source: U.S. Bureau of the Census, income, years A through J.

PERCENTAGE OF HOUSEHOLDS IN INCOME GROUPS

	Income (per household)	A	B	C	D	E
Year E						
Eastport	$12,124	23.3%	16.0%	35.4%	12.9%	13.4%
Midland	17,864	13.0	12.2	30.0	16.7	28.1
Westville	12,408	29.4	20.6	28.6	9.9	11.5
Year F						
Eastport	12,764	21.1	15.3	35.1	14.0	14.5
Midland	18,816	12.3	11.4	29.6	17.2	29.5
Westville	12,940	27.6	19.7	29.4	11.0	12.3

PERCENTAGE OF HOUSEHOLDS IN INCOME GROUPS (continued)

	Income (per household)	A	B	C	D	E
Year G						
Eastport	13,518	20.1	14.4	34.3	15.5	15.7
Midland	20,028	11.7	10.6	28.7	17.9	31.1
Westville	13,896	26.4	18.5	29.6	12.2	13.3
Year H						
Eastport	14,016	25.9	16.0	31.0	12.0	14.2
Midland	21,076	17.4	11.1	24.0	15.3	32.2
Westville	14,590	29.1	20.8	26.3	10.0	13.8
Year I						
Eastport	15,322	23.9	14.0	27.9	16.4	17.8
Midland	22,768	16.1	9.9	20.8	15.7	37.5
Westville	15,848	26.3	18.4	26.6	11.0	17.7
Year J						
Eastport	16,158	22.9	13.3	25.4	17.9	20.5
Midland	25,280	14.6	8.7	17.0	13.9	45.8
Westville	16,864	24.7	17.0	25.2	12.2	20.9

Key to columns: A = $0–4,998, B = $5,000–7,998, C = $8,000–13,998, D = 14,000–19,998, E = $20,000 and over.

Source: U.S. Bureau of the Census, income, years E through J.

RETAIL SALES ESTIMATES*
(in millions of dollars)

	Total	1*	2	3	4	5	6	7	8	9
Year E										
Eastport	$ 93.3	$23.9	$ 3.9	$13.5	$ 5.8	$ 5.0	$17.2	$ 7.4	$ 4.7	$ 3.6
Midland	92.1	23.7	5.4	7.7	6.4	5.7	18.8	8.7	6.5	2.2
Westville	85.8	19.2	4.6	12.1	4.6	3.8	19.2	6.8	5.6	2.9
Year F										
Eastport	98.5	25.0	5.3	11.5	6.0	6.9	21.4	6.3	3.1	4.4
Midland	102.3	23.8	8.0	9.8	8.8	5.2	21.8	8.1	4.5	7.9
Westville	95.6	18.8	5.0	15.8	5.4	4.0	21.5	7.5	6.7	3.3
Year G										
Eastport	113.1	28.2	6.2	13.5	7.2	7.6	26.0	7.1	3.5	5.1
Midland	106.5	24.2	8.5	10.4	8.6	5.2	24.0	8.3	4.7	8.2
Westville	104.5	20.1	5.6	17.6	5.6	4.2	24.8	8.0	7.2	3.6

RETAIL SALES ESTIMATES* (continued)
(in millions of dollars)

	Total	1*	2	3	4	5	6	7	8	9
Year H										
Eastport	126.8	33.4	7.6	10.7	8.9	9.2	29.6	8.4	4.1	6.1
Midland	122.4	27.7	10.0	12.5	10.2	6.1	26.4	9.5	5.1	9.7
Westville	113.7	21.6	6.2	19.8	6.2	4.7	25.7	8.6	7.5	4.0
Year I										
Eastport	123.8	30.1	7.5	15.6	8.8	8.7	26.5	8.3	3.9	5.8
Midland	120.1	26.6	11.0	12.4	9.8	6.1	25.2	9.4	5.1	9.9
Westville	111.0	20.8	6.7	19.7	6.2	4.7	24.5	8.2	7.5	4.6
Year J										
Eastport	130.1	30.8	8.0	16.4	9.1	9.1	28.9	8.5	4.1	6.1
Midland	128.9	27.8	12.1	13.4	10.6	6.6	28.0	9.6	5.3	10.4
Westville	117.3	21.4	7.8	20.9	6.5	5.0	26.8	8.6	7.7	4.3

Key to columns: 1 = food, 2 = eating and drinking places, 3 = general merchandise, 4 = apparel, 5 = furniture, household appliances, 6 = automotive, 7 = gas stations, 8 = lumber, building hardware, 9 = drugs

*Figures do not total due to rounding and because all categories of sales are not included.

OTHER ECONOMIC STATISTICS

	Building Permits Less Federal Contracts	Bank Debits (000s)	End-of-Month Deposits (000s)	Annual Rate of Deposit Turnover
Year E				
Eastport	$ 985,740	$ 74,264	$ 42,896	20.0%
Midland	2,501,520	147,623	105,785	16.2
Westville	332,141	71,141	51,603	16.6
Year F				
Eastport	219,975	70,605	43,474	18.4
Midland	2,512,850	162,675	118,912	16.0
Westville	613,725	69,731	50,942	16.1
Year G				
Eastport	176,641	75,516	43,954	20.7
Midland	3,925,225	144,885	113,779	14.9
Westville	309,380	81,926	56,841	17.3
Year H				
Eastport	625,081	76,505	50,708	19.0
Midland	611,250	150,030	114,020	15.1
Westville	516,144	84,011	60,098	16.9

OTHER ECONOMIC STATISTICS (continued)

	Building Permits Less Federal Contracts	Bank Debits (000s)	End-of-Month Deposits (000s)	Annual Rate of Deposit Turnover
Year I				
Eastport	195,233	78,848	47,221	20.3
Midland	673,340	162,396	123,199	15.1
Westville	561,818	96,911	60,999	18.4
Year J				
Eastport	376,684	80,144	53,265	18.6
Midland	453,730	190,100	132,734	16.9
Westville	414,703	105,911	63,706	19.2

3. *Deciding how Family Supermarkets, Inc., can effectively challenge entrenched competition in Centown, Any State.* Imagine that you are Willard Dayton, research director of Regional Marketing Surveys, 300–309 Professional Building, Metropolitan City, Any State. You are sitting at your desk glancing through a sheaf of questionnaire tabulations that has just been prepared by one of your assistants.

Three weeks ago, sitting at this same desk, you received a postconsultation letter from Mr. Roger Marcus Cochran, president, family supermarkets, Inc., 2801 Noblesse Street, Metropolitan City, Any State, authorizing you to go ahead with a research project you had previously discussed with him. Along with the letter came a check for $5,000—half of the $10,000 fee you had quoted Mr. Cochran.

Mr. Cochran's letter reviewed some of the things you had talked about. It reminded you of Family Supermarkets' intentions to establish a new chain store in Centown, Any State—provided that customer loyalty to existing stores is not entrenched too firmly. "Our policy," the letter said, "is to find out what our middle-class, essentially suburban customers really want and to adapt our stores accordingly." Mr. Cochran explained further that his chain's expansion strategy was to concentrate on locating in rapidly growing small cities with 20,000 to 50,000 population where existing supermarkets and grocery stores tended to be somewhat "small townish" and unprogressive. The idea, which had worked well in other places, was to challenge existing competitors by offering customers more modern, consumer-oriented facilities, merchandise, and services.

Will such a plan be successful in Centown? Do shoppers there have entrenched loyalty to any one store, or do they distribute their buying among a number of groceries? Are they pleased with the facilities, merchandise, and services offered by these stores? What faults do they find with the stores they patronize? Do they believe that local outlets are on a par with modern supermarkets in other cities? Are there any significant differences among shoppers' habits and opinions correlated with place of residence in Centown? These are some of the questions which Mr. Cochran in his letter asked you to answer.

"An even more important problem, though," he pointed out, "is to learn how we could best plan our own operations so as to give customers what they want." Here he emphasized the importance of determining their attitudes with respect to such things as the offering of nonfood items for sale, incorporating a bakery into the store, giving trading stamps, selling beer, cashing checks, and offering weekend specials. "Please make specific recommendations to guide us," added Mr. Cochran. "And if one part of the city looks best, we'd like site recommendations, too."

The day after you received this letter, you started your research. The first thing you did was to spend a day looking over Centown—an inspection which showed you that Family Supermarkets had four important supermarket competitors in your city. Your field trip also revealed that their customers came from four distinct neighborhoods, two being new suburban developments, one a mixed business-residential section in the center of the city, and the other an older suburban area developed before World War II.

Guided by your field insights, you next drafted a questionnaire designed to answer Mr. Cochran's questions. After pretesting it on 25 shoppers in Centown, you revised it and then sent four of your research people to Centown. Each researcher personally interviewed 50 shoppers, using a random-sampling method, in one of the four geographical areas. (You may use your own knowledge of research techniques to assume the specific method employed and described in your explanation of methodology.)

Now the findings have been tallied and compiled for you on one of the unused questionnaire forms. As you study the results, you begin to get a few insights into how the material should be organized. But, of course, there's much to be done before you can mail to Mr. Cochran an impressive, accurate, and attractive report that will show Family Supermarkets how to challenge existing Centown competition.

DISTRIBUTIONS OF CONSUMERS IN THE SAMPLE

Distribution by income classes	
Under $12,000 a year	100
$12,000 or more a year	<u>100</u>
	200
By areas	
Area 1	50
Area 2	50
Area 3	50
Area 4	50
By time in locality	
Less than 5 years	74
6–15 years	45
More than 15 years	81
By age	
Under 40 years	81
Over 40 years	<u>119</u>
	200

KEY TO NUMBERS OF EXISTING STORES

Store I	American Supermarkets
Store II	Shop-and-Save Stores
Store III	Convenient Stores, Inc.
Store IV	Shoppers' Day Stores

KEY TO AREAS

Area	Location	Neighborhood Type	19xx Census Tract Population
1	Northwest	New suburban	12,000
2	Northeast	New suburban	7,500
3	Central	Business-residential	3,500
4	South	Old residential	5,000
			28,000

ROUGH MAP OF AREA

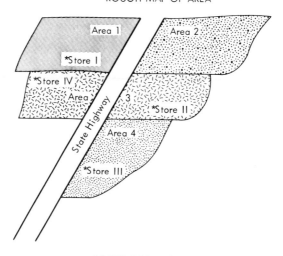

QUESTIONNAIRE

1. Please indicate whether you do or do not patronize any of the following stores.

		Stores		
	I	II	III	IV
Do patronize	82	116	120	110
Do not patronize	118	84	80	90
	200	200	200	200

Breakdown by areas:*

		Stores		
	I	II	III	IV
Do patronize				
Area 1	11	33	31	40
Area 2	14	28	36	37
Area 3	18	31	35	18
Area 4	39	24	18	15
	82	116	120	110
Do not patronize				
Area 1	37	17	19	11
Area 2	35	22	14	13
Area 3	31	19	15	32
Area 4	15	26	32	34
	118	84	80	90

* In the breakdown by areas, the question was asked both positively and negatively to determine whether the answers were exact opposites; some of the figures, you'll notice, do not quite add to 50.

Breakdown by income classes:

	Stores at Which Some Shopping Is Done			
	I	II	III	IV
Under $12,000	43	56	54	40
$12,000 or more	75	28	26	50

	Stores at Which Almost All or Most Shopping Is Done			
	I	II	III	IV
Under $12,000	38	43	38	29
$12,000 or more	65	17	14	38

2. Please indicate what you like best in each of the stores you do patronize.

	Stores			
	I	II	III	IV
Good prices	4	6	2	33
Good meats	6	11	30	5

	Stores			
	I	*II*	*III*	*IV*
Wide variety	5	26	9	5
Convenience	3	3	34	28
Nonfoods stocked	0	3	0	0
Clean, roomy store	8	18	13	1
Good brands	7	1	2	1
Friendly clerks	6	8	4	0
Good specials	0	8	4	4
Vegetables and fruit, fresh	1	8	4	1
Give trading stamps	1	3	1	0
Convenient packing	0	1	1	1
Fast checkout	1	0	0	0
Good frozen foods	0	0	3	2
Convenient hours	0	1	0	0
Easy-to-find items	3	1	0	0
No answer	<u>37</u>	<u>18</u>	<u>13</u>	<u>29</u>
	82	116	120	110

3. Please indicate what you like least in each of the stores you do patronize

	Stores			
	I	*II*	*III*	*IV*
Store is crowded	4	1	0	13
Store is dirty	0	1	1	15
Meat is of poor quality	1	0	2	14
Prices are high	3	7	3	1
Won't cash checks for more than purchase amount	0	0	0	1
Layout is poor	1	2	4	1
Not enough specials	0	2	0	0
Store is inconvenient	6	10	6	4
No carry-out service	0	0	6	4
Does not give stamps or gives unliked stamps	2	2	8	7
Fruits and vegetables are not fresh	1	2	1	1
Personnel are unfriendly	0	1	4	1
Poor checkout facilities	1	3	5	5
Narrow assortment	2	2	8	7
No answer	<u>60</u>	<u>83</u>	<u>72</u>	<u>36</u>
	82	116	120	110

4.   If you do not do any of your shopping at any of the stores listed at the left, please indicate where you do do your shopping.

Do Not Shop at	Do Shop at				
	I	II	III	IV	Combination
Store I (118)	—	23	47	42	6
Store II (84)	20	—	24	21	19
Store III (80)	15	15	—	24	26
Store IV (90)	20	22	25	—	23

5.   In your opinion, how do supermarket prices in your city compare with those in large cities?

They are much higher here.	9
They are somewhat higher here.	41
They are about the same here.	111
They are lower here.	37
They are much lower here.	2

Breakdown by areas:

	Much Higher	Higher	Same	Lower	Much Lower
1	3	13	22	11	1
2	0	9	26	14	1
3	3	10	29	8	0
4	3	9	34	4	0
	9	41	111	37	2

Breakdown by income classes:

	Much Higher	Higher	Same	Lower	Much Lower
Under $12,000	4	23	65	15	1
$12,000 and over	5	18	46	22	1
	9	41	111	37	2

Breakdown by time in city:

	Much Higher	Higher	Same	Lower	Much Lower
5 years or less	4	20	35	15	
6–15 years	0	12	24	9	0
Over 15 years	5	9	52	13	2
	9	41	111	37	2

6. If you bought nonfood items (e.g., bath towels or cosmetics) at a local supermarket, how would you expect the price you paid to compare with prices charged by other kinds of retail stores?

	Under $12,000	$12,000 Plus	All Classes
Supermarket price would be much lower	1	1	2
Supermarket price would be somewhat lower	25	21	46
Prices would be about the same	57	56	113
Supermarket price would be somewhat higher	17	22	39
Supermarket price would be much higher	0	0	0
	100	100	200

7. In your opinion, are local supermarkets more, or less, modern than those in larger cities?

	Under $12,000	$12,000 Plus	All Classes
Local supermarkets are much more modern	0	0	0
Local supermarkets are somewhat more modern	0	0	0
Local supermarkets are about the same as those in larger cities	42	20	62
Local supermarkets are less modern than those in larger cities	40	60	100
Local supermarkets are much less modern than those in larger cities	18	20	38
	100	100	200

8. To what extent do you agree or disagree with the statement that "local supermarkets offer a wide variety of groceries to choose from"?

Breakdown by income classes:

	Under $12,000	$12,000 Plus	Both Classes
Strongly agree	4	5	9
Agree	82	79	161

	Under $12,000	$12,000 Plus	Both Classes
Neither agree nor disagree	4	9	13
Disagree	9	6	15
Strongly disagree	1	1	2
	100	100	200

Breakdown by age levels:

	Under 40	40 Plus	Both
Strongly agree	4	5	9
Agree	66	95	161
Neither agree nor disagree	5	8	13
Disagree	6	9	15
Strongly disagree	0	2	2
	81	119	200

Breakdown by areas:

	1	2	3	4	Total
Strongly agree	6	0	1	2	9
Agree	33	48	41	39	161
Neither	4	1	4	4	13
Disagree	6	1	3	5	15
Strongly disagree	1	0	1	0	2
	50	50	50	50	200

Breakdown by time in locality:

	5 Years or Less	6–15 Years	Over 15 Years	Total
Strongly agree	3	2	4	9
Agree	63	36	62	161
Neither	1	5	7	13
Disagree	7	2	6	15
Strongly disagree	0	0	2	2
	74	45	81	200

9. To what extent do you agree or disagree with the statement that "a supermarket should sell beer"?

Breakdown by income classes:

	Under $12,000	$12,000 Plus	Both Classes
Strongly agree	4	7	11
Agree	7	10	17
Neither	22	25	47
Disagree	35	48	83
Strongly disagree	32	10	42
	100	100	200

Breakdown by areas:

	1	2	3	4	Total
Strongly agree	3	2	1	5	11
Agree	5	3	2	7	17
Neither	10	7	13	17	47
Disagree	23	22	22	16	83
Strongly disagree	9	16	12	5	42
	50	50	50	50	200

Breakdown by time in locality:

	5 Years or Less	6–15 Years	Over 15 Years	Total
Strongly agree	7	3	1	11
Agree	5	5	7	17
Neither	17	7	23	47
Disagree	29	19	35	83
Strongly disagree	16	11	15	42
	74	45	81	200

10. To what extent do you agree that the supermarket should have trading stamps?

Breakdown by income classes:

	Under $12,000	$12,000 Plus	Both Classes
Strongly agree	2	2	4
Agree	25	20	45
Neither	23	20	43
Disagree	40	40	80
Strongly disagree	10	18	28
	100	100	200

Breakdown by areas:

	1	2	3	4	Total
Strongly agree	2	1	0	1	4
Agree	9	13	13	10	45
Neither	13	9	12	9	43
Disagree	19	20	20	21	80
Strongly disagree	7	7	5	9	28
	50	50	50	50	200

Breakdown by time in locality:

	5 Years or Less	6–15 Years	Over 15 Years	Total
Strongly agree	1	0	3	4
Agree	10	14	21	45
Neither	17	9	17	43
Disagree	32	16	32	80
Strongly disagree	14	6	8	28
	74	45	81	200

11. To what extent do you agree or disagree with the statement that "a supermarket which gives trading stamps charges prices higher than do stores that do not give trading stamps"?

	All Respondents
Strongly agree	16
Agree	80
Neither agree nor disagree	20
Disagree	74
Strongly disagree	10
	200

12. If you agree or strongly agree that a supermarket charges higher prices if it gives trading stamps, what reasons can you give to account for the higher prices?

Responses	116 Respondents
Stamps cost the store money	20
Stamps are advertising like any other kind of promotion	15
Nothing comes free	70
Stamp companies must be paid whether or not stamps are redeemed	11
	116

13. To what extent do you agree or disagree with the statement that "supermarkets should cash checks for amounts greater than the amount of the grocery bill"?

Breakdown by income classes:

	Under $12,000	$12,000 Plus	Both Classes
Strongly agree	3	1	4
Agree	30	23	53
Neither	19	14	33
Disagree	41	52	93
Strongly disagree	7	10	17
	100	100	200

Breakdown by areas:

	1	2	3	4	Total
Strongly agree	0	0	4	0	4
Agree	5	19	15	14	53
Neither	14	5	8	6	33
Disagree	22	22	23	26	93
Strongly disagree	9	4	0	4	17
	50	50	50	50	200

Breakdown by time in locality:

	5 Years or Less	6–15 Years	Over 15 Years	Total
Strongly agree	2	0	2	4
Agree	23	7	23	53
Neither	11	13	9	33
Disagree	33	19	41	93
Strongly disagree	5	6	6	17
	74	45	81	200

14. To what extent do you agree or disagree with the statement that "it would be an advantage to customers if all supermarkets had a bakery"?

Breakdown by income classes:

	Under $12,000	$12,000 Plus	Both Classes
Strongly agree	8	10	18
Agree	53	70	123
Neither	15	9	24
Disagree	22	11	33
Strongly disagree	2	0	2
	100	100	200

Breakdown by areas:

	1	2	3	4	Total
Strongly agree	7	4	4	3	18
Agree	38	30	25	30	123
Neither	0	8	10	6	24
Disagree	5	8	10	10	33
Strongly disagree	0	0	1	1	2
	50	50	50	50	200

Breakdown by time in locality:

	5 Years or Less	6–15 Years	Over 15 Years	Total
Strongly agree	10	3	5	18
Agree	50	29	44	123
Neither	6	3	15	24
Disagree	6	10	16	33
Strongly disagree	2	0	1	2
	74	45	81	200

15. To what extent do you agree or disagree with the statement that "supermarkets in this locality have plenty of weekend specials"?

	All Respondents
Strongly agree	25
Agree	137

	All Respondents
Neither agree nor disagree	9
Disagree	29
Strongly disagree	0
	200

SUGGESTED REPORT TOPICS

Yes-or-No Decisions

1. Whether or not a successful family corporation should offer securities to the public.

2. Whether or not a company should accept a merger candidate.

3. Whether or not a firm should launch a new product line. Such a report could be based on a consumer survey.

4. Whether or not a large department store in a selected city should add a fancy-food department (or some other type not in operation).

5. Whether or not a large department store should discontinue its fancy-food department (or other type).

6. Whether or not a selected location will support a new savings institution, a new bank, a new department store, or other suitable business entity.

7. Whether or not a prospering firm should establish a branch (or an additional plant for a new product line) at a selected location.

8. Whether or not a business should launch a giveaway promotion—such as stamps, coupons, or new-account gifts.

9. Whether or not a business should furnish attractive uniforms for its personnel.

10. Whether or not a company should purchase an executive airplane.

11. Whether or not key administrators should be furnished company automobiles.

12. Whether or not a savings institution should adopt for home loans a flexible interest rate by which to adapt to economic changes.

13. Whether or not a city should initiate a speedy mass-transit system.

14. Whether or not a city hospital should discontinue its nursing school, which has proved quite costly to operate and has traditionally turned out graduates who go elsewhere to work.

Comparative-Evaluation Investigations

1. Whether a business should borrow money or issue stock to finance a proposed expansion.

2. Which of several alternative locations would be superior for the establishment of a new business or of a new branch.

3. Whether a city should purchase and operate a bus system or execute a management contract providing a guaranteed income with the present bus company, which is threatening to terminate service at the end of the current contract.

4. Whether to buy or lease needed equipment.

5. An evaluation of various possible ways of acquiring knowledge a business needs, such as either setting up a company staff to generate the knowledge or employing the services of a management consulting firm.

6. An appraisal of several ways in which a manufacturing firm might handle its waste or pollution problem.

7. An examination of various possible contributions a firm can make toward solving the hard-core unemployment problems in its environment.

8. Ranking the efficiency of alternative methods of distribution for a company line.

9. Making recommendations for a construction firm as to the best type of apartment buildings to develop, such as high-rise, townhouse, or condominium.

10. Whether a company should buy or manufacture a certain component necessary for product assembly.

11. An evaluation of various proposals for financing an expensive project.

12. An appraisal of the efficiency of two or several accounting procedures for a specific project.

Descriptive-Analytic Studies

1. An investigation of a number of manufacturing industries for which the raw materials are available, with recommendations as to which might be most successfully exploited in your state or in a selected city. *Standard & Poor's Industry Surveys* and Studley, Shupert's industry reviews might be suitable starting points.

2. An evaluation of various service industries which would be appropriate for starting a small business at a selected site on a stated amount of capital. Publications of the Small Business Administration offer possibilities of fruitful ideas.

3. Devising a plan that would afford maximum tax advantages for

the members of a family business when the founder approaches retirement age.

4.   Suggesting possible solutions for a company that has sustained substantial losses during the last several years.

5.   Finding ways to invest for satisfactory return on a $200,000 trust fund handled by a law firm or bank. The client's major objective is income production, with an inflation hedge as a desirable by-product.

6.   Developing a program for handling change for a company anticipating a major changeover. Orienting personnel could well be the prime objective.

7.   Describing consumer attitudes toward a product line (such as rugs, stoves, refrigerators, or automobiles) developed from a consumer survey, with recommendations for improved operating or advertising strategy.

8.   Planning ways in which a company can improve its image, win greater community acceptance.

9.   Building an organization chart for a new business or revising one for an old business with difficulties.

10.   Formulating ways in which a company establishing a large plant in a small community can help that community absorb the new plant with minimum chaos.

11.   Developing an advertising campaign for launching a new product, a new business, or a new branch.

12.   Devising a financial plan by which a symphony orchestra (or some other nonprofit organization) can break even instead of operating at a loss.

8

Gathering Information
for Business Decisions

*When you can measure what you are writing about
and express it in numbers, you know something
about it.*

Lord Kelvin

The analyst at this point is fully aware of the nature of the problem being investigated. Tentatively prescribed are the significant issues upon which the decision may hinge. A research guide has been set up for the filing of facts and statistics as they are found. And whether to use primary or secondary research techniques or a combination of the two is also a decided fact. This chapter then explores the following areas designed to make the search fruitful and efficient, step IV of the agenda for decision-making research projects:

1. Assembling data from secondary sources.
   a. Steps to follow in locating the desired information.
   b. Efficient notetaking and filing.
2. Collecting data by survey.
   a. Obtaining a list of respondents.
   b. An overview of sampling theory.
   c. Preparing the request letter.
   d. Drafting the interrogation instrument.

ASSEMBLING DATA FROM SECONDARY SOURCES

Despite plans to use library research as the prime data source, the investigator will dip into other sources as they apply to the decision. A review of company historical data, already discussed, is an important first step in any business study. Informal interviews with authorities in the field and by talking with people engaged in the same sort of work may also enrich insights. Historical data from the files of other companies similarly engaged may be all the researcher needs to solve the problem—but requests for such data are more often than not denied. With a justifiable wariness, competing firms will not give out more than surface information. It would be more foolhardy than cooperative for them to release their cost-of-doing business figures or their profit ratios. Here is a barrier the analyst must overcome with derivations from known figures, logical assumptions, and often shrewd guesses. The publications from trade associations in the problem field frequently give consolidated cost-of-doing-business and operating ratios that offer a way around the barrier. Dun & Bradstreet also issues periodically factor publications that furnish ratio data on many lines of business. Whether generating primary data or pursuing it from previously recorded sources, the analyst's first task is assembling a bibliography of publications dealing with a particular problem.

Steps to Follow in Locating Desired Information

A nucleus of a bibliography has already been built with the preliminary survey of the literature in the field as a means of defining the problem and formulating a research design. The analyst will now try to locate data to support the criteria of his or her decision with the hope of substantiating or rejecting the hypothesis.

Many libraries have computer search capabilities to make the analyst's data gathering faster, easier, and more complete than ever. Among these are (1) INFORM data base (a monthly awareness service printout of some 400 major journal citations and abstracts); (2) the business index (325 business periodicals); and (3) CIS (computer-based information services). The last includes on-line search of 150 or more data bases available through Lockheed Information Systems' DIALOG, System Development Corporation's ORBIT, and Bibliographic Retrieval Services, Inc. Most data bases include records for the last five to ten years, updated monthly. The data bases are computerized versions of important indexing and abstracting publications already available in printed form in most libraries. Searches are done on a partial-cost-recovery basis. The following steps, however, are suggested to make efficient work for those using a manual process:

1. Consult the subject card catalog of the library for books pertinent to the investigation, indicating call numbers as you go. Company and association names are usually found in the author rather than the subject file.

2. Check the *Cumulative Book Index* (called the *United States Catalog* prior to 1928), a guide to all books in print in the United States since 1912. Each book is listed under the author, title, and subject that describes the content of the book. Monthly supplements are bound into six-month and yearly indexes, with annual indexes accumulated into three- and five-year releases. Knowing the publication year or even the date within five years simplifies the researcher's problem. With no knowledge of the date, the analyst may have to go through several volumes. Full bibliographical data are given only under the *author listing*.

3. Locate the indexes most likely to provide a cataloging of material in the chosen field. A thoroughly useful source is *Ulrich's Periodicals Directory*, published in New York by the R. R. Bowker Company. This directory is a guide, classified by subject field, to a list of current domestic and foreign periodicals—and the coverage is quite comprehensive. The following indexes listed in Ulrich (with starting publication date indicated) may prove useful to the business researcher:

Bibliographical Index, since 1938. A cumulative bibliography of bibliographies; annual and larger cumulations (New York: H. W. Wilson Company). A starting bibliography for a study may be found here to be supplemented by more current listings from other sources.

Business Periodicals Index, since 1958. A cumulative subject index to periodicals in the fields of accounting, advertising, banking and finance, general business, insurance, labor and management, marketing and purchasing, office management, public administration, taxation, specific businesses, industries, and trades (New York: H. W. Wilson Company).

Funk & Scott Index of Corporations & Industries, since 1960. This index enables the executive, investor, and researcher to locate and keep abreast of analyses, opinions, forecasts, and newsworthy items appearing in a wide variety of publications. Each week approximately 2,500 items are classified by company and industry. Abstracts from articles appearing in all major business magazines, newspapers and investment advisory services (Cleveland, Ohio: Investment Index Company).

The New York Times Index, since 1913. A master-key to all newspapers. By subject and paper issue, as well as particular articles (New York: *The New York Times*).

Public Affairs Information Service, since 1915. A selective subject list of the latest books, pamphlets, government publications, reports of public and private agencies and periodicals relating to economic and social conditions, public administration, and international relations, published in English throughout the world. (New York: Public Affairs Information Service). This is the most comprehensive of the indexes and perhaps the most generally valuable.

Vertical File Index, since 1932. A subject and title file to selected pamphlet material (New York: H. W. Wilson Company).

The Wall Street Journal Index, New York edition, since 1960 (New York: *The Wall Street Journal*).

4. Examine the indexes, recording full documentation for pertinent publications.

5. Consult the *Directory of National Trade Associations,* published by the U.S. Department of Commerce, and any available state trade association directories to locate places to write for information and leads to house organs which could prove helpful. Many trade associations release annual statistical publications that are widely useful. Illustrative are such as these: *Annual Statistical Report of the American Iron and Steel Institute, Petroleum Facts and Figures* from the American Petroleum Institute, *Gas Facts* from the American Gas Association, *Automobile Facts and Figures* from the American Automobile Association, and *Life Insurance Fact Book* from the Institute of Life Insurance.

6. Check any of the following publisher's services which seem pertinent to your study.

Commerce Clearing House. Includes information on federal taxes, state taxes, banking, labor, social security, securities, carriers, utilities, and so on (New York: Commerce Clearing House, Inc.).

Congressional Quarterly Weekly Reports. Weekly reports on activities of Congress and the government. Yearly bound volumes (Washington, D.C.: Congressional Quarterly, Incorporated).

Dun & Bradstreet Credit Service
(1) *Reference Book*—updated regionally every 60 days.
(2) Publications dealing with 14 important ratios for numerous industries.

Factual Analyses of Corporate Securities. This company issues, in addition, composite studies of selected industries (Boston: Studley, Shupert & Co., Inc.).

Labor Arbitration Reports. Indexed by guide numbers (Washington, D.C.: The Bureau of National Affairs).

Moody's Investors Service. Divided into five parts: (1) transportation, (2) industrials, (3) public utilities, (4) bank and finance, (5) municipal and government.

(1) *Moody's Stock Survey.* Presents weekly stock data, including recommendations for purchase, sale, or exchange of individual stocks, and industry trends and developments.

(2) *Moody's Bond Survey.* Presents the same information for bonds. The latest reports of this publication are contained in two periodicals: *Barron's,* published weekly, and *Commercial and Financial Chronicle,* published twice weekly.

(3) *Moody's Dividend Record.* Published twice weekly, presenting dividend declarations, payment dates, ex-dividend dates, stock splitups, and so on.

Prentice-Hall Tax Service. Current loose-leaf publications covering the latest laws, rules, and regulations with interpretations and comments by the authors on many areas, including federal taxes, cumulative changes in the internal revenue code, tax regulations, and regulations on income and excess-profits taxes.

Quality Control and Applied Statistics including Operations Research. Abstract Service. A review of the most important journals in the field (New York: Interscience Publishers, Inc.).

The Real Estate Analyst Service. Current and historical data. Microfilm publication of materials (St. Louis: Roy Wenzlick Research Corporation).

Selected Securities Guide, including the Market Times. Published twice weekly (New York: International Statistical Bureau, Inc.).

Standard & Poor's Corporation Services

(1) *Standard & Poor's Corporation Records.* Information on capitalization, financial statements, properties and locations, officers, price range of securities, dividends, and so on. Covers approximately 6,000 major and 5,000 minor corporations.

(2) *Railroad Securities.* Up-to-date information on security issues of railroads.

(3) *Stock Reports for Over-the-Counter and Regional Exchanges.* Data for unlisted or regional stocks.

(4) *Facts and Forecast Service.* Daily sheets covering recommended stocks, stock market policy, stock price indexes, trading activity, and so on.

(5) *Listed Stock Reports, Bond Reports.* Much statistical and comparative data included.

(6) *Industry Surveys.* Provides a current and a basic analysis for some 45 major industries of interest to investors, with more than 1,000 companies regularly covered. Major industries subdivided into numerous components. Revisions appear weekly.

7. Check the *Monthly Catalog of U.S. Government Publications* for government releases useful to your problem. The Bureau of the Census issues statistics on agriculture, business, housing, manufacturing and

mineral industries, and population, with supplements published during the ten-year intervals.

The *Statistical Abstract of the United States*, issued annually, presents summary statistics in industrial, social, political, and economic fields in the United States. Subject matter includes area and population, vital statistics, education, climate, employment, military affairs, social security, income, prices, governments, banking, transportation, agriculture, forests, fisheries, mining, manufacturers, and commerce. Supplements to the *Abstract*, such as *The Cities Supplement* (selected data for cities of over 25,000 inhabitants), *The County Data Book*, and *Historical Statistics of the United States* (3,000 statistical time series extending back to 1789) are often useful.

The *Survey of Current Business*, issued monthly, gives facts on industrial and business activity in the United States, with up-to-date information provided in weekly supplements.

8.   Check any of the following sources which may be productive of valuable information for particular problems:

a. *Government Publications*

Banking and Monetary Statistics. Published by the Board of Governors of the Federal Reserve System, dealing with financial developments since 1914. Updated by the *Federal Reserve Bulletin*, the Board's monthly release.

Business Cycle Development. Reports issued by the U.S. Department of Commerce, available about the twentieth of each month and designed for specialists in business-cycle analysis.

The Congressional Directory. Issued by the U.S. Government Printing Office, giving names and biographical sketches of Senators and Representatives, committee memberships, special agencies and commissions, main government departments, important officials and their duties, and specific information about the Capitol.

The Congressional Record. An account of the proceedings and debates of the Congress of the United States.

Economic Report of the President. Following the Employment Act of 1946, the president submits regularly to Congress reports on the economic situation and recommended legislation, updated by the monthly release, *Economic Indicators.*

The Federal Register. Published daily except Sundays, Mondays, and days following holidays by the National Archives, containing all regulatory matter issued by the various national agencies and government bodies.

Handbook of Labor Statistics. Issued at intervals of several years by the Bureau of Labor Statistics, covering employment, payrolls, wages, working conditions, commodity prices, housing conditions, and so on. Updated by the *Monthly Labor Review.*

Market Research: A Guide to Information on Domestic Marketing, issued by the Department of Commerce.

b. *Private Sources*

The Commercial Atlas and Marketing Guide. Published annually since 1869 by Rand McNally & Co. Numerous maps and statistics in these areas: (1) general U.S. information; (2) agricultural analysis by states; (3) communications; (4) manufacturing analysis by states and metropolitan areas; (5) population; (6) Ranally metropolitan areas; (7) retail trade, trading areas, and principal business centers; (8) transportation; and (9) state maps and statistics.

Commodity Yearbook. Published by The Commodity Research Bureau, Inc. Data on commodities of use to business people.

The Economic Almanac. Published annually by the National Industrial Conference Board, giving significant statistical data most useful to business executives, labor leaders, students, and journalists. Subject areas: prices, savings, consumption and the standard of living, public debt, construction, transportation, labor force, foreign trade, international economic statistics, and wages.

Editor and Publisher Market Guide. Published in New York by *Editor and Publisher.* Contains economic and marketing data for more than 15,000 cities in the United States and Canada.

Survey of Buying Power. Accumulates yearly estimates of population, income, and retail and wholesale sales for United States and Canadian counties and cities.

c. *Releases of Regulatory Bodies*

The Federal Communications Commission.
Federal Communications Commissions Reports
Statistics of the Communications Industry

The Federal Trade Commission.
Federal Trade Commission Decisions
Trade Practice Rules
Antitrust and Trade Regulation Report

The Interstate Commerce Commission.
Decisions of the Commission
Reports of the Commission

The Securities and Exchange Commission.
Decisions and Reports of the Securities and Exchange Commission
The Work of the Securities and Exchange Commission

Numerous other sources of a specialized nature could be cited; those given, however, should provide a wealth of material for many business problems.

Efficient Notetaking and Filing

With bibliography cards (and perhaps library call cards in many cases) made out, you are now ready to gather the data to fill in the predetermined research scheme. Before you proceed to the library or to other data sources, you should have clearly in mind the documentation items that you will need for footnoting and for bibliography construction. If you fail to record a necessary entry, you may be delayed in finding the particular printed material again. The following basic items should be included on bibliography cards.

To identify a book reference, you must include

1. The name of the author or the names of all co-authors, if any, as well as any special titles, such as "editor."
2. The name of the book, underscored.
3. If other than the original printing, an indication of the edition in abbreviated form, not underscored: 2nd ed., rev. ed., or such.
4. The city of publication, including the state if the city is not well known.
5. The name of the publisher.
6. The publication date.
7. The exact pages from which material is extracted. (Bibliographies may call for the total number of prefatory pages in small Roman numbers and the number of pages in the work; your professor's preference in this respect should be determined.)

To identify an article from a periodical, you must include

1. The name of the author or names of co-authors and any special titles. (The names of societies, trade associations, and government bureaus appear in the author's place.)
2. The name of the article, in quotation marks.
3. The name of the publication, underscored.
4. The page numbers from which material is used and the total number of pages in the article.

To identify data from unpublished sources, you must include

1. The name, title, and address of the person contributing the material.
2. The city from which the material issued, if not the same as the address of the contributor.
3. The date when the contact took place.
4. The nature of the contribution: letter, interview, address, excerpts from the company files, minutes of a board meeting, or such.

Notetaking is a personal affair, and it should be accomplished in the way best suited to the individual investigator. Index cards (3″ by 5″ or 4″ by 6″) to fit in a file box are generally preferred; loose-leaf pages from a properly indexed notebook may prove equally efficient. As an investigator, you may transcribe verbatim the material of particular interest, placing quotation marks around it; you may summarize as you go; or you may use a combination of the two methods. Verbatim copying is probably better at this stage, for many a researcher finds that, when referring back to notes, the summaries are not too meaningful or an important point vaguely remembered was skipped. Summaries may best be made at the point of writing up the report. (Copiers and computer-searched abstract printouts provided by many libraries are a boon to modern researchers.) If the verbatim copier feels that a paragraph or more is not important to the report, the omission may be indicated in the three center-spaced periods (ellipses) between paragraphs. For omissions of less than a paragraph, ellipses—three double-spaced periods preceded or followed by appropriate punctuation mark, if applicable—indicate the omission. The researcher's own comments are inserted in brackets [ ].

Only a single fact or kind of related facts should be recorded on a card or loose-leaf page to facilitate later shuffling in the organization process. At the top of the card or sheet, the library call number should be recorded, as well as the code for placing it in the file, such as "Demand (a major discussion area) Consumption Pattern" (one area of evidence to support the Demand premise) from the flour-mill problem (page 335). A single item of data with its ramifications may well take more space than is afforded on the front and back of a single card. The carry-over portions should be carefully identified, with source and "Continued" placed at the top of the card. The combined material may be clipped together as a single entry in the file. A lengthy table may be reproduced, the sheet folded and clipped to a card. An illustrative note sequence appears in Sample Form 8-1.

COLLECTING DATA BY SURVEY

If a business needs information about its environment (not supplied by its records and statistical data issued by government and private publishing agencies), some form of original research may be initiated. The survey is an important tool for gathering facts not available elsewhere and is usually conducted in one or more of the following ways: (1) by telephone, (2) by interview, (3) through panels of respondents, or (4) by the mailed questionnaire. Planning the research effort for gathering data by all of the alternatives involves about the same processes:

```
(Filing Code)                              Library Call
DEMAND, Consumption Pattern                  Number

Bronson, David H.  The Milling Industry.  New York:
    Forsyth Press, 19xx.  x + 465 pp.

Page 98:

    "The flour-milling industry, beset with lagging
sales, has industriously tried to bolster its profit
position with careful processing of by-products and
with product diversification. . . .  Only 33 percent
of Consolidated Mills's sales came from flour in 19xx
as compared with 72 percent ten years ago."
```

```
DEMAND, Consumption Pattern

Bronson, David H.  The Milling Industry (Continued)

Page 102:

"The sale of ready-mixes has risen since their intro-
duction in 1946 to a phenomenal volume of $300 million
last year.  The giant slice of sales comes from cake
and biscuit mixes.
                    . . .
Consolidated and Amish, holding about 60 percent of
the market (Page 103) have been able to crowd out of
the picture small factors, such as Preek-Dane and
Marselle."
```

Sample Form 8-1   Suggested format for notetaking cards

1. Obtaining a list of respondents.
2. Choosing an appropriate sample.
3. Preparing the request letter.
4. Designing the interrogation format.
5. Analyzing the returns.

Obtaining a List of Respondents

The scope of the survey obviously determines the universe of respondents to be sought. If a list of survey respondents of the type the analyst has in mind is not readily available, the analyst might first consult the *Guide to American Directories,* published in New York by B. Klein and Company. This publication gives information on approximately 2,300 U.S. and foreign directories indexed alphabetically according to more than 250 categories. The *Directory of Mailing List Houses,* published by the same firm, lists more than 700 such companies and the types of lists provided by each. The following general-purpose directories are available in most libraries.

Dun & Bradstreet Middle Market Directory (New York: Dun & Bradstreet, Inc.). Issued annually. Compiled from the files of Dun & Bradstreet, Inc., showing nearly 18,000 business enterprises in the United States with an indicated worth of $500,000 to $999,999. Three kinds of lists are supplied: (1) businesses alphabetically arranged, (2) businesses by geographical location, and (3) businesses by product classification. Addresses, kinds of products, the principal officers, number of employees, and sales are given for each firm listed.

The Fortune Directory (New York: Times, Inc.). Published annually since 1954. Covers the 500 largest United States industrial corporations and the 50 largest banks, merchandising, transportation, life insurance, and utility companies, and the 200 largest foreign industrial corporations. For the industrials, information on headquarters, sales, assets, net profit, invested capital, number of employees, and profit as a percentage of sales and of invested capital is given. For the banks, assets, deposits, capital funds, earnings, and earnings as a percentage of capital funds are provided. Similar important statistics appear for the other types of firm. Indexed alphabetically by company.

MacRae's Blue Book (Chicago: MacRae's). An annual publication listing under product headings the names of manufacturers, producers, and wholesalers supplying each kind of material; trade names and the firms owning them are supplied in a second section.

Polk's Bank Directory (Nashville, Tenn.: R. L. Polk & Co.). Provides data in these areas: (1) a complete bank directory of each state of the United States, Canada, and foreign countries, arranged alphabetically by states, cities, and banks within the city; (2) lists of investment dealers and brokers in the United States and Canada; (3) general data on Federal Reserve Banks, government financial agencies, national associations, statistics, and so on.

Poor's Register of Directors and Executives of the United States and Canada (New York: Standard & Poor Corporation). Gives names of executives and directors of manufacturing and mining companies, utilities, railroads, banks and insurance companies, partners of financial and investment institutions and law firms. Seven main sections are provided: (1) the Product Index; (2) the Classified Index of Corporations under 200 industry classifications; (3) the Corporation Directory, giving names of officers, directors, and other important executive personnel, number of employees, and principal products under alphabetic listing of corporations; (4) the Register of Directors, with brief sketches of men and women listed; (5) the Obituary Section; (6) the New Names Section, indicating names appearing for the first time; and (7) the New Individuals Section.

Thomas' Register of American Manufacturers (New York: Thomas Publishing

Company). An annual publication of names and addresses of manufacturers, producers, and other sources of supply in all lines and all sections of the United States, except those with local distribution only. Product listing with symbol for minimum capital for each firm.

Trade directories for many business fields are published on both the national and state levels. Membership rosters for associations and organizations on the local, state, regional, and national level often provide the investigator with the sort of list needed. City and telephone directories are valuable on the local level, as are city maps set off by blocks or census tracts. Some ingenuity or outlay of capital may be called for, but the investigator may be fairly well certain of obtaining the kind of list needed for almost any sort of investigation. With list in hand, however, the researcher may be frustrated with the size of it. Scientific sampling procedure can provide needed relief.

An Overview of Sampling Theory

That a scientifically chosen sample drawn from an aggregate of items which have a common characteristic (the population, or universe) can be used to estimate specific properties of the aggregate body is a well-accepted precept of research methodology. Thus, obtaining information from a sample often provides for the business manager decision data that are sufficiently precise (and at times more precise than those resulting from a survey of an entire large universe) at a portion of the cost that would be incurred if the entire universe were surveyed. Precision in responses is reflected by the difference between the results obtained from surveying the universe and those derived from surveying just a sample.

Universe sizes are labeled as *infinite* (of infinitely large proportions) or *finite* (for which it is feasible to make a numerical count of the items composing it). For a large proportion of business surveys, universes of finite dimensions prevail: the 500 largest industrials in the United States, the membership of State Automobile Dealers Association, the males between ages 20 and 25 in Sussex County, and so on. To know rather accurately the error of your estimates from the sample, you must choose it in such a way that each item in the universe has a *known* probability of being selected—*probability sampling*. Statistical measures are available for measuring the risks of error. For *nonprobability* samples, usually designated as judgment or quota sampling, which are sometimes resorted to for practical reasons, the analyst may use sample results to make estimates as with probability samples, but with no scientific way of estimating the error. In practice, the business analyst, often deriving data from non-probability samples, takes care to provide at least *effective* randomness.

A	B	C
3̲5̲6756	519371	679389
700770	781547	916968
2̲7̲9584	733750	487151
862434	481154	391464
1̲9̲9585	167701	170778
0̲4̲8736	514507	977406
815218	609732	629295
643021	527212	492869
1̲6̲4332	245407	517804
1̲7̲4303	085157	308590
1̲3̲6325	414066	452293
117780	407444	426115

The households on your list bearing the numbers 34, 42, 6, 35, 27, 19, 4, 16, 17, and 13 will be interviewed.

Tables of random numbers are usually arranged in rows and columns, broken into groups containing the same number of items as digits in the individual numbers. Selection may go across the page or down the rows.

The Systematic Random Sample. A more efficient method of obtaining virtually the same results as those derived from simple random sampling comes with the *systematic* random sample. Using the example cited, you will number your households through 50 in the same way. If you wish to survey 10 of the households, divide 50 by 10, which process gives you 5. Thus every *fifth* household will be selected. You start the random process by randomly selecting a number from 1 through 5. If your random selection is 4, then these will be the numbers of the households to be interviewed: 4, 9, 14, 19, 24, 29, 34, 39, 44, and 49.

Selecting a mailing list from a membership roster of 500 names alphabetically arranged may be achieved in the same way. If you choose to survey one tenth of the list, or 50 names, select randomly a number from 1 through 10 and then designate every tenth name from there as part of your sample. If 7 is your initial random number, names 7, 17, 27, and so on until 50 names are selected will make up your sample. For this arrangement, you may merely count and circle every tenth name without numbering the items in the universe. The systematic sample has the advantage of insuring that chosen items will be evenly distributed throughout the population list.

Stratified Random Sampling. If the universe is known to fall naturally into distinct groups or classes, more precise results may be obtained for a set budgeted expenditure from stratifying the sample in the same way that the universe is stratified. For any array of people, obvious classifications occur, such as age, sex, occupation, or other characteristics that might affect

An Exploration of Probability Sampling

The only way in which a known positive probability of selection c
assured is by a *random* selection. There are four types of random, or
ability, samples.

Simple Random Sampling. In simple random sampling every it
the universe must have an *equal* chance of being chosen. Selecting a s
list of respondents under this restriction may be achieved by writin
names of all the people in the appropriate universe on cards, shufflin
cards thoroughly, and drawing names from the pack until a sample c
correct size to give a desired level of precision is reached. Ideally, si
random sampling calls for replacement into the pack of each item di
prior to subsequent drawings—a simulation of an infinite universe. S
replacement creates the possibility of drawing a name more than once, i
survey samples discard the replacement practice and consequently shc
as a general working rule, employ the finite-universe multiplier (expla
later in the chapter) in determining the sample size if more than 5 per
of the universe is queried.

For business surveys based on large universes, the use of a publis
table of random numbers produces a random selection equally as accepta
as the drawing process described above. The procedure runs like this: If
wish to interview 10 out of a list of 50 households, you will number
households on your list from 1 to 50. On the table of random numbers
may start at any arbitrary point, selecting the first ten numbers under
discarding any number which appears more than once and any number lar
than the total count of the universe—50. If the representation of the univ
consists of items numbered 00 through 99, two columns are used; thro
999 items, three columns; through 9,999, four columns; and through 99,0
five columns. Thus your sample chosen from the following arbitrarily selec
portion of a table of random numbers will be composed of the numb
indicated:[1]

A	B	
345769	953810	627
549075	004410	059
423480	950812	197
554518	514280	950
797165	670995	79
062730	163375	60

[1] H. N. Broom, "New Random Sampling Numbers," *Baylor Business Studies*
1 (Waco, Tex.: The School of Business, Baylor University), excerpt from Rows A, B
C of First 1,512 Random Digits.

the phenomenon under investigation. If one is studying the propensity of the population to buy a luxury, high-cost item, stratifying the sample according to income ranges would very likely give more precise results than would a simple random sample of the same population. A *proportionate* random sample is arrived at by putting the same proportion of each group in the sample as prevails in the universe. If one-tenth of the universe has an income of $25,000–40,000, then a random selection of one-tenth of the people in this income classification goes into the sample. If three-fifths have incomes from $10,000–17,000, then a random selection of three-fifths of these people is chosen for the sample. A random sample constructed in this way reflects the proportionate makeup of the universe.

In some cases, however, it is more efficient to use a *nonproportional* stratified sample. Two situations seem to warrant its use: (1) when wide variations occur among the strata, and (2) when survey costs may be reduced by questioning a greater number in some strata than in others. An example of the first situation might be the task of arriving at the per capita income of a city. Fewer people in the population would have incomes in the $25,000–40,000 bracket; yet this group would represent a large proportion of the city's total income; thus it might be well to include as many as 100 percent of the people in this stratum. A large number of the people would be in the $8,000–10,000 category, but the proportion of the city's total income represented by this group might be small. Thus a smaller number would be randomly selected from such a stratum. From a sample structured in this manner, the per capita income for the population is estimated by multiplying the per capita income in each stratum by the proportion of the population in that stratum. The weighted numbers thus resulting are then added and divided by the number in the population to compute the per capita income for the city.

An example of the second situation could be an interview survey of the graduates of a college or university who reside within the state. It is likely that more of the former students currently live in the college domicile city. These former students close at hand can be interviewed more economically than can those whose homes are at quite a distance; thus more students in this stratum would be interviewed than would those at greater distances. The results would be weighted in much the same manner as that indicated for the preceding example.

Cluster Sampling. In cluster sampling, instead of working with individual items, the analyst considers as basic units the normal groupings into which the population falls: city blocks, counties, or other political or geographical subdivisions. If you are to survey by questionnaire a sample from a large membership represented by a directory, the pages in the directory may be considered as clusters. For single-stage cluster sampling, you will randomly select enough pages in the directory to give the sample size you need. Let us suppose that the directory has 60 pages with approximately 25 names to a page, thus composing a 1,500-unit universe. At this point you may think that perhaps using more pages and fewer names to the page will distribute the sample more evenly through the universe; so you decide to employ two-stage sampling. If you want to survey one-tenth of the universe, you may choose to use 5 names from the 25 on each page; thus you will need 30 pages from the directory. You will randomly choose 30 out of the 60 pages as the first stage. Then you will randomly select 5 names from each page as the second stage. Ways of deciding on sample sizes appear later in this chapter.

The example just cited is the simplest kind of cluster sampling and subsampling, for the clusters are all of equal size. In many cases, though, the clusters are not so advantageously set up. The departments in a large organization form natural clusters for an interviewing program, but it is unlikely that all departments have the same number of employees. For the subsampling, the analyst may choose an equal number of employees from each cluster or a proportional number.

The Characteristics
of Nonprobability Sampling

Nonprobability samples, chosen according to convenience or judgment rather than by random selection, are usually termed *quota* or *judgment* samples. They are used widely and successfully in business, despite the fact that their precision cannot be measured exactly. A quota sample is one in which a certain number of individuals is surveyed, with no attention paid to random selection. An interviewer is told to interview a certain number of college students passing by a certain intersection. He or she interviews each student passing until the quota is reached.

A judgment sample for a particular purpose sometimes is more efficient than a probability sample. If a manufacturer of diet pills is considering possible locations for branch factories, better results will be obtained by selecting cities where people known to be interested in reducing live—such as Hollywood—or those with high incomes (under the assumption that people with more money eat better than those with less) than will be by a random selection from a list of cities with a certain population. Choosing a sample from a group known to be typical according to a certain characteristic under the assumption that, if they are typical in this respect they will be typical with respect to the aspect under investigation, is another form of judgment sampling. As an illustration, a publisher will conduct an opinion poll on a quality economics magazine that he or she intends to launch. The publisher chooses the sample from those individuals with doctor of philosophy degrees, under the assumption that, if respondents are alike in educational qualifications, they will be alike in other respects.

The Sample Size

The size of sample the individual chooses depends upon the degree of confidence to be placed in the results of the survey. If the decision to be based upon the findings of the investigation is highly significant—one that involves a substantial amount of money, or one that might have a crucial effect on the firm's operations if the decision turns out to be a bad one—the analyst must scientifically select a sample size that will approximate closely the results obtained if the entire universe were surveyed. In general, for probability samples, the larger the size of the sample, the more precise the answers. For many business decisions, however, a reasonable range of values may be all that the executive needs to implement action, in which case a smaller sample is indicated. In addition, the analyst must also resolve the problem of how precise an answer will be secured for a budgeted amount of money. A sophisticated treatment of sampling theory is beyond the scope of this book; so the analyst with no statistical background has three choices: (1) to survey the entire universe; (2) to query a sufficiently large sample, say, 20 to 25 percent of the universe, to minimize errors; or (3) to employ formulas mechanically, even though the user has little understanding of their origins. A review of formulas for determining sample size (descriptive statistics, related group) appears as an appendix to this chapter; see the appendix at the end of the next chapter also.

Preparing the Information Request and Questionnaire Cover Letter

Requesting access to the information your respondents may give is a difficult procedure, and effective handling often marks the difference between success and failure for the survey. The way the request is drafted depends upon the size of the proposal and the writer's knowledge of his or her readers: their education and cultural level, their prejudices and biases, their preferences, and the many facets of their world as they see it. One approach may work quite well with one type of reader and may provoke a negative reaction in another. The psychology of request making, covered in other chapters of this book, should be reviewed as background for reader appraisal and for adapting the tone and style to the particular audience.

Obtaining permission for an on-the-premises investigation of a company's operations, policies, marketing strategies, linear-programming techniques, and so forth is often most difficult, for management is justifiably wary of allowing such information to fall into alien hands. Two elements of assurance are essential: (1) evidence of your own integrity and (2) affirmation that the company's connection with the data will be withheld, not only by name but also by elimination of references that could lead to shrewd identity guesses.

Arrangements for an interview about business policies, peculiar problems of the industry, or whatever makes up the nature of the inquiry, may, of course, be made by telephone or by unannounced personal visit to the respondent's headquarters. Success in such procedures, though, depends heavily on careful preplanning of the interview and on superior personal presentation. Unless you are quite well informed as to the nature of the firm's activities, the timing of your call or visit may be ill chosen. In many cases, therefore, a well-written request preceding the personal contact has the advantages of allowing the respondent to consider your proposal at a suitable time, to reread it at leisure, or to consult with other people involved. In addition, the written form permits you the opportunity to phrase your proposal to the best advantage and to revise it until you are satisfied that each sentence makes its own effective contribution.

Requests that the respondent fill in attached questionnaires are more likely to receive a favorable reply than are other approaches; yet a high percentage of returns is so important to the accuracy of the findings that such requests merit careful planning. The writer's appraisal of reader characteristics or the stereotyped characteristics of the group to which he or she belongs will serve as a guide for which approach to use. For some readers a persuasive sales approach might be desirable, whereas to other readers it would appear offensive. On occasion, a direct, cards-on-the-table treatment would be called for; at other times, an inductive, climactic arrangement would serve best. The following are some general suggestions for drafting request letters that may be adapted, as the occasion requires, to your own particular problem.

The Direct-Style Plan of Presentation.   The direct plan of presentation is used when the writer thinks the reader would prefer to know what is expected of her or him at once—without any buildup or explanatory preamble. Suggested treatment of the parts is given here.

The opening should make clear the crux of what the writer wants and why it is wanted. Since covering all phases of the request in the opening may be difficult, this initial treatment presents the overall aspects, with the details to be worked out as the letter progresses. The question-request form is usually the most forceful for its interest-arousing value. Telling the reader *why* the request item is desired lends significance to his or her efforts in responding. The more worthy your purpose seems, the more likely you are to get a favorable response. The importance to be derived from the research itself should be stressed rather than the fact that you need the information to complete a class assignment—though that detail may appear later in the letter as part of the sponsorship. Another type of direct-style plea attempts a charmingly frank admission that the writer actually is doing some of the things the reader might object to and asks for his or her indulgence.

Elements of coverage in the main body of the letter embrace the following phases, with variations according to specific studies:

1. A transition into the aspects of the request or inquiry that plays up the significance the writer thinks the study will have or why the reader was chosen.

2. An explanation of the sponsorship—the company conducting the survey or, for the student, the supervising professor's name, the identity of the course under which the study is undertaken, or both. The supervisor's signature as well as the writer's may induce better response.

3. A concise explanation of the chosen procedures.

4. A clear delineation of the details of what the reader is expected to do. This is probably the most difficult task. Operations vary greatly; names for things may be different in different situations. If samples, models, or examples are desired, the writer should think the problem through carefully so that sufficient alternative suggestions can be provided to get what is wanted in spite of possible variations. If one is asking for access to an individual operation, the reader should be alerted precisely to the type of examination to be made at the plant, how long the study will take, suggested times possible to the investigator, and so on. If the reader is to answer an attached questionnaire, the writer should try to create an interest in the research instrument—its comprehensiveness, its brevity, any special ways in which it is arranged. Instructions for filling it in should appear on the questionnaire or as a separate sheet attachment.

5. Promise of anonymity, if such is desirable, and an explanation as to how it will be provided.

6. Any ways in which the reader might profit from the study, including a findings summary, if the writer honestly intends to furnish one. The graciousness with which the reader is made to feel a part of the project improves the researcher's chances of getting what is wanted.

The close is the writer's gracious leave-taking, an appreciation of the reader's contribution, a final goodwill-building effort. Here some kind of deadline for the reader's answer should be tactfully set. If the timing is too close, the reader may despair of replying in view of a busy schedule. If too much time is given, the receiver may postpone response and eventually not answer at all. A reasonable deadline should be selected and a reason given for it. Injecting a note of courtesy into the deadline request, possibly phrasing it as a question or placing a sincere value on the reader's compliance at the set time, is an effective device.

The Inductive, Climactic Treatment. The inductive pattern of organization is used when you think that you will have better success at obtaining the reader's cooperation if it is possible to interest the person in the project before the person is told what is expected. The larger the size of the request and the greater reader resistance anticipated, the more important the techniques of persuasion. Here are some suggestions for writing the persuasive-request letter.

The opening should capture the reader's interest with a remark or question that plays up something significant about the field of inquiry, his or her concern with it, her or his desire to contribute to its long-range progress, some unusual feature of it. The opening attempts to establish *rapport* between the writer and the respondent. Whatever material is chosen for this opening remark or question should somehow set the theme for the entire letter. If the reader is aroused or startled with ideas not related to the purpose of the message at least indirectly, he or she may feel cheated and may justifiably offer resistance. The opening, therefore, moves over into the reader's field of interest with something he or she can feel good about or neutral toward, without revealing the real purpose of the message, yet serving as an introductory lead into it.

The elements of coverage are the same as for the direct style; the treatment is somewhat different. Here the writer tries to build, a step at a time, reasons why the reader will want to comply with the request, working the elements of coverage into the argument: why the study is important, why the reader is a likely contributor, how he or she may profit, how the project will be executed. By the time this portion is completed, the reader has been carried through varying phases of agreement so that he or she is prepared for the request—may even feel that it is inevitable if the writer is skillful enough. Then comes the request itself and the details of what the reader is expected to do.

The closing words are essentially the same as for the direct presentation. Sample Form 8-2 is an example of the inductive-style request.

Drafting the Interrogation Instrument

Questionnaires are generally of two types or a combination of them.

1. The *closed* form, in which the respondents merely make choices among the alternatives and check their answers. Some provision is usually made for write-in choices. Often these voluntary answers are more significant than the alternatives the analyst has been able to draft in preplanning the instrument.

2. The *open*, or *free*, form, which calls for free response in the answerer's own words with no clues provided. This type is more efficient at getting at the real heart of the subject, but more difficult to tabulate and summarize.

Closed-form questions are of two types: multiple choice and dichotomous. In the multiple-choice arrangement, the analyst thinks through the question, anticipating possible answers and enumerating them for the respondent's choice. A final selection not designated (labeled in some such way as "other" or "none of these") moves over into free-form territory by asking the reader

---

PLACEMENT OFFICE
COLLEGE OF BUSINESS ADMINISTRATION, SOME UNIVERSITY
Some City, Your State

June 1, 19xx

Mr. David B. Tarlton
Personnel Director
National Aerospace Company
Chicago, Illinois 24591

Dear Mr. Tarlton:

When two job candidates with approximately the same qualifications write prospecting letters to the same firm, why does one applicant receive a more favorable response from the prospective employer than does the other?

Under the supervision of Mrs. Jerry Moore, Placement Director, College of Business Administration, Some University, I am attempting a study of application letters with the hope of isolating a few effective techniques that may enable future graduates to give a better account of themselves in the job hunt. A successful conclusion to the project may, in turn, provide you and other employers with more efficiently written applications to evaluate.

The scheme for the study centers around the two attached prospecting letters written by applicants with the same qualifications for jobs in your accounting department. Neither applicant has had significant experience in the accounting field. Since the test letters will be sent to 150 eminent personnel directors over the country, specific references to your particular company, though desirable, were necessarily omitted. Your answers to the questionnaire sheet in front of the letters will be a real contribution toward getting an evaluation of the writing techniques employed.

Trial runs on the questionnaire took ten to fifteen minutes. Won't you please give us that much of your time? We're eager to have your answers included in the data that we hope to assemble in time to place in the hands of September job candidates.

Sincerely yours

(Mrs.) Jerry Moore
(Mrs.) Jerry Moore

Daniel A. Hilliard
Daniel A. Hilliard

Sample Form 8-2   Questionnaire cover letter

to fill in an applicable response. Space for this free-form answer probably should be provided, even though it adds to the analyst's tabulating difficulties, for herein may lie the depth of the study—an added insight and perception. Another common variation gives multiple choices for the reader to rate as first, second, and so on. Certainly, providing too many things for the respondent to rate will result in meaningless and inaccurate answers. After the first few ratings, the recipient grows tired and confused and is likely to put down anything that occurs to him or her for the rest. Dichotomous questions ask the reader to choose between two things: "yes" or "no," "this" or "that." A third choice should be provided for the "undecided," lest answers be biased by forcing the respondent to go one way or the other. A blank calling for an elaboration of the "indecisive" part, free-form style, is valuable here also.

These basic ideas on questionnaire preparation and administration may prove helpful to the investigator in getting valid returns:

1. Choose the sample of respondents carefully according to their ability to answer questions on the subject.

2. Try to establish *rapport* with the readers from the beginning through an extra note of graciousness, capturing their interest, or imparting a feeling of ease in answering. Beginning with a striking question or a remarkably easy one is a good device.

3. Arrange the questions in logical sequence so that they grow out of each other naturally. Asking respondents to skip about only confuses and irritates them. If there is a series of questions they will fill in if their answer is "yes" and another series if their answer is "no," put the two series together.

4. Avoid complicated rating scales of indicated factors.

5. Avoid asking questions requiring mathematical computations, averages, or percentages.

6. Avoid questions that rely on the respondent's memory.

7. Define words that may have a different meaning for the researcher and the respondent. Avoid abstract words whose meaning may vary from person to person, such as *seldom, often, generally*. Ask for specific counts.

8. Eliminate words that might cast an emotional, political, or social bias on the answers. Rephrase with words of greater universality.

9. Ask for what has taken place or is present rather than for future intentions, unless you are a highly skilled researcher.

10. Strive for clarity of statement and then try the questionnaire out on some willing respondents before the final draft. In addition, make a pilot run of the completed form to see whether it is designed correctly to get the desired responses.

11. Beware of double negatives. Confusing: "Would you not find it desirable to make no decision prior to personality-test screening?" A single negative is almost as bad: "Is it not desirable to postpone decisions until personality tests have been administered?"

12. Be careful to provide adequate alternatives.

13. Avoid the double-barreled question, such as "Are you satisfied with the results of this program and do you plan to enlarge it in the future?"

14. Phrase questions so that they are appropriate for *all* respondents. Arrange so that all answers will be in the same basic units.

15. Make questions objective, with no leading suggestions as to the response desired. Leading: "Don't you consider this truck-replacement procedure to be the best for maximizing profits?"

16. Cut the size to a bare minimum. If the size can be reduced through printed format, the expense may be worthwhile.

17. Make the questionnaire (a) attractive, (b) easy to read, and (c) simple to answer. Leave readers enough space for free form answers, but do not overwhelm them with so much blank space that respondents will feel that their meager thoughts are probably of small consequence.

18. Provide all questions an equal chance by keeping them in parallel form.

19. Take into consideration the bias resulting from the fact that first choices are most often checked.

20. To probe for motives, ask a series of questions rather than a sudden "Why?"

Interviews are of various sorts: planned or unplanned, depth, or the sort used in motivational research. Unless the interviewer is highly skilled, better results are usually obtained from a carefully planned interview schedule, provided that asking definite questions will not defeat the purpose of the study. An investigation for which only a free-flow response is desirable might be an appraisal of discriminatory practices in labor unions. It is simple enough to imagine the outcome if the union manager were asked: "What discriminatory practices prevail in your union?"

Interview schedules vary according to their nature and the means of recording data. If the tape recorder is the chosen medium, the interviewer may need to make the respondent feel at home with the machine by pointing out that both will talk in their normal speaking voice and noting any special manipulations that will have to be made in the course of the conversation. Perhaps a trial talk of no real significance to the study will be helpful in setting the scene. Tape-recorded interviews are quite effective for getting at motivations and opinions where little quantification is possible. They are also beneficial in preserving accuracy.

The fact that the interviewer is writing down answers as the respondent speaks also might provoke some nervousness, self-consciousness, or wariness. A gracious explanation is apropos to put the respondent at ease. The planned interview procedures should be written down in rather complete detail. Adequate space should be provided for unanticipated developments which could have real meaning for the study. Any alternatives for the interviewee to choose from should be typed on cards for the respondent to look at, particularly if the list runs to more than three. If the interviewer prefers not to record answers during the course of the conversation, he or she should certainly record them immediately afterward. Sample excerpts from questionnaires for critical evaluation are Sample Forms 8-3 and 8-4.

APPENDIX: A REVIEW OF FORMULAS FOR DETERMINING SAMPLE SIZE

The applications for two equations designed to determine sample size are given here. The statistically inclined will recognize their origins. The mathematically uninitiated may very well employ them mechanically.

Probability Sample Size Gauged by the Mean

If the analyst is interested in knowing the mean value of the cases in a distribution of findings, the following equation may be employed for estimating the sample size needed to derive accurate answers.

$$n = \frac{\hat{\sigma}^2}{\hat{\sigma}^2_{\bar{x}}} \qquad (1)$$

where

n = the number of cases to be included in the sample

$\hat{\sigma}$ = an estimate of the standard deviation of the universe

$\hat{\sigma}_{\bar{x}}$ = the standard error of the mean of the sample

For illustrative purposes, suppose that you wish to survey a sample of the 10,000 members of the American Executive Secretaries Association to determine, among other things, the average annual salary. Sending questionnaires to the complete list of 10,000, with subsequent laborious calculations to be made, seems inordinately costly and time consuming; so you would like to know how many secretaries you must query as to their annual salary so that the *average* figure from the replies would approximate the *average*

WILL YOU PLEASE HELP US EVALUATE THE EFFECTIVENESS OF THE TWO
ATTACHED LETTERS BY ANSWERING THESE QUESTIONS?

1. Which of the two letters would more probably result in a job offer from you?
   Letter No. 1 [   ]   Letter No. 2 [   ]
   In what way or ways do you consider the letter of your choice superior?

2. Which of the opening paragraphs produces the more desirable effect on you?
   Letter No. 1 [   ]   Letter No. 2 [   ]
   Why?

3. Both letters report these facts of qualification:
   --A B.B.A. degree from Some University in August.
   --The technical skill acquired from a major in industrial accounting.
   --High scores on American Institute of Accountants tests and a B average.
   --Supplementary courses in liberal arts.
   --A writing skill rewarded with A's in business-communications courses.
   --24 years of age, married, with two children.
   --A stable, adaptable personality.
   --Military service covered.
   In your opinion, do these facts constitute adequate coverage for a pros-
   pecting application letter designed to arouse interest in the writer?
   Yes [   ]   No [   ]
   What other facts of qualification do you think should have been included?

   Since space is important, which facts of qualification would you omit?

   Which of the two letters handles these facts of qualification the more effectively?   Letter No. 1 [   ]   Letter No. 2 [   ]

4. Both candidates offer to start at the bottom of the accounting department:
   "The steady progress and the conserva-   "Have I made the preliminary
   tive policies of your company make it   hurdle of the challenge a
   quite desirable to me to pitch in as   starting job with you offers?"
   a clerk, if necessary, and let you be
   the judge the rest of the way."

   Which of the two ways of handling this portion do you consider to be the
   better?   Letter No. 1 [   ]   Letter No. 2 [   ]
5. Both letters make an appeal for an expression of interest from the employer:
   "I'll be happy to furnish a complete   "I'd like very much to present a
   data sheet and reference if you like."   detailed account of my qualifica-
                                               tions and references to support my
                                               claims. May I hear from you?"
   Which of the two produces the more desirable effect on you?
   Letter No. 1 [   ]   Letter No. 2 [   ]
   Please use the back of this   SIGNED:_____
   sheet for additional comments.

   _____

Sample Form 8-3   One page questionnaire

salary of the 10,000 members. You will also need to set some standard as to how much error you will tolerate, but first let us look into ways of substituting figures for the formula symbols.

THE CHASE MANHATTAN BANK N.A. SURVEY OF COLLEGE
AND UNIVERSITY ECONOMISTS

1. What do you consider the most pressing economic problem now facing the
U. S.?

   a. Unemployment   [ ]

   b. Inadequate growth   [ ]

   c. Balance-of-payments
      deficit   [ ]

   d. Automation   [ ]

   e. Other (please specify)
      _____

2. Do you favor a cut in federal taxes
at the present time?

   Yes [ ]   No [ ]

3. What is the major reason for our
persistent high rate of unemployment?

   a. Inadequate demand   [ ]

   b. Structural problems (e. g.,
      minimum wage laws, lack of
      education, automation, etc.)
                                      [ ]

   c. Other (please specify)

4. What is the most effective way of
dealing with automation?

   a. Improve rate of economic
      growth   [ ]

   b. Retrain workers with
      federal aid   [ ]

   c. Slow up the introduction of au-
      tomated equipment   [ ]

   d. No specific measures neces-
      sary   [ ]

5. In general are you satisfied with
the U. S. economic growth rate--
that is, are you willing to let it
proceed at the present rate without
advocating major government action?
   Yes [ ]   No [ ]

What do you think is the most prac-
ticable and effective way of speed-
ing growth?

   a. Increased federal
      expenditures   [ ]

   b. Tax reductions   [ ]

   c. Change in tax structure   [ ]

   d. Less government direc-
      tion of business ac-
      tivity   [ ]

   e. More government direc-
      tion of business ac-
      tivity   [ ]

   f. Other (please specify)

6. Do you think there is a conflict
between (1) solving the balance-
of-payments problem, and (2) achieving full employment?
   Yes [ ]   No [ ]

   If your answer is "yes," do you
   think:
   a. More emphasis should be put on
      correcting balance-of-payment
      difficulties?   [ ]

   b. More should be put on reaching
      full employment?   [ ]

   c. Present policies hit just
      about the right balance?   [ ]

7. Is inflation likely to be a major
problem within the next few years?
   Yes [ ]   No [ ]

   If inflationary pressures do develop,
   how should they be contained?

   a. General fiscal and monetary
      policy   [ ]

   b. Selective price controls   [ ]

   c. Selective credit controls   [ ]

   d. Other (please specify)

Sample Form 8-4   Combination multiple-choice and dichotomous questions, economy of arrangement

Since you know nothing about the salary ranges of the universe, or how the average or mean salary might vary between successive samples drawn from this universe, you must find some way of estimating the standard deviation of the universe—ở in the formula. One way of doing so is to make a pilot run of a small sample drawn from the universe, using the information thus obtained in estimating the standard deviation of the universe. Let us say, then, that you randomly select ten names from the Association membership list and send these ten people questionnaires to be answered. With the ten salary figures derived from this pilot run arranged in a list, you may proceed to find the standard deviation of individual salaries from the mean salary of the distribution with this formula:

$$s^2 = \frac{\sum x^2}{n} - \left(\frac{\sum x}{n}\right)^2 \tag{2}$$

where

s = the standard deviation of the sample

$\sum$ = the sum of

x = the value of individual items in the sample

   (the annual salaries of the 10 secretaries in the sample pilot run)

Let us say that x and x^2 of the pilot run of the questionnaires array in this fashion:

Individual Annual Salaries (x)	Individual Annual Salaries Squared (x²)
$ 16,000	$ 256,000,000
15,500	240,250,000
14,800	219,040,000
14,200	201,640,000
15,000	225,000,000
14,800	219,040,000
15,500	240,250,000
16,000	256,000,000
15,000	225,000,000
14,800	219,040,000
$151,600	$2,301,260,000

Filling these numbers into formula 2 gives

$$S^2 = \frac{\$2,301,260,000}{10} - \left(\frac{\$151,600}{10}\right)^2$$

$$= \$300,400$$

The s, of course, is the square root of 300,400—a needless calculation, since this figure is used in the next formula in squared form. Let us go back now to the basic assumption with which we began: that the standard deviation of the universe will be approximately the same as the standard deviation of the sample. Under this assumption, then, the value for s^2 (300,400) just derived may be substituted into

$$\hat{\sigma}^2 = s^2 \left(\frac{n}{n-1}\right) \tag{3}$$

where

$\hat{\sigma}$ = the estimated standard deviation of the universe

s = the standard deviation of the sample

Substituting sample figures into the formula, we find the standard deviation of the universe to be

$$\hat{\sigma}^2 = 300,400 \times \frac{10}{9}$$

$$= 333,777.77$$

The value 333,777.77 can now be substituted into formula 1 in place of $\hat{\sigma}$. At this point all that is left to do is to set limits on the degree of precision with which we need to know the average annual secretarial salary; and the sample size is sensitive to the required degree of precision. Cutting the range of error in half roughly calls for quadrupling the sample size, as is demonstrated in the following computations.

The $\hat{\sigma}_{\bar{x}}$ in formula 1 (the standard error of the mean of the sample) is set at the discretion of the researcher in that he or she can select it to yield a given probability that the mean of the universe will fall within plus or minus some numbers of $\hat{\sigma}_{\bar{x}}$'s of the $\bar{x}$ (mean) value. Let us say that, as a base for a preliminary estimation of survey costs, we would like to know the average annual secretarial salary within two ranges of precision, within $50 either way, ±$50, and within $100 either way, ±$100. If the means of numerous samples drawn from the universe were plotted, the resulting distribution would be, according to statisticians, approximately normal as in the following illustrative graph. Under this assumption, certain conclusions about this distribution may be drawn:

1. Approximately 68 percent of the samples drawn from the population should have means that fall within plus or minus one standard error of the mean, $\hat{\sigma}_{\bar{x}}$.

2. Approximately 95 percent of the samples drawn from the universe should have means that fall within ± 1.96 standard errors of the mean.

3. Approximately 99 percent of the samples drawn from the universe should have means that fall within ± 2.58 standard errors of the mean.

NORMAL DISTRIBUTION

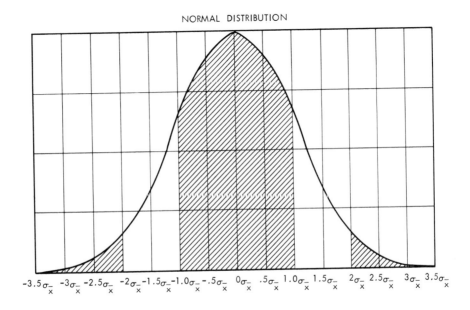

In view of these observations, $\hat{\sigma}_{\bar{x}}$ (the standard error of the mean of the sample) at different probability levels runs like this:

At the 68% level	$1\hat{\sigma}_{\bar{x}} = \$50$	$1\hat{\sigma}_{\bar{x}} = \$100$
	$\hat{\sigma}_{\bar{x}} = \$50$	$\hat{\sigma}_{\bar{x}} = \$100$
At the 95% level	$1.96\hat{\sigma}_{\bar{x}} = \$50$	$1.96\hat{\sigma}_{\bar{x}} = \$100$
	$\hat{\sigma}_{\bar{x}} = \dfrac{\$50}{1.96}$	$\hat{\sigma}_{\bar{x}} = \dfrac{\$100}{1.96}$
At the 99% level	$2.58\hat{\sigma}_{\bar{x}} = \$50$	$2.58\hat{\sigma}_{\bar{x}} = \$100$
	$\hat{\sigma}_{\bar{x}} = \dfrac{\$50}{2.58}$	$\hat{\sigma}_{\bar{x}} = \dfrac{\$100}{2.58}$

To demonstrate the difference in sample sizes according to the degree of accuracy required at different confidence levels, let us compute the sample size required to determine the average secretarial salary within $\pm \$50$ and within $\pm \$100$, according to formula 1. The value of $\hat{\sigma}^2$ (the standard deviation of the universe squared) has already been calculated to be 333,777.77.

	Within $\pm \$50$ Accuracy	Within $\pm \$100$ Accuracy
	$n = \dfrac{\hat{\sigma}^2}{\hat{\sigma}^2_{\bar{x}}}$	$n = \dfrac{\hat{\sigma}^2}{\hat{\sigma}^2_{\bar{x}}}$
At 68% confidence	$n = \dfrac{333{,}777.77}{(50/1.00)^2}$ $= 134$	$n = \dfrac{333{,}777.77}{(100/1.00)^2}$ $= 33$
At 95% confidence	$n = \dfrac{333{,}777.77}{(50/1.96)^2}$ $= 513$	$n = \dfrac{333{,}777.77}{(100/1.96)^2}$ $= 128$
At 99% confidence	$n = \dfrac{333{,}777.77}{(50/2.58)^2}$ $= 889$	$n = \dfrac{333{,}777.77}{(100/2.58)^2}$ $= 222$

From these examples the generalization that, to achieve 50 percent greater accuracy, it is necessary to quadruple the sample size becomes apparent. Rounding in the calculations accounts for the fact that the sample sizes on the left are not exactly four times those on the right.

The computations above concern the sample size to be drawn from a 10,000-number universe—one that for practical purposes may be considered *infinite*. For finite universes, random samples chosen without replacement, and samples that are likely to be more than 5 percent of the universe, the finite multiplier $\sqrt{1 - n/N}$ is added to the equation:

$$\hat{\sigma}_{\bar{x}} = \frac{\hat{\sigma}}{n}\left(1 - \frac{n}{N}\right) \tag{4}$$

Thus

$$n = \frac{\hat{\sigma}^2}{\hat{\sigma}^2_{\bar{x}} + \hat{\sigma}^2/N}$$

where N = the size of the universe.

The sample size for a finite universe of 1,000 secretaries with the accuracy level for average annual salary set at $\pm \$50$ and $\pm \$100$ runs like this:

	Within ±$50	Within ±$100
At 68% confidence	$n = \dfrac{333,777.77}{(50/1.00)^2 + (333,777.77/1,000)}$ $= 118$	$n = \dfrac{333,777.77}{(100/1.00)^2 + (333,777.77/1,000)}$ $= 32$
At 95% confidence	$n = \dfrac{333,777.77}{(50/1.96)^2 + (333,777.77/1,000)}$ $= 340$	$n = \dfrac{333,777.77}{(100/1.96)^2 + (333,777.77/1,000)}$ $= 114$
At 99% confidence	$n = \dfrac{333,777.77}{(50/2.58)^2 + (333,777.77/1,000)}$ $= 471$	$n = \dfrac{333,777.77}{(100/2.58)^2 + (333,777.77/1,000)}$ $= 182$

Probability Sample Size from the Standard Error of Percentage

If the answers on the questionnaire will be arranged in proportions or percentages of individual cases with a certain characteristic or attribute, the following formula may be used to estimate the sample size:

$$\hat{\sigma}_p = \sqrt{\frac{\pi(1 - \pi)}{n}} \tag{5}$$

where

$$\pi = \text{the proportion of the population having the characteristic}$$

$$1 - \pi = \text{the proportion of the population remaining}$$

Therefore,

$$n = \frac{\pi(1 - \pi)}{\hat{\sigma}_p^2}$$

Since the proportion of the universe having the characteristic is not known, a pilot run of a small sample or the proportions from similar studies may be substituted for the proportion of the universe. If one of the questions on the questionnaire to secretaries was "Have you passed the Certified Professional Secretary Exam?" and 0.20 of the respondents in the pilot run of 10 answered "yes," then this proportion can be substituted for π and the equation solved on a trial basis. Let us assume also that you would like to know the proportion of the secretaries having a CPS certificate within 5-percent accuracy. The formula is then filled in much the same way employed for determining sample size by mean relationships.

At the 95% confidence level,

$$n = \frac{0.20 \times 0.80}{(0.05/1.96)^2}$$

$$= 246$$

Sample sizes at the other confidence levels can be computed in the same manner. A suitable number of other questions should be tested to see whether the sample size computed for the first one is approximately the same for all questions. In cases of differences, some adjustment should be made in the final choice of sample size. It may be noted at this point that the size of the sample determined on the basis of answers to the question "What is your annual salary?" at the 95-percent confidence level within $50 accuracy was 340 and within $100 accuracy was 114. The sample size 246 computed with the proportion formula, then, is a little more than halfway between the ranges. If obtaining the average salary range is fairly important, perhaps it is best to use the 340 sample size. The proportion answers will, as a by-product, achieve somewhat greater accuracy.

9

Shaping the Decision

Collecting data isn't difficult; breathing life into the facts to make them meaningful for the reader is.

In the early chapters of this book the communication setting is described as originating with an individual possessed of a purpose: a communicator with something to say. Before an idea can be transferred successfully from one brain to the brain of another, the communicator will need a full understanding of the message's aspects and how they fit together. The process of formulating the communication for maximum effectiveness, regardless of the medium employed, involves an examination of the information available, followed by decisions as to the implied meaning of the data and how this meaning may best be imparted. Although the emphasis of this chapter lies with the shaping of a decision to be recorded in a formal, analytical business report, many of the suggested procedures are equally applicable to other communication forms.

Webster's defines a decision as "a settling, or terminating, as of a controversy, by giving judgment on the matter; also a conclusion after consideration." The situation from which a decision arises is characterized inevitably by a state of conflicting interests—a doubt as to which of two or several possible courses of action may be best for the enterprise in question. Each of the conflicting interests involves a train of possible consequences—good and bad—that must be evaluated if the decision is to be a sound one. The problem is further complicated by the fact that the business entity is inseparable from the environment in which it operates. Not only must internal influences be considered, but also those external forces that affect the organization: the general economic and social elements of the business environment and the competitive climate that affects business survival. Thus we cannot merely envision the decision maker as poised between two or several courses of action, spontaneously making a choice from infinite wisdom. Long and laborious analyses go into the process. The systematic application of the critical and creative powers of the analyst to assembled facts makes up the content of this chapter, stage V of the agenda.

The investigator, following the decision stages set out in this book, has thus far intellectualized the uncertainties of the problem into a question to be answered by research, identified the overall decision criterion embodied in the hypothesis, established the critical components of that decision criterion, and completed the search activity designed to provide data for the solution to the problem. The analyst is now ready to shape a rational decision from this welter of assembled data, some of it incomplete and conflicting, with full knowledge that the work is worth its cost only to the extent that it reduces the penalty of a bad decision.

Assistance is proposed for this formidable task through discussion of the following elements:

1. Some basic ideas on decision planning.
2. Decision-making techniques for the yes-or-no problem.
3. Framing the decision for the comparative evaluation.
4. The decision design for the analytic-descriptive investigation.

SOME BASIC IDEAS ON DECISION PLANNING

The area of decision making is currently burgeoning with new concepts, leaving the business manager and the scholar in a state of some perplexity as to what to make of all the information and methods at their disposal. For the purposes of this book, a fairly simple general-purpose decision maker (Figure 9-1) was synthesized from the ideas of the many writers consulted. The analyst may further elaborate it according to his or her own degree of sophistication in the field. Six basic steps are provided:

I. Data processing.
II. The prediction system.
III. The value system.
IV. Measurement by the decision criterion.

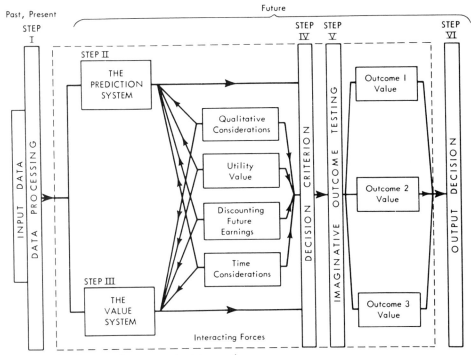

Figure 9-1   A general-purpose decision maker

    V. Imaginative testing of outcomes.
    VI. The decision.

The discussion below concentrates on basic considerations of value to all decision makers, whether they will apply intuitive judgment or quantitative measurement to their answers. Some applications of quantitative decision making (descriptive statistics) are provided in the appendix to this chapter.

Data Processing

Present-day decision makers have more mechanical aids at their disposal than did their predecessors, who nevertheless were able to come up with good strategies, often history making in effect. For the modern executive, the computer can process in minutes calculations that previously might have taken years of painstaking effort. Through translation of the aspects of the problem into the numbers, symbols, and words of mathematical formulae and computer language, today's analyst can derive mechanically certain binary and sequential decisions of a complexity unmanageable by the unaided finite mind and of greater accuracy than those resulting from business judgment alone.

Humans have made the computer in their own image, though, with potentialities for comparison, association, and word and number manipulation similar to those possessed by the humans who plan the programming. Business people may still prefer to apply their experience and judgment to the mastery of their uncertainties rather than to mechanize them; but it is likely that intuitive decisions will become less and less useful in an era of growing complexity and rapid technological change. Whether the analyst will convert aspects of the problem to mathematical formulae or apply personal analytical powers toward the answer, the preliminary thinking focused on the data has a common core.

In the original evaluation of the problem according to the steps outlined in Chapter 7, the analyst determined the kinds of data needed for the acceptance or rejection of the hypothesis in a yes-or-no, a comparative-evaluation, and a descriptive-analytic decision. Whichever type of answer is pursued, the six basic steps in the decision maker are followed. Points of divergence of the three types of problems are explained in later sections of this chapter.

As a first step the analyst will try to abstract all possible meaning from the assembled data, to search diligently for all clues as to what sort of action should be taken on the proposed venture. The data may be in quantitative form, from which fairly objective subjudgments on the components of the decision may be reached through statistical measures, or the data may be qualitative, calling for a subjective appraisal created, perhaps subconsciously, from a configuration of accumulated knowledge and past experiences. Prior to any form of processing, the analyst should scrutinize the data for (1) relevance, (2) reliability, and (3) repeatability. If the analyst has followed the suggested procedure of gathering facts and statistics according to their pertinence to the decision criterion embodied in the hypothesis, he or she should be fairly sure at this point of their *relevance* to the problem's solution. The insight gained in the process, however, may lead to discarding some types of data originally considered important and to adding others that at the point of conceiving the research design were unknown.

The *reliability* of data is measured according to the way in which they were gathered: the acceptability of the sampling procedures and research techniques employed, the conscious elimination of bias, possible falsification, concealed or misleading facts, and the authoritativeness of secondary sources consulted. *Repeatability* implies that the data are facts that all people see the same way: the results would be identical if another investigator undertook the same research activity. Data derived from secondary sources should be subjected to the same careful scrutiny as is the analyst's own primary accumulation.

Assembled quantitative data must first be ordered, that is, classified into groups according to common characteristics and organized. Manual tabulation may be possible for small numbers of items. For numerous items, punch cards or magnetic tape entry for electronic processing enable the decision maker to scan data in a fraction of the time required for manual tabulation, to make different runs of the data by varying classifications, and to retrieve them readily. Translating them for computer processing makes for even greater speed and depth of analysis.

The *summarization* the report writer makes of the data is dependent upon the type of analysis the data will be subjected to and upon the reporter's expertise. Almost universal in use are the conversion of data to percentages or ratios and the determination of the mean, median, and mode. The sophisticated statistician may proceed to estimate dispersion, set up correlations between variables, apply tests of significance to answers, make break-even analyses, and so on. If the analyst is not skilled in mathematical procedures, a generalized review presentation would not be of much help here. If such knowledge is already a part of his or her educational equipment, no explanation is necessary. This chapter merely sets up a basic decision scheme that the investigator can simplify or elaborate according to personal talents and sophisticated expertise.

Thus far the discussion has been concerned with *what is* and what *has been,* as evidenced from accumulated data. Since action will be taken in the future, though, the analyst plotting a decision must take the data through the next two interacting stages of the general-purpose decision maker: the prediction system (stage II) and the value system (stage III).

The Prediction System

In processing the problem data, the analyst forms a configuration of perceived situation reality for the past and for the present. Although his or her comprehension of the situation may differ widely from its reality, it still may be a remarkably accurate concept compared with the divergence of what the analyst thinks will happen in the future from what actually does happen. Since action will be implemented past the point of empirical observation in many cases, the analyst must forecast as accurately as possible future activity of the components of the decision with only past experience, accumulated knowledge, and history as a guide.

How far back into the past should one look? No definite guidelines are available. For some problems, the full circle of the business cycle may be critical. For others, going back to a point of external, environmental change, such as the passage of a new government regulation, the cessation or beginning of war, or the start of an economic era may fix the appropriate time interval. Internally, the progress of the company may be divisible into stages that do and do not have any bearing on the present problem. If new management has taken over at a certain point, for example, creating a marked change from conservative to aggressive policies, historical data prior to the change may have small value. With each case different, the analyst applies critical thought to ascertaining the past time interval having greatest relevance to the forecasts. Past company experience is more useful for short-run than for long-run planning. For long-range forecasts the researcher may have to draw on competitor and industry experience as well.

How far into the future may one safely predict? Unfortunately, predictions do not come with safety guarantees. The prudent analyst will extend the forecast time period to the point where all clues as to future activity surrounding the object of investigation are exhausted. Marketing research departments have been known to forecast demand for a product over a 10- to 15-year time interval. Ordinarily 2 to 5 years gives a new venture time to get through the expected net-loss period and indicate its chances of survival and progress, with long-range plans revised at set intervals in line with experience. Short-run forecasts may be made with some confidence, since dramatic changes in the company's financial picture are not likely to take place. But for capital investments with, say, a 20-year life expectancy, the analyst must be able to predict component activity for the life of the investment, with uncertainties mounting as the years ahead pile up.

Whatever future time interval the analyst deems crucial to a particular problem, predictions are subject to inaccuracies; yet to act without consideration of what the future will be like is behaving more impulsively than a business person should behave. Even inaccurate predictions have some value as planning guides. The forecaster's major problems are devising ways to discount for time and modifying the figures in line with preconceived eventualities, even eventualities he or she is unable to envision, none of which offer the comfort of certainty.

Some Prediction Considerations.   As the analyst looks back over the history of the activity for a decision criterion component and notes that there has been little or no change over a suitable period of years, he or she may predict the future of that component on the premise that there will be no change. A group of investors appraising the financial feasibility of an additional savings and loan association for the county might note from the published statements of existing institutions that the average increment of assets for each has been approximately $100,000 a month. They might note also that the entry of two new institutions into the competitive arena within the time period studied has had little effect on the average monthly deposits of institutions existing at the time the new ones opened. Other factors would enter into the calculations, but on the basis of *persistence*, the investors might hope for an average $100,000 a month in new assets for their proposed institution under the assumption that there would be no change in pattern.

If the analyst examining the history of activity for component A, B, or C notes that the *extent* of change has been relatively stable, say, an increase of 1 percent every 2 years for 20 years, it may be predicted rather safely that, barring unforeseen circumstances, there will be an increase of 1 percent in the next two years. Beyond the next time interval, however, this type of reasoning is fraught with danger, for a leveling-off period or an upswing may appear momentarily. If the activity of a component has been almost static for a time interval and suddenly enjoys a dramatic upsurge of some years' duration, the analyst will look for possible causes of the upsurge and evaluate the possible persistence of the causes before assessing the activity of the component for the next time interval.

Historical data over long time periods may reveal that *cycles* of activity for a component have been virtually repeated. The analyst may then plot future activity of the component through a similar cycle.

If the activity of a component is known to be sensitive to fluctuations in an outside causal force, such as the stock market, the gross national product, or political situations, the analyst may choose to predict the future of a component on the basis of the activity of the causal condition. If one lacks historical data for a new venture, this form of prediction may be the only recourse.

In possession of inadequate company historical data for predicting the activity of a component, possibly because of the novelty of the proposal under consideration, the analyst may look into the performance of a similar entity as a guide. In the Harley Mills problem [page 331], the analyst might examine the success of other similarly situated millers with the production of ready mixes. If one is concerned with predicting the portion of the consumer dollar that will go to savings in estimating anticipated savings volume for a new savings bank—and is unable to track down the figure for the particular locale—one may, with reasonable modifications, base a forecast on national figures or those available for other similar areas. There is always the possibility, also, of constructing a miniature model, either physical or mathematical, for observation as a means of predicting the activity of the real model.

Predicting future activity for the components of a decision is difficult and frustrating. Even after forecasts have been delivered by one or several of the methods suggested, the analyst may still need to modify them in line with the uncertainties of the internal and external environment in which the component operates.

Possible Environmental-Change Adjustment.   When the analyst arrives at a preliminary forecast of exceptionally good activity for a component of the decision, there is concern with the probability of the activity's ever reaching the forecast state. This researcher is well aware that adjusting figures to compensate for unforeseen eventualities is a necessary measure. Numerous formulas for so doing are currently available, with others expected as probability theory develops. Whether the analyst is able to place precise monetary, sociological, or psychological values on changes that could affect the forecasts, every effort should be made to consider all eventualities in weighing the components of a decision.

The decision models provided in this chapter are generalized, fitting specialized cases only with adaptation. The questions that follow are offered as typical of considerations that could influence forecasts in many different kinds of decisions—springboards for analyst thought—and perhaps not suited in their entirety to any one problem. The analyst may answer those pertinent to a particular project and think up other similar questions more precisely adapted to her or his own area of investigation.

External Eventualities

1. What *social* changes could affect my forecast of component A, B, or C activity?

  a.   What would happen if the status or prestige value for this product changed drastically in the foreseeable future?

  b.   What implications would there be if the early-marriage, early-family custom (or other evidence of the mores of the times) should change?

  3.   What influence would a reduction in family size have on the trend line?

  d.   What influence will increased life expectancy exert?

  c.   What chances are there in the market area of sizeable immigration or emigration?

  f.   Are changes in consumer buying and saving habits likely?

  g.   How long may consumer tastes be expected to last? Current value systems?

  h.   Could the production of a superior competing product wipe out the demand for this item as I have pictured it?

2. What *political* changes could conceivably influence my forecast?

  a.   What would be the impact of a change from Democratic to Republican power—or the reverse?

  b.   What effect might social legislation have on my plan?

  c.   What effect could antitrust action against this company or against its competitors have?

  d.   What anticipated changes in tax structure could affect my forecast?

  e.   What government regulations could affect activity of this component?

  f.   What effect would the adverse location of a new dam, reservoir, or transportation system have?

3. What *economic* changes could alter my present outlook on the future of this component?

a.   What effect would initiation or cessation of war have?

b.   Would my financial forecast still be reasonable in a deflated instead of an expected inflated economy?

c.   Could the competitors survive a temporary depression better than this company could?

d.   What unfavorable labor situation could develop?

e.   What changes in the import-export picture could affect my forecast?

f.   What would be the effect of changes in supply and demand in the money market?

4.   What *uninsurable acts of nature* could impair the validity of this forecast?

a.   What would happen if the nearby raw-material supply were temporarily or permanently destroyed?

b.   What effect would continued unfavorable weather have?

5.   What *technological* developments could affect this forecast?

Internal Eventualities

1.   What changes in management personnel could affect the presence of component A, B, or C?

2.   What human factors within the company could change in relation to this component?

3.   What changes in the company's financial position could affect the forecast potential of this factor?

4.   What other company decisions in related or unrelated areas could influence this decision determinant?

5.   What changes in company policy would have impact on this component?

6.   What internal labor problems could influence the projection?

The more knowledge one has, the more alert one is to the complexity of interrelationships in the internal and external environment, the better able that person is to imagine happenings for the future. When your reflection has conceptualized the good and bad influences that might alter the future course of a decision component, you may refine the analysis further by formulating in your own mind what the chances are of realizing the predictions.

The Value System

The value system, step III in Figure 9-1, is, in effect, simultaneous and interacting with the prediction system just covered; and both in turn are affected by the forces leading into examination of the findings against the decision criterion: step IV. Through the value system the analyst tries to find some method of measuring the anticipated outcomes against each other on the way to an ultimate choice. Money is the most celebrated measuring stick in the marketplace. Certainly the analyst should convert projections to monetary values, if it is convenient to do so. So many subjective factors enter the deliberations, however, that this translation is exceedingly difficult. The human factors in a situation, for example, do not lend themselves readily to monetary conversion. Or one or more of the components may serve as feeder systems for the financial analysis that is made for many business decisions, thus being convertible to money values only in contributory effect. As an illustration, the competition that the firm faces may be appraised with word values, such as "extremely difficult to meet," "a moderate hazard to the success of the venture," or "virtually negligible in the market area." Monetary values may not be placed on the competition factor per se. The monetary value may come when the analyst tries to estimate the portion of the market the company can hope to capture in view of the competitive picture, an element of vital concern to the financial analysis.

For many business decisions, evaluating subjective elements in quantitative terms may lead to such large margins of error that expending the time and money necessary for complex mathematical computations are unwarranted. Thus, as analyst, you may on numerous occasions find it expedient to place educated judgments on the activity of all the components of your decision and on the final answer (using your own intuitive concept for the size of the risk involved). The decision stages presented here are applicable whether you, personally, choose the mathematical or the educated judgment route. Putting data through the value system in Figure 9-1 is concerned with the probability that a decision component will behave in the manner forecast in the prediction system (step II).

Assignment of Probability Levels. The lay decision maker solving a personal problem goes through informal probability reasoning when he or she says "It is *highly likely* that this even will happen," "There is a *fair* chance," or "The chances are *extremely poor*." As has been implied in the preceding section, some business managers insist on working with such word levels of probability on the theory that probabilities of future events cannot be assigned precisely. If the entrepreneur's thinking coincides with this theory, he or she will mull over the data in the light of internal and external influences and formulate subdecisions on the components according to whether they have a *good, moderate,* or *poor* chance of behaving in the manner that circumstances seem to indicate. With such appraisals of value in mind, this researcher will then move on to other analyses before formulating a final answer.

Time Considerations. Time is the dictator of business decisions, for the competitive climate is dynamic, with rival agents continually alert to grasp opportunities at the psychological moment. The answers to such questions as the following may be significant to the analyst in settling probabilities of money values.

1. Will adequate performance of this decision component be achieved within the time limits of problem requirements?

2. Is the projected time period under analysis of sufficient duration?

3. What influence will the maximum time consideration have on the answer? Should demand for the product decline before the life of the investment expires, are there other possible uses for the plant and equipment?

4. Is there a chance of product or equipment obsolescence before the payout period has elapsed?

5. Is the firm interested in short-run security or long-range profit?

6. How long can the firm tolerate losses in anticipation of future gains?

7. Is this a fad product or service with a short-lived big volume? Or will it have a moderate volume over a long life?

8. What is the impact of time on tax considerations?

9. How does the planned time schedule compare with that of any known competition?

10. Is the time schedule for initiating this venture favorable or unfavorable?

Time is money to the business entity. If it is anticipated, for example, that a product cannot be launched until two months after the market entry date of a competitor's similar product, all the elements of cost for those two months will probably figure as a loss deduction from anticipated income. Any possible delays and other pertinent time considerations may, with some ingenuity, be converted to money values. It is feasible, at certain stages, to "buy" accelerated timing. The analyst may ask such questions as these: "How much is this company willing to pay to stimulate maximum demand within a short period?" "How much in overtime pay necessary to complete a project ahead of schedule or on schedule is the firm willing to bear?" "Will the cost of accelerated timing pay out in accelerated profits?"

Perhaps the most important time consideration for the business analyst comes with the assessing of value for future dollars—a decision process deemed worthy of consideration in a separate division.

Determining Present Value of Future Dollars. The discussion thus far has rather neatly bypassed the question of the value of future dollars; in many problems, however, this direction is not wise. How to settle this uncertainty may depend on the analyst's background and preferences, for no pat answer is apparently available. C. Jackson Grayson, in his study of how oil companies make the decision to drill or not drill a well, presents these observations:

> How, for example, should a barrel of oil or gas in the ground be valued? At today's prices? No, for only a portion of the oil or gas can be produced and sold today . . . .
>
> Future prices, then? If so, what price? Here is an uncertainty.
>
> Here also is a complexity. For now the time value of money must be accounted for by discounting. And what discount rate should be used: Cost of borrowed money, cost of capital, opportunity rate . . .? And what yardsticks are appropriate and accurate? Payout? Discounted cash flow? Profitability index? I found that payout and ultimate return on investment ("I want a minimum 2-year payout and 2 for 1 on my money") are currently the most widely used yardsticks. But I also saw increasing attention being given to the use of discounting.[1]

Churchman's view is epitomized in this selection:

> Discounting for time is essentially an opportunity cost. If I receive the dollar today rather than tomorrow, I can invest it today, and tomorrow I will not only have the dollar but also the return on the investment. For this reason, discounting for time looks like a comparison of annuities. The suggestion is that the company should adopt that policy which has payoffs that provide the highest annuity rate. . . . Why is a policy based on the highest annuity rate compelling? Indeed, it is not hard to find examples where it would not be. Perhaps by adopting a policy of a loss for ten years, the company can eventually make so much money that the corresponding annuity is maximum. But few companies would follow such a course of action. Discounting for time involves a consideration of certain psychological properties, such as patience, which may quite outweigh favorable annuity rates. In sum, there is no obvious and simple way of generating an adequate discounting function.[2]

There is some support in actual business practice for the projection of *current* production costs and selling prices into the future, with the decision maker's full realization that the resulting balance sheet is a "guesstimate." The guesstimate, however, has a calculated background, lending a more accurate decision foundation than mere qualitative considerations. Unless the report writer has an extensive knowledge of accounting and statistics, this sort of projection is the safest course. Other ways of arriving at the value of future dollars are discussed in the appendix.

Utility Value.   The risk potential of a decision is measured in terms of the attitudes, policies, and financial position of those individuals who bear

[1] C. Jackson Grayson, Jr., *Decisions Under Uncertainty, Drilling Decisions by Oil and Gas Operators* (Cambridge, Mass.: Harvard University, Division of Research, Graduate School of Business Administration, 1960), pp. 17–18.

[2] C. West Churchman, *Prediction and Optimal Decision*, Philosophical Issues of a Science of Values (Englewood Cliffs, N.J.; Prentice-Hall, Inc., 1961), p. 53.

the risk. With monetary values placed on anticipated outcomes, a gain and a loss of the same dollar amount may not have equal value. A gain of $50,000 may not wield sufficient impact on the company's financial position to affect it appreciably; but a $50,000 loss might provoke critical consequences. Or the first $30,000 of net income may be substantially significant, with the next $30,000 only marginal in importance. Thus the *utility value* of risk enters the picture.

The analyst may gain an insight into the risk potential of a problem through answers to questions such as these, as applicable to the specific situation:

1. How well and how long can the company stand estimated probable losses?

2. How important is it to the firm to initiate this venture? How much is it willing to pay?

3. Is asset growth more important than the price paid for it?

4. Is the enterprise security oriented, moderately security oriented, or speculative?

5. What property, assets, status, security, or prestige may be lost if a "yes" decision is a poor one?

6. What property, assets, status, security, or prestige may be lost by *not* undertaking this venture?

7. Is the company's financial status ascending or descending?

8. Is the risk isolated or sequential? Are there points within the forecast period at which adjustments can be made?

9. What is the nature of the people bearing the risk?

10. Is management willing to gamble on unfavorable odds at the chance of large winnings?

11. What recovery steps are available to the company if the venture fails?

12. Is this a one-shot decision? Or will it be made periodically?

13. What by-product consequences not related directly to the problem are likely if the decision is a good one? A poor one?

14. What good or bad chain reactions might result from implementing this decision?

The assessing of risk involved calls for greater reflective thinking ability than do other stages of the decision process. Here the analyst summons her or his imagination into full power to uncover hidden snares that might go unnoticed by the casual observer.

Qualitative Considerations. Mathematical calculations are reputedly productive of more accurate decisions than are those based on qualitative deliberations alone; yet there is no stage in the decision process that can be separated from the analyst's judgment. Judgment goes into the assignment of probabilities, into the estimate of future prices, into an appraisal of the accuracy of predictions. In many problems, also, there are elements that do not lend themselves directly to numerical conversion, even though they may exert an influence on the numerical statement of other elements. For example, certain psychological and sociological factors contribute to the declining market for flour products and the increasing demand for ready mixes:

1. Mechanized labor has lowered the need for energy from 3,500 calories a day to 2,000.

2. Diet-conscious Americans concentrate on consumption of milk, vegetables, fruit and meat instead of flour products.

3. Consumers have demonstrated a firm acceptance of convenience foods.

4. Young marrieds interested in easy household maintenance create an added market for ready mixes.

5. The increasing number of women in the labor force is a favorable factor for production of convenience foods.

Converting such factors to plus and minus dollars on the balance sheet might call for more ingenuity than is reasonable; yet they are worthy of consideration in setting other monetary values in the problem.

Certain psychological factors important to a decision were suggested in the risk-potential section. What prestige values might be lost if the company decides not to implement a proposed venture? Will the company risk losing its position of leadership in the industry if it fails to move in this direction? If its competitors decide to make this move and the company under investigation does not, will the effect be advantageous or disadvantageous? Disadvantageous for the short run and advantageous for the long run? What effect will this decision have on the internal relations within the enterprise? Will the recommendations resulting from this decision run counter to the company's long-established policies and practices? The imaginative analyst measuring the values of decision components puts together all possible combinations of elements in the search of consequences and measures the cause-effect relationships of changing mixtures of ingredients.

Since measuring the data for the components of the decision against the overall decision criterion and evaluating different possible outcomes vary considerably with the type of answer pursued, the remaining stages of the General-purpose decision maker introduced at the beginning of this chapter are discussed only as they apply to specific problem types: Step IV, Measurement by the Decision Criterion; Step V, Imaginative Testing of Outcomes; and Step VI, the Decision. The problem types are those outlined in Chapter 7: the yes-or-no decision, the comparative-evaluation investigation, and the descriptive-analytic investigation.

DECISION-MAKING TECHNIQUES
FOR THE YES-OR-NO PROBLEM

The yes-or-no, or binary, decision has already been described as one that determines whether a course of action shall be implemented: Shall Harley Mills undertake ready-mix product diversification? Shall Valley Mining Company purchase a plant for milling Mexican barite? Shall the Majex Corporation set up a separate organizational planning department? Each of these problems involves an alternative action either implied or explicitly stated; but overall the purpose is to determine whether or not to do something, whether or not the proposed venture will prove feasible in operation.

The decision design for the yes-or-no decision (Figure 9-2) picks up at the bottom level of the research scheme set out in Figure 7-2: the data are gathered and filed under the proper components of Decision Criterion D. The analyst has subsequently carried the data for each of the components through the first three stages of the General-purpose decision maker: data processing, the prediction system, and the value system. With the data processed and the deliberations regarding them complete, the analyst is ready to evaluate the syllogism with which he or she began.

Major Premise:	If A, B, and C are true, D will occur,
Minor Premise:	A, B, and C are true:
Therefore:	D will occur.

Measurement by the Decision Criterion

That "D will occur" was the statement in the hypothesis that contained the analyst's overall decision criterion; for example, the addition of ready mixes to the product lines will prove *profitable* to Harley Mills, the construction of a new plant will be *financially feasible*, the establishment of a separate organization-planning department will add to the *efficiency* of Majex Corporation. Degrees of criterion D may have been part of the problem requirements: a *profit* of 8 percent of gross sales, a *return* of 2 to 1 on capital investment with a two-year payout, or such. Thus the data collection and decision processes from the first were planned around decision criterion D. The final stages involve the acceptance of minor premises A, B, and C on the basis of Decision Criterion D: Are A, B, and C in fact true?

Because it is easier to deal with symbols in terms of the realities they represent, let us fill in with the decision components of the ready-mix problem: A is demand; B is competition; and C is manufacturing costs and profit potential. The analyst's first decision point comes with placing judgment on evidence 1, 2, 3, and 4 for components A, B, and C. Evidence A^1, A^2, A^3, and A^4, for example, may be thought of as current and forecast population in the market area, eating habits that point toward the acceptance of convenience foods, a per capita income sufficient to encourage the purchase of ready mixes, and other favorable sociological factors. Let us suppose that the analyst's configuration looks like that pictured in Figure 9-2 in the yes-or-no decision design, with X's at the appropriate decision points. For component A, there are "yes" answers for evidence A^1, A^2, and A^4, and a "no" answer for

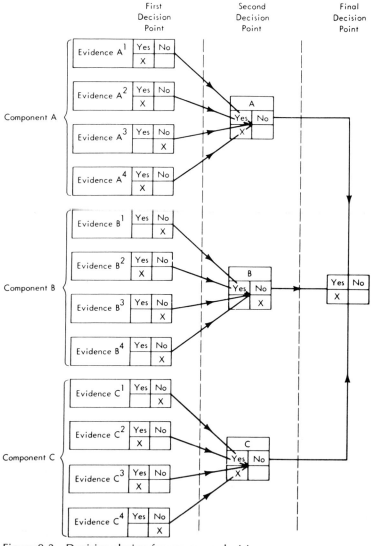

Figure 9-2   Decision design for yes-or-no decision

A^3: population, customer acceptance, and sociological elements look good, but per capita income does not. By sheer weight, then, the analyst might arrive at a "yes" subdecision for component A at the second decision point. The presence of that single opposing answer, though, is a signal for caution. Is that opposing answer powerful enough to negate the favorable effects of three positive answers? Or is it of minimal importance? How can it be by-passed or compensated for? Apparently the analyst decided that the presence of A is assured in spite of negative evidence A^3, for he or she comes up with a "yes" answer for component A at the second decision point: A is true.

For component B (the competition), there are three "no" answers and a single "yes", B^2. The analyst proceeds to apply a set of weights and balances to these conflicting interests, but it is likely that the subdecision here must be "no," for anyone would have considerable "explaining away" to do to offset three negatives with a single positive. Therefore, B is not true.

Component C (the cost-profit analysis) calls for a high degree of judg-ment, for there is an even balance of "yes" and "no" answers. The analyst finally decides that the positive evidence C^2 and C^3 outweigh negative evi-dence C^1 and C^4 and that a positive decision somehow can be implemented in spite of them. Therefore, C is true.

At the final decision point (the blending of the yes-or-no answers for A, B, and C derived at the second decision point into an overall answer), the analyst is still in a state of uncertainty, for components A and C are present in adequate measure and component B is not. The analyst may now need to engage in additional calculations to determine whether it is prudent to act on a positive decision in spite of negative B. Subdecision for the competition factor is that three giants of the industry control 90 percent of the market and that they are so well established and capitalized that the entry of a newcomer would meet with extremely hazardous conditions. One might rea-son further, though, that demand for a product does not merely exist—it must be created. President Bentley is an aggressive individual who likes a fight and is in a position for the loss not to be crucial; consequently, he may be willing to pay the price of extensive initial advertising to gain the necessary share of the market. Advertising costs can be set up on a declining scale as the foothold in the market grows. Thus this report arrives at a still tentative final decision. Therefore, D will occur—the manufacture of ready mixes will be profitable for Harley Mills.

Imaginative Testing of the Outcomes

The deliberations thus far in the yes-or-no decision process have concentrated on whether the proposed venture set out in the hypothesis will work. A further refinement of the analyst's decision comes from measuring the outcomes of implementing the proposal against the outcomes of *not* implementing it—in effect, a comparative evaluation of two courses of action, the subject matter of the next section of this chapter.

Somewhere in the investigator's creative thinking about the decision comes the idea of minimizing the maximum loss—the "minimax" standard, which holds the decision maker's maximum loss to a minimum. Unfortunately, however, the choice is never between taking a risk of whatever size and taking no risk, for the analyst must count on some risk, no matter which way he or she moves. Dwelling too long on minimizing maximum loss may mean taking no action at all. As a result, the firm may be out of business.

Nevertheless, the wise analyst carefully weighs possible outcomes before arriving at a final answer: a concentrated "what if" kind of thinking. What will happen if Harley Mills sets up for production of ready mixes and the project fails, despite favorable advance indications that it will succeed? What will happen if Harley Mills does not take this step? Would it be preferable to liquidate the business and invest whatever money can be recovered? What is the maximum loss that might be sustained through either course of action? The minimum loss? What are the minimum and maximum gains that may be anticipated from both courses of action? Here the analyst may again engage in some of the considerations that were suggested for the prediction system. When the best reflective thinking the analyst is capable of has been applied to the problem, a course of action should be selected and implemented with a positive attitude—no looking back.

FRAMING THE DECISION
FOR THE COMPARATIVE EVALUATION

The thinking developed in some detail for the General-purpose decision maker and for the yes-or-no answer is also applicable for the comparative-evaluation study and will not be repeated here. Only essential differences in approach are pointed up. The research scheme set up in Chapter 7 for the comparative-evaluation decision indicated that the choice of an alternative among two or several is based on the criteria of desirable performance of the class of entity under investigation. For an entrepreneur attempting to choose a plant site from among several locations, the operational requisites, such as raw material availability, transportation facilities, and so on become the criteria by which the sites are evaluated. A rapidly expanding firm may be interested in the decision of whether to purchase a computer for inventory control or to use a Kardex system. *Efficiency* of inventory control is the overall decision criterion. But what makes for *efficiency* in this case?

Speed may be one component of efficiency. The *human factors* involved in the choice may be another. A *cost comparison* may be a third. Thus such components of the overall decision criterion become the bases by which the choices are judged. The underlying assumption is that one of the choices will be superior to the others according to criteria A, B, and C. The data are gathered and filed to show which of the choices is superior according to A, B, and C. The input data are placed in the decision maker by the components of that decision; that is, evidence covering component A for choices 1, 2, and 3; evidence of component B for choices 1, 2, and 3; and evidence of component C for choices 1, 2, and 3. On first thought the analyst might have set the data up by choices; that is, evidence of A, B, and C for choice 1; evidence of A, B, and C for choice 2; and so on. Such an arrangement places the whole burden of comparison on the conclusions. Fixing the emphasis on the components sets the comparison in motion at once: Data for raw material availability for choice 1 are assembled; so are such data for choices 2 and 3. Then a sub-decision can be made as to which choice has the best raw-material supply (and so on for the other decision criteria).

Techniques for stages I and II—data processing and the prediction system—are virtually the same as for the yes-or-no decision design. When the analyst arrives at stage III, the value system, there may be some differences. As an illustration, let us say that an Iowa corn factory is planning to build a $25,000,000 plant for sorghum processing in one of three cities: Lubbock, Fort Worth, or Houston. The availability of an adequate supply of sorghum is Component A, by which the choices may be measured. The analyst will consider sorghum production figures for a suitable past period in an economic area surrounding the three cities and predict sorghum production for each area as far ahead as it is safe to do so—perhaps for the life of the investment. For the value system, the analyst may engage in some probability estimating as to the correctness of the predictions and attempt conversion to money or utility values by answering the question "How much is it worth to the company to have this much sorghum available?" A further step may be achieved by determining how much sorghum will have to be shipped in or stored to ensure year-round operation. Shipping and storage costs will certainly enter into the calculations. Instead of converting to money values at this point, the analyst may prefer to place rank-order desirabilities on the choices, such as the fact that Lubbock ranks first in sorghum availability, Fort Worth second, and Houston third. These rankings may serve as the base for an ultimate decision or as a feeder system for the financial analysis made as the culmination of the decision.

The next criterion may be the transportation facilities available to the three cities. Here the analyst ranks Houston first, Fort Worth second, and Lubbock third—a complexity! Lubbock is far ahead in sorghum availability, but poorest in transportation; and Houston, with the poorest sorghum supply, has the best transportation facilities. Fort Worth ranks second in both. These rankings are recorded in the decision design for the comparative-evaluation study, Figure 9-3. From the rankings just developed, it becomes evident to the analyst that a system of weights must be devised to resolve conflicts for the final answer. Is it more important to have sorghum nearby or transportation for servicing the market? By how much? Probably an income statement for each of the cities for the forecast period based on, perhaps, unit production and distribution costs measured against a going sales price for the finished product will have to be prepared.

Let us say that the analyst's configuration by the rank-order method is that appearing in Figure 9-3. If the ranks were of equal value, choice 3—Houston in the sorghum problem—is the choice for the new plant. It will be remembered, however, that Houston had a poor sorghum supply, the lifeblood of the operation. Before the decision maker chooses Houston, therefore, a decision must be made whether adequate grain can be moved in at a cost that will not be so great as to offset transportation, tax, burden, and other advantages evident from the financial analysis of the operations, which resulted in Houston as the first choice according to this component. Cheap in-transit freight rates for grain from Lubbock to Houston could well be the

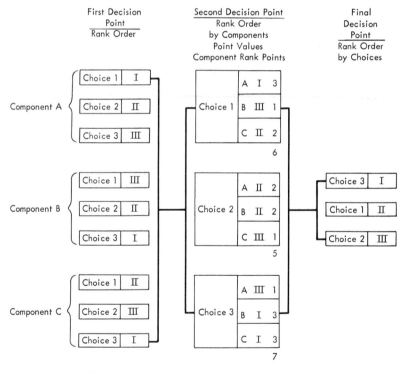

NOTE: The configuration here is based on the assumption that the components are of equal value. The analyst may develop a weighted mathematical scheme with components of weighted value: Component A, .40, Component B, .35, and Component C, .25, for example; then he may multiply the rank points by the weighted value to determine the final ranking.

Figure 9-3   Decision design for the comparative-evaluation study

factor that would enable a plant at Houston to take advantage of the two highly favorable factors. Before making the final decision, the researcher should enter into the same sort of "What would happen if" thinking employed for other types of decisions. Weights given to the ranks for the different components might also be assigned in developing a point system.

For example, consider that, out of a total of 1.00 for the three determinants, A was worth .40, B, .35, and C, .25, as suggested at the bottom of Figure 9-3. The analyst can multiply each rank value for A by .40 (with or without the decimal) to establish point value. Subsequently, B values will be multiplied by .35 and C values by .25 and the totals for all three added for final rank values of the choices. Such calculations may add refinement to the thinking, with the ultimate choice still dependent upon reasoning and judgment. As before, the examples are simplified to a few pertinent criteria to facilitate explanation and to provide a basic plan for selecting one out of several alternatives. Any analyst may elaborate on this simple plan according to personal background expertise.

DECISION DESIGN FOR THE DESCRIPTIVE-ANALYTIC STUDY

The major objective of the descriptive-analytic study is to examine the operation of a phenomenon under investigation and analyze the phases of it. The analyst may seek to determine the good and bad features of an entity as measured against a chosen criterion or standard. One may be interested in knowing what accounts for the good and bad features and what measures may be initiated to remedy the defects and to maintain the favorable aspects. As another approach the analyst may try to envision the operation of a phenomenon yet to be initiated: What sort of advertising budget would be best for launching turkey sausage in a test city? What kind of personnel department would best serve a chain of small department stores? What type of management policies should be adopted to promote good union-management relations? In such cases, the analyst follows the same type of reasoning as that used in the first type of problem just described; yet the ideas are projective. As the investigator, you study the good and bad features of entities already engaged in the type of project you have in mind and seek the opinions of authorities in the field; then you try to project them onto the operation you are faced with where the problem has developed. A researcher sets a goal for the phenomenon to achieve, examines the current situation, and decides what will have to be done for the goal to be realized.

The descriptive-analytic investigation usually begins with the hypothesis or key idea, as do other sorts: "Excessive middle-management turnover results from the company's failure to provide an objective merit-rating plan";

"The expensive electronic data-processing installation is not being used to its economic capacity"; or "The limited funds for a year's advertising for a successful launching of turkey sausage in a test city should be directed toward audiences in the upper-middle- and upper-income levels." Thus the hypothesis gives the analytic-descriptive analysis many of the same qualities of the yes-or-no decision. Is the hypothesis true—"yes" or "no"? Consequently, many of the same decision techniques described in prior sections are applicable here.

It is likely that the data assembled for a descriptive study will be qualitative, represented by such statements as "The poor work of the employees in Division III is attributable to feelings of job insecurity brought about by the computer installation" or "The bottleneck in the assembly line results from the failure of Machine 622 to function at advertised capacity." It is possible, obviously, to quantify such findings—a procedure that should be followed if feasible. Through adroit questioning, the investigator might find out that *60 percent* of the employees in Division III were fearful that an automated computer system would eliminate their jobs. Or, by means of carefully planned observation, it might be determined that machine 622 failed to perform *40 percent* of the operations scheduled for it. In view of the possibility of quantification, data processing makes up step I of the decision design in Figure 9-4 as it did for the other designs: the analyst performs whatever calculations that may be necessary or classifies qualitative findings according to their relevance to the decision criterion of the hypothesis.

As the analyst moves into stage II, concern is with the implications the data have for the analytic description of the object of investigation. What does it mean that the computer is idle 5 days of the 20-day working month? What are the implications of the fact that production has risen 20 percent with a computer inventory control? What about the finding that a Kardex system could control inventory efficiently at 40-percent cost reduction? Is it possible that the company's volume might in a short while reach a capacity too large for the Kardex system to handle so that the outlay for a computer in anticipation of long-run production might still be the more economical procedure?

Satisfied that the implications of the data are clearly in mind, the analyst moves into step III—subconclusions for the aspects chosen to describe the object of investigation. These subconclusions may range from "Yes, if only the evidence accumulated for aspect A is considered, the working hypothesis is true"; to "No, there is no indication from the evidence under aspect A that the hypothesis is tenable"; or to "According to evidence analyzed for aspect A, this situation exists." In the process, the analyst may also be pinpointing defects that will make up the diagnostic conclusions, step V, and be setting aside suggestions for practices that it would be well to perpetuate. Since the descriptive-analytic classification covers such a wide range of business problems, it is difficult to set specific decision guidelines. With

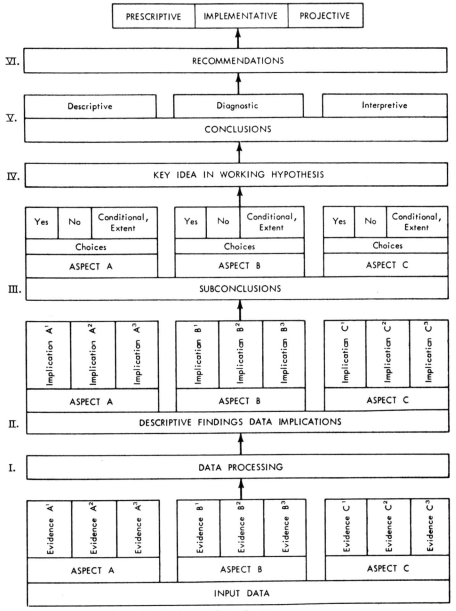

Figure 9-4   Design for a descriptive-analytic decision

the suggestions given here as a basis, we believe that the individual analyst can devise a suitable plan.

In step III the decision maker measures subconclusions in terms of the key idea embodied in the working hypothesis (step IV). In step V he or she arrives at conclusions that may be descriptive, diagnostic, or a combination of the two: descriptive as to what it will take to convert the present situation to meet the requirements of an initially set goal, diagnostic as to what is bad or good about the current situation. The recommendations made in step VI may be prescriptive (what it will take to remedy defects), implementative (how the recommendations may be put into effect), or projective (the future of the object of investigation in line with the findings of the study).

The decision maker following the thought processes outlined in this chapter may arrive at a good answer to a problem through a series of educated judgments. Then, with the aspects of the decision well in mind, the analyst may proceed to record the investigation findings in a carefully planned report, according to suggestions provided in Chapters 10 and 11.

The appendix which follows offers some applications of quantitative decision making as the basis for the business report for those interested in such procedures.

APPENDIX: SOME APPLICATIONS OF QUANTITATIVE DECISION MAKING (Descriptive Statistics)

With the increasing emphasis being placed on quantitative methods in collegiate schools of business today, it is likely that the advanced student, honors candidate, the entrepreneur using this book on a review basis, and participants in executive development seminars may have at their command some highly sophisticated mathematical techniques for analyzing data and arriving at decisions more dependable than those evolved from intuitive judgments. Consequently, we think it appropriate to explore some procedures that analysts may fit into the decision designs discussed in this text according to their own talents.

Summarization of Data

When the data have been assembled and are ready for processing (step I in the general-purpose decision maker, Figure 9-1), the investigator will summarize them according to the type of analysis these data are to be subjected to. Some of the simpler forms of statistical analyses are

1. Converting the items in a table to *percentages*—relative rather than absolute values—is a simple and widely used process of summarization. Percentage of change in a time series is often more meaningful to the investigator than is the amount of change. Almost any enterprise with a product or service to sell finds its demand sensitive to population growth. With the hope of forecasting the population in the market area for the next five to ten years, the analyst may calculate the yearly percentage of population increase or decrease for a suitable past time period in search of a stable pattern by which to estimate future activity. If the product is interesting only to a certain age group, say, 16–20, the analyst will concentrate on the percentage of the total market population that this group has comprised in the past as a base for forecasting future demand. A frequent concern also is in knowing what percentage of the population lies within the income level suitable for the purchase of a particular product or service.

2. *Ratios* showing the relative magnitude of one quantity to another are also useful to managers. If the amount of water available for industrial consumption is four times as great in one city as in another, the entrepreneur hunting a factory site for which water is a main production item has an important statistic for a decision. Ratios of assets to liabilities, gross or net profit to capital investment, sales to inventory, and such are important for financial analyses.

3. Summarizing an array of figures into *measures of central tendency* is valuable in providing a common standard for comparison. The per capita, or *average* income of an area is at times more significant than is the total income. In addition, the per capita incomes of several geographical divisions may be compared, despite differences of population among them. The three most widely used measures of central tendency are the *mean*, the *median*, and the *mode*—all ways of summarizing a number of cases into one figure. Averages are usually computed in search of the typical case. If that is the purpose, the researcher must examine the disparity among the individual cases, for the arithmetic mean of widely different magnitudes does not produce a typical case. The *median* is the middle case in an array of figures arranged in rank order—half the cases smaller and half larger than the median. For an uneven number of cases, say, 99, the middle case is 50, with 49 cases smaller and 49 larger. For an even-numbered array, say, 100, the median is located halfway between the two middle numbers, 50 and 51. The *mode* is the value that has the highest concentration of cases. If an array of figures, when plotted, makes a symmetrical curve, the mean, median, and mode have approximately the same value. The more complex formulas for computing the mean, the median, and the mode of frequency distributions may be obtained from basic statistics texts, in case the analyst's memory is not entirely dependable.

4. Estimating the *dispersion* of estimated measures of typical size from the individual items is one way of evaluating their reliability. This process involves assessing the consistency or homogeneity of the data.

The simplest method of measuring dispersion is through examination of the largest and smallest values in the distribution: *the range of the data*. For example, let us say that in an array of people grouped according to age the youngest age is represented as 10 and the oldest as 14, with the mean set at 12. This view of the scatter of the distribution makes possible the comparison of its makeup with that of other similar distribution.

Another measure of dispersion comes from dividing the distribution data into four parts. The first *quartile* point is that at which one-fourth of the cases are smaller and three-fourths, larger; the second quartile is the median, half smaller and half larger; and the third quartile has one-fourth of the cases larger and three-fourths smaller. The distance between the third and first quartile is known as the *interquartile* range.

5.   The *correlation* of the performance between two or several variables is a means of estimating a cause-and-effect relationship, though not dependably so. Correlations, arrived at mathematically or through scatter diagrams, may result in these possibilities with regard to cause-and-effect relationships.

a.   A high correlation between two series may result, with no reason for its doing so other than chance.

b.   The fluctuation in one series may actually cause the fluctuations in another. If a correlation is run between the birth rate and the age of the population, the age of the population may well account for fluctuations in the birth rate, and vice versa.

c.   The fluctuations in two series may in truth be the result of some outside causal agent. The price of automobiles may vary with the price of aluminum, but the prices of both may be fluctuating in proportion to some economic change which affects them both.

Although correlation charts may be useful in determining a causal relationship, they do not within themselves indicate that the independent variable affects the activity of the dependent variable. The decision is ultimately made through the analyst's reasoning powers.

6.   *Tests of significance* are applied to the estimates of certain characteristics of the universe to determine whether these estimates can be used as reliable evidence that a stated hypothesis should be accepted or rejected. Basic to sampling theory is the assumption that there will be some difference between the sample estimate of the universe—say, the mean—and the true value of the universe parameter obtained if the entire universe were surveyed. If the sample were chosen according to the probability standards given in Chapter 8, however, we know enough about the confidence interval of the sample estimate to be able to draw conclusions about the universe parameters. The analyst may test a hypothesis and make a decision on the basis of sample statistics and the concept of standard error, which was discussed with sampling. In making the decision, the analyst may also estimate the likelihood that it is a correct one.

7.   If the investigator making a financial analysis of a proposed venture would like to know the range of volume necessary for profitable operation, a *break-even analysis* or *scatter plot* of total costs involved versus anticipated sales volume can be constructed. The point at which sales and costs are exactly equal is the break-even point. Sales above this point represent varying degrees of profit. Accounting, finance, and management texts provide formulas for calculating the break-even point as well as for plotting cost and sales curves to determine their meeting point.

Numerous other more sophisticated measures that are a part of the analyst's background may be used to add depth to his or her work.

Converting Aspects of the Decision to Money Values

A decision maker may choose to estimate the probability that predictions are accurate through the application of word values: a *good, bad,* or *fair* chance that a component of the decision would perform in a certain prescribed manner. In decision-making literature there are strong proponents for the practice of converting such qualitative judgments to numbers. In the process, the analyst assigns numerical values to the probabilities that any forecast estimates made are right.

Instead of merely deciding on a single probability level for the performance of component A, B, or C the analyst's deliberations have led him or her to forecast, the analyst gives decision-making powers greater latitude by setting several probabilities that the given component will behave in the forecast fashion. Three sorts of levels may suffice: an optimistic probability that a set value for a decision criterion will occur; a pessimistic probability that a set value for a decision criterion will occur; and a moderate—average or acceptable—probability that a set value will prevail. Since none of these probabilities will occur simultaneously, the probabilities are additive: a total of 1.00. These probabilities may be expressed in decimal fractions and added in this fashion:

Optimistic probability level	0.60	3 chances in 5 you are right
Pessimistic probability level	0.10	1 chance in 10 you are right
Moderate probability level	0.30	3 chances in 10 you are right
Total	1.00	

The decimal fractions chosen here were arbitrarily selected for illustrative purposes and are not designed to set a pattern. Each analyst chooses probability fractions according to whatever insight he or she has into a particular problem.

As a further refinement of the value system in the decision maker, the analyst may use probability levels to convert certain aspects of the decision process to money values—the prime measuring stick in the marketplace. By way of illustration, let us look at ways in which some of the phases of the Harley Mills decision to add ready mixes to the product line may be converted to money values. The criteria for profitability (the components of the decision) for the firm were set up previously as demand, competition, and financial feasibility. A consumer survey sampling in the market area with 18,000,000 population and 6,000,000 households reveals that 70 percent of the households currently buy cake, pancake, and biscuit mixes. Overall industry trends have led the analyst in the case to believe that, at the end of the next five years, 90 percent of the households will be purchasing ready mixes—an increase evenly distributed at 5 percent a year. The analyst has also predicted that the population will increase 3 percent a year, with a proportional increase in the number of households.

Harley Mills plans to market initially simple cake, pancake, and biscuit mixes that currently retail at 33, 25, and 22 cents a pound, respectively. (Packages vary in poundage; so for figuring convenience, retail prices are reduced to those per pound.) It will be necessary, obviously, to calculate values for each line separately; the initial step is to determine the size of the cake-mix market with householders predicted to purchase at the conservative average rate of 12 pounds a year. The manufacturer's selling price is set at 30 cents a pound. Calculations at this point look like this:

Year	Population (Increasing 3% Yearly)	Households	Percentage Buying	Number Purchasing	Pounds Purchased (12 lbs per household)	Gross Sales (30 cents a pound)
A	18,000,000	6,000,000	70	4,200,000	50,400,000	$15,120,000
B	18,540,000	6,180,000	75	4,635,000	55,620,000	16,686,000
C	19,096,200	6,365,400	80	5,092,320	61,107,840	18,332,352
D	19,669,086	6,556,362	85	5,572,908	66,874,896	20,062,469
E	20,259,159	6,753,052	90	6,077,747	72,932,964	21,879,889

These calculations have obvious limitations, one of which is that, in addition to an increase in the number of households purchasing cake mixes, each household might purchase a greater number of pounds. In view of the health and weight consciousness of the citizenry, though, the current amount was carried through the forecast period.

The analyst now has a picture of total gross sales for manufacturers in the market area. Next comes the most important question: What are Harley Mills' chances of getting a profitable share of the market? To answer this question, the analyst examines the competitive climate revealed in the consumer surveys undertaken in seeking a problem solution. Interviews were conducted for cake, pancake, and biscuit mixes, which sought the answers to the question: "What brand did you buy last?" The summary of the replies will give the researcher a basis for estimating the type of competition to be faced.

Distribution of Purchases

Brand	Cake Mix		Brand	Pancake Mix		Brand	Biscuit Mix	
	This Year	Last Year		This Year	Last Year		This Year	Last Year
GM	56.9%	54.2%	QO	62.9%	59.7%	GM	54.5%	58.3%
PM	22.6	24.8	PM	20.0	23.5	PFM*	22.2	20.7
GF	10.0	9.3	GM	6.6	5.0	PM	8.8	6.8
FM*	5.1	2.8	PFM*	4.5	3.5	FM*	6.2	3.0
NBC	2.4	4.2	FM*	1.4	0.6	CMC	2.3	3.6
CMC	1.7	2.3	CMC	0.9	1.6	OTF	0.8	1.5
FC	0.6	0.5	FC	0.3	1.3	B	0.5	1.7
JT	0.6	1.2	Others	—	0.6	Others	—	—
AP	0.2	—	Unknown	3.0	2.2	Unknown	4.7	3.0
Others	—	0.4						
Unknown	2.6	2.0						

*Independent manufacturers with headquarters in this state.

The figures for cake mixes reveal to the analyst that three of the industry giants control about 90 percent of the market, with one controlling better than 50 percent. Three manufacturers control from 85 to 90 percent of the pancake and biscuit market, with better than 50 percent going to one in each case. FM is the only state-owned cake-mix manufacturer, with 2.8 percent of the market last year and 5.1 percent this year. For pancake and biscuit mixes, state-operated mills are closer to the top. The analyst might begin to reason that, in view of the long, successful history of the industry giants, the probability of their controlling the market for the next five years is virtually 1.00. Thus, Harley Mills may have to wrest the major portion of its market share from the approximate 10 percent now held by other manufacturers. After some reflection, the researcher may assess the probabilities of Harley Mills' market share in this way:

Level	Market Share	Probability
Optimistic	5%	0.25
Pessimistic	1	0.45
Moderate	2	0.30
		1.00

According to these estimates, there is a 100-percent chance that the company will gain 5, 1, or 2 percent of the market. The analyst will next be interested in the expected money value of Harley Mills' market share so that other cost and income calculations can be figured. The expected value may be derived from this formula:

$$E = P \times MV$$

where

$$E = \text{expected value}$$
$$P = \text{probability}$$
$$MV = \text{market value}$$

(In this case the market value with which he is concerned will be the value of the total market multiplied by the percentage share he hopes to get.)

The expected value at three (or any number of probabilities) will be the mean value derived from adding the values at the different probabilities, since the variables will not occur simultaneously.

On the basis of the total gross-sales values for the entire market calculated, the expected value of Harley Mills' market share will be as shown in the calculations which follow:

Year	Market Share	Gross Sales in Market Area	Probability	Expected Value
A	0.05 X	$15,120,000 X	0.25	= $ 189,000
	0.01	15,120,000	0.45	68,040
	0.02	15,120,000	0.30	90,720
		Mean value	1.00	$ 347,760
B	0.05	16,686,000	0.25	208,575
	0.01	16,686,000	0.45	75,087
	0.02	16,686,000	0.30	100,116
		Mean value	1.00	$ 383,778
C	0.05	18,332,353	0.25	229,154
	0.01	18,332,353	0.45	82,496
	0.02	18,332,353	0.30	109,994
		Mean value	1.00	$ 421,644
D	0.05	20,062,469	0.25	250,781
	0.01	20,062,469	0.45	90,281
	0.02	20,062,469	0.30	120,375
		Mean value	1.00	$ 461,437

Year	Market Share	Gross Sales in Market Area	Probability	Expected Value
E	0.05	21,879,889	0.25	273,499
	0.01	21,879,889	0.45	98,460
	0.02	21,879,889	0.30	131,279
		Mean value	1.00	$ 503,238
		Grand Total		$2,117,857

The calculations can be carried on through 10, 15, 20 years, however many the analyst is interested in, but these five will serve for illustrative purposes.

With an expected value in mind from the breakdown given, the analyst is now ready for the culminating phase of the calculations—the preparation of an income statement. At the going manufacturer's selling price of 30 cents a pound, Harley Mills must make $0.009 on each pound to realize its goal of 3 percent of gross sales. The $50,000 in capital equipment for the ready mixes may likely be spread over 10 years, making $5,500 with interest at 10 percent to be liquidated each year. For convenience, let us say that this cost is divided evenly between cake, pancake, and biscuit production. Thus cake-mix manufacture will cover $1,833 of this amortization cost. To get a foothold in the market, high expenditures for advertising will be necessary, at least for two years. That the giants might decide to eliminate Harley Mills and other pretenders through price wars is unlikely; yet the possibility may be worthy of consideration in setting the amount for operating reserves. As volume increases, there will also be some economy of scale.

Unit-cost figures for the five-year period are set, after some deliberation, to run like this:

Year A	Year B	Year C	Year D	Year E
$0.31	$0.30	$0.291	$0.29	$0.286

Then the income statement can be calculated as shown in the table.

HARLEY MILLS INCOME STATEMENT FOR CAKE MIXES
years A through E

Year	No. of Units	Gross Sales	Costs	Yearly Income	Cumulative Income
A	1,159,200	$ 347,760	$ 359,352	− $11,592	− $11,592
B	1,279,260	383,778	383,778	000	− 11,592
C	1,405,480	421,644	408,995	12,649	1,057
D	1,538,123	461,437	446,056	15,381	16,438

Year	No. of Units	Gross Sales	Costs	Yearly Income	Cumulative Income
E	1,677,460	503,238	476,894	26,344	42,782
Total	7,059,523	$2,117,857	$2,075,075	$42,782	

If the total income of $42,782 were spread evenly over the 5-year period, the $8,556.40 average income provides approximately 17 percent of the $50,000 capital investment for ready mixes annually. If the accountants were to allocate to cake mixes $195,000 of the total capital investment (original $625,000 for building and equipment plus $50,000 for ready mixes), cake-mix production would give about a 4.4-percent annual return ($8,556.40 divided by $195,000). The income from pancake and biscuit mixes is yet to be considered. The company also realizes its desired income of 3 percent of gross sales ($12,649 divided by $421,644) at the end of the third year and pays out approximately 16 percent of its $50,000 capital investment plus interest at the end of the fifth year.

The examples given here are segmented and simplified to illustrate the thinking in which an analyst may engage in converting the components of a problem to money values. Other important forces, such as the time considerations, utility values, and qualitative elements discussed in the preceding chapter exert a strong influence on both the analyst's assignment of probability levels and subsequent assignment of money values. Different accounting procedures might also produce different answers.

Determining Present Value of Future Dollars

If the analyst wishes a more accurate estimate of future costs and sales volume than is possible through the projection of *current* costs and selling prices into the years ahead, then the techniques employed in the preceding section may be used by forecasting what costs and sales prices will be for each year of the forecast interval at three probability levels and adding them together as an expected value for each year. The tabulation given here is illustrative of the calculation of the future cost of some input item with a unit price of $5 on the basis of these assumptions:

The price will rise by 4% per year for 5 years	50% chance
The price will remain stable for 5 years	25% chance
The price will fall by 3% per year for 5 years	25% chance
The price will rise by 4%, fall by 3%, or remain stable for 5 years	100%

The expected price for the item can then be computed in this manner:

Year	Price	Probability	Expected Price	Expected Price
1	$5.00	1.00	$5.00	$5.00
2	5.20	0.50	2.60	
	5.00	0.25	1.25	
	4.85	0.25	1.21	5.06
3	5.4080	0.50	$2.70	
	5.0000	0.25	1.25	
	4.7045	0.25	1.18	5.13

Costs and prices thus arrived at can be put into the calculations of other aspects of the problem.

Another of the simpler methods of assessing the value of future dollars is discounting at the rate the company could invest the capital involved during the forecast period through the present value formula:

$$PV = \frac{A_1}{(1 + r)^1} + \frac{A_2}{(1 + r)^2} + \frac{A_3}{(1 + r)^3} + \cdots + \frac{A_n}{(1 + r)^n}$$

where

A = the amount accumulated each year over the n-year period

r = the interest rate

Thus if the ten-year forecast of earnings for a company is $1,000,000 (accumulated at the uniform rate of $100,000 annually) and the interest rate is 10 percent, the present value of this return is $614,457, approximately.

$$PV = \frac{\$100,000}{(1 + 0.10)^1} + \frac{\$100,000}{(1 + 0.10)^2} + \frac{\$100,000}{(1 + 0.10)^3} + \cdots + \frac{\$100,000}{(1 + 0.10)^{10}}$$

$$= \frac{\$100,000}{1.10} + \frac{\$100,000}{1.21} + \frac{\$100,000}{1.331} + \cdots + \frac{\$100,000}{2.5937}$$

$$= \$614,457$$

This discussion of discounted future earnings is included only to illustrate its importance and is by no means definitive, for that is a book in itself. The method to be employed is dependent upon the degree of educational sophistication in mathematics and accounting possessed by the analyst. If the problem is one involving income—as most business decisions are—the analyst should provide a financial accounting for all the years of the forecast period according to a method of his or her own choice.

Imaginative Testing of the Outcomes

In addition to engaging in the "what if" kind of thinking already suggested for testing the outcomes of *acting* on a proposal and of *not acting* on it, the analyst may refine the decision process further by plotting the financial return on the two possible courses and making a choice from anticipated money values. Using the Harley Mills problem again, the analyst may calculate the return from the sale of cake, biscuit, and pancake mixes and the return on the $50,000 used for equipment if it were invested at 10 percent, for five years in the manner illustrated below. (Figures are based on the assumption that the income from cake mixes constitutes one-half the total income from ready mixes.)

Year	Cumulative Return on Ready Mixes	Return on $50,000 at 10 Percent
A	− $ 23,184	$ 5,000
B	− 23,184	5,500
C	2,114	6,050
D	32,876	6,655
E	85,564	7,321
		$30,526
	+ 25,000*	+ 50,000†
	$110,564	$80,526

* $50,000 machinery 50% depreciated at end of 5 years.
† Original $50,000 still on hand at end of 5 years.

On this basis, it is considerably better to market ready mixes than to invest the $50,000 at 10 percent, not compounded.

The flour-mill problem is further complicated, though, by the fact that *all* of Harley Mills, currently valued at $625,000, might be sold and the money invested at 10 percent. If the plant can be sold at a conservative $500,000 and ready mixes make up 60 percent of gross income with flour and corn meal accounting for the rest, the five-year financial rundown might look like this:

Year	Gross Sales of Ready Mixes	Gross Sales of Flour and Meal	Gross Sales of All Products	Income, Flour and Meal (3% of gross sales)
A	$ 695,720	$463,813	$1,159,533	$13,914
B	767,556	511,704	1,279,260	15,351

Year	Gross Sales of Ready Mixes	Gross Sales of Flour and Meal	Gross Sales of All Products	Income, Flour and Meal (3% of gross sales)
C	843,288	562,192	1,405,480	16,866
D	922,874	615,249	1,538,123	18,457
E	1,006,476	670,984	1,677,460	20,130
				$84,718

Year	Cumulative Income from Flour, Meal	Cumulative Income from Ready Mixes	Total	Return from $500,000 at 10% Interest
A	$13,914	− $23,184	− $ 9,270	$ 50,000
B	29,265	− 23,184	− 6,081	105,000
C	46,131	2,114	48,245	165,500
D	64,588	32,876	97,464	232,050
E	84,718	85,564	170,282	305,255

On this basis, it is considerably better to sell the plant and invest the money than it is to continue production with the addition of ready mixes. Carrying the calculations through 20 years might give a different picture, however. Whether the $500,000 will realize a uniform 10-percent investment return throughout the time interval is also a matter of conjecture. These examples are given to illustrate the kind of thinking the analyst might use in an effort to anticipate profit potential. The sophisticated financial analyst and accountant will, of course, add further refinements to the calculations in line with their preparation.

The return on several alternatives for any comparative-evaluation study involving money may be calculated and evaluated in much the same way.

10

Preparing the Prefatory Report Parts

*Disorganized, illogical writing reflects a
disorganized, illogical (and untrained) mind.*

Anonymous

At this point, steps I through V of the agenda for decision-making research projects pictured in Figure 7-1 are completed: statement of the project, defining the problem, planning the research design, the search for data to support or reject the hypothesis, and shaping the decision. The analyst is now ready to refine and formalize reflective thinking through the preparation of certain prefatory portions of the report, the first phase of step VI.

As orientation, a capsule presentation of the parts of the full-scale analytical report with appropriate paging is given in Ex. 10-1. Even though some of the parts will not be drafted until the report is completed, suggestions for preparing all of them are covered here for convenience in reference. In this chapter, the following elements are included:

1. Page format.
2. The title fly.
3. The title page.
4. The authorization letter or memorandum.
5. The letter of transmittal.
6. The table of contents.
7. The list of illustrations.
8. The abstract or epitome.

```
         COVERAGE AND SEQUENCE                          PAGINATION

1.   The Prefatory Parts
     Title fly--a page containing only
        the report title, typed in solid
        capitals, underscored, lines
        centered in inverted-pyramid
        fashion, riding approximately
        an inch above the vertical
        middle of the sheet.  Sample
        Form 10-2.                                 Counted but not numbered
     Title page--a three-level identifi-              on page faces
        cation that shows the title,
        the authorizer's name, title,
        and address, the writer's name,
        title, and address, and submittal
        date.  Sample Form 10-3.
     Authorization memorandum or
        letter--Sample Form 10-4.
     Letter of transmittal--Sample
        Form 10-5.

     Table of contents--Sample Forms
        10-6, 10-7, 10-8, and 10-9.
     List of tables--Sample Form 10-10.
     List of figures--Sample Form           Numbered with small roman numbers
        10-10.
     Epitome or abstract--Sample Form
        10-11.

2.   The Text
     The introductory chapter or chapters
        (part or parts for short reports)--
        Sample Forms 11-1 and 11-2.
     The succession of content chapters--
        Sample Form 11-3.
     The summary, conclusions, and
        recommendations chapters or parts.    Numbered with arabic numerals

3.   The Appended Parts
     The appendix or appendices.
     The bibliography (sequence of
        appendix and bibliography may be
        reversed).
     The index (for published material
        only).
```

Exhibit 10-1   The makeup and pagination of the business report

Specific writing applications for report parts may well be supplemented with principles developed in other pertinent portions of the text.

PAGE FORMAT

Arranging the report in proper format makes its own contribution to the quality of the report, for a presentation with a good appearance is an indication of a craftsmanlike job. At this point only the requirements for setting up the page properly are given, with treatment of captions, footnotes, and indented blocks reserved for Chapter 11, which is concerned with the writing of the body of the report.

Margins

The page guide shown in Sample Form 10-1 was constructed by first marking off to the left the amount of space to be taken up by the report binder, usually varying from one-half to two-thirds of an inch. Uniform right and left margins of 1¼ inches were arranged to keep the pages from seeming crowded and to allow note space for the reader, should that be needed. The 1½-inch bottom margin provides flexibility for pages, some of which must necessarily be longer than others. For the first page of every major division, a 2-inch top margin is provided above the title. The parts that constitute separate divisions (to be started on new pages) are these: the table of contents, the lists of illustrations, the epitome, each individual chapter (if the report is divided into separate chapters instead of parts), separate divisions of the appendix, the bibliography, and the index (if any). Pages starting new sections are numbered 1 inch from the bottom, centered, as in the small box on the guide sheet. On pages not starting a new section an inch margin at the top is recommended, with the page number placed flush with the right margin a double space above the first line of type (line 5 for most typewriters). The center of the sheet is measured from the binding-space line at the left out to the right page boundary. Drafting a page guide according to these instructions will help you to place the prefatory parts of your report attractively.

Spacing

Formal papers traditionally call for the text to be double-spaced (or space and a half) with footnote entries single-spaced. For the formal business report, single-spacing affords greater compactness and is acceptable or even preferable. Consequently, the sample pages for this text are set up in single-spaced format. You may well choose, however, to employ double-spacing. If the report is to be published, the typescript copy is usually double-spaced to allow for the proofreader's marks.

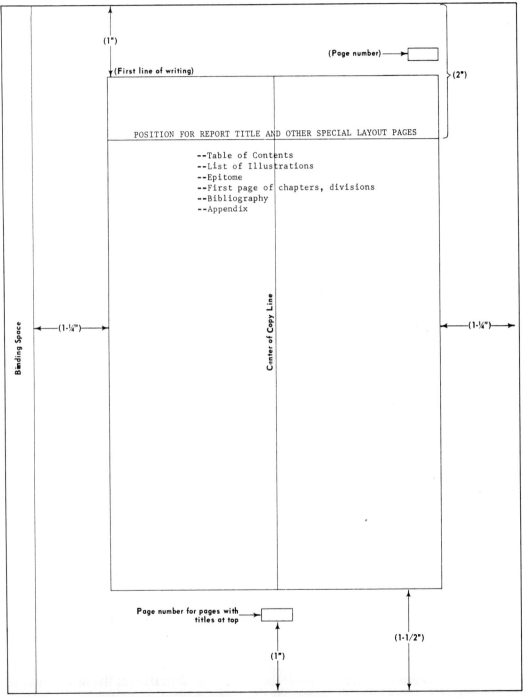

Sample Form 10-1 Page guide

Single-spaced copy may have blocked or indented paragraphs, according to the writer's preference, but in either case double spaces come between successive paragraphs to set off the end of one and the beginning of another. For double-spaced copy, paragraphs must be indented five to ten spaces, with the same indentation plan used for all other indented elements, such as footnotes, quotations, and enumerations. Special spacing instructions for separate prefatory parts are given with each separate element.

THE TITLE FLY

As one stage in further clarifying the problem, the writer begins to frame the boundaries of the investigation in a well-worded title. Complete coverage in most cases includes the *why, who, what, where, when,* and *how* of journalism news stories:

1. The *why* involves the overall purpose: to study, evaluate, analyze, appraise, recommend, describe, or such. Since the purpose is the most important element, this part usually merits placement in the first line of the title, the point of greatest impact.

2. The *who* is the people involved in the study. For business reports, the company, institution, or association name for whom the analysis is done makes up this part and also is worthy of placement in the first line. It is possible that only a portion of long names may be worked in.

3. The *what* is the subject matter: what is being investigated, the value to be derived from the answer.

4. The *where* is the geographical location with which the study is concerned. For market analyses, both the production center and the distribution area likely should be identified.

5. The *when* is the time interval investigated. If the investigation is current—as most business studies are—an indication of the present year or of the range of years (including the present) represented by internal or published statistics may serve.

6. The *how* is the basic data-gathering procedure: experimental, survey, observation, research from published economic data, or whatever.

The title should be reduced to the fewest words that will carry the content. Tight writing may be achieved by the elimination of repeated or unnecessary words or by making possessives or adjectives out of prepositional phrases. If two major units are linked by *and*, it is possible that economy may result from the subordination of one phrase to the other. The title in no way reflects the answer; it merely covers all the significant objectives of the investigation. The following titles are submitted for your critical evaluation.

(when)   *(why)*   *(who, where)*   *(what)*
A 19xx APPRAISAL FOR HARLEY MILLS OF THE PROFIT POTENTIAL

OF READY-MIX PRODUCT DIVERSIFICATION DERIVED FROM
(how)
A MARKET-AREA CONSUMER SURVEY

(why)   *(who)*
A COMPARATIVE EVALUATION FOR RENICK-DORN REFINING
(where)
COMPANY OF LUBBOCK, FORT WORTH, HOUSTON, AND
(what)
GALVESTON AS SORGHUM-PROCESSING SITES
(when)   *(how)*
BASED ON 19xx–19yy PUBLISHED DATA

(why)   *(what)*
AN EVALUATION OF THE MERCHANDISING PRACTICES OF
(who)   *(how)*
SAYLOR DEPARTMENT STORE THROUGH SAMPLE
(when)
SHOPPING IN THE SPRING
19xx SALES CAMPAIGN

(why)   *(who)*   *(where, what)*
A PROPOSED SITE FOR OLD SOUTH'S LOUISIANA REFINERY
(when)
FOR COTTON OIL BASED ON 19xx–19yy COTTON YIELDS,
(how)
LIVING CONDITIONS, COMPETITION,
AND TRANSPORTATION

(why)   *(who)*
A RECOMMENDATION FOR NORTHERN GAS COMPANY ON
(what)   *(where)*
THE PURCHASE OF THE MILVILLE PLANT FOR THE
MANUFACTURE OF ANHYDROUS AMMONIA BASED
(how, when)
ON 19xx–19yy PUBLISHED DATA

The title is first displayed in the title fly, with lines broken into natural groupings, centered in inverted-pyramid fashion, with the middle line about 1 inch above the center sheet, as in Sample Form 10-2. Titles of three lines or less are double-spaced; those of four lines or more, single-spaced. If chapter or division headings in the report are to be typed in solid capitals, some sort of typographical distinction should be given the title, possibly the use of underscoring, as in the sample form. The first line should be spread out well toward the margins to avoid piling up too many short lines. It is best not to

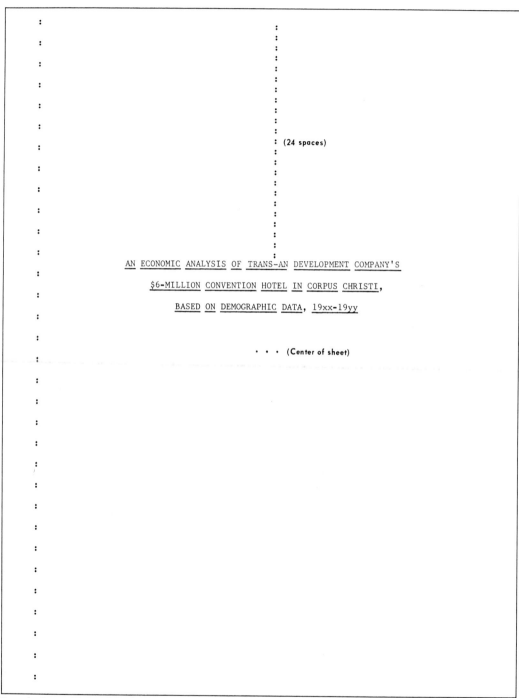

: (24 spaces)

AN ECONOMIC ANALYSIS OF TRANS-AN DEVELOPMENT COMPANY'S

$6-MILLION CONVENTION HOTEL IN CORPUS CHRISTI,

BASED ON DEMOGRAPHIC DATA, 19xx-19yy

· · · (Center of sheet)

Sample Form 10-2   Title fly

divide words at line ends. Typing the title fly over the guide sheet you have prepared will position it right to be bound in with the report.

THE TITLE PAGE

The title page has three levels displaying the report title and supplying data regarding its destination (the name and identification facts of the person for whom it was written) and facts about the writer (name, address, title of the writer, and the date on which the report is submitted). When the recipient and the writer are from the same company and the same address, put only the firm name for the recipient, reserving the full address to go with the firm name in the writer's identification block. A properly proportioned title page is pictured in Sample Form 10-3.

THE AUTHORIZATION LETTER
OR MEMORANDUM

Authorization to initiate a full-scale investigation is often made orally in the business scene, and in no other way. An oral authorization is not particularly desirable from the reporter's point of view for three reasons. (1) In case dissatisfaction with the end product arises, there is no tangible way of pinpointing responsibility anywhere but on the writer. (2) Oral authorization may result in misunderstandings that could be avoided if the major aspects of the proposed study were placed on paper for extended examination. (3) An oral authorization may lack the clarity and detail that would be present if the authorizer had transferred his or her thoughts into written form. If the authorization is given orally, the investigator as a matter of self-protection should write down the elements of the study as he or she interprets them for the authorizer's approval before any work is begun on the report.

The authorization letter or memorandum is virtually an order for services, thus forming the first stage of a contract. The writer, therefore, should make clear, as in any order, exactly what is wanted, the maximum delivery date beyond which the contract becomes invalid, how much will be paid for the service involved in the report (if applicable), and when payment will be made (the whole amount on delivery, a certain portion down with so much on delivery and so much 30 days after acceptance, or other businesslike arrangement).

Writing the authorization is not the report writer's responsibility; yet it is so much a part of the project that experience in drafting it is provided here. Detailed background for composing requests that the reader will have

```
:                              :
:                              :
:                              : (9 spaces)
:                              :
:                              :
:              AN ECONOMIC ANALYSIS OF TRANS-TEX DEVELOPMENT COMPANY'S
:
:              $6-MILLION CONVENTION HOTEL IN CORPUS CHRISTI,
:
:              BASED ON DEMOGRAPHIC DATA, 19xx-19yy
:                              :
:                              :
:                              :
:                              :
:                              : (13 spaces)
:                              :
:                              :
:                              :
:                          Prepared for
:
:                   MR. W. H. MACREA, JR., PRESIDENT
:                   Trans-Tex Development Company
:                      900-915 Republic Building
:                         Any City, State
.                              :
:                              :
:                              :
:                              :
:                              : (15 spaces)
:                              :
:                              :
:                              :
:                              :
:                          Prepared by
:
:                  David B. Winton, Research Analyst
:                  Metropolitan Research Associates
:                      1691-1698 Martin Tower
:                         Any City, State
:                          April 3, 19xx
:
:
:
:
```

Sample Form 10-3   Title page

no objections to complying with and for letters designed for systematically imparting information appears in Chapters 2 and 3. Thus, only ideas especially oriented to research authorizations are suggested. The letter or memorandum includes five main areas: (1) specific authorization in the opening; (2) a clear delineation of what is wanted; (3) an elaboration of any background facts affecting the study; (4) a businesslike treatment of costs, payment, and dates; and (5) a gracious close. Often the authorizer and the analyst have engaged in numerous conferences prior to the actual issuing of the authorization. The authorizer, however, includes all pertinent phases to keep the record straight, even though the analyst may have a good understanding of them already. The executive requesting an investigation should bear in mind that certain of the facts being delineated are common knowledge between the two of them and not to be presented as though they were introduced into the situation for the first time. Simple phrases such as "In line with our previous conversations" or even "As you know" puts the information into proper perspective.

The *opening* should move straight to the major issue of the message: definite authorization for the report writer to proceed. Compatible with the innate courtesy of the knowledgeable business manager, this request for services may be phrased in a polite imperative or question-request:

> In line with the plans we've made in the past few months, *please find out* for us whether the addition of ready mixes to our product lines will prove profitable.

> To serve as a base for a sound decision on the purchase of the Milville plant, *will you please go ahead* with your appraisal of it as a site for the production of anhydrous ammonia?

Thus *what* is to be investigated and the purpose of the study are clearly set out in the opening words. A dependent structure at the beginning of the sentence, as in the examples, is functional in softening the *command* aspects of the authorization. Other essential phases, such as the deadline, quality, or size standards for the report or a reference to previous plans may be worked in here or in other convenient spots in the message.

What the authorization writer wants may include such things as the following.

1. The areas of investigation, perhaps an explicit statement enumerating the decision components or specific questions for which an answer is sought.

2. Any boundaries set upon the study: a delimitation of the marketing area or other geographical limits, any aspects that may be excluded from consideration, how large a sample should be used, what income percentage is expected of the venture and how soon, and so on.

3. What the report will be used for—any aspects of the main purpose not included in the opening and any collateral purposes, such as to serve

as the basis of an appeal to the Securities Exchange Commission, for consideration of the board of directors, or as the foundation for a preliminary decision, with a larger study in the offing.

4. Some idea of the desired size for the report.

Itemizing the main phases of the analysis, either as part of a sentence or arranged in an indented block, emphasizes the authorizer's expectations, allows the analyst to perceive them more readily, and makes it easy for check off as each phase is completed. Courtesy and respect for the analyst's capabilities might call for a casual statement that any other pertinent aspects should be considered as well.

Background facts having a bearing on the interpretation of the findings and on the conclusions of the study should be elaborated.

1. The initiating force for the investigation, which may be an informal statement of the hypothesis. "When Cool-Air Heating and Cooling Company was put on the market for $50,000, the management of Newton Industries decided to look into the possibilities of short-term income and long-term capital growth to be derived from purchasing and managing this potentially sound small business."

2. Vital elements of the history of the project up to the point of the investigation.

3. Any applicable action already taken, such as

a. A decision on the amount of money to be involved in the venture.

b. Any land or building options established.

c. Financing plans already made.

d. The anticipated size of the project: output capacity, number of workers, sales expected, the length of the production year, or such.

Taking care of *costs* also involves a clear delineation of

1. Personnel or other types of assistance to be provided for the investigator, if any.

2. Expense or travel money afforded, if any, and how and when it will be paid.

The analyst will get the report together either for a fee or as part of the job; in both cases an obligation and a willingness are implied. Yet the writer of the authorization inspires superior performance with a tone of friendly encouragement, perhaps in *the close.* Subtly picturing the report performing its intended purpose in some effective way releases an image of quality craftsmanship in the reader's mind—something to live up to: "We're looking forward to your report as an excellent base for a sound decision when the Board of Directors meets on April 6."

Injecting a note of courtesy into establishing the delivery date may be achieved by placing a value on the writer's presentation by the deadline (as in the sentence just given) or by phrasing the request in question form:

> May I have the report by April 4 so we may make immediate plans to implement the venture by May 1, according to the procedure your findings suggest?

Giving the reader a reason for the deadline is also a subtle way of inducing appropriate action—an item that may be placed at any point where it fits well into the fabric of the message.

Since the analyst will want to keep the original authorization for contractual reasons, a copy of it is generally placed in the report. The typescript of the copy, then, will be shifted to the right of the page by the amount of the binding space to match in margin placement the remainder of the report pages. It should also be labeled as a COPY in some convenient way, with an indication that the original was signed by the authorizer. An authorization to an outside consultant takes the letter format; one going to a staff member is prepared as a memorandum in the TO, FROM, SUBJECT, DATE form suggested in Chapter 6. A sample authorization letter in proper format is given in Sample Form 10-4.

THE LETTER OF TRANSMITTAL

The transmittal note is the report writer's last task: "Here is the report you asked for; preparing it was a rewarding experience." The idea in the latter portion of the sentence is perhaps optional; yet it is certainly advantageous to the writer to generate at least a minimum of enthusiasm for the project, whether the work was done for a fee or as part of regular job performance. Some sort of transmittal message accompanies the delivery of almost all assigned written jobs in the business office.

The analyst may here consult the instructions for preparing the favorable answer outlined in Chapter 3, as well as the other background chapters on the communication process. The transmittal note specifically includes these elements:

1. Delivery of the report in the opening words, which picture it performing its intended purpose, a functional value. The authorization date and manner are worked in incidentally: "The report, authorized in your memorandum of March 1, should provide the Board of Directors with many avenues of discussion when they meet on April 7 to decide whether to establish the barite mill in Hidalgo." What the report is about—its purpose—and the authorization date and manner are included for identification. Nowhere in the transmittal is the decision answer revealed for the formal report.

2. Some interesting talk about the report and its preparation: any

```
                              TRANS-AN DEVELOPMENT COMPANY
                                 900-915 Republic Building
                                     Any City, State


          C O P Y                                      February 19, 19xx


          Mr. David B. Winton
          Research Analyst
          Metropolitan Research Associates
          1691-1698 Martin Tower
          Any City, State

          Dear Mr. Winton:

          In line with our recent discussion concerning the construction of
          a $6-million convention hotel in Corpus Christi, will you please
          proceed with a brief preliminary study to serve as a base for
          our decision on the feasibility of the project?

          As you recall, we have a 90-day option expiring May 1 to purchase
          a filled-in peninsula directly on the bay for $300,000.  Located
          just off Ocean Drive, this site is to be connected to the main-
          land by a $200,000 causeway.  With the completion of the struc-
          ture at a cost of $4,500,000 and an additional $750,000 outlay for
          furnishings, the new hostelry can provide luxurious accommodations
          for both tourists and convention delegates.

          The enclosed preliminary financial schedule is still in the plan-
          ning stage; so please make any adjustments you think necessary.
          Also included on the same sheet, you will notice, are the number
          and size of planned bedrooms and their apportional rates.  With a
          total of 500 bedrooms, a maximum of 850 guests can enjoy a swank
          private club, two swimming pools, five smart lobby shops, three
          dining rooms, and underground parking facilities.  Bedrooms fea-
          ture built-in radio-and-television units and dressers.  Eleven
          meeting rooms and a grand ballroom which seats 2,500 (with a capa-
          city of 1,500 for convention banquets) are provided.  Mediterranean
          decor prevails throughout.

          In the initial stages, Trans-An will operate the hotel, employing
          an experienced hotel manager and a French chef internationally
          known for his exotic cuisine.
```

Sample Form 10-4   Authorization letter

Mr. David B. Winton, Research Analyst, February 19, 19xx, page 2

So that a sound decision may result, will you please probe into
all areas of patronage to determine the expected demand and possible competition, including a projected income analysis of operations? Any additional information which you think will assist
the directors in making their decision will be appreciated.

Because your report is to be considered at our April 15th Board
of Directors meeting, will you please limit your analysis to one
which concentrates on specifics and can be read within an hour?
As previously agreed, you will find your $1,000 retainer enclosed,
with the additional $1,500 to be mailed on receipt of your report.
Reimbursement for travel expenses not exceeding 3 percent of the
total fee will also be made at that time.

With your careful study of this possible development in Corpus
Christi, we will be in a much better position to make a sound decision concerning the economic prospects of such an interesting
project.

Cordially yours

(Signed)

W. H. Macrea, Jr.
President

Sample Form 10-4   Continued

specifically helpful ways in which it is arranged, unusual incidents connected with the gathering of data, the comprehensiveness with which data were pursued, the logic of certain assumptions under which you operated, the accuracy of the data, an explanation of certain difficult or surprising features, the ingenuity with which you derived or tracked down elusive facts, or such. The attitude is one of modest confidence in the report for its intended purpose. No digest of the findings is given when a separate synopsis is included.

The transmittal is the one report part that may be written in a friendly, conversational, personal style instead of in the objective, impersonal manner employed for other portions. Since most transmittals are written to someone in a superior position, the letter is preferable to the memo format. As in the authorization message, the copy is pushed to the right of the page for horizontal centering by the width of the binding space. A typical transmittal letter is shown in Sample Form 10-5.

ORGANIZING THE OUTLINE

The formal, analytical business report either contains a business decision in its pages or serves as the basis for one, depending on the writer's level of authorization. Therefore, the whole effort should be so arranged that it is geared to the executive's greatest need at any point it is examined.

The outline, then, assumes sizable importance in informing the reader at once of the scope and coverage of the investigation—the first report part turned to. In addition, the effectiveness of the outline, the writer's organizational blueprint, has more influence on the ultimate quality of the report itself than has any of the other preliminary portions or activities. Here the analyst tries to reflect the essence of her or his decision-making deliberations resulting from the stages elaborated in Chapter 9.

Selecting a Contents Format

The report outline gives a clear indication of these things: (1) the coverage, (2) the sequence of the items, and (3) the relative importance of the parts. The table of contents goes a step farther, showing where the parts may be found by page number. The interrelationship of the parts may be exhibited in two ways: (1) through a system of numbering, lettering, or a combination, which indicates sequence, weight, and relationship; and (2) through variations in typography for different levels of importance. Outline formats for the traditional combination of numbers and letters and for the decimal system begin on page 446.

```
                    HARLEY FLOUR MILLS
                    1968 East 14th Street
                    Any City, State 06123


                                              July 17, 19xx


        Mr. Thomas Y. Bentley, President
        Harley Flour Mills
        1968 East 14th Street
        Any City, State 06123

        Dear Mr. Bentley:

        This report, authorized in your June 26th memorandum,
        should give you a sound basis for a tentative decision
        on Harley Mills's proposed entry into the ready-mix
        field.

        An examination of the financial statements of the prime
        contenders--General Mills, Pillsbury, and Quaker Oats--
        generates an illusion of a steady stream of profits
        flowing from the manufacture of such convenience items.
        The writers of these stockholders' reports, however,
        are understandably reticent to disclose unit production-
        cost figures for the giants, an aspect that would have
        proved most helpful.  You will notice, though, that I
        managed to derive estimates to measure against the
        projected cost figures for Harley Mills cake, pancake,
        and biscuit mixes submitted by Jack Alderson in Pro-
        duction.  The recorded history of the State competitors
        (Fant and Pioneer) were particularly revealing, I think.

        I found making this analysis an absorbing undertaking.
        Should there be any areas that need further investiga-
        tion, I'll be happy to go to work on them.

                                Sincerely yours

                                Morris Iverson

                                Morris Iverson
                                Product Analyst
```

Sample Form 10-5   Transmittal letter

Traditional Pattern with Varying Typography	Decimal System with Uniform Typography
I. SOLID CAPITALS	1. First level of importance
A. <u>Initial Capitals Underlined</u>	1.1 Second level
1. Initial Capitals Not Underlined	1.11 Third level
a. First word only capitalized	1.111 Fourth level
(1) First word only capitalized	1.1111 Fifth level
(2) First word only capitalized	1.2 Second level
b. First word only capitalized	1.21 Third level
2. Initial Capitals Not Underlined	2. First level of importance
B. <u>Initial Capitals Underlined</u>	2.1 Second level
II. SOLID CAPITALS	2.2 Second level
	2.3 Second level
	3. First level of importance

In the traditional pattern to the left, certain of the typographical gradations may be skipped if the writer chooses, but none should be used out of sequence. Some style manuals use roman numbers with first-level divisions and omit the numbers and letters with subsequent levels, indicating the degree of importance with variations in typography and suitable indentation for sublevels. Double spaces may appear before and after the first two levels, with third- and subsequent-level entries single-spaced, except that double spaces appear before the first and after the last item of single-spaced blocks. Carried-over lines of single-spaced groups should be indented an extra two or three spaces, as in (1) and (2) above, so that the start of each new entry is clearly visible. The decimal system format has uniform typography and uniform double-spacing throughout. Sample outlines typed in proper format are interspersed in the text of the following pages in appropriate spots to illustrate other techniques for good outlining.

Construction of the Topical and the Descriptive Outline

Two plans for phrasing the outline captions prevail: (1) the topical and (2) the descriptive. The topical caption indicates the coverage and the relationship of the parts through the use of *impact* words; the descriptive caption includes the coverage, the significance of its relationship to the investigation decision, and the main supporting facts and figures. Each plan has its own peculiar merits, with descriptive captions having the advantage of providing executives with the meat of the investigation if they read no other part of the report than the outline. The distinctions between the two types are elaborated below by major outline section.

The Introduction. The first-level caption identifying the introduction to the report indicates that the boundaries of the problem are set out here. It may consist of the traditional word *Introduction* or be based around other cue words of a similar nature, such as these:

Preview of	The Situation
Setting the Scene for	The X Company's Need for
Orientation to	Boundaries Set for
Background Affecting	Purpose and Scope of

For the topical outline, the addition of *the study, the investigation, the analysis, the decision,* or other suitable terminology completes the main introductory caption. (A topical outline with decimal numbering is illustrated in Sample Form 10-6.) For the descriptive outline the writer goes a step further by adding to the cue words the company name (since only the words *Contents* or *Table of Contents* appear at the top of the page) and the purpose of the study (which implies the hypothesis) so that the reader may at once be oriented to the basic problem without flipping back.

The writer makes a selection of coverage for the introduction subcaptions from the following areas, identified with a brief resumé of what they will present when the report is written.

A. *Authorization and Submittal Data.* This section includes the primary and collateral purposes; the authorization date and manner; the names, titles, and addresses of the writer and reader; and the submittal date.

B. *Background History.* The text of this portion covers any material from the company's financial picture having a bearing on the decision; the initiating force of the investigation; any facts from industry history or operations which are pertinent; and any company planning or work done on the subject prior to the study.

C. *Scope and Boundaries of the Analysis.* Report elaboration will call for a delineation of particular products, services, projects, or plans to be investigated; any areas to be omitted from consideration; any limits on procedures or sample size; geographical limits; ideas as to the size of the report desired, money to be spent, and so on.

D. *Definitions and Explanation of Terms.* The writer may include a section defining technical terms which may not be readily understood by all readers or explaining any terms used in other than the ordinary sense. This portion may be skipped in cases in which the writer and reader(s) are both well versed in the intricacies involved; or a minimum amount of definition may become a part of C.

CONTENTS

Part		Page
Synopsis		xi
1.	Perspective of the report	2
	1.1 Authorization and purpose of the investigation . . .	2
	1.2 Prior planning and activity	2
	1.3 Data sources and the research scheme	3
	1.4 Scope and limitations of the study	3
	1.5 Financial feasibility, demand, and competition in that order as the major criteria	4
2.	The financial prospects for the proposed hotel	4
	2.1 The outlook based on a three-year projection of financial operations	5
	2.2 Difficulties arising from partial financing through a common-stock issue	6
	2.3 The impact on the hotel industry of increasing costs since 19xx	7
	2.31 The necessity of higher rates to offset declining occupancy	7
	2.32 The results of capitalization ratios at an 18-year low	8
3.	The implications of present and future demand for convention facilities in Corpus Christi	8
	3.1 An appraisal of the capacity of existing accommodations	9
	3.2 The significance of present and future Chamber of Commerce convention listings	10

viii

Sample Form 10-6   Topical outline, decimal system, impact words used

ix

Part	Page
3.3 The influence of city promotional activities on hotel-convention demand	11
3.4 The anticipated advantages of area industrial expansion	12
4. The competition posed by other convention-oriented entities	13
4.1 Location and transportation facilities of Corpus Christi	14
4.2 The status of entertainment activities	14
4.3 The capacity of Corpus Christi to compete with lodging accommodations in rival cities	15
4.4 The effect of local motor hotels on the success of the project	15
5. Improbable success for convention hotel because of intense competition and projected financial difficulties	16
5.1 An estimated net loss of $48,280 through 19xx as a most unfavorable element	16
5.2 Promising demand conditions outweighed by doubtful financial feasibility and strong competition . . .	17
5.3 Corpus Christi's location, inadequate transportation and entertainment facilities as competitive handicaps	17
5.4 The luxury motor hotels in the area as the greatest threat to the project	18
5.5 Declining industry profits an inauspicious consideration	19
Appendix	20
Bibliography	25

Sample Form 10-6   Continued

E.   *Sources and Procedures.* This part of the presentation is the writer's description of the research scheme, the procedure in getting data, the details of experimental design, how sample and interrogation format were set up, an analysis of returns, the names of the main printed sources drawn from, any special methods of organizing, arranging, or interpreting. This material for certain reports may be extensive enough to warrant placement in a separate, first-level section.

F.   *Limitations.* This section tells what is good about the report, in what ways it might have been improved, or what further research might be called for. Material in this section may be combined with that in C.

G.   *The Principal Criteria of Evaluation.* The text of the report will identify the critical discussion areas or the criteria for evaluating the working hypothesis, a justification for the choices, and the sequence in which they appear.

H.   *A Preview of the Organizational Plan.* The reader here is guided to the sequential development of the report. G and H are frequently combined into a single section.

Basic to the writer's choice of coverage for the introduction subcaptions is a concept of the size of the final report. All the main divisions of the work should be approximately the same in size. If there are six first-level captions, the text to develop each should make up about one-sixth of the wordage, for example. Coverage for the introduction will be viewed for proportion and for possible combinations and eliminations. As suggested, it may be feasible to skip the definitions section or to include what few seem necessary in another appropriate division if the report is written for a person who knows a great deal about the subject matter. The scope and limits might be combined with the background history. Sources and procedures might be grouped with limitations; or the preview of the organizational plan might be derived from the criteria section with a little additional wording to indicate sequence. Trying to balance economy with adequate coverage, the writer makes this decision of choices.

For the topical outline the reporter merely identifies areas of discussion; for the descriptive form the salient features of the report background are specifically identified.

Topical	*Descriptive*
INTRODUCTION	I. PREVIEW OF VALLEY MINING COMPANY'S ANALYSIS OF THE FEASIBILITY OF MILLING BARITE IN HIDALGO
A. Authorization and Submittal Data	
B. Background Information	
C. The Research Plan	A. President Crashaw's Authorization of a Study of the Probable Success of the Proposed Plant
D. Basic Research Sources	
E. Limitations of the Study	B. Preliminary Financial and Organizational Planning
F. The Organizational Plan	

C. Appraisal of Census, Market, and
Financial Publications as the Basic
Method

D. Limitation of the Report to Highlight Aspects

E. Demand, Competition, and Profit
Potential in That Order as the Main
Criteria

The Critical Discussion Areas. Captions for the critical discussion area
or the criteria for evaluating the hypothesis reveal the components of the
business decision. The difference in phrasing for the topical and descriptive
outlines is illustrated with first-level captions for the Harley Mills yes-or-no
problem:

Topical	*Descriptive*
The Demand Criterion	
II. THE SIGNIFICANCE OF DEMAND FOR READY MIXES IN THE MARKET AREA	II. A 300-PERCENT INCREASE IN DE-MAND FOR READY MIXES BY 19xx A FAVORABLE FACTOR FOR HARLEY MILLS PRODUCTION
The Competition Determinant	
III. THE INFLUENCE OF COMPETITION	III. THREE READY-MIX GIANTS WITH 85 PERCENT OF THE MARKET AS A HANDICAP TO A NEW ENTRY TO THE FIELD
The Cost Factor	
IV. THE EFFECT OF BIG-VOLUME PRODUCTION COSTS AND PROMO-TION CAPACITY	IV. THE INABILITY OF HARLEY MILLS TO MATCH PRODUCTION COSTS AND ADVERTISING EXPENDITURES OF VOLUME PRODUCERS
The Decision	
V. CONCLUSIONS	V. POOR PROSPECTS FOR HARLEY MILLS IN THE READY-MIX FIELD IN VIEW OF INTENSE COMPETITION

The roman captions to the left identify the determinant and its relationship
to the overall decision with the impact words *significance, influence,* and
effect. The captions on the right show whether the subdecision for each criterion is yes or no with the words *favorable, handicap,* and *inability;* in addition, these subdecisions are supported with significant facts and figures
developed in the analysis, where feasible. Roman V names the report decision,
supported by a justifying reason. A complete outline for a yes-no decision
appears in Sample Form 10-7.

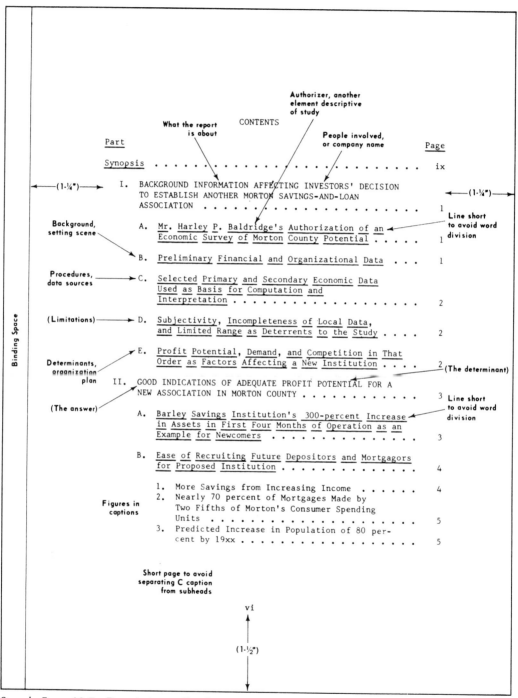

Binding Space

Authorizer, another element descriptive of study

What the report is about

CONTENTS

People involved, or company name

Part

Page

Synopsis   ix

←(1-¼")→

I.   BACKGROUND INFORMATION AFFECTING INVESTORS' DECISION
     TO ESTABLISH ANOTHER MORTON SAVINGS-AND-LOAN
     ASSOCIATION   1

←(1-¼")→

Background, setting scene

A. Mr. Harley P. Baldridge's Authorization of an
    Economic Survey of Morton County Potential   1

Line short to avoid word division

B. Preliminary Financial and Organizational Data . . .   1

Procedures, data sources

C. Selected Primary and Secondary Economic Data
    Used as Basis for Computation and
    Interpretation   2

(Limitations)

D. Subjectivity, Incompleteness of Local Data,
    and Limited Range as Deterrents to the Study   2

Determinants, organization plan

E. Profit Potential, Demand, and Competition in That
    Order as Factors Affecting a New Institution   2

(The determinant)

(The answer)

II. GOOD INDICATIONS OF ADEQUATE PROFIT POTENTIAL FOR A
     NEW ASSOCIATION IN MORTON COUNTY   3

Line short to avoid word division

A. Barley Savings Institution's 300-percent Increase
    in Assets in First Four Months of Operation as an
    Example for Newcomers   3

B. Ease of Recruiting Future Depositors and Mortgagors
    for Proposed Institution   4

Figures in captions

1. More Savings from Increasing Income   4
2. Nearly 70 percent of Mortgages Made by
    Two Fifths of Morton's Consumer Spending
    Units   5
3. Predicted Increase in Population of 80 per-
    cent by 19xx   5

Short page to avoid separating C caption from subheads

vi

(1-½")

Sample Form 10-7   Descriptive outline for yes-or-no decision

Part   Page

    C. Projected Cost Analysis of New Operation as
        Indicant of Future Stability 6

      1. High Projected Assets after One Year as
          an Assurance of Continued Progress 6

The answer ⟶

      2. Only $31,500 Income Needed to Meet Expenses
          the First Year 7

  III. GOOD SAVINGS AND MORTGAGE MARKETS AS EVIDENCE OF   ⟵ **The determinant**
      STABILITY AND INCREASING SUPPLY OF AND DEMAND FOR
      LOANABLE FUNDS IN MORTON COUNTY 7

    A. The Dynamic Expansion of the Local Savings
        Market 9

      1. A 350-percent Increase of Savings Deposits
          in Local Associations in Eight Years. 9
      2. Undeposited Funds in 19xx Approximately
          $317,000 9

    B. Favorable Conditions in the Future Mortgage
        Market 11

      1. An Anticipated 50-percent Increase in
          Volume of Morton County Mortgages by
          19xx 11
      2. Morton's Lead in State Building Statistics 11
      3. Favorable Effects from Possible Democratic

The determinant ⟶

          Power 11

  IV. COMPETITION AS MAJOR HINDRANCE TO THE PROPOSED
      ASSOCIATION'S SURVIVAL 13

    A. Approximately 40 percent of Morton County's New
        Savings Acquired by Existing Association 13

    B. High Concentration of Firms in Downtown Morton 13

    C. Mortgages Controlled by Existing Associations
        15 percent above High-Competition Level . . . . 14 ⟶ **Report answer**

  V. MORTON COUNTY SEEN AS FAVORABLE SITE FOR ADDITIONAL   ⟶ **Supporting reason**
      SAVINGS-AND-LOAN ASSOCIATION DESPITE COMPETITION ⟵
      DISADVANTAGE 14

    A. High Projected Profits of $30,000 after One Year
        as the Deciding Factor 15

Short page for
reasons of spacing

Sample Form 10-7 Continued

Part

Re-evaluation of
conclusions ranked
in descending order—
not in sequence in
which they were
discussed

B. Competition Secondary in View of 50-percent
   Expansion of Supply and Demand for Loanable
   Funds 15

C. Barley Savings Institution's Early Success
   in Tripling Assets in Four Months as an
   Example of County Potential 15

D. Rising Income and Population Growth of 80 percent
   in the Next 20 Years as Insurance for Continued
   Success. 15

E. Suburb Location to Combat Concentration of
   Institutions in Downtown Morton. 16

F. Morton's Present Lead in Building Construction
   as Indication of Future Success 16

Appendix 18

Bibliography 23

Taking care of
negative feature

Sample Form 10-7   Continued

First-level captions for the comparative-evaluation descriptive outline identify the bases of comparison and which of the items compared is superior according to the indicated measuring criteria. The second-level captions rank the alternatives in line with the bases of comparison, supported with facts and figures. A comparative-evaluation outline is shown in Sample Form 10-8.

Guides for the arrangement of first-level captions for both topical and descriptive outlines are as follows.

1. The caption should clearly indicate the critical discussion area or decision criterion.

2. The critical discussion areas or decision criteria should be of approximately equal value to the investigation decision.

3. The phrasing of the caption should somehow cover all the material to be discussed under it.

4. The wording should be reduced to the minimum that will carry the content—generally no more than two or three typed lines.

5. All the first-level captions should be in the same grammatical form—all noun phrases or all sentences.

6. The sequence of captions should build up to the decision, either in descending or in the logical order of interrelatedness.

7. The lines between the captions should be so clearly drawn that there is no overlapping, no duplication of similar material in more than one caption.

These requisites, in addition, are indicated for descriptive outlines, as applicable to particular studies.

8. The caption should make clear what the answer is according to the decision criterion and make explicit the subdecision embodied in the coverage.

9. It should relate the subdecision to the main problem answer.

10. It should contain any possible significant figures.

A good test of whether the roman headings are successful in meeting their goals is to set them down in order and evaluate their decision progress in this way:

I. PREVIEW OF THE ANALYSIS OF THE POSSIBILITY OF SUCCESSFULLY MILLING BARITE IN HIDALGO	Introduction caption sets scene, names the hypothesis
II. A 150-PERCENT INCREASE IN BARITE DEMAND BETWEEN 19xx and 19yy AS A FAVORABLE FACTOR	The demand is good. If this were the only decision determinant, the barite mill would probably succeed

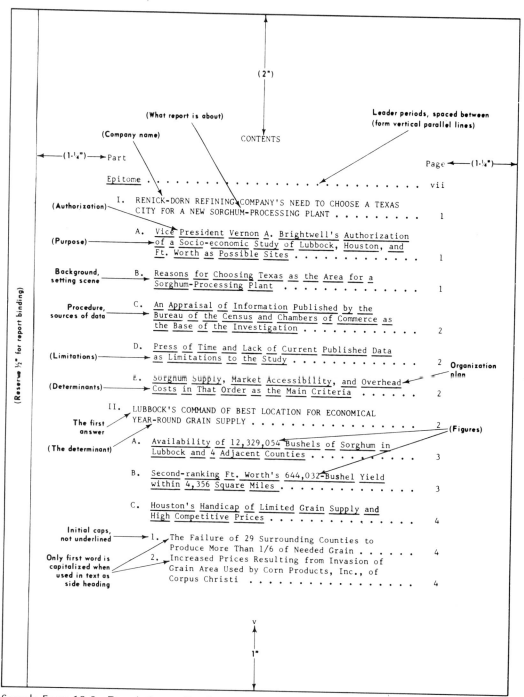

(2")

(What report is about)

(Company name)

Leader periods, spaced between
(form vertical parallel lines)

CONTENTS

(1-¼") → Part   Page ← (1-¼")

Epitome vii

(Authorization) →   I. RENICK-DORN REFINING COMPANY'S NEED TO CHOOSE A TEXAS
                        CITY FOR A NEW SORGHUM-PROCESSING PLANT   1

(Purpose) →   A. Vice President Vernon A. Brightwell's Authorization
                           of a Socio-economic Study of Lubbock, Houston, and
                           Ft. Worth as Possible Sites   1

Background,   B. Reasons for Choosing Texas as the Area for a
setting scene   Sorghum-Processing Plant   1

Procedure,   C. An Appraisal of Information Published by the
sources of data   Bureau of the Census and Chambers of Commerce as
                           the Base of the Investigation   2

(Limitations) →   D. Press of Time and Lack of Current Published Data
                           as Limitations to the Study   2   Organization

(Determinants) →   E. Sorghum Supply, Market Accessibility, and Overhead ← plan
                           Costs in That Order as the Main Criteria   2

                   II. LUBBOCK'S COMMAND OF BEST LOCATION FOR ECONOMICAL
The first   YEAR-ROUND GRAIN SUPPLY . . . .   2 (Figures)
answer

(The determinant)   A. Availability of 12,329,054 Bushels of Sorghum in
                           Lubbock and 4 Adjacent Counties   3

                       B. Second-ranking Ft. Worth's 644,032-Bushel Yield
                           within 4,356 Square Miles   3

                       C. Houston's Handicap of Limited Grain Supply and
                           High Competitive Prices   4

Initial caps,   1. The Failure of 29 Surrounding Counties to
not underlined   Produce More Than 1/6 of Needed Grain   4

Only first word is   2. Increased Prices Resulting from Invasion of
capitalized when   Grain Area Used by Corn Products, Inc., of
used in text as   Corpus Christi   4
side heading

v

1"

Sample Form 10-8   Descriptive outline for comparative evaluation

(Reserve ½" for report binding)

456

(The second answer) (Significant figure) vi line 5 from top

Part   Page

(Determinant)

III. HOUSTON'S SUPERIORITY WITH 50-PERCENT GREATER
      ACCESSIBILITY TO DISTRIBUTION OUTLETS   5

   A. Flexibility of Houston's Distribution Outlets by
       Rail, Water, and Truck   5

       1. Service to Houston by 6 Major Railway Systems
           Covering All Parts of the United States   5
       2. Sea-train and "Fishy-Back" Facilities out of
           Houston as a Plus Value   5
       3. Operation of 33 Truck Lines Spanning the
           Entire Country   5

   B. Ft. Worth's Position at "Hub of the Southwest" as
       the Reason for Close-second Rating in Distribution
       Adequacy   6

The third
answer

   C. Lubbock's Lack of Access to Major Distribution
       Outlets as Chief Drawback   6

IV. HOUSTON AS THE CHOICE FOR LOW OVERHEAD COST   6   (Determinant)

   A. Houston's Utility Rates Twice as Reasonable as
       Those of Closest Competitor   7

   B. Tax Savings of $33,600 in Houston over Figures for
       Second-ranking Ft. Worth   7

   C. Houston's Access to Semiskilled Labor at Prices
       Comparable to Those of Ft. Worth and Lubbock   7

The report
answer given
in conclusion
caption and
hint at why

V. RANKING OF HOUSTON, FT. WORTH, AND LUBBOCK IN THAT
    ORDER ACCORDING TO RELATIVE WEIGHTING OF THE CHOSEN
    FACTORS   8

   A. Houston as the Preferred Site Because of
       Distribution Flexibility and Low Overhead Expense . .   8

       1. Good In-transit Rates as the Possible
           Compensation for Houston's Inferior Grain
           Supply.   8
       2. Sea-train and "Fishy-Back" Service a
           50-percent Plus Value over Ft. Worth's Good
           Inland Transportation Accommodations   8
       3. Equal Wage Costs and 100-percent Better
           Utility Rates as Extra Determinants   9

   B. The Second-ranking of Ft. Worth for Adequate Grain
       and Market Proximity   9

   C. The Third Choice for Lubbock in Spite of Superior
       Sorghum Supply   10

Sample Form 10-8   Continued

III. UNFAVORABLE MARKET DUE TO COMPETITION FROM MAJOR COMPANIES AND BARITE SUBSTITUTES

The market looks bad. If this were the only consideration, project should be abandoned

IV. LOW BREAK-EVEN POINT AT SLIGHTLY MORE THAN ONE-THIRD CAPACITY AS AN INDICATOR OF SUCCESS

The profit picture projects favorably; if one looked only at possible income, the company should proceed

V. FAVORABLE PROSPECTS FOR VALLEY MINING COMPANY IN VIEW OF INCREASING DEMAND AND LOW PRODUCTION COSTS

THEREFORE, the company should mill barite at Hidalgo because a tremendous forecast demand and low-cost production offer ways of overcoming an unfavorable market picture

The next two captions could not appear compatibly as first-level entries in the same outline because they are not parallel in structure:

A Phrase: A 300-PERCENT INCREASE IN THE DEMAND FOR READY MIXES BY 19xx AS A FAVORABLE FACTOR FOR HARLEY MILLS

A Sentence: THREE READY-MIX GIANTS WITH 85 PERCENT OF THE MARKET STRONGLY CHALLENGE THE NEWCOMER

If two headings such as those following turn up in an outline, the chances are that the analyst has not drawn the lines around the critical discussion areas with sufficient care:

II.   LOW PRODUCTION *COSTS* AS A FAVORABLE INDICATOR FOR THE ESTABLISHMENT OF THE BARITE MILL AT HIDALGO

III.   HIGH TRANSPORTATION *COSTS* AS THE MAJOR DETERRENT FOR THE PROPOSED OPERATION

Could not both of these cost factors be grouped under a single comprehensive heading that would include them both?

Second- and Subsequent-Level Captions.   The progress of the critical discussion areas or decision criteria, with each of the subdecisions clearly announced, is but the initial step in convincing the reader of the soundness of that decision. The writer has merely set up the areas of argument for which proof must be produced. These guides for achieving conviction in second- and subsequent-level captions in both the topical and descriptive outline are pertinent.

1.   Ample evidence must be submitted. Two second-level captions (A and B or 1.1 and 1.2) in a short report may be adequate if each or one is subheaded with third-level captions (1, 2, 3 or 1.11 and 1.12). Three or four second-level entries are probably better, depending on the size of the report. In the comparative-evaluation report, the number of sec-

ond-level captions is determined by the number of things compared: if there are three choices, there will be three A–B–C–level captions (appropriately subdivided), with A showing which choice ranks first, B which ranks second, C which ranks third, and so on.

2.   Second-level captions should be arranged in descending order of significance to the subdecision set out in the first-level caption above them. If the first-level caption says that demand is favorable, A should present the most favorable statistics to prove it, B the next most favorable, and on down the line.

3.   Any factors unfavorable to the subdecision set out in the first-level caption should be given honest and adequate treatment. They will probably appear at the end of the list if arranged in descending order; or they may be covered as subheads of the appropriate second-level caption.

4.   The subcaptions, taken together, should leave the feeling that the subdecision has indeed been substantiated.

5.   All subcaptions in one spot in the outline should be phrased in the same grammatical form—which may or may not be the same as that in the first-level caption which introduces them. In other words, the II may be a phrase with the ABC's under it, sentences, or in the reverse relationship. Any third- or subsequent-level subdivisions may be sentences or phrases regardless of the form under which they are arranged, just so that all are alike. And the form for second-level captions is not necessarily the same under all first-level divisions throughout the outline: They may be sentences under II and phrases under III. They must merely be alike in one spot. A writer, of course, avoids parallelism problems by writing all captions as noun phrases, the most universally acceptable format.

6.   It is not feasible to have only a single subdivision under any heading. If at least two are not possible, there is no logical reason to subdivide.

7.   Each subdivision must be capable of producing at least a paragraph in the report. If little more can be said about the subject than appears in the caption, then probably the material should be discussed under the heading without appearing as a specific subdivision. More than one paragraph is possible for a heading, of course; but each heading should be capable of producing at least one.

For the descriptive outline, these ideas may be added:

8.   Significant *figures* should be woven into the text of the captions so that the executive may get the true picture without reading the report. If a first-level caption has subdivisions of a different nature under it, the figures will likely go in the subdivisions, as in II in the savings and loan yes-no decision, Sample Form 10-7. The executive's profit-conscious mind will want to know not only whether a phase is good or bad but also how good or bad it is. The figures should be oriented as an increase or decrease, as a portion or percentage of something, as a deviation

from a standard of some sort; for figures by themselves are seldom meaningful. It is also important to remember that comparisons should be made in the same sort of units.

9. If the citing of figures is not feasible, generalities should be supported with significant facts.

It is always interesting to note that two analysts can take the same determinant and, with different proof statistics, come up with different answers, as illustrated below:

II. A 150-PERCENT INCREASE IN BAR-ITE DEMAND BETWEEN 19xx AND 19yy AS A FAVORABLE FACTOR

    A. Oil Well Drilling-mud Needs to Increase 180 Percent by 19xx

        1. Increase in oil well depth of about 50 percent in the last 10 years

        2. Sharp increase in multiple drilling in the market in the last two years

        3. Forecast increase in oil well drilling of 2 percent per year

    B. Other Uses of Barite to Continue Increasing in the Coming Years

        1. Increased sales of barium chemicals to consumers other than drillers

        2. Barite use as an aggregate in high-density concrete mixes for nuclear research

        3. Growing use of barite in electrical systems for rockets

II. DECREASE IN DEMAND FOR BAR-ITE OFFERS UNFAVORABLE MARKET OUTLOOK FOR VALLEY MINING COMPANY

    A. Market Area Notes 26.8 Percent Decrease in Oil Well Completions

    B. A 4.6-Percent Decrease in New Area Wells is Forecast for the Next 10 Years

    C. Air Drilling Replaces Mud Drilling in Many New Operations

        1. Sales of air-drilling equipment increased sevenfold in a single year

        2. Air drilling cuts well costs 35 percent

    D. New Mud Technology Reduces Quantity of Drilling Mud Used

Both analysts present some rather convincing supporting facts and figures for different answers. With the possibility that different data may produce different decisions, the analyst's obligation is to dig deep and to weigh carefully the significance of the data to the decision.

Tying up the Decision in Conclusions and Recommendations

Since the concluding sections of the outline are another place the executive looks for the meat of the study, these portions should be written in the same manner, whether the outline is basically topical or basically descriptive.

Framing the captions for the conclusions and recommendations and second-level subcaptions follows the same principles as those just set forth for the body of the decision. Second-level subdivisions should be even more specific and more laden with significant figures than they are for the determinants, since this is another spot management's eye is trained to look. The findings of the report should be here in a nutshell.

Second-level subdivisions of the conclusions do not merely retrack each criterion discussion, for the conclusions to a decision-making business report are not merely a summary—they are the synthesis of reasoning into a decision with all the supporting aspects. Here the major subdecisions arrived at in the entire study are presented in a descending order of importance of their own, no matter where they appear in the report body. More than one important idea could certainly come from a single determinant. (One exception to this sort of reasoning is the comparative-evaluation study, in which the choices are ranked in the second-level captions, with supporting data given in third- and subsequent-level subdivisions.) In the second-level captions of the conclusions there should also appear consideration of factors in opposition to the direction of the overall problem answer, with some indication of offsetting factors or how the adverse conditions may be overcome, if applicable. (Note captions B and E in the savings and loan problem outline, Sample Form 10-7).

The recommendations first-level caption should give an idea of what, in essence, is being recommended and at least a hint as to why. The second-level subdivisions should implement the recommendations as specifically as possible, fulfilling the requirements of other second-level subdivisions throughout the entire outline. Adaptations for the descriptive-analytic outline are presented in Sample Form 10-9.

Format and Typing Suggestions

All pages in the report that start a new section have two-inch margins at the top; so CONTENTS or TABLE OF CONTENTS is centered appropriately in solid capitals on line 13 from the top of the sheet. A double space below, the word *Part* or *Chapter* goes against the left margin, and the word *Page* against the right. These words may be indicated with initial capitals underlined, as they are in the sample outlines illustrated here, or typed in solid capitals. The *Synopsis* or *Epitome*, the only prefatory part listed in the table of contents, appears a double space below *Part* or *Chapter*, with an initial capital, underlined. Another double space below, the outline begins.

In the traditional pattern, first-level (I, II, III) captions are typed in solid capitals. It is best not to divide words at line ends; so some lines may necessarily be short. Second-level captions (A, B, C) have initial capitals (first and last words and all other words except articles, prepositions, and conjunctions) underlined either by words or with unbroken underlining. This second level of typographical gradation may be skipped and simply typed

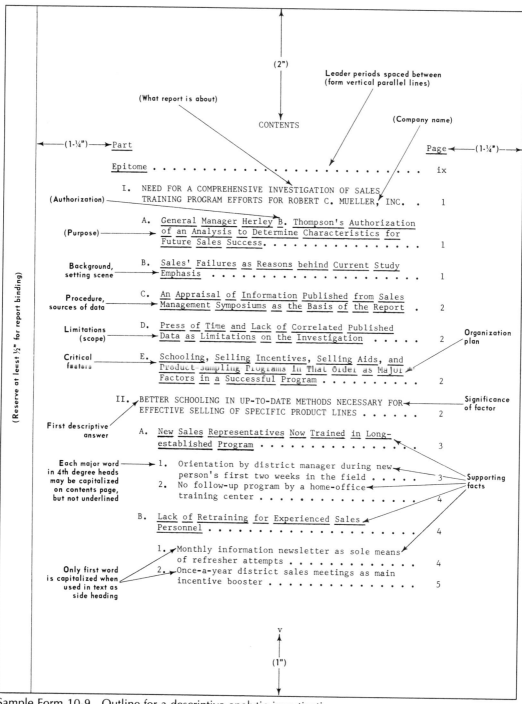

(2")

Leader periods spaced between
(form vertical parallel lines)

(What report is about)

CONTENTS

(Company name)

(1-¼") → Part

Page ← (1-¼")

Epitome   ix

I.   NEED FOR A COMPREHENSIVE INVESTIGATION OF SALES
(Authorization) ──   TRAINING PROGRAM EFFORTS FOR ROBERT C. MUELLER, INC. .   1

(Purpose) ──────→   A.   General Manager Herley B. Thompson's Authorization
of an Analysis to Determine Characteristics for
Future Sales Success.   1

Background,
setting scene ──────→   B.   Sales' Failures as Reasons behind Current Study
Emphasis   1

Procedure,
sources of data ──────→   C.   An Appraisal of Information Published from Sales
Management Symposiums as the Basis of the Report   .   2

Limitations
(scope) ──────→   D.   Press of Time and Lack of Correlated Published
Data as Limitations on the Investigation   2

Organization
plan

Critical
factors ──────→   E.   Schooling, Selling Incentives, Selling Aids, and
Product Sampling Programs In That Order as Major
Factors in a Successful Program   2

II. BETTER SCHOOLING IN UP-TO-DATE METHODS NECESSARY FOR ←
EFFECTIVE SELLING OF SPECIFIC PRODUCT LINES   2

Significance
of factor

First descriptive
answer

A.   New Sales Representatives Now Trained in Long-
established Program   3

Each major word ──→   1.   Orientation by district manager during new
in 4th degree heads   person's first two weeks in the field   3
may be capitalized   2.   No follow-up program by a home-office
on contents page,   training center   4
but not underlined

Supporting
facts

B.   Lack of Retraining for Experienced Sales
Personnel   4

1.   Monthly information newsletter as sole means
Only first word   of refresher attempts   4
is capitalized when   2.   Once-a-year district sales meetings as main
used in text as   incentive booster   5
side heading

v

(1")

Sample Form 10-9   Outline for a descriptive-analytic investigation

462

Line 5
from top

Second descriptive
answer

vi

Part   Page

III. STIMULATING SELLING INCENTIVES RECOMMENDED TO PRODUCE
      OUTSTANDING SALES PERSONNEL   5

      A. Well-defined Bonus Programs to Provide Attractive
          Rewards, Enlarged according to Needs   5

      B. Field Promotions Postulated on a Point System
          Based on Sales Performance   6

IV.   SELLING AIDS ADEQUATELY GEARED TO SALES EFFORT NEEDED
      FOR EFFECTIVE SUPPORT   6

      A. Designing and Procuring Plastic Scale Models of
          Each Product Unit   6

      B. Devising Compact Visual Aids for Each Program . . .   7

      C. Creating Lucid Descriptive Literature   7

      D. Utilizing Leave-behinds After Each Sales Visit . .   7

V.   EXPANDED PRODUCT-SAMPLING PROGRAMS ESSENTIAL FOR
      BETTER CONTROL   8

      A. Granting Increased Supplies of Samples for Each
          Sales Representative   8

          1. Monthly personal selection of samples for
              shipment to suit individual territorial
              needs   8
          2. Follow-up reports to indicate final use and
              disposition of samples in line with sales
              secured   9

      B. Gearing Additional Quotas of Samples to
          Individual Sales Accomplishments   9

VI.   INCREASED SALES LIKELY TO RESULT FROM BETTER
      INTEGRATED TRAINING AND PROMOTION CAMPAIGNS FOR
      INDIVIDUAL PRODUCTS   9

      A. Advertising Can Be Better Coordinated with
          Quarterly Sales Efforts   10

          1. Journal advertisements can be planned and
              executed six months in advance of scheduled
              appearance to help sales people push specific
              lines   10
          2. Direct-mail pieces can be sent with greater
              frequency during planned periods of
              individual product emphasis to a more
              carefully screened mailing list   10

Significance
of factor

Third descriptive
answer

(Significance)

(Significance)

Fourth descriptive
answer

The report answer
given in conclusion
caption and hint
at why

Sample Form 10-9   Continued

vii

Part   Page

       3. Sales personnel can be provided in advance
           with full advertising schedules as well as
           copies of individual ads and mail pieces
           prior to release for use in personal
           selling   10

    B. Establishing a Home Office Sales-training Center
        Is Needed for Initial Training and for Refresher
        Courses   11

       1. New sales representatives can spend second two
           weeks in home office center for additional
           orientation and familiarization   11
       2. Experienced sales people need to undergo sales-
           retraining refresher course following
           eighteen months in the field   11

Appendix   12

Bibliography   15

Sample Form 10-9   Continued

464

without underlining. According to some style manuals, third-level captions (1, 2, 3) are written with initial capitals, as in the second level. Others say that all levels below the second capitalize only the first word and proper nouns and adjectives—the practice followed here.

The leader periods to guide the eye out to the page numbers are spaced between and kept in vertical parallel lines. A period is not placed immediately after the last letter of the last word. Periods continue out to within three or four spaces of the word *page.*

The contents marks the first page to have a small roman number on its face. The title fly, title page, authorization message, and the transmittal are counted but not numbered. If each of these items is made up of one page, the first page of the contents is *v*, centered an inch from the bottom of the sheet. Succeeding pages of the outline are numbered on line 5 at the top right of the sheet, as are other succeeding pages in the report. The words *part* or *chapter* and *page* are reproduced on succeeding pages.

The listing for the *appendix* and the *bibliography* is typed with initial capitals and underlined, in the same way that the *synopsis* is listed. Since these parts are not portions of the report proper, presenting them in this way rather than in solid capitals (as some style manuals do) sets them apart.

THE LIST OF ILLUSTRATIONS

A list of the tables and graphic presentations, which picture in easily readable form the principal findings of the investigation, starts a new page right after the table of contents, with small roman numbers identifying the page sequence. If the report contains only a few such items, the writer may well prepare but a single list to cover both tables and graphics calling it some such inclusive title as *List of Illustrations.* For convenience, illustrations made up of rows and columns are labeled *tables* and all other forms, such as maps, charts, or graphs, are labeled *figures* to avoid a multiplicity of subdivisions in the list. The writer, though, may list each type separately at his or her discretion.

As for the table of contents, the list title is centered in solid capitals 2 inches from the top of the sheet, with the page number centered an inch from the bottom. The word *Table* goes against the left margin and the word *Page* against the right. The table numbers and titles are arranged under *Table* typed with initial capitals and with leader periods guiding the eyes from the last word out to the page number. Individual entries of more than one line are usually single-spaced, with double spaces before and after each entry.

When the list of tables is complete, the word *Figure* appears against the left margin a triple space below the last line of the tables list. Figure numbers and titles are typed in the same form as that employed for tables. Proper arrangement is demonstrated in Sample Form 10-10. If an extensive number

LIST OF ILLUSTRATIONS

Table   Page

I.   Capacities and Rental Charges for Auditoriums and
Convention Halls in Corpus Christi and Selected Texas
Cities, 19xx   12

II.   Major Convention Hotel Facilities and Capacities in
Corpus Christi, 19xx   16

III. Projected Income Statement for First Five Years of
Trans-An Development Company's $5-million Convention
Hotel in Corpus Christi   18

Figure

1.   Population Increase in Corpus Christi, Texas, and the
United States, 19xx to 19yy   4

2.   Disposable Personal Income in Corpus Christi and the
United States, 19xx to 19yy   6

3.   Texas and Houston Hotel Occupancy Trends, 19xx to 19yy   8

4.   Major City Headquarters of 380 State-based Trade and
Professional Associations, 19xx   9

5.   Number of Convention Delegates in Selected Texas
Cities during 19xx   10

6.   Average Daily Convention Expenditure of the 19xx
Delegate in San Antonio, Dallas, Austin, and Corpus
Christi   14

7.   Analysis of Anticipated Break-even Point for Trans-An
Development Company's $5-million Convention
Hotel.   20

Sample Form 10-10   List of illustrations

466

of tables and graphic presentations are employed, the writer may prefer to make a separate list, starting on separate pages, for each type.

THE ABSTRACT OR EPITOME

Right after the list of illustrations (and listed as the first entry on the table of contents) appears a synopsis of the complete report. This report part carries various names: *précis, digest, synopsis, abstract, epitome* but *not summary*. The writer makes the choice. This epitome differs from a summary in that it is a compressed version of the *complete* report rather than merely a digest of the findings. A convenient reduction ratio is one to ten: for ten pages of report text there will be one page of epitome; for a 3,500-word report, there will be approximately 350 words in the epitome.

The epitome is a very important report item, for the writer may spend six months getting the report together only to find that the epitome is the only part top management reads. Thus the epitome may be the reporter's one opportunity to exhibit excellence; consequently the writer's best efforts should be directed toward making this portion of the work superior in every respect.

The epitome is included for the reason given (for management's convenient appraisal) and also to inform the casually interested reader of the report's content. Frequently in the business scene the epitome is reproduced and distributed separately to persons or groups concerned with the findings, even up to the board of directors. In addition, the epitome serves as a guidepost for subsequent reading of the report and a means of review and recall when the reading is done.

The epitome may be written in one of two forms:

1. The *inductive* style, which retracks the report as it was developed, beginning with the introductory portions and working through the findings up to the report answer.

2. The *deductive* presentation, which gives the conclusions and recommendations first. A transition is then made back to the beginning of the report, followed by subsequent development of the findings as support for the opening generalization up to a reiteration of the conclusions and recommendations.

With the complexity of activities in the management environment and the speed with which decisions must be made and implemented, the deductive presentation is the more advantageous. Thus, a plan for writing a deductive epitome follows:

1. Present the essence of the report answer (supplemented by the principal recommendation if applicable) in the first few words. "That

Smylie Automobile Corporation should enter the small-economy-car field (the report answer) through an alliance with a foreign manufacturer (the principal recommendation) is the conclusion of this analysis submitted to President August Smylie, Smylie Automobile Corporation, 2619 Dearborn Road, Detroit, Michigan."

2.   Work in the most pertinent introductory facts in proportionately reduced size.

a.   Authorization and submittal data—the authorizer's name, title, and address, authorization date and manner; the writer's name, title, and address (if other than the authorizer's) and the submittal date; and any collateral uses the report may have.

b.   Any relevant background action—what got the study under way; any financing, organization, or other plans made prior to the investigation.

c.   The research plan.

d.   The principal data sources.

e.   The limitations.

f.   The major decision criteria or critical discussion areas.

3.   Reduce proportionately the findings of each major discussion area, pinpointing the most significant *figures* and facts played up in the body of the report.

a.   Begin each major area with a strong topic sentence that reports the major finding or relates the significance of the material to the problem answer.

b.   Bring each section to a close with a concluding statement which emphasizes the subdecision reached and its impact on the problem answer.

4.   Reiterate the overall decision in a different manner from that used to introduce the epitome and summarize the main supporting arguments.

5.   Compress the principal recommendations, if any are made, to proportionate size.

Compressed writing is usually good writing, for the author is forced to make a single forceful word take the place of several of lesser impact and to cut until each word remaining makes a tangible contribution to the presentation. A tentative epitome may be drafted before the reporter begins writing; but the real meat of the analysis can be captured only after the report is completed. An example of effective epitome writing appears in Sample Form 10-11.

EPITOME

(Triple space) ← → (The answer)

That the Morton investment group should not establish an additional savings-and-loan association is concluded in this report prepared by the Management Research League, Morton, for Mr. Harley P. Baldridge, 9619 Massey Drive, Morton, Anystate, in compliance with his letter of June 23, 19xx.

Authorization, submittal data

(The introduction)

Ample secondary information was procured from such reliable sources as the Bureau of the Census and Banking Redbook on necessary economic data. The Bureau of Business Research proved invaluable in supplying local financial information. The lack of divulged internal statistics as well as press of time limited the study somewhat. The feasibility of Morton's support of an additional savings-and-loan firm was determined through investigation of the elements of demand, competition, and other economic factors.

(Data sources)

(Limitations)

Decision criteria

Summary of first criterion

Demand was arrived at by analysis of population, disposable income, and the savings and mortgage markets. The population in Morton County has increased by 50,000 from 19xx to 19yy. This population increase stimulated the savings market to a $56,000,000 increase over this 10-year period. The total volume of savings not acquired by existing institutions and therefore available for a new association has decreased by 18.4 percent in this time interval. Even with this decline, an ample 19xx volume of approximately $30,000,000 was still available. This savings-market increase was paralleled by the mortgage market. The mortgage market in Morton County gained $42,000,000 over this period. In Morton alone, new construction increased in the last five years by approximately $8,000,000. These figures depict an ample savings and mortgage market arising from population and income increases.

Topic sentence

Supporting statistics

Concluding statement

Second criterion

The competition is sufficient to cause serious detriment to local market success. This competition comes in declining degrees of severity from the existing institutions, local commercial banks, insurance companies, and mortgage companies. The existing institutions have, for the past ten years, averaged holding over 40 percent of the local mortgage market--a highly competitive portion. The commercial banks rank second with 20 percent of a $15,000,000 volume from the mortgage market in 19xx. Life-insurance companies held on to only $1,000,000 of the market in 19xx, which fact limits their importance considerably. The new institution will find the competitive factors to be its main barrier to success.

Topic sentence— major finding

Supporting statistics

Concluding statement

xii

Sample Form 10-11 An example of epitome writing

Third criterion

The other economic factors that may detract from the success of the organization are the cost to compete, financial trends, and national monetary and fiscal policy. The cost to compete has been projected for a three-year period, with no visible profit shown. The financial trends will continue on the upgrade but show signs of leveling off in intensity by late 19yy. The two factors above and the national monetary and fiscal policy of "tight money" or anti-inflation may have a limiting effect on the market potential for the newly proposed institution.

Topic sentence

(Support)

Concluding statement

The conclusions

Despite a favorable ten-year forecast of ample savings and a rising mortgage market, the Morton investment group could use its pledged funds to better advantage than placing them in a new savings association in Morton County. The high degree of competition existing in this area is the main limiting factor to long-term success. A projected financial statement showing a slow trend of expected profit, coupled with an anticipated unfavorable national fiscal policy, combine to render the establishment of a new association at this time unfeasible.

Topic sentence

Reiteration of opening decision

Sample Form 10-11   Continued

11

Convincing Presentation of the Findings

Communication is one of the great crossroads
where many pass but few tarry.

Anonymous

In the beginning, the analyst faced with shaping a consequential decision finds it necessary to break the elements of the problem into a hierarchy of subproblems until a level that can be solved is found. Working through a series of solutions and subdecisions, the analyst finally synthesizes subanswers into the overall problem answer. The researcher following the successive stages of the analytical process presented thus far in this book has that part of the work completed: the decision is made and its aspects set up in a well-constructed outline. Now the reporter is ready to record the decision in such a way as to convince the wary reader with a vested interest in the outcome of the soundness of the findings and the good judgment of the ultimate choices—the second step in stage VI of the agenda introduced in Chapter 7, writing the main body of the report.

The reflective thinking that led to the decision was a cumulative process, snowballing into a compact entity of interacting forces, which does not at this point lend itself well to segmentation. The isolation of a single segment minimizes its meaning through removal from its context; the remaining segments as well suffer in continuity and integrity. Yet the finite mind of the report reader, unable to handle the compact entity in its entirety, will find understanding only through the recording of the successive stages of that decision. The level of sophistication of the recording process depends upon the sophistication of the reader. If the reader has only a surface knowledge of mathematics and statistics, the report writer may find it necessary to abandon the machinery of computations and present findings in the realm of the reader's anticipated level of comprehension. The reporter may have to forego the use of such words as *standard deviation, significance tests, trajectory prediction,* finding simpler ways of explaining what has been discovered. Much of the elaborate work may necessarily be relegated to an appendix so that the reader or readers may check according to individual capacities and interests.

The communications skills of the report writer assume parallel importance with his or her analytical abilities, for if the analyst is unable to impart the elements of a decision in a convincing and effective manner, the results are minimized. This chapter blends the report writer's decision-making and communication skills through consideration of the following segments:

1. Writing the introduction.
2. Report format and style.
3. Tabular and graphic illustration.
4. Drafting the contents sections.
5. The concluding portions.
6. Report writing style.
7. Scholarly documentation—footnotes and bibliography.
8. The appendix or appendices.

WRITING THE INTRODUCTION

The introduction should clarify the intention of the report for the main reader and for possible auxiliary readers of varying classifications now and for the future. Choices of makeup for the introduction are given on pages 447–450 of Chapter 10. Filling in the details through the writing of the introduction may also be helpful in clarifying the analyst's thinking about the problem and in making sure that all the boundaries set for the investigation by the authorizer have been considered. Elaboration for writing the divisions is given only where significant suggestion seems pertinent.

Authorization and Submittal Data

The title of the section or chapter and the second-level caption to head this division are transferred from the outline to the text according to instructions given in Exhibit 11-1, typographical gradations for captions. The purpose of the investigation is the most important introductory element and worthy of

First level   CHAPTER III

1. Chapter number and title, two
   inches from top, solid capi-   UNFAVORABLE MARKET DUE TO COMPETITION FROM
   tals, centered by line, tri-
   ple space between chapter num-   MAJOR COMPANIES AND SUBSTITUTES
   ber and title, double-spaced
   for continued lines, inverted
   pyramid, triple space to first . . . .
   line of writing. . . . .
               OR   (triple space ahead)
2. Part number followed by a peri-   III. UNFAVORABLE MARKET DUE TO COMPETITION
   od, part title in solid capi-
   tals, centered by line, triple   FROM MAJOR COMPANIES AND
   space ahead and double space
   after.   BARITE SUBSTITUTES

  . . . .
  . . . .

Second level   (triple space ahead)
                A. Control of 85 Percent of the Market
Centered heading, underlined, ini-
tial capitals, double-spaced for   by Five Major Companies
continued lines, inverted pyramid,
triple space ahead of caption, ...
double space after. . . . .

Third level   (triple space ahead)
              1. Trend toward Company Retail Stock Points
Centered heading, not underlined,
initial capitals, double spaced . . . .
for continued lines, inverted pyra- . . . .
mid, triple space ahead of caption, ...
double space after. . . . .

Fourth level   (double space ahead)
            (a) Mineral substitutes hold
1. Flush with left margin, under-   small share of market
   lined, first words and proper
   words capitalized, single- . . . .
   spaced for continued lines, ...
   lines broken at approximately . . . .
   the line center, double space . . . .
   before and after caption. . . . .
               OR   (double space ahead)
2. Caption typed in boxed cut-ins   (a) Mineral substitutes . . . .
   (of same width throughout the   hold small share . . . .
   report), underlined, first   of market . . . .
   word and proper words capital-   . . . .
   ized, single-spaced for con- . . . .
   tinued lines, double space be- . . . .
   fore and after caption.

Exhibit 11-1   Typographical gradations for captions

<u>Fifth</u> <u>level</u>

Same as fourth level except
not underlined.

(1) Technical disadvantages
        of iron ore and galena

. . . .
. . . .

<u>Sixth</u> <u>level</u>   (double space ahead)

Heading run into paragraph followed
by a period or a period and dash,
underlined, first and proper words
capitalized.

(a) <u>Employment of air drilling</u>. . . . . . .
. . . .
. . . .
. . . .

NOTE: The writer may skip any caption level if he or she chooses, but no level should
        be used out of sequence. If levels are skipped, the letter-number sequence
        will be different from that pictured here; for example, if A- or second-
        level form is skipped, the 1-level becomes the A-level, and so on.

        The writer may also elect to skip the letter-number labels from all levels
        except the first.

Exhibit 11-1   Continued

474

placement in the first sentence. Several good ways of phrasing the purpose are available:

1. *A well-phrased question that highlights the value to be derived from the findings:* "Will the addition of ready mixes to the product line of Harley Mills be an effective way to bolster lagging sales? To aid in answering this question, this report, orally authorized on June 26, 19xx, by Mr. Thomas Y. Bentley, president, is submitted by Morris H. Iverson, product and market analyst, on July 17, 19xx."

2. *An infinitive phrase:* "To determine the best distribution system for freshly chilled orange juice to Eastern Seaboard Markets from Orlando, Florida, is the purpose of this study, authorized by President Max Hendricks, Fresh Juice, Inc. Presented on July 17, 19xx, by Henry Talbot, research analyst, Market Research Associates, 810–816 Perry Brooks Building, Orlando, this analysis was made in line with the requirements set out in Mr. Hendricks's letter of June 22."

3. *A declarative statement:* "Determining the financial feasibility of the proposed Hidalgo plant for the processing of Mexican barite is the purpose of this study authorized by President David Crashaw, Valley Mining Company, 231 Market Road, Encino, California, in a December 1, 19xx, memorandum."

Other essential elements of the authorization and submittal data are the authorizer's name, title, address, and the authorization date and manner (by letter, memorandum, telephone, orally, or such, as in the examples given); and the writer's name, title, address (if different from the authorizer's), and the submittal date. Any collateral purposes the report may serve should be worked in:

Should the answer prove favorable, the material in this report may furnish the data for an appeal to the Securities Exchange Commission for permission to issue stock.

If the collateral purposes involve dates or other restrictions, they, too, should be specified as part of the background orientation.

The writing style is impersonal in the formal report: no first- or second-person references, such as *I, we, our, you* and no third-person references to "the writer" or "the reporter." Eliminating such personal references minimizes bias by placing the burden of proof on report findings rather than on the opinions of the writer and reader. A report dealing with current data for an immediately anticipated decision logically takes the present tense (or present-tense derivatives) as the typical time viewpoint. Obviously, antecedent and future action will be phrased in the proper tense; but current activity, permanent truth, and references to report parts are appropriately couched in present tense. (Further suggestions for effective writing style are covered under the discussion of the content areas later in this chapter.)

The Background History

Background history usually begins with a statement of the initiating force, which, as a by-product, plays up the significance of the study:

> The fact that no national manufacturer of luxury home furnishings operates in this state prompted Vanhedron, Inc. to look into the possibilities of producing quality living-, dining-, and bedroom furniture for a five-year trial run in the surrounding five-state market.

Since business reports are concerned with brevity for management's quick use, the sentences should be both functional and informative—functional in achieving their intended purpose and informative in packing background data into the fabric as facts already of record instead of recounting them in flat narrative style. The inept writer might be guilty of introducing the facts for the sentence just given in a primer arrangement such as this:

> No national manufacturer of luxury home furnishings operates in this state; therefore Vanhedron, Inc. decided to look into the possibilities of introducing its quality lines here. It will produce living-, dining-, and bedroom furniture. The company plans a five-year trial run. The products will be distributed in the surrounding five-state market.

The skilled writer bypasses the narrative stage by weaving accomplished facts into the fabric of a single functional sentence that moves ahead with the subject.

If no current effect is based on past history, there is no justification for including it. The background material for a business report generally embraces the preliminary organizational and financial planning undertaken by the company on the project prior to the investigation: a description that demonstrates size, volume, aspects to be covered, and such; whether the venture will be financed from current assets, through borrowed capital, through a stock issue, or how; the market limits of the product or service; the expected profit potential and the timing. These ideas are suggested as thought springboards; each writer determines the essential ideas for the particular problem.

Most of the information that makes up the introduction is set out in the authorization instrument; but in the interest of making each report section autonomous and of keeping the record straight, the report writer outlines here the background of the problem. The trick of good treatment is the same packing of detail into the fabric of the functional sentence already illustrated:

> With the rental of a 20,000-square-foot plant at Mayhew protected with a 90-day option, the profit potential of the manufacturer of 5,000 units annually is ready for investigation.

The writer has, in addition, the problem of deciding which of the background facts should go under preliminary organization and financial planning and which are part of the limits and scope of the investigation. These decisions are of minimal importance, as long as all pertinent data are recorded. Any elaborate schedules or exhibits presenting detailed plans should probably be referred to here and placed in an appropriate appendix. Small maps, organization charts, tables, or other sorts of illustrative material are appropriately placed at strategic points in the introduction. If an illustration appears opposite the first page of the introduction, the first page of the text of the report is thus numbered 2—a plain Arabic number.

Data Sources and the Research Scheme

The complexity of the research scheme determines whether the writer will describe it in the main introductory division or whether a separate first-level introductory section will be needed. For survey data, these things will ordinarily need to be delineated:

1.   What directories or mailing lists were used, what random- or non-random-sampling procedures were employed, the confidence level assigned, a statement that the entire universe was surveyed, or such. Part of the treatment will justify the methods selected and the sample size.

2.   The thinking behind the questionnaire preparation or the interview check list, authority or justification for designing it in the particular way chosen, any special features of its arrangement. A copy of the questionnaire will appear here or in the appendix.

3.   The plan followed in drafting the cover letter. The writer will also include a copy of it here or in the appendix.

4.   An explanation of follow-up procedures and their productivity.

5.   An analysis of questionnaire returns, along with the statistical measures employed to estimate the margin of error, or such. The writer will describe the sample as it now stands, compare it to the sample originally designed, and point up implications the present sample may have on the findings.

If secondary research is the chosen method, the reporter writer will

1.   Tell what indexes were consulted or what people were talked to or written to in the search for data.

2.   Name the principal publications consulted (not a complete bibliography, obviously) to give the reader a measure for evaluating the quality of the work done.

3.   Delineate the plan of attack: the statistical measures employed, what criteria the findings were measured against, how the data were put together in usable form for the report—in short, a detailed outline of the procedures followed.

If special research approaches are employed for different report divisions for either primary or secondary research, the writer may prefer to tell about them at the beginning of each division.

Defining the Limits and Limitations of the Study

Whether the reporter chooses to have a separate second-level division to define the limits of the study or to combine such material with the limitations, some phase of the introduction will narrow the treatment down to size: the geographic area covered, the alternatives to be investigated in the comparative-evaluation study and why, the specific level of a complex entity to be analyzed, the time period involved, or whatever means were used to limit the study to manageable proportions. It may be necessary to identify the assumptions under which the writer worked and to show why the assumptions are considered logical. Any gaps in available information should be pointed out—and how they were compensated for or why they were significant or insignificant. Thus the writer defines for the readers the boundaries within which the findings of the study are valid. Attitude toward the work should be one of confidence in the report for its intended purpose, lest the authorizer develop a reluctance to part with the promised compensation.

In addition, the writer must frankly admit ways in which the study might have been improved, suggest other areas of research that might be helpful in substantiating the conclusions, point up ways in which changes in the social-political-economic-technological climate could affect the answers, or name hypotheses growing from the study which seem worthy of further investigation. (The writer may incorporate some of this material into recommendations, if that seems more preferable.)

The size of the report may be limited by circumstances—for example, too little money or time. Since the writer does not want to deprecate the work effort needlessly, it is best in many cases to frame such deficiencies in some positive fashion:

> The validity of the conclusions might have been improved with a parallel consumer survey, for which no funds were budgeted in preliminary planning.
>
> The study focuses on only the essential determinants within its limitations and should serve as a sound basis for a tentative decision.
>
> The current nature of the data necessitated a decision before the latest statistical compilations were available.

Some adverse circumstance might actually have occurred to impede the investigation; the writer should report it. Care should be taken to keep the limitations from sounding like excuses and from making the authorizing company seem to be at fault in *not* supplying adequate money, allowing sufficient time, or such.

Critical Discussion Areas and Preview of the Organizational Plan

In a separate second-level introductory division or as a part of the description of the sequential development of the report, the writer (1) names specifically the criteria by which the working hypothesis is tested or the critical-discussion areas into which the subject matter is divided, (2) justifies their selection, (3) indicates (possibly by part or chapter number) the sequence in which they appear, and (4) justifies the sequence unless the reason for it is obvious. An extra sentence or so points toward the rounding out of the report in conclusions and recommendations (if needed).

Even though the decision determinants are set up in the caption for this part of the introduction—as they are in the descriptive outline—the opening paragraph of the preview names them, as though the caption were omitted altogether. Throughout the report, the opening paragraph sentences are written so that they do not depend upon the captions for their meaning. In referring to report parts, the writer employs the present tense: "An evaluation of anticipated profit potential *appears* in Part IV." It *appears* there now and forever. A sample introduction for critical evaluation is exhibited in Sample Form 11-1 (completed in Sample Form 11-2).

REPORT FORMAT

Typing the body of the report with paper placed over the page guide prepared for the prefatory parts assures margin and arrangement uniformity throughout the presentation. Ways of transferring the captions from the outline to the text (including proper spacing, typography, and capitalization) are explained fully in Exhibit 11-1, typographical gradations for captions. If the report sections will be short (not more than five or six pages of text each), you will probably prefer to write it continuously, dividing the material into *parts* rather than *chapters*. In such a case, the first page will be set up as in Sample Form 11-1. When you have completed a roman section, simply triple space after the last line of writing and type in the number and caption for the next roman section as in Sample Form 11-2. If a new section happens to fall at the top of the page, place the caption on line 7 instead of dropping it 2 inches from the top.

For long reports separated into chapters, omit the report title on the first page of the introduction, placing CHAPTER I in solid capitals two inches from the top of the sheet, with the chapter caption appearing a triple space

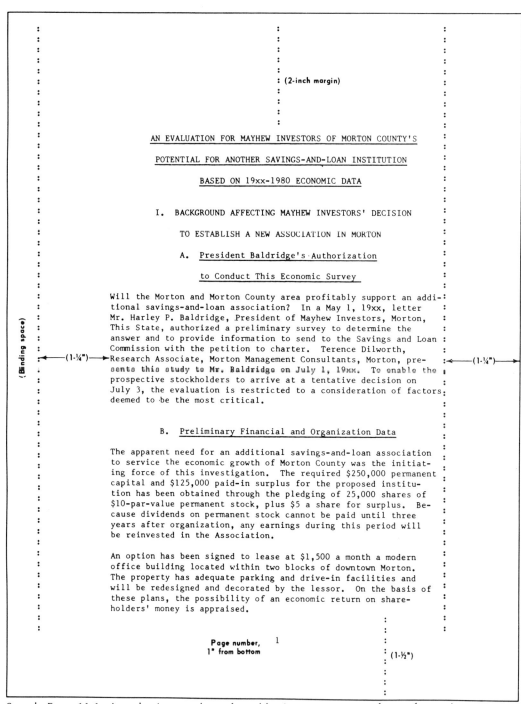

AN EVALUATION FOR MAYHEW INVESTORS OF MORTON COUNTY'S

POTENTIAL FOR ANOTHER SAVINGS-AND-LOAN INSTITUTION

BASED ON 19xx-1980 ECONOMIC DATA

I. BACKGROUND AFFECTING MAYHEW INVESTORS' DECISION

TO ESTABLISH A NEW ASSOCIATION IN MORTON

A. President Baldridge's Authorization

to Conduct This Economic Survey

Will the Morton and Morton County area profitably support an additional savings-and-loan association? In a May 1, 19xx, letter
Mr. Harley P. Baldridge, President of Mayhew Investors, Morton,
This State, authorized a preliminary survey to determine the
answer and to provide information to send to the Savings and Loan
Commission with the petition to charter. Terence Dilworth,
Research Associate, Morton Management Consultants, Morton, presents this study to Mr. Baldridge on July 1, 19xx. To enable the
prospective stockholders to arrive at a tentative decision on
July 3, the evaluation is restricted to a consideration of factors
deemed to be the most critical.

B. Preliminary Financial and Organization Data

The apparent need for an additional savings-and-loan association
to service the economic growth of Morton County was the initiating force of this investigation. The required $250,000 permanent
capital and $125,000 paid-in surplus for the proposed institu-
tion has been obtained through the pledging of 25,000 shares of
$10-par-value permanent stock, plus $5 a share for surplus. Because dividends on permanent stock cannot be paid until three
years after organization, any earnings during this period will
be reinvested in the Association.

An option has been signed to lease at $1,500 a month a modern
office building located within two blocks of downtown Morton.
The property has adequate parking and drive-in facilities and
will be redesigned and decorated by the lessor. On the basis of
these plans, the possibility of an economic return on shareholders' money is appraised.

Page number, 1
1" from bottom

(1-½")

Sample Form 11-1   Introduction to a long, formal business report, page format for sections

C. Selected Secondary Economic Data as

the Base of the Study

Important sources of nationwide statistics for this report were publications of the Bureau of the Census, Department of Commerce, and the Federal Reserve Board. Sales Management, The State Banking Redbook, published financial statements of Morton savings-and-loan associations, and Percentage Summaries for Savings-and-Loan Associations released by the Federal Home Loan Bank of Little Rock provided valuable state and local data. In addition, interviews with Mr. B. Y. Mathis of the Department of Planning of the Morton Chamber of Commerce and with Dr. Jack Cashin, Executive Vice President of the State Savings and Loan League, proved quite fruitful. Trend-analysis techniques were employed to project current trends of population, mortgage demand, effective buying income, and growth of existing associations. Finally, the chances of success of a new association in the county were measured against data thus assembled.

D. Geographical Boundaries, Derived Data, and

Restricted Scope as Limiting Factors

(1-¼")

Confining the scope of this report to the geographical limits of Morton County rather than to the 100-mile radius legally permitted for an association's operation and restricting the coverage to criteria of greatest impact wield a minimizing influence on the validity of the decision. In addition, national statistics were modified in line with area economic conditions in cases for which local figures were not available. The comprehensiveness of the analysis and the care with which interpretations were made should provide a sound base for a tentative decision when the stockholders meet on July 3.

(1-¼")

E. Demand, Competition, and Profitability

in That Order as the Major Criteria

The most important variables affecting a decision to establish another savings-and-loan institution are demand, competition, and cost-profit potential. The demand factor, discussed in Part II, covers primarily an appraisal of the demand for residential mortgage funds resulting from the continued growth of residential construction in Morton County and the anticipated supply of loanable funds to be derived from an increase in population and effective buying income. The influence of the competition on the new institution's ability to capture its proportionate share of the market, considered to be the next most critical decision factor,

(1-½")

Sample Form 11-1   Continued

is presented in Part III. The capacity of the new firm to realize a satisfactory profit within a reasonable time is evaluated in Part IV. A final section pulls together the findings of the report into conclusions as to what sort of action Mayhew Investors should take.

II. DYNAMIC GROWTH IN DEMAND FOR AND SUPPLY OF LOANABLE

FUNDS AS EVIDENCE OF PROBABLE SUCCESS

The potential demand for an additional facility to provide residential mortgage funds and to act as a public depository for consumer savings is based upon historical data of actual mortgage requirements and savings tendencies during previous years. The growth trend of the mortgage market is examined first; next comes an appraisal of Morton's position in the business-activity index; and finally, an analysis of growth trends in the number of households and in consumer savings as they relate to mortgage requirements and savings characteristics for Morton and Morton County now and for the future.

← (1-¼") →   ← (1-¼") →

A. 130-percent Growth in Mortgage Volume Since 19xx

as Indication of Expanding Demand

One of the primary determinants of the success of a savings-and-loan association is the potential market of residential mortgages available to the association. The subsequent analysis of the status of mortgage demand is illustrative of the exploding growth of residential construction in Morton and Morton County, as shown by the 130-percent growth of the mortgage volume in Figure 1.

1. $559 million increase
    projected in mortgage
    volume by 19xx

The growth of the residential-construction mortgage volume from $32.3 million in 19xx to an anticipated volume of $121.7 million, shown in Figure 2, will result in a total $559 million in additional construction for Morton and Morton County during the 19xx-19yy period, under the assumption that the present growth trend will remain stable. This increased building activity will, in addition to stimulating the local economy, require funds not currently available through present banking facilities. This unfulfilled need will be accommodated by financial institutions foreign to the local area, thereby leading to greater outside influence over the local economy unless additional financial facilities are established in Morton.

**Short page—no room for caption
and at least two lines of text**

Sample Form 11-2   Succession of divisions for report not divided into chapters, box-cut-in arrangement

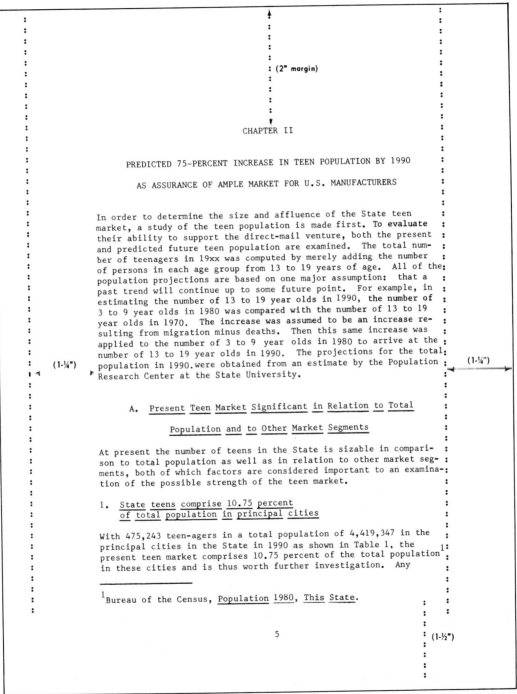

(2" margin)

CHAPTER II

PREDICTED 75-PERCENT INCREASE IN TEEN POPULATION BY 1990

AS ASSURANCE OF AMPLE MARKET FOR U.S. MANUFACTURERS

In order to determine the size and affluence of the State teen market, a study of the teen population is made first. To evaluate their ability to support the direct-mail venture, both the present and predicted future teen population are examined. The total number of teenagers in 19xx was computed by merely adding the number of persons in each age group from 13 to 19 years of age. All of the population projections are based on one major assumption: that a past trend will continue up to some future point. For example, in estimating the number of 13 to 19 year olds in 1990, the number of 3 to 9 year olds in 1980 was compared with the number of 13 to 19 year olds in 1970. The increase was assumed to be an increase resulting from migration minus deaths. Then this same increase was applied to the number of 3 to 9 year olds in 1980 to arrive at the number of 13 to 19 year olds in 1990. The projections for the total population in 1990.were obtained from an estimate by the Population Research Center at the State University.

(1-¼")

A. Present Teen Market Significant in Relation to Total

Population and to Other Market Segments

At present the number of teens in the State is sizable in comparison to total population as well as in relation to other market segments, both of which factors are considered important to an examination of the possible strength of the teen market.

1. State teens comprise 10.75 percent
    of total population in principal cities

With 475,243 teen-agers in a total population of 4,419,347 in the principal cities in the State in 1990 as shown in Table 1, the present teen market comprises 10.75 percent of the total population[1] in these cities and is thus worth further investigation. Any

_____

[1]Bureau of the Census, Population 1980, This State.

5

(1-½")

Sample Form 11-3   First page of chapter, third-level caption, footnote indication below, as in Sample Form 11-3. Each new chapter will start in the same manner on a new page.

Arabic numbers are used from the first page of the report proper through the last page of the appended parts. Pages with titles at the top are numbered at the bottom; those that do not start new sections are numbered two-thirds of an inch from the top, line 5, flush with the right margin.

All indented blocks (such as those used for enumerations and quotations of four lines or more) are indented five to ten spaces from right and left margins, with the same indentation plan used for all indentations. Spacing suggestions for footnotes and quotations are given in the discussion of scholarly documentation, pages 522–527.

TABULAR AND GRAPHIC PRESENTATION

When the report writer is ready to present the reader an assemblage of quantitative findings, the data are already classified and tabulated and the statistical analyses are completed. The analyst may choose to display the data in the tables into which they were originally classified, organized, and processed, or to picture them in some form of graphic illustration. For simplicity, rows and columns are designated as *tables* and other forms of illustration may be indicated with the overall label *figure,* to avoid a multiplicity of divisions in the list of illustrations.

Since brevity in the business report is a requisite, pinpointing the data to be presented to those most essential to the decision becomes the guiding force as to what to include. Complete tabulations (general-purpose tables) and computations may be placed in the appendix, with excerpts and summarizations developed from them interspersed in appropriate spots in the text. Text tables, then, are special-purpose displays rather than mere repositories of data.

Tables may be the choice when exact representations are pertinent, for graphics may be read only in approximations. Graphics are preferable to tables in providing the reader with a quick grasp of relationships, provided that the number of classifications is not too great for adequate picturization. How much tabular or graphic illustration to include is a matter of individual judgment. An illustration is employed to make the text easier to understand, to emphasize a point made, to carry the gist of the findings for the casual reader, and perhaps for the pedestrian reason of making the report more inviting. Certainly, too many tabular and graphic presentations tend to break the continuity of the writing. As a sort of working-rule minimum, the writer should include at least one illustration for each major point (major factor or component). From there on, additional enrichment illustrations are a matter of individual preference.

In view of the broad coverage of this book, treatment of tabular and graphic presentation is limited to that which is generally most useful. For specialized forms, the analyst may need to consult a more comprehensive reference.

Statistical Tables

The following suggestions are designed to aid the writer in displaying tables in good order and in making the most of the meaning contained in the data.

Spacing According to Size.   Tables with as many as three columns including the stub (the left-hand line indicators) should occupy the same line width as that used for the rest of the text. Tables with only the stub and one column, though, will have an appropriately reduced line width for easier reading, unless the stub lines are rather long. Leader lines to guide the eye from the end of the stub to the column aid reading, as in Exhibit 11-2.

For tables with many columns, margins on both sides may be extended horizontally outside the regular text line width, if doing so will make possible display of material on the regular size of paper. In such a case, the left margin should never be less than one inch nor the others less than one-half inch to escape the binder's blade. Tables with still too many columns to fit on a page lengthwise may be typed sideways, as in Exhibit 11-3.

If it is necessary to display the tables on larger sheets than are used for the text, the large sheets should be placed flush with the top and left edges of the page assembly, folded up from the bottom and in from the right side. From the left edge of the fold-up a strip one inch wide should be trimmed so that this left edge will not be caught in the binding. The folds from the bottom up and from the right in should be made one-half inch short of the regular page dimensions to avoid having the folded portions cut in the trimming process. If more than one right fold-in is necessary, the first fold should be made one-half inch from the right edge of the page assembly; for the second, the fold should be made two inches from the binding edge; and successive folds should be arranged parallel with the first one. The same type of procedure may be employed for successive bottom-up folds.

Tables typed lengthwise or sideways that are too long vertically may be continued on to successive pages with appropriate labeling, as in Exhibit 11-4. If there are not too many columns, half the table may appear on the left half of the sheet and half on the right, as in Exhibit 11-5. Tables too large for any of these suggested methods may be reduced photographically.

Tabular Identification.   Tables are numbered consecutively throughout the report, including those in the appendix. Since tables are usually read downward, they are customarily labeled at the top. TABLE typed in solid capital letters, plus an appropriate Arabic or roman number, is centered at the top of the tabular illustration. Arabic numbers are probably easier to

TABLE 2

ESTIMATES AND PROJECTIONS OF THE POPULATION OF THE
UNITED STATES BY AGE AND SEX, 1970-1995

(in thousands)

Age Group	1970	1975	1980	1990	1995	% Increase 1970-1995
			Males			
Under 5	10,352	10,838	12,245	15,602	16,877	63.0%
5-9	9,572	10,374	10,851	13,944	15,597	62.9
10-14	8,595	9,601	10,394	12,269	13,956	62.3
15-19	6,814	8,612	9,609	10,873	12,266	80.0
Total	35,333	39,425	43,099	52,688	58,696	66.0
			Females			
Under 5	10,013	10,403	11,746	14,955	16,171	61.5
5-9	9,254	10,046	10,426	13,383	14,964	61.7
10-14	8,314	9,288	10,075	11,791	13,407	61.2
15-19	6,651	8,365	9,331	10,496	11,829	77.8
Total	34,232	38,102	41,578	50,625	56,371	64.6
TOTAL	69,565	77,527	84,677	103,313	115,067	65.4

SOURCE: For the 1970-1995 data, see U.S. Department of Commerce, Bureau of the Census, Current Population Reports--Population Estimates, Series P-25, No. 279 (February 4, 1978), pp. 6,7.

Exhibit 11-2   Standard table format, illustrating cut-in headings, leader periods, subtotals, and total

TABLE 3

COMPARISON OF CHARACTERISTICS OF FEDERAL RESERVE MEMBER BANK LOANS TO NEW FIRMS WITH CHARACTERISTICS OF LOANS MADE TO ALL FIRMS AND TO OLDER FIRMS

Type of Firm	All Loans		Type of Maturity				Secured Loans	
			Short-term Loans[a]		Intermediate and Long-term Loans[b]			
	Amount	Percent	Amount	Percent	Amount	Percent	Amount	Percent
			Number of Loans (in thousands)					
All business firms	$1,281	100.0	$801	62.5	$479	37.4	$856	66.8
New firms[c]	107	100.0	66	61.3	41	38.7	77	72.0
Older firms	1,174	100.0	736	62.7	438	37.3	779	66.3
Firms with assets of less than $250,000	999	100.0	621	62.2	378	37.8	669	67.0
New firms	94	100.0	...	...	...	...	...	...
Older firms	905	100.0	...	...	...	...	...	...
			Amount of Loans (in billions)					
All business firms	$40.6	100.0	$25.2	62.1	$15.4	37.9	$20.4	50.2
New firms	2.0	100.0	1.1	54.1	0.9	45.9	1.5	76.0
Older firms	38.6	100.0	24.1	62.4	14.5	37.6	18.9	49.0
Firms with assets of less than $250,000	6.7	100.0	4.1	61.2	2.6	38.8	5.2	77.6
New firms	0.6	100.0	...	...	...	...	...	...
Older firms	6.1	100.0	...	...	...	...	...	...

[a]Maturity of less than one year.
[b]Maturity of over one year.
[c]Those firms established within the preceding twenty-four months period.

SOURCE: Federal Reserve System.

Exhibit 11-3   Table typed sideways, spanner and cut-in headings

TABLE 6

YEARLY VOLUME FOR CRITICAL AND NONCRITICAL PRODUCTS,
BANLON COMPANY, 19xx

Product Number	Cases Sold	Price per Case	Dollar Volume
	Critical Products		
1	87,996	$ 7.20	$ 633,571
2	16,917	7.40	125,186
3	68,203	5.20	354,656
4	12,376	5.60	69,306
5	92,945	9.60	892,272
6	17,418	10.25	178,535
7	48,900	7.00	342,300
8	6,673	12.40	82,745
9	25,964	12.95	336,234
10	15,433	2.80	43,212
11	92,797	7.20	668,138
12	84,055	4.85	407,667
13	20,526	4.15	85,183
14	9,132	7.20	65,750
15	103,682	2.20	228,100
16	131,968	4.85	640,045
17	13,664	13.20	180,365
18	9,569	13.20	126,311
19	4,138	14.80	61,242
20	76,759	5.60	429,850
21	11,773	6.60	77,702
22	7,316	5.70	41,701
23	13,029	7.60	99,020
24	28,613	3.90	111,591
25	2,605	15.60	40,638
Total	1,002,451	--	$6,321,320

Exhibit 11-4   Vertical table continued on to second page

488

TABLE 6--Continued

Product Number	Cases Sold	Price per Case	Dollar Volume
		Noncritical Products	
26	6,900	$ 3.48	$ 24,012
27	9,397	4.00	37,588
28	3,788	5.60	21,213
29	1,320	9.00	11,880
30	3,723	10.35	38,533
31	490	11.50	5,635
32	4,300	4.92	21,156
33	3,058	7.80	23,852
34	4,290	7.00	30,030
35	1,978	11.50	22,747
36	1,881	14.50	27,275
37	910	16.50	15,015
38	3,828	3.78	14,470
39	6,650	4.20	27,930
40	1,045	12.00	12,540
41	1,090	4.32	4,709
42	465	8.70	4,045
43	2,906	3.88	11,275
44	2,543	3.78	9,620
45	115	5.90	679
46	177	5.10	903
47	208	7.30	1,518
48	2,875	8.35	24,006
49	922	3.20	2,950
50	1,554	3.20	4,973
51	3,115	3.60	11,214
52	9,221	3.90	35,962
53	1,143	12.40	14,173
54	100	5.85	585
55	1,925	7.60	14,630
56	817	24.95	20,384
57	1,019	21.50	21,909
58	2,454	5.22	12,810
Total	86,209	--	$ 530,221
GRAND TOTAL	1,088,660	--	$6,851,541

SOURCE: Company file data.

Exhibit 11-4   Continued

TABLE 6

NUMBER OF COMMUNITIES IN THE UNITED STATES WITH
INDUSTRIAL DEVELOPMENT CORPORATIONS
BY GEOGRAPHIC DIVISION, 19xx

TOTAL	1,801			
		South Atlantic (Continued)		
New England	103	Virginia	55	
Maine	23	West Virginia	39	
New Hampshire	29	North Carolina	70	
Vermont	11	South Carolina	c	
Massachusetts	22	Georgia	123	
Rhode Island	3	Florida	26	
Connecticut	15			
		East South Central	145	
Middle Atlantic	105	Kentucky	41	
New York	53	Tennessee	92	
New Jersey	a	Alabama	3	
Pennsylvania	52	Mississippi	9	
East North Central	345	West South Central	248	
Ohio	49	Arkansas	118	
Indiana	25	Louisiana	15	
Illinois	24	Oklahoma	44	
Michigan	79	Texas	71	
Wisconsin	168			
		Mountain	39	
West North Central	461	Montana	3	
Minnesota	109	Idaho	7	
Iowa	99	Wyoming	3	
Missouri	149	Colorado	9	
North Dakota	11	New Mexico	1	
South Dakota	13	Arizona	11	
Nebraska	33	Utah	4	
Kansas	47	Nevada	1	
South Atlantic	325	Pacific	30	
Delaware	b	Washington	7	
Maryland	12	Oregon	10	
		California	13	

[a]A recently enacted law authorizes the establishment of local business development corporations in New Jersey.

[b]The promotion of industrial development is carried on by the governor's Committee to Promote Delaware, Inc., and by local chambers of commerce.

[c]Development activities are carried on by county development boards, local chambers of commerce committees, and private community development.

SOURCE: U. S. Department of Commerce, Office of Area Development.

Exhibit 11-5   Two halves of table typed in parallel columns

read when many illustrations are presented. A double space below the table number, the table title is centered in solid capitals. If more than one line is necessary, single space the extra lines in inverted-pyramid fashion. The table title should be so completely self-identifying that no reference to the table itself is necessary for the reader to know what it contains. The *who* or *what*, *when*, and *where* of other types of titles should be included in as few words as are feasible to carry the content. No abbreviations are permissible in the main caption of a table or graphic. Complete identification in the list of illustrations is particularly helpful to executives who may have time only for scanning the report parts that are of special concern to them.

For tables typed sideways on right-facing pages, the number and title go toward the binding edge so that they may be read by turning the page clockwise. For a table placed opposite the text reference to it, and thus on a left-facing page, the identification goes toward the free edge. It is consequently important to plan in advance where the tables will go so that the extra binding space may be added in the right place. A single space below the last line of the table title, a double line is made with the typewriter underliner.

When tables are continued on successive pages, continuations are identified with only the table number, a dash, and the word *Continued* centered at the top: TABLE 2—*Continued*, as in Exhibit 11-4. All the box headings should be repeated on every page in precisely the same way that they appear on the first page. For sidewise tables continued on successive pages, the *continued* indication and the box headings need not be repeated for facing pages, and the bottom rule is omitted on all pages except the last.

For tabular material borrowed from other sources, full credit should in fairness be given to the original compiler. The authoritative nature of the original compilation in addition may lend prestige to your reasoning. Data from universally known sources, such as the Bureau of the Census and other government publications widely available, may be cited rather generally. Citations from less well-known publications merit the full footnote treatment discussed later in this chapter. Footnote with small arabic letters any word item or entry in the data display that may not be readily meaningful to the reader as in Exhibit 11-3: "Short-term loans,[a]" "New firms.[c]"

A double space below the last line of the table or its last footnote, the word *Source* (either in solid capitals or with an initial capital underlined) followed by a colon is placed at the left margin of the table. The source itself is typed with initial capitals and underlined for a book or periodical reference. Carried-over lines may either be indented five spaces or placed even with the first word of the source citation. A period closes the entries. The source properly arranged appears in the sample tables, Exhibits 11-2 through 11-5.

Arranging the Box Headings. With the top double rule drawn a single space under the number and title, the box headings are then arranged over the stub and over the columns. At least one space should be left between the top rule and the first line of the box heading. The caption for the stub usually is placed flush with the left margin of the table. Each line in each column heading is centered from the midpoint of the space devoted to the column. With varying numbers of lines vertically in the headings, the bottom lines are usually aligned. For spacing reasons in tables with many columns, the box heading should be approximately the same width as the data recorded under it. If overly long, the heading can be typed broadside or diagonally, although these arrangements should be avoided if possible. A consistent capitalization plan should be followed. The most usual practice is to capitalize the first and last words and all other words except articles, prepositions, and conjunctions. Generally only the first word and proper nouns and adjectives in the stub lines are capitalized. If the items in the table are all of the same measuring unit, the unit used should be indicated in the overall table caption. If different units appear among the columns, the appropriate unit should be indicated in each box heading. Abbreviations, usually forbidden in the report text and in the table caption, are permissible as spacesavers in the box headings and in the columns.

On occasion the box will include spanner heads, with subdivisions under the main entry, as in Exhibit 11-3. A line will be drawn over the subdivisions to indicate how much is covered or the subitems will be enclosed in side rules. When the box headings are completed, a line is drawn a single space below the last line of the captions.

Constructing the Columns.   Items in the table may be single-spaced or double-spaced, whichever practice makes for the more attractive appearance on the individual page. Even though the table is basically single spaced, double spaces may appear where distinct breaks in the continuity occur. Carried-over lines in the space devoted to the stub should be indented two or three spaces, as in Exhibit 11-3. For large numbers of stub lines, reading is facilitated if they are separated into groups by double spaces after a chosen number of lines, say, five. Subheads under a stub line should be indented, as well as the words *total, mean,* or others indicating summaries of data given above. Leader periods [. . .] out to the next column may be used anywhere that the copy is difficult for the eye to follow. At least two blank spaces should be left, horizontally, between each column. A single or double rule at the bottom completes the table.

These instructions are useful for constructing the columns:

a. Align decimal points.

b. Place a zero in front of a column of decimal fractions before the first and last numbers only.

c. Align figures in which no decimals occur on the right, as if for addition.

d. Align plus, minus, and plus-minus signs.

e. Place dollar signs, percentage symbols, and the like before the first entry in a column and before totals. Keep them aligned.

f. Indicate omissions in columns with a blank space, by dashes, or by leader periods, without spaces between them. Use zero (0) only when the value is actually zero. If reasons for omissions are needed, give them in a footnote.

Placement Suggestions.   If a table or graphic occupies as much as three-fourths of a page, it should be placed on a separate sheet. Smaller tables appear in the text with triple spaces above and below them, as in Exhibit 11-6. It is not a good idea to break a paragraph to insert an illustration. If the paragraph and the illustration cannot be completed on a page, the text should be continued to the bottom of the sheet and on to the next page. The illustration may come at the end of the first paragraph on the continued sheet. As to vertical placement of tables and graphics on separate pages, it is best to leave a little more space for the bottom margin than for the top, since the eye seems to lower tables that ride through the middle of the sheet. A good proportion is a ratio of 2 : 3 for top and bottom margins.

Ideally, the table is placed as close as possible to the text reference introducing it. In the long, formal (left-side-bound) business report, which is geared to management's easiest use, it is often quite helpful to put the table on a left-facing page opposite the text reference so that the reader may consult it in reading the report writer's analysis of the data. Since the text is generally typed on only one side of the page, a double sequence of blank pages thus occurs. The report writer may leave the double blank pages, numbering the page for the table on the back of the illustration in the same position as for other pages with (Obverse) in parentheses centered a double space below the page number:

6

(Obverse)

Or the blank pages may be pasted together or placed in clear plastic notebook envelopes so that they turn as one. Right-facing tables have pages numbered in the same position as do other report sheets. Left-facing tables (*for two pages turning together only*) carry the page number in the upper left corner, flush with the margin, on line five from the top.

Vertical Ruling.   Tables of more than two columns call for vertical ruling according to most authorities. Since vertical lining is rather difficult either on the typewriter or with a pen, lines may be omitted in cases in which no confusion results. Vertical rulings should extend from the double rule at the top (or from the rule indicating spanner headings) to the ruling at the bottom of the table. No vertical side rulings to enclose the table at the left and right are necessary.

The change of the United States to a net importer of petroleum gas was brought about by continued discoveries of large reserves in South America and Canada and a series of dramatic discoveries in the Middle East. Large discoveries in North Africa soon followed. As a result, proved world reserves on January 1, 19xx, were distributed as in Table 2.

TABLE 2

ESTIMATED PROVED WORLD OIL RESERVES, JANUARY 1, 19xx

Area	Proved Reserves (billion barrels)	Percent of World
United States	31.4	10.1
Other North American Reserves.	7.1	2.3
Total North America .	38.5	12.4
South America	21.7	7.0
Western Europe	1.6	0.5
Eastern Europe.	29.9	9.7
Africa	12.3	4.0
Middle East	194.0	62.7
Far East.	11.6	3.7
World Total	309.6	100.0

SOURCE: *Petroleum Facts and Figures*, 19xx Edition, American Petroleum Institute, New York.

The rapidity of the shift in relative positions with respect to reserves is illustrated by the fact that in 1944 the United States held 39.6 percent of world proved reserves. By January 1, 19xx, this percentage had slipped to 10.1. In 1944 the Middle East held 30.6 percent of world reserves. By January 1, 19xx, this percentage had more than doubled. Africa in 1944 had 0.2 percent of world reserves compared with 4.0 percent in 19xx.

Exhibit 11-6   Small table inserted in the text, reduced line width

494

Graphic Illustration

A good graphic illustration is generally preferable to a table in enabling the busy executive to grasp relationships at a glance. In the business report such graphic presentation may be actual pictures, charts, graphs, maps, pictograms, or diagrams.

Graphic illustrations, usually read upward, are more appropriately labeled at the bottom than at the top. Current usage, though, sanctions identifying figures as well as tables at the top, in which case the same procedure for the identification and the source is followed, except that Figure is substituted for Table. Figures have a numbering sequence of their own, beginning with arabic number 1.

Figures may be labeled at the bottom in two ways, with the source placed in parentheses right after the title:

FIGURE 8

POPULATION OF YOUR STATE (IN THOUSANDS), 1900–19xx, WITH YEARLY IN-CREASE (FROM U.S. BUREAU OF THE CENSUS, POPULATION, 19xx)

or

Figure 8. Population of Your State (in thousands), 1900–19xx, with Yearly Percentage Increase (From U.S. Bureau of the Census, Population, 19xx.)

Figure 8. Population of Your State (in thousands), 1900–19xx, with Yearly Percentage Increase. (From U.S. Bureau of the Census, Population, 19xx.)

The same placement suggestions offered for tables apply to figure arrangement. It is likely, though, that all graphics may be more conveniently placed on separate pages than interspersed in the text, since they are difficult to prepare. If an error is made in the drafting, it thus becomes necessary to retype the page as well as to redo the graphic. Several small graphics may be assembled on a single sheet—an arrangement that is particularly desirable if reference is made to more than one graphic on a single page of text. Graphic presentations should be enclosed with a line border on all four sides.

Bar Charts. Bar charts are a versatile form of graphic presentation in that they are equally effective in vertical or horizontal form. Vertical bars are generally the choice for time-series and frequency distributions. They are particularly valuable for showing magnitude fluctuations of a single factor through a time series, as in Exhibit 11-7, or for showing varying magnitudes of several items, as in Exhibit 11-8.

Effective bar chart presentation is dependent upon a carefully planned

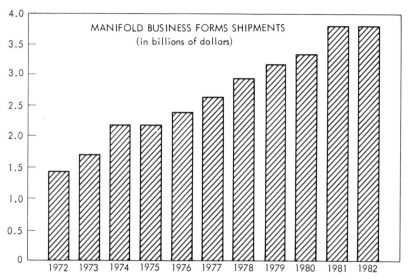

Source: Bureau of Domestic Commerce; Standard & Poor's Corp.

Chart 1. Value of business forms shipments annually.

(From Standard & Poor's Industry Surveys, 1981.)

Exhibit 11-7   Simple bar chart, time series

scale, with proper labeling of parts, either on the chart itself or in a legend below it. Guidelines should be drawn across the chart to indicate the units of scale, with vertical and horizontal axes specifically labeled. The classes of items compared should be indicated at the left of horizontal bars and at the bottom of vertical bars, as in Exhibits 11-8 and 11-9. For bar charts exhibiting discrete numbers, spaces of smaller size than the bars themselves appear between the bars, as in Exhibits 11-7, 11-8, and 11-9. For continuous variables with no gaps between the class limits, the bars are contiguous, as in Exhibit 11-10. Such charts are called *histograms*.

If the items compared are uniformly made up of the same components of varying proportions, bars may be subdivided, as in Exhibits 11-9 and 11-11, with different proportions shown by the use of shading, cross-hatching, or color. Comparisons of two or three variables within a single bar chart may also be achieved through the use of shading, cross-hatching, or color, as in Exhibit 11-11. Color may be applied with draftsman's crayons, with Zip-a-tone—commercially prepared cellophane sheets of tape with adhesive backing—or with adhesive strips. For releases directed to mass audiences, bar charts may be converted easily to pictograms: varying piles of dollars instead of different sizes of bars for income; pictures of cars for automobile production figures, and so on.

Pie Charts.   If the report writer is interested in showing the relative proportions of the parts of a whole, the pie chart is an effective device (see

Exhibit 11-12). Six slices in the pie are an approximate maximum for easy comprehension. Usual practice begins division of the pie at the 12 o'clock position with the largest portion, proceeding clockwise in descending order of the magnitude of the slices. Since it is difficult to estimate the proportions of the slices visually, it is a good idea to type the exact percentages for each slice on the graphic itself. Each slice may be differentiated from the others with shadings or color, as for other types of charts.

Line Charts. Line charts (Exhibits 11-13 through 11-15) are useful to show time-series fluctuations of a single item or of several items, usually no more than six. Such charts are usually plotted on graph paper, with time on the X, or horizontal, axis and values on the Y, or vertical, axis. The graphs may subsequently be traced onto paper used in the rest of the report, indicating only the main divisions of the scales. Xeroxing or other forms of sharp reprography will also provide a professional-appearing version of the original drawing.

The size of the scale to use may call for commonsense judgment in relation to the overall impression desired. Small spaces for large numbers will show much sharper fluctuations than will large spaces for the same

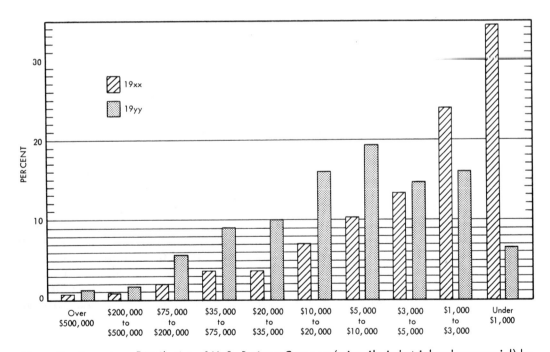

Figure 2.   Percentage Distribution of U.S. Business Concerns (primarily industrial and commercial) by Tangible Net Worth Groups, 19xx to 19yy. (From U.S. Bureau of the Census.)

Exhibit 11-8   Vertical bar chart, more than one variable

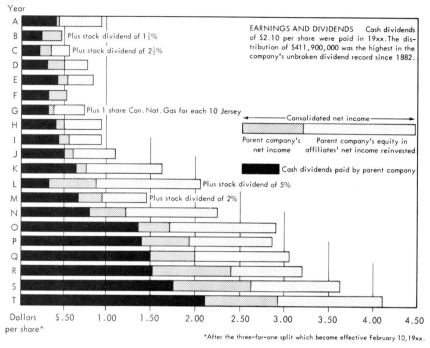

Figure 3. Earnings and Dividend Record, (From the 19xx Annual Report.)

Exhibit 11-9   Horizontal bar chart, subdivided

values. Since arithmetic rather than logarithmic grids are most often used in the business report, they are the only ones considered here.

If time is given in years, the recording month may have some significance as to where the plot dots are to be placed. January 1 figures may be plotted on the line on which the year is indicated. July 1 figures may be plotted at the midpoint of the interval between two successive year indications on the scale. Some types of graph paper are marked off by months on the time series—a particularly valuable type for break-even analyses.

The lines for different items should have distinctive features, such as color or form (dots and dashes in suitable combinations) with identification for the different forms labeled on the graphic itself or explained in a legend below. The Y axis must always begin with zero; consequently, when figures are rather high, it is acceptable to let the first unit on the Y scale represent a much larger value than is represented by successive intervals, with an indication that the scale is broken, probably with two parallel lines cutting through the Y axis at an appropriate spot.

Maps and Diagrams.   The report writer may purchase many kinds of maps already made, often calling for little more than the addition of the figure number and title. Or a commercial map may be used as a foundation,

498

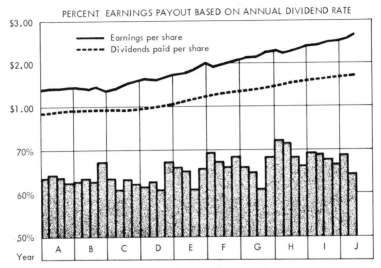

Exhibit 11-10   Continuous-data bar chart labeled at the top

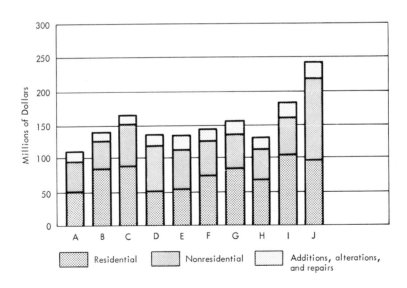

Residential   Nonresidential   Additions, alterations,
and repairs

Chart 4.   Construction Authorized in Dallas, Texas, by Type, 19-A – 19-J.
(From the Bureau of Business Research, The University of Texas.)

Exhibit 11-11   Subdivided bar chart

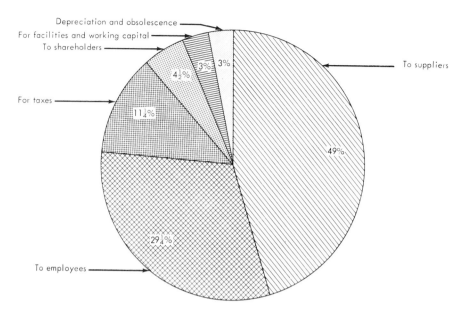

Figure 8. Distribution of Mayhew Corporation's Money during 19xx.
(From the 19xx Annual Report to Stockholders.)

Exhibit 11-12   A pie chart

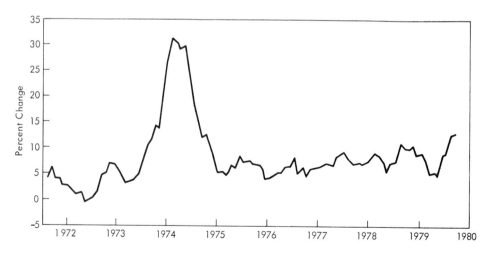

Chart 6. Inflation rate for capital equipment, 1972–80. Quarterly changes seasonally adjusted at
annual rates for the producer price index for capital equipment. (From U.S Department
of Labor, Bureau of Labor Statistics.)

Exhibit 11-13   Simple line chart

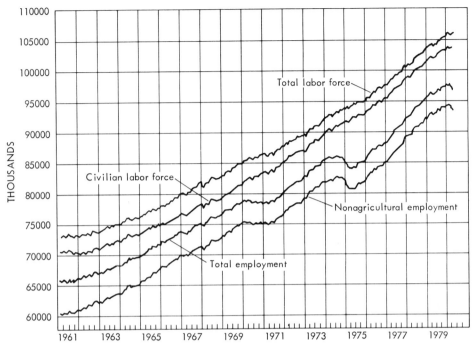

Source: *Employment and Earnings*, U.S. Department of Labor, Bureau of Labor Statistics, Vol. 27, no. 5 (May 1980), p. 7.

Chart 1. LABOR FORCE AND EMPLOYMENT (Seasonally adjusted)

Exhibit 11-14 Line chart with multiple variables

with the writer's additions of outlines for areas, shading, or coloring to indicate differences among the areas. Organization or flow charts and other sorts should be drawn with permanent ink in professional style as in Exhibit 11-16. A photographic process of reproduction may be necessary to procure the requisite number of copies of any sort of graphic illustration.

Interpreting Illustrations

A table or figure is supposedly introduced into the text because it includes necessary data to prove a point. Logically, the illustration has some bearing on the working hypothesis and on the major discussion area established for the particular section or chapter in which it appears. The statement used, then, to introduce the illustration (and, logically, prior to its actual appearance in the text) should make clear its relationship, its importance to the overall presentation. Instead of saying "Table 6 shows" the writer places the emphasis where it belongs—on the significant idea being developed. The table number itself will be picked up in some incidental, subordinate fashion.

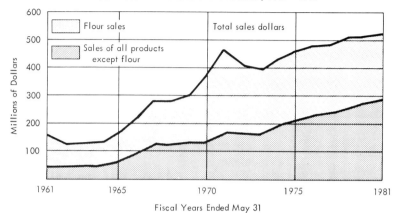

FIGURE 9

CONSOLIDATED MILLS SALES RECORD, 1961 – 1981

SOURCE: 1981 Annual Report to stockholders.

Exhibit 11-15   Line chart showing trend components

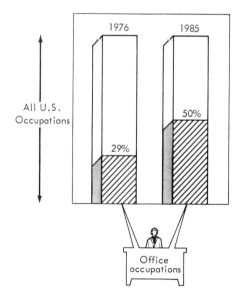

Source: Bureau of Labor Statistics

Figure 2.   Office occupations as a percentage of
all U.S. occupations

Exhibit 11-16   Pictogram incorporating
subdivided bar chart

If the table appears on the opposite or the following page, the page number is not an essential part of the reference. Tables or figures on pages in other parts of the study are identified by number and the page on which they appear.

An appropriate introductory statement for an illustration might run like this: "The trading volume of Aerodynamics more than doubled the day after the effective stock-split date, from $55,000 to $127,000, as seen in Figure 10." What should be said about the data varies with the type of data, but here is a checklist of things to look for and use as applicable.

1. Array extremes.
2. The mean, median, and mode or modes.
3. Other applicable statistical measures.
4. Any sharp fluctuations or other unusual features. (The reader is due some sort of interpretation as to *why* these unusual features happened and *what implications* they have for the area under discussion.)
5. The relationship these data have to other data.
6. Any notable trends or tendencies.
7. Conditions in the environment in which these data occur that could have influenced them.
8. What effect any anticipated changes in the environment might have on the figures.
9. How the data are related to the working hypothesis or the objectives of the section of the paper in which they appear.

The entire burden of presenting the data should never be left to the table or graphic. The writer should point out the essential features specifically, citing the figures to back them up. The text and the illustrations have both a separate and an interrelated function to perform. The table or figure should be so constructed that anyone reading only the table or figure will capture the significance of the data. The text covering the illustration should elaborate completely the vital aspects so that full understanding would result if the illustration were omitted.

WRITING THE DECISION-COMPONENT OR CONTENT SECTIONS

When the graphic and tabular presentations are prepared, the report writer is ready to record the components of the decision developed in the stages of Chapter 9 and blueprinted in the outline constructed through the suggestions made in Chapter 10. The analyst records not only the findings themselves, but their interpretation—the implications they have for the ultimate decision so that the reader may be led to accept this reasoning. The sequence of the roman sections and their subdivisions in relation to the overall decision has already been set up in the construction of the outline. In the following paragraphs, two elements of the writing of the content divisions are considered: (1) the makeup and (2) the reporting style.

In each of the critical discussion areas of the body of the report, these phases are included: (1) a section or chapter preview or introduction, (2) the findings and their interpretation, and (3) a concluding statement for the section. The first-level, or roman, caption is transferred from the outline to the text in the manner suggested in Exhibit 11-1. If a topical outline is used, the reader is thus made aware of the nature of the content and its impact on the overall decision. In the case of a descriptive outline, anyone using the report is alerted to the subdecision for the section or chapter by the explicit wording of the caption.

The Section or Chapter Preview

The business report is so written that the executive mainly concerned with evaluating the decision arrived at (or the basis thereof) may be oriented with minimum effort to the trend of reasoning at whatever point attention is focused. Thus at the beginning of each content division (between the main caption and its first subdivision, as in Sample Forms 11-2 and 11-3, the writer provides a preview of the coverage that includes

> 1.   The relationship of the material to the overall hypothesis or objective or to what has gone immediately before.
>
> 2.   A brief justification of the choice of material covered here.
>
> 3.   An explanation of special procedures or techniques, if any, employed in this section.
>
> 4.   A statement of the purpose of this part, which delineates at least the second-level subdivisions presented.
>
> 5.   An indication of their sequence and the reason for it.

In effect, this chapter or section preview is a transitional device, which in no way summarizes the findings: It merely points out the sequential development of the section for the reader's easy assimilation. As is characteristic of all transitions, the first sentence in the preview looks backward and points the way forward. For the first content division, the writer has no choice other than that of tying the material covered to the overall decision criterion or the main purpose of the study. For other sections, however, the content is tied either to the overall report objective or to the immediately preceding material. Basic for the writing throughout the report is that the first sentence under a caption must not depend on the caption itself for meaning. This sentence should be written as though the caption were omitted altogether.

The section previews below, taken from the sorghum-processing study explored previously, indicate a steady march of the decision components of this comparative-evaluation toward the decision in the ways indicated by side notations.

II. (First Decision Component)

Because the nearby *availability* of at least 6,000,000 bushels of *sorghum* is a primary requirement for the proposed plant, that factor is given primary attention. In the subsections that follow, each of the four areas evaluated (Lubbock, Fort Worth, Houston, and Galveston) is ranked according to the quantity of grain it could make available to a Renick-Dorn plant. Facts about the sorghum supply available to the competitive Bluebonnet Plant at Corpus Christi are also given as standards against which the production figures of the chosen areas may be compared.

Tie-in with the decision criterion (plant location factors), the identification of the component (the availability of 6,000,000 bushels of sorghum)

The section or chapter purpose

Second-level subdivisions: one for each of the four areas

The fifth second-level subdivision

III. (Second Decision Component)

Next to raw-material supply, the factor of greatest importance is *market accessibility*. This factor is measured by two indexes: (1) the average airline distance of the four cities from nine key Southwestern manufacturing centers shown in Table 3 and (2) the number of livestock in the home and adjacent counties of the potential sites as an outlet for the by-products of sorghum processing. Evaluations according to these criteria are presented in the order indicated.

Tie-in with immediately preceding section

Identification of component, justification section or chapter purpose

Identification of second-level subdivisions

Sequence indication

No special procedures were employed in these sections of this particular study. If special procedures are used, they should be explained here.

A Record of the Findings and Their Interpretation

With the plan for the first-level subdivision set out in the preview, the writer proceeds to record the subdecision arrived at for this section and to justify it through elaboration of specific findings. Since the content divisions are all written in much the same way, a basic plan applicable to all of them is set forth here. The A or other second-level caption under the roman section is transferred from the outline to the text draft according to suggestions given in Exhibit 11-1. Thus the reader is alerted to the nature of the coverage and its relationship to the problem answer if a topical outline is employed or to the specific nature of its contribution to the subdecision reflected in the roman caption above in descriptive outline treatment. Again following the plan of writing for management's easiest use, the reporter begins each paragraph with a strong topic sentence. The executive may then scan the report more readily: By reading the first sentence in each paragraph, he or she can learn at once the gist of the coverage.

Such topic sentences, to be used alternately as the situation dictates, are of two sorts: (1) one that points up the significance of the subject matter to be treated or (2) one that reports the major findings of the section. Paragraphs developed from the first type are generally arranged in climactic fashion, leading up to the major finding or conclusions. Those built from the second type present, deductive fashion, the supporting evidence that led to the major conclusion or finding set out in the topic sentence.

The analyst has already assembled the facts and figures to support the decision and has appraised the direction toward which they tend. Readers with vested interest in the outcome of the decision will certainly want an understanding of the reasoning behind the choices. If the writer has used elaborate statistical measures to abstract the meaning from the data, part of the problem may be explaining answers in terms that an executive or other reader with little mathematical background may comprehend. Computations should be put in the appendix for ready checking, certainly; in the text itself the reporter tells in simple language what the data mean and how far they can be depended upon. Much of the data may appear in tables, graphic illustrations, or financial exhibits; the text should pick up the significant figures and interpret them: What do they mean, so far as the purposes of the report are concerned? What internal or external environmental factors might have influenced them? What about the future of this trend? What elements could impair the validity of this conclusion?

Appropriately interspersed among the findings and interpretations should be a clear delineation of the assumptions under which the analyst operated (if any) and a defense of their logic, any method for bridging gaps in available data, and the way of resolving conflicting facts and figures. The limits of the research and sample designs should also be taken into consideration in the evaluation of data so that more significance is not claimed for them than their origin warrants. The analyst thus makes his or her thought processes explicit, for the manager who may budget money for implementation is as much concerned with how the decision was evolved as with the decision itself.

Any third- or subsequent-level subdivisions are transferred from the outline to the text, preceded by an appropriate introductory statement (illustrated in the annotated report sections in the next few pages). This introductory statement does not necessarily preview the coverage as does the chapter preview. It is merely a transitional device between second- and third-level treatment. At the end of each paragraph, at whatever level, comes a concluding statement that indicates the importance of this analyzed material to section or chapter objectives and thus, perhaps indirectly, to the proof or disproof of the working hypothesis or to the measurement in terms of the decision criterion.

When all the subdivisions of a roman section are complete, the writer still has the task of tying the subdivisions together into a subdecision for that roman section in line with the overall decision criterion. It may be done in a separate unnumbered paragraph or paragraphs (see the example on page 514). This portion is not a summary in the usual sense. It is more of an evaluative or concluding statement that relates the significance of the material covered to the overall problem answer—an explicit wording of the subdecision arrived at in the section.

Following are two roman sections (the demand and competition components) from a business report that decides whether or not Valley Mining Company of McAllen should exercise its 90-day option to purchase a Hidalgo plant. This plant would process Mexican barite—a weighting substance used primarily in the production of oil well drilling mud. The emphases are on whether the plant would prove financially feasible. Tables and graphics are omitted purposely so that you may judge whether the text tells the story completely. To augment the useful life of the material, specific dates are masked and time periods summarized as the last ten years or the next ten years. A report writer actually doing this project would, of course, include specific dates.

II. DEMAND FOR BARITE TO INCREASE BY 150 PERCENT BETWEEN 19xx AND 19yy

	Section Review
In order to base an opinion on the financial success of Valley Mining Company's barite plant, it is important to study the present and future demand for barite. A survey of the needs of the oil industry is considered first, because barite is used primarily in oil well drilling mud. As a result of modern technology, many other fields have been opened to barite, and the extent to which this mineral is used in these fields is the next area of discussion. From these areas a com-	Backward look—tying section to problem objective
	Justification of subject matter
	Identification of first subdivision
	Identification of second subdivision
	Purpose of the section

posite forecast of barite demand for the next ten years is determined.

A. Needs for Oil Well Drilling Mud to Increase 150 Percent Between 19xx and 19yy

The trend line for sales of crushed and ground barite, pictured in Figure 2, has advanced an approximate 180 percent in the last ten years, paralleling the rising consumption by oil and gas well drillers.

Topic sentence—pinpointing the major finding

In view of a proportionate anticipated rise in national population and income figures, energy shortages, and automobile and plane production, the demand for barite is forecast conservatively to increase by 150 percent in the next ten years (also shown in Figure 2).

Justifying forecast figure

An abrupt change from a cold to a fighting war in this period could only result in augmented demand to provide additional fuel and energy for a military economy.

Consideration of environmental factors

The possibility of the powering of automobiles and planes with fuel other than gasoline was taken into consideration, but was not deemed a significant deterrent to demand within the forecast period.

Delineation of an assumption

Various trends within the industry tend to justify the forecast demand increase of 150 percent in the next ten years as reasonable.

Importance of material to follow

Certain activities of oil and gas well drillers, who use 95 percent of all crushed and ground barite sold,[1] exert an important influence on the demand for barite:

Specific statistics to justify reasoning

Increases in oil well depth, in multiple drilling, and in the actual number of wells drilled.

Identification of subdivisions for caption A

1. Increase in oil well depth of about 50 percent in the last ten years

Although the average number of drilling rigs in operation in 19xx was the lowest since wartime 1943, the penetration rate set an all-time high. As illustrated in Figure 3, the average depth per hole drilled

Topic sentence—highlighting major finding for subdivision

---

[1] U.S. Department of Interior, Bureau of Mines, *Barite* (Washington, D.C.: U.S. Government Printing Office, 19xx), p.3.

was 5,775 feet, an increase of 7.2 percent over last year's figures. According to estimates released by the International Petroleum Institute, drilling mud for an 8,500-foot well costs approximately $7,500, and mud for a 15,000-foot well, $100,000. Thus, mud needs accelerate sharply as the depth increases. The trend in oil wells toward greater depth augments the possibilities of encountering high-pressure formations, with a consequent increase in the requirements for a weighting agent such as barite.

Statistics to support topic sentence

Concluding statement for subdivision

2. Sharp increase in multiple drilling in the state in 19xx

The abrupt rise in the number of multiple completions is making the total number of wells drilled an antiquated yardstick for measuring drilling activity. The average number of holes drilled per rig has shown a rising trend, up to 12.6 in 19xx.[2] The net effect of the multiple drilling is to decrease the total number of tests drilled in the state in 19xx by 1,965. Drilling in the United States would have totaled 48,715, or 4.2 percent above the actual number of holes drilled, if multiples in the state had been conventionally drilled as singles.[3] In line with this trend toward more multiples, the need for drilling mud is greater because of the added depth and increased size of the hole. "The trend toward multiples is hurting the drilling contractor—not the equipment supplier."[4]

Topic sentence which summarizes most significant finding

Interpretation of the effects of the statistics

Concluding statement for subdivision 2

3. Increase in oil well drilling of 2 percent per year

Anticipated energy needs in 19xx will be met by the oil and gas industry in increasing amounts, as shown in Figure 4. By 19yy the world demand for crude oil will be around five billion barrels annually. By completely replacing present

Topic sentence significance of section 3

Statistic supporting topic sentence statement

---

[2] "Drilling Reaches New Low," *Petroleum Chronicle*, May 19xx, p. 13.

[3] "Multiples Blast Drilling Total," *Petroleum Chronicle*, June 19xx, p. 14.

[4] Ibid.

reserves, which will be depleted by then, the world would be left with a supply for only 15 years. This prediction means that the oil industry will need to find more than 275 million barrels by 19yy. The volume of oil well drilling is forecast to increase by 2.8 percent per year, with most of the increased volume to be located in the Gulf Coast Region of the state. "There is no likelihood of a letup	Implications of the statistics
in the constant search for new pools and fields in the State Gulf Coast."[5]	Concluding statement for section 3

B. Other Uses of Barite to Continue Increasing in the Coming Years

Although other uses of barite consume only 5 percent of the total production,	Main finding of section B
sales of barium chemicals to consumers other than oil well drillers are expected to increase along with the rise in the number of products that use barite. Advances in nuclear-reactor development should boost barite demand as an aggregate used in high-density concrete mixes. Barite in the form of rubarite, as an additive to asphalt and barium titanite used in the electrical systems of rockets and missiles, will gain wider acceptance. Favorable results of preliminary research on the use of barite in whiteware ceramic bodies indicate that further investigation is warranted. The use of barite in glass, paint, and rubber industries is expected to continue at the previous consumption	Facts supporting the topic sentence statement
levels shown in Table I.[6] As described above, the increase in other uses of barite are sure to add to overall demand for the product.	Concluding statement for section B
Although barite has many uses, sales rise and fall in almost direct proportion to increases and decreases in oil well drilling activity. Deeper wells, coupled with predictions for higher drilling activity and more multiples, are sure to mean a steadily growing market for barite.	Concluding statement for roman section II—the determinant "demand" related to the hypothesis that the plant will prove profitable is favorable

[5] "Midyear Report," *The Drillers Journal*, July 6, 19xx, p. 8.

[6] Ibid.

III. UNFAVORABLE MARKET DUE TO COMPETITION FROM MAJOR COMPANIES AND BARITE SUBSTITUTES

Even though there is an anticipated thriving demand for barite in the next decade, the competitive nature of the industry might well affect Valley Mining Company's success in the new venture. It is therefore wise to evaluate the impact of the major competitors—Baroid, Magcober, and Milwhite—as well as competition from barite substitutes in determining the Company's possible share of the market.

A. Three Major Companies Control 85 Percent of the Market

Leaders in the mud field are Baroid, a division of National Lead Company; Magnet Cove Barium Corporation, Magcobar Division; and Milwhite Mud Sales Company, a division of Mississippi River Fuel Corporation. These three companies have about 85 percent of the total mud business, and all three are located in Bayville. Other big mud companies are Mud Control Labs, Incorporated, at Oklahoma City, and Macco Corporation at Paramont, California. Mud Control and Macco probably have 2 percent of the market. In addition to these, 150 to 200 local companies split the remaining 13 percent.[7] State mud companies are dispersed throughout the area, as illustrated in Figure 5. Since Valley Mining Company intends to sell its entire output to firms in Bayville, the presence of the three market leaders in this area indicates a need for caution.

A noticeable trend among mud companies is to put in their own retail stock points. "The capital needed for large warehouses with necessary servicing equipment is more than small distributors can afford; so they are rapidly passing out of the picture."[8] Baroid's products

Section Preview

Transition tying discussion to immediately preceding section

Reference to problem objective

Justification of section content
Identification of second-level subdivisions

Topic sentence significance

The most important finding

Supporting statistics

Concluding statement for paragraph

Significance of section

[7] "Big Profits for Drilling-mud Makers," *Chemical Journal*, August 8, 19xx, p. 33.

[8] Ibid., p. 37.

are now 100 percent company distributed, and Magcobar sells about 80 percent of its output through its 400 outlets.[9] Milwhite is also moving in the direction of owning its own distribution facilities. In addition, field engineering services offered by large companies also help strengthen their positions in the market. Since more than 95 percent of mud used is mixed at the well site, drillers view these services as a price reduction; the services are included in the mud contract for the job. Generally, oil companies award a mud contract for the entire requirements of each well. Because such engineering services are offered by the three big companies, it is the considered opinion of this report that local companies will have difficulty competing in the future. Magcobar, Milwhite, and Baroid mill barite ore in Brownsville, Bayville, and Corpus Christi; and, since these companies market their own products, they are not likely to buy milled barite from Valley Mining Company. Because of the field engineering services and the company-owned retail stock points, the three big companies are able to provide stiff competition for the independents.

Effect of findings

Concluding statement—relating material to overall problem decision

Concluding statement for all of section A—competition determinant of financial feasibility unfavorable to the hypothesis

B. Drilling Mud Substitutes Offer Little Competition

In addition to appraising the influence of competition from other mud manufacturers, it is important to examine the effects of competition from mud-drilling substitutes for barite. The share of the market held by mineral substitutes, the practice of mud recovery, and the employment of air drilling are considered below as the major types of drilling mud substitutes.

Justification of content

Identification of third-level subdivisions

1. Mineral substitutes hold small share of the market

Barite is not absolutely essential in some of its uses. In its larger use, as a weighting

Topic sentence significance

[9] "Multiple Services of Mud Makers," *Oil and Gas Chronicle*, September 19xx, p. 69.

agent in drilling muds, barite is preferred over other materials: It is clean to handle, relatively inexpensive, nonabrasive, inert, and with a relatively high specific gravity. Although celestite has a lower specific gravity, it has been used in the past as a substitute when a royalty was charged on the use of barite. Celestite does not now compete in this field.

Some iron ores are heavier and in the same price range as barite. Even though there are no technical reasons why they cannot be substituted, these ores are not used extensively because they soil personnel and equipment. Galena, with a specific gravity of 7.4 to 7.6, is much more expensive and has some technical disadvantages.[10] Strontium sulphate, a lighter material, has been used to some extent in wells where anticipated pressures are not excessive. The trend toward deeper wells indicates, however, that the use of this substitute will not gain wide acceptance.[11] It appears that competition from mineral substitutes is not a significant factor.

Factor complicating overall negative trend of competition determinant

Concluding statement

2. Mud recovery is not widely practiced

A substantial portion of used barite could be recovered and reused. Some of the drilling mud is lost in porous formations, but most is returned to mud ponds on the surface where it is usually abandoned after completion of the well. Although recovery of barite for further use is possible, the practice has not been widely adopted.[12]

Topic sentence significance

Concluding statement in opposition to overall negative competition trend

3. *Air drilling is only employed in northern section of the state*

Air drilling is a unique method of exploration which does not require any mud because normal gas pressures are checked

Topic sentence

---

[10] U.S. Department of Interior, Bureau of Mines, *Barium* (Washington, D.C.: U.S. Government Printing Office, 19xx), p. 4.

[11] Interview with Marlon P. Brandon, research analyst, Independent Petroleum Engineers of America, Washington, D.C., October 5, 19xx.

[12] Ibid.

with air pressure. This method is employed somewhat in the northern section of the state but is inapplicable in the southern half, for extreme gas pressures are encountered at all depths in these areas. As established previously, future drilling activities will be concentrated in the southern sectors of the state; hence, there is no major threat to the mud industry from air drilling.

Concluding statement

Even though competition from barite substitutes is insignificant, efforts by three major companies to increase their 85-percent share of the market indicate an unfavorable outlook for Valley Mining Company's new plant. Additional warehouse locations and engineering services offered by Baroid, Milwhite, and Magcobar are causing rising hardships for local companies.

Concluding statement for all of Section III—competition is an unfavorable determinant despite favorable elements

In the financial analysis that follows, then, the portion of the market Valley Mining Company may hope to expect is optimistically set at 2 percent with a minimum level of 0.5 percent.

Transition into roman IV

In the comparative-evaluation study, again dictated by the outline set up previously, the second-level (A) subdivisions rank the choices according to the decision criterion set out in the roman caption. The topic sentence under each second-level caption, then, names the choice and its rank; the subsequent development produces supporting evidence as to why the choice was accorded that rank. The topic sentences for the ABC sections for the raw-material criterion in the sorghum-processing problem and the concluding statement that makes explicit the subdecision of the whole roman section are offered as illustration.

II. LUBBOCK'S COMMAND OF BEST LOCATION FOR ECONOMICAL YEAR-ROUND GRAIN SUPPLY

(Preview Previously cited)

A. *Availability of 12,329,054 Bushels of Sorghum in Lubbock and Four Adjacent Counties*

When the four cities are ranked in order of the amount of sorghum they can make available to a Renick-Dorn plant, Lubbock clearly takes first place. . . .

Topic sentence

B. *Second-ranking Ft. Worth's*
644,032-Bushel Yield within
4,356 Square Miles

Ft. Worth is situated near the second-
largest grain supply, as shown by Figure
1. . . .

Topic sentence

C. *Houston's Handicap of Limited*
Grain Supply and High
Competitive Prices

The grain-supply situation for Houston
and Galveston, two cities drawing on the
same production area, is even worse
than that at Ft. Worth. . . .

Topic sentence

. . .

A Renick-Dorn plant located at Ft. Worth,
Houston, or Galveston, therefore, would
be at a competitive disadvantage. If the
plant were located at Lubbock, on the
other hand, it would have an even
greater supply of easily obtained sorghum
than does the Bluebonnet rival. Lubbock
alone would be able to compete in terms
of raw-material costs.

Concluding statement for roman II—explicit statement of the subdecision according to the raw material criterion

The analytic-descriptive main divisions are developed along the same
lines. The topic sentence either introduces the criterion against which the
phenomenon under investigation is being measured or the major diagnostic,
descriptive, prescriptive, or implementative finding arrived at in the subdivision. The concluding statement for the roman section blends the findings
of the subdivisions into an analytic-descriptive subanswer of the type
indicated.

THE CONCLUDING PORTIONS

The final sections of the business report are not *summaries* in the sense that
we generally think of them. Since a decision will be implemented as a result
of the data presented in the report, merely retracking the findings as they
were developed minimizes their effectiveness. All data presented must be
looked at in the light of the overall decision reached. The analyst might even
do well to pause in the writing at this point for a germinating period; for,
even though the findings may not be entirely decisive, some sort of action
will be taken as a result of them. Thus, consider thoughtfully again the "what
if" reasoning and the imaginative testing of the outcomes of alternatives

suggested in Chapter 9 in a search for what to tell readers as justification of this overall answer. The concluding portions are the most important phase of the treatment, for the manager, pressed for time, may turn first to the conclusions. You as writer are thus obligated to record the essence of your reasoning and the most important facts and figures developed in the entire report. If no recommendations were asked for by the authorizer, the final part of the report may go under a single caption which reflects the conclusion and the major reason that conclusion emerged. If recommendations make up only a minor portion of the last phase, you may choose to blend conclusions and recommendations under a single roman caption. If recommendations are a substantial part of your study, you may have one section for conclusions and another for recommendations.

Drawing Conclusions for the Yes-or-No Answer

For the conclusions to a yes-or-no answer, the analyst has already arranged second-level captions in descending order of importance to the overall answer in the outline made according to ideas suggested in Chapter 10. The report answer is reflected in the caption for this section:

MORTON COUNTY SEEN AS FAVORABLE SITE FOR ADDITIONAL

SAVINGS AND LOAN ASSOCIATION DESPITE

COMPETITION DISADVANTAGE

RANKING OF HOUSTON, FT. WORTH, AND LUBBOCK IN THAT

ORDER ACCORDING TO THE RELATIVE WEIGHTING OF

THE CHOSEN FACTORS

IMPROBABLE SUCCESS FOR CONVENTION HOTEL BECAUSE OF

INTENSE COMPETITION AND POTENTIAL

FINANCIAL DIFFICULTIES

Under this definitive-answer caption, the analyst *introduces* argument by stating the conclusion and indicating that the answer is supported by the findings that follow—or words to that effect:

Despite strong evidence of an unfavorable competitive position, the preponderance of evidence indicates that Harley Mills will succeed in realizing 17 to 20 percent of its capital investment and 3 percent of gross sales through the manufacture and marketing of ready mixes. Supporting data justifying this decision are presented in the paragraphs that follow.

The same procedure of beginning with a strong topic sentence whose meaning is independent of the caption statement and ending with a concluding remark that wraps up the argument is suitable for the writing of the second-level sections here, as it is elsewhere.

The writer should be careful to record the significant facts and figures and to show what they mean: what inferences are drawn from them, what implications they have in relation to the working hypothesis or to other chosen criteria, what will happen as a result of them. Statistics documented in the body of the report need not be documented here—merely presented as proof. The relative effects of the conditional or opposing findings are particularly important, as well as their qualification: what conditions account for them, what influence they have on implementation, how they may be circumvented, and so forth. The writer should also make clear any assumptions that affect the interpretation of the findings. No new data are introduced in the conclusions; yet additional documentation may serve a useful purpose here if needed to justify implementation suggestions or to show how other similar entities have overcome a negative element.

When the chief evidence has been enumerated and interpreted, the writer may end with a concluding statement for the whole report, unnumbered and uncaptioned, that says in effect that the objectives set for the study have been accomplished. (If recommendations are to be cited, this summing up comes at the end of the recommendations.)

The Conclusions for the Comparative Evaluation

The number of second-level subdivisions in the conclusions of the comparative-evaluation study is dictated by the number of choices that were evaluated: one concluding section for each choice. The purpose here is to give a final ranking of the choices according to *all* the criteria against which they were measured. In making a choice according to suggestions in Chapter 9, the writer very likely may discover that no one choice is superior according to all the criteria. It then is necessary to apply a weighting system to arrive at an ultimate selection. Naturally, then, the analyst will proceed in the same manner outlined for the yes-or-no decision by considering the criteria in descending order: the criterion in which the first choice was most favorable at the head of the list and on down. There will be as many areas of discussion under each choice as criteria employed. A very important part of the writing job is pointing up ways in which elements unfavorable to the choice may be overcome or in showing why the negative element is relatively insignificant to implementation of this choice. With these essential differences in mind, the writer develops conclusions in the same way advocated for the yes-or-no decision.

Conclusions for the Descriptive-Analysis Study

Since the descriptive-analytic investigation includes such a wide variety of approaches, the best general procedure is to gear the conclusions to the hypothesis with which the study began. Thus the major findings will be arranged in descending order according to whether the hypothesis proves favorable or unfavorable. If the findings are diagnostic, the most significant defect of the phenomenon under investigation will appear first—and on down. For prescriptive answers, the most effective remedy comes at the top, as does the most vital implementation suggestion. Paragraphs are developed in the same way as for other studies.

The Recommendations

The first sentence under the recommendations heading characterizes the overall trend of what the writer is proposing and introduces the reasoning to follow:

> It is proposed that Marlin Motors enter the small-economy-car field through an alliance with a foreign manufacturer. Ways of implementing this alliance follows.
>
> . . .
>
> Harley Mills should launch its ready mixes through an expenditure of 50 percent of anticipated first-year sales for advertising, concentrating on a single unique feature of the company's product. Advertising-money budget allocations and possible advertising approaches are outlined below.

Subdivisions that name the specific recommendations are transferred from the outline to the text. Carefully planned details or general guidelines allowing for flexibility in implementation may be set out. The recommendations have some origin in the reasoning developed in the body of the report and thus should be supported with facts and figures previously established wherever possible. Additional documentation as to the wisdom of recommendations may add to their quality. Recommendations may also require exhibits, tables, maps, or other types of visual aids employed elsewhere. The report closes with a wrapup summation that gives a sense of completeness to this investigative effort . . . a final suggestion as inducement to action.

REPORT-WRITING STYLE

The basic framework for writing the sections of the reports presented above is further enhanced by incorporating the following ideas.

1. *Build your report as you would the arguments in a debate, for report writing is argumentative writing.* Basically the debater advances each premise in support of the opening resolution, backs it up with what he or she considers to be incontrovertible evidence, refutes arguments that opponents either have advanced or might offer in opposition to the premise, and pulls his or her own argument together in a final appeal to the judges. The success of the presentation is dependent upon something no book can provide: the writer's individual sense of logic.

Those concerned with teaching writing techniques invariably say "Be concise, be clear, be forceful." Often the person reading such advice is as bewildered as if told to "be brave, be beautiful, be happy." No one would question the desirability of these attributes. If the person so admonished knew how to go about realizing them, though, there would probably be no need for help from anybody. It is perhaps equally frustrating, then, to offer still another suggestion that takes precedence over all others: "Be logical."

One hopeful aspect of the problem is that one's eclectic powers can be sharpened through exercise—perhaps the basis for all educational endeavors. The best advice for a self-administered program aimed in this direction is "*Think* as you write." Then, when you have finished a section, go back and check for logic by asking yourself these questions:

"Does the last part of this sentence match the first part?"

"Is the sequence of these sentences logical? Or would the sixth sentence be more effective in second position?"

"Are my sentences related to each other in a way that is readily apparent to the reader?"

"Does this sentence actually say what I mean to say?"

"Will this reference seem surprising or disoriented to my reader?"

"Is adequate explanation given for the reader's easy comprehension?"

"Have I jumped about in the time sequence—from yesterday to tomorrow and then back to today?"

"Is my treatment of space or geographical sequence coherent? Or have I leaped about over the terrain without reason or warning?"

Since few people can depend upon the spontaneous outpourings of their own genius, considerable rewriting may be necessary to achieve a creditable piece of work. Even professional writers often revise whole books many times before releasing them.

Most people who are called upon to prepare a business report handle the technicalities of grammar and punctuation well enough; the prime criticism is that their writing lacks logic. For example, the sentences that follow are not sharply deficient in grammatical construction. But what impression of the writer's thinking powers do they leave?

> Marcus Hindman, president of Marseille-Montandon Railway, has accomplished more in a few years than most railroad executives do in a lifetime, since he learned the railroad business as he went along.
>
> . . .
>
> All successful companies go through stages, thus accounting for Milestone Freightway's ultimate transition into the committee form of management.

In the next selection, all the sentences show some relationship to a common subject, but little relationship to each other:

> The business of Nuclear Engineering, Inc. is built upon the Volstead accelerator, a machine devised before World War II by Dr. Maylan Volstead, who is still chief scientist at Nuclear Engineering. The proton machines are used in physics to break up the nuclei of atoms.
>
> Many are now being used to study the effect of radiation in space on people and things. The most practical use of all, however, from the point of view of profits, is the large new market in industry. Industrial use of electronic radiation has been held back until recently. Two years ago Nuclear Engineering began producing a new kind of electron machine called an insulating core transformer.

Quite a frustrating bit of reading. Yet it is the sort that often emerges from writers who fail to direct their logic to the sequence of arrangement and to visualize what the reader needs to know to understand their ideas.

2. *Read your work aloud to determine whether you have achieved rhythmic balance.* Balance can be effected through variety in sentence length, in sentence patterns, and in wording. Writers who admonish you to keep your sentences short may be a bit shortsighted. Certainly a sentence that is too long runs the risk of being obscure in meaning. But a business report made up entirely of short sentences might arouse some doubt in the reader's mind as to the writer's authority to speak—beyond the primary department.

3. *Write in third-person, impersonal style.* So that the burden of proof may be placed on the findings instead of on the writer's opinions, do not use references to *I, we you, us,* and *our.* Certainly the writer's attempt to mask first-person usage with the coy subterfuge "the writer" or "the investigator" is to be avoided. Keep yourself out of the treatment. If an opinion must be

labeled as such, instead of saying "in this report writer's judgment," qualify the statement with phrases such as "it is likely that," "it is possible," "perhaps," "apparently," and the like. Following the impersonal style rules out also using imperatives, such as "See Figure 6."

4. *Avoid the use of contractions.*

5. *Keep the tense sequence consistent.* For business reports, usually dealing with current data, the present is the typical tense viewpoint: "X company *manufactures* three types of lenses." Thus present-perfect derivatives will indicate antecedent action: "Management *has allocated* 50 percent of anticipated first-year sales to the launching of Harley Mills ready mixes." Certainly the present tense will be used for permanent truth and for talk about report parts: "Discussion of the leverage factor in the Company's proposed financing *appears* in the next section." Future activity will necessarily be described appropriately in the future tense, even though the typical tense is the present.

Some authorities contend that, since the report will be read in the future, the typical tense should be the past. A writer may follow this procedure, but with the customary short lapse of time between the writing of the report and the action taken on it, the present tense seems more desirable.

6. *Try to find synonyms for words that occur continually.* Do not start several sentences in sequence with the same word.

7. *Make your writing as* definite *as possible, with full use of concrete figures and facts.* Beware of generalizations without adequate evidence to back them up. Only statements that are common knowledge may go unsupported by either an explanation of the reasoning behind them or citations from authorities.

8. *Remember that figures are not much good except by comparison.* Compare them with those of a similar preceding period, to a standard set up as good, to the figures for another similar operation, or to something of which they are a part. Summarize changes in figures as percentages or proportions more or less:

> During the year 19xx Manhattan builders had completed or under construction 132 new office buildings containing 44,700,000 square feet, half as much as all the existing office-building space ten years before.

9. *Put life into your statistics.* Think as you write about the realities behind them. Back of the percentage of business failures in 19xx are battered and broken men and women who grope for a hopeful solution to their dilemmas. Back of population increases are newborn babies, proud and optimistic parents, a whole new market for consumer goods. You may not want to put these ideas into the report itself, but just thinking about the realities encourages you to write in a more interesting fashion.

Picking out the statistics to play up in the writing is a process of selecting those which have the greatest validity for the reader of the report, considering what that person expects to do with the data. Make these ideas stand out in the copy with forceful wording so that the executive concerned with implementing the decision does not have to grope for needed information.

SCHOLARLY DOCUMENTATION— FOOTNOTES AND BIBLIOGRAPHY

This section on footnoting and bibliography is included in this chapter because the quality of the authority cited does much to lend credence to a generalization the report writer is developing. Documentation has the further purpose of protecting the writer against charges of plagiarism. Most entries in footnotes are subsequently placed in the bibliography; there is some variation in arrangement of the two.

The Techniques of Footnoting

You, as writer, have an obligation to give full credit for ideas that are not fully your own. Thus you footnote all direct quotations from other writers or speakers and all borrowed ideas, even though they are paraphrased in your presentation. Ordinarily, the specific words of an author are quoted when it is important to reproduce ideas *exactly* so that no misinterpretation will result, when they are useful in illustrating a point the writer is attempting to make, when they lend authority to a conclusion, and when they are so aptly phrased that retention in their original form seems desirable.

Quotations of three lines or less are introduced right into the text and enclosed in double quotation marks. When the quotation is a part of the writer's sentence, the first word is not capitalized. When the quotation is a sentence or more, it is usually preceded by a colon, with the first word capitalized. The period and comma go inside the end quotation mark; the semicolon and colon go outside.

> The report of the Comptroller of Public Accounts indicates that "the state government derives one-fourth of its revenues from Washington." [*The* preceding *state* was capitalized in the original.]

> The new president's concern may be summed up in these figures from the company annual report: "Debt has risen to $60 million, 450 percent higher than it was ten years ago." [*Debt* was not capitalized in the original.]

Quotations of four lines or more appear in indented blocks with no quotation marks around them. Quotations within such quotations, therefore, will be enclosed in double quotation marks [" "]. A five-space indentation from right and left page margins is generally preferable as a space saver, although wider indentations are acceptable if the writer prefers. The same indentation plan should be used for all indentations—paragraphs, enumerations, and quotations—throughout the paper.

Generally, quotations are held to a length of a half page or less, with a page as a possible maximum. Any portions of a quotation not directly applicable to the point the writer is making should be omitted. Certainly any phrases that would detract from the report's purposes would be skipped. For omissions within a sentence, three periods with spaces before, after, and in between [. . .]—ellipses—are used. Punctuation marks preceding the ellipses are placed right next to the word. If a new sentence follows an ellipsis, a period is placed after the preceding selection, even though it does not appear in the original. Omissions of a paragraph or more are indicated by three periods (ellipses) spaced centered in the width of the quotation lines:

> Further extensions of market potential are substantiated in this selection:
>
> In the next few years Nuclear Engineering may find substantial business in a more profitable market—private industry. A smaller, different type of NE accelerator . . . has industrial applications in the treatment of surfaces. . . . It can be used for instant curing of paints and coatings on plywood, plaster-board, paper, textiles, automobile bodies, and home appliances.
>
> . . .
>
> "The world is full of surfaces," says President Marleborough, "and it is surfaces that are attacked by weather and rot, by bacteria and molds."

Quotations should be reproduced exactly in the same form that they appear in the original source as to wording, spelling, and punctuation. The quoter may disclaim responsibility for errors by placing the Latin *sic* in brackets after the error: "The accomodations [*sic*] are modern in the true sense." The writer's interpolations within a quotation should be enclosed in brackets [ ], never in parenthesis. If the typewriter has no bracket symbols, suitable brackets may be drawn carefully with a ruler.

The reader is alerted to the presence of a footnote by a superscript (raised number) placed after the last word of paraphrased or quoted material. The superscript is placed after the end quotation mark in selections quoted along with the text. The footnote arabic number is elevated by turning the platen backward approximately a half-line space. It is generally better to start numbering footnotes with "1" at the beginning of each new chapter. Reports not divided into chapters will have footnotes numbered continuously throughout.

The most widely accepted plan is that of placing the footnote references at the bottom of the sheet on which they are introduced so that the executive interested in the source may merely look down to find it. A line 1½ inches long made with the underliner one space below the last line of writing on a page separates the text from the footnotes. The first line of the footnote rests a double space below this separation line, with the arabic number elevated. No space is left between the superscript and the first word of the footnote. Blocked paragraphs call for blocked footnotes and indented paragraphs, for indented footnotes. Proper footnote form is illustrated here:

[1] Abram C. Zeiger, *The Computer in Industry* (Chicago: The Meredith Press, 19xx), p. 96 [blocked form].

[2] Martin P. Henderson, "The Manager Looks at Delegation," *Business Times*, Vol. 13, no. 8 (August 19xx), 16–20 [indented form].

A blank line is left between successive footnotes. Ideally, the last line of the last footnote entry rests inside the bottom margin set for report pages, with a permissible latitude of two or three lines short or long.

Two styles of footnote arrangement are presented here, our preference resting with the form advocated for formal research papers, which places the publication facts in parentheses.

1. Proper footnote coverage, sequence, and form for a book:

a. The author's name in its normal order: given name (or names) or initials followed by family name and separated by a comma from the title, which follows.

b. The title of the book italicized (underlined by words or with a solid line, just so a consistent scheme is followed). A comma separates the title from any following footnote parts except publication information. Publication facts are enclosed in parentheses immediately following the title, with a comma after the final parenthesis. Example:

[16] Robert Moreland Conrad, *Probability Theory* (New York: The Meredith Press, 19xx), pp. 19–20.

c. The editor or translator, if any, is indicated in third position (after the author and title), separated from the title by a comma. Example:

[17] Herman Schoenfeldt, *The New English*, trans. Otto Friedrich (New York: The Meredith Press, 19xx), p. 46.

[18] Mayo King, *Symposium on Decision Theory*, ed. Muriel Farnsworth (New York: The Meredith Press, 19xx), pp. 101–116.

d. The total number of volumes, if such inclusion is significant, the edition number, and the series title, if significant, are set off by commas.

e. Publication information to be enclosed in parentheses immediately following a–d with no punctuation before first parenthesis.

(1) The publication city and state, (if city is not well known), followed by a colon.

(2) The publisher's name, followed by a comma.

(3) The publication date, followed by parenthesis and comma.

f. The volume number, if any, is set in capital roman numerals, followed by a comma.

g. Page number or numbers are followed by a period.

[19] David A. Tomlinson, *The Executive and the New Decision Theory*, 2 vols., 3rd ed., "The Mayhew Lecture Series" (New York: The Meredith Press, 19xx), II, 91.

2. Proper footnote coverage, sequence, and form for an article in a periodical:

a. The author's name in its normal order, followed by a comma.

b. The title of the article enclosed in quotation marks, followed by a comma (inside final quotation mark).

c. The name of the magazine in italics (underlined), followed by a comma.

d. The date of the publication, followed by a comma.

e. The page number or numbers, followed by a period.

In the interest of simplicity, references to popular periodicals may be identified by date only, even though the volume and issue number are known.

If you include the volume and issue numbers, however, Vol. is recorded in arabic numerals, the issue in arabic following no., and the date of publication is enclosed in parentheses as in the Martin Henderson citation. If the specific date is not cited, no comma is placed between the month and the year: December 1970. If the day of the month is included, the comma is used: December 12, 1970. There is a trend toward writing the date in the European or military fashions: 12 December 1970; in such case no comma appears. There is adequate sanction in business usage, however, to write the date in traditional fashion, the practice followed here. (For references to scholarly journals, you will need to consult a more comprehensive style manual.) It is often easier (and perfectly correct) to write out the full numbers for pages than to try to remember which digits may be omitted: pp. 400–402; pp. 140–142; pp. 60–61. Most eliminations and abbreviated formats are initiated as a matter of convenience. One never errs by writing in more than is necessary. Examples:

[20] Stanley A. Ryan, "The Auditor and the Computer," *Commerce Digest*, July 19xx, p. 3.

[21] "Stock Dividends on the Upgrade," *Finance Weekly*, December 19xx, pp. 116–118.

[22] Jackson H. Taylor, "A Review of PERT," *Marketing Chronicle*, February 2, 19xx, p. 28.

3. Proper footnoting of letters, interviews, information from company files, and speeches, with these factors as needed:

a. The nature of the contact, such as interview with, letter from.

b.   The name, title, and official connection of the person involved, followed by commas.

c.   The company name with appropriate identification, if needed separated by commas.

d.   The date, followed by a period.

[23] Letter from Nat Henderson, business manager, Toltec Enterprises, Hauteville, Indiana, April 1, 19xx.

[24] Interview with P. B. Calcasieu, vice president, Bank of the Midwest, St. Louis, Missouri, November 19, 19xx.

[25] Minutes of the Quarterly Meeting of the Board of Directors, March 31, 19xx, Marlon Corporation, Paterson, New Jersey (in the company files).

4.   Citing a U.S. government document:

[26] U.S., Congress, House, Final Report of the Select Committee on Small Business, *Review of Small Business*, 82d Cong., 2d sess., 1952, H. Rept. 2513 pursuant to H. R. 33, p. 37. [H. R. stands for House Resolution.]

[27] U.S. Department of Commerce, Bureau of the Census, *Census of Agriculture*, General Report (Washington: U.S. Government Printing Office, 1981), II, 10.

5.   Legal citations:

[28] U.S., *Internal Revenue Code of 1954*, Sec. 305 (a).

[29] U.S., *Defense Production Act of 1950* (as amended by Public Law 96, 82d Cong.), Sec. 714.

6.   Form for unpublished theses or dissertations:

[30] Marion Joseph Stahl, "The Influence of the Health Issue on the Operations of U.S. Tobacco Companies" (unpublished master's thesis, College of Business Administration, The University of Maine, 19xx), pp. 100–103.

7.   Citation of the immediately preceding reference:

[31] Ibid. [Refers to the Stahl thesis, same page as the immediately preceding entry. In line with current trends, ibid. is not italicized.]

[32] Ibid., p. 96. [Refers to the immediately preceding entry in all respects except for a different page. If a number of pages intervene between the references, it is better to write out the citation. You never err by writing in too much.]

8.   Reference to the work of an author previously cited, with other references intervening:

[33] Stahl, "The Influence of the Health Issue," p. 16. [This citation may also be written out in full, and should be if the original reference is many pages back. The Latin form op. cit. may still be used here to mean the work of Stahl previously cited but a different page: Stahl, op. cit., p. 16. Loc. cit.,

another of the traditional forms, means that the citation is exactly the same as that of the author previously cited, including the page number: Thompson, loc. cit. Through extensive usage, these two abbreviations have also achieved status as acceptable English words and are not italicized. When two references from the same author have been cited, citing an abbreviated title will let the reader know specifically which work of the author is referred to here.

9. Content footnote interspersed in the numbering sequence:

[34] In the closed-circuit or wire system of TV broadcasting the program is piped through a coaxial cable network from a central studio to the subscriber's home.

10. A book with more than one author with a subtitle:

[35] Bedell Moore, Marian Spooner, Samuel T. Green, and Walter S. Sivers, *The Behavioral Approach to Business*, A Practical Treatise (New York: The Meredith Press, 19xx), p. 280. [Authors after the first may be indicated by "and others," or "et al.": Bedell Moore and others. Subtitles may be italicized or not, so long as a consistent pattern is followed.]

11. A book, no author given, indication of series:

[36] *The Mighty Force of Research*, "Fortune" (New York: McGraw-Hill Book Company, 1956), pp. 92–94.

12. Article from a periodical with association as author:

[37] National Retail Grocers Association, "Volume Sales Are Consumer Oriented," *The Grocer's Journal*, December 15, 19xx, p. 14.

13. Periodical article with no author given:

[38] "The Impact of a Buyer's Market," *The Wholesaler*, July 6, 19xx, p. 16.

The Bibliography

In the search for data, the investigator may have listed bibliographical entries that prove to be relatively worthless when the publications are read. In the bibliography at the end of the work, the writer will exclude these irrelevant items, concentrating on those found to be useful. As one looks through the bibliography cards, ways of classifying the entries will very likely occur.

Interviews, public addresses, and radio and TV talks, although not actually bibliographical entries, are usually included. It is possible to categorize entries according to the nature of the release, such as books, periodicals, government publications, documents, interviews—or perhaps a general designation such as miscellaneous sources, under which might be ranged single entries of a varied classification. A subject matter classification and chronological development are other choices.

When the writer has established the appropriate categories, the entries are arranged under each in alphabetic sequence by the author's last name. For this reason, the author's name is inverted—family name, comma, given name, period. With more than one author, only the first author's name is inverted. Some style authorities, however, advocate inversion of all of the authors' names, possibly for uniformity. If no author is given, the title of the publication is alphabetized by the first important word, skipping *A*, *An*, or *The*. The articles, however, are typed in. The coverage and sequence of bibliographical entries is the same as for footnotes. According to the formal research paper format, a period separates the author's name from the title, and another period separates the title from the publication facts, which are not enclosed in parentheses as in the footnotes. If the alternate footnote format is used, entries are recorded in the same order, with commas separating bibliographic items, just as in the footnotes.

The total number of pages in publications and pamphlets is included at the writer's discretion. Proper indication of total pages gives the number of prefatory pages in small roman numbers plus the pages in the book itself in arabic numerals: pp. x + 687. The total number of pages an article from a periodical occupies is given, whether or not total pages for books are included. The bibliography is preferably typed with overhanging indentation, single spaced, with double spacing between separate entries. A bibliography in proper format is shown in Sample Form. 11-4.

THE APPENDIX OR APPENDICES

Typical appendix entries include the following items.

1. Data too lengthy to present in the report itself but which add to the understanding or appreciation of the paper.

2. Large tabulations that are broken into sections for discussion at appropriate points in the text.

3. Extensive computations or other types of work sheets which may be checked for accuracy.

4. A copy of the questionnaire and its cover letter.

5. A tabulated summary of complete survey data.

6. Other schedules or forms used in collecting data.

7. Copies of documents or statutes relevant to the investigation.

8. Illustrative materials.

: (2" margin)

BIBLIOGRAPHY

Books

King, Mayo. Symposium on Decision Theory, ed. Muriel
    Farnsworth. New York: The Meredith Press, 19xx.

The Mighty Force of Research, "Fortune." New York: McGraw-Hill
    Book Company, 19xx.

Moore, Bedell, Marion Spooner, Samuel T. Green, and Walter S.
    Sivers. The Behavioral Approach to Business, A Practical
    Treatise. New York: The Meredith Press, 19xx.

Schoenfeldt, Herman. The New English, trans. Otto Fried-
    rich. New York: The Meredith Press, 19xx.

Tomlinson, David A. The Executive and the New Decision Theory,
    2 vols., 3rd ed., "The Mayhew Lecture Series." New York:
    The Meredith Press, 19xx.

Zeiger, Abram C. The Computer in Industry. Chicago: The Meredith
    Press, 19xx.

Articles and Periodicals

"The Dow-Jones Averages," The Wall Street Journal, New York ed.,
    January 23, 19xx, p. 21.

Henderson, Martin P. "The Manager Looks at Delegation," Business
    Times, August 19xx, pp. 16-20.

National Retail Grocers Association. "Volume Sales Are Consumer
    Oriented," The Grocer's Journal, December 15, 19xx, pp. 13-18.

"Stock Dividends on the Upgrade," Finance Weekly, December 19xx,
    pp. 116-118.

Public Documents

U. S. Congress, House. Review of Small Business. Final Report of
    the Select Committee on Small Business. 82nd Cong., 2d sess.,
    1952. H. Rept. 2513.

←——(1·¼")——→ (appears at left margin) ←—(1·¼")—→ (appears at right margin)

36

Sample Form 11-4   Bibliography prepared in proper format

37

U. S. Department of Commerce, Bureau of the Census. <u>Census of
   Agriculture</u>. General Report. Washington, D.C.: U.S. Government
   Printing Office, 19xx.

Miscellaneous

Calcasieu, P. B., business manager, Bank of the Midwest, St. Louis,
   Missouri. Letter dated April 1, 19xx.

Henderson, Nat, Business Manager, Toltec Enterprises, Hauteville,
   Indiana. Interview on November 19, 19xx.

Marlon Corporation. Minutes of the Quarterly Meeting of the
   Board of Directors, Paterson, New Jersey, March 31, 19xx.
   (In the company files.)

U.S., <u>Defense Production Act of 1950</u>(as amended by Public Law 96,
   82nd Cong.), Sec. 714.

U.S., <u>Internal Revenue Code of 1954</u>, Sec. 305(a).

Sample Form 11-4   Continued

9. Case studies.
10. Interview transcripts.

All items in the appendix must be titled or classified so they may be listed in the table of contents descriptively. If several related items occur, separate categories should be set up, appropriately identified. Since chapters or sections are labeled with roman numbers, it is preferable to indicate appendices with ABC's in this manner:

APPENDIX A. Questionnaire Preparation
    Sample Selection
    Cover Letter
    The Mailing List
    The Questionnaire
APPENDIX B. Master Tabulation of Survey Returns
APPENDIX C. Standard-error Computations

A division page for each appendix should contain appendix designation and title typed in solid capitals, centered, an inch above the vertical middle of the sheet. Full identification of all appendix parts will appear in the table of contents.

Part III

RESOURCE MATERIAL FOR PERSONAL USE

If you do not know where you are going, any road will get you there.

The Talmud[1]

---

[1] From the *Newsletter*, Center for Teaching Effectiveness, The University of Texas at Austin, Vol 2, No. 4 (January 1981), p. 1.

12

Career Planning as the Focus in the Job-Getting Process

A job is just that, a task. One's career, however, is a lifetime investment requiring a careful plan at the outset and periodic assessment toward successful achievement.

Career planning is a process that will eventually account for approximately 100,000 hours of your lifetime—a rough estimate of the time you will spend working. Shouldn't it involve more than mere job hunting? Shouldn't it mean more than a haphazard look at what is available or just settling for the job easiest to get? Getting yourself into the right job is the climax of your education career—the sale of the finished product.

As a college graduate you will have acquired both a general and a professional fund of knowledge. You will have learned how to approach life situations and problems logically. You will have acquired social intelligence, and the ability to adjust to many different types of people. You will have acquired skills important for your personal happiness and *essential* to your vocational success. Now you are ready to plan a career that will offer you satisfaction from a sense of service, professional pride in accomplishment, happiness, and enjoyment. But your college education—to be most valuable to you—must be properly directed.

The college degree alone does not guarantee success; it *does* guarantee opportunity. Statistics indicate your earnings can be double to triple those who are not college trained. Getting that degree is big business on an individual basis. The cost is estimated to be about $35,000. Add to this figure the recruiting, selecting, and training cost of the employer for a single college graduate (from $5,000 to $50,000) and you begin to see what a sizable investment it is. Salaries of noncollege graduates recently have been rising more rapidly than have those for college graduates. College graduates, however, still earn more; there is simply less disparity now.

No longer are employers content to hire for a job with the survival of the fittest becoming the executive crop. They can't wait that long or take the kind of chances inherent in such a procedure. They have to plan now for developing the potential they will need in the years ahead and to cope with the proportional shift in future human resource requirements. One of the major problems facing us in this decade and probably continuing on throughout the remainder of the twentieth century will be the decreasing and phasing out of the so-called "traditionally dominant" industries in this nation. Already, projections made more than a decade ago that manufacturing would decline as a major source of jobs in the flowing transition from an agricultural to industrial to service economy in the United States have proved true. Emerging industries such as those concerned with pollution, quality of the environment, health care, food, and technology now require more and more professional and highly trained personnel.

Your own intelligent approach to career planning should be long-range—about 20 years, for in 20 years from now, you should reach the peak of your career. Will you have had 20 years' of professional experience or one year's experience 20 times?

How do you plan for this career development? First, you start with yourself by selecting your goals. You then organize your job campaign. Once the right job and company have been selected and you have landed the job, the third phase—evaluating your progress—takes over.

This chapter takes you through the first two phases and offers some guidelines for the third.

APPRAISING YOURSELF

You must learn who you really are, what you want, and what you have to offer before you can think about where you are going. This self-appraisal is the basic foundation for the entire application procedure. Answering three basic questions will help determine your personal inventory or as it is sometimes called, your self-analysis:

1. Who am I?
2. What do I want to do?
3. What am I prepared to do?

Self-confession is said to be good for the soul, but it is more than just that here. It is a chance for you to really take an honest, objective, frank look at yourself, often for the first time in your life. There is no other course or place, short of a psychiatrist's couch, where you are encouraged, in fact, *urged* to do so.

In writing a self-analysis, we take a page from the sales representative's own handbook. Just as that professional is better able to promote sales of the firm's product or service by knowing it inside out—its weaknesses, strong points, appeals, and *likeliest customers*—so we, too, come to know ourselves in the self-appraisal.

We know what our strong points are. We know what weaknesses we must overcome or live with. And, we can then discover our likeliest sources of employment for assuming a successful career. But the self-appraisal cannot be done in a few minutes' time, for it is yet another example of problem solving and decision making requiring careful analysis.

Who Am I?

You can start with detailing your family background. Was your family life prior to college a happy, stable one? What specifically accounted for it? What things caused you to be upset or frustrated? What did you dislike most in your relationships with each member of your family? Were you perhaps responsible for it? What did you like most? Why? Such answers will begin to tell you how well you get along with others, but it is a biased picture at this point. To get a broader, truer perspective, look at your extracurricular activities. Have you ever been elected to a responsible position in any student organization? Were you a key worker? Do you prefer to lead—or to follow someone else's direction? How well have you gotten along with your college roommates and your fellow classmates? Do you make friends easily? Do you have lots of friends or only a few close ones? What in your life—right now— seems to give it the most purpose? a sense of meaning?

What prejudices and biases do you have? What things irk you? Are they really minor incidents, or are they likely to play a big role in your future relationships with others? Using the techniques from the justification report format, your honest appraisal here will set the pros against the cons in parallel columns—one headed *valuable traits*, the other *shortcomings*.

Valuable Traits	*Shortcomings*
Responsible; like to be my own boss	Prefer to be closely supervised; told what
Even-tempered, calm	to do (this trait could be highly desirable for some jobs, of course)
Work well under pressure	Can't work under pressure

Make decisions quickly	Find it difficult to motivate others to work with me
Can teach and train others	Easily irritated, quick-tempered
Motivate others to work for and with me	Moody

To make the listing of real help to yourself, you need to add (parenthetically) an example or two from your background to support each trait.

What interests and hobbies do you have? Do you tend to start many new interests only to give them up after a short, enthusiastic beginning? Why? You might include in this particular phase of your analysis those activities you want to pursue but haven't yet had time or money for.

What are your recreational interests and pursuits? How do you use your free time? Do your activities reveal constructive interests of the mind and body, such as reading a good book or following a planned physical exercise program, or do they fall more into the category of enjoying the sheer pleasure of loafing or of being kind of lazy? The entertainment choices you make absolutely freely and the overt points in your self-appraisal begin to give you a picture of yourself the way others see you. And it should tell you a lot about who you really are.

What Do I Want to Do?

By grouping similar things together in all the phases of your self-inventory, you can begin to see what they indicate about your direction and viewpoint. Are you inclined to work with detail or do you prefer to plan and let others take over to complete a project? Do you prefer working with your hands or with your mind, with numbers or with people? Are you creative, innovative? An idea-generating person who wants a chance to brain storm; problem solver? You want a chance to travel? Really use your talents and abilities? Would you be happy in a job rigidly restricting your free movement—one in which you must discipline yourself to the routine because of the confinement in performing the job? Would you be content tied to a desk? Or do you prefer a job offering more freedom of movement where responsibility is left more to you?

What Am I Prepared to Do?

With an idea now of what kind of an individual you are and what interests you have, your next step is detailing and assessing the qualifications you have to offer a prospective employer. You need to include both your own evaluation and the comments of others.

Start with your education. The list will include (working back from the most recent) the schools you have attended and your academic achievements—both general and specific. Backtrack all the way to high school. What subjects did you enjoy most? Least? Did your interests run to scientific subjects or more to skill-building courses? Did your grades match these interests—that is, did you make your best scholastic achievement in your favorite subjects? Has this pattern continued in college?

Review your work experience—every bit you have had—to see what you learned from your jobs. Did you develop particular skills? Handle some duties more efficiently and with more pleasure than others? Did you dread some duties and do you know why? Were you able to use your initiative on some jobs? Evaluate your overall performance critically.

Have you served in the military? If so, you'll want to appraise your experience to see what you learned from it that will prove valuable in your future work. In a national emergency when you face a tour of duty, you must recognize this requirement perhaps as a limitation in seeking employment. Some companies do not want to hire graduates only to lose them to the military service even for a short while. With other organizations it makes little or no difference. But keep this point in mind when you do your company analysis if military obligation is a potential fact of life for you.

What opportunities have you had for self-expression? Have you written for publication, served as a member of a team in completing some bit of significant research, invented a device, composed or conducted music, acted in or directed drama, received an honor or award, developed competence in a particular area? How well are you able to express yourself in both writing and speech? Your aptitudes and capacity are important factors in trying to determine your career selection.

Your numerical and scientific skills, your problem-solving ability, your organizational and supervisory skills, your ability to work under pressure, your aptitude and capacity for leadership, will serve you well in seeking employment if you can appraise how you stand in these areas. Add to your own analysis what others have to say about your capacities and abilities.

How physically fit are you? Different jobs and different organizations make different demands on your energy and physical stamina. Just because you feel you are in excellent physical health does not mean that you are equipped to take on *any* job. If you haven't stood on your feet, walking constantly all day, don't be misled into thinking you could handle a floor-walker's job in a department store or milling operation. Having tried a part-time job behind a retail sales counter can answer this point for you quickly.

The abilities and capacities revealed from a review and analysis of your education and experience may still produce no clear-cut career plans. So your next step is to seek professional assistance.

Your faculty advisor or a professor you know well may help you to formulate your objectives and goals. Most large institutions have counseling and testing services with highly trained psychologists and counselors available to serve students at no cost; they require a modest fee for the general public's use. There are many reputable public vocational centers you can use. A particularly helpful source in locating them is the *Directory of Vocational Counseling Services,* American Personnel, and Guidance Association, 1605 New Hampshire Avenue, N.W., Washington, D.C. ($2.50). Also see if your school has a career planning and placement office that can help you explore career possibilities. Many colleges and universities now have such a service.

The skilled counselor's responsibility is to review with you your inventory, suggest additions and revisions, and outline the basic fields that would best utilize your combination of abilities and interests. This person will help you discover more fully your assets and liabilities, to accept those that cannot be changed, and to make wholesale emotional, educational, and vocational adjustment to them.

Vocational counseling is based upon a battery of tests selected to provide multidimensional information about your intelligence, achievement, aptitude, interest, and personality. But there is no test or battery of tests that will reveal the one occupation you are best fitted for. The tests usually associated with vocational counseling and the measures sought are indicated in Exhibit 12-1.

Selection of a vocational objective is at best a difficult task. That, however, is the purpose of any self-appraisal—not to find yourself just a job, but to find *the occupational field* that will best make use of your education, special training talents, and interests (which in turn help you to achieve your career objective in the most efficient way possible).

Calvert and Steele point out the importance of your deciding this objective early by indicating that you now have more than 30,000 kinds of positions for a career selection and that "the occupation you choose will determine the kind of life you lead, your mode of living, and your circle of friends."[1] You *can* of course complicate your planning by searching exclusively for career fields suggested by your college major. Nevertheless, a general vocational objective helps to narrow or focus the choice.

FITTING YOUR QUALIFICATIONS TO THE JOB REQUIREMENTS AND THE HIRING ENTITY

As a part of defining your vocational goal you need to analyze employers in general, by industry or service, size, geographical locations, and other features. The occupation and company analyses should be no less thorough than that of your self-appraisal. Your placement office with its wealth of occupational monographs and brochures is a good place to start. From there you

[1] Robert Calvert and John E. Steele, *Planning Your Career* (New York: McGraw-Hill Book Company, 1963) p. 16.

Exhibit 12-1
Tests Used in Vocational Counseling

Type of Test	Measures	Examples
1. Intelligence	Capacity for mastering problems (generally referred to as IQ, or intelligence quotient)	Wonderlic Personnel Test Otis Self-Administering Tests of Mental Ability Wechsler-Bellevue Scales of Mental Ability
2. Achievement	Extent of knowledge or skill in a particular subject	Iowa Placement Examinations Typing or shorthand examinations College midterm or final examinations
3. Aptitude	Facility and speed with which new information or skills may be learned	Army General Classification Test Purdue Pegboard Minnesota Clerical Test
4. Interest	Pattern of likes and dislikes in various activities	Kuder Preference Record Strong Vocational Interest Blank
5. Personality	Emotional stability and personal adjustment	Bernreuter Personality Inventory Minnesota Multiphasic Personality Inventory Thurstone Temperament Schedule

Source: Robert Calvert, Jr., and John E. Steele, *Planning Your Career* (New York: McGraw-Hill Book Company, 1963), p. 14.

can conduct your own survey from current publications. Here is a listing of the best available sources, some of which will also be available in many placement offices.

Bolles, Richard N., *What Color Is Your Parachute?*, rev. ed., 1980, published by Ten Speed Press, P.O. Box 7123, Berkeley, California.

Career, published annually by Career, Inc., 15 West 45th Street, New York. Describes employment opportunities in about 60 leading organizations.

Career Information Service, Box 51, Madison Square Station, New York.

Careers Research Monographs, published by the Institute for Research, 537 South Dearborn Street, Chicago. Covers 224 occupational fields.

College Placement Annual, published by the College Placement Council, 35 East Elizabeth Street, Bethlehem, Pennsylvania. Contains an alphabetical listing and brief description of more than 1,800 organizations in the United States and Canada including information on openings and the name, title, and address of the proper person to contact.

College Placement Directory, published by the Industrial Research Service, Dover, New Hampshire. Contains an alphabetical listing of more than 1,500 employers, including name, location, type of business, name of personnel officer, and types of graduates sought; like the *College Placement Annual*, it has an occupational and geographical index.

Foreign Operations, published by Foreign Operations, Inc., New Haven, Connecticut. Describes overseas employment opportunities in U.S. business organizations and government agencies.

Forrester, Gertrude, *Occupational Literature*, published by the H. W. Wilson Company, New York. Lists occupational pamphlets and where they may be obtained.

Hawes, Gene R., *Careers Tomorrow*, published by Times Mirror, New York, 1979 (geared to college graduates). Describes a large number of career tracks, predicts future demand, and offers strategy for reaching career goals.

Insurance World, published by the Yale Daily News, Box 241, Yale Station, New Haven, Connecticut. Describes the nature, scope, and functions of career opportunities in life and property insurance.

Journal of College Placement, published quarterly by the College Placement Council, 35 East Elizabeth Street, Bethlehem, Pennsylvania. Contains articles on career opportunities, employment techniques, and descriptive career ads from leading employers.

The Occupational Outlook Handbook, published by the Bureau of Labor Statistics, the U.S. Government Printing Office, Washington, D.C. Summarizes employment opportunities in a number of fields.

Pitt, Gavin A., *The Twenty-Minute Lifetime: A Guide to Career Planning*, published by Prentice-Hall, Inc., Englewood Cliffs, New Jersey. Contains pertinent information about careers in many fields.

Smith, Leonard J., *Career Planning*, published by Harper & Row, Publishers, Inc., New York. Contains fields of interest alphabetized for easy reference.

Wall Street 20th Century, published by the Yale Daily News, Box 241, Yale Station, New Haven, Connecticut. Describes career opportunities in the securities industry.

In detailing the job requirement coverage you ought also to be guided by a list of your own salient specifications predetermined from your career objectives. Answers to the following series of questions can bring your self-analysis and job requirements into focus at this point.

1. What are the future prospects for the occupational field I want to enter? (Some technological changes make many jobs obsolete; new product discoveries open even wider horizons. The U.S. Department of Labor estimates that approximately 1.8 million persons are replaced each year by technological advances.)

2. Is the field a part of a growing industry?

3. Is money a major objective of mine? (A study of approximately 3,300 alumni from seven different colleges and schools at the Ohio State University revealed that graduates who had placed income as their

primary objective actually were earning less than those who emphasized other criteria.)[2]

4. Am I aiming for the right level? Surveys have indicated that of college graduates in industry

a. three quarters of the top executives are college trained. (So with your BBA degree, you have merely passed the entrance exam.)

b. seventy-five percent may reach middle management—currently $30,000–60,000 income. (Of this 75 percent only a fourth will go higher than levels paying $60,000 or more.)

The fact remains that there is *not* always room at the top.

5. Does the occupation choice offer me the best chance for maximum personal happiness? Does it offer a challenge? (You will be happier as one of the best in your field than as a mediocre performer in an area in which you cannot achieve top status professionally. Of course this assessment does not mean throttling your ambition, but it does mean assessing demands of various positions and appraising opportunities realistically. The job must be satisfying and worthwhile, utilizing your abilities.)

6. Do I have the temperament and patience to reach my ultimate goal? A majority of current positions, especially in larger organizations, require lengthy training programs prior to advancement of any sort, proved performance in interim associated positions, and indoctrination and knowledge gained from full company exposure.

7. Does this proposed job provide me with skills that could help me in gaining subsequent jobs? Statistics show that you will change career areas four to seven times before reaching retirement age.

Several large banks with 1,500 or more employees are now using computerized human resource information systems to help match employees' skills with various jobs and promotions as they come open. Some use a skills inventory system for exempt employees which stores personnel data, such as pay and performance information. Others, like Bank of America, are going even farther and are automating their job posting systems. Employee attitude surveys are being computerized by Citibank so the bank will know how employees feel about various job-related topics. Computerized employee information has also helped in producing annual employment information reports required by the EEO Commission. Career pathing—dividing skills and jobs into families as a prelude to job posting—is computerized as well. All these computerized systems have helped to reduce turnover and have promoted upward mobility and job satisfaction.

For describing the occupational field you are considering, the National Vocational Guidance Association has recommended a 16-point analysis as shown in Exhibit 12-2. In looking for the job for which you are best

[2] Ibid., p. 20.

suited, one of the most important decisions you will need to make is whether you should seek out a small organization or a larger one. Each has its advantages.

Advancement possibilities are perhaps greater in larger companies. In small companies, advancement may hinge upon retirement and replacement of senior employees—sometimes a slow process. Closer contacts and ties, however, more often are achieved in smaller companies than in larger ones, where personal relationships are harder to establish.

Larger companies, because of diversity, greater financial strength to weather depressions and technological changes, and more extensive training programs, usually offer better security, more proportional opportunities and fringe benefits, and the starting salary is often higher. Going into business on your own is a rewarding experience, if you have the temperament for it, but if you are security oriented, such an entrepreneurial venture is not for you. It takes a wider knowledge to run a small business than a large one because of the multiplicity of functions that one person has to perform.

Large companies emphasize long, more specialized careers. Small companies allow fewer opportunities for specialization and job requirements

Exhibit 12-2

Coverage Recommended by the National Vocational Guidance Association for Occupational Surveys

1. History of the occupation.
2. Importance of the occupation and its relation to society.
3. *Duties:* Definition of the occupation; nature of the work.
4. Number of workers engaged in the occupation: number, distribution, trends.
5. *Qualifications:* Age, sex, special qualifications or skills, scores on tests for employment, legislation affecting the occupation.
6. *Preparation:* General education, special training, experience.
7. Methods of entering.
8. Time required to attain skill.
9. *Advancement:* Lines of promotion, opportunity for advancement.
10. Related occupations.
11. Earnings: Beginning wage range; wage range of largest number of workers; maximum, median, and average salary; annual versus life earnings; regulations; benefits, other rewards.
12. *Conditions of work:* Hours, regularity of employment, health and accident hazards.
13. Organizations: Employees, employers.
14. Typical places of employment.
15. Advantages and disadvantages not otherwise enumerated.
16. *Supplementary information:* Suggested reading; trade and professional journals; visual aids; other sources; list of associations, firms, or individuals who may provide further information.

Source: Robert Calvert, Jr., and John E. Steele, *Planning Your Career* (New York: McGraw-Hill Book Company, 1963), p. 19.

have a broader base. If it is versatility, mobility, and variety you seek in an occupational objective, the smaller company rates second choice to the larger one. But small companies may offer greater prominence for an outstanding employee, more opportunity to benefit from the growth of the organization, and the possibility of eventual ownership. Advancement, consequently, is often quite fast in the small company where competition may be less.

You can increase your odds of success by deciding what you prefer before you go into an organization. Actually, however, the "perfect job" doesn't exist. So be ready to compromise. Location of the company offering the promising vocational objective you are seeking often forces a compromise. Would you be willing to live in a large, industrialized city, even though you have lived all your life in small towns, or *must* you live only in the sunny Southwest—not the northern states with severe cold winters. Your health often will dictate or affect geographical location. For some, in order to enter the field of your choice, it will be necessary to compromise on the type of position you accept.

Once you have a fairly clear idea of the employer field, find out as much as you can about the particular companies you would like to work for:

1. The character of a number of unique entities.
2. Their way of doing business.
3. Their strategies of competition.
4. Their plans for expansion.
5. Their likely future of survival in view of technological change, environmental factors, governmental actions.

You can find out about small organizations from professors, bankers, your professional contacts and friends, professional organizations, and community-supplied information. For larger organizations, there are numerous published sources: *Moody's Industrials, Standard & Poor, McRae's Blue Book, The Wall Street Journal;* you can also scan trade publications and spend some time in your own placement office files.

Educational requirements are on the upgrade for good jobs. As more and more job candidates enter the field with a bachelor's degree, the economics of supply and demand enter the picture. So the candidate with an advance degree has a favorable plus value. If you can stay on now for a master's degree, perhaps it is best to do so, although some MBA programs are now requiring work experience prior to accepting applicants for admission. Chances that you will come back after five or ten years to get it are rather slim—you will be making too much money to give up your job, and your family responsibilities may have progressed to the point where you cannot afford to. Corporations, too, are often impressed these days by students who take an advanced degree in a field other than their undergraduate majors. The fact that starting salaries are more than $300 to 500 a month higher for master's degree graduates—both for nontechnical and technical degrees—may lend some inducement to your acquiring more schooling now. Your school's placement office can supply you with average starting figures of graduates and undergraduates from your own college and field of study for comparative purposes. Probably available also in your placement office will be a copy of the College Placement Council's average monthly starting salary offers (published each June) for both master's and bachelor's degree candidates nationwide. We think you will find it time well spent to make a quick comparison between the national figures and those of your own school.

SELLING YOUR ABILITIES

Having now selected a vocational target, your next step in the career-planning process is pulling together your qualifications and planning a successful job campaign presentation through the resumé, the interview and employer application blank, and the letter.

Most employment contacts come about in the form of letter applications or interviews. Applicants quite naturally need to know what they should do, how they should act, what they should say, how they can put their best foot forward, and whether they should attempt to be humorous or witty *before* going to the interview or writing an application letter.

The Resumé

The tool used universally by skilled job seekers both with their application letters and with their job interviews is the resumé—a digest of qualifications for a job. It may be a tailored form prepared for a specific application, or it may be a general sheet obtained in multiple copies through a placement office. Both types have advantages and disadvantages.

The general sheet—the results of registering with your placement service and completing a preliminary form prebuilt to a standard plan—serves a definite purpose. Interviewing companies find it useful when it is necessary to compare qualifications among a number of candidates. But the general resumé sometimes falls short because it does not tell a specific company what it needs to know about the applicant, particularly when unique qualifications are called for.

The individually tailored resumé overcomes this gap, since the company's needs are investigated first and the applicant's qualifications to fill these needs are emphasized in this data sheet makeup.

It will pay you to put real effort into toning up your resumé, for, no matter what kind of employment you may be seeking, you are in competition. You need to get your best licks in fast. A well-written summary of your experience will help you do just that. According to employment specialists queried by *Changing Times*, you will find that a resumé is particularly important in these situations:

1. When you are seeking a professional, semiprofessional, or highly skilled job.

2. When the job you want requires special knowledge such as a foreign language or operation of complicated office technology.

3. When your experience is so diverse that when you talk about it you run the risk of seeming aimless.

4. When there is likely to be heavy competition for the job. The greater the competition, the greater your need for a personally adapted resumé.

Even if your job problem doesn't fit any of the categories, a resumé can be extremely useful. For one thing, it helps you organize your central sales message (from the self-inventory, job, and company analyses) for the all-important personal interview. For another, it focuses the interviewer's attention on your best qualifications. And it is something tangible to leave behind as a reminder of who you are and what you can do.

Here are suggestions from *Changing Times* for constructing an effective resumé:

1. Keep it short. One page is best. (Placement service data sheets are restricted to one page because of the volume of registrants handled, cost, and multiple copies provided for your personal use—usually 100 at a cost of $20.) Two pages are all right; anything longer is likely to be too much for a prospective employer to plow through. For your own tailored sheet, get everything important in. This resumé is supposed to be a rather complete catalog of facts about you which are too numerous to go into a letter. Let your first draft run as many pages as you need to get all the facts down. Then rewrite and cut ruthlessly. You'll be surprised at how much of the content you can cover in fewer words.

2. Keep it neat. Your resumé is likely to be the very first glimpse a prospective employer gets of how you do things. Don't jazz it up with fancy trimmings. Keep it conservative. Avoid using carbon copies; sharply reproduced copies from an original, however, are quite acceptable.

3. Keep it factual. What you have *done* counts, not what you *think*. Long statements proclaiming your supreme confidence in yourself are out of place; so are declarations of your business philosophy. The latter are more appropriately a part of a letter.

4. Keep it on target. You have supposedly at this stage already selected your vocational objective; so put the job title at the beginning.

Don't fake. Employers will check details, and faking will automatically rule you out. You do have a right, though, to put your best foot forward; in fact, it is expected that you will. If you are qualified for different types of jobs, it is best to write separate resumés for each.

Increasingly, resumés now begin with a short *summary of career objectives.* Such a statement may summarize both the short- and long-range goals of the applicant in an attempt to provide a favorable first impression on a prospective employer. The resumé's job, however, is primarily to give a statistical picture of the applicant as a potential employee.

In addition to name, address, and other identifying points such as your voluntary photograph, which helps to personalize your resumé, cover your education, experience, personal factors, and references. Arrange the material you include in descending order of importance or usefulness for the entry job level. If your education is more promising than your experience, this is a good place to begin. If you can only give a line or so of experience, why not make up a caption that will cover both education and experience so that the small amount of experience will not stand out all alone and exposed by itself? Military service might also be combined with work experience to show stronger qualifications.

Education and Special Training.   Some employers are interested in where and when you graduated from high school. Security-risk employers frequently go back as far as your first-grade record. But for ordinary purposes, your high school record is sufficient. Record when and where your college degree or degrees were earned, including any special features, such as highest honors, scholastic standing, your college major, scholarships, or prizes.

Many graduates dwell excessively on the fact of college training. This accomplishment you share with millions of others; special qualifications need the emphasis. Make a division of the courses you have had according to (1) those which contribute directly to the kind of work and vocational objective you are seeking and (2) those which offer supplementary background. If the catalog listing of the course is self-explanatory, you will need no further elaboration. If the content of the course is important to the job, and may not be entirely clear from the course name, explain applicable content briefly. If you made outstanding grades in your major field, it is worth recording. If you say 3.1, indicate it is 3.1 out of 4—or call it a "B" average. Grade-point bases vary.

Employment Record.   Give jobs by dates (with immediate supervisor's name), either chronologically or in reverse order. Have dates stand out from the copy. Another way to classify your record is *functionally.* For example, if you want a job as sales manager, it might be helpful to group past positions under headings like these: *sales promotion, retail selling, market research, advertising.* Include these things:

1. The period of employment, the name of the firm. Rounded month or year figures will do. Label part-time and summer work as such.

2. Your actual duties and responsibilities. It is your highest-level experience in each job that means most. Lower positions may be mentioned to show how you went up the ladder or to demonstrate that you have mastered certain skills. But don't waste precious space describing them in detail. Put the stress on what you yourself did, not on what the firm did, unless a word about the company's reputation, size, or method of operating is needed to clarify your role.

3. Your accomplishments and commendations. If you installed a new system of inventory control that reduced cost by 10 percent, say so. If you received a letter of commendation for a particular job, quote a line or two. But don't make big, flowery statements about yourself.

Personal Facts and Other Qualifications. Include date of birth, marital status and dependents, family background if it has a bearing, height, weight, health or physical limitations (if any), organization memberships (including offices you have held), participation in extracurricular activities, honors and awards, and your social security number. Something should be included also about your physical activities such as jogging, fitness exercising, participative sports (e.g., tennis or organized team), and so on.

If you have traveled widely, know several languages, or have published articles in your field, this is the place to include them. Any hobbies or special interests may well be included, but be sure that the information has some relevance to the job you are seeking. The fact that you manage the local cub scout nine or collect butterflies doesn't count, unless, of course, you want to be a recreation director or a lepidopterist.

References. List from three to six. Give names, titles, phone numbers, and addresses, but check with those whom you plan to use before you include them on your resume—this is common business courtesy. Get references from several functional areas if you can: work references, academic references, and personal references. It is helpful to include both business and home telephone numbers.

More and more resumés are omitting a list of references and are placing at the bottom of the sheet: "References available on request." Many of the best authorities still recommend listing references, however; they also recommend that references be varied. Ideally, those whose names you use should be at the same professional level as your potential employer, but you must select people who are familiar with your capabilities.

Three types of responsible community leaders usually make poor references so far as employers are concerned. Members of the clergy, rather than concentrating on employment assets and liabilities, tend to dwell on ethical or moral standing. Politicians know many people, but few of them well enough to give a specific reference. Seasoned politicians have also wisely learned the lesson of avoiding negative remarks. Physicians and dentists are acquainted with your physical health, but not necessarily vocational potential.

In summary, there are several ways to increase the mileage from your resumé:

1. List the companies you think you would like to work for; write to a top official by name if possible, by title otherwise, and enclose the data sheet. (The letter should be short, portraying your unusual characteristics. For the essentials, see the suggestions of what to include in the following discussion on letters.) Also send a copy to the top personnel officer or the top college recruiting officer, just in case someone forgets to pass it along.

2. Remember, whenever you do send the resumé through the mail, not to skip the covering letter. Time it to arrive in the middle of the week, not on a hectic Monday or Friday.

3. Give copies of your resumé to relatives, friends, and acquaintances. You may be surprised at how little they know about your experience—and how helpful many of them can be.

4. Use the resumé, along with a covering letter, to answer ads.

5. Send copies to everyone whom you intend to use as a reference with your letter requesting permission and to everyone who might be asked about you.

6. Be sure that the resumé figures in every personal interview. If you have not sent a copy ahead, produce one as soon as the interview begins. Leave one or two behind as a reminder or to be passed on to other company officials.

Examples of typical, standard data sheets—mass produced as a result of registering with a placement office and completing its form requirements—appear in Exhibits 12-3 and 12-4. An individually typed resumé designed especially for use with a specific job application is shown in Exhibit 12-5.

Many placement offices now put together resumé books which are sent to firms planning interview trips to campus. Resumés are then screened prior to campus visits. As placement services get more and more into teleconferencing (Slo-scan screens or voice-activated cameras), these resumé books will take on an increasingly important role in the job-getting process.

Application Letters

Because letters of application are read, compared, and used to screen candidates for employment, as well, your letter—if well written—is the most efficient way for you to present your qualifications to a busy executive. Do

Bruce McCombs

Bachelor of Business Administration
May 1981

Present Address

703 W. Crestland
Austin, Texas 78752
(512) 452-2498

Permanent Address

811 N. Plymouth
Dallas, Texas 75211
(214) 337-9495

Career Objective

An entry-level position in sales - strategically located with an innovative firm - leading to a position in sales/marketing management based on initiative and performance.

Educational Experience

University of Texas at Austin, 1978 to the present
Marketing Major:
   Grade Point Average in Major 4.00/4.00
Course Work:
   Major - Information and Analysis, Sales Management, and Market Area Analysis
   Outside of Major - Intermediate Business Statistics, Computer and Statistical Analysis (Mini Tab), Motivational Psychology, and Business Report Writing.

Work Experience   **Dates**

H.E.B., Austin, Texas; Checker and Provide Managerial   July 1979 to the
Supervision   present
   Responsibilities include, cash control in excess of
   $20,000, coordination of service area employees-
   determining and defining task to be performed, and
   act as liaison for customer complaints for a
   facility that has $14 million in sales annually.

Swensen's Ice Cream, Austin, Texas; Supervisor   September 1978 to
   In charge of quantity control for product sold in   July 1979
   addition to managing store operations during
   manager's absence.

Swensen's Ice Cream, Arlington, Texas;   Summer 1978
Assistant Manager
   Initiated a reduction in employee work hours by
   55% while increasing productivity 40%.

Fox Photo, Dallas, Texas; Film Salesperson   November 1976 to
   Personal performance, increased overall store sales   May 1978
   by an estimated 58%.

Percent of College Expenses Earned: 85% to 90% while working 25 hours weekly

Additional Information

Participated in a feasibility study for condominium development for local developer.

References available upon request.

Exhibit 12-3   Format of standardized duplicated resumé, undergraduate

KATHRYN CLOUGH KELLY
Master of Business Administration
May 1981

PRESENT ADDRESS
P.O. Box 7561
Austin, Texas 78712
(512) 471-3322, 476-1159

PERMANENT ADDRESS
5833 Burning Tree
El Paso, Texas   79912
(915) 581-0397

OBJECTIVE
A sales position leading to management with a dynamic multinational
corporation in the field of Telecommunication and Information Systems.

EDUCATION
Master of Business Administration, The University of Texas, Austin,
  Texas, May 1981, Concentrating in Accounting and Business Communications
  with special emphasis in Data Processing and Information Systems.
  3.4/4.0 GPA
Master of Arts, The University of Texas, Austin, Texas, August 1977,
  Majoring in Applied Linguistics, Thesis dealt with Computer Assisted
  Instruction. 3.4/4.0 GPA
Bachelor of Arts, The University of Texas, Austin, Texas, May 1975,
  Majoring in Linguistics. 3.3/4.0 GPA

COMPUTER LANGUAGES
BASIC & COBOL

FOREIGN LANGUAGES
French & Thai (rusty)

EMPLOYMENT
The University of Texas, Austin, Texas
  Teaching Assistant II, Department of General Business, August 1979-
  Present, Taught technical writing skills to students in the Graduate
  School of Business; staffed graduate Writing Laboratory.
  Research Assistant II, Department of Management, July - August 1979,
  Developed instructional material for Behavior Theory course.
  Program Specialist I & II, The Intensive English Program, June 1975 -
  August 1977, Taught English language classes to foreign students.
Telemedia Inc., Tehran, Iran.
  Instructor, November 1977 - February 1978, Taught English language
  classes to Iranian government personnel.
The Royal Thai Language Center, Bangkok, Thailand.
  Instructor, January - August 1974, Taught English language and culture
  classes to Royal Thai Navy Commanders and Admirals.

AWARDS & ACTIVITIES

Scholarship awarded by Department
  of Accounting, 1980.
Member, Curriculum Committee,
  Department of Linguistics.
Representative, School of Social
  and Behavioral Sciences Council.

Vice-president, Foreign
  Language Education
  Center Student
  Association.
Member, Mensa.

          Scholarship and earnings constituted 100% of college
          expenses for both Master's degrees.

PERSONAL
Outside interests include bicycling, karate, theater, gemology, and travel.
Have lived in France, Thailand, India, Iran, and Bangladesh.
Location preferences are California, Florida, and Southeast Asia, flexible.

REFERENCES FURNISHED UPON REQUEST

Exhibit 12-4   Format of standardized, duplicated resumé, graduate

not be deceived, however. Your chances of landing a job solely on the basis of a letter of application are practically nil. The letter's job is to create a favorable impression of you and to interest the prospective employer enough

QUALIFICATIONS OF MARK G. LORD FOR PARKS AND RECREATION WORK

Permanent Address: 3500 Hillbrook Drive
                    Austin, Texas 78731
                    (512) 459-5367

Vocational Objective: To acquire a position which leads to
                       administrative responsibility in Parks
                       and Recreation Services.

Social Security Number: 465-86-2157

PREPARATION AND TRAINING

1976: Graduated from L. C. Anderson High School (Austin, Texas)

1981: Completed five years' specialized study in Physical
       Education and Economics at The University of Texas at
       Austin. Awarded a Bachelor of Science Degree in
       Physical Education and a Texas Teaching Certificate
       for Secondary Schools. (Available May 1981)

SPECIALIZED COURSES CONTRIBUTING TO RECREATION QUALIFICATIONS

(Racket Sports and Individual Sports as areas of concentration)

Racket Sports: Tennis--Beginning and High Intermediate
                Racquetball
                Badminton--Beginning and Intermediate

Individual Sports: Bowling
                    Archery
                    Golf
                    Conditioning--Cardiovascular Physical Fitness

COURSES AND SKILLS PERTAINING TO GENERAL RECREATION KNOWLEDGE

SOCCER   SOFTBALL   FOOTBALL   GYMNASTICS--DEVELOPMENTAL

RELEVANT COURSES IN HUMAN PHYSICAL AND NEUROLOGICAL FUNCTIONS

Basic Human Anatomy, Physiology of Exercise, Motor Learning
Kinesiology--Bio-mechanics of Sports, Basic Neurological Motor
  Control

SPECIAL COURSES IN TRAINING AND SKILLS

Football Coaching, Baseball Coaching, Athletic Training; Varsity
Football Manager 1976-1981; National Flag Football Association
Umpire; United States Tennis Association--Associate Umpire.

Exhibit 12-5   An individually tailored, typed resumé

1977-1978: PARD Specialist II--National Junior Tennis League
            Instructor (Austin Parks and Recreation Department)
1979:   Supervisor for 8 Playgrounds--National Junior Tennis
            League (Austin Parks and Recreation Department)
1980:   Director, National Junior Tennis League--Austin Program
            (Austin Parks and Recreation Department)

PERSONAL DETAILS AND EXTRACURRICULAR ACTIVITIES

Age: 22
Height: 5 feet, 7 inches
Weight: 145 pounds
Health: Excellent; no physical handicaps
Birthplace: Champaign, Illinois; July 29, 1958
Marital Status: Single
Church Affiliation: Baptist

COLLEGE ORGANIZATION MEMBERSHIPS

Sigma Nu Fraternity (social)--Officer; University of Texas
  Football Team Manager

HONORS RECEIVED

Athletic Scholarship 1979-80; 1980-81; Senior Head Manager, The
  University of Texas Football Team, 1979-80; Texas Letterman
  Who's Who in America, High School

REFERENCES (BY PERMISSION)

Mr. Bill Ellington   Mr. Prenis Williams
Athletic Director   Superintendent of Athletics,
The University of Texas   Aquatics, and Tennis
Austin, Texas 78712   Austin Parks and Recreation
                                    Department
Dr. Gaylord A. Jentz, Chairman   P. O. Box 1088
Department of General Business   Austin, Texas 78767
The University of Texas
Austin, Texas 78712
                                  Dr. Waneen W. Spirduso
Mr. Anthony B. Luttrell   Chairperson, Department of
President, General Office   Health & Physical Education
  Equipment Company   The University of Texas
P. O. Box 4005   Austin, Texas 78712
Austin, Texas 78767

Exhibit 12-5   Continued

to investigate your qualifications and to make contact with you. Most employers won't hire until they have had a personal interview.

Even if a letter doesn't lead to an interview immediately, it still may help you. The good letter written by a promising candidate is filed away for future references. This situation is especially true for employers who do not advertise job openings or make regular recruiting trips. Rather, they rely on carefully screened unsolicited applications.

In this situation, your application letter offers two distinct, positive advantages: (1) presenting your writing and organizational skills, it can quickly set you apart from your competition on these two important elements pertinent to most positions, and (2) it is often easier to present outstanding achievements in writing than in an oral interview.

As you plan for the letter portion of your campaign for the job of your choice, keep in mind there are several kinds of application letters you may have to write.

1. *The "blind ad" application*—Answering a blind ad is usually one of the last sources of a job for the college graduate. The identity of the company is usually unknown. Ads in newspapers, magazines, journals, and teletype releases telling of a job opening are typical. Only very general and limited information about the job is revealed with a box number address for your reply.

2. *Prospecting application*—The writer, *without knowledge of whether a job opening exists*, sends this kind of letter to a company of his or her choice attempting to create interest and, hopefully, a job. Generally, there has been no previous contact between the company and the applicant. But from the applicant's already accomplished company analyses, he or she is quite certain such a company normally requires people with his or her qualifications. Although the best way to write such a letter is to learn as much as you can about the company, its policies, its key personnel, its history, and its future plans, it is possible to write a pattern letter that may be adapted to several companies offering similar types of employment.

If you will write many such letters, the pattern piece becomes virtually an economic necessity. The fact that it is a pattern letter must not be allowed to show through, however. An appearance of carrying on a direct-mail campaign might imply that you are rather desperate for a job. Prospecting applications have the following advantages over those where a job exists:

a. You have a greater choice of companies and locations.

b. You have a chance to be considered for jobs that are often not advertised.

c. You can sometimes create a job for yourself where none existed before.

d. You do not have as much competition as for an advertised job.

e. Often it is the only way for you to get the exact kind of work you want to do.

f. It is the tool for paving the way for a better job a few years later after you have gained some experience.

Any notice in the newspapers, magazines, or trade journals of expansion plans indicates the need for additional personnel. What chance will you have of getting one of the top jobs in expanded operations? Very little, since key people are usually moved in. But there is a chance to get in at the beginning of a growing concern.

What sorts of jobs could you create for yourself? What sorts of added services could you talk the company into adding that you could initiate for them? A good way to begin, for there will be no older people ahead of you who may stand in the way of your progress.

3. *Follow-up*—Initial application contacts sometimes draw no (or only routine) response. The follow-up letter may be written to revive or heighten the reader's interest in the applicant.

4. *The note of appreciation*—Common business courtesy dictates a "thank you" following an interview. It is particularly appropriate after you have made an expense-paid trip to the prospective employer's office or plant. So often this is the kind of letter the applicant forgets to write, but—because of its rarity—is so much appreciated by the receiver. This goodwill message contact is yet another example of the favorable impression the applicant makes in following up on the job campaign.

5. *Follow-through*—After an employer has shown an initial spark of interest, the follow-through letter may be required. Such a letter is frequently requested at the end of a personal interview or as a result of the first application letter. The employer sometime asks for more information or reflections of your thought on certain issues or points raised.

6. *The job-offer postponement*—In your process of company interviewing, particularly through a college placement office, it is quite likely you may receive a job offer from one or more firms before you have completed all interviews, or before you hear from a company you are especially interested in. Your task, then, is to postpone a decision temporarily.

7. *The job-offer turndown*—Although not really an application letter per se, the job refusal still may hold potential for future employment. Your best approach is the positive, goodwill, leave-the-door-open ploy recommended in Chapter 5, page 190 in handling negative responses.

8. *The job-offer acceptance*—With your campaigning done, and the job of your choice decided, the last letter is your official acceptance. Enthusiasm and pleasure are the keynotes for this direct-style, informative message.

To be effective, all letters of application should be personalized and follow certain basic principles.

Always address the letter with the employer's name whenever possible—the personnel manager, department superintendent, vice president, or president by title when you cannot find names from placement offices, employment agencies, or directories. Care should be taken for correct spelling and title.

The opening should be fairly direct, but the applicant needs to do something more than just say: "Here I am. I want a job with your company." After all, the first paragraph of *this* persuasive message, too, should attract the reader's attention, tell why the letter is written, and be specific about the job-entry area being applied for. In the case of the prospecting letter, the applicant sometimes *needs to create a job* as well and a routine opening just will not do that.

In a simple, natural way, you as writer move into the reader's field of interest with talk about employment in the firm. Why you picked this particular company to write to, the name of a person who recommended that you write and that person's connection with the company, or special qualifications you may have for doing the job are all possibilities for the opening. Many candidates begin letters with a question. It should not be coy or *too* provocative. In subtly catching the reader's interest and showing that you have some understanding of the business, you want to take care *not* to lecture the reader or say what the company needs. By the same token, don't offer yourself as a superhuman, the answer to all of the firm's problems.

Although a good introductory paragraph may raise some questions in the mind of the reader (which the middle paragraphs should answer), its content should fit you into the image the employer has of his or her own organization.

Here are two example openings revealing the candidates' research on the employer.

> Greenfield Construction Company's successful bids on contracts for the new Post Office Building and the Stratford High-Rise Office-Apartment complex undoubtedly make it the envy of the industry. I am seeking an opportunity to put my abilities to use in the engineering department of your on-the-go firm.
>
> . . .
>
> After studying your company, using your products, and talking with your retailers, I am much impressed with your engineering skills, sound marketing procedures, and progressive management policies. I'd now appreciate the chance to use my qualifications on a job in your accounting department.

As you move straight into the details that will demonstrate you can do the job your opening talks about, beware of the selfish tone, as in the following:

> For four years my thoughts and studies have been fixed on the day when my degree in Public Accounting from the University of _____would help place me in a large, nationally known, respected concern where I could advance rapidly.

Such a turn focuses only on the writer. You must present the effects of, as well as facts about, your qualifications and preferably in terms of how they apply specifically to the job to be done for the prospective employer. Play up your university major as a *foundation for starting*. But aim at one particular type of work in the company. Your supplementary qualifications on your resumé will enable the prospective employer to determine where you could fit in if there are no openings in the field you are applying for—and in case you look too good to pass up. Specific examples—adapting your qualifications to fit job requirements—develop a clear and interesting picture of your accomplishments and capabilities.

Positive statements are much more helpful than are negative ones in pointing out how your background fits the requirements of the job. Consider such common weaknesses as "inexperience," "too young," or "a follower, not a leader." Positively, lack of experience might be thought of as flexibility. The inexperienced person can absorb an employer's procedures without having to unlearn past experiences or habits.

To counteract your youth, you may be able to demonstrate by your past accomplishments, your ambition, your willingness to learn, your record of hard work, and your acceptance of responsibility and maturity, that you are not too young for the job.

The ability to follow intelligently and resourcefully is an asset of interest to most employers, for no matter how far up the organizational structure you move, some following is necessary. Even the president of the firm must follow most of the recommendations of his or her operative supervisors and staff consultants. And the CEO is always aware that his or her actions are being reviewed and appraised by the board of directors, the stockholders, or the general public.

Work in something of your personal characteristics and your attitude toward the job or career. (Wanting to build a career with the company, if you give convincing reasons, is perhaps the best-liked attitude as far as personnel administrators are concerned.) Tell something about your family status, background, whether you have earned all or part of your college expenses, and so on.

Play up any qualifications other candidates might not have—such as knowledge of a foreign language for border or overseas jobs, having grown up in the industry you are interested in entering, or in a place where it is concentrated, excellent training and grades in closely related academic fields. Personnel interviewers are always interested in grades, for better or for worse.

Despite the shining exceptions that disprove the rule, a good academic record usually correlates with later financial success. But if your scholastic record is low, don't search for excuses. Instead, look for qualities that make grades less important. Look at the courses in which you excelled to determine what point or points you can stress. Good grades in English or business communication, for example, give you an obvious chance to demonstrate your writing ability in the application letter itself. This fact, correlated with evidence of high scores on verbal achievement tests, tends to confirm a specialized ability to communicate effectively—a valuable trait for any applicant to possess. A good grade-point average in your major subject can also demonstrate your ability to excell in other specific areas.

Sometimes low grades result from an individual's having worked his or her way through school. The fact that you were ambitious enough to do just that and succeeded by earning the degree is pretty strong evidence of your determination and willingness to work hard.

If you are employed at the time you write the letter of application, tell why you are seeking another position. Again, this statement should be presented positively—without any negative reference to your present employer. Perhaps the reason may be that you have reached the top plateau for some time to come in your present company. Maybe your interests and career objectives have changed legitimately since you have had a chance to try your first career choice, or from association with other professions.

Your application letter is an attempt to get further negotiations underway. It should end with a statement or question that invites an expression of interest. Your close may ask the reader to investigate your qualifications by contacting your references for an outside opinion about you. It may be your offer to supply additionally requested information. You may ask for an interview if the distance is not too great, or for an application form.

When you do ask for an interview appointment, it is always appropriate to suggest when, in general, you will be available for it. For long distances, the company generally arranges transportation; so you should wait for the offer.

Stay away from *if* closings: "*If* my qualifications suggest to you the type of person who . . . ." Avoid the no-choice of alternatives begun with *when*: "When may I see you to discuss my prospects for. . . ." (Such a close implies that the recipient has no choice but to see you.)

Some friction is caused, too, by the applicant who closes with the statement that he or she will call the employer's secretary to schedule an interview appointment . . . quite presumptuous on the applicant's part. If an employment possibility exists, most employers will be pleased to contact you.

An effective application letter can usually be limited to a single page, for the resumé carries the burden of additional information. But blend the letter with the resumé. The letter must tell something about the writer and attract interest so the resumé will be read.

Slanting your letter's message to the employer's needs is just as important in the letter as it is in the tailored resumé. Your job is to make your letter tell what you can do for the employer—as such it stresses the *interests of the reader*, not the writer. Excessive use of first-person pronouns reflects lack of skill in communicating and detracts from the impression the applicant seeks to create with this letter. Spend part of your polishing of the letter copy, therefore, editing excessive pronouns. To eliminate them completely, however, will make your letter unnatural and less smooth than it should be. Work for a tone of modest self-confidence in your entire presentation.

The finished job should invite reading by being well typed and on white, plain stationery; generous margins; no errors, strikeovers, or messy erasures; grammatically and mechanically correct. Sending a carbon gives the impression of not caring enough about any particular employer to send a personal letter and reveals the fact you are mass mailing.

Exhibits 12-6 and 12-7 illustrate many of the principles set forth in the preceding discussion for effective initial application contacts.

The Interview and Application Form

Good job interviews do not just happen. The applicant has a responsibility to prepare for the interview, both physically and mentally. The *College Placement Annual* suggests that you

1.   Take pains to be physically presentable, prompt, and courteous.

2.   Absorb adequate information about the company from information sheets and brochures.

3.   Develop a general alertness to what is going on in the business world and the world at large through a planned reading program.

4.   Work at the ability to converse in a free-flowing and grammatically correct manner. The successful candidate is usually characterized by good personal presence and effective oral communication.

5.   Make the most of any *demonstrated* capacities for leadership. The candidate who has actively sought responsibility in campus activities, or at least has accepted such responsibility when thrust upon him or her is a better bet to achieve a successful career than one who has neither sought nor accepted opportunities to develop and exercise administrative knowhow.

Good grooming is, of course, vital. Hair combed, fingernails clean, shoes shined—these are basic. Expensive clothing is not essential. Dress neatly, attractively—and reasonably conservatively. You want to make just the right impression.

What about mental preparation? Never go into an interview cold. You cannot afford to be in the dark about a company's operations, products, size, and special features. Do your research before the interview so that you can talk intelligently about the company.

Informally, at least, prepare a list of questions on things you want to know about the company. While you no doubt will have specifics you want to ask about, consider the following questions, particularly if your company research effort hasn't produced answers prior to the interview:

2506 Pearl Street
Knoxville, Tennessee 37922
November 15, 19xx

Mr. James J. Campbell, Manager
Southern Accounting Division
J. C. Penney Company
3454 Ross Avenue
Atlanta, Georgia 30310

Dear Mr. Campbell:

Certainly the overwhelming success and growth of the J. C. Penney Company
from 1901 to 19xx is evidenced by the 1700 Penney stores now stretching
across the nation. In the mammoth accounting systems and control operations you maintain in running your division smoothly, I would like to
apply my talents and ability for hard work.

During my studies for a BBA degree at the University of Tennessee, accounting has been my special field of interest. Thirty hours in this one area
have included basic accounting courses, cost, tax, auditing, and others,
with special emphasis on corporate and systems accounting. With such a
background, I believe I am not only well versed in accounting theory and
principles, but that I can readily comprehend the magnitude of accounting
operations for a company the size of the J. C. Penney organization.

I have maintained high grades (a 2.4 overall out of 3.0) while partici-
pating in several social and student government activities. As an officer
in Sigma Phi Epsilon social fraternity, I assumed responsibilities of
leadership. In student government I was a member of the CBA Council
representing the Junior Class as Vice-president, and I worked actively on
other Challenge and Round-Up Committees.

For the past few summers I have worked in the Knoxville Penney Store under
the direction of Mr. Lloyd Dennis. The valuable knowledge of a local
store's operations thus gained should enable me to understand and appreciate the separate entity and to coordinate accounting procedures with
all-store operations in the Southern Accounting Division. I realize that
I have a lot yet to learn. With the company's training and guidance and
my own determination, I know that I can become a useful and valuable
member of the Penney accounting team.

A complete detailing of my personal history, complementary courses studied,
and references are presented on the attached data sheet for your consideration.

Since I shall be eligible for employment after graduation in January, I
should welcome the opportunity for discussing my qualifications further
with you at your convenience. In the meantime, I shall be pleased to
provide any additional information you need.

Sincerely yours

Robert L. Adair, III

Robert L. Adair, III

Exhibit 12-6 An effective initial-contact application

1.   This is the way I understand the position (present it); then follow with: Is that the way you see the job?
2.   What career paths are open at _____(company)?
3.   What makes your company different from others in the industry?

3500 Hillbrook Drive
Austin, Texas   78731

February 7, 19xx

Ms. Sharon Prete, Director
Parks and Recreation Department
214 East Main Street
Round Rock, Texas   78664

Dear Ms. Prete:

With Round Rock's unprecedented population growth in new, young families, no doubt you are now considering the necessary expansion in city services to keep pace. Can you use a young person with solid credentials in recreation and a genuine desire to work for the up-and-growing City of Round Rock?

Strongest of the area programs that I could bring to you and the citizens of Round Rock is a completely implemented Tennis League--from the 8-year-old through adult levels. I successfully directed the National Junior Tennis League, Austin Program, last year. Currently, I am an NJTL Field Representative for Central Texas. Additionally, I have the knowledge to organize, implement, and operate city leagues for a variety of team sports. Parks and recreation programs have been an integral part of my working life for the past 5 years while earning a degree in Physical Education and Economics. I am certified by the State for teaching.

Other details of my education, experience, and flexibility, shown on the enclosed resumé, will allow me, I believe, to adapt quickly to new, changing, and different situations. As I'm sure you are finding out, a city with the fast growth rate Round Rock experiences certainly may encounter such at any time. Because I am young, healthy, accustomed to long hours, eager, and willing to work where the community needs in recreation exist, you will find me a sound addition to your parks and recreation personnel. I plan to make a career in this field.

May I have an appointment for an interview with you soon to discuss the possibilities of my joining the Round Rock City Team? Please call me at home (512) 459-5367 where a message can be taken while I'm completing my practice teaching assignments in Physical Education for the Austin Independent School District this spring.

Sincerely yours

Mark Gregory Lord

Exhibit 12-7   An initial-contact application letter combining two areas of study

4.   What do you predict as future interests and/or involvements of your company?

5.   If, after three or four years I decided to leave your company, what marketable advantages will I have gained from employment with ____ (company)?

6.   Will this position we are discussing involve using my _____(specific major) coursework/graduate coursework?

7.   What are the company benefits offered new employees?

8.   What is the (cost of living, climate, housing, transportation facilities) where your firm is located?

9.   How large is the organization? How long has it been in business? What is the reputation of the company? What are its products/services? What are its management policies? Where are its branch offices? (Surely your research on the company should have provided some of this information. You might phrase a question as follows: I understand that your company employs approximately 3,500 individuals, but how many branch operations do you have and in what cities are they located?)

10.   Do you think I have the qualifications you are looking for?

Show your interest. You will have an opportunity to ask questions. And if you don't, the interviewer will think that you are not interested.

Anticipate what the interviewer will want to know about you. Be prepared to take advantage of your strong points and to handle your weaker ones skillfully.

Here is a list of questions frequently asked of college graduates in employment interviews taken from the updated Endicott survey, Northwestern University:[3]

1.   In what school activities have you participated? Why? Which did you enjoy the most?

2.   What courses did you like best? Least? Why?

3.   How much money do you hope to earn at age 30? 35?

4.   What do you think determines a person's progress in a good company?

5.   Are you primarily interested in making money, or do you feel that service to your fellow human beings is a satisfactory accomplishment?

6.   Tell me a story.

7.   What interests you about our product or service?

8.   Have you ever changed your major field of interest while in college? Why?

9.   When did you choose your college major?

[3] *Placement Manual*, Published for The University of Texas at Austin School of Business by University Communications, Inc., Rahway, NJ, 1981, pp. 12, 18, 48.

10.   If you were given a chance to work for our company, how do you think you could be of most value to us?

11.   Why do you think you might like to work for our company?

12.   Do you think that your extracurricular activities were worth the time you devoted to them? Why?

13.   Would you prefer a large or a small company? Why?

14.   Are you willing to go where a company sends you?

15.   What is your major weakness?

16.   Which of your college years was the most difficult? Why?

17.   Have you ever had any difficulty getting along with fellow students or faculty?

18.   What kind of a boss do you prefer?

19.   How do you feel about your family?

20.   How do you spend your spare time? What are your hobbies?

21.   What other kinds of preparation will you need to be a success with our company?

22.   What qualifications do you have that make you feel you will be successful in your field?

23.   How do you feel about traveling?

24.   What would you consider to be routine work?

25.   What kind of people irritate you the most? How do you get along with them?

27.   Tell me what you have done from your junior year in high school until now.

28.   How would you react to being asked to do something that was not a part of your normal job?

29.   What causes you to lose your temper?

30.   What do you do to keep in good physical condition?

31.   What job in the company would you like to work toward?

32.   What have you done that shows initiative and your willingness to work?

33.   What have you learned from any jobs that you have held?

34.   How old were you before you became self-supporting?

35.   What would you like to learn to do that you cannot do now?

Surely, too, you will want to take note of the following list of negative factors mentioned in the same survey that led most frequently to rejection of the applicant. The list was composed by personnel officers of 153 companies:

1.   Poor personal appearance.

2.   Overbearing, aggressive, conceited.

3. Poor use of English.
4. Overemphasis on money, open to highest bid.
5. Poor scholastic record, just got by.
6. Lack of courtesy, ill-mannered.
7. Limp, fishy handshake.
8. Failure to look interviewer in the eye.
9. Sloppy application blank.
10. Lack of planning career, no goals.
11. No interest in company, industry.
12. Cynical.
13. Radical ideas.
14. Late to interview without reason.
15. Never heard of the company.
16. Asked no questions about the job.
17. Indefinite response to questions.
18. Failure to express thanks for interview.

Remember, you never get a second chance to make a first impression. The first two-to-five minutes of any employment interview are usually the most crucial—especially in terms of subjective decisions that take place during the interview. To some extent you can have an instrumental role in determining the success of that interview:

Management of the Employment Interview

The order of items in an interview cannot easily be predetermined. The prospective employer is, of course, in control. You, however, need to

1. Clarify the job requirements.

2. Show *why* you are applying: for this job (or type of work), at this time, with *this company.*

3. Present your qualifications in these terms: you have something of value to offer the company (assuming that *you* are convinced of this truth).

a. Deal as much as possible in specific details and examples—job experiences, avocations, travel, activities, offices held, organizations, school work, special assignments, honors, and so on. (In other words, be freely responsive; avoid curt "yes" and "no" answers. On the other hand, don't "gas off" forever!)

b. Don't be reluctant to admit potential "weaknesses." Under no circumstances should you attempt to bluff or fake on these.

c. But: Wherever possible, make a transition from a "weakness" to a strength; or at least, when the facts justify it, show some good extenuating circumstances for the weakness, if possible. Avoid supplying alibis or excuses.

d. Try to summarize and to leave a strong, clear impression on the *main reason(s)* you should be qualified to hold a certain type of job with this firm.

e. Do not depend merely on a "smooth front" (appearance, smile) to "sell yourself." Provide full information to the prospective employer for your mutual benefit.

4. Deal as much as possible in factual, neutral terms about yourself; avoid vague or evaluational adjectives. (A bad example: "I had an *excellent* experience in my job with the Smith Manufacturing Company.")

5. Get as much information as possible on such "sensitive" matters as salary (usually in terms of *a range* or of the "going average") in the middle or later portions of the interview. Avoid giving the impression (a) that you expect a soft, high-paying job, (b) that your chief concern is with money, or (c) that you expect to be hired immediately as a supervisor or executive.

6. Don't play up the "training period" so much that it sounds as though your main concern is to keep on going to school, or that you won't really be qualified, in terms of basic essentials, to hold the job (until the company completely reeducates you).

7. Let the employer set the "tone" or atmosphere of the interview. Be a little more formal than usual—but not a stuffed shirt.

8. Watch the opening moments of the interview: Avoid making any remark that may create a negative context for the rest of the interview, for example, starting off with a remark such as "I'm really not sure that my background will be appropriate for your company or for this job" or "I'm sorry to say I haven't had any experience along these lines."

9. Be informed on the company: its history, geographical locations, general methods of doing business, reputation, and so on. Make an extra effort to learn the spelling of the firm's name and the interviewer's name and official title with absolute accuracy.

10. Try never to have an interview concluded without some sort of understanding about where you stand, what is to happen next, who is to contact whom, and such. (This last point, however, does not mean that you are to push the prospective employer against the wall and force a definite commitment!)

Most personnel managers see the job interview as a learning experience. It's an opportunity for the employer to get information about the applicant and for the applicant to find out about the position and the company. In recent years, however, the traditional job interview has come under attack; minority groups have complained that some of the questions that are asked are irrelevant to the job and can be used as screening tools by prejudiced individuals or firms.

The result is that the federal government now lists 42 questions that should not be asked of an applicant during the preemployment interview. Naturally, some of the questions will be asked after the applicant is hired so that personnel and payroll records can be set up. Here are sample questions:

1. Asking the applicant his or her marital status.

2. Asking the applicant his or her religious preference (unless job related).

3. Asking "What holidays do you observe?"

5. Asking the applicant if his or her parenting will interfere with job commitments and responsibilities.

5. Asking the applicant about pregnancy or family planning.

6. Asking the applicant if he or she has an established credit rating.

7. Asking the applicant if he or she is a homosexual.

8. Requesting any preemployment information from female applicants that is not requested from male applicants.

9. Using any test such as an IQ exam for preemployment selection if it is not directly job related.

10. Asking questions concerning the applicant's status as the head of the household or as the principal wage earner.

Some personnel recruiters seemingly make no written notations during the course of an interview for one reason or another. They neither want to distract you unnecessarily by appearing to take down every word you say or to put you on the defensive and have you puzzled over what you said (that you shouldn't have, perhaps) or didn't say and should have. Make no mistake, however; the recruiter will compile a written record of the cogent points in the interview as soon as he or she is alone and can do so without interruption.

Other interviewers will follow a carefully planned, printed form, checking each item as you respond to their questioning. Such a form gives the recruiter a much more accurate, comprehensive basis for later comparisons and evaluations of all the prospective candidates interviewed than does relying on memory notations made *after* each interview has been completed.

Your letter of application and data sheet have interested the employer in your qualifications to get you this far. But before you are actually hired for a position—even before you are interviewed on some occasions—most employers require you to fill out a detailed application blank. Some forms are extensive and probing in the information sought, frequently 4–7 pages in length. The completed form and seeming minutia asked for may even be subjected to the probing eye of the company's psychologist.

Before you start to fill out any application blank, you should first read the instructions *carefully*. Some employers prefer that you type the information in, others prefer that you print it, and still others want the data in your own handwriting. Look over the entire form before you begin; some questions may be related.

Fill the blanks carefully and completely. Many job seekers carry detailed information with them to the company so that they will be able to list the required facts quickly, accurately, and easily. Should you be hired, your application blank will be placed permanently in your personnel file, or it may even become your master personnel record. It will be read and used many times, especially when your name comes up for merit raises or promotion. Every form will include questions not pertinent to your background. It is best to respond to these with an "NA" (not applicable), indicating that you have read the question but that it does not apply to you. A sloppy application blank hints at careless work habits and lack of interest in the employer. Sometimes, too, the original application forms are used later for weeding out prospects for special assignments after otherwise highly qualified candidates have been hired and are on the job.

An increasing number of application blanks have been designed by psychologists and are reviewed and evaluated by them. Typical of the items added by psychologists are questions soliciting essay responses on such topics as your attitude toward former employers, your self-concept, and your preference for various types of people. Don't attempt to outguess the psychologists; do answer questions carefully and completely. Your responses provide still another measure of your qualifications, and they help assure the prospective employer that you will fit the job's requirements.

Your attempt to land the right job with the right company that in turn will help you ultimately attain your career objective most efficiently should be planned and controlled just as carefully as any other research project. A useful tool in this process is the contact-control record. You may have half a dozen or more applications in process at one time. Because it is difficult to keep tabs on what stage each one is in at any given moment, a control record is indispensable to an efficient effort. Illustrated in Exhibit 12-8, this form or some variation of it should be maintained rigorously as each stage of the separate applications you have underway develops.

What Personnel Officers Have to Say

Because personnel officers receive far more letters from applicants than they can interview, they use a weeding-out process for the likeliest candidates to follow up on. Trick letters are the first to be thrown out—like the one written upside down to Marshall Field & Co., Chicago, some years ago, or the one with pennies pasted across the top that begins: "I want to be sure and get my two cents worth in." Most employers, in response to survey questioning, tell us they like a letter that is natural and direct, not clever or cute but still individual.

Carelessness, vagueness, and egotism in letters will also help personnel officers pare their list to prime candidates for interviews. A worn ribbon or dirty typeface, bad layout, misspellings, strikeovers, general statements with no specifics—no clear indication of what kind of job the applicant wants, or why, or when—keep letters from receiving a fair reading. Here are typical comments made by these busy executives:

We assume that the applicant is writing us the best letter he or she knows how to write. If candidates are careless about it, when could we ever trust them to be careful?

Without specific evidence, we can't make even a preliminary judgment about the applicant. It just takes too long to find out what's there.

Some applicants seem to know too much to learn anything more. We prefer a person who knows that he or she doesn't know everything.

Executives who do the hiring do give consideration to letters offering efficient organization of the material presented, those giving evidence of distinctive facts, and those revealing the writers' own personality and writing ability. A typical comment is this one:

RECORD OF EMPLOYER CONTACTS	INTERVIEWER — Ron Jones / EMPLOYER — XYZ CORPORATION												
Date and Time of Interview	10/5 8:30												
Application Submitted	11/9												
Inquiry or Application Letter	11/12												
Interview or Plant Visit Offer	11/24												
Plant Visit Taken	12/17												
Job Offer Received	1/10 $790												
Rejection Letter Recieved													
Contact Terminated	SAMPLE												

Exhibit 12-8   Control record of employer contacts

We think we can usually tell whether the tone of a letter is genuine or phony. If it reads like a real person talking, we usually take an interest. If it reads like all the others in the pile, we lose interest, quickly.

A study made by Dan Hillard[4] of IBM resulted in the idea that personnel officers are more interested in a down-to-earth, straightforward presentation of qualifications than in one with perhaps more literary quality. One hundred personnel directors scattered over the country and in various industries were asked to evaluate two prospecting letters for accounting jobs: one was the best of its kind a business communication teaching staff could cook up in the direct style, asking immediately for a place with the company and then showing why the applicant could fill that job. The other was more subtle, trying to create an interest in the applicant, inductive fashion, in good writing style.

Sixty-eight percent of the respondents preferred the more direct approach, 21 percent the inductive. The study revealed that the better educated a personnel officer was, the more likely that person was to prefer the inductive application. If they like it at all, they like it very much.

The opinions run pro and con as might be expected. Here are some of the comments from that study.

G. F. Irvin, Household Finance Corporation: "In writing a letter of application, a college graduate should not strive to intrigue the reader with literary ploys. Instead, facts should be given in as simple, uncluttered, unencumbered, plain a fashion as possible."

James H. Logan of Dun & Bradstreet: "My appraisal of an applicant would be based. . . on factual information provided by the applicant on a completed application for employment form, by additional facts elicited during the interview, and by background investigation."

J. L. Neill, Libby-Owens-Ford Fibers Company: "As our company operates in every section of the country, employment opportunities may be a considerable distance from the applicant's home. A positive statement of willingness to relocate if necessary gives us something to go on in fitting the applicant into the organization."

Carl G. Strub, Colgate-Palmolive Company: "Personally, I favor the letter-resumé combination. In the letter I look for the source of reference to the company, the applicant's reason for selecting the company, the general field of work desired, and an estimated salary requirement. Other pertinent information is best presented, I feel, in a brief outline-type resumé."

P. A. Carlstone, International Harvester Company: "It is our feeling that it would be better to submit a shorter letter of application and include ·

[4] As a graduate student at The University of Texas, Dan Hillard conducted a nationwide research study, and wrote an analytical report on personnel directors' preferences in the letter of job application.

personal data information on a separate sheet rather than require a company to write for the personal data sheet after it receives the original employment letter."

R. M. Bielstein, Celanese Corporation of America: "Get to the point of interest without the thought-provoking question. I am not one to subscribe to the question approach. Try to create reader interest without overwhelming."

A. A. Henderson, Texas National Bank of Houston: "The letter should be brief and simple, covering the following points:

1. Date and why available.
2. Express a sincere interest in entering my business.
3. Request an appointment if I am interested, giving dates available for an interview.

Attach a fairly complete resumé of the following:

1. Education—showing college scholastic record, honors, athletic and extracurricular activities.
2. Family—including marital status.
3. Military experience and status, if applicable.
4. Health.
5. Work experience—including temporary and part-time.
6. Any other pertinent information."

J. E. Glassgow, Bemis Brother Bag Company: "No letter would result in a job offer since we would never employ a person without using a multiple interview system."

Alan B. Kamman, Director of College Recruiting: "The Bell Telephone System does not hire anyone except on the basis of a personal interview . . . both of your applicants would have been offered the opportunity of visiting us. Summed up, our feeling is that an application *per se* is not necessarily a hallmark of character or initiative. We need to talk with the individual personally."

The Colgate-Palmolive Company response also included this remark:

There is a volume of applications and resumés which must be examined daily. We require all applicants to complete and submit one of our standard application forms as well, and we usually reserve any consideration until that is received and reviewed. For these reasons, we welcome the brief and direct approach in application letters.

And Ellis Gladwin, former communications specialist for Connecticut Mutual Life Insurance Company, quotes the personnel director of a huge corporation this way:

Recently we interviewed over 100 college graduates to fill a post calling for knowledge of good English. None of them made the grade. None of them knew the rules of good writing, and none of them could express . . . clear, simple forthright English sentences.[5]

Norman Cousins, in a provocative editorial in *Saturday Review*, adds weight to the employer's desire for hiring people who can communicate:

It makes little difference how many university courses or degrees a person may have. If he or she cannot use words to move an idea from one point to another, that person's education is incomplete. Taking in a fact is only part of the educational process. The ability to pass it along with reasonable clarity and even distinction is another. The business of assembling the right words, putting them in proper sequence, enabling each one to pull its full weight in the conveyance of meaning—these are the essentials.[6]

There seem to be, then, certain characteristics that business executives look for in the potential employee of their firms—the formula personnel heads believe to be indicative of future business success:

1. *A balance between classroom performance and extracurricular activities.*
2. *A balance between specific abilities and a well-rounded personality.*

Companies look with great favor on students who are active on campus. They look with even greater favor on active students who can get "B's" and a few "A's". Although candidates who have superior academic averages to display to potential employers can take considerable comfort from their attainments, it is extremely important to realize that grades are far from "the whole show." The top scholar with little else to offer may find the competition with top scholars possessing other strong qualities somewhat disconcerting. Moreover, some employers do not emphasize the highest grades, and others require high grades only in some of the areas for which they recruit. Thus it is possible for a top scholar to lose out in competition for the most attractive offers to those with more modest academic attainments who can present important nonscholastic qualities.

With modern life dominated by electronics and business more and more quantitatively oriented, however, it is probable that good grades are taking on increased importance. A mistake of a decimal point, personnel heads point out, can have catastrophic results. So the person with good grades takes on stature as one who is careful, one with the desire "to get it right."

3. *Mental ability.*

Often "brains" are not placed first in the list of qualifications for executives; yet follow-up studies show that of the country's outstanding executives:

[5] *Letter Logic*, Connecticut Mutual Life Insurance Company, Hartford, September 1965.

[6] Ibid.

a.   Three-fourths had above-average scholastic records

b.   One-fourth had average

c.   None were below average.

Marked intelligence would appear to make a person alert to the importance both of doing a job well and of getting along with colleagues—a talent most often listed first by recruiters.

4.   *Spouses.*

Spouses of candidates are gaining increasing importance all the time, particularly for certain types of jobs. If you have not yet made your selection, think about whether your chosen mate actually has the potential to advance with you as far as you have in mind to go. For jobs that require a lot of travel, the attitude of the one left at home during those long periods of absence can be crucial.

5.   *Mobility.*

Your willingness to go wherever the company can make best use of your services is very important. Some recruiters criticize midwestern graduates because they all want to work in the Midwest, or Texas graduates because they all want to work in Texas. True, Texans—like Midwesterners—are an ethnocentric lot. But if you really want to get somewhere with a large corporation, you will need to demonstrate flexibility in job location.

Most authorities agree that the starting salary is relatively unimportant. Ed Smith of Armstrong Cork Company says, for example,

Look for future opportunity, not initial salary. Your starting salary is only a temporary one. You will eventually be paid as much as you are worth. Too much interest in salary may hurt your career chances.

When you are asked point-blank about salary, your response might well be:

Salary is important, of course, but secondary to opportunity. I'd like to discuss the future in the position rather than its beginning salary.

Many organizations consider training one of their most valuable investments in the future, for training programs are designed to accomplish three things for them:

1.   Integrating most efficiently the large number of new graduates hired each year.

2.   Providing new graduates with background information on the organization similar to that gained in the past by employees who worked their way up.

3.   Making high-salaried new college graduates productive as soon as possible.

Westinghouse Electric's philosophy is typical: "We hire nearly all of our inexperienced young professional personnel for our Graduate Training Program rather than for a specific job."

Guidelines for Assessing Progress

It is often difficult, when working in a group situation, to identify a particular person with a particular idea. Often the development of a plan involves different people contributing ideas that build on each other. "Idea people" often have proprietary feelings about their ideas and feel—rightly or wrongly—that without their initial inspiration the total workable target program would not exist. Therefore, it would be helpful to take a closer look at your interactions with your boss and your co-workers to determine whether your boss is taking unfair advantage of you or whether you are simply experiencing the dynamics of the creative process as part of a group.

Put yourself in your boss's position. If the boss is basing a total presentation on ideas from a number of people—as well as his or her own ideas—it may be very impractical to footnote and credit each one. Your primary concern, in this case, is whether at review time the boss knows where the idea for his or her programs originated. Keep in mind that one of the most effective ways to advance in any organization is to help your boss move up the ladder ahead of you. Your superior is judged on how well his or her area as a whole performs. The boss may already appreciate your contributions without having told you directly. But how do you ensure receiving credit and recognition for your ideas? The more completely and thoroughly you present your ideas, the harder it will be for anyone to claim credit for them.

How do you *present* your ideas? Do you throw out an idea and let others run with it, or do you think it through first and present it in a more complete way with your stamp on it? As Thomas Edison said, genius is one percent inspiration and ninety-nine percent perspiration. If you have a lot of good ideas but leave them at that—without developing them, thinking through the problems, and considering the operational aspects—you shouldn't expect to get all the credit. If you're not doing this work, then others probably are, and they should receive credit.

The presentation of your ideas is important. If you present them orally, it is very easy for people to forget their origin or for your ideas to get lost in the creative process. Writing a memo or a short report would help. This task can be difficult if a lot of work is done in open brainstorming sessions—you can't hold back in order to write a memo with your name on it later—but, where appropriate, you might be able to follow up a meeting with a memo or a short report or recommendation.

If you present your ideas cogently and thoroughly in discussions, and put your thoughts into writing whenever possible and practical, the source of the ideas will be much clearer, harder to refute. In short, your objective should be to develop your ideas to the point where it is almost superfluous for your boss to do any more work on them. Your boss should be able to take one of your memos and do nothing more than put a cover note on it before passing it on or call you into a presentation to discuss whatever aspects of the program you developed. You'll advance as a result.

Robert Calvert and John Steele in their fine paperback, *Planning Your Career,* offer specific steps in evaluating progress after a job has been accepted: from the training period, to developing professional status, through weathering the crucial thirties. They suggest that your career timetable go like this:[7]

Age	Career Stage
22–24	Training program (military service, if applicable)
25–30	Internship (experience on a journeyman's level)
31–35	Supervisory (getting work done through others)
36–40	Managerial or minor executive (responsibility for several units of work)
41–on	Executive (peak years of performance)

"You do not help a man," Abraham Lincoln said, "when you do for him what he can and should do for himself." And most employers agree. Though they speak of their responsibility for executive development, when pressed, they will admit that individuals they want to promote will really develop themselves.

If you are to succeed in your career objective, it means broadening your perspective in each stage of job performance, completing minor as well as major assignments, improving interpersonal relationships, developing a satisfactory life outside the firm, seeking additional education—through the company or through outside sources, making your own breaks, crystallizing a personal philosophy, and taking a personal inventory at each step along the way. Answering the following questions posed by *Planning Your Career* will tell you how well you are doing.

1. Does your work challenge all of your abilities? Do you really enjoy going to work in the morning? Do you feel able to handle the even more difficult assignments to which advancement would lead?

2. Are you able to make the decisions necessary in your field? Do you obtain and use accurate background information to help in making decisions?

3. Are you able to accept the criticism which accompanies advancement? Do you have enough inner drive, strength of conviction, and enthusiasm for your work to move forward confidently despite external criticism?

[7] Calvert and Steele, *Planning Your Career,* p. 127

4.   Are you able to sort out important ideas and present them tactfully and effectively? Do you practice economy in words, both written and spoken? (Loquaciousness is a common handicap of the unsuccessful.)

5.   Are you succeeding without undue dependence upon argument? You must ration your use of argument or run the risk of being tagged as basically disagreeable. Or are you so careful to avoid controversy that you never take a stand for a position in which you believe?

6.   Are you able to space your activities? One can't operate at high speed all year long. Lefty Gomez, the former major-league pitching star, once said, "A big-league pitcher must bear down on every batter—but harder on some than on others."

7.   Are you able to rate others effectively? This is an essential management skill. You will succeed only if you select the right people to work under and with you.

8.   Are you performing your present duties and responsibilities to the best of your ability? Do you relate well with your superiors, colleagues, and subordinates?

9.   Are you moving? Standing still may be the equivalent of going downhill. Reflect on the old Italian proverb, "If there is no gain, the loss is obvious."[8]

At each stage, you should not expect the same rate of progress that marked your early career years. Promotions become more significant, but are spaced farther apart. Early advancements are often scheduled as part of a career development plan. Later promotions depend more upon availability of suitable openings, the growth and vitality of your organization, and the general economic climate. But how long must you wait to get to the top? One way to compare your own path to success with similar jobs elsewhere comes from a survey done by *Dun's Review.* Simply locate your job function on the scales, and you will see how long the average person must wait to get to the top—*or to the first-choice spot.*

The really important thing for you to consider, however, is not how many years it will take for you to get "there," but whether you are first choice, second choice, or farther down the line.

A GENERAL CHECKLIST FOR THE PROSPECTING APPLICATION MESSAGE

Opening

A 10   Subtly catch the reader's interest and show an understanding of the business.

11   Fit yourself into the image that the reader has of his or her company.

12   Make your wording fit just this one case—*why* you picked the company, persons referring you, or special qualifications for the work you have in mind.

13   Aim at some specific area of work rather early in the letter.

[8] Ibid., pp. 135–136.

Your Present Job Function	Average Wait to Top Job—First-Choice Person	Average Wait to Top Job—Second-Choice Person
Corporate planning	0 years*	9 years
General administration	3 years	6 years
Sales or Marketing	4 years	5 years
Finance	6 years	10 years
Purchasing	4 years	10 years
Personnel administration	8 years	9 years
Production	5 years	9 years
Research	7 years	12 years
Accounting	6 years	8 years
Traffic	− 3 years†	0 years*
Engineering	7 years	9 years
International	7 years	8 years
Legal	9 years	15 years
Advertising and promotion	6 years	11 years
Public Relations	8 years	17 years

* 0 years doesn't mean that he or she has arrived. It means that the person is probably as close to retirement age as the boss.

† − 3 years means that on the average the individual is that much older than the boss! Reprinted by special permission from *Dun's Review & Modern Industry* (June 1966). Copyright 1966, D&B Publication Corporation.

14 Don't lecture the employer on what he or she needs or present yourself as a superhuman.

15 Your opening as an initial contact lacks conviction, plausibility, or logicalness.

16 Improve and adapt for better tone and interest.

Coverage

A 20 *Introduce the idea that you're presenting your qualifications; then move into the details.*

21 *The sentence at the turn here lacks smoothness of connection.*

22 *Try to talk about the job* as sentence subjects; lead from the job *to your ability to do it.*

23 Your highlight coverage of points should play up at least three of the following:

a. Your education.

b. Your experience.

c. Your personal characteristics.

d. Your attitude toward job, career.

e. Your special qualifications which might distinguish you and give you a competitive edge over other candidates.

24 Somewhere let your letter show the logical effects of your qualifications.

25 Treatment is too vague, general, or "universal." Wouldn't what you say fit just as well if you changed the address to almost any other company?

26 Be modest when you talk of your accomplishments.

27 Concentrate on one particular type of work, with supplementary qualifications carried in the resumé.

28 Point interestingly and construc-

tively to something significant in your résumé.

29 Assume that your reader knows the obvious; avoid bald, flat-out assertions.

A 30 Your coverage is too brief to adequately interest this employer in you as a potential employee.

31 This one is too detailed, drawn out, over done.

32 Better reader adaptation is possible.

33 For an adequate treatment of this problem, your analysis should

a. Make the job look more valuable to the firm as a result of your filling the position and satisfying the requirements.

b. Express your ambitions and interests as being compatible with those of the company.

c. Make the tone of your wording bespeak sincerity.

d. Make the reader see you in relation to his or her needs and his or her job.

e. Introduce nothing that might undermine your positive salesmanship.

f. Reflect an image of yourself (by word choice) that the company will want to recruit.

Close

A 40 Invite an expression of interest from your reader.

41 Make the appeal for action on his or her part appropriate, tactful, courteous.

41 Work for more originality in your close.

43 Avoid the negative *if* alternative and the no-alternative *when* constructions.

44 Let your wording positively infer a response: "In the meantime, I shall be glad to . . ."

45 No high pressure, please.

46 Your wording here seems to take the matter out of the reader's hands.

Tone, Style, Format as marked
Your Grade _____

A GENERAL CHECKLIST FOR THE RESUMÉ

Heading

DS 10 The main caption ought to identify in an original way the purpose of your sheet, your name, the job, and the company.

11 This one strives too hard for originality, thus giving an effect that is not altogether pleasing.

12 Make your caption say something more helpful than a catalog listing would give.

13 Keep clean precision in your words. Merchandise manager is a person, but the work is the managership or work of the manager.

14 This caption is too wordy for true effectiveness. Trim the title down to those words that move your case forward, omitting such phraseology as "position as" and such.

15 Use open punctuation and inverted pyramid style for the caption.

16 Adding a statement of your vocational objective following the caption may add clarity to your sheet and orient your reader more easily.

Coverage

DS 20 Your resumé data should be grouped according to likeness of items with your most applicable factors relative to the job requirements appearing first on the sheet.

21 If your experience is better, then emphasize it by primal position. If it's your training that sells you best, put it at the top.

22 Superior listing of experience makes an effort to interpret the work performed on jobs.

23 Interpreting the intensity of work done on courses is a help, too.

24 Be sure to highlight courses and experience that are specific preparation for the particular job you want.

25 In tabulating courses, name them by general fields, showing pertinent content of course study. Such words as *elementary, intermediate,* or *advanced* do little to inform as to course content.

26 Preferably use small letters for the course names unless using the titles exactly from the catalog with initial capitals for the main words.

27 Select descriptive wording to picture training and experience.

"Degree earned" shows more action than "degree granted," and "techniques mastered" is more forceful than "courses taken." Grades and honors may be interpreted as evidence of achievement.

28 Identify your jobs completely: dates, places, companies.

29 If experience is part time, honesty requires that you list it so.

30 Highlight any unusual qualification that gives you an edge on your competition.

31 Include your physical and social characteristics with an indication of military status, if applicable.

32 Give, by name and title, three to five references with complete addresses.

33 Toward the end of a school year, you do well to list two addresses: your school address and a permanent home address.

Style and Layout

DS 40 Your margins give the effect of a page that is too crowded. Top and sides should be at least one inch and the bottom a little wider.

41 Center captions (for the separate groupings of your qualifications) are perhaps more effective and balance the page better.

42 This heavy, solid-left-wall effect makes hard reading. As a basic practice, if you have to carry over part of a tabulated item to a second line, *do not block the carried-over portion.* Instead indent it two spaces.

43 Preferably, though, do not break up the items. Keep each on the same line it starts on if you can.

44 In a tabular sheet, tabulate. A solid paragraph of items run end on end is hard to read, looks bad, obscures emphasis.

45 Don't number the captions or individual items unless the numbers serve a special purpose. Their relationship and sequence on the single page or two is obvious at a glance.

46 The data sheet is an objective presentation of facts about an applicant. The first- and second-person pronouns are, therefore, out of place, and so are imperatives.

47 Use the same grammatical pattern in any one division for listed items. Noun phrases are a conventional best choice but adjectives and fast-traveling verbs may set a good pattern, too. Just be consistent throughout each level.

Your Grade _____

A TYPICAL PROBLEM ASSIGNMENT IN
APPLICATION COMMUNICATIONS*

Using the prospecting application as an opening wedge to the job of your choice. In times when jobs are scarce, it may be useful to solicit interest in your qualifications through writing directly to the company or organization of your choice. This letter, then, must be interesting enough to arrest attention even though the time of its arrival may not be altogether fortunate. The personnel director (1) may have filled all available spots with competent people, (2) may have regular avenues of recruitment, or (3) may be in a particularly foul mood as a result of some business upheaval. Your letter could easily seem an unwelcomed intrusion.

How can you arouse this personnel director's interest in you in spite of possible unfavorable circumstances? First, any person responsible for hiring will very likely be impressed if you have taken the trouble to find out something about the company— its policies, its expansion proposals, its special features. Second, the prospective employer will probably like you better if your message is short and straightforward— certainly no more than a single page which highlights only your special qualifications with details presented in an accompanying resumé. You may need to consider whether you'd prefer to start with a large, national organization where the possibilities of advancement are almost limitless or with a smaller concern where the chances of becoming a small cog in a big machine are less.

Select a company or organization in your major field for which you'd like to work. Choose the qualifications in your own background that seem especially fitted to this firm or organization in view of what you know about it. Prepare a resumé to go along with the letter. Write a letter that will create an interest in you which could lead to an interview and to your eventual employment.

---

* Other application problem situations appear at the end of Chapters 2, 3, 4, 5, and 6 as informative, persuasive, or negative writing exercises.

Appendix A—Useful Guide Forms

The sample forms on the following pages will help you to familiarize yourself with the parts of the business letter and their proper placement, and will also help you set up your own guide sheets that will keep everything in proper proportion.

To construct your own guide block for a letter with a letterhead, and for one without, take two sheets of regular typing paper and follow the measurements indicated for each form. Use heavy lines for all the blocks you draw on each sheet so that they can easily be seen through the sheet of paper you type on. Select the rectangle you think will hold your copy and type the letter. It may be a trial-and-error approach at first.

The reason for giving so much attention to the block and the spacing of parts is that most of us need some help at first in getting proper placement for that "just right" appearance. These blocks are designed to achieve that end. After you have practiced this placement, you will find you do not need a guide at all. Your eye is a good judge for proper layout; you can tell quickly whether the letter copy rides too high or too low on the page. After all, it is a favorable impression that counts—not whether you run one line over or two short on the block. The right and left side block lines also help you get good proportioning. You do not want your letters to be too wide for their height or too narrow for their length.

As an illustration of a finished letter using an imitated letterhead, look closely at Sample Form 2-1. If you could take that letter and place the form

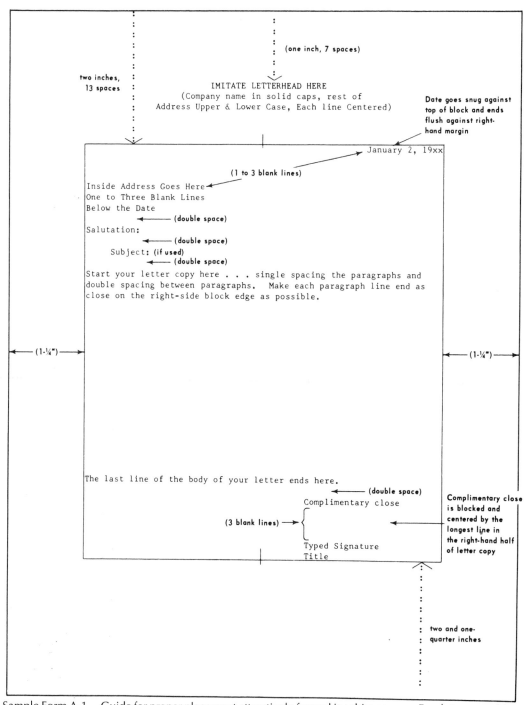

Sample Form A-1   Guide for proper placement attractively framed in white space.   For letters requiring less space, move in ¼-inch from sides, top, and bottom of block and draw additional smaller blocks.

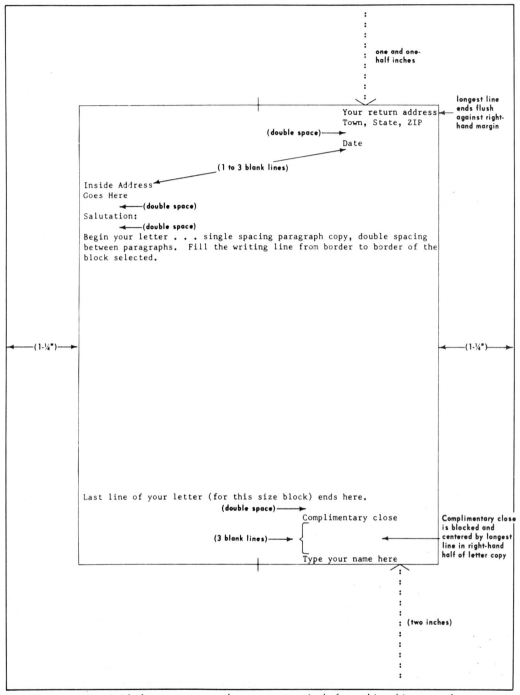

one and one-
half inches

longest line
ends flush
against right-
hand margin

Your return address
Town, State, ZIP
(double space)→
Date

(1 to 3 blank lines)

Inside Address
Goes Here
←(double space)
Salutation:
←(double space)
Begin your letter . . . single spacing paragraph copy, double spacing
between paragraphs. Fill the writing line from border to border of the
block selected.

←(1-¼")→

←(1-¼")→

Last line of your letter (for this size block) ends here.
(double space)→
Complimentary close

(3 blank lines)→

Type your name here

Complimentary close
is blocked and
centered by longest
line in right-hand
half of letter copy

(two inches)

Sample Form A-2   Guide for proper copy placement attractively framed in white space for personal
business letters with no letterhead.

guide behind it, you would see that the letter is ½-inch smaller than the guide form.

INSTRUCTIONS FOR SETTING UP A LETTER
NEATLY AND ATTRACTIVELY

1- a.   For uniformity, imitate a printed letterhead with a compact three- or four-line heading centered at top and symmetrically balanced, with solid-capital typing for firm name and lower-case for remainder.

b.   Begin the letterhead an exact inch from the top of the sheet (line 7).

c.   To fit the typed mass to the shape of the white space, use your letterhead guides for routine letters. For prefatory letters in reports, note that the essential binding margin narrows the white space; shape copy to fit.

(1)   Layout is too wide for height here.

(2)   Layout is too tall for width.

(3)   Placement is too high on the page.

(4)   Placement is too low.

(5)   Follow the arrow as marked.

d.   For handling the standard letter parts:

(1)   End of date line marks average margin.

(2)   Allow one to three free lines between date and inside address (double-, triple-, or quadruple-space, the rule says).

(3)   Use a complete inside address:
First, the courtesy title Mr., Mrs.;
Next, the reader's correct name;
Third, his title of position;
Fourth, his firm name;
Fifth, address: street, box, or office building; city, state, and ZIP code
(Group the elements to make balanced lines.)

(4)   Salute the reader by name if known.

(5)   Otherwise, use Dear Sir (or Madam), for one; Gentlemen [not Dear Sirs] or Ladies, for plural.

(6)   With the friendly "name" salutation, use a "Sincerely yours" form of close (Yours sincerely, Very sincerely yours). Capitalize the first word only.

(7)   With the impersonal (no-name) salutation, use a "Yours truly" form (Very truly yours; or Yours very truly).

(8)   The comma after the close serves no purpose any longer. With "open" style of punctuation for other parts, omit that vestigial comma.

(9)   For signature, the firm name is rarely needed. If required by house practice or for legal authenticity, it is included, in solid capitals (see 13 for spacing).

(10)   On the fourth line below complimentary close (or firm name), type the writer's name (for clarity), and his official title (for legal responsibility and as a courtesy to the reader: he got a letter from someone in authority).

(11)   Put name and title on same or on separate lines for best balance. If a long title is too long for a good line and you have to split it, indent the carried-over part two spaces from the left block of the other parts.

(12)   Sign every letter with a neat signature (in the space between close and typed name), as a courtesy to the reader.

(13)   For format: double-space below last line of text for the complimentary close. Double-space below close for firm name if used. Quadruple-space (three free lines) below close or firm name for typed signature. Single-space title below typed name.

(14)   Set this whole unit of close and signature so that its longest typed line rides half-way between the center of the layout and the right-hand margin.

2- a.   A two-page letter should be split about 50-50 between the two pages. (Avoid a heavy first page and a scant second one.) Plan ahead to use a shorter first page. Use the same layout guide rectangle for the second as for the first page.

b.   Identify the second sheet in the simplest authentic form: Type first line of inside address (or reader's name), the date, and page 2 in a single running line (items separated with commas) as top line of the layout.

c.   On the fourth line below, start typing the carried over text of the letter.

Index

Abstract (*see* Epitome)
Acceptance of persuasive
    message by reader,
    157
Accusation, avoiding, 186
Acknowledging reader's
    letter by date, 102
Acronym:
  SOAR (Short Operational
    Analytical Report),
    244
Adaptation to reader (*see*
    Reader adaptation)
Adapting to the reader,
    105–6
Adaptive management, an
    organized approach,
    213
Adjectives, 154
Administration as a
    communication

process, 16
Agenda for decision-making
    research project,
    step-by-step guide,
    325–26
Analysis of reader (*see*
    Reader analysis)
Analyst (report):
  posing alternative
    solutions to the
    problem, 329
  pulling the research
    plans into final focus,
    339–40
Analyzing data, 219
*Annual Statistical Report of
    the American Iron
    and Steel Institute*,
    366
Anticipated reader reaction
    in informative

communication, 94
*Antitrust and Trade
    Regulation Report*,
    369
Apology, avoiding in
    persuasive writing,
    151
Appearance:
  characteristics of,
    33
  of a letter, 33–40
Appendix, appendices:
  in contents table, 465,
    531
  make up, 528, 531
Applicant (*see* Job
    applicant)
Application (*see* Job
    applicant; Job
    application)
Application blank, 568

Applied research, defined, 320
Argumentative style of writing, 236
Assembling facts, for accomplishing message's purpose, 48–49
Associated Credit Bureaus and consumer credit reporting, 188
Attention-interest factors in persuasive writing, 146
Attention line, placement of, 39
Attitude:
    manager's tolerance toward other's errors, 185
    work, 2
    writer, 4
Audience, writing down to, 5
Authorization instrument:
    letter or memorandum, 437–41
    sample letter, 442–43
    ways of beginning, 100
Automated information, management problem, 24
Automation, 18
Automobile Facts and Figures, 366

Baker, George, 136
Banking and Monetary Statistics, 368
Barnard, Chester I., 16
Barrier:
    to analyst in data assembly, 364
    in informative communication, 91
Barriers:
    caused from writer's

conflicts and pressures, 98
communication, 9
Basic appeals in persuasive messages, 146
Behavior:
    consistency in assignment of meaning, 141
    dyadic systemization of, 87
    feedback, 88
    influences of, 87
    motivational research and depth interviewing in, 339
    as a process of interaction, 87
Behavior patterns, 139
Behavioral scientists' view of management authority, 244–45
Beliefs, roles of in persuasive writing, 141–43
Bibliographical Index, 365
Bibliography:
    accumulation, 364–69
    arrangement, 527, 528
    article reference, 370
    book reference, 370
    composition, 527
    coverage sequence of entries, 528
    example, 529–30
    spacing, 528
    unpublished sources, 370
Brackets, use of, 371
Brevity, 16
Buried negative, technique in written messages, 176
Business communication:
    application, 1
    not an end in itself, 1
Business Cycle Development, 368
Business-decision research

projects:
agenda for:
    defining the problem, 324–32
    designing the research scheme, 333–40
Business Periodical Index, 365
Business problem, analysis of, 7
Business reports (*see also* Reports):
    indispensable ally of economic management, 317
    information system for plotting strategies, 317
"Bypassing," 14

Calvert, Robert, 540
Caption format for short operational report, 220–21, 261
Career:
    as a lifetime investment, 535
    attaining objective, 568
    planning, 535
        long-range, 536
        pulling together qualifications and job campaign, 546
    progress, 536
    sources of information, 540–41
Career Information Service, 541
Career pathing, 543
Central idea in simple sentences, 46
Change, 17
    importance of, 17
Changing Times, 547
Checklists:
    basic fundamentals in good writing, 76–77

constructive, informative
    messages, 115–16
goodwill messages, 77–78
informing under adverse
    conditions, 116–17
the justification report,
    285
negative messages,
    199–200
persuasive messages, 160
prospecting application,
    576, 577–78
the resumé, 578–79
the short analytical
    report, 285–88
writing:
    readability, 76
    tone, style, appearance,
        76
Choosing the format for
    short operational
    reports, 221
Chronological arrangement,
    organizational form
    of short reports, 220
Churchman, C. West, 406
Claims:
    and adjustments, 56
    opening sentences, 100
Clarity:
    achievement, 16
    thought, 41
Clichés, avoiding in
    writing, 108
Close:
    clinching action in
        persuasive writing,
        150–51
    for informative messages,
        108–9
    tone, 151
    ways of appealing for
        action, 151
Closings:
    fitting situation, 96
    nature of, 96
    paragraphs, suggestions
        for writing, 108–9

writing, 95
Code of symbols,
    communication, 9
Cognition, 32
Coherence, method of
    achieving, 219
College Placement Annual,
    541
College Placement Directory,
    541
Commerce Clearing House,
    366
The Commercial Atlas and
    Marketing Guide, 369
Commodity Yearbook, 369
Communication (see also
    Business
    communication):
and administration, 16,
    18
affectors in written
    messages, 14
barriers, 9
    in informative writing,
        91
as a catalyst, 14
classifications, 29–30
    by purpose, 29
competence, 7
as a decision-making
    tool, 1
defined, 2, 8, 16
effect in informing and
    influencing, 7
effective results, 7
effectiveness, 4, 5, 16
essence of, 86
focus of, 2
as a form of behavior,
    86–87
four fundamentals of,
    16–17
and information, 17
    problems, 18
kinds, 2
manager's skill in, 17
media, 8
misconception, 15

nature of nonpersuasive,
    135
network, 22
pacesetter, 2
paradox, 7
patterns, influence of,
    18
as perception, 16–17
planning, importance of,
    6
problem solving and
    decisions, 245
process, 8, 86, 88
    barriers to, 88
    components of, 8
purpose, 13
role:
    in influencing, 7
    in informing, 7
    in operational
        efficiency, 1, 18
    in organization
        advancement, 7
skills:
    and proficiency, 7
    in the work
        environment, 7
tool of management, 9
Communication gap,
    25
    between employee,
        employer, 3
    in management
        information, 25–26
Communication/
    information
    specialist, 25
Communication specialists,
    28
    shortage, 21
Communication systems,
    grapevine, 13
Communication technology,
    18
Communicators,
    performance of, 4
Company analysis in job-
    getting, 540, 544–45

Company policy:
  as the basis of refusal,
    181
  handling, 177
  negative connotation,
    199
  reasons for, 107
Comparative-evaluation
    investigations,
    261–63, 412–15, 505,
    514–15
  research method of, 323
Complaint, fast action for,
    186
Compliendings, 38
Components:
  data search, 258
  problem, 258
Computer:
  communication expert,
    20
  communication
    technology, 19
  office, 19
  and data processing for
    long, formal report,
    397
  effectiveness in
    management
    information systems,
    23
  impact, 24
  on communication, 18
  information storage and
    retrieval, 19–20
  interface, 24
  people and machines,
    24
  and linear programming
    in descriptive-
    analytic solutions,
    323
  managers:
    and communication
    work stations, 19
  office automation, 19
  role in information
    systems, 23–27

  shortage of office
    employees, 19
  sources of data gathering,
    364–65
Computerized human
    resource information
    systems, 543
Conciseness, 41
  confusion with brevity,
    16
Concluding sections, long
    report, 515–19
  comparative-evaluation,
    517–18
  descriptive-analytic
    study, 518
  yes-no answers, 516–17
Conclusion, drawing of,
    330
Conclusion caption in
    working outline:
  comparative-evaluation
    refined for overall
    answer, 263, 266
  parenthetically
    phrasing
    requirements, 261
  phrased as
    achievement of goal
    in introduction
    caption, 261
  phrased from step 3 in
    problem formulation,
    261
The Congressional Directory,
    368
*Congressional Quarterly
    Weekly Reports*, 366
The Congressional Record,
    368
Content sections:
  report:
    findings,
    interpretations,
    505–15
  makeup, 503–15
  section, chapter
    preview, 504–5

Controlled reader action in
    persuasive writing,
    150
Conveying technical
    information, 97
Cordial contacts:
  characteristics, 71–72
  results from, 72
Cost of poor
    communication, 5
Coverage captions:
  working outline:
    formulated from
    components of
    problem formulation,
    259–60
  refined after report
    draft to reveal
    ranking choice for
    each component in
    comparative
    evaluation, 263
Creating belief with words,
    153
Credit grant, four C's rule-
    of-thumb evaluation,
    188
Credit Interchange Bureau,
    mercantile credit
    check, 188
Credit reputation,
    managing, 189
Credit Research
    Foundation: ten
    factors influencing
    credit decisions,
    187–88
Cue words for stating the
    SOAR problem as a
    question, 251
Customer complaints, 180

Data (*see also* Primary;
    Secondary):
  analysis, prediction
    system of, 399
  analyst:

abstracting meaning, 398

first task in assembling, 364

systematic application of critical and creative powers, 396

assembling, 20

barrier to analyst, 364

bibliography nucleus from preliminary survey of literature in field, 364

computer search capabilities, 364

government publications, 368

interview, 385–86

methods of computer search, 364–65

monthly catalog of government publications, 367–68

private sources, 368

publishers' services, 366–67

regulatory bodies, 369

secondary sources, 364–71

steps in locating secondary, 364–70

steps in manual process, 365

steps in planning the research effort, 371–72

useful indexes to business researcher, 365–66

ways of efficient notetaking and filing, 370–71

burden of presenting, 503

classifying, 398–99

displays in SOAR, mistaken belief, 267

interpretation and things to look for, 503

problem of isolating kinds through syllogistic reasoning, 334–35

processing:

break-even analysis, 399

correlation between variables, 399

determination of mean, median, and mode, 399

estimating dispersion, 399

percentages, ratios, 399

tests of significance, 399

relevancy, 398

reliability, 398

repeatability, 398

summarization, 399, 418–21

three further categories, 321

Database:

data communications, 24

sources for management reports, 247

Data processing/ information specialist, 20

Data search, components of, 258

Data sheet (see Resumé)

Data system, defined, 24

Data System Concept, 24

Decision (see also Conclusion):

defined, 395

occurrence, 16

planning, 396

shaping for analytical reports, 395

significant issues, 363

Decision-component sections (see Content sections)

Decision criterion:

short comparative-evaluation study, 262

short descriptive-analytic inquiry, 268

in problem solving, 334

yardstick in the report's decision, 251

short yes-no study, 257

Decision design:

for comparative-evaluation investigation, 414

for descriptive-analytic inquiry, 417

for yes-no problem, 410

Decision makers:

basic considerations of value to, 397

long-run survival of, 317

Decision making:

data processing for, 397–99

imaginative testing of the outcomes, 411, 415, 428–29

quantitative applications, 418–29

reflective thinking, 471

short analytical report, 244

subordinates' input to, 245

techniques:

for the comparative-evaluation, 412–15

for the descriptive-analytic inquiry, 415–18

measurement by the decision criterion in comparative-evaluation investigation, 412–14

measurement by the decision criterion in descriptive-analytic inquiry, 416–18

Decision making,
   techniques (*cont.*)
   measurement by the
      decision criterion in
      yes-no study, 409–11
   for the yes-no problem,
      409–12
   testing the outcomes
      with "minimax"
      standard, 412
   uncertainties, 398
Decision-making reporting,
   7
Decision-making reports:
   analytical nature, 245
   common characteristics,
      245
*Decisions and Reports of
   the Securities and
   Exchange
   Commission*, 369
Decisions made by hunch,
   317
*Decisions of the
   Commission*, 369
Declining order requests,
   reasons for, 181–82
Deemphasizing the "no,"
   techniques in
   negative messages,
   176–77
Defining the problem:
   cue words in phrasing
      question, 250–51
   key in phrasing question
      according to nature
      of decision, 247
Denied negative, 60
   examples, 154
   trap for writers, 154
Dependent structure, use
   of, in openings, 100
Descriptive-analytic
   inquiry, 266–67,
   415–18
   use of linear
      programming, 337
   research methods, 323

Descriptive research (*see*
   Research method)
Direct style of writing, 94
Directories:
   The Congressional, 368
   *Directory of National
      Trade Associations*,
      366
   *Directory of Vocational
      Counseling Service*,
      540
   *Dun & Bradstreet Middle
      Market*, 373
   The Fortune Directory,
      373
   MacRae's Blue Book, 373
   Mailing List Houses, 373
   Polk's Bank Directory, 373
   *Poor's Register of
      Directors and
      Executives of the
      United States and
      Canada*, 373
   *Thomas' Register of
      American
      Manufacturers*, 373
Disarming reader:
   in negative messages, 175
   psychology behind, 175
Drawing conclusions in
   inconclusive
   messages, 12
Drucker, Peter:
   on functioning
      communication, 25
   fundamentals of
      communication,
      16–17
Dun & Bradstreet as
   principal reporting
   agency for
   mercantile credit,
   188
*Dun & Bradstreet Credit
   Service*, 366

The Economic Almanac, 369

*Economic Report of the
   President*, 368
*Editor and Publisher Market
   Guide*, 369
Effective communication,
   test of, 6
Efficiency:
   and attitude, 2
   and competitiveness, 2
Efficient communication, 5,
   9
Ego:
   need for strengthening in
      negative
      transmissions, 174
   reinforcement, 174
Ego-involvement, 51, 54
Electronic mail, 19
Ellipses, 523
Emotion:
   in persuasive writing,
      137
   and reason, 143
Emphasis:
   of ideas in informative
      messages, 174
   methods of achieving, 43,
      219
   through one-sentence
      paragraphs, 104
Employee:
   ability to communicate,
      572
   characteristics sought by
      employers, 572–73
   communication,
      dissemination of, 9
   evaluation of progress,
      575–77
   interaction with boss,
      574
   job performance, 575
   as manager's eyes, ears,
      and scouts, 245
   as an opinion molder, 13
   presentation of ideas, 574
   promotions, 575
   psychological needs, 98

questions about
advancement, 575–76
receiving credit and
recognition for ideas,
574
say in decisions affecting
work and working
conditions, 245
training programs,
573–74
visibility in an
organization through
written reports, 245
Employment (*see also* Job
application):
application form, 567–68
application letter, 546
interviews, 546
Epitome, 465, 467–68 (*see
also* Abstract):
deductive presentation,
467
example, 469–70
importance, 467
inductive style, 467
reasons for, 467

Face-saving, 199
Fact presentation in
operational
efficiency, 6
Facts in decision making, 7
*Factual Analyses of
Corporate Securities*,
366
Factual evidence in
communication, 8
Failure to listen, 12
Featherbedding, 2
*Federal Communication
Commission Report*,
369
The Federal Register,
368
*Federal Trade Commission
Decisions*, 369

Feedback, 9, 88
anticipated in persuasive
messages, 138
anticipated reader
resistance, 138
Fielden, John S., 8
Figures, defined, 484 (*see
also* Graphics)
"Fire-and-brimstone"
messages, 185–86
Five-step problem-
formulation model,
248
short operational
analytical report use,
246–55
Follow-up message, change
of pace approach,
159
Footnoting (*see also*
Quotations):
article, 525
association author,
527
date, no volume, 525
no author, 527
blocked form, 524
book, 524
more than one author,
527
no author, 527
series indication, 524
subtitles, 527
company files, 525–26
dissertations, 526
edition, 524
editor, edited by, 524
explanatory, 527
Ibid., 526
immediately preceding
reference, 526
indented form, 524
with intervening
references, 526
interviews, 525–26
legal citations, 526
letters, 525–26
loc. cit., 526–27

necessary occasions,
522
numbering, 523
op. cit., 526
placement, 522, 523–24
previously cited author,
526
reasons for, 522
spacing, 524
speeches, 525
superscript, 523–24
theses, 526
translator, 524
U.S. Government
document, 526
volume, number of
volumes, 524, 525
Forecasting (*see* Prediction)
Format for short
operational reports,
221
Form letters, 74–75
how to use, 75
justification for using,
74
reader objections, 74
Four C's of Credit, granting
or refusing, 188
Framing ideas
constructively,
samples, 106
Free enterprise, 12
Fuchs, Walter, 17
*Funk & Scott Index of
Corporations &
Industries*, 365

General-purpose decision
maker, 397
six basic steps for
shaping decisions,
396–97
interacting stages:
the prediction system,
399
the value system, 399
General semantics, 9

Goal, direction, and boundaries provided by SOAR problem formulation and working outline, 267
Good news, ways of emphasizing, 101
Goodwill, 33
  achievement, 33
  appreciation message, 62, 64
  congratulatory notes, 64–66
  in the firm, 7
  notes of condolence and apology, 66–68
  objectives:
    in apology, 67
    thank-you letter, 63
  reader, negative message, 173
  role in communication, 61
  suggestions, seasonal messages, 68–69
  ways of achieving, 61–62
Goodwill letters, 61–74
  cordial contacts, 71–73
  invitations to special events, 70–71
  to new customers, 73
  reasons for form use, 74
  seasonal greetings, 68–70
Grapevine, 3, 13
Graphics (*see also* Illustrations):
  bar chart, 495–96
    continuous data, 496, 499
    discrete numbers, 496
    horizontal, 496, 498
    legend, 496
    preparation, 495, 496
    simple, 495, 496
    subdivided, 496, 498, 499, 502
    verticle, 496, 497
  color in, 496, 497

crosshatching, 496
diagrams, 501
histograms, 496
labeling, 495
line chart, 497–98
  legend, 498
  multiple variables, 497, 501
  overview, 497
  preparation, 497, 498
  simple, 497, 500
  trend components, 497
  uses, 497
maps, 498, 501
pictograms, 496, 502
pie charts, 496–97
  preparation, 497
  uses, 496, 500
placement, 495
ruling, 495
shading, 496
uses, 484, 495, 497
Grayson, C. Jackson, 405, 406

Handbook of Labor Statistics, 368
Headings (*see* Captions)
Herzberg, Frederick, 244
Hoke, Henry, 34
How to Write a Report, Commonwealth Edison Company, 216
Human information processing, 20
Human nature:
  employing the you-attitude persuasively, 140
  guideposts, 140
Human relations, overcentralization of, 5
Hypothesis (*see also* Working hypothesis):
  working:

decision criterion in, 334
statement of, 333
testing soundness of, 324

Ibid., 526
Id, 51
Idea:
  development, 218
  methods of presenting, 574
  people, 574
  putting in writing to receive credit, 574
Illustrations (*see also* Graphics; Tables):
  interpreting, 501, 503
  introductory statement, 501, 503
  labeling, 495
  obverse placement, 493
  purpose, 484, 495, 501
  quantity to use, 484
  in short reports, 244
  text reference to, 501, 503
Illustrations list, 465
  sample, 466
  Image building, 33
  factors, 33
  role of planning, 48–61
  with words, 11
Image of firm or organization, 56
Indexes, 477
  Bibliographical, 365
  Business Periodicals, 365
  Funk & Scott Index of Corporations & Industries, 365
  The New York Times, 365
  Public Affairs Information Service, 366
  Vertical File, 366
  The Wall Street Journal, 366

Inductive strategy (*see also* Writing):
 persuasive messages, 146–47
 writing,
  building a case, 147
  revealing proposal, 147–48
Inductive style (*see also* Writing):
 negative transmissions, 174
 writing, 135
The industrial infrastructure, 21
Ineffective communication, results of, 7
Ineffective reports, result of overemphasis upon form, 245
Inference and reasoning, 219
Information:
 abundance, 25
 control nets, 18
 crisis, 2
 and decision making, 27
 demands, 3
 explosion, 24
 and fact, 90
 flow, 2, 18
  model, 18
 as logic, 17
 overload, 24
 organizing, 220
 as prelude to decision making, 27–29
 problems, 27
 processing, 19
 quality, 27
 reader acceptance, 90
 reporting, 27
 retention, 11
 subsystems, 22
 system, 25
 types, 27
 usefulness, 27

Information systems:
 adequacy, 23
 automated job posting, 543
 business, 1
  competitiveness, 2
  improving, 4
 career pathing, 543
 computerized human resources, 543
 concept, 21–22
 defined, 21–22
 effectiveness, 24
 employment reports, 543
 ingredients, 21
 management, 21
 network, 22
 research, 22
Information theory, 17, 25
 defined, 20
 and telecommunication, 20
Informational report, objectives of, 218
Informative communication:
 defined, 89
 nature, 91
 planning:
  designing close to build goodwill, 95
  getting off to a good start, 94
  giving only essential information, 95
 process, 89
 situations, 89–90
 types, 89–90
Informative message:
 adjustment granting, 107
 authorization for investigation, 100
 authorization instrument for report investigation, 437–41
 direct, polite style, 99
 emphasis of ideas, 174
 favorable replies, 101

framing ideas constructively, 106–8
 giving the crux of the message in opening words, 99
 granting credit, 107
 organizing for best sequence of ideas, 105
 orienting reader with background information, 103
 progression of directness examples, 102
 three occasions for pseudo-direct approach, 100
 two kinds of direct-style answers, 101
 use of topic-sentence leadoff in paragraphs, 104
 writing, 27
Informative messages under adverse conditions, 109–15
 avoiding point-blank assertions, 114
 bypassing communication barriers, 112
 calculating sequence of ideas, 110–12
 case example, 109
 constructive aspects, 113
 contrasting examples, keeping reader on writer's side, 115
 letting reader save face, 112–13
 playing up constructive rather than destructive aspects, 113–14
 sample response, 114
 winning support with right tone, 108–9

Interaction, 86, 574
  of communicator and
    audience, 87–89
  defined, 88
  influence of environment,
    87
  and problem solving, 89
  process, 88
  role of language in, 89
Internal communication,
    defined, 318
Internal short reports:
  difficulties in writing,
    216
  movement, 214
  requirements, 216–17
Interpretation, analyzed
    data, 219
Interview in job
    applications, 560,
    562–65
  frequently asked
    questions, 563–64
  handling salary, 566, 573
  impressions, 565, 566
  managing, 565–66
  mental preparation, 560
  negative factors, 564–65
  personnel manager's
    views, 566
  planning, 560
  points to consider, 560
  questions forbidden in
    preemployment, 567
Interviewers, 567
Interviewing, questions to
    ask interviewer, 560,
    562–63
Introduction caption,
    phrasing to
    incorporate the
    report's objective,
    259
Introduction, long report:
  authorization, submittal
    data, 472, 475
  background history,
    476–77

coverage, 479
data sources, 477–78
example, 480–82
limitations, 478–79
organizational preview,
    479
research scheme, 477–78
scope, 478–79
Introduction section,
    minimal
    requirements of
    coverage for short
    operational
    analytical report, 259
Inverse order, use of in
    short report, 220

Job analysis, 540–44
Job applicant:
  advanced degree
    consideration, 545
  communication skills,
    572
  educational cost, 535
  educational opportunity,
    535
  educational
    requirements, 545
  and employment
    contacts, 546
  knowledge of English,
    571–72
  letter, 550, 553–60
    advantages, 555
    appearance, 560
    basic principles,
      557–60
    closing, 559
    effective, 556, 559
    example, 561, 562
    future use, 554–55
    kinds of, 555–56
    opening, 557
    prospecting, 555
    task, 553
    tone, 557, 560
    unsolicited, 555

mental ability, 572
mobility, 573
objectives and goals,
    539–40
  formulating, 539
personal interview, 554,
    560, 562–63
qualifications, 538–40
  advanced degree and
    salary, 546
  assessing, 538–39
  educational
    requirements, 545
  fitting to job
    requirements, 540
  professional assistance,
    539
resumé, 546–550
salary, 546
  college graduate,
    536
  noncollege, 536
self-appraisal, 536–40
  objective, 540
  personal inventory,
    536–37
  as problem solving and
    decision making, 537
  short comings, 537–38
  three questions to
    answer, 537–38
  valuable traits, 537–38
vocational objectives:
  attainment, 543
  career changes, 543
  counseling, 540
  difficulties in deciding,
    539–40
  employer analysis,
    540–41
  future assessment for
    occupational field,
    542
  importance of goals,
    540
  level, 543
  money considerations,
    542

personal
considerations, 543
planning a successful
job campaign, 546
testing services, 539
tests, 541
Job application:
contact-control record,
568
example, 569
planning, 568
turndown, considerations
in, 189
Job getting:
company analysis:
considerations, 544,
545
factors in selecting
large or small,
544–45
sources of information,
545
Job offer:
postponement, 189
refusal, 190
turndown, 189
Job requirements, 540–44
occupational field, 16-
point analysis of,
543–44
use of placement office,
540
and self-analysis, 542–43
sources, 541–42
Job resignation, 190–91
Jobs:
computer use in locating,
543
kinds, 540
sources, 536
Justification report:
as a comparative-
evaluation study, 236
emphasis on evidence,
235
illustration, 237–39
instructions for writing,
536, 540

use of parallel arguments
for and *against*, 236
reasons for use, 235–36
three-level form, 236
what it does, 235
when to use, 236
frequently writer
originated, 236

Korzybski, Alfred, 9
Kozmetsky, George, 21

Labor Arbitration Reports,
366
Lack of resistance of sales
reps to other sales
reps' pitch, 138
Language:
abusive, reaction to, 186
avoiding words and ideas
with poor
connotation, 198–99
expressing ideas
appropriately, 106
function, 17
use of impersonal style
under adverse
circumstances, 111
meaning, 9
not spoken writing, 9
standards, 4
usage, 4
in writing, 86
Letter:
achieving clarity in, 41
achieving conciseness, 41
achieving economy, 41
complimentary closes,
38–39
punctuation, 39
correct dress for, 35
defined, 40–41
devices for distinction, 34
favorable reception, 34
impression, 34, 35
interest-plus factor, 34
personality, 34, 108

physical appearance, 33
placement of indentions,
35
planning, 33
salutations, 39
punctuation, 38
sample:
modified block form,
36
two page, 37
second page
identification, 35
special parts of, 39
attention line, 39
postscripts, 39
subject line, 39
standard parts, 35
complimentary closes,
38
inside address, 35
placement, 35
placement of inside
address, 35
the salutation, 35, 38
signature block, 39
style considerations, 33,
41
success of, 41
tests of, 41
tone, 33
as the workhorse of
business, 40
Letterhead, considerations,
34
The letter report, 240
headings in, 140
illustrations, 241, 243
informal style in, 240
management functions
of, 240–43
as operational or
evaluative
instrument, 240
on oral reporting, 240
types, 240–43
Life Insurance Fact Book,
366
Likert, Renis, 244

Listener, role in
     nondirective
     counseling, 12
Listening, 10
  failure, 5, 12
  mental set, 11
  retention, 11
Loc. cit., 526–27
Logic:
  deductive reasoning, 333
  inductive reasoning, 333
Logical arrangement of
     organization form for
     short report, 220

Major premise as basis for
     judging relevancy of
     data, 252–53
Management:
  attitude as key to
     effective
     communication, 12
  and authority, 244–45
  and change, 17–18
  and communication, 2
  control function, 241–42
  environment, 11
  functions of information
     system control, 24
  and inefficient
     communication, 7
  information, 23
  information crisis, 24
  information system,
     22–23
  newsletter, 243
  role in communication,
     13
  shared decision making,
     244
  theory, 244
Management
     communication:
  and demand for
     information, 26
  with employee, 3
  gap, 25

role, 15
Manager:
  concern with four types
     of information, 246
  functions, 18, 240–43
  tolerance toward others'
     errors, 185
Managing the employment
     interview, 565–66
Market Research: A Guide to
     Information on
     Domestic Marketing,
     369
Mathematical techniques,
     418–29
Matthies, Leslie H., 227
Meaning, 9, 88
  assignment of, 10
  how individuals assign,
     140–41
  impact from poor timing,
     141
  of words, 153
Measurable information, 17
Measures of effective
     communication, 6
Memoranda:
  no complimentary close
     in, 224
  general uses, 221–22
  information concerns of,
     222
  requiring signature:
     accountant's audit, 224
     employee evaluation,
        224
     recommendation for
        dismissal, 224
  signing of, 224
  two specific forms of, 224
     the justification report,
        235–40
     the playscript
        technique for
        procedures, 224
The memorandum, 221
  distinguishing elements,
     222

for down- or cross-
     channel reporting,
     221
least formal of short
     report formats, 221
narrative message,
     example, 223
one subject, one memo
     restriction, 222
problem-solving
     illustration, 225–26
as record to the file, 222
short informational
     report form, 218
two types of, 221
Mental set:
  jumping to conclusions,
     12
  occurrence, 12
Mercantile credit as basis
     of decision for
     negative response,
     187
Message:
  acceptance, 15
  ambiguity, use of, 16
  categorizing, 56
  credibility, 56
  determinants of
     reception, 47
  form, 90
  influence, 86
  presentation,
     effectiveness of, 6
  semantics, 57
  understanding, 15
Messages for which no
     reader resistance is
     anticipated, 98–109
Modular classroom, 20
Monthly Catalog of U.S.
     Government
     Publications, 367
Moody's Investor Service,
     366
Motivation:
  use in communication,
     135

reader, 50–52

Narrative memo, 221–22
    purposes, 221
Nature of people, 128
Negative elements in
    persuasive writing,
    149
Negative-ladened closing
    threats, 186
Negative material, avoiding
    paragraph-end
    emphasis, 176
Negative message (*see also*
    Techniques/strategy
    in persuasion):
    avoiding negative words
    and reference, 176
    contrasting ways of
        returning the
        unearned-discount
        check, 184–85
    coping with angry
        reactions, 185
    counter suggestion,
        196
    declining order requests,
        181–82
    denying claims, 180
    disarming upset reader,
        175
    example:
        refusal for free
            services, 191–92
        refusal to accept
            partial payment, 187
        two ways of refusing a
            consumer claim,
            180–81
    fire-and-brimstone,
        characteristics of,
        186
    goodwill refusal of
        unsolicited
        suggestions, 191
    humor in, 197–98
    hurried reactions to, 185

job-applicant turndown,
    189
job-offer turndown, 189
job resignation, 190–91
light, impersonal
    statements, 197–98
misunderstandings over
    discounts, credit
    terms, exchanges,
    185
neutral material in, 174
objectives, 173
office memo, illustration,
    182–83
phrasing ideas positively,
    176
planning strategy, 192–98
poor appraisal of
    employee
    performance, 182
problem of misleading
    reader in opening,
    175
reader acceptance, 176
reader reaction, 174
refusals:
    adjustment, 186
    consumer claim when
        company is not
        responsible, 180
    credit terms, 186
    partial payment,
        186–87
    reasons for, 180
    request, 180
    request for free
        services, 191
    restoring goodwill,
        186
    side-by-side illustrations,
        182–83
    situations requiring
        tactful refusals,
        179–92
    taking the reader by
        surprise, 185
    techniques for writing,
        176–77

tracking a sample case
    through various
    stages of strategy,
    192–96
types, 180, 184, 185, 186,
    190–91
unreasonable requests,
    180
writer's disadvantaged
    position in, 173–74
Negative references,
    absence of, in
    informative writing,
    108
Negative, special form of,
    60
    the challenging question,
    60
Negatives, avoidance of,
    154
The New York Times, 328
The New York Times Index,
    365
Nondirective counseling, 5
Nonverbal communication,
    9–14
No-resistance messages (*see
    also* Informative
    messages):
    claims, 99
    inquiries, 99
Notetaking and filing:
    efficient system in
        research, 370–71
    suggested format sample,
        372
Nouns and verbs, 154

*The Occupational Outlook
    Handbook*, 542
Occupational surveys, 544
Office automation, 18
The office of tomorrow, 20
One-sentence paragraphs,
    104
    as a means of emphasis,
    104

On being understood, 107

One-way communication, written, 14

Op. cit., 526

Opening:
danger of misleading reader, 175
difficulty in getting reader's acceptance, 175
direct-style writing, 100
informative message, 94
direct-style of, 94
negative message, 175
selecting initial point of contact, 149–50
subordinating reference to letter in reply, 94
wedge in persuasive writing, 146–47

Operational efficiency, role of reporting in, 6

Oral communication, 9–14, 88
management's policies, 14
management's stake in, 14
media, 14
problem in, 10
problem of, 9

Oral instructions or orders, weaknesses in, 221

Oral reporting, 240–43

Oral reports, 245

Organization, defined, 16

Organizational patterns in short operational reports:
chronological, 220
logical, 220
psychological, 220

Organizing information (see also Outlining):
considerations, 221
points for best sequence of ideas, 105

Orienting reader with background information, 103
samples, 103

Outline, samples of, 448–49, 452–57, 462–64 (see also Working outline for SOAR)

Outlining:
captions, 447, 450–60
overlapping, 455, 458
parallelism, 455–57, 458–59
significant facts and figures in descriptive style, 451
single subdivision, 459
conclusions and recommendations, 460–61
coverage, 444, 446, 450
critical-discussion areas, 451–460
decimal system, 446, 448–49, 458
descriptive, 446–47, 450–51, 455, 459–60
effectiveness, 444
format, 461, 465
interrelationship of parts, 444
the introduction, 447–48, 450–51
second- and subsequent-level captions, 458–60
spacing, 446
topical, 446–51
traditional pattern, 444, 446–47, 452, 456, 462
short report, working, 259–61, 263–66, 267, 269–70

Paragraph:
as a thought unit, 104

one-sentence length, 104
one-topic rule, 105

Passive voice, situation for, 198

Paving the way for the persuasive request, 138

Peg statement:
function, 218
as lead sentence in short operational report, 218
reasons for position, 218–19
reshaping of, 218

Perception, 17
factors, 17
of reader, 17
authoritarian oriented, 52
inner directed, 52
of writer by reader, 52–53
in written communication, 91

Personal interview, 8

Personnel officers:
characteristics looked for in potential employee, 572–73
interests in application letters, 570
remarks about job candidates, 568–72
weeding-out process of applicants, 568

Persuasibility, 50
as a content-free factor, 50
of low-esteem person, 53

Persuasion:
defined, 137
degree of resistance, 137–38
in formal reports, 138
as influence of reader's attitude, 135

nature of, in any
communication, 135
role in business
communication, 49
situations for use, 137–38
tools of, 139
Persuasive argument,
planning of, 148
Persuasive messages:
anticipated reader
reaction, 138
anticipating feedback,
138
behavior patterns in,
139–40
blending informative
techniques through
annotated example,
157–58
use of emotion and
reason, 143
factors to overcome, 138
barriers, 138
reader indifference, 138
reader predisposition,
138
feedback, 138
follow up to, 159
paving the way, 138
plan for writing, 136–37
poor timing, for effective
meaning, 141
psychological placement
of request, 150
reader appeals, 145
reader benefits, 145
role of beliefs, 141
task, 135
techniques:
in contrasting
examples, 156–57
in illustrated example,
155–56
types:
adjustments, 139
collections, 137, 139
disappointing answers
to requests, 137

fund raising, 137
job applications, 139
job-offer postponement,
189
mass communication,
137
political, 137
requests, 137
sales, 137, 139
Persuasive strategy as
parallel of syllogistic
research model, 151
Persuasive writing:
making the request, 150
sample case, 148–52
*Petroleum Facts and
Figures*, 366
Planning:
considerations in writing,
91–98
informative, 91
process, 91
the message, 48–61
analyzing the reader,
49–61
assembling facts,
48–49
purpose, 48
reader adaptation,
role playing, 61
wording, positive vs.
negative, 58
the you-attitude, 60–61
the research design,
333–40
role, 91
for successful image
building, 48
three purposive strategies
in, 48
Playscript procedure:
characteristics, 227–28
examples, 229–33
policy statement in, 228
in short operational
reports, 224–35
suitable subjects for,
228

vital factor of *when*,
228
Playscript technique, for
writing procedures,
224
Poor communication:
cost of, 5
two types of
informational
reporting, 28
Positive suggestion:
power of, 139
technique, 139
Positive versus negative
phrasing, 58–60
Postscripts, 39–40
defined, 39
impact, 40
use, 40
Predicament-to-remedy
appeal in persuasive
writing, 145
Prediction:
basic considerations,
399–401
by causal condition,
400–401
by cycle, 401
discounting for time,
404–6
environmental
adjustment, 401
expected value, 424–25
extent of change, 400
market value, 424
by performance of
similar entity, 401
persistence base, 400
present value, 405–6,
426, 427
probability assignment,
401, 404–5, 426–27
system in the decision
maker, 397
time interval, future, 400
time interval, past, 399
Prentice-Hall Tax Service,
367

Preplanning the short
operational
analytical report,
246–47
Price, handling of, from
reader's point of
view, 107
Primary data, definition,
320
Primary research:
computer and probability
theory, great
flexibility of, 320
methods, 320
Problem:
authorizer's hypothesis
of, 324
defining, 324, 326–31
alternate solutions, 329
analyzing possible
readers, 329
company situation,
324, 326–27
competitive climate,
327
cost of doing business,
327
critical discussion
areas, 334
designing research
scheme, 333
exploring general
literature in field,
327–29
financial aspects, 324
framing elements into
a question to be
answered by
research, 334
for Harley Flour Mills,
331–32
managerial features,
326
for the short report,
217–18, 246, 247,
249, 257, 262, 267
question statement of,
247, 249

solution, 329
Problem formulation model
for decision making,
246–55
Salem-Harcourt Office
Equipment Company
case, 262–63
nature of the decision,
262
illustration, 268
State Department
Employee Turnover
case, 266–67
nature of the decision,
267, illustration,
268
Westside Roofing
Company case,
257–58
nature of the decision,
257, illustration,
257
Problem solving:
employees' knowledge of
and skill in, 245
in the interaction
process, 89
memo, 221
illustration, 225–26
purposes, 222
steps for short
operational reports,
217
Procedure:
graphic concept, 227
handling explanation in
credit messages, 107
required degrees of
coverage, 228
Procedures (*see also*
Playscript):
instructions for
rebuilding, 230, 235
job of, 224, 227
prose style, 230, 231–32
team pattern in, 224, 227
technique for pulling
together, 227

writing,
making team patterns
clear, 227
Psychological arrangement
of organization form,
short report, 220
Psychological needs of
employees, 98
Psychological plan for
successful, inductive
request making,
136–37
*Public Affairs Information
Service,* 366
Public relations, 5
Pure research, defined, 320
Purpose, focus in writing,
95

*Quality Control and Applied
Statistics Including
Operations Research,*
367
Quantitative decisions,
418–29 (*see also*
Decision making)
discounting for time, 427
expected value, 424–25
market value, 424
present value, 426, 427
probability assignment,
426–27
Questionnaires (*see also*
Survey;
Interrogation
instrument):
basic ideas on
preparation and
administration,
384–85
illustrations, 387–88
two types of, 382
Quotations:
capitalization, 522
errors in, 523
footnoting, 523
four-plus lines, 522

indented blocks, 522–23
maximum length, 523
omissions from, 523
paraphrased, 522
punctuation, 522
within quotations, 522
within sentence, 522
three or fewer lines, 522
verbatim, 522, 523
writer's interpolations in,
    523

Readability, 41–47
constructing simple
    sentences for, 46
four ways of emphasizing
    an idea, 42
material arrangement
    for, 42
role of style, 41
rules for, 272–73
sentence techniques, 46
word selection, 42–45
as verbal waste, 43–45
Reader (see also Receiver;
    Recipient):
acceptance, 157
in informative
    messages, 90
adaptation, 58–61, 96–98
analysis, 34, 49–58,
    96–98
assumptions about
    environment, 53
perception of the
    writer, 52
anticipated reaction,
    persuasive message,
    138
promise of reward and
    ego-involvement, 50
psychological maturity,
    54
reader-writer role
    relationships, 55–58
appraisal, 380
assumptions, 88

avoiding conflict in mind
    of, 153
basic needs of, 90, 146
effects of beliefs, 140
benefit, 50
in persuasive writing,
    144–45
building up ego, 113
consideration in short
    reports, 220
considerations in writing,
    95
conviction achieved in
    second- and
    subsequent-level
    outline captions,
    458–59
defense, 175
desires, 142
ego, 51
expectations, 87
expressing understanding
    of, 113
gaining acceptance in
    persuasive message,
    144
getting on common
    ground with, 175
indifference factor, 138
inertia, 142
influence, 93, 98
interest in persuasive
    writing, 146
as most logical source of
    information, 107
mood established for, 47
motivation:
    extrinsic, 51
    intrinsic, 51
need:
    basis in persuasive
        writing, 146
    face-saving in negative
        message, 175
    for information, 27
obstacles, 34
orienting with you-
    attitude sentences,

103
perception, 88, 91
predisposition factor, 138
psychological impact,
    from disappointing
    news, 176
reaction, 49
anticipating, 97
relating facts for
    understanding, 92
relationship to writer, 87
report, sophistication of,
    as determiner of
    recording process,
    471
response to writer, 88
review of justification
    report in thirds, 236
role that beliefs play, 141
satisfaction with status
    quo, 142
self-image, 141
three ways of using
    mental power, 47
The Real Estate Analyst
    Service, 367
Reason:
and emotion as tools of
    persuasion, 143
in persuasive writing,
    137
Reasoning:
in arriving at the most
    likely decision
    criterion, 257
in major premise to
    establish conditions
    and extent of
    components, 252
testing the logic of, 252
Receiver (see also Reader):
appraisal, 96–98
by assessing
    environment, 98
from intellect and
    culture, 96–97
by reaction to message,
    97

Receiver, appraisal
(*cont.*)
by relationship to
writer, 97
role, 15
Recipient as the *one* who
communicates, 17
Refusal:
credit grant, four C's as
basis, 188
example, functional
comments in the
margin, 178–79
making it reasonably
pleasant, 174
preparing reader for it,
174
psychology behind,
174–79
softening effect of,
174
use of two types of
reasoning, 174–75
value of convincing
explanation, 174
Refusing an unknown
person, two ways of,
178
Refusing the request of a
well-known person,
178–79
Relevancy of data
determined by
problem formulation
and working outline,
267
Report:
analysts with different
proof statistics
reaching different
answer for same
determinant, 459
authorization
instrument, 437–41
classifying uses, 330
decision:
minimized results of,
472

successive stages of,
471
format, 479
chapter, first page,
479–80
chapters, 479, 483
sections, 479, 480–82
introduction,
clarifying intention of
report for reader, 472
long formal:
makeup, pagination,
431
oral authorization for,
437
outline, 444, 446–65
page format, 432
page guide, 433
page numbering, 493
title, 434–35
title page, 437–38
reader, trained eye for
meat of study in
concluding sections
and second-level
subdivisions, 460
title page for short
analytical report, 274
*Reporter of Direct Mail
Advertising*, 34
Reports:
according to nature of
the decision:
the comparative-
evaluation
investigation, 323
the descriptive-
analytical inquiry,
323
problems with yes-or-
no answers, 322–23
analytical, defined, 319
classification:
according to decision-
making status, 318
according to the nature
of the business
decision, 322

for decision makers,
requirements, 29
and the decision-making
process, 28
sound bases for, 28
division of, internal or
external, 318
as element of executive
function, 28
employment of, outside
professional
consultant on, 318
external:
defined, 318
functions, 318
five forms of, 319
gearing research to
management's
greatest need, 322
importance, 27
informational, 220
defined, 318
internal:
movement, 318
origination, 318
relationship to
management's
decision-making
prerogative, 318
interpretative, defined,
319
letter, 240
management need for
information not
available within the
organization, 318
persuasion in, 138
research, 7
short operational
analytical, 244–70
topics:
comparative-evaluation
investigations, 361
descriptive-analytic
inquiries, 361–62
yes-no decisions, 360
Reports of the Commission,
369

Report writer (*see also* Writer; Analyst; Investigator):
activities, 320
analytical skills, 472
communication skills, 472
factors of good communication and essentials of sound management, 246
four basic steps in organized approach to decision making, 245–46
as information generator, 27
as *key* communicator, 29
presenting findings in the realm of reader's anticipated level of comprehension, 472
research activity, 320
according to prevailing goal—pure or applied, 320
responsibility, 28
pointing out essential features in illustrations, 503
as specialist, 27
value in mastering basic techniques and strategies in decision making, 245
Report writing:
fact presentation, 6
inadequacy, 6
style, 519–22
Request, public utility concept, 191
Research:
activities:
agenda, 325–26
overlapping classifications, 323
classification:

in line with research method, 321
as primary or secondary, 320
as pure or applied, 320
definitive answer for, 330
design:
from combination of inductive and deductive logic, 333
comparative-evaluation inquiries, 335–36
descriptive-analytic investigation, 337–38
short operational analytical report, 267
for yes-no studies, 334–35, 336
designing scheme, 333–34
on human behavior, 339
method:
descriptive, defined, 321
experimental, 339
five kinds relevant to business studies, defined, 321–22
historical, defined, 321
observation, defined, 339
operations, defined, 322
prognostic, defined, 321–22
sociological, defined, 321
model:
comparative-evaluation inquiry, 337
descriptive-analytic investigation, 338
yes-no decision, 336
plans, pulling into final focus, 339–40
primary sources, 339
Research projects (*see* Business-decision research projects)

secondary sources, 338–39
selecting appropriate tools and procedures for, 338–40
Respondents list, ways of obtaining, 372–74
Resumé, 546–50
example, 551, 552, 553–54
parts of, 548–49
purpose, 546, 547
suggestions for constructing, 547–48
types of, 546
usage, 546, 547, 550
Rewriting, 520
Role playing, 61, 87, 146, 574
in informative communication, 86
through language, 89
Role relationships, reader and writer, 55

The Salem-Harcourt Office Equipment case, problem background against which 5-step model applied, 261–62
Salutopenings, 38
Sampling:
determining sample size, 379
formulas for, 386–94
effective randomness, 374
error of estimate, 374
measuring the risks of error, 374
nonprobability, 374
characteristics, 378
judgment quota, 378
overview of theory, 374–79
probability, 374
cluster, 377

Sampling, probability
(*cont.*)
random selection, 375
simple random, 375
size (mean), 386–93
size (percentage),
393–94
stratified random, 376
systematic random,
376
Saying "no" pleasantly, 177
Secondary data:
defined, 320–21
sources, 321
Section, chapter preview,
504–5
*Selected Securities Guide
including the Market
Times*, 367
Semantics, 9, 17
Sentence,
developing central idea,
46
length, 46
one-idea rule, 105
simple, 46
structure, progression of
directness, 102
Self-analysis, 536–40
Service to the reader, 95
attitude, 60
benefit, examples, 103
Sharpening (in listening),
defined, 11
Short operational reports:
characteristics, 216
choosing the format, 221
functions, 214–17
need for, at three levels
of management:
administrative, 214
departmental and
supervisory, 214
operative, 214
organization strategy,
217–21
peg sentence function,
218

reader expectations, 217
thinking and planning
processes, 213
three formats of, 221
uses, 220
as workhorses of
business, 213
writing requirements,
218
writing tasks, 215
[*sic*], 523
Silicon-chip technology, 19
Simple words and short
sentences:
in informative
communication, 103
writing, 95
SOAR:
acronym for short
operational
analytical report, 244
application of model to
three types of
problems, 255
careful writer of, 245
determining the nature of
the problem decision,
247–48, 250
employees' contributions
to ongoing success in
an organization, 245
employees' vehicle for
selling an idea to
management, 245
employees' visibility in
an organization, 245
5-step model in problem
formulation, 246–55
step 1—stating the
problem as a
question to be
answered by the
investigation, 247
step 2—isolating the
decision criterion,
251
step 3—the working
hypothesis, 251

step 4—components of
the decision
criterion, 251
step 5—syllogistic
reasoning of the
problem elements,
251–53
four basic points in an
organized approach
to decision making,
245–46
full illustration, with
marginal notations of
analyst/writer
functions, 274–84
ineffective results,
overemphasis upon
form, 245
key to defining problem,
247
length, 244
limited use of lab test
data and field
observations, 244
particular short report
formats for employee
use, 244
prefatory items, 244
quality of firm's
operations
determined by, 245
relationship to long,
formal investigation,
244
restricted scope,
244
similarities and
differences to long,
formal report, 244,
246, 267
tables, graphics in,
244
title page, 244
transmittal note, 244
types of information
needed, 246
Spacing for long, formal
report 432, 434

Staff report:
  classified as to physical
    characteristics, 215
  defined, 214
  kinds, external, 214–15
  kinds, internal, 214
*Standard & Poor's
    Corporation Services*,
    367
*Standard & Poor's Industry
    Surveys*, 328
State Department
    Employee Turnover
    case, problem
    background against
    which 5-step model
    applied, 266–67
Stating the problem as a
    question for the
    descriptive-analytic
    inquiry, 268
Stating the problem as a
    question for the
    comparative-
    evaluation, 262
Stating the problem as a
    question for yes-no
    study, 257
  incorporating the cause
    and effect, 257
*Statistical Abstract of the
    United States*, 368
Statistical analyses (*see*
    Data summarization)
Statistics, descriptive,
    418–21
Statistics of the
    Communications
    Industry, 369
Steele, John E., 540
Stereotype:
  message, 6
  verbiage, 42–43
Stereotypes, 11
Stereotyping, 56–57
Style:
  clarity, 41
  defined, 41

  in a letter, 41
  mood created, 47
  qualities, 41
  readable, 47
  selecting words for, 46
  writing, 45
    argumentative, 236
    functional prose, 46
    simple words for, 45,
    46
Subject line, reasons for,
    39
Subordinating reference to
    reader's letter, 94
Success consciousness in
    persuasive writing,
    139
Successful business
    communication, 8
Supervisor, concept of, as
    absolutely autocratic
    (or parental)
    monarch, 245
Survey of Buying Power,
    369
Survey of Current Business,
    328, 368
Survey:
  data collection,
    371
  direct-style request
    letter:
    suggestions for
      drafting, 380–81
  inductive-style request
    letter,
    suggestions for
      drafting, 382
  interrogation instrument:
    basic ideas on
      questionnaire
      preparation and
      administration,
      384–85
    closed form, 382
    drafting, 382
    free form, 383–84
    open form, 382

  providing for third
    choice in
    dichotomous
    questions, 384
  sample cover letter,
    383
  two types of closed
    form, 382–83
interviews, types of,
    385
on-the-premises
    investigation, 379
preparing the
    information request
    and questionnaire
    cover letter, 379–86
inductive, climatic
    treatment, 381
two elements of
    assurance for on-the-
    premises
    investigation, 379–80
ways of conducting, 371
Syllogism, hypothetical in
    persuasive strategy,
    151
Syllogistic reasoning:
  problem elements in the
    descriptive-analytic
    study, 258, 337
  problem elements in the
    comparative-
    evaluation inquiry,
    263, 335
  problem elements in the
    yes-no decision, 258,
    334–35, 409–11
  pseudoscientific form in
    business problem
    solving, 334–35
Syllogistic research model,
    151, 334, 409
Symbols, reaction to, 60
Synopsis (*see* Epitome)
Systems analyst, role of, 22
Systems approach, for
    plotting operational
    strategies, 322

Systems cycle, in
procedures writing,
227–28

Tables:
abbreviations in, 491
in appendix, 484, 485
box headings, 491–92
capitalization in
headings, 485, 492
columns, 491, 492–93
continued, 485, 488–89,
491
cut-in headings, 486–89
defined, 484
documentation, 491
folding large exhibits,
485
format, standard, 486,
488
identification, 485–95
coverage, 484, 488, 491,
492
placement, 485
sidewise format, 491
leader periods, 486,
492
left-facing, 491, 493
numbering, 485
with parallel columns,
485, 490
placement, 491, 493
in relation to text, 493,
494
in text, 493, 494
on separate page, 493
vertical, 493
ruling, vertical, 493
sidewise, 485, 487, 491
source, 486, 487, 489–91
spacing by size, 485
spanner headings, 487,
492
use, 484
Technical information,
conveying, 97
Technical writing, 219

Techniques in negative
writing, 177
Teleconferencing, 19, 20
Terms, handling
explanation of in
credit grants, 107
Thayer, Lee O., 90
Three basic organizational
patterns of short
reports, examples,
220
Timing in persuasive
writing, 138, 147–48
Title:
formulated from SOAR
problem stated as
question, 259
samples of analytical
report, 435
suggestions for
formulating for long,
formal report, 434
Title fly, long report,
434–35
example, 436
Title page:
make up, for long, formal
report, 437
sample (long), 438
sample (short), 274
Tolerance in claims and
complaints, 185
Tone and spirit in the letter
makeup, 41
Topic sentence:
samples, 104
use as leadoff statement,
104
Trade Practice Rules,
369
Training programs, 573–74
Transmittal letter, 441,
443–44
function in short
operational
analytical report, 244
sample, 445
as synopsis in SOAR, 244

Turn down of prospective
job-applicant,
example, 189
Two-way communication,
oral and nonverbal,
14
Two-ways of saying "yes,"
101
Typing:
box cut-ins, 491–92
footnotes, 522–26
illustration list, 465
indented blocks, 484
leader periods, 492
the outline, 444, 446
report sections, 479–84
tables, 485, 488, 491–93
typographical gradations
for captions, 473–74

Unity, method of achieving,
219
Universe:
finite, 374
finite multiplier, 375, 392
infinite, 374, 392
Unpleasant ideas, stripping
emphasis of, 174

Value system, 403–8
discounting for time,
404–6
present value, 405–6
probability assignment,
404, 426–27
qualitative
considerations,
407–8
utility, risk value, 406–7
Verbal waste, 43–45
Verbiage, absence of, in
informative writing,
108
Verbs, 154
Vertical File Index, 366

The Wall Street Journal, 328

The Wall Street Journal Index, 366
Ways of saying "no" pleasantly, 177
The Westside Roofing case, problem background against which to apply 5-step model, 256–57
Word processing, 19
Words:
of accusation, 186
creating belief, 153
defined, 152
of fact, 154
forceful, 468
as fragments of experience, 151
and ideas,
examples, 198–99
with poor connotation, 198–99
as image makers, 11
impact, 153, 446, 451
limitation, 9
meanings, 153
negative,
avoiding accusation, 186
inferences, 175–76
negatives to be avoided, 154
of opinion, 154
picture making, 153–54
power of, 152
usage, 10
Word-world problems, 9, 10
The Work of the Securities and Exchange Commission, 366
Working hypothesis:
avoiding naming choice as possible bias, comparative-evaluation investigation, 262
defined, 257, 333

determining components for the statement to hold true, 258, 262–63, 334–35
for the SOAR descriptive-analytic inquiry, 268
for the SOAR comparative-evaluation investigation, 262
for the SOAR yes-no study, 257
three characteristics of, 251
Working outline:
for descriptive-analytic inquiry constructed from problem formulation, 267
for comparative-evaluation investigation constructed from problem formulation, 263
flexibility, 259
as a means of further understanding the problem's ramifications, 259
parenthetically stating what each caption section must cover, 259–61
sample illustrations, 260, 264–65, 269–70
section captions phrased as statement of writer's intent, 259
for yes-no study constructed from problem formulation, 259
Writer (*see also* Analyst; Researcher):
adapting language to reader, 141
adapting to reader needs

in persuasive message, 146
appraisal of reader, 380
assumptions, clear delineation, 506
barriers from conflicts and pressures, 98
beginning message with the turn down, 177–78
competence in short reports, 217
expectations, 87
finesse in declining requests, 181
job of, 8
obligation in making a decision, 330
perception by reader, 52
prestige, 54
problem with information, 27
qualities, 245
reinforcing reader's ego prior to giving disappointing news, 174
research:
method for personal comments in quotations, 371
verbatim material indicating omission of paragraph or more, 371
responsibility for objectivity in reporting, 251
responsibility for ordering facts, 92–93
responsibility for wording captions in reports, 261
skill in problem solving and communication of decisions in defensible written and oral reports, 245

Writer (*cont.*)
useful tools, 245
Writing:
addressing reader's
feelings, not words,
108
analysis and
interpretations in
reports, 267, 271–73
argumentative, 236, 519
the authorization
instrument for the
report, 437–41
bad news messages two
ways, 182–83
calculating effect in
arranging ideas,
105–6
and changing personality,
108
conveying facts merely as
news under adverse
condition, 113
dependent structure in
opening, 100
direct style:
informative messages,
94
survey request letter,
380–81
discipline as a problem
area for many, 271
inductive style, 174
persuasive messages,
143–52
survey request letter,
381–82
informative, emphasizing
point with topic
sentence, 104
the job-application letter,
557–60
the job-offer refusal, 190
and job performance, 7
and job skills, 7
justification report:
deductive style, 235
persuasiveness in, 240

style, 236
using the language of the
reader, 86
logic, 519, 520
Writing, long report:
concluding sections,
515–18
comparative-
evaluation, 517–18
descriptive-analytic,
518
yes-no, 516–17
content sections,
503–15
chapter, section
preview, 504–5
concluding statements,
507
interpreting findings,
505–15
topic sentence leads,
506
introduction,
472–479
plan for deductive
epitome, 467–68
recommendations,
518–19
style, 519–522
Writing, management, 5
Writing, negative:
burying disappointing
news, 176
deemphasizing the "no,"
176
employee job
performance, 182
expressions that set
reader and writer on
same side, 175
limiting words to achieve
positive wording, 176
making the refusal
unmistakeably clear,
176
misunderstandings, 185
questionable "softener"
effect phrases, 176

refusing to accept
unearned discount,
184
ways of saying "no," 177
when claim falls outside
warranty period, 180
when claim is unjustified
because of abusive
product treatment,
180
when request is
unreasonable in size,
180
Writing, persuasive:
appealing for action in
close, 151
arousing reader interest,
144
avoiding negatives, 154
close for action, 150
connotation of diction,
155
denied-negative trap, 154
first step in, 148
handling negative
elements, 149
inductive strategy for,
147–49
obstacles to, 142
using one major appeal,
145
opening wedge in,
146–47
use of passive voice in
negative situations,
198
use of reader benefits,
145
use of reader desires,
142–43
use of reader needs as an
appeal, 146
request for action,
150–51
role of beliefs in, 141
role of emotion and
reason, 143
situations for, 135

strategy for, 144–52
tools, 139
tracking through a
    typical problem,
    148–52
transitions in, 147
use of you-attitude, 140
Writing, procedures, 224
    (*see also* Playscript)
simplification of, 227
Writing, rules:
readability, 272–73
receiving credit for ideas,
    574

recommendations, 236
requirements, 218
rewriting, 520
simple words, 95
strategies, 192–98
style, 15–16, 45–47, 90,
    135, 519
topic sentences, 104
transitions, 504

Yes-no decision:
also called *binary*, 322
as smallest bit of
    information, 20

Yes-no problem, 257
Yes-or-no report studies:
hypothesis, 322
research method, 322–23
studies, 409–412, 507–14
The you-attitude, 60 (*see
    also* Service for the
    reader)
You viewpoint, 51
for transitional turn in
    persuasive writing,
    150